KU-547-822

**PHILIP'S**

# ESSENTIAL
# WORLD
# ATLAS

# PHILIP'S

# ESSENTIAL
# WORLD
# ATLAS

## THIRD EDITION

**IN ASSOCIATION WITH**
**THE ROYAL GEOGRAPHICAL SOCIETY**
WITH THE INSTITUTE OF BRITISH GEOGRAPHERS

# CONTENTS

Cartography by Philip's

Text
Keith Lye

Picture Acknowledgements
© Corbis /Stephen Frink, cover top right, / Hans
Georg Roth, cover bottom right
Courtesy of NPA Group, Edenbridge, UK 1
Image Bank /Lionel Brown 10
Images Colour Library /cover bottom left
Rex Features /Sipa 6, 24
Still Pictures 26, /Anne Piantanida 8, /Chris
Caldicott 16, /Mark Edwards 18, 20, /Hartmut
Schwarzbach 14, 22, /Luke White 4, /Francois Pierrel
cover top left
Tony Stone Images /Kevin Kelley 2, /Art Wolfe 12

First published in Great Britain in 1996
under the title Philip's Desk Reference Atlas

This edition first published in 1998 by
George Philip Limited, a division of
Octopus Publishing Group Limited,
2–4 Heron Quays, London E14 4JP

Third edition 2001

© 2001 George Philip Limited

A CIP catalogue record for this book is available
from the British Library.

ISBN 0–540–07888–3

Printed in Hong Kong

Details of other Philip's titles and services can be
found on our website at: www.philips-maps.co.uk

## WORLD STATISTICS

vi–ix     Countries

x–xi      Cities

xii–xv    Physical

xvi       Climate

## THE EARTH IN FOCUS

2–3       The Universe and Solar System

4–5       The Changing Earth

6–7       Earthquakes and Volcanoes

8–9       Water and Ice

10–11     Weather and Climate

12–13     Landforms and Vegetation

14–15     Population

16–17     Languages and Religions

18–19     Agriculture and Industry

20–21     Trade and Commerce

22–23     Transport and Travel

24–27     International Organizations

28–29     Regions in the News

30–32     World Flags

Philip's is proud to announce that its World Atlases are now published
in association with The Royal Geographical Society (with The Institute
of British Geographers).

The Society was founded in 1830 and given a Royal Charter in 1859
for 'the advancement of geographical science'. It holds historical collections
of national and international importance, many of which relate to the
Society's association with and support for scientific exploration and
research from the 19th century onwards. It was pivotal in establishing
geography as a teaching and research discipline in British universities close
to the turn of the century, and has played a key role in geographical and
environmental education ever since.

Today the Society is a leading world centre for geographical learning –
supporting education, teaching, research and expeditions, and promoting
public understanding of the subject.

The Society welcomes those interested in geography as members.
For further information, please visit the website at: www.rgs.org

# WORLD MAPS

| | | | |
|---|---|---|---|
| 1 | General Reference | 54–55 | North-west Africa |
| 2–3 | Northern Hemisphere | 56–57 | Central Africa |
| 4–5 | Southern Hemisphere | 58–59 | Southern Africa |
| 6–7 | Europe | 60–61 | Australia |
| 8–9 | Scandinavia | 62–63 | South-east Australia |
| 10–11 | British Isles | 64–65 | New Zealand, Central and South-west Pacific |
| 12–13 | France | | |
| 14–15 | Germany and Benelux | 66–67 | North America |
| 16–17 | Central Europe | 68–69 | Eastern Canada |
| 18–19 | Spain and Portugal | 70–71 | Western Canada |
| 20–21 | Italy and the Adriatic | 72–73 | North-east USA |
| 22–23 | Greece and the Balkans | 74–75 | South-east USA |
| 24–25 | Eastern Europe | 76–77 | North-central USA |
| 26–27 | Asia | 78–79 | Southern USA |
| 28–29 | Western Russia and Central Asia | 80–81 | North-west USA |
| | | 82–83 | South-west USA |
| 30–31 | Eastern Siberia | 84–85 | Mexico |
| 32–33 | Japan | 86–87 | Caribbean and Central America |
| 34–35 | China | | |
| 36–37 | South-east Asia | 88–89 | South America |
| 38–39 | Philippines and Eastern Indonesia | 90–91 | South America – North-west |
| 40–41 | Eastern India, Bangladesh and Burma | 92–93 | South America – North-east |
| 42–43 | Western India and Pakistan | 94–95 | South America – South |
| 44–45 | Iran, the Gulf and Afghanistan | | |
| 46–47 | The Middle East and Turkey | 96 | Antarctica |
| 48–49 | Arabia and the Horn of Africa | | |
| 50–51 | Africa | | |
| 52–53 | North-east Africa | 97–160 | **Index to World Maps** |

# WORLD STATISTICS – COUNTRIES

Listed below are the principal countries of the world; the more important territories are also included. If a territory is not completely independent, then the country it is associated with is named. The area figures give the total area of land, inland water and ice. Annual income is the GNP per capita. The figures are the latest available: usually 1998.

| Country / Territory | Area (1,000 sq km) | Area (1,000 sq mls) | Population (1,000s) | Capital City | Annual Income US$ |
|---|---|---|---|---|---|
| **Afghanistan** | 652 | 252 | 26,511 | Kabul | 800 |
| **Albania** | 28.8 | 11.1 | 3,795 | Tirana | 810 |
| **Algeria** | 2,382 | 920 | 32,904 | Algiers | 1,550 |
| **Andorra** | 0.45 | 0.17 | 49 | Andorra La Vella | 18,000 |
| **Angola** | 1,247 | 481 | 13,295 | Luanda | 340 |
| **Argentina** | 2,767 | 1,068 | 36,238 | Buenos Aires | 8,970 |
| **Armenia** | 29.8 | 11.5 | 3,968 | Yerevan | 480 |
| **Australia** | 7,687 | 2,968 | 18,855 | Canberra | 20,300 |
| **Austria** | 83.9 | 32.4 | 7,613 | Vienna | 26,850 |
| **Azerbaijan** | 86.6 | 33.4 | 8,324 | Baku | 490 |
| **Azores (Portugal)** | 2.2 | 0.87 | 238 | Ponta Delgada | – |
| **Bahamas** | 13.9 | 5.4 | 295 | Nassau | 20,100 |
| **Bahrain** | 0.68 | 0.26 | 683 | Manama | 7,660 |
| **Bangladesh** | 144 | 56 | 150,589 | Dhaka | 350 |
| **Barbados** | 0.43 | 0.17 | 265 | Bridgetown | 7,890 |
| **Belarus** | 207.6 | 80.1 | 10,697 | Minsk | 2,200 |
| **Belgium** | 30.5 | 11.8 | 9,832 | Brussels | 25,380 |
| **Belize** | 23 | 8.9 | 230 | Belmopan | 2,700 |
| **Benin** | 113 | 43 | 6,369 | Porto-Novo | 380 |
| **Bhutan** | 47 | 18.1 | 1,906 | Thimphu | 1,000 |
| **Bolivia** | 1,099 | 424 | 9,724 | La Paz/Sucre | 1,000 |
| **Bosnia-Herzegovina** | 51 | 20 | 4,601 | Sarajevo | 1,720 |
| **Botswana** | 582 | 225 | 1,822 | Gaborone | 3,600 |
| **Brazil** | 8,512 | 3,286 | 179,487 | Brasília | 4,570 |
| **Brunei** | 5.8 | 2.2 | 333 | Bandar Seri Begawan | 24,000 |
| **Bulgaria** | 111 | 43 | 9,071 | Sofia | 1,230 |
| **Burkina Faso** | 274 | 106 | 12,092 | Ouagadougou | 240 |
| **Burma (= Myanmar)** | 677 | 261 | 51,129 | Rangoon | 1,200 |
| **Burundi** | 27.8 | 10.7 | 7,358 | Bujumbura | 140 |
| **Cambodia** | 181 | 70 | 10,046 | Phnom Penh | 280 |
| **Cameroon** | 475 | 184 | 16,701 | Yaoundé | 610 |
| **Canada** | 9,976 | 3,852 | 28,488 | Ottawa | 20,020 |
| **Canary Is. (Spain)** | 7.3 | 2.8 | 1,494 | Las Palmas/Santa Cruz | – |
| **Cape Verde Is.** | 4 | 1.6 | 515 | Praia | 1,060 |
| **Central African Republic** | 623 | 241 | 4,074 | Bangui | 300 |
| **Chad** | 1,284 | 496 | 7,337 | Ndjaména | 230 |
| **Chile** | 757 | 292 | 15,272 | Santiago | 4,810 |
| **China** | 9,597 | 3,705 | 1,299,180 | Beijing | 750 |
| **Colombia** | 1,139 | 440 | 39,397 | Bogotá | 2,600 |
| **Comoros** | 2.2 | 0.86 | 670 | Moroni | 370 |
| **Congo** | 342 | 132 | 3,167 | Brazzaville | 690 |
| **Congo (Dem. Rep. of the)** | 2,345 | 905 | 49,190 | Kinshasa | 110 |
| **Costa Rica** | 51.1 | 19.7 | 3,711 | San José | 2,780 |
| **Croatia** | 56.5 | 21.8 | 4,960 | Zagreb | 4,520 |
| **Cuba** | 111 | 43 | 11,504 | Havana | 1,560 |

| Country / Territory | Area (1,000 sq km) | Area (1,000 sq mls) | Population (1,000s) | Capital City | Annual Income US$ |
|---|---|---|---|---|---|
| Cyprus | 9.3 | 3.6 | 762 | Nicosia | 13,000 |
| Czech Republic | 78.9 | 30.4 | 10,500 | Prague | 5,040 |
| Denmark | 43.1 | 16.6 | 5,153 | Copenhagen | 33,260 |
| Djibouti | 23.2 | 9 | 552 | Djibouti | 1,200 |
| Dominica | 0.75 | 0.29 | 87 | Roseau | 3,010 |
| Dominican Republic | 48.7 | 18.8 | 8,621 | Santo Domingo | 1,770 |
| Ecuador | 284 | 109 | 13,319 | Quito | 1,530 |
| Egypt | 1,001 | 387 | 64,210 | Cairo | 1,290 |
| El Salvador | 21 | 8.1 | 6,739 | San Salvador | 1,850 |
| Equatorial Guinea | 28.1 | 10.8 | 455 | Malabo | 1,500 |
| Eritrea | 94 | 36 | 4,523 | Asmara | 200 |
| Estonia | 44.7 | 17.3 | 1,647 | Tallinn | 3,390 |
| Ethiopia | 1,128 | 436 | 61,841 | Addis Ababa | 100 |
| Fiji | 18.3 | 7.1 | 883 | Suva | 2,110 |
| Finland | 338 | 131 | 5,077 | Helsinki | 24,110 |
| France | 552 | 213 | 58,145 | Paris | 24,940 |
| French Guiana (France) | 90 | 34.7 | 130 | Cayenne | 6,000 |
| French Polynesia (France) | 4 | 1.5 | 268 | Papeete | 10,800 |
| Gabon | 268 | 103 | 1,612 | Libreville | 3,950 |
| Gambia, The | 11.3 | 4.4 | 1,119 | Banjul | 340 |
| Georgia | 69.7 | 26.9 | 5,777 | Tbilisi | 930 |
| Germany | 357 | 138 | 76,962 | Berlin/Bonn | 25,850 |
| Ghana | 239 | 92 | 20,564 | Accra | 390 |
| Greece | 132 | 51 | 10,193 | Athens | 11,650 |
| Grenada | 0.34 | 0.13 | 83 | St George's | 3,170 |
| Guadeloupe (France) | 1.7 | 0.66 | 365 | Basse-Terre | 9,200 |
| Guatemala | 109 | 42 | 12,222 | Guatemala City | 1,640 |
| Guinea | 246 | 95 | 7,830 | Conakry | 540 |
| Guinea-Bissau | 36.1 | 13.9 | 1,197 | Bissau | 160 |
| Guyana | 215 | 83 | 891 | Georgetown | 770 |
| Haiti | 27.8 | 10.7 | 8,003 | Port-au-Prince | 410 |
| Honduras | 112 | 43 | 6,846 | Tegucigalpa | 730 |
| Hong Kong (China) | 1.1 | 0.40 | 6,336 | – | 23,670 |
| Hungary | 93 | 35.9 | 10,531 | Budapest | 4,510 |
| Iceland | 103 | 40 | 274 | Reykjavik | 28,010 |
| India | 3,288 | 1,269 | 1,041,543 | New Delhi | 430 |
| Indonesia | 1,905 | 735 | 218,661 | Jakarta | 680 |
| Iran | 1,648 | 636 | 68,759 | Tehran | 1,770 |
| Iraq | 438 | 169 | 26,339 | Baghdad | 2,400 |
| Ireland | 70.3 | 27.1 | 4,086 | Dublin | 18,340 |
| Israel | 27 | 10.3 | 5,321 | Jerusalem | 15,940 |
| Italy | 301 | 116 | 57,195 | Rome | 20,250 |
| Ivory Coast (Côte d'Ivoire) | 322 | 125 | 17,600 | Yamoussoukro | 700 |
| Jamaica | 11 | 4.2 | 2,735 | Kingston | 1,680 |
| Japan | 378 | 146 | 128,470 | Tokyo | 32,380 |
| Jordan | 89.2 | 34.4 | 5,558 | Amman | 1,520 |
| Kazakstan | 2,717 | 1,049 | 19,006 | Astana | 1,310 |
| Kenya | 580 | 224 | 35,060 | Nairobi | 330 |
| Korea, North | 121 | 47 | 26,117 | Pyŏngyang | 1,000 |
| Korea, South | 99 | 38.2 | 46,403 | Seoul | 7,970 |

| Country / Territory | Area (1,000 sq km) | Area (1,000 sq mls) | Population (1,000s) | Capital City | Annual Income US$ |
|---|---|---|---|---|---|
| Kuwait | 17.8 | 6.9 | 2,639 | Kuwait City | 22,700 |
| Kyrgyzstan | 198.5 | 76.6 | 5,403 | Bishkek | 350 |
| Laos | 237 | 91 | 5,463 | Vientiane | 330 |
| Latvia | 65 | 25 | 2,768 | Riga | 2,430 |
| Lebanon | 10.4 | 4 | 3,327 | Beirut | 3,560 |
| Lesotho | 30.4 | 11.7 | 2,370 | Maseru | 570 |
| Liberia | 111 | 43 | 3,575 | Monrovia | 1,000 |
| Libya | 1,760 | 679 | 6,500 | Tripoli | 6,700 |
| Lithuania | 65.2 | 25.2 | 3,935 | Vilnius | 2,440 |
| Luxembourg | 2.6 | 1 | 377 | Luxembourg | 43,570 |
| Macau (China) | 0.02 | 0.006 | 656 | Macau | 16,000 |
| Macedonia (F.Y.R.O.M.) | 25.7 | 9.9 | 2,157 | Skopje | 1,290 |
| Madagascar | 587 | 227 | 16,627 | Antananarivo | 260 |
| Madeira (Portugal) | 0.81 | 0.31 | 253 | Funchal | – |
| Malawi | 118 | 46 | 12,458 | Lilongwe | 200 |
| Malaysia | 330 | 127 | 21,983 | Kuala Lumpur | 3,600 |
| Maldives | 0.30 | 0.12 | 283 | Malé | 1,230 |
| Mali | 1,240 | 479 | 12,685 | Bamako | 250 |
| Malta | 0.32 | 0.12 | 366 | Valletta | 9,440 |
| Martinique (France) | 1.1 | 0.42 | 362 | Fort-de-France | 10,700 |
| Mauritania | 1,030 | 412 | 2,702 | Nouakchott | 410 |
| Mauritius | 2.0 | 0.72 | 1,201 | Port Louis | 3,700 |
| Mexico | 1,958 | 756 | 107,233 | Mexico City | 3,970 |
| Micronesia, Fed. States of | 0.70 | 0.27 | 110 | Palikir | 1,800 |
| Moldova | 33.7 | 13 | 4,707 | Chişinău | 410 |
| Mongolia | 1,567 | 605 | 2,847 | Ulan Bator | 400 |
| Morocco | 447 | 172 | 31,559 | Rabat | 1,250 |
| Mozambique | 802 | 309 | 20,493 | Maputo | 210 |
| Namibia | 825 | 318 | 2,437 | Windhoek | 1,940 |
| Nepal | 141 | 54 | 24,084 | Katmandu | 210 |
| Netherlands | 41.5 | 16 | 15,829 | Amsterdam/The Hague | 24,760 |
| Netherlands Antilles (Neths) | 0.99 | 0.38 | 203 | Willemstad | 11,500 |
| New Caledonia (France) | 18.6 | 7.2 | 195 | Nouméa | 11,400 |
| New Zealand | 269 | 104 | 3,662 | Wellington | 14,700 |
| Nicaragua | 130 | 50 | 5,261 | Managua | 390 |
| Niger | 1,267 | 489 | 10,752 | Niamey | 190 |
| Nigeria | 924 | 357 | 105,000 | Abuja | 300 |
| Norway | 324 | 125 | 4,331 | Oslo | 34,330 |
| Oman | 212 | 82 | 2,176 | Muscat | 7,900 |
| Pakistan | 796 | 307 | 162,409 | Islamabad | 480 |
| Panama | 77.1 | 29.8 | 2,893 | Panama City | 3,080 |
| Papua New Guinea | 463 | 179 | 4,845 | Port Moresby | 890 |
| Paraguay | 407 | 157 | 5,538 | Asunción | 1,760 |
| Peru | 1,285 | 496 | 26,276 | Lima | 2,460 |
| Philippines | 300 | 116 | 77,473 | Manila | 1,050 |
| Poland | 313 | 121 | 40,366 | Warsaw | 3,900 |
| Portugal | 92.4 | 35.7 | 10,587 | Lisbon | 10,690 |
| Puerto Rico (US) | 9 | 3.5 | 3,836 | San Juan | 9,000 |
| Qatar | 11 | 4.2 | 499 | Doha | 17,100 |
| Réunion (France) | 2.5 | 0.97 | 692 | Saint-Denis | 4,800 |

| Country / Territory | Area (1,000 sq km) | Area (1,000 sq mls) | Population (1,000s) | Capital City | Annual Income US$ |
|---|---|---|---|---|---|
| Romania | 238 | 92 | 24,000 | Bucharest | 1,390 |
| Russia | 17,075 | 6,592 | 155,096 | Moscow | 2,300 |
| Rwanda | 26.3 | 10.2 | 10,200 | Kigali | 230 |
| St Lucia | 0.62 | 0.24 | 177 | Castries | 3,410 |
| St Vincent & Grenadines | 0.39 | 0.15 | 128 | Kingstown | 2,420 |
| Samoa | 2.8 | 1.1 | 171 | Apia | 1,020 |
| São Tomé & Príncipe | 0.96 | 0.37 | 151 | São Tomé | 280 |
| Saudi Arabia | 2,150 | 830 | 20,697 | Riyadh | 9,000 |
| Senegal | 197 | 76 | 8,716 | Dakar | 530 |
| Sierra Leone | 71.7 | 27.7 | 5,437 | Freetown | 140 |
| Singapore | 0.62 | 0.24 | 3,000 | Singapore | 30,060 |
| Slovak Republic | 49 | 18.9 | 5,500 | Bratislava | 3,700 |
| Slovenia | 20.3 | 7.8 | 2,055 | Ljubljana | 9,760 |
| Solomon Is. | 28.9 | 11.2 | 429 | Honiara | 750 |
| Somalia | 638 | 246 | 9,736 | Mogadishu | 600 |
| South Africa | 1,220 | 471 | 43,666 | C. Town/Pretoria/ Bloemfontein | 2,880 |
| Spain | 505 | 195 | 40,667 | Madrid | 14,080 |
| Sri Lanka | 65.6 | 25.3 | 19,416 | Colombo | 810 |
| Sudan | 2,506 | 967 | 33,625 | Khartoum | 290 |
| Surinam | 163 | 63 | 497 | Paramaribo | 1,660 |
| Swaziland | 17.4 | 6.7 | 1,121 | Mbabane | 1,400 |
| Sweden | 450 | 174 | 8,560 | Stockholm | 25,620 |
| Switzerland | 41.3 | 15.9 | 6,762 | Bern | 40,080 |
| Syria | 185 | 71 | 17,826 | Damascus | 1,020 |
| Taiwan | 36 | 13.9 | 22,000 | Taipei | 12,400 |
| Tajikistan | 143.1 | 55.2 | 7,041 | Dushanbe | 350 |
| Tanzania | 945 | 365 | 39,639 | Dodoma | 210 |
| Thailand | 513 | 198 | 63,670 | Bangkok | 2,200 |
| Togo | 56.8 | 21.9 | 4,861 | Lomé | 330 |
| Trinidad & Tobago | 5.1 | 2 | 1,484 | Port of Spain | 4,430 |
| Tunisia | 164 | 63 | 9,924 | Tunis | 2,050 |
| Turkey | 779 | 301 | 66,789 | Ankara | 3,160 |
| Turkmenistan | 488.1 | 188.5 | 4,585 | Ashkhabad | 1,630 |
| Uganda | 236 | 91 | 26,958 | Kampala | 320 |
| Ukraine | 603.7 | 233.1 | 52,558 | Kiev | 850 |
| United Arab Emirates | 83.6 | 32.3 | 1,951 | Abu Dhabi | 18,220 |
| United Kingdom | 243.3 | 94 | 58,393 | London | 21,400 |
| United States of America | 9,373 | 3,619 | 266,096 | Washington, DC | 29,340 |
| Uruguay | 177 | 68 | 3,274 | Montevideo | 6,180 |
| Uzbekistan | 447.4 | 172.7 | 26,044 | Tashkent | 870 |
| Vanuatu | 12.2 | 4.7 | 206 | Port-Vila | 1,270 |
| Venezuela | 912 | 352 | 24,715 | Caracas | 350 |
| Vietnam | 332 | 127 | 82,427 | Hanoi | 330 |
| Virgin Is. (US) | 0.34 | 0.13 | 135 | Charlotte Amalie | 12,500 |
| Western Sahara | 266 | 103 | 228 | El Aaiún | 300 |
| Yemen | 528 | 204 | 13,219 | Sana | 300 |
| Yugoslavia | 102.3 | 39.5 | 10,761 | Belgrade | 2,300 |
| Zambia | 753 | 291 | 12,267 | Lusaka | 330 |
| Zimbabwe | 391 | 151 | 13,123 | Harare | 610 |

# WORLD STATISTICS – CITIES

Listed below are all the cities with more than 600,000 inhabitants (only cities with more than 1 million inhabitants are included for Brazil, China and India). The figures are taken from the most recent censuses and surveys, and are in thousands. As far as possible the figures are for the metropolitan area, e.g. greater New York or Mexico City.

| | Population (1,000s) | | Population (1,000s) | | Population (1,000s) | | Population (1,000s) |
|---|---|---|---|---|---|---|---|
| **Afghanistan** | | Ottawa–Hull | 1,022 | **Dominican Republic** | | Vishakhapatnam | 1,052 |
| Kabul | 1,565 | Edmonton | 885 | Santo Domingo | 2,135 | Varanasi | 1,026 |
| **Algeria** | | Calgary | 831 | Santiago | 691 | Ludhiana | 1,012 |
| Algiers | 2,168 | Québec | 693 | **Ecuador** | | **Indonesia** | |
| Oran | 916 | Winnipeg | 677 | Guayaquil | 1,973 | Jakarta | 11,500 |
| **Angola** | | Hamilton | 643 | Quito | 1,487 | Surabaya | 2,701 |
| Luanda | 2,418 | **Chile** | | **Egypt** | | Bandung | 2,368 |
| **Argentina** | | Santiago | 5,067 | Cairo | 9,900 | Medan | 1,910 |
| Buenos Aires | 11,256 | **China** | | Alexandria | 3,431 | Semarang | 1,366 |
| Córdoba | 1,208 | Shanghai | 15,082 | El Gîza | 2,144 | Palembang | 1,352 |
| Rosario | 1,118 | Beijing | 12,362 | Shubra el Kheima | 834 | Tangerang | 1,198 |
| Mendoza | 773 | Tianjin | 10,687 | **El Salvador** | | Ujung Pandang | 1,092 |
| La Plata | 642 | Hong Kong (SAR)* | 6,502 | San Salvador | 1,522 | Bandar Lampung | 832 |
| San Miguel de | | Chongqing | 3,870 | **Ethiopia** | | Malang | 763 |
| Tucumán | 622 | Shenyang | 3,860 | Addis Ababa | 2,112 | Padang | 721 |
| **Armenia** | | Wuhan | 3,520 | **France** | | **Iran** | |
| Yerevan | 1,248 | Guangzhou | 3,114 | Paris | 9,319 | Tehran | 6,750 |
| **Australia** | | Harbin | 2,505 | Lyon | 1,262 | Mashhad | 1,964 |
| Sydney | 3,770 | Nanjing | 2,211 | Marseille | 1,087 | Esfahan | 1,221 |
| Melbourne | 3,217 | Xi'an | 2,115 | Lille | 959 | Tabriz | 1,166 |
| Brisbane | 1,489 | Chengdu | 1,933 | Bordeaux | 696 | Shiraz | 1,043 |
| Perth | 1,262 | Dalian | 1,855 | Toulouse | 650 | Ahvaz | 828 |
| Adelaide | 1,080 | Changchun | 1,810 | **Georgia** | | Qom | 780 |
| **Austria** | | Jinan | 1,660 | Tbilisi | 1,300 | Bakhtaran | 666 |
| Vienna | 1,595 | Taiyuan | 1,642 | **Germany** | | **Iraq** | |
| **Azerbaijan** | | Qingdao | 1,584 | Berlin | 3,470 | Baghdad | 3,841 |
| Baku | 1,720 | Fuzhou, Fujian | 1,380 | Hamburg | 1,706 | Diyala | 961 |
| **Bangladesh** | | Zibo | 1,346 | Munich | 1,240 | As Sulaymaniyah | 952 |
| Dhaka | 6,105 | Zhengzhou | 1,324 | Cologne | 964 | Arbil | 770 |
| Chittagong | 2,041 | Lanzhou | 1,296 | Frankfurt | 651 | Al Mawsil | 664 |
| Khulna | 877 | Anshan | 1,252 | Essen | 616 | **Ireland** | |
| **Belarus** | | Fushun | 1,246 | Dortmund | 600 | Dublin | 952 |
| Minsk | 1,700 | Kunming | 1,242 | **Ghana** | | **Israel** | |
| **Belgium** | | Changsha | 1,198 | Accra | 949 | Tel Aviv-Yafo | 1,502 |
| Brussels | 948 | Hangzhou | 1,185 | **Greece** | | **Italy** | |
| **Bolivia** | | Nanchang | 1,169 | Athens | 3,097 | Rome | 2,775 |
| La Paz | 1,126 | Shijiazhuang | 1,159 | **Guatemala** | | Milan | 1,369 |
| Santa Cruz | 767 | Guiyang | 1,131 | Guatemala | 1,167 | Naples | 1,067 |
| **Brazil** | | Ürümqi | 1,130 | **Guinea** | | Turin | 962 |
| São Paulo | 16,417 | Jilin | 1,118 | Conakry | 1,508 | Palermo | 698 |
| Rio de Janeiro | 9,888 | Tangshan | 1,110 | **Haiti** | | Genoa | 678 |
| Salvador | 2,211 | Qiqihar | 1,104 | Port-au-Prince | 1,255 | **Ivory Coast** | |
| Belo Horizonte | 2,091 | Baotou | 1,033 | **Honduras** | | (Côte d'Ivoire) | |
| Fortaleza | 1,965 | Hefei | 1,000 | Tegucigalpa | 813 | Abidjan | 2,500 |
| Brasília | 1,821 | **Colombia** | | **Hungary** | | **Jamaica** | |
| Curitiba | 1,476 | Bogotá | 6,004 | Budapest | 1,885 | Kingston | 644 |
| Recife | 1,346 | Cali | 1,985 | **India** | | **Japan** | |
| Pôrto Alegre | 1,288 | Medellin | 1,970 | Mumbai (Bombay) | 12,572 | Tokyo– | |
| Manaus | 1,157 | Barranquilla | 1,157 | Kolkata | 10,916 | Yokohama | 26,836 |
| Belém | 1,144 | Cartagena | 812 | Delhi | 7,207 | Osaka | 10,601 |
| Goiânia | 1,004 | **Congo** | | Chennai (Madras) | 5,361 | Nagoya | 2,152 |
| **Bulgaria** | | Brazzaville | 937 | Hyderabad | 4,280 | Sapporo | 1,757 |
| Sofia | 1,116 | **Congo (Dem. Rep. of the)** | | Bangalore | 4,087 | Kyoto | 1,464 |
| **Burkina Faso** | | Kinshasa | 1,655 | Ahmadabad | 3,298 | Kobe | 1,424 |
| Ouagadougou | 690 | Lubumbashi | 851 | Pune | 2,485 | Fukuoka | 1,285 |
| **Burma (Myanmar)** | | Mbuji-Mayi | 806 | Kanpur | 2,111 | Kawasaki | 1,203 |
| Rangoon | 2,513 | **Costa Rica** | | Nagpur | 1,661 | Hiroshima | 1,109 |
| **Cambodia** | | San José | 1,220 | Lucknow | 1,642 | Kitakyushu | 1,020 |
| Phnom Penh | 920 | **Croatia** | | Surat | 1,517 | Sendai | 971 |
| **Cameroon** | | Zagreb | 931 | Jaipur | 1,514 | Chiba | 857 |
| Douala | 1,200 | **Cuba** | | Coimbatore | 1,136 | Sakai | 803 |
| Yaoundé | 800 | Havana | 2,241 | Vadodara | 1,115 | Kumamoto | 650 |
| **Canada** | | **Czech Republic** | | Indore | 1,104 | Okayama | 616 |
| Toronto | 4,344 | Prague | 1,209 | Patna | 1,099 | **Jordan** | |
| Montréal | 3,337 | **Denmark** | | Madurai | 1,094 | Amman | 1,300 |
| Vancouver | 1,831 | Copenhagen | 1,362 | Bhopal | 1,064 | Az-Zarqā | 609 |

X

| | Population (1,000s) | | Population (1,000s) | | Population (1,000s) | | Population (1,000s) |
|---|---|---|---|---|---|---|---|

**Kazakstan**
Almaty . . . . . . . . . . . . 1,150
**Kenya**
Nairobi . . . . . . . . . . . . 2,000
Mombasa . . . . . . . . . . . 600
**Korea, North**
Pyŏngyang . . . . . . . . . . 2,639
Hamhung . . . . . . . . . . . 775
Chŏngjin . . . . . . . . . . . 754
Chinnampo . . . . . . . . . 691
**Korea, South**
Seoul . . . . . . . . . . . . . 11,641
Pusan . . . . . . . . . . . . . 3,814
Taegu . . . . . . . . . . . . . 2,449
Inchon . . . . . . . . . . . . . 2,308
Taejŏn . . . . . . . . . . . . 1,272
Kwangju . . . . . . . . . . . 1,258
Ulsan . . . . . . . . . . . . . . 967
Sŏngnam . . . . . . . . . . . 869
Puch'on . . . . . . . . . . . . 779
Suwŏn . . . . . . . . . . . . . 756
**Latvia**
Riga . . . . . . . . . . . . . . . 846
**Lebanon**
Beirut . . . . . . . . . . . . . 1,900
**Libya**
Tripoli . . . . . . . . . . . . . 1,083
**Madagascar**
Antananarivo . . . . . . . 1,053
**Malaysia**
Kuala Lumpur . . . . . . . 1,145
**Mali**
Bamako . . . . . . . . . . . . 800
**Mauritania**
Nouakchott . . . . . . . . . 735
**Mexico**
Mexico City . . . . . . . 15,048
Guadalajara . . . . . . . . 2,847
Monterrey . . . . . . . . . 2,522
Puebla . . . . . . . . . . . . 1,055
León . . . . . . . . . . . . . . . 872
Ciudad Juárez . . . . . . . . 798
Tijuana . . . . . . . . . . . . . 743
Culiacán Rosales . . . . . . 602
Mexicali . . . . . . . . . . . . 602
**Moldova**
Chişinău . . . . . . . . . . . 700
**Mongolia**
Ulan Bator . . . . . . . . . . 627
**Morocco**
Casablanca . . . . . . . . . 3,079
Rabat-Salé . . . . . . . . . 1,344
Fès . . . . . . . . . . . . . . . . 735
Marrakesh . . . . . . . . . . 621
**Mozambique**
Maputo . . . . . . . . . . . . 2,000
**Netherlands**
Amsterdam . . . . . . . . 1,101
Rotterdam . . . . . . . . . 1,076
The Hague . . . . . . . . . . 694
**New Zealand**
Auckland . . . . . . . . . . . 997
**Nicaragua**
Managua . . . . . . . . . . . 864
**Nigeria**
Lagos . . . . . . . . . . . . 10,287
Ibadan . . . . . . . . . . . . 1,365
Ogbomosho . . . . . . . . . 712
Kano . . . . . . . . . . . . . . 657
**Norway**
Oslo . . . . . . . . . . . . . . 714

**Pakistan**
Karachi . . . . . . . . . . . 9,863
Lahore . . . . . . . . . . . . 5,085
Faisalabad . . . . . . . . . 1,875
Peshawar . . . . . . . . . . 1,676
Gujranwala . . . . . . . . . 1,663
Rawalpindi . . . . . . . . . 1,290
Multan . . . . . . . . . . . . 1,257
Hyderabad . . . . . . . . . 1,107
**Paraguay**
Asunción . . . . . . . . . . . 945
**Peru**
Lima–Callao . . . . . . . . 6,601
Callao . . . . . . . . . . . . . 638
Arequipa . . . . . . . . . . . 620
**Philippines**
Manila . . . . . . . . . . . . 9,280
Quezon City . . . . . . . 1,989
Davao . . . . . . . . . . . . 1,191
Caloocan . . . . . . . . . . 1,023
Cebu . . . . . . . . . . . . . . 662
**Poland**
Warsaw . . . . . . . . . . . 1,638
Lódz . . . . . . . . . . . . . . 825
Kraków . . . . . . . . . . . . 745
Wrocław . . . . . . . . . . . 642
**Portugal**
Lisbon . . . . . . . . . . . . 2,561
Oporto . . . . . . . . . . . 1,174
**Romania**
Bucharest . . . . . . . . . . 2,060
**Russia**
Moscow . . . . . . . . . . 9,233
St Petersburg . . . . . . . 4,883
Nizhniy Novgorod . . . . 1,425
Novosibirsk . . . . . . . . 1,400
Yekaterinburg . . . . . . . 1,300
Samara . . . . . . . . . . . . 1,200
Omsk . . . . . . . . . . . . . 1,200
Chelyabinsk . . . . . . . . 1,100
Kazan . . . . . . . . . . . . . 1,100
Ufa . . . . . . . . . . . . . . . 1,100
Volgograd . . . . . . . . . 1,003
Perm . . . . . . . . . . . . . 1,000
Rostov . . . . . . . . . . . . 1,000
Voronezh . . . . . . . . . . . 908
Saratov . . . . . . . . . . . . 895
Krasnoyarsk . . . . . . . . . 869
Togliatti . . . . . . . . . . . . 689
Simbirsk . . . . . . . . . . . . 678
Izhevsk . . . . . . . . . . . . 654
Krasnodar . . . . . . . . . . 645
Vladivostok . . . . . . . . . 632
Yaroslavl . . . . . . . . . . . . 629
Khabarovsk . . . . . . . . . 618
**Saudi Arabia**
Riyadh . . . . . . . . . . . . 1,800
Jedda . . . . . . . . . . . . . 1,500
Mecca . . . . . . . . . . . . . 630
**Senegal**
Dakar . . . . . . . . . . . . . 1,571
**Singapore**
Singapore . . . . . . . . . 3,104
**Somalia**
Mogadishu . . . . . . . . . 1,000
**South Africa**
Cape Town . . . . . . . . 2,350
East Rand . . . . . . . . . . 1,379
Johannesburg . . . . . . . 1,196
Durban . . . . . . . . . . . . 1,137
Pretoria . . . . . . . . . . . 1,080

West Rand . . . . . . . . . . 870
Port Elizabeth . . . . . . . 853
Vanderbijlpark–
Vereeniging . . . . . . . . 774
**Spain**
Madrid . . . . . . . . . . . . 3,029
Barcelona . . . . . . . . . . 1,614
Valencia . . . . . . . . . . . . 763
Sevilla . . . . . . . . . . . . . . 719
Zaragoza . . . . . . . . . . . 607
**Sri Lanka**
Colombo . . . . . . . . . . 1,863
**Sudan**
Omdurman . . . . . . . . . 1,267
Khartoum . . . . . . . . . . 925
Khartoum North . . . . . 879
**Sweden**
Stockholm . . . . . . . . . 1,744
Göteborg . . . . . . . . . . 775
**Switzerland**
Zürich . . . . . . . . . . . . . 1,175
Bern . . . . . . . . . . . . . . 942
**Syria**
Aleppo . . . . . . . . . . . . 1,591
Damascus . . . . . . . . . . 1,549
Homs . . . . . . . . . . . . . . 644
**Taiwan**
Taipei . . . . . . . . . . . . . 2,653
Kaohsiung . . . . . . . . . . 1,405
Taichung . . . . . . . . . . . . 817
Tainan . . . . . . . . . . . . . 700
**Tanzania**
Dar-es-Salaam . . . . . . . 1,361
**Thailand**
Bangkok . . . . . . . . . . . 5,572
**Togo**
Lomé . . . . . . . . . . . . . . 590
**Tunisia**
Tunis . . . . . . . . . . . . . 1,827
**Turkey**
Istanbul . . . . . . . . . . . . 7,490
Ankara . . . . . . . . . . . . 3,028
Izmir . . . . . . . . . . . . . 2,333
Adana . . . . . . . . . . . . . 1,472
Bursa . . . . . . . . . . . . . 1,317
Konya . . . . . . . . . . . . . 1,040
Gaziantep . . . . . . . . . . . 930
Icel . . . . . . . . . . . . . . . 908
Antalya . . . . . . . . . . . . . 734
Diyarbakir . . . . . . . . . . . 677
Kocaeli . . . . . . . . . . . . . 661
Urfa . . . . . . . . . . . . . . . 649
Kayseri . . . . . . . . . . . . . 648
Manisa . . . . . . . . . . . . . 641
**Uganda**
Kampala . . . . . . . . . . . . 773
**Ukraine**
Kiev . . . . . . . . . . . . . . 2,630
Kharkiv . . . . . . . . . . . . 1,555
Dnipropetrovsk . . . . . 1,147
Donetsk . . . . . . . . . . . 1,088
Odesa . . . . . . . . . . . . . 1,046
Zaporizhzhya . . . . . . . . 887
Lviv . . . . . . . . . . . . . . . 802
Kryvyy Rih . . . . . . . . . . 720
**United Kingdom**
London . . . . . . . . . . . 8,089
Birmingham . . . . . . . . 2,373
Manchester . . . . . . . . 2,353
Liverpool . . . . . . . . . . . 852
Glasgow . . . . . . . . . . . . 832

Sheffield . . . . . . . . . . . . 661
Nottingham . . . . . . . . . 649
Newcastle . . . . . . . . . . 617
**United States**
New York . . . . . . . . . 16,329
Los Angeles . . . . . . . 12,410
Chicago . . . . . . . . . . . 7,668
Philadelphia . . . . . . . . 4,949
Washington, DC . . . . . 4,466
Detroit . . . . . . . . . . . . 4,307
Houston . . . . . . . . . . . 3,653
Atlanta . . . . . . . . . . . . 3,331
Boston . . . . . . . . . . . . 3,240
Dallas . . . . . . . . . . . . . 2,898
Minneapolis–St Paul . . . 2,688
San Diego . . . . . . . . . . 2,632
St Louis . . . . . . . . . . . . 2,536
Phoenix . . . . . . . . . . . 2,473
Baltimore . . . . . . . . . . 2,458
Pittsburgh . . . . . . . . . . 2,402
Cleveland . . . . . . . . . . 2,222
San Francisco . . . . . . . 2,182
Seattle . . . . . . . . . . . . 2,180
Tampa . . . . . . . . . . . . . 2,157
Miami . . . . . . . . . . . . . 2,025
Newark . . . . . . . . . . . 1,934
Denver . . . . . . . . . . . . 1,796
Portland (Or.) . . . . . . . 1,676
Kansas City (Mo.) . . . . 1,647
Cincinnati . . . . . . . . . . 1,581
San Jose . . . . . . . . . . . 1,557
Norfolk . . . . . . . . . . . . 1,529
Indianapolis . . . . . . . . . 1,462
Milwaukee . . . . . . . . . 1,456
Sacramento . . . . . . . . 1,441
San Antonio . . . . . . . . 1,437
Columbus (Oh.) . . . . . . 1,423
New Orleans . . . . . . . 1,309
Charlotte . . . . . . . . . . 1,260
Buffalo . . . . . . . . . . . . 1,189
Salt Lake City . . . . . . . 1,178
Hartford . . . . . . . . . . . 1,151
Oklahoma . . . . . . . . . . 1,007
Jacksonville (Fl.) . . . . . . 665
Omaha . . . . . . . . . . . . . 663
Memphis . . . . . . . . . . . 614
**Uruguay**
Montevideo . . . . . . . . 1,378
**Uzbekistan**
Tashkent . . . . . . . . . . . 2,107
**Venezuela**
Caracas . . . . . . . . . . . . 2,784
Maracaibo . . . . . . . . . . 1,364
Valencia . . . . . . . . . . . 1,032
Maracay . . . . . . . . . . . . 800
Barquisimeto . . . . . . . . 745
**Vietnam**
Ho Chi Minh City . . . . 4,322
Hanoi . . . . . . . . . . . . . 3,056
Haiphong . . . . . . . . . . . 783
**Yemen**
Sana . . . . . . . . . . . . . . . 972
**Yugoslavia**
Belgrade . . . . . . . . . . . 1,137
**Zambia**
Lusaka . . . . . . . . . . . . . 982
**Zimbabwe**
Harare . . . . . . . . . . . . 1,189
Bulawayo . . . . . . . . . . . 622

\* SAR = Special Administrative Region of China

xi

# WORLD STATISTICS – PHYSICAL

Under each subject heading, the statistics are listed by continent. The figures are in size order beginning with the largest, longest or deepest, and are rounded as appropriate. Both metric and imperial measurements are given. The lists are complete down to the > mark; below this mark they are selective.

## Land and Water

| | km² | miles² | % |
|---|---|---|---|
| The World | 509,450,000 | 196,672,000 | – |
| Land | 149,450,000 | 57,688,000 | 29.3 |
| Water | 360,000,000 | 138,984,000 | 70.7 |
| | | | |
| Asia | 44,500,000 | 17,177,000 | 29.8 |
| Africa | 30,302,000 | 11,697,000 | 20.3 |
| North America | 24,241,000 | 9,357,000 | 16.2 |
| South America | 17,793,000 | 6,868,000 | 11.9 |
| Antarctica | 14,100,000 | 5,443,000 | 9.4 |
| Europe | 9,957,000 | 3,843,000 | 6.7 |
| Australia & Oceania | 8,557,000 | 3,303,000 | 5.7 |
| | | | |
| Pacific Ocean | 179,679,000 | 69,356,000 | 49.9 |
| Atlantic Ocean | 92,373,000 | 35,657,000 | 25.7 |
| Indian Ocean | 73,917,000 | 28,532,000 | 20.5 |
| Arctic Ocean | 14,090,000 | 5,439,000 | 3.9 |

## Seas

| Pacific Ocean | km² | miles² |
|---|---|---|
| South China Sea | 2,974,600 | 1,148,500 |
| Bering Sea | 2,268,000 | 875,000 |
| Sea of Okhotsk | 1,528,000 | 590,000 |
| East China & Yellow | 1,249,000 | 482,000 |
| Sea of Japan | 1,008,000 | 389,000 |
| Gulf of California | 162,000 | 62,500 |
| Bass Strait | 75,000 | 29,000 |

| Atlantic Ocean | km² | miles² |
|---|---|---|
| Caribbean Sea | 2,766,000 | 1,068,000 |
| Mediterranean Sea | 2,516,000 | 971,000 |
| Gulf of Mexico | 1,543,000 | 596,000 |
| Hudson Bay | 1,232,000 | 476,000 |
| North Sea | 575,000 | 223,000 |
| Black Sea | 462,000 | 178,000 |
| Baltic Sea | 422,170 | 163,000 |
| Gulf of St Lawrence | 238,000 | 92,000 |

| Indian Ocean | km² | miles² |
|---|---|---|
| Red Sea | 438,000 | 169,000 |
| The Gulf | 239,000 | 92,000 |

## Mountains

| Europe | | m | ft |
|---|---|---|---|
| Elbrus | Russia | 5,642 | 18,510 |
| Mont Blanc | France/Italy | 4,807 | 15,771 |
| Monte Rosa | Italy/Switzerland | 4,634 | 15,203 |
| Dom | Switzerland | 4,545 | 14,911 |
| Liskamm | Switzerland | 4,527 | 14,852 |
| Weisshorn | Switzerland | 4,505 | 14,780 |
| Taschorn | Switzerland | 4,490 | 14,730 |
| Matterhorn/Cervino | Italy/Switzerland | 4,478 | 14,691 |
| Mont Maudit | France/Italy | 4,465 | 14,649 |
| Dent Blanche | Switzerland | 4,356 | 14,291 |
| >Nadelhorn | Switzerland | 4,327 | 14,196 |
| Grandes Jorasses | France/Italy | 4,208 | 13,806 |
| Jungfrau | Switzerland | 4,158 | 13,642 |
| Barre des Ecrins | France | 4,103 | 13,461 |
| Gran Paradiso | Italy | 4,061 | 13,323 |
| Piz Bernina | Italy/Switzerland | 4,049 | 13,284 |

| Europe (cont.) | | m | ft |
|---|---|---|---|
| Eiger | Switzerland | 3,970 | 13,025 |
| Monte Viso | Italy | 3,841 | 12,602 |
| Grossglockner | Austria | 3,797 | 12,457 |
| Wildspitze | Austria | 3,772 | 12,382 |
| Monte Disgrazia | Italy | 3,678 | 12,066 |
| Mulhacén | Spain | 3,478 | 11,411 |
| Pico de Aneto | Spain | 3,404 | 11,168 |
| Marmolada | Italy | 3,342 | 10,964 |
| Etna | Italy | 3,340 | 10,958 |
| Zugspitze | Germany | 2,962 | 9,718 |
| Musala | Bulgaria | 2,925 | 9,596 |
| Olympus | Greece | 2,917 | 9,570 |
| Triglav | Slovenia | 2,863 | 9,393 |
| Monte Cinto | France (Corsica) | 2,710 | 8,891 |
| Gerlachovka | Slovak Republic | 2,655 | 8,711 |
| Torre de Cerredo | Spain | 2,648 | 8,688 |
| Galdhöpiggen | Norway | 2,468 | 8,100 |
| Hvannadalshnúkur | Iceland | 2,119 | 6,952 |
| Kebnekaise | Sweden | 2,117 | 6,946 |
| Ben Nevis | UK | 1,343 | 4,406 |

| Asia | | m | ft |
|---|---|---|---|
| Everest | China/Nepal | 8,850 | 29,035 |
| K2 (Godwin Austen) | China/Kashmir | 8,611 | 28,251 |
| Kanchenjunga | India/Nepal | 8,598 | 28,208 |
| Lhotse | China/Nepal | 8,516 | 27,939 |
| Makalu | China/Nepal | 8,481 | 27,824 |
| Cho Oyu | China/Nepal | 8,201 | 26,906 |
| Dhaulagiri | Nepal | 8,172 | 26,811 |
| Manaslu | Nepal | 8,156 | 26,758 |
| Nanga Parbat | Kashmir | 8,126 | 26,660 |
| Annapurna | Nepal | 8,078 | 26,502 |
| Gasherbrum | China/Kashmir | 8,068 | 26,469 |
| Broad Peak | China/Kashmir | 8,051 | 26,414 |
| Xixabangma | China | 8,012 | 26,286 |
| Kangbachen | India/Nepal | 7,902 | 25,925 |
| Jannu | India/Nepal | 7,902 | 25,925 |
| Gayachung Kang | Nepal | 7,897 | 25,909 |
| Himalchuli | Nepal | 7,893 | 25,896 |
| Disteghil Sar | Kashmir | 7,885 | 25,869 |
| Nuptse | Nepal | 7,879 | 25,849 |
| Khunyang Chhish | Kashmir | 7,852 | 25,761 |
| Masherbrum | Kashmir | 7,821 | 25,659 |
| Nanda Devi | India | 7,817 | 25,646 |
| Rakaposhi | Kashmir | 7,788 | 25,551 |
| Batura | Kashmir | 7,785 | 25,541 |
| Namche Barwa | China | 7,756 | 25,446 |
| Kamet | India | 7,756 | 25,446 |
| Soltoro Kangri | Kashmir | 7,742 | 25,400 |
| Gurla Mandhata | China | 7,728 | 25,354 |
| >Trivor | Pakistan | 7,720 | 25,328 |
| Kongur Shan | China | 7,719 | 25,324 |
| Tirich Mir | Pakistan | 7,690 | 25,229 |
| K'ula Shan | Bhutan/China | 7,543 | 24,747 |
| Pik Kommunizma | Tajikistan | 7,495 | 24,590 |
| Demavend | Iran | 5,604 | 18,386 |
| Ararat | Turkey | 5,165 | 16,945 |
| Gunong Kinabalu | Malaysia (Borneo) | 4,101 | 13,455 |
| Yu Shan | Taiwan | 3,997 | 13,113 |
| Fuji-San | Japan | 3,776 | 12,388 |

| Africa | | m | ft |
|---|---|---|---|
| Kilimanjaro | Tanzania | 5,895 | 19,340 |
| Mt Kenya | Kenya | 5,199 | 17,057 |
| Ruwenzori | Uganda/Congo (D. Rep.) | 5,109 | 16,762 |
| Ras Dashan | Ethiopia | 4,620 | 15,157 |

| Africa (cont.) | | m | ft |
|---|---|---|---|
| Meru | Tanzania | 4,565 | 14,977 |
| Karisimbi | Rwanda/Congo (D. Rep.) | 4,507 | 14,787 |
| Mt Elgon | Kenya/Uganda | 4,321 | 14,176 |
| Batu | Ethiopia | 4,307 | 14,130 |
| Guna | Ethiopia | 4,231 | 13,882 |
| Toubkal | Morocco | 4,165 | 13,665 |
| Irhil Mgoun | Morocco | 4,071 | 13,356 |
| Mt Cameroon | Cameroon | 4,070 | 13,353 |
| Amba Ferit | Ethiopia | 3,875 | 13,042 |
| Pico del Teide | Spain (Tenerife) | 3,718 | 12,198 |
| Thabana Ntlenyana | Lesotho | 3,482 | 11,424 |
| Emi Koussi | Chad | 3,415 | 11,204 |
| Mt aux Sources | Lesotho/South Africa | 3,282 | 10,768 |
| Mt Piton | Réunion | 3,069 | 10,069 |

| Oceania | | m | ft |
|---|---|---|---|
| Puncak Jaya | Indonesia | 5,029 | 16,499 |
| Puncak Trikora | Indonesia | 4,750 | 15,584 |
| Puncak Mandala | Indonesia | 4,702 | 15,427 |
| Mt Wilhelm | Papua New Guinea | 4,508 | 14,790 |
| Mauna Kea | USA (Hawaii) | 4,205 | 13,796 |
| Mauna Loa | USA (Hawaii) | 4,169 | 13,681 |
| Mt Cook (Aoraki) | New Zealand | 3,753 | 12,313 |
| Mt Balbi | Solomon Is. | 2,439 | 8,002 |
| Orohena | Tahiti | 2,241 | 7,352 |
| Mt Kosciuszko | Australia | 2,237 | 7,339 |

| North America | | m | ft |
|---|---|---|---|
| Mt McKinley (Denali) | USA (Alaska) | 6,194 | 20,321 |
| Pierre Elliott Trudeau | Canada | 5,959 | 19,551 |
| Citlaltepetl | Mexico | 5,700 | 18,701 |
| Mt St Elias | USA/Canada | 5,489 | 18,008 |
| Popocatepetl | Mexico | 5,452 | 17,887 |
| Mt Foraker | USA (Alaska) | 5,304 | 17,401 |
| Ixtaccihuatl | Mexico | 5,286 | 17,342 |
| Lucania | Canada | 5,227 | 17,149 |
| Mt Steele | Canada | 5,073 | 16,644 |
| Mt Bona | USA (Alaska) | 5,005 | 16,420 |
| Mt Blackburn | USA (Alaska) | 4,996 | 16,391 |
| Mt Sanford | USA (Alaska) | 4,940 | 16,207 |
| Mt Wood | Canada | 4,848 | 15,905 |
| Nevado de Toluca | Mexico | 4,670 | 15,321 |
| Mt Fairweather | USA (Alaska) | 4,663 | 15,298 |
| Mt Hunter | USA (Alaska) | 4,442 | 14,573 |
| Mt Whitney | USA | 4,418 | 14,495 |
| Mt Elbert | USA | 4,399 | 14,432 |
| Mt Harvard | USA | 4,395 | 14,419 |
| Mt Rainier | USA | 4,392 | 14,409 |
| Blanca Peak | USA | 4,372 | 14,344 |
| Longs Peak | USA | 4,345 | 14,255 |
| Tajumulco | Guatemala | 4,220 | 13,845 |
| Grand Teton | USA | 4,197 | 13,770 |
| Mt Waddington | Canada | 3,994 | 13,104 |
| Mt Robson | Canada | 3,954 | 12,972 |
| Chirripó Grande | Costa Rica | 3,837 | 12,589 |
| Mt Assiniboine | Canada | 3,619 | 11,873 |
| Pico Duarte | Dominican Rep. | 3,175 | 10,417 |

| South America | | m | ft |
|---|---|---|---|
| Aconcagua | Argentina | 6,960 | 22,834 |
| Bonete | Argentina | 6,872 | 22,546 |
| Ojos del Salado | Argentina/Chile | 6,863 | 22,516 |
| Pissis | Argentina | 6,779 | 22,241 |
| Mercedario | Argentina/Chile | 6,770 | 22,211 |
| Huascaran | Peru | 6,768 | 22,204 |
| Llullaillaco | Argentina/Chile | 6,723 | 22,057 |
| Nudo de Cachi | Argentina | 6,720 | 22,047 |
| Yerupaja | Peru | 6,632 | 21,758 |
| N. de Tres Cruces | Argentina/Chile | 6,620 | 21,719 |
| Incahuasi | Argentina/Chile | 6,601 | 21,654 |
| Cerro Galan | Argentina | 6,600 | 21,654 |
| Tupungato | Argentina/Chile | 6,570 | 21,555 |

| South America (cont.) | | m | ft |
|---|---|---|---|
| Sajama | Bolivia | 6,542 | 21,463 |
| Illimani | Bolivia | 6,485 | 21,276 |
| Coropuna | Peru | 6,425 | 21,079 |
| Ausangate | Peru | 6,384 | 20,945 |
| Cerro del Toro | Argentina | 6,380 | 20,932 |
| Siula Grande | Peru | 6,356 | 20,853 |
| Chimborazo | Ecuador | 6,267 | 20,561 |
| Cotapaxi | Ecuador | 5,896 | 19,344 |
| Pico Colon | Colombia | 5,800 | 19,029 |
| Pico Bolivar | Venezuela | 5,007 | 16,427 |

| Antarctica | m | ft |
|---|---|---|
| Vinson Massif | 4,897 | 16,066 |
| Mt Kirkpatrick | 4,528 | 14,855 |
| Mt Markham | 4,349 | 14,268 |

## Ocean Depths

| Atlantic Ocean | m | ft |
|---|---|---|
| Puerto Rico (Milwaukee) Deep | 9,220 | 30,249 |
| Cayman Trench | 7,680 | 25,197 |
| Gulf of Mexico | 5,203 | 17,070 |
| Mediterranean Sea | 5,121 | 16,801 |
| Black Sea | 2,211 | 7,254 |
| North Sea | 660 | 2,165 |
| Baltic Sea | 463 | 1,519 |

| Indian Ocean | m | ft |
|---|---|---|
| Java Trench | 7,450 | 24,442 |
| Red Sea | 2,635 | 8,454 |
| Persian Gulf | 73 | 239 |

| Pacific Ocean | m | ft |
|---|---|---|
| Mariana Trench | 11,022 | 36,161 |
| Tonga Trench | 10,882 | 35,702 |
| Japan Trench | 10,554 | 34,626 |
| Kuril Trench | 10,542 | 34,587 |
| Mindanao Trench | 10,497 | 34,439 |
| Kermadec Trench | 10,047 | 32,962 |
| New Guinea Trench | 9,140 | 29,987 |
| Peru–Chile Trench | 8,050 | 26,410 |

| Arctic Ocean | m | ft |
|---|---|---|
| Molloy Deep | 5,608 | 18,399 |

## Land Lows

| | | m | ft |
|---|---|---|---|
| Dead Sea | Asia | −411 | −1,348 |
| Lake Assal | Africa | −156 | −512 |
| Death Valley | North America | −86 | −282 |
| Valdés Peninsula | South America | −40 | −131 |
| Caspian Sea | Europe | −28 | −92 |
| Lake Eyre North | Oceania | −16 | −52 |

## Rivers

| Europe | | km | miles |
|---|---|---|---|
| Volga | Caspian Sea | 3,700 | 2,300 |
| Danube | Black Sea | 2,850 | 1,770 |
| Ural | Caspian Sea | 2,535 | 1,575 |
| Dnepr (Dnipro) | Black Sea | 2,285 | 1,420 |
| Kama | Volga | 2,030 | 1,260 |
| Don | Black Sea | 1,990 | 1,240 |
| Petchora | Arctic Ocean | 1,790 | 1,110 |
| Oka | Volga | 1,480 | 920 |
| Belaya | Kama | 1,420 | 880 |

| Europe (cont.) | | km | miles |
|---|---|---|---|
| Dnister (Dniester) | Black Sea | 1,400 | 870 |
| Vyatka | Kama | 1,370 | 850 |
| Rhine | North Sea | 1,320 | 820 |
| North Dvina | Arctic Ocean | 1,290 | 800 |
| Desna | Dnepr (Dnipro) | 1,190 | 740 |
| Elbe | North Sea | 1,145 | 710 |
| Wisla | Baltic Sea | 1,090 | 675 |
| Loire | Atlantic Ocean | 1,020 | 635 |
| West Dvina | Baltic Sea | 1,019 | 633 |

| Asia | | km | miles |
|---|---|---|---|
| Yangtze | Pacific Ocean | 6,380 | 3,960 |
| Yenisey–Angara | Arctic Ocean | 5,550 | 3,445 |
| Huang He | Pacific Ocean | 5,464 | 3,395 |
| Ob–Irtysh | Arctic Ocean | 5,410 | 3,360 |
| Mekong | Pacific Ocean | 4,500 | 2,795 |
| Amur | Pacific Ocean | 4,400 | 2,730 |
| Lena | Arctic Ocean | 4,400 | 2,730 |
| Irtysh | Ob | 4,250 | 2,640 |
| Yenisey | Arctic Ocean | 4,090 | 2,540 |
| Ob | Arctic Ocean | 3,680 | 2,285 |
| Indus | Indian Ocean | 3,100 | 1,925 |
| Brahmaputra | Indian Ocean | 2,900 | 1,800 |
| Syrdarya | Aral Sea | 2,860 | 1,775 |
| Salween | Indian Ocean | 2,800 | 1,740 |
| Euphrates | Indian Ocean | 2,700 | 1,675 |
| Vilyuy | Lena | 2,650 | 1,645 |
| Kolyma | Arctic Ocean | 2,600 | 1,615 |
| Amudarya | Aral Sea | 2,540 | 1,575 |
| Ural | Caspian Sea | 2,535 | 1,575 |
| Ganges | Indian Ocean | 2,510 | 1,560 |
| Si Kiang | Pacific Ocean | 2,100 | 1,305 |
| Irrawaddy | Indian Ocean | 2,010 | 1,250 |
| Tarim–Yarkand | Lop Nor | 2,000 | 1,240 |
| Tigris | Indian Ocean | 1,900 | 1,180 |
| Angara | Yenisey | 1,830 | 1,135 |
| Godavari | Indian Ocean | 1,470 | 915 |
| Sutlej | Indian Ocean | 1,450 | 900 |
| Yamuna | Indian Ocean | 1,400 | 870 |

| Africa | | km | miles |
|---|---|---|---|
| Nile | Mediterranean | 6,670 | 4,140 |
| Congo | Atlantic Ocean | 4,670 | 2,900 |
| Niger | Atlantic Ocean | 4,180 | 2,595 |
| Zambezi | Indian Ocean | 3,540 | 2,200 |
| Oubangi/Uele | Congo (Dem. Rep.) | 2,250 | 1,400 |
| Kasai | Congo (Dem. Rep.) | 1,950 | 1,210 |
| Shaballe | Indian Ocean | 1,930 | 1,200 |
| Orange | Atlantic Ocean | 1,860 | 1,155 |
| Cubango | Okavango Swamps | 1,800 | 1,120 |
| Limpopo | Indian Ocean | 1,600 | 995 |
| Senegal | Atlantic Ocean | 1,600 | 995 |
| Volta | Atlantic Ocean | 1,500 | 930 |
| Benue | Niger | 1,350 | 840 |

| Australia | | km | miles |
|---|---|---|---|
| Murray–Darling | Indian Ocean | 3,750 | 2,330 |
| Darling | Murray | 3,070 | 1,905 |
| Murray | Indian Ocean | 2,575 | 1,600 |
| Murrumbidgee | Murray | 1,690 | 1,050 |

| North America | | km | miles |
|---|---|---|---|
| Mississippi–Missouri | Gulf of Mexico | 6,020 | 3,740 |
| Mackenzie | Arctic Ocean | 4,240 | 2,630 |
| Mississippi | Gulf of Mexico | 3,780 | 2,350 |
| Missouri | Mississippi | 3,780 | 2,350 |
| Yukon | Pacific Ocean | 3,185 | 1,980 |
| Rio Grande | Gulf of Mexico | 3,030 | 1,880 |
| Arkansas | Mississippi | 2,340 | 1,450 |
| Colorado | Pacific Ocean | 2,330 | 1,445 |
| Red | Mississippi | 2,040 | 1,270 |

| North America (cont.) | | km | miles |
|---|---|---|---|
| Saskatchewan | Lake Winnipeg | 1,940 | 1,205 |
| Snake | Columbia | 1,670 | 1,040 |
| Churchill | Hudson Bay | 1,600 | 990 |
| Ohio | Mississippi | 1,580 | 980 |
| Brazos | Gulf of Mexico | 1,400 | 870 |
| St Lawrence | Atlantic Ocean | 1,170 | 730 |

| South America | | km | miles |
|---|---|---|---|
| Amazon | Atlantic Ocean | 6,450 | 4,010 |
| Paraná–Plate | Atlantic Ocean | 4,500 | 2,800 |
| Purus | Amazon | 3,350 | 2,080 |
| Madeira | Amazon | 3,200 | 1,990 |
| São Francisco | Atlantic Ocean | 2,900 | 1,800 |
| Paraná | Plate | 2,800 | 1,740 |
| Tocantins | Atlantic Ocean | 2,750 | 1,710 |
| Paraguay | Paraná | 2,550 | 1,580 |
| Orinoco | Atlantic Ocean | 2,500 | 1,550 |
| Pilcomayo | Paraná | 2,500 | 1,550 |
| Araguaia | Tocantins | 2,250 | 1,400 |
| Juruá | Amazon | 2,000 | 1,240 |
| Xingu | Amazon | 1,980 | 1,230 |
| Ucayali | Amazon | 1,900 | 1,180 |
| Marañón | Amazon | 1,600 | 990 |
| Uruguay | Plate | 1,600 | 990 |
| Magdalena | Caribbean Sea | 1,540 | 960 |

## Lakes

| Europe | | km² | miles² |
|---|---|---|---|
| Lake Ladoga | Russia | 17,700 | 6,800 |
| Lake Onega | Russia | 9,700 | 3,700 |
| Saimaa system | Finland | 8,000 | 3,100 |
| Vänern | Sweden | 5,500 | 2,100 |
| Rybinskoye Reservoir | Russia | 4,700 | 1,800 |

| Asia | | km² | miles² |
|---|---|---|---|
| Caspian Sea | Asia | 371,800 | 143,550 |
| Lake Baykal | Russia | 30,500 | 11,780 |
| Aral Sea | Kazak./Uzbek. | 28,687 | 11,086 |
| Tonlé Sap | Cambodia | 20,000 | 7,700 |
| Lake Balqash | Kazakstan | 18,500 | 7,100 |
| Lake Dongting | China | 12,000 | 4,600 |
| Lake Ysyk | Kyrgyzstan | 6,200 | 2,400 |
| Lake Orumiyeh | Iran | 5,900 | 2,300 |
| Lake Koko | China | 5,700 | 2,200 |
| Lake Poyang | China | 5,000 | 1,900 |
| Lake Khanka | China/Russia | 4,400 | 1,700 |
| Lake Van | Turkey | 3,500 | 1,400 |
| Lake Ubsa | China | 3,400 | 1,300 |

| Africa | | km² | miles² |
|---|---|---|---|
| Lake Victoria | East Africa | 68,000 | 26,000 |
| Lake Tanganyika | Central Africa | 33,000 | 13,000 |
| Lake Malawi/Nyasa | East Africa | 29,600 | 11,430 |
| Lake Chad | Central Africa | 25,000 | 9,700 |
| Lake Turkana | Ethiopia/Kenya | 8,500 | 3,300 |
| Lake Volta | Ghana | 8,500 | 3,300 |
| Lake Bangweulu | Zambia | 8,000 | 3,100 |
| Lake Rukwa | Tanzania | 7,000 | 2,700 |
| Lake Mai-Ndombe | Congo (D. Rep.) | 6,500 | 2,500 |
| Lake Kariba | Zambia/Zimbabwe | 5,300 | 2,000 |
| Lake Mobutu | Uganda/Congo (D. Rep.) | 5,300 | 2,000 |
| Lake Nasser | Egypt/Sudan | 5,200 | 2,000 |
| Lake Mweru | Zambia/Congo (D. Rep.) | 4,900 | 1,900 |
| Lake Cabora Bassa | Mozambique | 4,500 | 1,700 |
| Lake Kyoga | Uganda | 4,400 | 1,700 |
| Lake Tana | Ethiopia | 3,630 | 1,400 |
| Lake Kivu | Rwanda/Congo (D. Rep.) | 2,650 | 1,000 |
| Lake Edward | Uganda/Congo (D. Rep.) | 2,200 | 850 |

| Australia | | km² | miles² |
|---|---|---|---|
| Lake Eyre | Australia | 8,900 | 3,400 |
| Lake Torrens | Australia | 5,800 | 2,200 |
| Lake Gairdner | Australia | 4,800 | 1,900 |

| North America | | km² | miles² |
|---|---|---|---|
| Lake Superior | Canada/USA | 82,350 | 31,800 |
| Lake Huron | Canada/USA | 59,600 | 23,010 |
| Lake Michigan | USA | 58,000 | 22,400 |
| Great Bear Lake | Canada | 31,800 | 12,280 |
| Great Slave Lake | Canada | 28,500 | 11,000 |
| Lake Erie | Canada/USA | 25,700 | 9,900 |
| Lake Winnipeg | Canada | 24,400 | 9,400 |
| Lake Ontario | Canada/USA | 19,500 | 7,500 |
| Lake Nicaragua | Nicaragua | 8,200 | 3,200 |
| Lake Athabasca | Canada | 8,100 | 3,100 |
| Smallwood Reservoir | Canada | 6,530 | 2,520 |
| Reindeer Lake | Canada | 6,400 | 2,500 |
| Nettilling Lake | Canada | 5,500 | 2,100 |
| Lake Winnipegosis | Canada | 5,400 | 2,100 |
| Lake Nipigon | Canada | 4,850 | 1,900 |
| Lake Manitoba | Canada | 4,700 | 1,800 |

| South America | | km² | miles² |
|---|---|---|---|
| Lake Titicaca | Bolivia/Peru | 8,300 | 3,200 |
| Lake Poopo | Peru | 2,800 | 1,100 |

# Islands

| Europe | | km² | miles² |
|---|---|---|---|
| Great Britain | UK | 229,880 | 88,700 |
| Iceland | Atlantic Ocean | 103,000 | 39,800 |
| Ireland | Ireland/UK | 84,400 | 32,600 |
| Novaya Zemlya (North) | Russia | 48,200 | 18,600 |
| West Spitzbergen | Norway | 39,000 | 15,100 |
| Novaya Zemlya (South) | Russia | 33,200 | 12,800 |
| Sicily | Italy | 25,500 | 9,800 |
| Sardinia | Italy | 24,000 | 9,300 |
| North-east Spitzbergen | Norway | 15,000 | 5,600 |
| Corsica | France | 8,700 | 3,400 |
| Crete | Greece | 8,350 | 3,200 |
| Zealand | Denmark | 6,850 | 2,600 |

| Asia | | km² | miles² |
|---|---|---|---|
| Borneo | South-east Asia | 744,360 | 287,400 |
| Sumatra | Indonesia | 473,600 | 182,860 |
| Honshu | Japan | 230,500 | 88,980 |
| Sulawesi (Celebes) | Indonesia | 189,000 | 73,000 |
| Java | Indonesia | 126,700 | 48,900 |
| Luzon | Philippines | 104,700 | 40,400 |
| Mindanao | Philippines | 101,500 | 39,200 |
| Hokkaido | Japan | 78,400 | 30,300 |
| Sakhalin | Russia | 74,060 | 28,600 |
| Sri Lanka | Indian Ocean | 65,600 | 25,300 |
| Taiwan | Pacific Ocean | 36,000 | 13,900 |
| Kyushu | Japan | 35,700 | 13,800 |
| Hainan | China | 34,000 | 13,100 |
| Timor | Indonesia | 33,600 | 13,000 |
| Shikoku | Japan | 18,800 | 7,300 |
| Halmahera | Indonesia | 18,000 | 6,900 |
| Ceram | Indonesia | 17,150 | 6,600 |
| Sumbawa | Indonesia | 15,450 | 6,000 |
| Flores | Indonesia | 15,200 | 5,900 |
| Samar | Philippines | 13,100 | 5,100 |
| Negros | Philippines | 12,700 | 4,900 |
| Bangka | Indonesia | 12,000 | 4,600 |
| Palawan | Philippines | 12,000 | 4,600 |
| Panay | Philippines | 11,500 | 4,400 |
| Sumba | Indonesia | 11,100 | 4,300 |
| Mindoro | Philippines | 9,750 | 3,800 |

| Asia (cont.) | | km² | miles² |
|---|---|---|---|
| Buru | Indonesia | 9,500 | 3,700 |
| Bali | Indonesia | 5,600 | 2,200 |
| Cyprus | Mediterranean | 3,570 | 1,400 |

| Africa | | km² | miles² |
|---|---|---|---|
| Madagascar | Indian Ocean | 587,040 | 226,660 |
| Socotra | Indian Ocean | 3,600 | 1,400 |
| Réunion | Indian Ocean | 2,500 | 965 |
| Tenerife | Atlantic Ocean | 2,350 | 900 |
| Mauritius | Indian Ocean | 1,865 | 720 |

| Oceania | | km² | miles² |
|---|---|---|---|
| New Guinea | Indon./Papua NG | 821,030 | 317,000 |
| New Zealand (South) | New Zealand | 150,500 | 58,100 |
| New Zealand (North) | New Zealand | 114,700 | 44,300 |
| Tasmania | Australia | 67,800 | 26,200 |
| New Britain | Papua NG | 37,800 | 14,600 |
| New Caledonia | Pacific Ocean | 19,100 | 7,400 |
| Viti Levu | Fiji | 10,500 | 4,100 |
| Hawaii | Pacific Ocean | 10,450 | 4,000 |
| Bougainville | Papua NG | 9,600 | 3,700 |
| Guadalcanal | Solomon Is. | 6,500 | 2,500 |
| Vanua Levu | Fiji | 5,550 | 2,100 |
| New Ireland | Papua NG | 3,200 | 1,200 |

| North America | | km² | miles² |
|---|---|---|---|
| Greenland | Atlantic Ocean | 2,175,600 | 839,800 |
| Baffin Is. | Canada | 508,000 | 196,100 |
| Victoria Is. | Canada | 212,200 | 81,900 |
| Ellesmere Is. | Canada | 212,000 | 81,800 |
| Cuba | Cuba | 110,860 | 42,800 |
| Newfoundland | Canada | 110,680 | 42,700 |
| Hispaniola | Atlantic Ocean | 76,200 | 29,400 |
| Banks Is. | Canada | 67,000 | 25,900 |
| Devon Is. | Canada | 54,500 | 21,000 |
| Melville Is. | Canada | 42,400 | 16,400 |
| Vancouver Is. | Canada | 32,150 | 12,400 |
| Somerset Is. | Canada | 24,300 | 9,400 |
| Jamaica | Caribbean Sea | 11,400 | 4,400 |
| Puerto Rico | Atlantic Ocean | 8,900 | 3,400 |
| Cape Breton Is. | Canada | 4,000 | 1,500 |

| South America | | km² | miles² |
|---|---|---|---|
| Tierra del Fuego | Argentina/Chile | 47,000 | 18,100 |
| Falkland Is. (East) | Atlantic Ocean | 6,800 | 2,600 |
| South Georgia | Atlantic Ocean | 4,200 | 1,600 |
| Galapagos (Isabela) | Pacific Ocean | 2,250 | 870 |

# WORLD STATISTICS – CLIMATE

For each city, the top row of figures shows total rainfall in millimetres; the bottom row shows the average temperature in ° Celsius or centigrade. The total annual rainfall and average annual temperature are given at the end of the rows.

| | Jan. | Feb. | Mar. | Apr. | May | June | July | Aug. | Sept. | Oct. | Nov. | Dec. | Total |
|---|---|---|---|---|---|---|---|---|---|---|---|---|---|
| **Europe** | | | | | | | | | | | | | |
| Berlin, Germany | 46 | 40 | 33 | 42 | 49 | 65 | 73 | 69 | 68 | 49 | 46 | 43 | 603 |
| Altitude 55 metres | 1 | 0 | 4 | 9 | 14 | 17 | 19 | 18 | 15 | 9 | 5 | 1 | 9 |
| London, UK | 54 | 40 | 37 | 37 | 46 | 45 | 57 | 59 | 49 | 57 | 64 | 48 | 593 |
| 5 m | 4 | 5 | 7 | 9 | 12 | 16 | 18 | 17 | 15 | 11 | 8 | 5 | 11 |
| Málaga, Spain | 61 | 51 | 62 | 46 | 26 | 5 | 1 | 3 | 29 | 64 | 64 | 62 | 474 |
| 33 m | 12 | 13 | 16 | 17 | 19 | 29 | 25 | 26 | 23 | 20 | 16 | 13 | 18 |
| Moscow, Russia | 39 | 38 | 36 | 37 | 53 | 58 | 88 | 71 | 58 | 45 | 47 | 54 | 624 |
| 156 m | -13 | -10 | -4 | 6 | 13 | 16 | 18 | 17 | 12 | 6 | -1 | -7 | 4 |
| Paris, France | 56 | 46 | 35 | 42 | 57 | 54 | 59 | 64 | 55 | 50 | 51 | 50 | 619 |
| 75 m | 3 | 4 | 8 | 11 | 15 | 18 | 20 | 19 | 17 | 12 | 7 | 4 | 12 |
| Rome, Italy | 71 | 62 | 57 | 51 | 46 | 37 | 15 | 21 | 63 | 99 | 129 | 93 | 744 |
| 17 m | 8 | 9 | 11 | 14 | 18 | 22 | 25 | 25 | 22 | 17 | 13 | 10 | 16 |
| **Asia** | | | | | | | | | | | | | |
| Bangkok, Thailand | 8 | 20 | 36 | 58 | 198 | 160 | 160 | 175 | 305 | 206 | 66 | 5 | 1,397 |
| 2 m | 26 | 28 | 29 | 30 | 29 | 29 | 28 | 28 | 28 | 28 | 26 | 25 | 28 |
| Bombay (Mumbai), India | 3 | 3 | 3 | <3 | 18 | 485 | 617 | 340 | 264 | 64 | 13 | 3 | 1,809 |
| 11 m | 24 | 24 | 26 | 28 | 30 | 29 | 27 | 27 | 27 | 28 | 27 | 26 | 27 |
| Ho Chi Minh, Vietnam | 15 | 3 | 13 | 43 | 221 | 330 | 315 | 269 | 335 | 269 | 114 | 56 | 1,984 |
| 9 m | 26 | 27 | 29 | 30 | 29 | 28 | 28 | 28 | 27 | 27 | 27 | 26 | 28 |
| Hong Kong, China | 33 | 46 | 74 | 137 | 292 | 394 | 381 | 361 | 257 | 114 | 43 | 31 | 2,162 |
| 33 m | 16 | 15 | 18 | 22 | 26 | 28 | 28 | 28 | 27 | 25 | 21 | 18 | 23 |
| Tokyo, Japan | 48 | 74 | 107 | 135 | 147 | 165 | 142 | 152 | 234 | 208 | 97 | 56 | 1,565 |
| 6 m | 3 | 4 | 7 | 13 | 17 | 21 | 25 | 26 | 23 | 17 | 11 | 6 | 14 |
| **Africa** | | | | | | | | | | | | | |
| Cairo, Egypt | 5 | 5 | 5 | 3 | 3 | <3 | 0 | 0 | <3 | <3 | 3 | 5 | 28 |
| 116 m | 13 | 15 | 18 | 21 | 25 | 28 | 28 | 28 | 26 | 24 | 20 | 15 | 22 |
| Cape Town, South Africa | 15 | 8 | 18 | 48 | 79 | 84 | 89 | 66 | 43 | 31 | 18 | 10 | 508 |
| 17 m | 21 | 21 | 20 | 17 | 14 | 13 | 12 | 13 | 14 | 16 | 18 | 19 | 17 |
| Lagos, Nigeria | 28 | 46 | 102 | 150 | 269 | 460 | 279 | 64 | 140 | 206 | 69 | 25 | 1,836 |
| 3 m | 27 | 28 | 29 | 28 | 28 | 26 | 26 | 25 | 26 | 26 | 28 | 28 | 27 |
| Nairobi, Kenya | 38 | 64 | 125 | 211 | 158 | 46 | 15 | 23 | 31 | 53 | 109 | 86 | 958 |
| 1,820 m | 19 | 19 | 19 | 19 | 18 | 16 | 16 | 16 | 18 | 19 | 18 | 18 | 18 |
| **Australia, New Zealand & Antarctica** | | | | | | | | | | | | | |
| Christchurch, New Zealand | 56 | 43 | 48 | 48 | 66 | 66 | 69 | 48 | 46 | 43 | 48 | 56 | 638 |
| 10 m | 16 | 16 | 14 | 12 | 9 | 6 | 6 | 7 | 9 | 12 | 14 | 16 | 11 |
| Darwin, Australia | 386 | 312 | 254 | 97 | 15 | 3 | <3 | 3 | 13 | 51 | 119 | 239 | 1,491 |
| 30 m | 29 | 29 | 29 | 29 | 28 | 26 | 25 | 26 | 28 | 29 | 30 | 29 | 28 |
| Mawson, Antarctica | 11 | 30 | 20 | 10 | 44 | 180 | 4 | 40 | 3 | 20 | 0 | 0 | 362 |
| 14 m | 0 | -5 | -10 | -14 | -15 | -16 | -18 | -18 | -19 | -13 | -5 | -1 | -11 |
| Sydney, Australia | 89 | 102 | 127 | 135 | 127 | 117 | 117 | 76 | 73 | 71 | 73 | 73 | 1,181 |
| 42 m | 22 | 22 | 21 | 18 | 15 | 13 | 12 | 13 | 15 | 18 | 19 | 21 | 17 |
| **North America** | | | | | | | | | | | | | |
| Anchorage, Alaska, USA | 20 | 18 | 15 | 10 | 13 | 18 | 41 | 66 | 66 | 56 | 25 | 23 | 371 |
| 40 m | -11 | -8 | -5 | 2 | 7 | 12 | 14 | 13 | 9 | 2 | -5 | -11 | 2 |
| Kingston, Jamaica | 23 | 15 | 23 | 31 | 102 | 89 | 38 | 91 | 99 | 180 | 74 | 36 | 800 |
| 34 m | 25 | 25 | 25 | 26 | 26 | 28 | 28 | 28 | 27 | 27 | 26 | 26 | 26 |
| Los Angeles, USA | 79 | 76 | 71 | 25 | 10 | 3 | <3 | <3 | 5 | 15 | 31 | 66 | 381 |
| 95 m | 13 | 14 | 14 | 16 | 17 | 19 | 21 | 22 | 21 | 18 | 16 | 14 | 17 |
| Mexico City, Mexico | 13 | 5 | 10 | 20 | 53 | 119 | 170 | 152 | 130 | 51 | 18 | 8 | 747 |
| 2,309 m | 12 | 13 | 16 | 18 | 19 | 19 | 17 | 18 | 18 | 16 | 14 | 13 | 16 |
| New York, USA | 94 | 97 | 91 | 81 | 81 | 84 | 107 | 109 | 86 | 89 | 76 | 91 | 1,092 |
| 96 m | -1 | -1 | 3 | 10 | 16 | 20 | 23 | 23 | 21 | 15 | 7 | 2 | 11 |
| Vancouver, Canada | 154 | 115 | 101 | 60 | 52 | 45 | 32 | 41 | 67 | 114 | 150 | 182 | 1,113 |
| 14 m | 3 | 5 | 6 | 9 | 12 | 15 | 17 | 17 | 14 | 10 | 6 | 4 | 10 |
| **South America** | | | | | | | | | | | | | |
| Antofagasta, Chile | 0 | 0 | 0 | <3 | <3 | 3 | 5 | 3 | <3 | 3 | <3 | 0 | 13 |
| 94 m | 21 | 21 | 20 | 18 | 16 | 15 | 14 | 14 | 15 | 16 | 18 | 19 | 17 |
| Buenos Aires, Argentina | 79 | 71 | 109 | 89 | 76 | 61 | 56 | 61 | 79 | 86 | 84 | 99 | 950 |
| 27 m | 23 | 23 | 21 | 17 | 13 | 9 | 10 | 11 | 13 | 15 | 19 | 22 | 16 |
| Lima, Peru | 3 | <3 | <3 | <3 | 5 | 5 | 8 | 8 | 8 | 3 | 3 | <3 | 41 |
| 120 m | 23 | 24 | 24 | 22 | 19 | 17 | 16 | 17 | 18 | 19 | 21 | | 20 |
| Rio de Janeiro, Brazil | 125 | 122 | 130 | 107 | 79 | 53 | 41 | 43 | 66 | 79 | 104 | 137 | 1,082 |
| 61 m | 26 | 26 | 25 | 24 | 22 | 21 | 21 | 21 | 21 | 22 | 23 | 25 | 23 |

# THE EARTH IN FOCUS

> Landsat image of the
San Francisco Bay area.
The narrow entrance to
the bay (crossed by the
Golden Gate Bridge)
provides an excellent
natural harbour. The
San Andreas Fault runs
parallel to the coastline.

# THE UNIVERSE & SOLAR SYSTEM

RECENT ESTIMATES SUGGEST that around 12,5000 million years ago, the Universe was created in a huge explosion known as the 'Big Bang'. In the first $10^{-24}$ of a second the Universe expanded rapidly and the basic forces of nature, radiation and subatomic particles, came into being. The Universe has been expanding ever since. Traces of the original 'fireball' of radiation can still be detected, and most scientists accept the Big Bang theory of the origin of the Universe.

| The Nearest Stars ▾ | |
|---|---|
| The 20 nearest stars, excluding the Sun, with their distance from Earth in light-years.* | |
| Proxima Centauri | 4.25 |
| Alpha Centauri A | 4.3 |
| Alpha Centauri B | 4.3 |
| Barnard's Star | 6.0 |
| Wolf 359 | 7.8 |
| Lalande 21185 | 8.3 |
| Sirius A | 8.7 |
| Sirius B | 8.7 |
| UV Ceti A | 8.7 |
| UV Ceti B | 8.7 |
| Ross 154 | 9.4 |
| Ross 248 | 10.3 |
| Epsilon Eridani | 10.7 |
| Ross 128 | 10.9 |
| 61 Cygni A | 11.1 |
| 61 Cygni B | 11.1 |
| Epsilon Indi | 11.2 |
| Groombridge 34 A | 11.2 |
| Groombridge 34 B | 11.2 |
| L789-6 | 11.2 |
| *A light-year equals approximately 9,500 billion km [5,900 billion miles]. | |

> The Lagoon Nebula is a huge cloud of dust and gas. Hot stars inside the nebula make the gas glow red.

## GALAXIES

Almost a million years passed before the Universe cooled sufficiently for atoms to form. When a billion years had passed, the atoms had begun to form proto-galaxies, which are masses of gas separated by empty space. Stars began to form within the protogalaxies, as particles were drawn together, producing the high temperatures necessary to bring about nuclear fusion. The formation of the first stars brought about the evolution of the protogalaxies into galaxies proper, each containing billions of stars.

Our Sun is a medium-sized star. It is

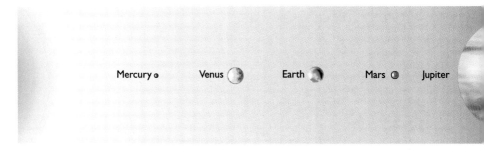

Mercury ◦    Venus ◯    Earth ◗    Mars ◐    Jupiter

**PLANETARY DATA**

|  | Mean distance from Sun (million km) | Mass (Earth = 1) | Period of orbit (Earth years) | Period of rotation (Earth days) | Equatorial diameter (km) | Escape velocity (km/sec) | Number of known satellites |
|---|---|---|---|---|---|---|---|
| **Sun** | – | 332,946 | – | 25.38 | 1,392,000 | 617.5 | – |
| **Mercury** | 58.3 | 0.06 | 0.241 | 58.67 | 4,878 | 4.27 | 0 |
| **Venus** | 107.7 | 0.8 | 0.615 | 243.0 | 12,104 | 10.36 | 0 |
| **Earth** | 149.6 | 1.0 | 1.00 | 0.99 | 12,756 | 11.18 | 1 |
| **Mars** | 227.3 | 0.1 | 1.88 | 1.02 | 6,787 | 5.03 | 2 |
| **Jupiter** | 777.9 | 317.8 | 11.86 | 0.41 | 142,800 | 59.60 | 16 |
| **Saturn** | 1,427.1 | 95.2 | 29.46 | 0.42 | 120,000 | 35.50 | 20 |
| **Uranus** | 2,872.3 | 14.5 | 84.01 | 0.45 | 51,118 | 21.30 | 15 |
| **Neptune** | 4,502.7 | 17.2 | 164.79 | 0.67 | 49,528 | 23.3 | 8 |
| **Pluto** | 5,894.2 | 0.002 | 248.54 | 6.38 | 2,300 | 1.1 | 1 |

one of the billions of stars that make up the Milky Way galaxy, which is one of the millions of galaxies in the Universe.

## THE SOLAR SYSTEM

The Solar System lies towards the edge of the Milky Way galaxy. It consists of the Sun and other bodies, including planets (together with their moons), asteroids, meteoroids, comets, dust and gas, which revolve around it.

The Earth moves through space in three distinct ways. First, with the rest of the Solar System, it moves around the centre of the Milky Way galaxy in an orbit that takes 200 million years.

As the Earth revolves around the Sun once every year, its axis is tilted by about 23.5 degrees. As a result, first the northern and then the southern hemisphere lean towards the Sun at different times of the year, causing the seasons experienced in the mid-latitudes.

The Earth also rotates on its axis every 24 hours, causing day and night. The movements of the Earth in the Solar System determine the calendar. The length of a year – one complete orbit of the Earth around the Sun – is 365 days, 5 hours, 48 minutes and 46 seconds. Leap years prevent the calendar from becoming out of step with the solar year.

> The diagram below shows the planets around the Sun. The sizes of the planets are relative but the distances are not to scale. Closest to the Sun are dense rocky bodies, known as the terrestrial planets. They are Mercury, Venus, Earth and Mars. Jupiter, Saturn, Uranus and Neptune are huge balls of gas. Pluto is a small, icy body.

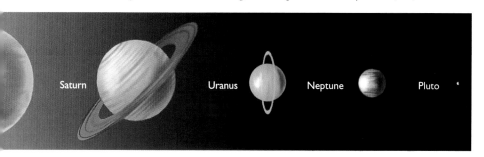

Saturn    Uranus    Neptune    Pluto

# THE CHANGING EARTH

THE SOLAR SYSTEM was formed around 4.7 billion years ago, when the Sun, a glowing ball of gases, was created from a rotating disk of dust and gas. The planets were then formed from material left over after the creation of the Sun.

After the Earth formed, around 4.6 billion years ago, lighter elements rose to the hot surface, where they finally cooled to form a hard shell, or crust. Denser elements sank, forming the partly liquid mantle, the liquid outer core, and the solid inner core.

## EARTH HISTORY

The oldest known rocks on Earth are around 4 billion years old. Natural processes have destroyed older rocks. Simple life forms first appeared on Earth around 3.5 billion years ago, though rocks formed in the first 4 billion years of Earth history contain little evidence of life. But

> Fold mountains, such as the Himalayan ranges which are shown above, were formed when two plates collided and the rock layers between them were squeezed upwards into loops or folds.

rocks formed since the start of the Cambrian period (the first period in the Paleozoic era), about 590 million years ago, are rich in fossils. The study of fossils has enabled scientists to gradually piece together the long and complex story of life on Earth.

## THE PLANET EARTH

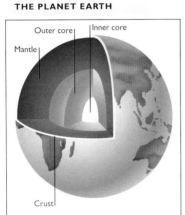

Outer core | Inner core
Mantle
Crust

**CRUST** The continental crust has an average thickness of 35–40 km [22–25 miles]; the oceanic crust averages 6 km [4 miles].

**MANTLE** 2,900 km [1,800 miles] thick. The top layer is solid, resting on a partly molten layer called the asthenosphere.

**OUTER CORE** 2,100 km [1,300 miles] thick. It consists mainly of molten iron and nickel.

**INNER CORE (DIAMETER)** 1,350 km [840 miles]. It is mainly solid iron and nickel.

## ELEMENTS

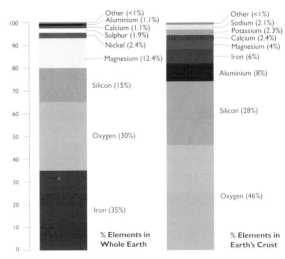

% Elements in Whole Earth:
Other (<1%)
Aluminium (1.1%)
Calcium (1.1%)
Sulphur (1.9%)
Nickel (2.4%)
Magnesium (12.4%)
Silicon (15%)
Oxygen (30%)
Iron (35%)

% Elements in Earth's Crust:
Other (<1%)
Sodium (2.1%)
Potassium (2.3%)
Calcium (2.4%)
Magnesium (4%)
Iron (6%)
Aluminium (8%)
Silicon (28%)
Oxygen (46%)

> The Earth contains about 100 elements, but eight of them account for 99% of the planet's mass. Iron makes up 35% of the Earth's mass, but most of it is in the core. The most common elements in the crust – oxygen and silicon – are often combined with one or more of the other common crustal elements, to form a group of minerals called silicates. The mineral quartz, which consists only of silicon and oxygen, occurs widely in such rocks as granites and sandstones.

## PLATE BOUNDARIES

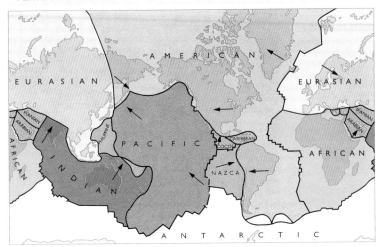

> The Earth's lithosphere is divided into six huge plates and several small ones. Ocean ridges, where plates are moving apart, are called constructive plate margins. Ocean trenches, where plates collide, are subduction zones. These are destructive plate margins. The map shows the main plates and the directions in which they are moving.

——— Plate boundaries

➤ Direction of plate movements

PACIFIC Major plates

## THE DYNAMIC EARTH

The Earth's surface is always changing because of a process called plate tectonics. Plates are blocks of the solid lithosphere (the crust and outer mantle), which are moved around by currents in the partly liquid mantle. Around 250 million years ago, the Earth contained one super-continent called Pangaea. Around 180 million years ago, Pangaea split into a northern part, Laurasia, and a southern part, Gondwanaland. Later, these huge continents, in turn, also split apart and the continents drifted to their present positions. Ancient seas disappeared and mountain ranges, such as the Himalayas and Alps, were pushed upwards.

## PLATE TECTONICS

In the early 1900s, two scientists suggested that the Americas were once joined to Europe and Africa. Together they proposed the theory of continental drift to explain the similarities between rock structures on both sides of the Atlantic. But no one could offer an explanation as to how the continents moved.

Evidence from the ocean floor in the 1950s and 1960s led to the theory of plate tectonics, which suggested that the lithosphere is divided into large blocks, or plates. The plates are solid, but they rest on the partly molten asthenosphere, within the mantle. Long ridges on

the ocean floor were found to be the edges of plates which were moving apart, carried by currents in the asthenosphere. As the plates moved, molten material welled up from the mantle to fill the gaps. But at the ocean trenches, one plate is descending beneath another along what is called a subduction zone. The descending plate is melted and destroyed. This crustal destruction at subduction zones balances the creation of new crust along the ridges. Transform faults, where two plates are moving alongside each other, form another kind of plate edge.

## GEOLOGICAL TIME SCALE

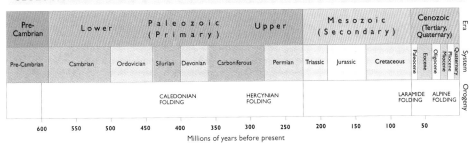

| Pre-Cambrian | Lower | | Paleozoic (Primary) | | | | Upper | Mesozoic (Secondary) | | | Cenozoic (Tertiary, Quaternary) | Era |
|---|---|---|---|---|---|---|---|---|---|---|---|---|
| Pre-Cambrian | Cambrian | Ordovician | Silurian | Devonian | Carboniferous | Permian | Triassic | Jurassic | Cretaceous | Paleocene / Eocene / Oligocene / Miocene / Pliocene / Quaternary | System |
| | | | CALEDONIAN FOLDING | | HERCYNIAN FOLDING | | | | LARAMIDE FOLDING | ALPINE FOLDING | Orogeny |

| 600 | 550 | 500 | 450 | 400 | 350 | 300 | 250 | 200 | 150 | 100 | 50 |

Millions of years before present

# EARTHQUAKES & VOLCANOES

PLATE TECTONICS HELP us to understand such phenomena as earthquakes, volcanic eruptions, and mountain building.

## EARTHQUAKES

Earthquakes can occur anywhere, but they are most common near the edges of plates. They occur when intense pressure breaks the rocks along plate edges, making the plates lurch forward.

### Major Earthquakes since 1900 ▼

| Year | Location | Mag. | Deaths |
|------|----------|------|--------|
| 1906 | San Francisco, USA | 8.3 | 503 |
| 1906 | Valparaiso, Chile | 8.6 | 22,000 |
| 1908 | Messina, Italy | 7.5 | 83,000 |
| 1915 | Avezzano, Italy | 7.5 | 30,000 |
| 1920 | Gansu, China | 8.6 | 180,000 |
| 1923 | Yokohama, Japan | 8.3 | 143,000 |
| 1927 | Nan Shan, China | 8.3 | 200,000 |
| 1932 | Gansu, China | 7.6 | 70,000 |
| 1934 | Bihar, India/Nepal | 8.4 | 10,700 |
| 1935 | Quetta, Pakistan | 7.5 | 60,000 |
| 1939 | Chillan, Chile | 8.3 | 28,000 |
| 1939 | Erzincan, Turkey | 7.9 | 30,000 |
| 1960 | Agadir, Morocco | 5.8 | 12,000 |
| 1964 | Anchorage, Alaska | 8.4 | 131 |
| 1968 | North-east Iran | 7.4 | 12,000 |
| 1970 | North Peru | 7.7 | 66,794 |
| 1976 | Guatemala | 7.5 | 22,778 |
| 1976 | Tangshan, China | 8.2 | 255,000 |
| 1978 | Tabas, Iran | 7.7 | 25,000 |
| 1980 | El Asnam, Algeria | 7.3 | 20,000 |
| 1980 | South Italy | 7.2 | 4,800 |
| 1985 | Mexico City, Mexico | 8.1 | 4,200 |
| 1988 | North-west Armenia | 6.8 | 55,000 |
| 1990 | North Iran | 7.7 | 36,000 |
| 1993 | Maharashtra, India | 6.4 | 30,000 |
| 1994 | Los Angeles, USA | 6.6 | 51 |
| 1995 | Kobe, Japan | 7.2 | 5,000 |
| 1997 | North-east Iran | 7.1 | 2,400 |
| 1998 | Takhar, Afghanistan | 6.1 | 4,200 |
| 1998 | Rostaq, Afghanistan | 7.0 | 5,000 |
| 1999 | Izmit, Turkey | 7.4 | 15,000 |
| 2001 | Gujrat, India | 7.9 | 20,000 |

> The earthquake that struck Kobe in January 1995 was the worst one experienced in Japan since 1923. Japan lies alongside subduction zones.

> The section between the Pacific and Indian oceans shows a subduction zone under the American plate, with spreading ocean ridges in the Atlantic and Indian oceans. East Africa may one day split away from the rest of Africa as plate movements pull the Rift Valley apart.

Earthquakes are common along the mid-ocean ridges, but they are a long way from land and cause little damage. Other earthquakes occur near land in subduction zones, such as those that encircle much of the Pacific Ocean. These earthquakes often trigger off powerful sea waves, called tsunamis. Other earthquakes occur along transform faults, such as the San Andreas fault in California, a boundary between the North American and Pacific plates. Movements along this fault cause periodic disasters, such as the earthquakes in San Francisco (1906) and Los Angeles (1994).

## VOLCANOES & MOUNTAINS

Volcanoes are fuelled by magma (molten rock) from the mantle. Some volcanoes, such as in Hawaii, lie above 'hot spots' (sources of heat in the mantle). But most volcanoes occur either along the ocean ridges or above subduction zones, where

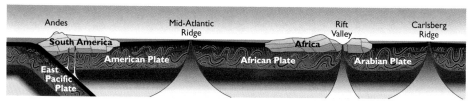

## EARTHQUAKES

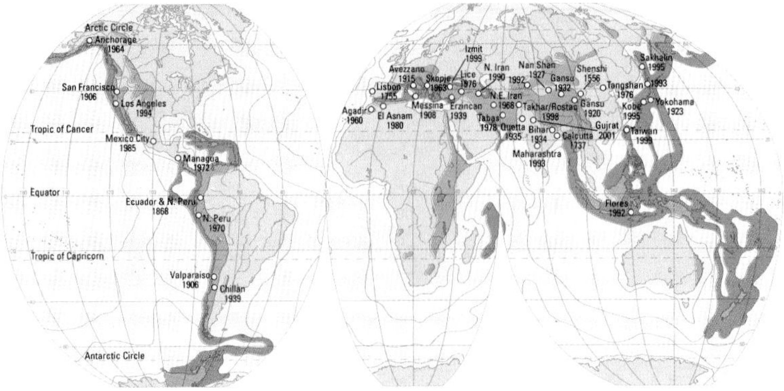

**Map labels (left globe):**
Arctic Circle
Anchorage 1964
San Francisco 1906
Los Angeles 1994
Tropic of Cancer
Mexico City 1985
Managua 1972
Equator
Ecuador & N. Peru 1868
N. Peru 1970
Tropic of Capricorn
Valparaiso 1906
Chillan 1939
Antarctic Circle

**Map labels (right globe):**
Izmit 1999
Avezzano 1915
Lisbon 1755
Lice 1975
Skopje 1963
N. Iran 1990
Nan Shan 1927
Shenshi 1556
Gansu 1932
Sakhalin 1995
Tangshan 1976
Agadir 1960
El Asnam 1980
Messina 1908
Erzincan 1939
N.E. Iran
Takhar/Rostaq 1998
Gansu 1920
Kobe 1995
Yokohama 1923
Tabas 1978
Quetta 1935
Bihar 1934
Gujarat 2001
Calcutta 2001 1737
Ottawa 1999
Taiwan 1999
Maharashtra 1993
Flores 1992

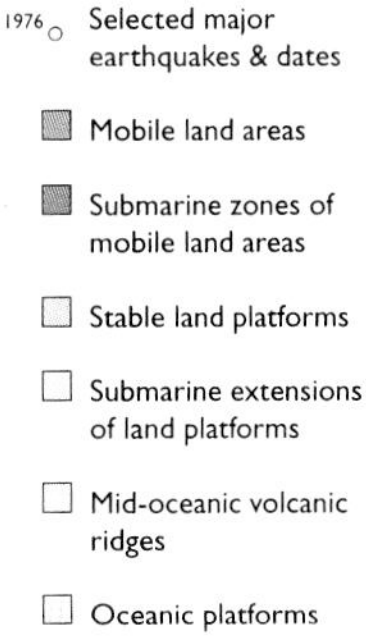

**Legend:**
1976 ○ Selected major earthquakes & dates
▨ Mobile land areas
▨ Submarine zones of mobile land areas
☐ Stable land platforms
☐ Submarine extensions of land platforms
☐ Mid-oceanic volcanic ridges
☐ Oceanic platforms

## VOLCANOES

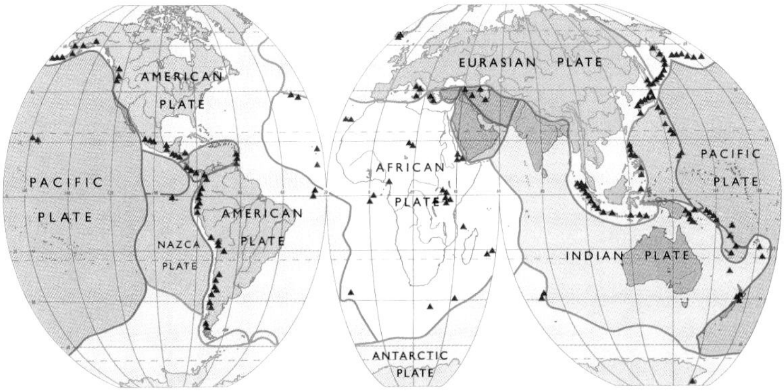

**Map labels (left globe):**
AMERICAN PLATE
PACIFIC PLATE
PACIFIC PLATE
AMERICAN PLATE
NAZCA PLATE

**Map labels (right globe):**
EURASIAN PLATE
AFRICAN PLATE
AFRICAN PLATE
PACIFIC PLATE
INDIAN PLATE
ANTARCTIC PLATE

**Legend:**
▲ Land volcanoes active since 1700
— Boundaries of tectonic plates

The maps show that the main earthquake zones follow plate edges. Most volcanoes are also in these zones, whereas some lie over 'hot spots', far from plate edges.

---

magma is produced when the descending plate is melted.

Volcanic mountains are built up gradually by runny lava flows or by exploded volcanic ash. Fold mountains occur when two plates bearing land areas collide and the plate edges are buckled upwards into fold mountain ranges. Plate movements also fracture rocks and block mountains are formed when areas of land are pushed upwards along faults or between parallel faults. Blocks of land sometimes sink down between faults, creating deep, steep-sided rift valleys.

> *Volcanoes occur when molten magma reaches the surface under pressure through long vents. 'Quiet' volcanoes emit runny lava (called pahoehoe). Explosive eruptions occur when the magma is sticky. Explosive gases shatter the magma into ash, which is hurled upwards into the air.*

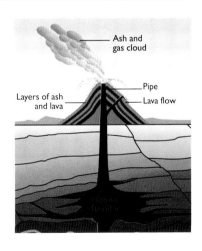

Ash and gas cloud
Layers of ash and lava
Pipe
Lava flow

7

# WATER & ICE

A VISITOR FROM outer space might be forgiven for naming our planet 'Water' rather than 'Earth', because water covers more than 70% of its surface. Without water, our planet would be as lifeless as the Moon. Through the water cycle, fresh water is regularly supplied from the sea to the land. Most geographers divide the world's water into four main oceans: the Pacific, the Atlantic, the Indian and the Arctic. Together the oceans contain 97.2% of the world's water.

The water in the oceans is constantly on the move, even, albeit extremely slowly, in the deepest ocean trenches. The greatest movements of ocean water occur in the form of ocean currents. These are marked, mainly wind-blown

## EXPLANATION OF TERMS

**GLACIER** A body of ice that flows down valleys in mountain areas. It is usually narrow and hence smaller than ice caps or ice sheets.

**ICE AGE** A period of Earth history when ice sheets spread over large areas. The most recent Ice Age began about 1.8 million years ago and ended 10,000 years ago.

**ICEBERG** A floating body of ice in the sea. About eight-ninths of the ice is hidden beneath the surface of the water.

**ICE SHEET** A large body of ice. During the last Ice Age, ice sheets covered large parts of the northern hemisphere.

**OCEAN** The four main oceans are the Pacific, the Atlantic, the Indian and the Arctic. Some

people classify a fifth southern ocean, but others regard these waters as extensions of the Pacific, Atlantic and Indian oceans.

**OCEAN CURRENTS** Distinct currents of water in the oceans. Winds are the main causes of surface currents.

**SEA** An expanse of water, but smaller than an ocean.

> Ice breaks away from the ice sheet of Antarctica, forming flat-topped icebergs. Researchers fear that warmer weather is melting Antarctica's ice sheets at a dangerous rate, after large chunks of the Larsen ice shelf and the Ronne ice shelf broke away in 1997 and 1998, respectively.

## JANUARY TEMPERATURE AND OCEAN CURRENTS

(Northern Hemisphere – Winter)

ACTUAL SURFACE
TEMPERATURE

°C
30
20
10
0
-10
-20
-30
-40

OCEAN CURRENTS
Cold  Warm  Speed (knots)
Less than 0.5
0.5 – 1.0
Over 1.0

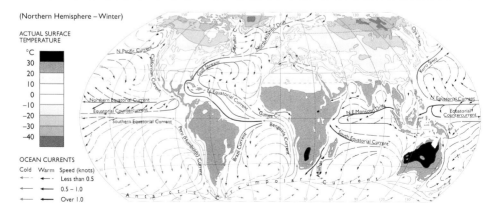

## CROSS-SECTION OF ANTARCTICA

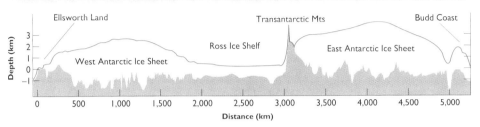

> This section across Antarctica shows the concealed land areas in brown, with the top of the ice in blue. The section is divided into the West and East Antarctic Ice Sheets. The vertical scale has been exaggerated.

movements of water on or near the surface. Other dense, cold currents creep slowly across the ocean floor. Warm and cold ocean currents help to regulate the world's climate by transferring heat between the tropics and the poles.

## ICE

About 2.15% of the world's water is locked in two large ice sheets, several smaller ice caps and glaciers. The world's largest ice sheet covers most of Antarctica. The ice is up to 4,800 m [15,750 ft] thick and it represents 70% of the world's fresh water. The volume of ice is about nine times greater than that contained in the world's other ice sheet in Green-land. Besides these ice sheets, smaller ice caps are found in northern Canada, Iceland, Norway and Spitzbergen, and

in several valley glaciers in numerous mountain areas.

Reports in the early 21st century sugg – ested global warming had begun to melt polar and glacier ice. If all the world's ice melted, sea level could rise by 100 m [330 ft], flooding islands and coastal areas and displacing tens of millions of people.

### Composition of Seawater ▾

The principal components of seawater, by percentage, excluding the elements of water itself:

| | | | |
|---|---|---|---|
| Chloride (Cl) | 55.04% | Potassium (K) | 1.10% |
| Sodium (Na) | 30.61% | Bicarbonate (HCO₃) | 0.41% |
| Sulphate (SO₄) | 7.69% | Bromide (Br) | 0.19% |
| Magnesium (Mg) | 3.69% | Strontium (Sr) | 0.04% |
| Calcium (Ca) | 1.16% | Fluorine (F) | 0.003% |

The oceans contain virtually every other element, the more important ones being lithium, rubidium, phosphorus, iodine and barium.

## JULY TEMPERATURE AND OCEAN CURRENTS

# WEATHER & CLIMATE

WEATHER IS A description of the day-to-day state of the atmosphere. Climate, on the other hand, is weather in the long term: the seasonal pattern of temperature and precipitation averaged over time.

In some areas, the weather is so stable and predictable that a description of the weather is much the same as a statement of the climate. But in parts of the mid-latitudes, the weather changes from hour to hour. Changeable weather is caused mainly by low air pressure systems, called cyclones or depressions, which form along the polar front where warm subtropical air meets cold polar air.

The main elements of weather and

### LIGHTNING

Lightning is a flash of light in the sky caused by a discharge of electricity in the atmosphere. Lightning occurs within cumulonimbus clouds during thunderstorms. Positive charges build up at the top of the cloud, while negative charges build up at the base. The charges are finally discharged as an electrical spark. Sheet lightning occurs inside clouds, while cloud to ground lightning is usually forked. Thunder occurs when molecules along the lightning channel expand and collide with cool molecules.

climate are temperature and rainfall. Temperatures vary because the Sun heats the Earth unequally, with the most intense heating around the Equator. Unequal heating is responsible for the general circulation of the atmosphere and the main wind belts.

Rainfall occurs when warm air containing invisible water vapour rises. As the rising air cools, the capacity of the air to hold water vapour decreases and so the water vapour condenses into droplets of water or ice crystals, which collect together to form raindrops or snowflakes.

> Lightning occurs in clouds and also between the base of clouds and the ground. Lightning that strikes the ground can kill people or start forest fires.

> The rainfall map shows areas affected by tropical storms, which are variously called hurricanes, tropical cyclones, willy willies and typhoons. Strong polar winds bring blizzards in winter.

### ANNUAL RAINFALL

| mm | |
|---|---|
| 3,000 | |
| 2,000 | |
| 1,000 | |
| 500 | |
| 250 | |

⇒ Paths of tropical storms and winter blizzards

BLIZZARDS November–March

HURRICANES August–October

CYCLONES June–November

TYPHOONS July–October

WILLY WILLIES January–March

## GLOBAL WARMING

The Earth's climates have changed many times during its history. Around 11,000 years ago, much of the northern hemisphere was buried by ice. Some scientists believe that the last Ice Age may not be over and that ice sheets may one day return. Other scientists are concerned that air

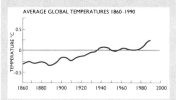

AVERAGE GLOBAL TEMPERATURES 1860–1990

pollution may be producing an opposite effect – a warming of the atmosphere. Since 1900, average world temperatures have risen by about 0.5°C [0.9°F] and increases are likely to continue. Global warming is the result of an increase in the amount of carbon dioxide in the atmosphere, caused by the burning of coal, oil and natural gas, together with deforestation. Short-wave radiation from the Sun passes easily through the atmosphere. But, as the carbon dioxide content rises, more of the long-wave radiation that returns from the Earth's surface is absorbed and trapped by the carbon dioxide. This creates a 'greenhouse effect', which will change the world's climates with, perhaps, disastrous environmental consequences.

## CLIMATE

The world contains six main climatic types: hot and wet tropical climates; dry climates; warm temperate climates; cold temperate climates; polar climates; and mountain climates. These regions are further divided according to the character and amount of precipitation and special features of the temperature, notably seasonal variations. Regions with temperate climates include Mediterranean areas with hot, dry summers and mild, moist winters. The British Isles have a different type of temperate climate, with warm, rather than hot, summers and rain throughout the year.

## CLIMATIC REGIONS

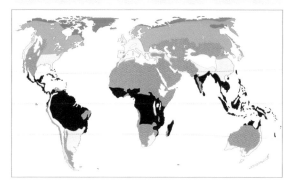

- ■ Tropical Climate (hot & wet)
- ■ Dry Climate (desert & steppe)
- □ Temperate Climate (warm & wet)
- ■ Continental Climate (cold & wet)
- ■ Polar Climate (very cold & wet)
- □ Mountainous Areas (where altitude affects climate types)

## WORLD CLIMATIC RECORDS

**Highest Recorded Temperature**
Al Aziziyah, Libya: 58°C [136.4°F] on 13 September 1922

**Highest Mean Annual Temperature**
Dallol, Ethiopia: 34.4°C [94°F] from 1960–66

**Lowest Mean Annual Temperature**
Polus, Nedostupnosti, Pole of Cold, Antarctica: –57.8°C [–72°F]

**Lowest Recorded Temperature (outside poles)**
Verkhoyansk, Siberia, Russia: –68°C [–90°F] on 6 February 1933

**Windiest Place**
Commonwealth Bay, Antarctica: gales often exceed 320 km/h [200 mph]

**Longest Heatwave**
Marble Bar, Western Australia: 162 days over 38°C [94°F], 23 October 1923 to 7 April 1924

**Driest Place**
Calama, northern Chile: no recorded rainfall in 400 years to 1971

**Wettest Place (average)**
Tututendo, Colombia: mean annual rainfall 11,770 mm [463 in]

**Wettest Place (24 hours)**
Cilaos, Réunion, Indian Ocean: 1,870 mm [73.6 in] from 15–16 March 1952

**Wettest Place (12 months)**
Cherrapunji, Meghalaya, north-east India: 26,470 mm [1,040 in], August 1860 to 1861. Cherrapunji also holds the record for rainfall in one month: 2,930 mm [115 in] in July 1861

**Heaviest Hailstones**
Gopalganj, central Bangladesh: up to 1.02 kg [2.25 lbs] in April 1986, which killed 92 people

**Heaviest Snowfall (continuous)**
Bessans, Savoie, France: 1,730 mm [68 in] in 19 hours over the period 5–6 April 1969

**Heaviest Snowfall (season/year)**
Paradise Ranger Station, Mt Rainier, Washington, USA: 31,102 mm [1,224 in] fell from 19 February 1971 to 18 February 1972

11

# LANDFORMS & VEGETATION

THE CLIMATE LARGELY determines the nature of soils and vegetation types throughout the world. The studies of climate and plant and animal communities are closely linked. For example, tropical climates are divided into tropical forest and tropical grassland climates. The tropical forest climate, which is hot and rainy throughout the year, is ideal for the growth of forests that contain more than half of the world's known plant and animal species. But tropical grassland, or savanna, climates have a marked dry season. As a result, the forest gives way to grassland, with scattered trees.

## CLIMATE & SCENERY

The climate also helps to shape the land. Frost action in cold areas splits boulders apart, while rapid temperature changes in hot deserts make rock surfaces peel away like the layers of an onion. These are examples of mechanical weathering.

Chemical weathering usually results from the action of water on rocks. For example, rainwater containing dissolved carbon dioxide is a weak acid, which reacts with limestone. This chemical process is responsible for the erosion of the world's most spectacular caves.

Running water and glaciers play a major part in creating scenery, while in

> The tropical broadleaf forests are rich in plant and animal species. The extinction of many species because of deforestation is one of the great natural disasters of our time.

## NATURAL VEGETATION

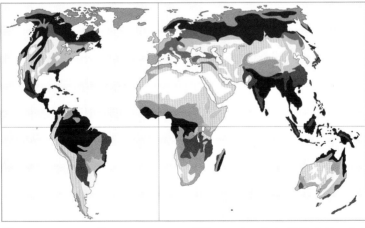

- ☐ Tundra & mountain vegetation
- ■ Needleleaf evergreen forest
- ☐ Broadleaf deciduous forest
- ■ Mixed needleleaf evergreen & broadleaf deciduous trees
- ☐ Mid-latitude grassland
- ☐ Semi-desert scrub land
- ☐ Evergreen broadleaf & deciduous trees & scrub
- ☐ Desert
- ☐ Tropical grassland (savanna)
- ■ Tropical broadleaf & monsoon rainforest
- ■ Subtropical broadleaf & needleleaf forest

> Human activities, especially agriculture, have greatly modified plant and animal communities throughout the world. As a result, world vegetation maps show the natural 'climax vegetation'.of regions – that is, the kind of vegetation that would grow in a particular climatic area, had that area not been affected by human activities. For example, the climax vegetation of western Europe is broadleaf, deciduous forest, but most of the original forest, together with the animals which lived in it, was destroyed long ago.

12

## DESERTIFICATION AND DEFORESTATION

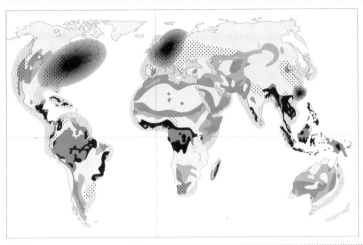

Pollution

☐ Polluted seas

▨ Main areas of sulphur & nitrogen emissions

■ Areas of acid rain

Desertification

☐ Existing deserts

▧ Areas with a high risk of desertification

▨ Areas with a moderate risk of desertification

Deforestation

■ Former areas of rainforest

▨ Existing rainforest

dry areas, wind-blown sand is a powerful agent of erosion. Most landforms seem to alter little in one person's lifetime. But geologists estimate that natural forces remove an average of 3.5 cm [1.4 in] from land areas every 1,000 years. Over millions of years, these forces reduce mountains to flat plains.

### HUMAN INTERFERENCE

Climate also affects people, though air conditioning and central heating now make it possible for us live in comfort almost anywhere in the world.

However, human activities are damaging our planet. Pollution is poisoning rivers and seas, while acid rain, caused by air pollution, is killing trees and acidifying lakes. The land is also harmed by such things as nuclear accidents and the dumping of toxic wastes.

Some regions have been overgrazed or so intensively farmed that once fertile areas have been turned into barren deserts. The clearance of tropical forests means that some plant and animal species are disappearing before scientists have had a chance to study them.

### MOULDING THE LAND

Powerful forces inside the Earth buckle rock layers to form fold mountain ranges. But even as they rise, the forces of erosion wear them away. On mountain slopes, water freezes in cracks in rocks. Because ice occupies more space than the equivalent amount of water, this 'frost action' shatters rocks, and the fragments tumble downhill. Some end up on or inside moving glaciers. Other rocks are carried away by running water. The glaciers and streams not only trans-port rock fragments, but they also wear out valleys and so add to their load. The eroded material breaks down into fragments of sand, silt and mud, much of which reaches the sea, where it piles up on the sea floor in layers. These layers eventually become compacted into sedimentary rocks, such as sandstones and shales. These rocks may eventually be squeezed up again by a plate collision to form new fold mountains, so completing a natural cycle of mountain building and destruction.

### MAJOR FACTORS AFFECTING WEATHERING

| | WEATHERING RATE | | |
|---|---|---|---|
| | ← SLOW | | FAST → |
| **Mineral solubility** | low (e.g. quartz) | moderate (e.g. feldspar) | high (e.g. calcite) |
| **Rainfall** | low | moderate | heavy |
| **Temperature** | cold | temperate | hot |
| **Vegetation** | sparse | moderate | lush |
| **Soil cover** | bare rock | thin to moderate soil | thick soil |

*Weathering is the breakdown and decay of rocks in situ. It may be mechanical (physical), chemical or biological.*

# POPULATION

THE ADVENT OF agriculture around 10,000 years ago had a great impact on human society. People abandoned their nomadic way of life and settled in farming villages. With plenty of food, some people were able to pursue jobs unconnected with farming. These developments eventually led to rapid social changes, including the growth of early cities and the emergence of civilization.

## THE POPULATION EXPLOSION

The social changes had a major effect on the world's population, which rose from around 8 million in 8000 BC, to about 300 million by AD 1000. The rate of population increase then began to accelerate further, passing the 1 billion mark in the 19th century, the 2 billion mark in the 1920s, and the 4 billion mark in the 1970s.

Today the world has a population of more than 6 billion and experts forecast that it will reach around 11 billion by 2200. However, they then predict that it will stabilize at this level or even begin to decline. Most of the expected increase will occur in developing countries in Africa, Asia and Latin America.

> Many cities in India, such as Mumbai (formerly called Bombay), have grown so quickly that they lack sufficient jobs and homes for their populations. As a result, slums now cover large areas.

### POPULATION PYRAMIDS

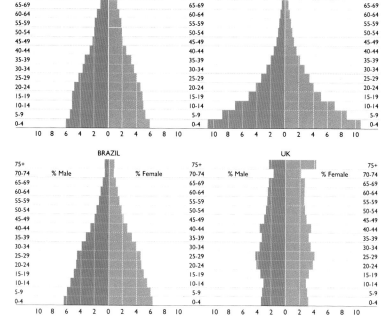

> The population pyramids compare the average age structures for the world with those of three countries at varying stages of development. Kenya, a developing country, had, until recently, one of the world's highest annual rates of population increase. As a result, a high proportion of Kenyans are aged under 15. Brazil has a much more balanced economy than Kenya's, and a lower rate of population increase. This is reflected in a higher proportion of people aged over 40. The UK is a developed country with a low rate of population growth, 0.3% per year between 1985–95, much lower than the world average of 1.6%. The UK has a far higher proportion of people over 60 years old.

14

### The World's Largest Cities ▼

Early in the 21st century, for the first time ever, the majority of the world's population lives in cities. Below is a list of the 20 largest cities (in thousands) based on latest available figures.

| | | |
|---|---|---|
| 1 | Tokyo, *Japan* | 26,836 |
| 2 | São Paulo, *Brazil* | 16,417 |
| 3 | New York, *USA* | 16,329 |
| 4 | Shanghai, *China* | 15,082 |
| 5 | Mexico City, *Mexico* | 15,048 |
| 6 | Bombay (Mumbai), *India* | 12,572 |
| 7 | Los Angeles, *USA* | 12,410 |
| 8 | Beijing, *China* | 12,362 |
| 9 | Seoul, *South Korea* | 11,641 |
| 10 | Jakarta, *Indonesia* | 11,500 |
| 11 | Buenos Aires, *Argentina* | 11,256 |
| 12 | Calcutta, *India* | 10,916 |
| 13 | Tianjin, *China* | 10,687 |
| 14 | Osaka, *Japan* | 10,601 |
| 15 | Lagos, *Nigeria* | 10,287 |
| 16 | Cairo, *Egypt* | 9,900 |
| 17 | Rio de Janeiro, *Brazil* | 9,888 |
| 18 | Karachi, *Pakistan* | 9,863 |
| 19 | Paris, *France* | 9,319 |
| 20 | Manila, *Philippines* | 9,280 |

This population explosion has been caused partly by better medical care, which has reduced child mortality and increased the average life expectancy at birth throughout the world. But it has also created problems. In some developing countries, nearly half of the people are children. They make no contribution to the economy, but they require costly education and health services. In richer countries, the high proportion of retired people is also a strain on the economy.

In the 21st century, for the first time in 10,000 years, the majority of people are no longer forced to rely on farming for their livelihood. Instead, nearly half of them live in cities where many of them enjoy a high standard of living. But rapid urbanization also creates problems, especially in the developing world, with the growth of slums and an increase in homelessness and crime.

### POPULATION BY CONTINENT

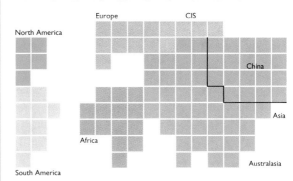

> The cartogram shows the populations of the continents in a diagrammatic way, with each square representing 1% of the world's population. For example, North America is represented by five squares, which means that it contains about 5% of the world's population, while Asia, the most populous continent even excluding the Asian part of the former USSR, is represented by 56 squares (China accounting for 19 of these). By contrast, Australasia is represented by less than half of a square because it contains only 0.45% of the world's population.

### WORLD DEMOGRAPHIC EXTREMES

| Fastest growing population; average annual % growth (1992–2000) | | Slowest growing population; average annual % growth (1992–2000) | |
|---|---|---|---|
| 1 | Nigeria ... 5.09 | 1 | Kuwait ... -1.39 |
| 2 | Afghanistan ... 4.21 | 2 | Ireland ... -0.24 |
| 3 | Ivory Coast ... 3.54 | 3 | St Kitts & Nevis ... -0.22 |
| 4 | Oman ... 3.52 | 4 | Bulgaria ... -0.13 |
| 5 | Syria ... 3.51 | 5 | Latvia ... -0.10 |

| Youngest populations; % aged under 15 years (1996) | | Oldest populations; % aged over 65 years (1996) | |
|---|---|---|---|
| 1 | West Bank/Gaza ... 51.7 | 1 | Sweden ... 17.3 |
| 2 | Uganda ... 48.6 | 2 | Italy ... 16.1 |
| 3 | Benin ... 48.4 | 3 | Greece ... 15.9 |
| = | Niger ... 48.4 | = | Norway ... 15.9 |
| 5 | Zambia ... 48.2 | 5 | Belgium ... 15.8 |

| Highest urban populations; % of population in urban areas (1996) | | Lowest urban populations; % of population in urban areas (1996) | |
|---|---|---|---|
| 1 | Singapore ... 100.0 | 1 | Bhutan ... 6.0 |
| = | Bermuda ... 100.0 | = | Rwanda ... 6.0 |
| 3 | Macau ... 99.0 | 3 | Burundi ... 8.0 |
| 4 | Kuwait ... 97.0 | 4 | Ethiopia ... 13.0 |
| 5 | Hong Kong ... 95.0 | = | Uganda ... 13.0 |

| Most male populations; number of men per 100 women (1997) | | Fewest male populations; number of men per 100 women (1997) | |
|---|---|---|---|
| 1 | Qatar ... 193.3 | 1 | Latvia ... 84.3 |
| 2 | United Arab Emirates ... 176.4 | 2 | Ukraine ... 86.8 |
| 3 | Bahrain ... 133.7 | 3 | Russia ... 88.0 |
| 4 | Saudi Arabia ... 125.1 | 5 | Estonia ... 88.7 |
| 5 | Oman ... 113.4 | 4 | Belarus ... 88.8 |

# LANGUAGES & RELIGIONS

ALL PEOPLE BELONG to one species, *Homo sapiens*, but within that species is a great diversity of cultures. Two of the main factors that give people an identity and sense of kinship with their neighbours are language and religion.

Definitions of languages vary and as a result estimates of the total number of languages in existence range from about 3,000 to 6,000. Many languages are spoken only by a small number of people. Papua New Guinea, for example, has only 4.2 million people but 869 languages.

The world's languages are grouped into families, of which the Indo–European is the largest. Indo–European languages are spoken in a zone stretching from

> Religion is a major force in South-east Asia. About 94% of the people in Thailand are Buddhists, and more than 40% of men over the age of 20 spend some time, if only a few weeks, serving as Buddhist monks. Confucianism, Islam, Hinduism, and Christianity are also practised in Thailand.

## THE WORLD'S LANGUAGES

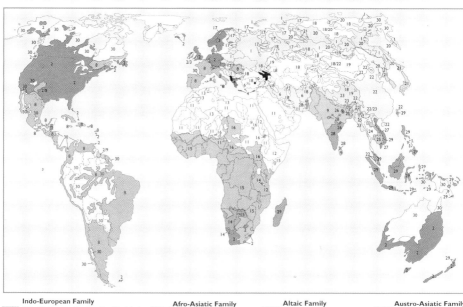

**Indo-European Family**
1. Balto-Slavic group (inc. Russian, Ukrainian)
2. Germanic group (inc. English, German)
3. Celtic group
4. Greek
5. Albanian
6. Iranian group
7. Armenian
8. Romance group (inc. Spanish, Portuguese, French, Italian)
9. Indo-Aryan group (inc. Hindi, Bengali, Urdu, Punjabi, Marathi)
10. **Caucasian Family**

**Afro-Asiatic Family**
11. Semitic group (inc. Arabic)
12. Kushitic group
13. Berber group

14. **Khoisan Family**

15. **Niger-Congo Family**

16. **Nilo-Saharan Family**

17. **Uralic Family**

**Altaic Family**
18. Turkic group
19. Mongolian group
20. Tungus-Manchu group
21. Japanese & Korean

**Sino-Tibetan Family**
22. Sinitic (Chinese) languages
23. Tibetic-Burmic languages

24. **Tai Family**

**Austro-Asiatic Family**
25. Mon-Khmer group
26. Munda group
27. Vietnamese

28. **Dravidian Family** (inc. Telugu, Tamil)

29. **Austronesian Family** (inc. Malay-Indonesian)

30. **Other Languages**

16

**NATIVE SPEAKERS**

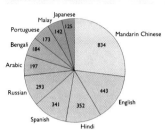

> The chart shows the native speakers of major languages in millions. Mandarin Chinese is the language of 834 million, as compared with English, which has 443 million speakers. However, many other people speak English as a second language.

| Religious Adherents ▾ | |
|---|---|
| The world's major religions, with the number of adherents in millions (latest available year) | |
| **Christian** | 1,669 |
| Roman Catholic | 952 |
| Protestant | 337 |
| Orthodox | 162 |
| Anglican | 70 |
| Other Christian | 148 |
| **Muslim** | 945 |
| Sunni | 841 |
| Shia | 104 |
| **Hindu** | 663 |
| **Buddhist** | 312 |
| **Chinese folk** | 172 |
| **Ethnic/local** | 92 |
| **Jewish** | 18 |
| **Sikh** | 17 |

> Most languages have alphabetic systems of writing. The Greek alphabet uses some letters from the Roman alphabet, such as the A and B. Russians use the Cyrillic alphabet, which is based partly on Roman and partly on Greek letters. The Cyrillic alphabet is also used for Bulgarian and some central Asian languages. Serbs use either the Cyrillic or the Roman alphabet to write Serbo-Croat.

Europe, through south-western Asia into the Indian subcontinent. In addition, during the period of European colonization, they spread throughout North and South America and also to Australia and New Zealand. Today about two-fifths of the world's people speak an Indo-European language, as compared with one-fifth who speak a language belonging to the Sino-Tibetan language.

The Sino-Tibetan language family includes Chinese, which is spoken as a first language by more people than any other. English is the second most important first language, but it is more important than Chinese in international affairs and business, because so many people speak it as a second language.

**RELIGIONS**

Christianity is the religion of about a third of the world's population. Other major religions include Buddhism, Islam, Hinduism, Judaism, Chinese folk religions and traditional tribal religions.

Religion is a powerful force in human society, establishing the ethics by which people live. It has inspired great music, painting, architecture and literature, yet at the same time religion and language have contributed to conflict between people throughout history. Even today, the cause of many of the conflicts around the world are partly the result of linguistic and religious differences.

**ALPHABETS**

**The Greek Alphabet**

Α Β Γ Δ Ε Ζ Η Θ Ι Κ Λ Μ Ν Ξ Ο Π Ρ Σ Τ Υ Φ Χ Ψ Ω
A V/B G D E Z E TH I K L M N X O P R S T Y F CH PS O

**The Cyrillic Alphabet**

А Б В Г Д Е Ё Ж З И Й К Л М Н О П Р С Т У Ф Х Ц Ч Ш Щ Ю Я
A B V G D E YO ZH Z I Y K L M N O P R S T U F KH TS CH SH SHCH YU YA

17

# AGRICULTURE & INDUSTRY

BECAUSE IT SUPPLIES so many basic human needs, agriculture is the world's leading economic activity. But its relative importance varies from place to place. In most developing countries, agriculture employs more people than any other activity. For example, the diagram at the bottom of this page shows that more than 90% of the people of Nepal are employed in farming.

Many farmers in developing countries live at subsistence level, producing barely enough to supply the basic needs of their families. Alongside the subsistence sector, some developing countries produce one or two cash crops that they export. Dependence on cash crops is precarious: when world commodity prices fall, the country is plunged into financial crisis.

In developed countries, by contrast, the proportion of people engaged in agriculture has declined over the last 200

> The cultivation of rice, one of the world's most important foods, is still carried out by hand in many areas. But the introduction of new strains of rice has greatly increased yields.

years. Yet, by using farm machinery and scientific methods, notably the selective breeding of crops and animals, the production of food has soared. For example, although agriculture employs only 3% of its workers, the United States is one of the world's top food producers.

## INDUSTRIALIZATION

The Industrial Revolution began in Britain in the late 18th century and soon spread to mainland Europe and other parts of the world. Industries first arose in areas with supplies of coal, iron ore and cheap water power. But later, after oil and gas came into use as industrial fuels, factories could be set up almost anywhere.

The growth of manufacturing led to an increase in the number of industrial cities. The flight from the land was accompanied by an increase in efficiency in agriculture. As a result, manufacturing replaced agriculture as the chief source of

### EMPLOYMENT

The number of workers employed in manufacturing for every 100 workers engaged in agriculture (latest available year)

- ■ Under 10
- □ 50 – 100
- ■ 200 – 500
- ■ 10 – 50
- □ 100 – 200
- ■ Over 500

### DIVISION OF EMPLOYMENT

- Agriculture
- Industry
- Services

Nepal   Nigeria   Pakistan   Brazil   Hong Kong   USA

18

## PATTERNS OF PRODUCTION

> The table shows how the economy breaks down (in terms of the Gross Domestic Product for 1997) in a selection of industrialized countries. Agriculture remains important in some countries, though its percentage share has steadily declined since the start of the Industrial Revolution. Industry, especially manufacturing, accounts for a higher proportion, but service industries account for the greatest percentage of the GDP in most developed nations. The figures for Manufacturing are shown separately from Industry because of their importance in the economy.

| Country | Agriculture | Industry (excl. manufacturing) | Manufacturing | Services |
|---|---|---|---|---|
| Australia | 3% | 24% | 12% | 61% |
| Austria | 1% | 24% | 14% | 61% |
| Brazil | 10% | 28% | 18% | 44% |
| Denmark | 4% | 7% | 20% | 69% |
| Finland | 5% | 3% | 28% | 64% |
| France | 2% | 20% | 13% | 65% |
| Germany | 1% | 8% | 24% | 67% |
| Greece | 17% | 13% | 23% | 47% |
| Hungary | 4% | 24% | 14% | 58% |
| Ireland | 8% | 7% | 3% | 82% |
| Italy | 3% | 8% | 21% | 68% |
| Japan | 1% | 28% | 19% | 52% |
| Kuwait | 0% | 46% | 9% | 45% |
| Mexico | 4% | 18% | 17% | 61% |
| Netherlands | 3% | 21% | 12% | 64% |
| Norway | 2% | 24% | 10% | 64% |
| Singapore | 0% | 29% | 17% | 54% |
| Sweden | 3% | 8% | 28% | 61% |
| UK | 2% | 8% | 23% | 67% |
| USA | 3% | 10% | 20% | 67% |

income and employment in industrialized countries, and rapidly widened the wealth gap between them and the poorer non-industrialized countries whose economies continued to rely on agriculture.

## SERVICE INDUSTRIES

Eventually, the manufacturing sector became so efficient that it could supply most of the things that people wanted to buy. Trade between industrialized countries also increased, so widening the choice for consumers in the developed world. These factors led to a further change in the economies of developed countries, namely a reduction in the relative importance of manufacturing and the growth of the service sector.

Service industries include such activities as government, transport, insurance, finance, and even the writing of computer software. In the United States, service industries now account for about two-thirds of the Gross National Product (GNP), while in Japan they account for just over half. But the wealth of both countries still rests on their massive industrial production.

## AGRICULTURE

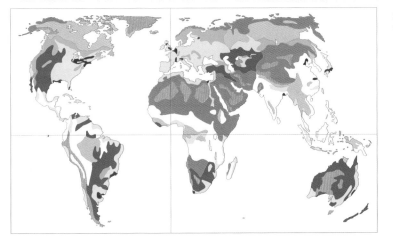

Predominant type of farming or land use

- Nomadic herding
- Hunting, fishing & gathering
- Subsistence agriculture
- Commercial ranching
- Commercial livestock & grain farming
- Urban areas
- Forestry
- Unproductive land

19

# TRADE & COMMERCE

TRADE HAS ALWAYS been an important human activity. It has widened the choice of goods available in any country, lowered prices and generally raised living standards. People regard any growth of world trade as a sign that the world economy is healthy, whereas a decline indicates a world recession.

Exports and imports are of two main kinds. Visible imports and exports include primary products, such as food and manufactures. Invisible imports and exports include services, such as banking, insurance, interest on loans, and money spent by tourists.

World trade, both visible and invisible, is dominated by the 29 members of the OECD (Organization for Economic Development), which includes the world's top trading nations, namely the United States, Japan, Germany, France, Italy and the United Kingdom, as well as Australia, New Zealand, Canada and Mexico. Hungary, Poland and South Korea joined in 1996.

> The new port of the historic Italian city of Ravenna is linked to the Adriatic Sea by a canal. The port has large oil refining and petrochemical industries.

## CHANGING EXPORTS

From the late 19th century to the 1950s, primary products, including farm products, minerals, natural fibres, timber and, in the latter part of this period, oil

## DEBT AND AID

International debtors and the development aid they receive (latest available year)

The provision of aid by rich countries to developing countries is part of international politics. But the grants made to developing countries are often dwarfed by the burden of debt which the countries are expected to repay. In 1990, the debts of Mozambique, one of the world's poorest countries, were estimated to be 75 times its entire earnings from exports.

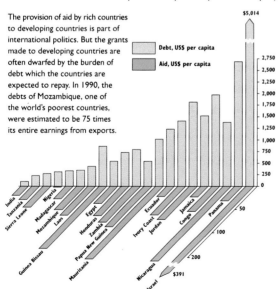

| The World's Largest Businesses ▾ | |
|---|---|
| The world's largest businesses in 1997 by sales, in billions of US$. | |
| 1 | General Motors, *USA* ............ 168.4 |
| 2 | Ford Motor, *USA* ............ 147.0 |
| 3 | Mitsui, *Japan* ............ 144.9 |
| 4 | Mitsubishi, *Japan* ............ 140.2 |
| 5 | Itochu, *Japan* ............ 135.5 |
| 6 | Royal Dutch/Shell Group, *UK/Neths* 128.2 |
| 7 | Marubeni, *Japan* ............ 124.0 |
| 8 | Exxon, *USA* ............ 119.4 |
| 9 | Summitomo, *Japan* ............ 119.3 |
| 10 | Toyota Motor, *Japan* ............ 108.7 |
| 11 | Wal-Mart Stores, *USA* ............ 106.1 |
| 12 | General Electric, *USA* ............ 79.2 |
| 13 | Nissho Iwai, *Japan* ............ 78.9 |
| 14 | Nippon Telegraph/Telephone, *Japan* 78.3 |
| 15 | Intl. business Machines, *USA* ............ 75.9 |
| 16 | Hitachi, *Japan* ............ 75.7 |
| 17 | AT&T, *USA* ............ 74.5 |
| 18 | Nippon Life Insurance, *Japan* ............ 72.6 |
| 19 | Mobil, *USA* ............ 72.3 |
| 20 | Daimler-Benz, *Germany* ............ 71.6 |

## TRADED PRODUCTS

The character of world trade has greatly changed in the last 50 years. While primary products were once the leading commodities, world trade is now dominated by manufactured products. Cars are the single most valuable traded product, followed by vehicle parts and engines. The next most valuable goods are high-tech products such as data processing (computer) equipment, telecommunications equipment, and transistors. Other items include aircraft, paper and board, trucks, measuring and control instruments, and electrical machinery. Trade in most manufactured products is dominated by the OECD countries. For example, the leading vehicle exporter is Japan, which became the world's leading car manufacturer in the 1980s. The United States, Germany, the United Kingdom, France and Japan lead in the production of data processing equipment.

and natural gas, dominated world trade.

Many developing countries still remain dependent on exporting mineral ores, fossil fuels, or farm products such as cocoa or coffee whose prices fluctuate according to demand. But today, manufactured goods are the most important commodities in world trade. The OECD nations lead the world in exporting manufactured goods, though they are being challenged by a group of 'tiger economies' in eastern Asia, notably Singapore, Hong Kong and Taiwan. Other rapidly industrializing countries in Asia include Thailand, Malaysia and the Philippines. Despite a recession during the late 1990s, these countries, with their generally low labour costs, are able to produce manufactured goods that compete with similar goods made in the Western world.

Private companies carry on most of the world's trade. The small proportion handled by governments decreased recently with the collapse of Communist regimes in eastern Europe and the former Soviet Union.

## SHARE OF WORLD TRADE

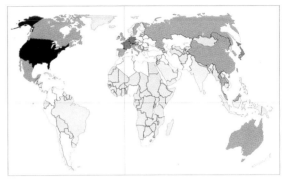

Percentage share of total world exports by value (1999)

- ■ Over 10%
- ▨ 1 – 5%
- ☐ 0.1 – 0.5%
- ■ 5 – 10%
- ☐ 0.5 – 1%
- ☐ Under 0.1%

## DEPENDENCE ON TRADE

Value of exports as a percentage of Gross Domestic Product (1997)

- ■ Over 50% GDP
- ☐ 30 – 40% GDP
- ☐ 10 – 20% GDP
- ■ 40 – 50% GDP
- ☐ 20 – 30% GDP
- ☐ Under 10% GDP

### Trade in Oil ▾

Major world trade in oil in millions of tonnes (1997)

| | | |
|---|---|---|
| Middle East to Asia (not Japan) | 294.4 | Mexico to USA | 68.0 |
| Middle East to Japan | 218.1 | W. Africa to W. Europe | 40.1 |
| Middle East to W. Europe | 187.9 | Western Europe to USA | 32.9 |
| S. and C. America to USA | 132.1 | Middle East to Africa | 32.0 |
| N. Africa to W. Europe | 97.9 | Middle East to South and Central America | 27.8 |
| CIS to Western Europe | 90.8 | |
| Middle East to USA | 86.9 | CIS to Central Europe | 31.8 |
| Canada to USA | 72.7 | Middle East to Central Europe | 19.3 |
| West Africa to USA | 68.3 | Total world trade | 1,978.9 |

21

# TRANSPORT & TRAVEL

ABOUT 200 YEARS ago, most people never travelled far from their birthplace. But adventurous travellers can now reach almost any part of the world.

Transport is concerned with moving goods and people around by land, water and air. Land transport was once laborious, and was dependent on pack animals or animal-drawn vehicles. But during the Industrial Revolution, railways played a vital role in moving bulky materials and equipment required by factories. They were also important in the opening up and development of remote areas around the world in North and South America, Africa, Asia and Australia.

Today, however, motor vehicles have taken over many of the functions once served by railways. Unlike railways, motor vehicles provide a door-to-door service and, through the invention of heavy trucks, they can also carry large loads. In the late-1990s, about 90% of inland freight in Britain was carried by road, while car and van travel accounted for 86% of passenger travel, as compared with 6% by buses and coaches, 5% by rail and less than 1% by air.

> Traffic jams and vehicle pollution have affected cities throughout the world. Many of Bangkok's beautiful old canals have been filled in to provide extra roads to cope with the enormous volume of traffic in the city.

## TRAVEL & TOURISM

Sea transport, which now employs huge bulk grain carriers, oil tankers and container ships, still carries most of the world's trade. But since the late 1950s, fewer passengers have travelled overseas by sea, because air travel is so much faster, though many former ocean liners now operate successfully as cruise ships.

Air travel has played a major part in the rapid growth of the tourist industry,

## AIR TRAVEL

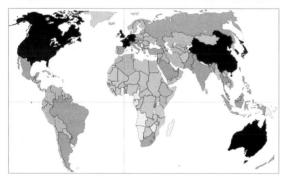

Number of passenger kilometres flown, in millions (1997). Passenger kilometres are the number of passengers (both international and domestic) multiplied by the distance flown by each passenger from airport of origin.

- ■ Over 100,000
- ■ 50,000 – 100,000
- ▨ 10,000 – 50,000
- ☐ 1,000 – 10,000
- ☐ 500 – 1,000
- ▨ Under 500

### The World's Busiest Airports ▼

Total number of passengers, in thousands (1997)

| | | |
|---|---|---|
| 1 | O'Hare Intl., *Chicago* | 70,295 |
| 2 | Hartsfield Atlanta Int., *Atlanta* | 68,206 |
| 3 | Dallas/Fort Worth Int., *Dallas* | 60,489 |
| 4 | Los Angeles Intl., *Los Angeles* | 60,143 |
| 5 | Heathrow, *London* | 57,975 |
| 6 | Haneda, *Tokyo* | 49,302 |
| 7 | San Francisco Intl., *San Francisco* | 40,500 |
| 8 | Frankfurt/Main, *Frankfurt* | 40,263 |
| 9 | Kimpo Intl., *Seoul* | 36,757 |
| 10 | Charles de Gaulle, *Paris* | 35,294 |
| 11 | Denver Intl., *Denver* | 34,973 |
| 12 | Miami Intl., *Miami* | 34,533 |
| 13 | Schiphol, *Amsterdam* | 31,570 |
| 14 | Metro Wayne County, *Detroit* | 31,521 |
| 15 | John F. Kennedy Intl., *New York* | 31,229 |

## The Longest Rail Networks ▾

Extent of rail network, in thousands of kilometres (latest available year)

| | | |
|---|---|---|
| 1 | USA | 243.3 |
| 2 | Russia | 87.1 |
| 3 | India | 62.9 |
| 4 | China | 56.7 |
| 5 | Germany | 40.8 |
| 6 | Argentina | 34.2 |
| 7 | France | 31.9 |
| 8 | Mexico | 26.5 |
| 9 | South Africa | 25.9 |
| 10 | Poland | 23.4 |

which accounted for 7.5% of world trade by the 1990s. Travel and tourism have greatly increased people's understanding and knowledge of the world, especially in the OECD countries, which account for about 8% of world tourism.

Some developing countries have large tourist industries which have provided employment and led to improvements in roads and other facilities. In some cases, tourism plays a vital role in the economy. For example, in Kenya, tourism provides more income than any other activity apart from the production and sale of tea and coffee. However, too many tourists can damage fragile environments, such as the wildlife and scenery in national parks, and also harm local cultures.

## THE IMPORTANCE OF TOURISM

Nations receiving the most from tourism, millions of US$ (1996)

| | | |
|---|---|---|
| 1 | USA | 64,400 |
| 2 | Spain | 28,400 |
| 3 | France | 28,200 |
| 4 | Italy | 27,300 |
| 5 | UK | 20,400 |
| 6 | Austria | 15,100 |
| 7 | Germany | 13,200 |
| 8 | Hong Kong | 11,200 |
| 9 | China | 10,500 |
| 10 | Switzerland | 9,900 |

Fastest growing tourist destinations, % change in receipts (1994–95)

| | | |
|---|---|---|
| 1 | South Korea | 49% |
| 2 | Czech Republic | 27% |
| 3 | India | 21% |
| 4 | Russia | 19% |
| 5 | Philippines | 18% |
| 6 | Turkey | 17% |
| 7 | Thailand | 15% |
| 8 | Poland | 13% |
| 9 | China | 12% |
| 10 | Israel | 12% |

Number of tourist arrivals, millions (1996)

| | | |
|---|---|---|
| 1 | France | 66,800 |
| 2 | USA | 49,038 |
| 3 | Spain | 43,403 |
| 4 | Italy | 34,087 |
| 5 | UK | 25,960 |
| 6 | China | 23,770 |
| 7 | Poland | 19,514 |
| 8 | Mexico | 18,667 |
| 9 | Canada | 17,610 |
| 10 | Czech Republic | 17,400 |

Overseas travellers to the USA, thousands (1997)

| | | |
|---|---|---|
| 1 | Canada | 13,900 |
| 2 | Mexico | 12,370 |
| 3 | Japan | 4,640 |
| 4 | UK | 3,350 |
| 5 | Germany | 1,990 |
| 6 | France | 1,030 |
| 7 | Taiwan | 885 |
| 8 | Venezuela | 860 |
| 9 | South Korea | 800 |
| 10 | Brazil | 785 |

## THE WORLD'S VEHICLES

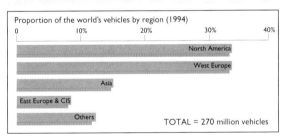

Proportion of the world's vehicles by region (1994)

North America
West Europe
Asia
East Europe & CIS
Others

TOTAL = 270 million vehicles

## CAR OWNERSHIP

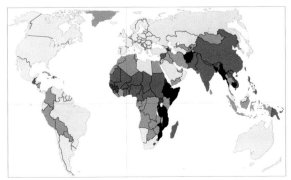

Number of people per car (1998)

- ■ Over 1,000
- ■ 500 – 1,000
- ■ 100 – 500
- ■ 25 – 100
- □ 5 – 25
- □ Under 5

Two-thirds of the world's vehicles are found in the developed countries of Europe and North America. Car ownership is also high in Australia and New Zealand, as well as in Japan, the world's leading car exporter. Car transport is the most convenient form of passenger travel, but air pollution caused by exhaust fumes is a serious problem in many large cities.

# INTERNATIONAL ORGANIZATIONS

IN THE LATE 1980s, people rejoiced at the collapse of Communist regimes in eastern Europe and the former Soviet Union, because this brought to an end the Cold War, a long period of hostility between East and West. But hope of a new era of peace was shattered when ethnic and religious rivalries led to civil war in Yugoslavia and in parts of the former Soviet Union.

In order to help maintain peace, many governments have formed international organizations to increase co-operation. Some, such as NATO (North Atlantic

*> In the early 1990s, the United Nations peacekeeping mission worked to end the civil war in Bosnia-Herzegovina and also to bring aid to civilians affected by the fighting.*

Treaty Organization), are defence alliances, while others aim to encourage economic and social co-operation. Some of the organizations such as the Red Cross are non-governmental organizations, or NGOs.

## UNITED NATIONS

The United Nations, the chief international organization, was formed in October 1945 and now has 188 member countries. The only independent nations that are not members are Switzerland, Taiwan and the Vatican City.

### UN Contributions ▾

In 1996–97, the top ten contributing countries to the UN budget, which was US$2.6 billion, were as follows:

| | | |
|---|---|---|
| 1 | USA | 25.0% |
| 2 | Japan | 15.4% |
| 3 | Germany | 9.0% |
| 4 | France | 6.4% |
| 5 | UK | 5.3% |
| 6 | Italy | 5.2% |
| 7 | Russia | 4.5% |
| 8 | Canada | 3.1% |
| 9 | Spain | 2.4% |
| 10 | Brazil | 1.6% |

## THE UNITED NATIONS

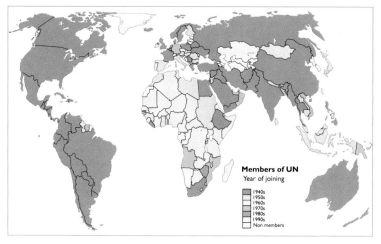

**Members of UN**
Year of joining
- 1940s
- 1950s
- 1960s
- 1970s
- 1980s
- 1990s
- Non members

*> The membership of the UN had risen from 51 in 1945 to 188 by the end of 2000. The first big period of expansion came in the 1960s when many former colonies achieved their independence. The membership again expanded rapidly in the 1990s when new countries were formed from the former Soviet Union and Yugoslavia. The most recent addition, Palau, is a former US trust territory in the Pacific Ocean and joined in 1994.*

The United Nations was formed at the end of World War II to promote peace, international co-operation and security, and to help solve economic, social, cultural and humanitarian problems. It promotes human rights and freedom and is a forum for negotiations between nations.

The main organs of the UN are the General Assembly, the Security Council, the Economic and Social Council, the Trusteeship Council, the International Court of Justice and the Secretariat.

The UN also operates 14 specialized agencies concerned with particular issues, such as agriculture, education, working conditions, communications and health. For example, UNICEF (the United Nations International Children's Fund), established in 1946 to deliver post-war relief to children, now aims to provide basic health care to children and mothers worldwide. The ILO (International Labour Organization) seeks to improve working conditions, while the FAO (Food and Agricultural Organization) aims at improving the production and distribution of food. The WTO (World Trade Organization) was set up as recently as January 1995 to succeed GATT (General Agreements on Tariffs and Trade).

## THE UNITED NATIONS

**THE GENERAL ASSEMBLY** is the meeting of all member nations every September under a newly-elected president to discuss issues affecting development, peace and security.

**THE SECURITY COUNCIL** has 15 members, of which five are permanent. It is responsible for maintaining international peace.

**THE SECRETARIAT** consists of the staff and employees of the UN, including the Secretary-General (appointed for a five-year term), who is the UN's chief administrator.

**THE ECONOMIC & SOCIAL COUNCIL** works with the specialized agencies to implement UN policies on improving living standards, health, cultural and educational co-operation.

**THE TRUSTEESHIP COUNCIL** was designed to bring several dependencies to independence. This work is now complete.

**THE INTERNATIONAL COURT OF JUSTICE**, or World Court, deals with legal problems and helps to settle disputes. Its headquarters are at The Hague, in the Netherlands.

## UN DEPARTMENTS

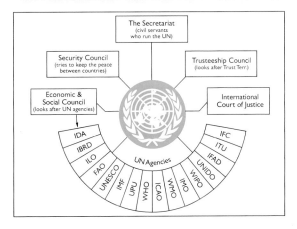

## UN PEACEKEEPING MISSIONS

The United Nations tries to resolve international disputes in several ways. It sends unarmed observer missions to monitor cease-fires or supervise troop withdrawals, and the Security Council members also send peacekeeping forces.

The first of these forces was sent in 1948 to supervise the cease-fire between Arabs and Jews in disputed parts of Palestine and, since then, it has undertaken more than 30 other missions. The 'Blue Berets', as the 25,650 UN troops are called, must be impartial in any dispute

and they can fire only in self-defence. Hence, they can operate only with the support of both sides, which leaves them open to criticism when they are unable to prevent violence by intervening.

By the mid-1990s, the UN was involved in 15 world conflicts, was policing the boundary in partitioned Cyprus, and was seeking to enforce a peace agreement in Angola after 20 years of civil war. Other UN missions were in Tajikistan, Georgia, the Israeli-occupied Golan Heights, Haiti, Kuwait, southern Lebanon, the India–

Pakistan border, Liberia, Mozambique, Western Sahara and the former Yugoslavia. A force known as UNPROFOR (UN Protection Force) had been operating in Bosnia-Herzegovina and, by 1995, it accounted for 60% of the total UN peacekeeping budget. In February 1996, the Secretary-General of the UN approved the setting up of a new force, the United Nations Mission in Bosnia-Herzegovina (UNMIBH). Its main objective was to help create the right climate for the elections held in September 1996.

## ECONOMIC ORGANIZATIONS

Over the last 40 years, many countries have joined common markets aimed at eliminating trade barriers and encouraging the free movement of workers and capital.

The best known of these is the European Union. Other organizations include ASEAN (the Association of South-east Asian Nations), which aims to reduce trade barriers between its ten members: Brunei, Burma, Cambodia, Indonesia, Laos, Malaysia, the Philippines, Singapore, Thailand and Vietnam.

APEC (the Asia-Pacific Co-operation Group) was founded in 1989 and in-

> The European Parliament, one of the branches of the EU, consists of 626 members. The number of members for each country is based mainly on population.

cludes the countries of East and South-east Asia, as well as North America, plus Australia, New Zealand and Chile. APEC aims to create a free trade zone by 2020.

Together the United States, Canada and Mexico form NAFTA (North American Free Trade Agreement), which aims at eliminating trade barriers within 15 years of its foundation on 1 January 1994. Other economic groupings link the countries of Latin America.

Another economic group with more limited aims is OPEC (Organization of Petroleum Exporting Countries). It works to unify policies concerned with the sale of petroleum on world markets.

The central aim of the Colombo Plan is to provide economic development assistance for South and South-east Asia.

## OTHER ORGANIZATIONS

Some organizations exist for consultation on matters of common interest. The Commonwealth of Nations grew out of the links created by the British Empire, while the OAS (Organization of American States) works to increase understanding throughout the Western hemisphere. The OAU (Organization of

### THE EUROPEAN UNION

At the end of World War II (1939–45), many Europeans wanted to end the ancient emnities that had caused such destruction and rebuild the shattered continent. It was in this mood that Belgium, France, West Germany, Italy, Luxembourg and the Netherlands signed the Treaty of Paris in 1951. This set up the European Coal and Steel Community (ECSC), the forerunner of the European Union.

In 1957, through the Treaty of Rome, the same six countries created the European Economic Community (EEC) and the European Atomic Community (EURATOM). In 1967, the ECSC, the EEC and EURATOM merged to form the single European Community (EC).

Another economic group, the European Free Trade Association (EFTA), was set up in 1960 by seven countries: Austria, Denmark, Norway, Portugal, Sweden, Switzerland and the United Kingdom. However, Denmark, Ireland and the UK left to become members of the EC in 1973, followed by Greece in 1981, Spain and Portugal in 1986, and Austria, Finland and Sweden in 1995. The expansion of the EC to 15 members left EFTA with just four members: Iceland, Liechtenstein, Norway and Switzerland.

In 1993, following the signing of the Maastricht Treaty, the EC was reconstituted

as the European Union (EU). The aims of the EU include economic and monetary union, a single currency for all 15 countries, and closer co-operation on foreign and security policies and also on home affairs. This step has led to a debate. Some people would like the EU to develop into a federal Europe, but others fear that this would lead to a loss of national identity. On 1 January 1999, 11 EU countries adopted the euro as their official currency, although euro coins and notes would not to come into use until 1 January 2002. On 1 January 2001, Greece also adopted the euro, leaving only Denmark, Sweden and the United Kingdom outside the euro zone.

## AUSTRALIA'S NEW ROLE

Most of the people who settled in Australia between 1788 and the mid-20th century came from the British Isles. However, the strong ties between Australia and Britain were weakened after Britain joined the European Community in 1973. Since 1973, many Australians have argued that their world position has changed and that they are part of a Pacific community of nations, rather than an extension of Europe. Some want closer integration with ASEAN, the increasingly powerful economic group formed by seven South-east Asian nations. But in 1995, the prime minister of Malaysia, Dr Mahathir Mohamad, argued that Australia could not be regarded as Asian until at least 70% of its people were of ethnic Asian origin.

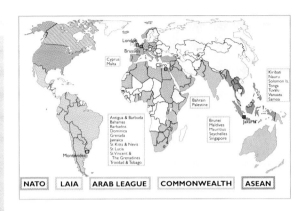

African Unity) has a similar role in Africa, while the Arab League is made up of Arabic-speaking North African and Middle Eastern states. The CIS (Commonwealth of Independent States) was formed in 1991 to maintain links between 12 of the former 15 republics in the Soviet Union.

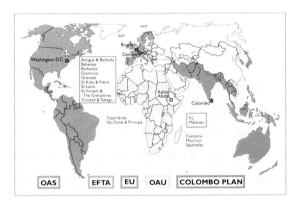

## NORTH–SOUTH DIVIDE

The deepest division in the world today is the divide between rich and poor nations. In international terms, this is called the North–South divide, because the North contains most of the world's developed countries, while the developing countries lie mainly in the South. The European Union recognizes this division and gives special trading terms to more than 60 former European dependencies, which form the ACP (African, Caribbean and Pacific) states. One organization containing a majority of developing countries is the Non-Aligned Movement. This Movement was created in 1961 during the Cold War as a political bloc allied neither to the East nor to the West. However, the aims of the 113 members who attended the movement's 11th gathering in 1995 were concerned mainly with economic matters. The 113 countries between them produce only about 7% of the world's gross output and they can speak for the poorer South.

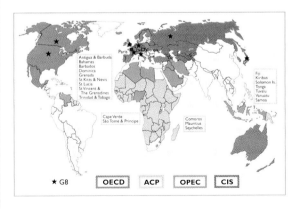

> The maps above show the membership of major international organizations. One important grouping shown on the bottom map is the Group of Eight (often called 'G8'). This group of eight leading industrial nations (comprising Canada, France, Germany, Italy, Japan, Russia, the United Kingdom and the United States) holds periodic meetings to discuss major problems, such as world recessions.

# REGIONS IN THE NEWS

## THE BREAK-UP OF YUGOSLAVIA

> The former Yugoslavia, a federation of six republics, split apart in 1991–92. Fearing Serb domination, Croatia, Slovenia, Macedonia and Bosnia-Herzegovina declared themselves independent. This left two states, Serbia and Montenegro, to continue as Yugoslavia. The presence in Croatia and Bosnia-Herzegovina of Orthodox Christian Serbs, Roman Catholic Croats and Muslims led to civil war and 'ethnic cleansing'. In 1995, the war ended when the Dayton Peace Accord affirmed Bosnia-Herzegovina as a single state partitioned into a Muslim-Croat Federation and a Serbian Republic. But the status of Kosovo, a former autonomous Yugoslav region, remained unresolved. Kosovo's autonomy was abolished in 1989 and Albanian-speaking, Muslim Kosovars came under direct Serbian rule. From 1995, support grew for the rebel Kosovo Liberation Army. War broke out, and NATO launched an offensive in 1999 that led to the withdrawal of Serbian troops from Kosovo. In 2000, President Slobodan Milosevic, whose policies were considered to be the cause of much of the ethnic conflict, was defeated in elections.

### Population Breakdown ▾

Population totals and the proportion of ethnic groups (1995)

**Yugoslavia** — 10,881,000
  Serb 63%, Albanian 17%, Montenegrin 5%, Hungarian 3%, Muslim 3%
Serbia — 6,017,200
  Kosovo — 2,045,600
  Vojvodina — 2,121,800
Montenegro — 696,400

**Bosnia-Herzegovina** — 4,400,000
  Muslim 49%, Serb 31%, Croat 17%

**Croatia** — 4,900,000
  Croat 78%, Serb 12%

**Slovenia** — 2,000,000
  Slovene 88%, Croat 3%, Serb 2%

**Macedonia (F.Y.R.O.M.)** — 2,173,000
  Macedonian 64%, Albanian 22%, Turkish 5%, Romanian 3%, Serb 2%

International borders

Republic boundaries

Province boundaries

Line of the Dayton Peace Accord

Muslim–Croat Federation

Serbian Republic

28

> Since its establishment in 1948, the State of Israel has seldom been out of the news. During wars with its Arab neighbours in 1948–49, 1956, 1967 and 1973, it occupied several areas. The largest of the occupied territories, the Sinai peninsula, was returned to Egypt in 1979 following the signing of an Egyptian–Israeli peace treaty. This left three Israeli-occupied territories: the Gaza Strip, the West Bank bordering Jordan, and the Golan Heights, a militarily strategic area overlooking south-western Syria.

Despite the peace agreement with Egypt, conflict continued in Israel with the PLO (Palestine Liberation Organization), which claimed to represent Arabs in Israel and Palestinians living in exile. Finally, on 13 September 1993 Israel officially recognized the PLO, and Yasser Arafat, leader of the PLO, renounced terrorism and recognized the State of Israel. This led to an agreement signed by both sides in Washington, DC. In May 1994, limited Palestinian self-rule was established in the Gaza Strip and in parts of the occupied West Bank. A Palestinian National Authority (PNA) was created and took over from the Israeli military administration when Israeli troops withdrew from the Gaza Strip and the city of Jericho. On 1 July 1994 the Palestinian leader, Yasser Arafat, stepped on to Palestinian land for the first time in 25 years.

Many people hoped that these developments would eventually lead to the creation of a Palestinian state, which would co-exist in peace with its neighbour Israel. But groups on both sides sought to undermine the peace process. In November 1995, a right-wing Jewish student assassinated the Israeli prime minister, Yitzhak Rabin, who was succeeded by Símon Peres.

In 1996, a right-wing coalition led by Binyamin Netanyahu was elected to power. Peace talks with the PLO were halted, but, in 1999, the Labour Party leader Ehud Barak was elected prime minister. Barak revived negotiations with the PLO and Middle Eastern leaders aimed at exchanging 'land for peace'. But agreement, especially on the status of Jerusalem, proved elusive and fighting broke out in 2000. In 2001, Barak was defeated in elections by the right-wing Ariel Sharon.

## Population Breakdown ▾

Population totals and the proportion of ethnic groups (1995)

**Israel** .................................................. **5,696,000**
 Jewish 82%, Arab Muslim 14%, Arab
 Christian 3%, Druse 2%
West Bank .................................................. 973,500
 Palestinian Arab 97% (Arab Muslim 85%,
 Christian 8%, Jewish 7%)
Gaza Strip .................................................. 658,200
 Arab Muslim 98%

**Jordan** .................................................. **5,547,000**
 Arab 99% (Palestinian Arab 50%)

**Syria** .................................................. **14,614,000**
 Arab 89%, Kurdish 6%

**THE NEAR EAST**

—·—·— 1949 Armistice Line

------ 1974 Cease-fire Lines (Golan Heights)

*Efrata*
●   Main Jewish settlements in the West Bank and Gaza Strip

Halhul   Main Palestinian Arab towns in the West Bank and Gaza Strip
□   – under Palestinian control since May 1994 (Gaza and Jericho)
   and 28 September 1995 (West Bank)

29

# WORLD FLAGS

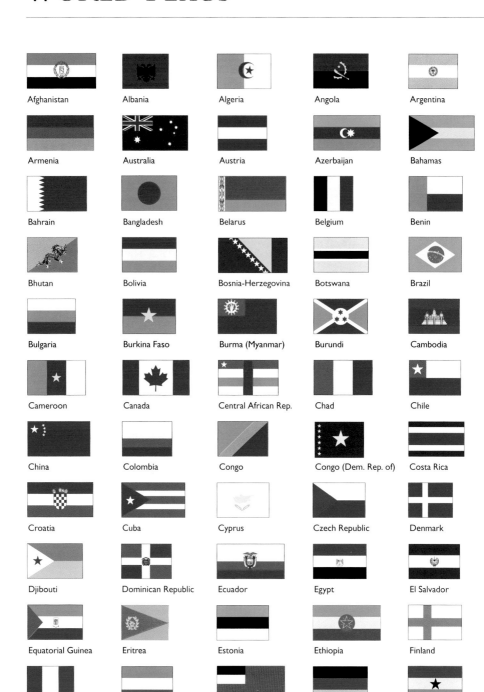

| | | | | |
|---|---|---|---|---|
| Afghanistan | Albania | Algeria | Angola | Argentina |
| Armenia | Australia | Austria | Azerbaijan | Bahamas |
| Bahrain | Bangladesh | Belarus | Belgium | Benin |
| Bhutan | Bolivia | Bosnia-Herzegovina | Botswana | Brazil |
| Bulgaria | Burkina Faso | Burma (Myanmar) | Burundi | Cambodia |
| Cameroon | Canada | Central African Rep. | Chad | Chile |
| China | Colombia | Congo | Congo (Dem. Rep. of) | Costa Rica |
| Croatia | Cuba | Cyprus | Czech Republic | Denmark |
| Djibouti | Dominican Republic | Ecuador | Egypt | El Salvador |
| Equatorial Guinea | Eritrea | Estonia | Ethiopia | Finland |
| France | Gabon | Georgia | Germany | Ghana |

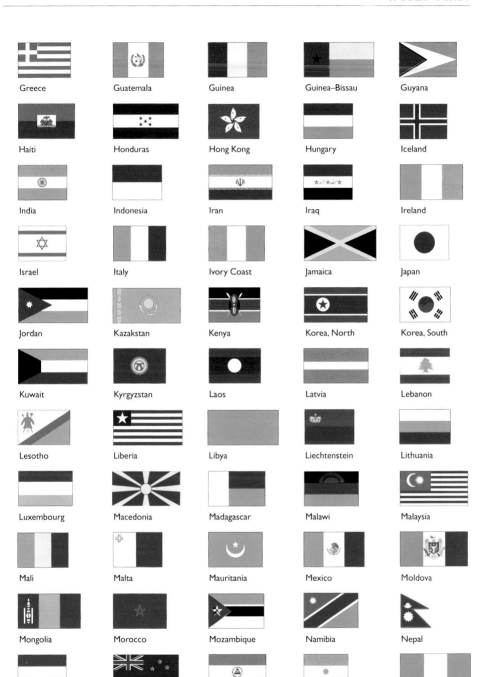

| | | | | |
|---|---|---|---|---|
| Greece | Guatemala | Guinea | Guinea–Bissau | Guyana |
| Haiti | Honduras | Hong Kong | Hungary | Iceland |
| India | Indonesia | Iran | Iraq | Ireland |
| Israel | Italy | Ivory Coast | Jamaica | Japan |
| Jordan | Kazakstan | Kenya | Korea, North | Korea, South |
| Kuwait | Kyrgyzstan | Laos | Latvia | Lebanon |
| Lesotho | Liberia | Libya | Liechtenstein | Lithuania |
| Luxembourg | Macedonia | Madagascar | Malawi | Malaysia |
| Mali | Malta | Mauritania | Mexico | Moldova |
| Mongolia | Morocco | Mozambique | Namibia | Nepal |
| Netherlands | New Zealand | Nicaragua | Niger | Nigeria |

Norway

Oman

Pakistan

Panama

Papua New Guinea

Paraguay

Peru

Philippines

Poland

Portugal

Puerto Rico

Qatar

Romania

Russia

Rwanda

São Tomé & Príncipe

Saudi Arabia

Senegal

Sierra Leone

Singapore

Slovak Republic

Slovenia

Somalia

South Africa

Spain

Sri Lanka

Sudan

Surinam

Swaziland

Sweden

Switzerland

Syria

Taiwan

Tajikistan

Tanzania

Thailand

Togo

Trinidad & Tobago

Tunisia

Turkey

Turkmenistan

Uganda

Ukraine

UAE

United Kingdom

USA

Uruguay

Uzbekistan

Vatican City

Venezuela

Vietnam

Yemen

Yugoslavia

Zambia

Zimbabwe

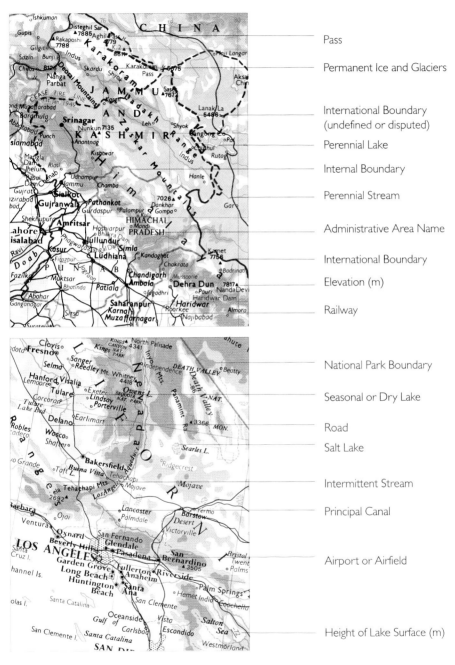

Pass

Permanent Ice and Glaciers

International Boundary
(undefined or disputed)

Perennial Lake

Internal Boundary

Perennial Stream

Administrative Area Name

International Boundary

Elevation (m)

Railway

National Park Boundary

Seasonal or Dry Lake

Road

Salt Lake

Intermittent Stream

Principal Canal

Airport or Airfield

Height of Lake Surface (m)

Settlements

Settlement symbols and type styles vary
according to the scale of each map and
indicate the importance of towns rather
than specific population figures.

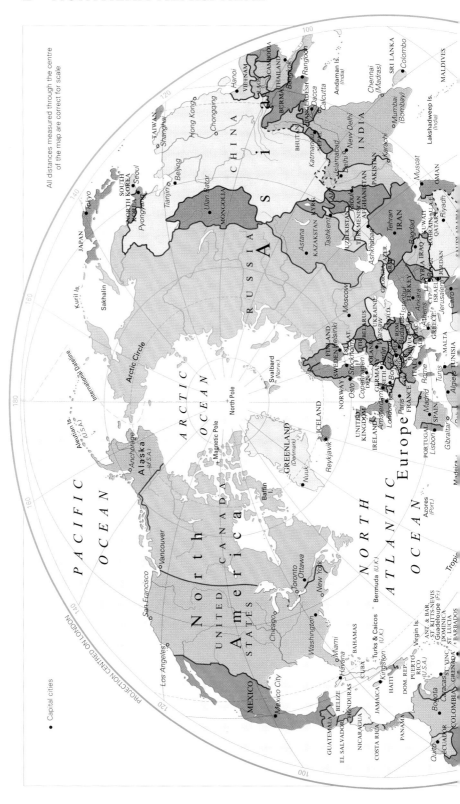

All distances measured through the centre of the map are correct for scale

PROJECTION CENTRED ON LONDON

• Capital cities

PROJECTION CENTRED ON CAPE TOWN

+8.00
+7.00

+8.00

East from Greenwich

+5.30

+5.00 +4.30
+4.00

+3.30 +6.00
+5.00

+3.00 +6.00
+2.00 +3.00

+3.00

Cape Town

+1.00

+2.00
+1.00

0.00

+South Pole

-3.00

-3.30
-3.00
-4.00
-5.00

West from Greenwich

COPYRIGHT GEORGE PHILIP LTD

CARTOGRAPHY BY PHILIP'S.

**TIME ZONES**

Zones using Greenwich Mean Time

Zones fast of Greenwich Mean Time

Zones slow of Greenwich Mean Time

Standard Time not the Zone hour

No Official Time

*OCEAN* (U.K.)

SEYCHELLES

MAURITIUS

Réunion (Fr.)
Antananarivo

MADAGASCAR

COMOROS
Mayotte (Fr.)

DJIBOUTI
SOMALIA
Addis Ababa
ETHIOPIA
Mogadishu

Khartoum
SUDAN
KENYA
Nairobi
UGANDA
RWANDA Dodoma
BURUNDI TANZANIA
Kampala

CENTRAL
AFRICAN
Bangui
CHAD
CAMEROON
Yaoundé
CONGO (DEM. REP. OF THE)
Kinshasa
CONGO
Brazzaville
GABON
Libreville

MALAWI
Lilongwe

ZAMBIA
Lusaka
MOZAMBIQUE
Harare
ZIMBABWE Maputo
SWAZILAND
Pretoria Johannesburg
LESOTHO

ANGOLA
Luanda

NAMIBIA
Windhoek
BOTSWANA
Gaborone
SOUTH AFRICA
Cape Town

NIGER
MALI
CHAD
NIGERIA
Abuja
BENIN
Niamey
BURKINA FASO
TOGO
GHANA
Accra
IVORY COAST
Yamoussoukro

ÉQUAT GUINEA
SÃO TOMÉ & P.

Tropic of Capricorn

MAURITANIA
Nouakchott
SENEGAL
Dakar
GAMBIA
Banjul
GUINEA BISSAU
GUINEA
Conakry
SIERRA LEONE
Freetown
LIBERIA
Monrovia

CAPE VERDE IS.

Equator

*SOUTH*

*ATLANTIC*

*OCEAN*

St. Helena (U.K.)

Ascension (U.K.)

East from Greenwich

West from Greenwich

SURINAM FRENCH GUIANA

South

America

BOLIVIA

BRAZIL
Brasília

São Paulo

Rio de Janeiro

Projection: Oblique Azimuthal Equidistant

PROJECTION CENTRED ON SAN FRANCISCO

West from Greenwich

Greenwich
0.00
-1.00
-2.00 -3.30
-3.00
-4.00
-4.00 -5.00
-1.00
-3.00 -5.00
-6.00
-7.00
San Francisco
-8.00

North Pole +

+3.00
+4.00
+5.00
+6.00
+7.00
+8.00
+9.00
+8.00 +9.00
-9.00
+10.00
+11.00
+12.00
-10.00

International Dateline

East from Greenwich

South America

PERU

BOLIVIA

CHILE

ARGENTINA

PARAGUAY

URUGUAY

BRAZIL

Santiago

Asunón

Buenos Aires

Montevideo

Falkland Is.
(U.K.)

South Georgia
(U.K.)

Antarctica

Byrd Land

Ellsworth Land

South Pole

Enderby Land

Queen Maud Land

Bouvet I.
(Norw.)

South
Sandwich Is.
(U.K.)

SOUTH

ATLANTIC

OCEAN

Kerguelen
(Fr.)

Heard I.
(Austral.)

Crozet I.
(Fr.)

Pr. Edward I.
(S. African)

PROJECTION CENTRED ON SHANGHAI

West from Greenwich

International Dateline

North Pole

Shanghai

Greenwich

Equator

East from Greenwich

−10.00

−9.00

−8.00

−7.00

−6.00

−5.00

−3.00

−1.00

0.00

+1.00

+2.00

+3.00

+4.00

+5.00

+6.00

+7.00

+8.00

+9.00

+10.00

+11.00

+12.00

+3.30

+4.30

+5.30

+6.30

+9.30

**TIME ZONES**

Zones using Greenwich Mean Time

Zones fast of Greenwich Mean Time

Zones slow of Greenwich Mean Time

Standard Time not the Zone hour

PROJECTION CENTRED ON CAIRO

East from Greenwich

North Pole

Greenwich

Cairo

Equator

West from Greenwich

−9.00

−7.00

−6.00

−5.00

−4.00

−3.00

−1.00

0.00

+1.00

+2.00

+3.00

+4.00

+5.00

+6.00

+7.00

+8.00

+9.00

+10.00

+11.00

+12.00

+3.30

+4.30

+5.30

+6.30

−3.30

C

Arctic Circle

ICELAND
•Reykjavik

*Norwegian*

*Sea*

60

Faroe Is.
(Den.)

D

SWED

Trondheim

Shetland
Is.

NORWAY

•Bergen

Oslo

Uppsala

Örebro

55

Stavanger

*Vänern*

Vättern
Jönköping

ATLANTIC

UNITED
KINGDOM

Hebrides

Aberdeen

SCOTLAND

Glasgow •Dundee

Edinburgh

Orkney
Is.

*North*

Skagerrak

Älborg

Göthenburg

Ba

Kattegat

E

IRELAND
•Belfast

N
IRELAND

DENMARK
Århus

Copenhagen •Malmö

Dublin

Newcastle-
upon-Tyne

*Sea*

•Kiel

Szczecin

Gdar

Cork

Manchester•
Liverpool •Leeds
•Sheffield

•Hamburg

•Bremen *Elbe*

•Berlin

Bydgoszcz

PO

WALES
Cardiff•

Birmingham
ENGLAND

Amsterdam•NETHER-
The Hague•LANDS
Rotterdam

Hannover•

Magdeburg

*Oder*

Poz

F

OCEAN

Plymouth

Southampton
•Bristol

LONDON

Antwerp

BELGIUM

GERMANY

•Dortmund

Halle

Dresden

Katow

*English Channel*

Le Havre

Lille

•Brussels

•Essen

•Cologne

Leipzig
•Chemnitz

Ostrav

Channel Is.
(U.K.)

Brest

Rouen

Bonn
•Wiesbaden

•Frankfurt
am Main

Prague•

CZECH REP.

*Seine*

PARIS

LU
Luxembourg

Strasbourg

•Nuremberg

Vienna

45

Nantes *Loire*

FRANCE

Dijon

*Rhine*

Stuttgart

•Munich

AUSTRIA

Linz

Br

G

*Bay of
Biscay*

Limoges•

Lyons•

SWITZERLAND
•Bern

LIECH
Vaduz

Innsbruck

Salzburg

Graz

HU

Bordeaux•
*Garonne*

St.-Étienne•

Zürich•

Geneva•

Milan•

SLOVENIA•

Ljubljana

•Zagreb

Vigo•

La Coruña

Toulouse

Grenoble•

Turin•

Venice•

Trieste

CROAT

40

Porto• *Douro*

Bilbao•

*Rhône*

Nice•

Genoa•

Bologna•

Valladolid•

ANDORRA•Andorra-
la-Vella

Marseilles•

MONACO

Florence•

SAN
MARINO

BOSN
HER

Lisbon•

Madrid•

Zaragoza•

Toulon•

Corsica

Split•

Saraje

H

PORTUGAL

*Tagus*

SPAIN

Barcelona•

Ajaccio•

ITALY

Rome•

Adriatic Sea

*Guadiana*

Valencia•

Balearic Is.
Palma

Minorca

Sardinia

Naples•

Bari

Seville•

Córdoba•
*Guadalquivir*

Murcia•

Ibiza

Majorca

Tyrrhenian

Taranto•

Granada•

Alicante•

*Sea*

35

Cádiz•

Málaga•

Gibraltar(U.K.)

Cagliari•

Palermo•

Messina•

Io

*Str. of Gibraltar*

Tangier•

Ceuta(Sp.)

*Mediterranean*

Sicily •Catania

S

Melilla(Sp.)

Algiers•

Annaba•

J

MOROCCO

*Af r i c a*

ALGERIA

Constantine•

*Sea*

Pantelleria
(Italy)

Tunis•

TUNISIA

MALTA• Valletta

1 : 20 000 000

100   0   100   200   300   400   500 miles
100   0   200   400   600   800 km

**11   12   13   14   15   16   17   18   19**

C

*Ob*

lammerfest

Murmansk

*White Sea*

Arkhangelsk

*N. Dvina*

D

uled

Kotlas

Nizhniy Tagil

Perm

**FINLAND**

*L. Onega*

Yekaterinburg

asa

Kirov

Chelyabinsk

re

Vyborg L. Ladoga

Turku

Vologda

Ufa

Helsinki

**ST. PETERBURG**

*Rybinsk Res.*

Kostroma

**R   U   S   S   I   A**

E

Magnitogorsk

Tallinn

*L. Chudskoye*

Yaroslavl

Ivanovo

Nizhniy Novgorod

Kazan

**ESTONIA**

**LATVIA**

Riga

*W. Dvina*

**MOSCOW**

Simbirsk

Samara

Orenburg

**LITHUANIA**

Vitebsk

Smolensk

Tula

Penza

*Volga*

Uralsk

ningrad

Kaunas

Vilnius

Mogilev

*Ural*

**K  A  Z  A  K  S  T  A  N**

F

tigl

Minsk

Orel

Tambov

Saratov

dystok

**BELARUS**

Gomel

Kursk

Voronezh

Atyraū

**N   D**

Brest

*Pripet*

Chernigov

Volgograd

arsaw

Lublin

Zhitomir

Kiev

*Dnieper*

Kharkov

*Don*

Astrakhan

ow

Lvov

**U K R A I N E**

Dnepropetrovsk

Donetsk

*Caspian Sea*

G

*Dniester*

Bug

Krivoy Rog

Zaporozhye

Taganrog

Rostov

EP

**MOLDOVA**

Nikolayev

Kherson

Stavropol

Makhachkala

oki

Debrecen

Cluj-Napoca

Kishinev

Odessa

Krasnodar

Cluj-Napoca

**R O M A N I A**

Brasov

Galati

*Crimea*

Timisoara

Ploiesti

Sevastopol

**GEORGIA**

Tbilisi

**AZERBAIJAN**

Baku

grade

Bucharest

Constanta

*Black   Sea*

**ARMENIA**

H

BIA

*Danube*

Varna

Yerevan

*Araks*

liš

**BULGARIA**

Sofia

*Bosporus*

Samsun

Erzurum

**T   U   R   K   E   Y**

Tabriz

VIA

Skopje

Plovdiv

EDONIA

**İSTANBUL**

Diyarbakır

**IRAN**

Thessaloniki

Bursa

Ankara

Kayseri

a

i

REECE

*Aegean Sea*

İzmir

Konya

**S   Y   R   I   A**

Aleppo

*Euphrates*

**IRAQ**

*Tigris*

J

Adana

Antalya

Patrai

Athens

**CYPRUS**

Nicosia

Baghdad

**10   Crete   11**          **12**          **13**          **14**          **15**

CARTOGRAPHY BY PHILIPS.

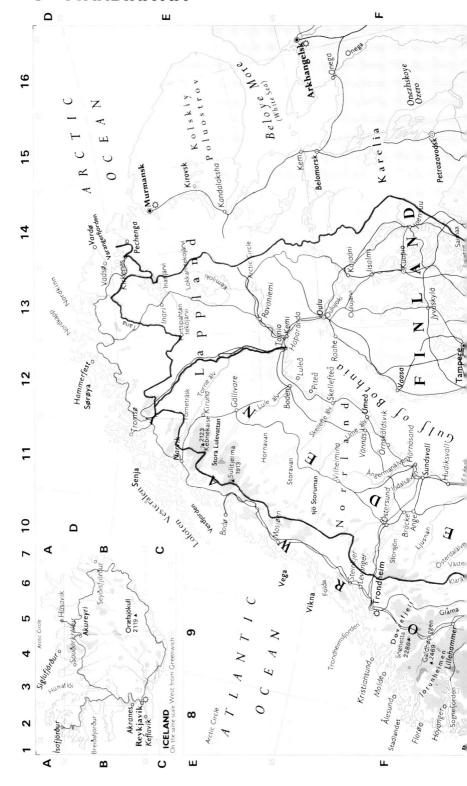

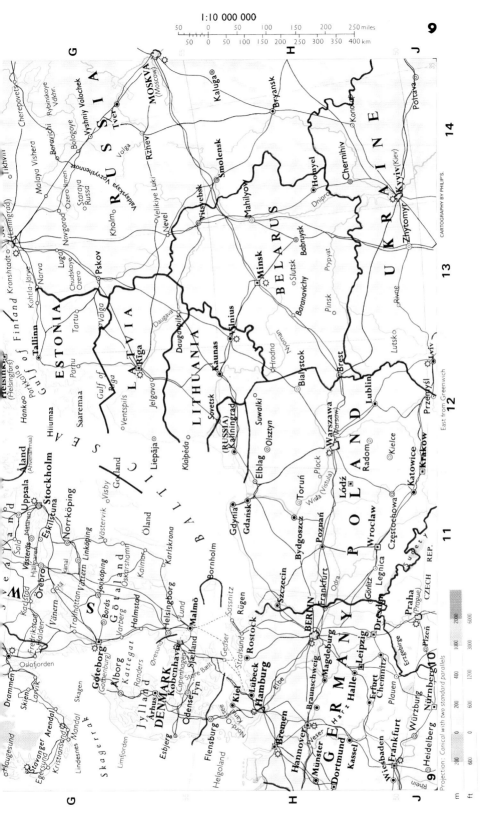

1:10 000 000

50    0    50    100    150    200    250 miles

50    0    50    100    150    200    250    300    350    400 km

CARTOGRAPHY BY PHILIP'S.

East from Greenwich

Projection: Conical with two standard parallels

G                    H                    J

14

13

12

11

10

9

**RUSSIA**

MOSKVA
(Moscow)

Kaluga

Bryansk

Tver

Rzhev

Smolensk

Vyazma

Vyshniy Volochek

Bologoye

Borovichi

Valday

Rybinskoye
Vdkhr.

Cherepovets

Tikhvin

Malaya Vishera

Ozero Ilmen

Novgorod

Staraya
Russa

Kholm

Velikiye Luki

Nevel

Vitsyebsk

Mahilyow

Homyel

Chernihiv

Kyiv(Kiev)

**UKRAINE**

Zhytomyr

Pottava

Konotop

Dnipro

Prypyat

Pinsk

Lutsko

L'viv

Przemyśl

Rivne

**BELARUS**

Minsk

Slutsk

Baranovichy

Babruysk

Brest

Hrodna

Vilnius

Kaunas

**LITHUANIA**

Sovetsk

Suwałki

Olsztyn

(RUSSIA)
Kaliningrad

Elbląg

Klaipėda

Liepāja

Ventspils

**LATVIA**

Riga

Jelgava

Daugavpils

Daugava

**ESTONIA**

Tallinn

Pärnu

Tartu

Võru

Saaremaa

Hiiumaa

Gulf of
Riga

Gulf of Finland

Kronshtadt

(Leningrad)

St Petersburg

Lugo

Pskov

Ozero
Chudskoye

Narva

Kohtla-Järve

Hanko

**Helsinki**
(Helsingfors)

**SWEDEN**

Stockholm

Uppsala

Åland
(Ahvenanmaa)

Eskilstuna

Norrköping

Gotland

Visby

Västervik

Öland

Kalmar

Karlskrona

Karlshamn

Bornholm

Oskarshamn

Jönköping

Linköping

Vänern

**Göta land**

Vättern

Örebro

Västerås

Sala

Hallstahammar

Mälaren

Trollhättan

Vänersborg

Borås

**Göteborg**
(Gothenburg)

Varberg

Halmstad

Helsingborg

Lund

Malmö

Kattegat

Frederikshavn

Ålborg

Århus

Randers

**DENMARK**

København
(Copenhagen)

Odense

Fyn

Sjælland

Flensburg

Kiel

Lübeck

Hamburg

Bremen

Hannover

Braunschweig

Magdeburg

**BERLIN**

Szczecin

Frankfurt

Rostock

Stralsund

Rügen

Sassnitz

Gedser

Store Bælt

Helgoland

Esbjerg

**Jylland**

Skagerrak

Kristiansand

Arendal

Egersund

Mandal

Lindesnes

Haugesund

Stavanger

Skien

Drammen

Oslofjorden

**NORWAY**

Münster

Dortmund

Kassel

Wiesbaden

Frankfurt

Heidelberg

Würzburg

Nürnberg

Plauen

Chemnitz

Erfurt

Halle

Leipzig

Dresden

Görlitz

Legnica

Wrocław

**GERMANY**

**CZECH
REP.**

Praha
(Prague)

Plzeň

Sudety

Ergebirge

Harz

Weser

Rhein

Elbe

**POLAND**

Warszawa
(Warsaw)

Łódź

Radom

Kielce

Częstochowa

Katowice

Kraków

Lublin

Wisła (Vistula)

Płock

Toruń

Bydgoszcz

Poznań

Gdańsk

Gdynia

Odra

m    200    0    200    400    1000    2000

ft    600    0    600    1200    3000    6000

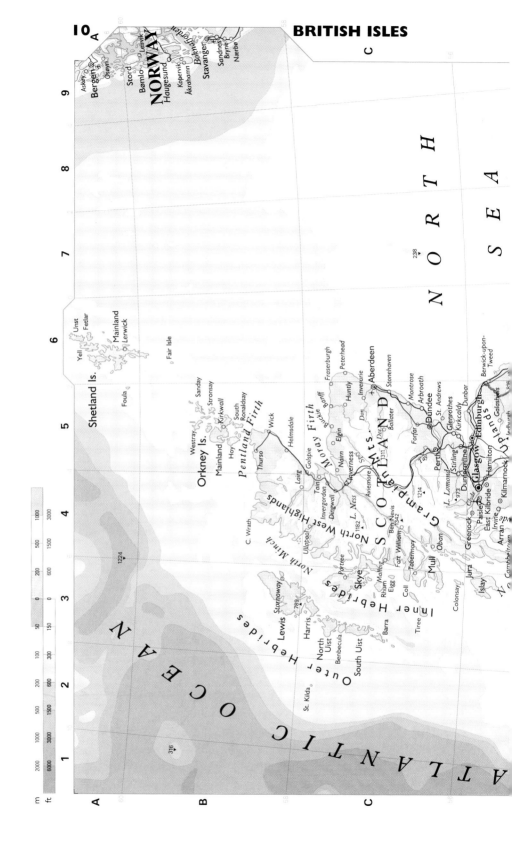

NORWAY

Askøy
Bergen
Osøyri
Stord
Bømlo
Haugesund
Kopervik
Åkrahamn
Stavanger
Sandnes
Bryne
Nærbø
Lerwick
Bokn

Shetland Is.

Yell
Unst
Fetlar
Mainland
Lerwick

Foula

Fair Isle

Orkney Is.

Westray
Sanday
Stronsay
Mainland
Kirkwall
Hoy
South Ronaldsay

NORTH SEA

Pentland Firth

C. Wrath
Thurso
Wick
Helmsdale
Golspie
Lairg
Ullapool
Dingwall
Invergordon
Tain
Inverness
Nairn
Elgin
Buckie
Banff
Fraserburgh
Peterhead
Aberdeen
Stonehaven
Huntly
Inverurie
Moray Firth
Aviemore

Stornoway
Lewis
Harris
North Uist
Benbecula
South Uist
Barra
St. Kilda

North Minch
North West Highlands
Skye
Portree
Rhum
Eigg
Coll
Tiree
Mull
Colonsay
Jura
Islay

Inner Hebrides
Outer Hebrides

L. Ness
Ben Nevis 1342
Fort William
Tobermory
Oban

SCOTLAND
Grampian Mts.
Ballater
Don
Dee
1214
L. Lomond
Greenock
Paisley
East Kilbride
Hamilton
Kilmarnock
Irvine
Arran
N.
Campbeltown

Forfar
Montrose
Arbroath
Dundee
St. Andrews
Glenrothes
Kirkcaldy
Dunbar
Perth
Stirling
Dunfermline
Glasgow
Clyde
Edinburgh
Galashiels
Jedburgh

Southern Uplands

Berwick-upon-Tweed

ATLANTIC OCEAN

238
1224
316
789
1182
3111
973

A B C
1 2 3 4 5 6 7 8 9

m
2000
1000
500
200
50
0

ft
6000
3000
1500
600
150
0

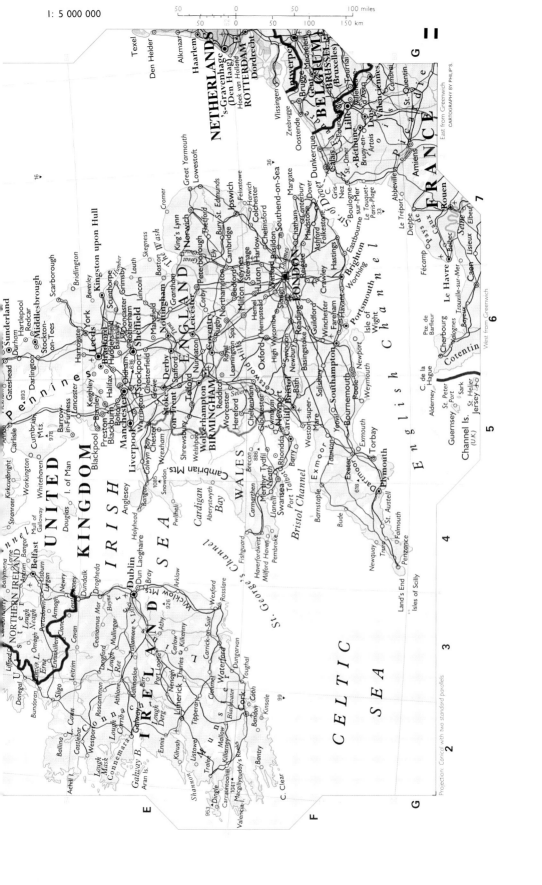

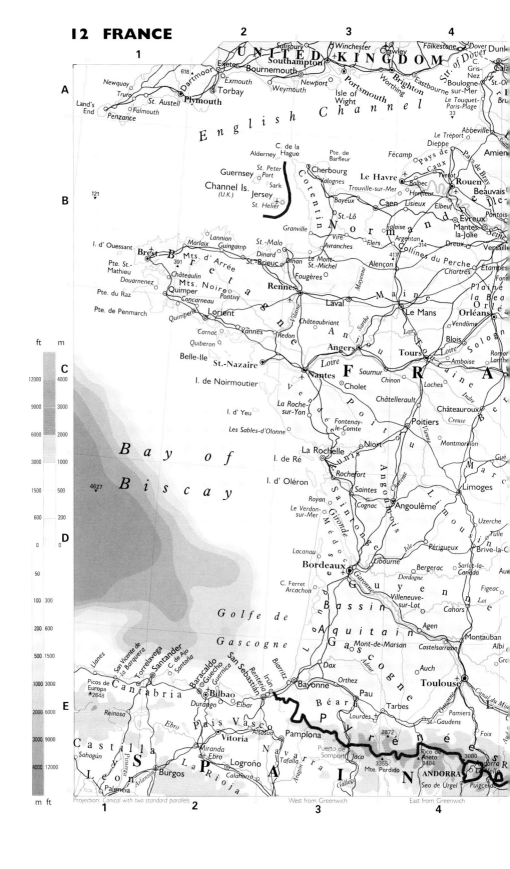

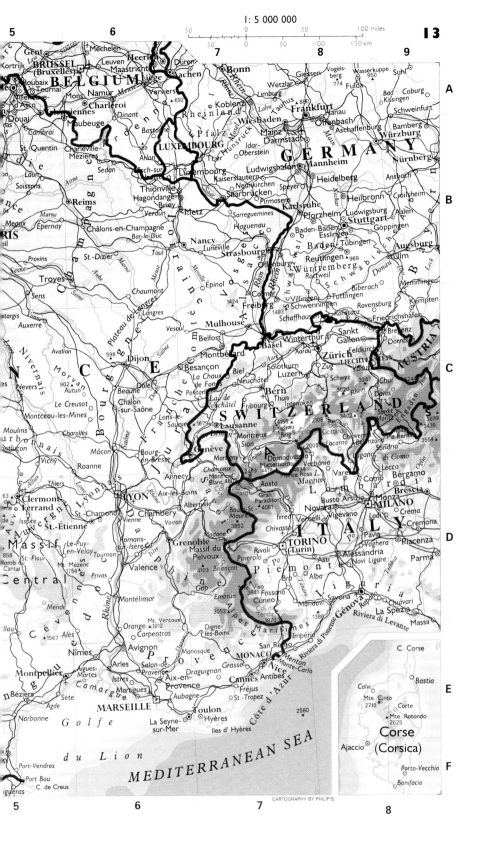

1: 5 000 000

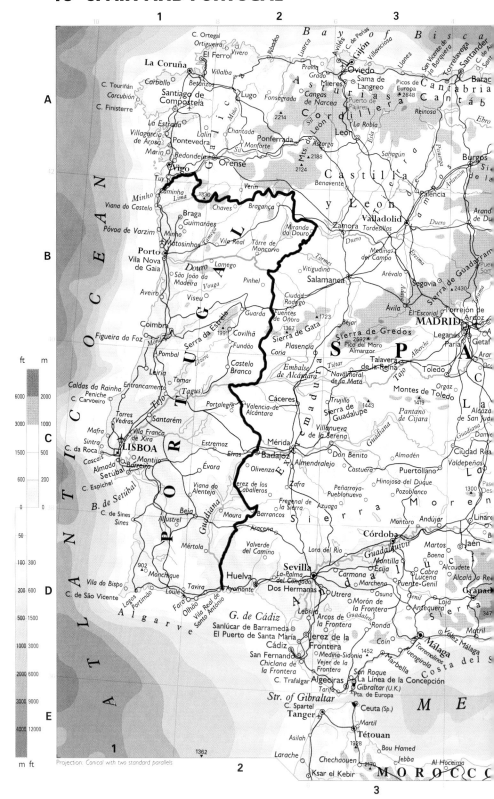

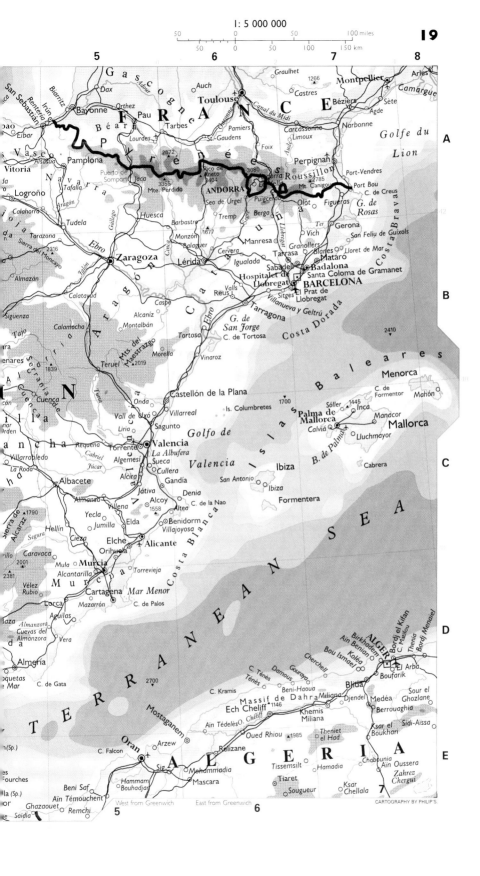

1: 5 000 000

50  0  50  100 miles
50  0  50  100  150 km

FRANCE

**5**     **6**     **7**     **8**

Graulhet   1266   Montpellier   Arles
Auch   Castres   Béziers   Camargue
San Sebastian   Biarritz   Dax   Adour   Cognne   Toulouse   Canal du Midi   Agde   Sète
Bilbao   Renteria   Irún   Bayonne   Orthez   Pau   Pamiers   Carcassonne   Narbonne
Eibar   Béarn   Tarbes   St-Gaudens   Limoux
Vasco   Lourdes   Foix   Aude   **Golfe du**
Vitoria   Alsasua   Pamplona   Puerto de   2872   Pyrénées   Perpignan   **Lion**
Navarra   Somport   Jaca   Rico de   3080   Andorra   Roussillon   Port-Vendres
Logroño   Tafalla   Aragón   3355   Aneto   404   **ANDORRA**   Mt. Canigou   2785   Port Bou
Calahorra   Mte. Perdido   Seo de Urgel   Puigcerdá   C. de Creus
Rioja   Tudela   Huesca   Tremp   Berga   Olot   Figueras   **G. de**
Tarazona   Gállego   Barbastro   1677   Ter   Gerona   **Rosas**
Sierra del Moncayo   2316   Monzón   Vich   San Felíu de Guixols
Ebro   **Zaragoza**   **Lérida**   Balaguer   Cervera   Manresa   Granollers   Blanes   Lloret de Mar   Costa Brava
Almazán   Aragón   Cinca   Igualada   Tarrasa   **Badalona**
Calatayud   Caspe   Valls   Sabadell   **BARCELONA**   Santa Coloma de Gramanet
Sigüenza   Alcañiz   Reus   Hospitalet de   El Prat de   Llobregat
Calamocha   Montalbán   Llobregat   Sitges   Villanueva y Geltrú
Tajo   Mts. del   Tortosa   **G. de**   Tarragona   **Costa Dorada**   2410
Siguenza   Maestrazgo   **San Jorge**   C. de Tortosa
Teruel   1839   2019   Morella   **Baleares**
Cuenca   Turia   Vinaroz   Menorca
Serranía   Onda   **Castellón de la Plana**   C. de   Formentor   Mahón
Villarrobledo   Vall de Uxó   Villarreal   Is. Columbretes   1700   Sóller   1445   Inca
La Roda   Liria   Sagunto   **Palma de**   Mancor
Requena   Torrente   **Valencia**   **Golfo de**   **Mallorca**   Calviá   **Mallorca**
Cabriel   Algemesí   La Albufera   Lluchmayor
Albacete   Júcar   Sueca   **Valencia**   B. de Palma
Almansa   Alcira   Cullera   **Ibiza**   Cabrera
Villena   Gandía   San Antonio
Sierra del   1790   Játiva   Denia   Ibiza
Alcaraz   Yecla   Alcoy   1558   C. de la Nao   **Formentera**
Hellín   Jumilla   Elda   Altea
Segura   Cieza   Benidorm
Caravaca   2001   Elche   Villajoyosa
2381   Mula   **Murcia**   Orihuela   **Alicante**
Vélez   Alcantarilla   **Murcia**   Torrevieja
Rubio   Lorca   **Cartagena**   Mar Menor
Baza   Mazarrón   C. de Palos
Almanzora   Aguilas
Cuevas del   Almanzora   Vera
Almería   **M E D I T E R R A N E A N  S E A**
Roquetas   C. de Gata
de Mar   2700   ALGIER
C. Ténés   Damous   Gouray   Cherchell   Bordj el Kifan   C. Matifou   Bordj Menaiel
C. Kramis   Ténès   Beni-Haoua   **ALGER**   Birkhadem   Thenia
Massif de Dahra   1146   Miliana   Aïn Benian   Koléa   El Arba
Mostaganem   Ech Cheliff   Bou Ismael   Boufarik
Aïn Tédelès   O. Chéliff   Khemis   **Blida**   Djendel   Medéa   Sour el
Oran   Arzew   Oued Rhiou   Miliana   Berrouaghia   Ghozlane
C. Falcon   Relizane   1985   Theniet   Ksar el   Sidi-Aïssa
Sig   Mohammadia   el Had   Boukhari
**A L G E R I A**
Mascara   Tissemsilt   Hamadia   Chabounia   Aïn Oussera
Beni Saf   Hammam   Tiaret   Zahrez
Aïn Témouchent   Bouhadjar   Sougueur   Ksar   Chergui
Ghazaouet   Remchi   Chellala
Saïdia

West from Greenwich    East from Greenwich   **6**

CARTOGRAPHY BY PHILIP'S

**A**    **B**    **C**    **D**    **E**

**5**     **6**     **7**

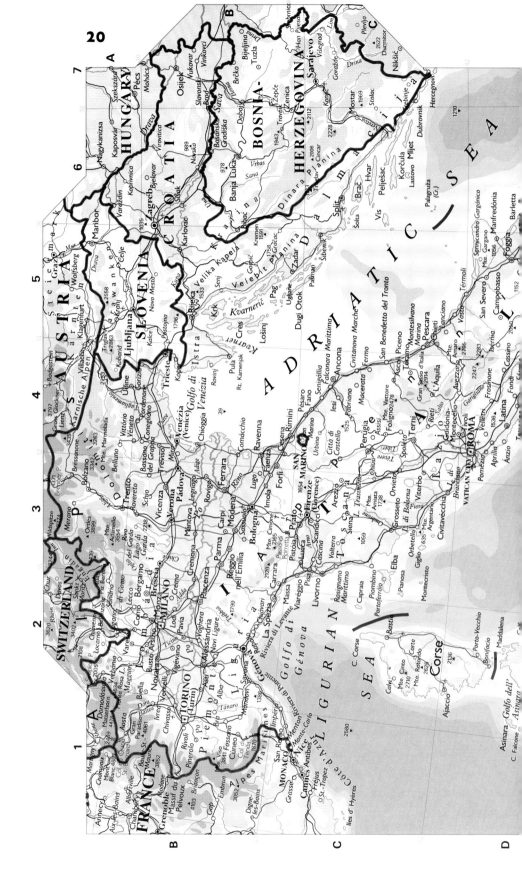

1: 5 000 000

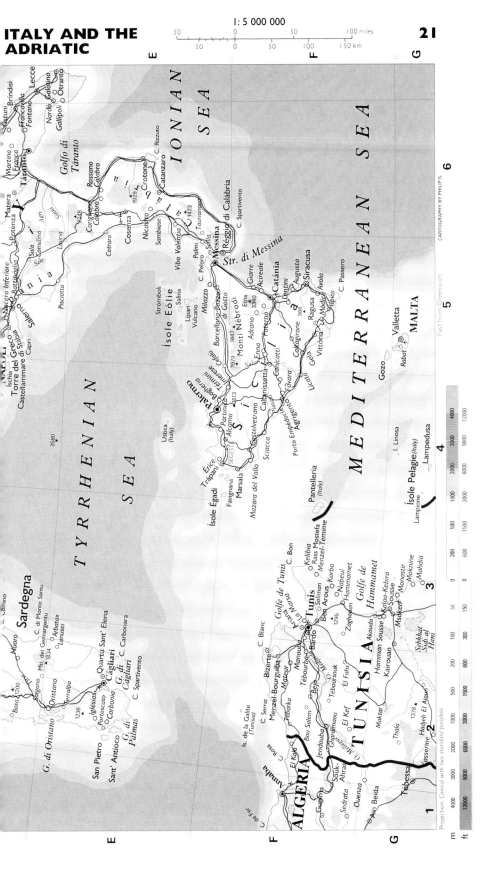

Projection: Conical with two standard parallels

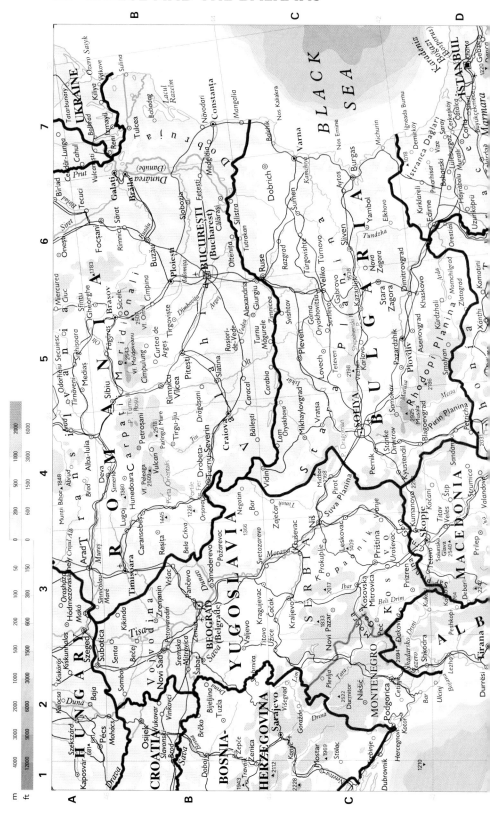

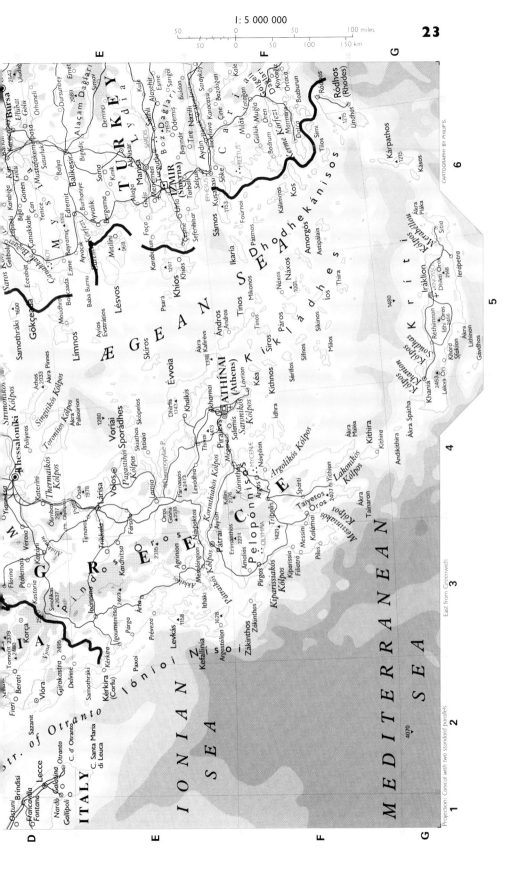

1: 5 000 000

50  0  50  100 miles

50  0  50  100  150 km

**23**

CARTOGRAPHY BY PHILIP'S.

Projection: Conical with two standard parallels

East from Greenwich

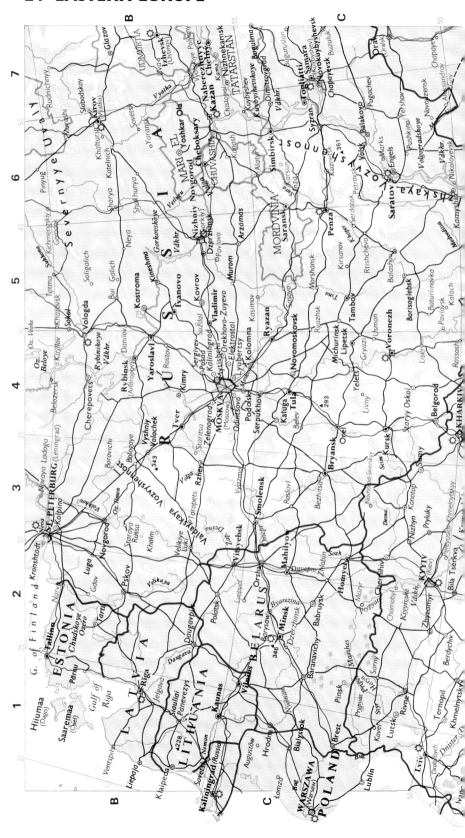

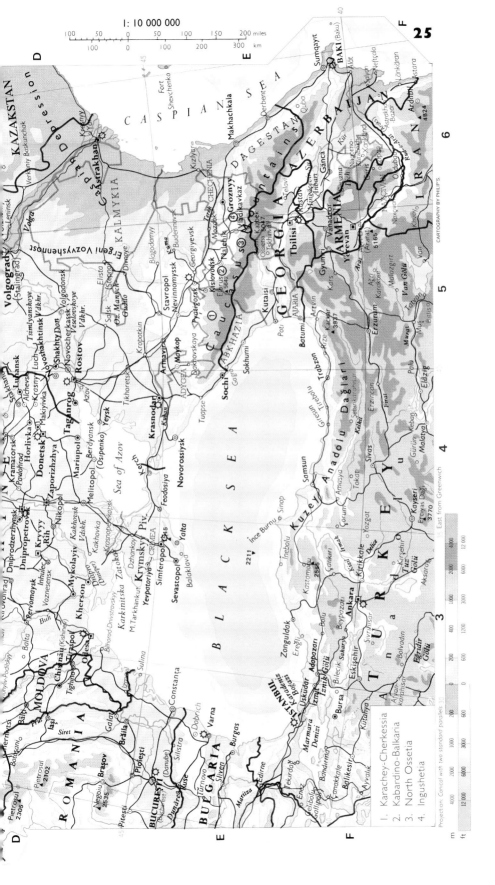

1: 10 000 000

100   50   0   50   100   150   200 miles
100   0   100   200   300 km

40° East from Greenwich

CARTOGRAPHY BY PHILLIPS.

Projection: Conical with two standard parallels

1. Karachey-Cherkessia
2. Kabardino-Balkaria
3. North Ossetia
4. Ingushetia

m   4000   2000   1000   400   200   0   200   1000   2000   4000
ft   12 000   6000   3000   1200   600   0   600   3000   6000   12 000

C  B  A

ATLANTIC OCEAN

GREENLAND

ARCTIC

ICELAND
Arctic Circle

Svalbard

Barents Sea
Novaya Zemlya
Kara Sea

UNITED KINGDOM

NORWAY

North Sea

Murmansk

Vorkuta
Salekhard

R U

LONDON
PARIS
FRANCE
GERMANY
Berlin
SWEDEN
FINLAND

ST. PETERSBURG

Nizhniy Novgorod
Perm
Yekaterinburg
Irtysh
Ob

Arkhangelsk
White Sea

Warsaw
Prague
Vienna
E u r o p e

MOSCOW
Kazan
Ufa
Chelyabinsk
Omsk

ITALY
Rome
Belgrade
UKRAINE
Odessa

Volga
Samara

Astana
Pavlodar

Don
Volgograd
Rostov
Astrakhan

KAZAKSTAN

Karaganda

Danube
Black Sea
ISTANBUL
Bursa
Athens

Mediterranean Sea

ISTANBUL
Ankara
Izmir
Konya
Adana
TURKEY
GEORGIA
Tbilisi
Yerevan
ARMENIA
AZERBAIJAN
Baku

Caspian Sea

Aral Sea
Syrdarya
UZBEKISTAN
L. Balkhash

Alma

Nicosia
CYPRUS
Beirut
LEBANON
Aleppo
SYRIA
Damascus
Euphrates
Mosul
Tabriz

TURKMENISTAN
Ashkhabad
Tashkent
Samarkand
Bishkek
KYRGYZSTAN

LIBYA

Alexandria
ISRAEL
CAIRO
Suez
Jerusalem
JORDAN
Amman
IRAQ
Baghdad
Basra

Mashhad
TEHRĀN
Eşfahān
IRAN
Herāt
Kābul
Islamabad
TAJIKISTAN
Dushanbe
Kashi

JAMMU & KASHMIR

EGYPT
Nile

Aswān
Red Sea

KUWAIT
Kuwait
The Gulf
Shīrāz
Zāhedān

AFGHANISTAN
Qandahār
Faisalabad
Lahore

DELHI

SUDAN

Khartoum

Port Sudan
Jedda
Medina
SAUDI ARABIA
Riyadh
Mecca

BAHRAIN
QATAR
Manāmah
Doha
UNITED ARAB EMIRATES
Abu Dhabi
G. of Oman

PAKISTAN
KARACHI
Indus

New Delhi
Jaipur
Lucknow
Kanpur
Vara

Muscat
OMAN

Ahmadabad
Vadodara
Indore
Bhopal
Surat
Na
MUMBAI
(Bombay)
Pune
Hyde

I N D

ERITREA
Şana'a
YEMEN
Aden
G. of Aden

Socotra
(Yemen)

Arabian Sea

DJIBOUTI
SOMALI
REP.

Addis Ababa
ETHIOPIA

Bangalore

Lakshadweep Is.
(India)

Madurai

A f r i c a

CONGO
(DEM. REP. OF THE)
UGANDA
L. Victoria
KENYA
Nairobi
Mogadishu
Equator

Colombo

MALDIVES
Male

I N D I A N   O

TANZANIA
Mombasa

Dar es Salaam

ZAMBIA
MALAWI

SEYCHELLES
Victoria

Aldabra Is.
(Seychelles)
Amirante Is.
(Seychelles)

Chagos Arch.
(U.K.)

Projection: Bonne

6  7  8  9  10  11

Hanoi ● Capital Cities

East from Greenwich

200   0   200   400   600   800   1000   1200 miles
200   0   400   800   1200   1600   2000 km

B                    C                    D

**OCEAN**   New Siberian   Wrangel I.

*Laptev Sea*

Khatanga   Verkhoyansk   Gizhiga

*Lena*   Okhotsk   Magadan

*Sea of Okhotsk*

S   I   A   Yakutsk

Sakhalin

Komsomolsk

Angara   Krasnoyarsk   Bratsk   L. Baikal

irsk   vokuznetsk   Irkutsk   Ulan Ude   Chita   Blagoveshchensk   Khabarovsk   Yuzhno-Sakhalinsk

*Amur*   Hailar   Qiqihar   Vladivostok   Hokkaidō   Sapporo

MONGOLIA   Ulan Bator   Harbin   Changchun   Honshū

Jilin   *Sea of Japan*   TŌKYŌ   JAPAN

Ürümqi   Hami   Baotou   SHENYANG   Anshan   NORTH KOREA   Kyōto   Nagoya   Yokohama

Yumen   BEIJING   TIANJIN   Jinzhou   Dalian   Pyongyang   SEOUL   SOUTH KOREA   Pusan   Hiroshima   Osaka

Lanzhou   Taiyuan   Jinan   SOUTH KOREA   Kitakyushu

C   H   I   N   A   Xi'an   Nanjing   SHANGHAI   *Yellow Sea*   Bonin Is. (Japan)

ET   Chengdu   *Yangtze*   Wuhan   HANGZHOU   *East China Sea*   Volcano Is. (Japan)

Lhasa   CHONGQING   Nanchang   Fuzhou   Tropic of Cancer

Changsha   Taipei   *Ryukyu*

Thimphu   Kunming   Si Kiang   GUANGZHOU   TAIWAN

BHUTAN   *Brahmaputra*   HONG KONG   Macau

BANGLADESH   BURMA   Hanoi   Haiphong

DACCA   Chittagong   (MYANMAR)   Hainan   Luzon

ITTA   *Irrawaddy*   *Salween*   LAOS   Vientiane   VIETNAM   MANILA   PHILIPPINES

*Bay of Bengal*   Rangoon   THAILAND   BANGKOK   *Mekong*   Cebu   FED. STATES OF MICRONESIA

Andaman Is. (India)   CAMBODIA   Phnom Penh   Ho Chi Minh City   *South China Sea*   Mindanao   PALAU

A   Nicobar Is. (India)   *G. of Thailand*   Palawan   *Sulu Sea*   Davao

Zamboanga

PEN. MALAYSIA   BRUNEI   SABAH   *Celebes Sea*   Manado   Halmahera   IRIAN JAYA

Medan   Kuala Lumpur   *Str. of Malacca*   SARAWAK   Bandar Seri Begawan

*AN*   SINGAPORE   Borneo   Ceram   Ambon   Ceram

Sumatra   Banjarmasin   Celebes   *Banda Sea*   *Arafura Sea*

Palembang   I   N   D   O   N   E   S   I   A   Ujung Pandang

JAKARTA   Semarang   *Java Sea*   Flores   Timor   *Timor Sea*   AUSTRALIA

Bandung   Surabaya   Sumba

Java

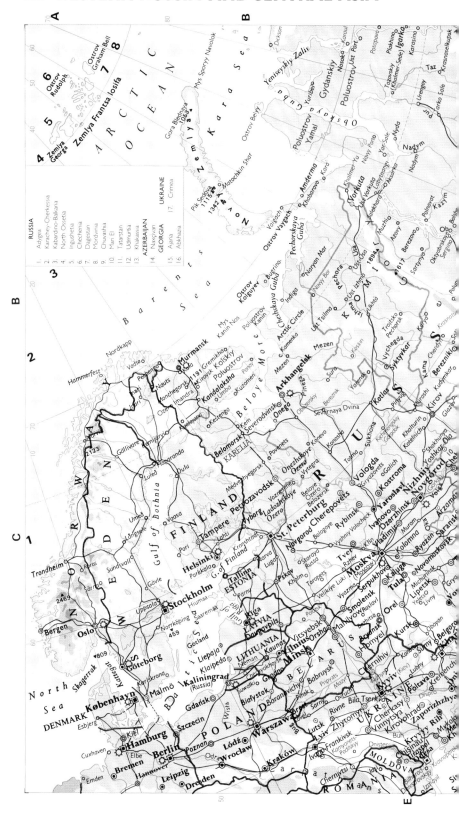

RUSSIA
1. Adygea
2. Karachev-Cherkessia
3. Kabardino-Balkaria
4. North Ossetia
5. Ingushetia
6. Chechenia
7. Dagestan
8. Mordovia
9. Chuvashia
10. Mari El
11. Tatarstan
12. Udmurtia
13. Khakassia
AZERBAIJAN
14. Naxçivan
GEORGIA
15. Ajaria
16. Abkhazia
UKRAINE
17. Crimea

1: 20 000 000

100   0   100   200   300   400   500 miles
100   0   200   400   600   800 km

CARTOGRAPHY BY PHILIP'S

Projection: Conical Orthomorphic with two standard parallels

East from Greenwich

m
ft

Projection: Conical Orthomorphic with two standard parallels

1 : 20 000 000

| 100 | 0 | 100 | 200 | 300 | 400 | 500 miles |
| 100 | 0 | 200 | 400 | 600 | 800 km |

14    B    15    16    Mys Dezhneva (East C.)    C

Ostrov Henrietta  Ostrov Jeanette
Ostrova Delong  Ostrov Zhokhova

Ostrova Faddeyevskiy    Ostrov Novaya Sibir

Chukchi Sea

Uelen

St. Lawrence I. (U.S.A.)

East Siberian Sea    Ostrov Vrangelya

Anadyrskiy Zaliv

Ostrov Malyy Lyakhovskiy  Ostrov Bolshoy Lyakhovskiy
Proliv Dmitriya Lapteva

Pevek    Chukotskoye Nagorye

Ostrova Medvezhi    ▲1853

Ambarchik

Bering Sea

Koryakskoye Nagorye    ▲2562

Nizhne Kolymsk    Bolshoy Anyuy    ▲1742

Srednekolymsk

Khrebet Cherskogo    Kolymskoye Nagore

D

Gizhiga    Penzhinskaya Guba    Sredinnyy

Verkhoyansk  ▲2389    Pobeda ▲3147

Gora Chen ▲2682  Ust Nera

▲2959

Magadan

Okhotsk

Poluostrov Kamchatka

Komandorskiye Ostrova

Ust-Kamchatsk

Petropavlovsk-Kamchatskiy

Yakutsk    Maya

I    A    Sea of Okhotsk

Neryungri

Stanovoy Khrebet    Ostrov Bolshoy Shantar

Nikolayevsk-na-Am.

Sakhalinskiy Zaliv    Okha

Sakhalin

Komsomolsk    ▲2078

Khrebet Sikhote Alin

Sovetskaya Gavan

Yuzhno-Sakhalinsk

E

Birobidzhan    Khabarovsk

Ostrov Iturup  Kurilsk

Blagoveshchensk

Qiqihar    Jiamusi

Harbin    Ussuriysk    Vladivostok    Nakhodka

Hokkaidō    Sapporo    Hakodate

JAPAN

9    10    11

CARTOGRAPHY BY PHILIP'S.

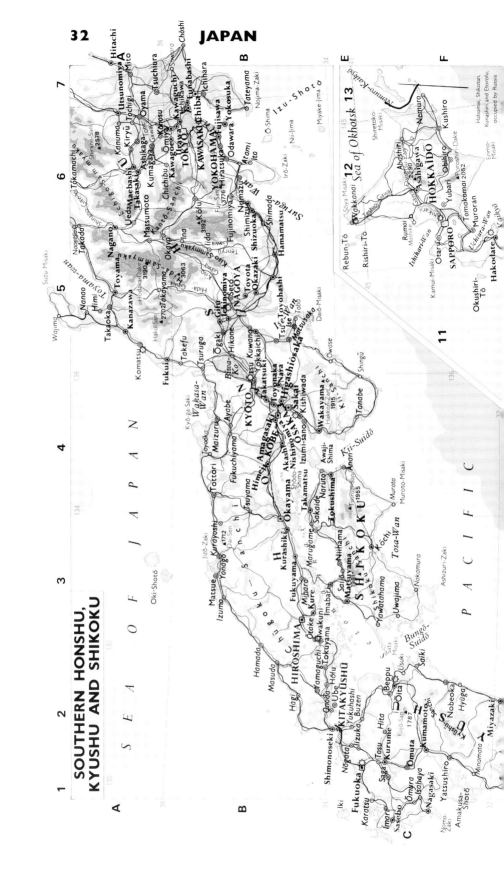

# SOUTHERN HONSHU, KYUSHU AND SHIKOKU

**JAPAN**

SEA OF

JAPAN

PACIFIC

OCEAN

EAST

CHINA SEA

CARTOGRAPHY BY PHILIP'S.

1:10 000 000

East from Greenwich

Projection: Bonne

0   50   100   150   200 miles

0   100   200   300   km

1:5 000 000

East from Greenwich

Projection: Conical with two standard parallels

25   0   25   50   75   100 miles

25   0   50   100   150   km

3

SOUTH
KOREA

Pohang
Taegu
Chungju
Chinju
PUSAN
Masan
Chŏnju
Iri
Chŏngju
Taejŏn
1915
Sunchon
Yŏsu
Suwŏn
Kunsan
Kwangju
Mokpo
Cheju Do
1950

Tsushima

**KYŪSHŪ**
**KITAKYŪSHŪ**
**FUKUOKA**
Shimonoseki
Ube
Sasebo
Ōmuta
Kumamoto
**Nagasaki**
Gotō-
Rettō
Nomo-Zaki
Ōmuta
Ōita
Saiki
Miyazaki
Koyá
Sendai
Kanoya
Kagoshima-Wan
**Kagoshima**
Ōsumi-Kaikyō
Tane-ga-
Shima
1935 Yaku-Shima
Ōsumi-
Shotō

**HIROSHIMA**
Kure
S.
Matsuyama **SHIKOKU**
Takamatsu
Tokushima
Kōchi
Tosa
Wan
Ashizuri-Zaki
Muroto-Misaki

**Okayama**
**KOBE**
**OSAKA**
Sakai
**KYOTO**
**Wakayama**
Kii
Shio-no-Misaki

Tottori
Yonago
Matsue
Oki-Shotō
Maizuru
Biwa-Ko
Wakasa-Wan
Komatsu

**Kanazawa**
**Toyama**
Noto-
Hantō
Suzu-Misaki
Wajima

**Niigata**
Sado
Nagaoka
Takada
**Takasaki**
**Maebashi**
Hida-San

**NAGOYA**
**Gifu**
Ise-Wan
**Hamamatsu**
**Toyohashi**
Iwata
**Shizuoka**
Fuji-San
2776

**TOKYO**
**YOKOHAMA**
Yokosuka
Tateyama
Bōsō-
Hantō
Nojima-Zaki
Ō-Shima
Miyake-Jima
Niī-Jima
Hachijō-Jima

**Kōriyama**
**Fukushima**
Mito
Utsunomiya
**Chōshi**
Inubō-Zaki

**Sendai**
**Iwaki**
Hitachi
Azuma-San
2024

**Yamagata**
Tsuruoka
Sakata
Mogami-Gawa

**Akita**
Hanamaki
Kitakami-Gawa
Iwate-San
2041
**Morioka**
Miyako
Kamaishi
Ishinomaki
Hiraizumi
Ōdate
Hirosaki
Oga-Hantō

▼ 7756
▼ 8412

Ōsumi-Kaikyō
Tane-ga-
Shima
1935
Nishino'omote
Ōsumi-
Shotō
Yaku-
Shima
Sata-Misaki

m   ft
8000  24 000
6000  18 000
4000  12 000
2000  6000
0   0
200   600
2000  6000
4000  12 000
6000  18 000
8000  24 000

3000  9000
2000  6000
1500  4500
1000  3000
400   1200
200   600
0   0

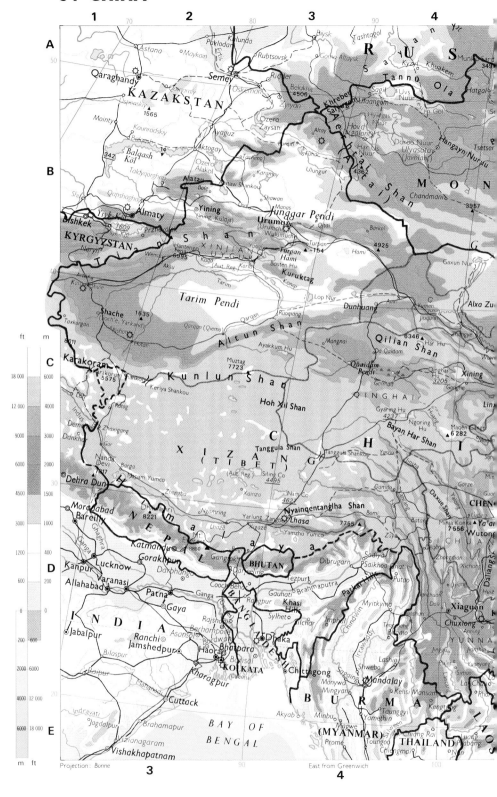

East from Greenwich

1: 20 000 000

100    0    100    200    300    400    500 miles
100    0    200    400    600    800 km

**37**

1:12 500 000

100    0    100    200    300   miles

100    0    100    200    300    400    500   km

CARTOGRAPHY BY PHILIP'S.

Projection: Mercator

East from Greenwich

NUSA TENGGARA BARAT

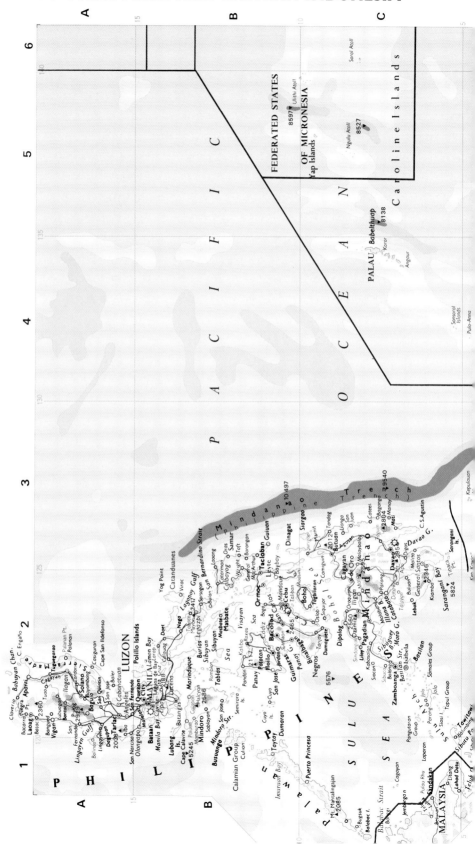

1:12 500 000

100 0 100 200 300 miles
100 0 100 200 300 400 500 km

CARTOGRAPHY BY PHILIP'S

PAPUA NEW GUINEA

Equator

CELEBES SEA

Kepulauan Sanghe
Pulau Sanghe

Manado 2022

SULAWESI (CELEBES)

UTARA

TENGAH

SELATAN

Ujung Pandang
Sungguminasa

Selat Makasar

FLORES SEA

Flores

Sumba

Sumbawa
Bima
Raba

NUSA TENGGARA BARAT

Lesser Sunda Islands

Sawu Sea

NUSA TENGGARA TIMUR
TIMOR

Alor

Lesser Sunda Islands

Roti

BANDA SEA

MALUKU

SERAM SEA

Halmahera

Morotai

Ternate
Tidore

Buru

Ceram

Ambon

Misool

Jazirah Doberai

Waigeo

Salawati

IRIAN JAYA

Pegunungan Maoke
Pegunungan Sudirman

Teluk Cenderawasih

Yapen

Biak

Kepulauan Mapia

ARAFURA SEA

Kepulauan Tanimbar

Kepulauan Kai

Kepulauan Aru

Merauke

Jayapura

Tanahmerah

East from Greenwich

Projection: Mercator

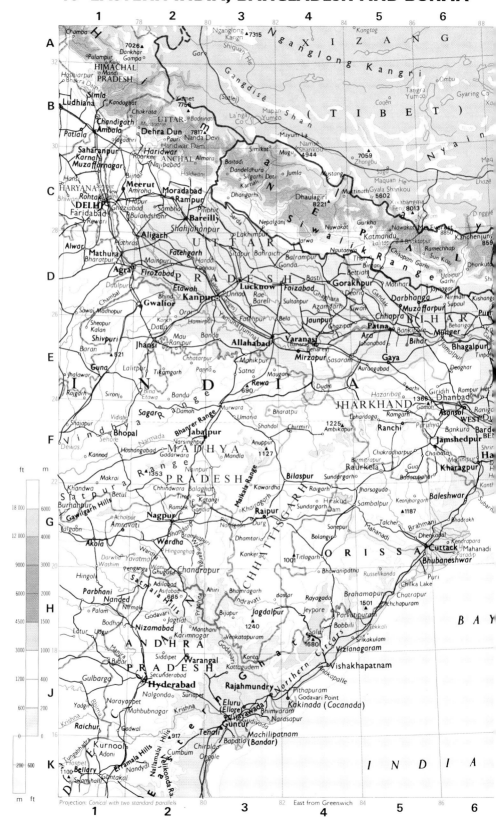

Projection: Conical with two standard parallels

East from Greenwich

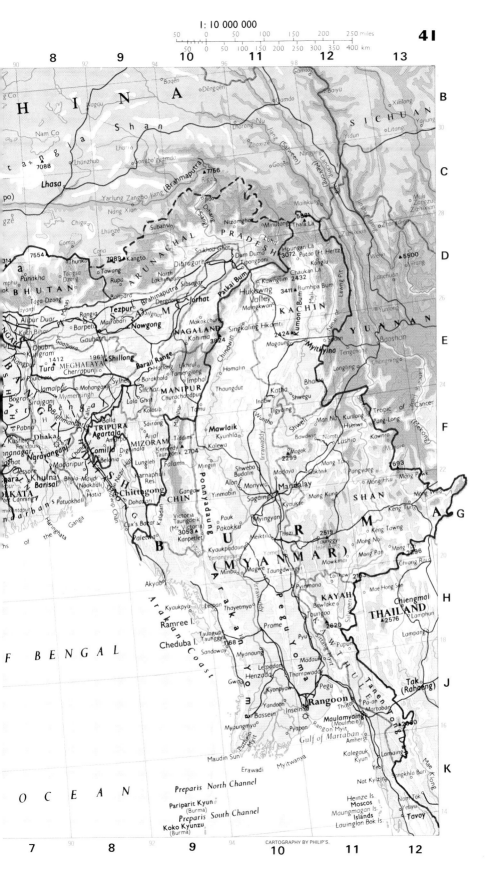

1: 10 000 000

50   0   50   100   150   200   250 miles
50  0  50 100 150 200 250 300 350 400 km

8        9        10        11        12        13

B

H   I   N   A
S   I   C   H   U   A   N

Baqên
Dêngqên
Qamdo
Baiyu
Xinlong

Nam Co
Ta n g l a   Shan
Nu   Jiang   (Salween)
Litang
Yalung

Zhaxize
Zhuoni
Gogên
Ningjing Lancang (Mekong)
Yidun

Co
7088
Lhünzhub
Lhorong
Yunqên

Lhasa
Lhari
Gongbo'gyamda
28

po)
Yarlung Zangbo Jiang (Brahmaputra)
Zhaxize
30

gzê
Nang Xian
Chigu
Jianchuan

C

A   R   U   N   A   C   H   A   L     P   R   A   D   E   S   H

▲7756
Rima

314
7554
Subansiri
Jido
Dihang (Siang)
Nizamghat
Minutang
5881
Thala La
Muli Zizixian

a
Chunku
7089
Kangto
Saikhoa Ghat
Dum Duma
Chaukan La
Weixi
▲5500

Punakha
Tangsa Dzeng
Towang
Rupa
North Lakhimpur
Dibrugarh
3072
Potao (Ft. Hertz)
Konglu
Jianchuan

B   H   U   T   A   N
Taga-Dzong
Bomdila
Brahmaputra
Sibsagar
Hpungan La
Kawngtim
2432
Bumhpa Bum
Yunfong

D

mphu
Alipur Duar
Rangia
Tezpur
Sila
Jorhat
Parkai Bum
Hukawng Valley
3411
K   A   C   H   I   N
Y   U   N   N   A   N

ok
Jalpaiguri
Barpeta
Mairabari
Mokokchung
Maingkwan
Kumon Bum
Baoshan

Kach Bihar
Goalpara
Gauhati
N A G A L A N D
Singkaling Hkamti
2424
Myitkyina
Tengchung

Dhubri
Kuriqram
1412
Kohima
3824
Mogaung
Longling
Changning

Rangpur
Tura
MEGHALAYA
1961
Shillong
Barail Range
Chindwin
Homalin
Bhamo
E

Dinajpur
Phulbari
Cherrapunji
Haflong
Ukhrul
Tamenglong
Katha
Shwegu

Jamalpur
Mohanganj
Sylhet
Barakhola
Imphal
Thaungdut
Indaw
Tigyaing
24

Bogra
Mymensingh
Silchar
MANIPUR
Churachandpur
Shweli
Man Na
Kunlong
Tropic
of
Cancer

Sirajganj
Lala Ghat
Tamu
Wuntho
Mogok
Bawdwin
Namtu
Hsenwi
Pang-Long
F

Pabna
Kolasib
Sairang
Mawlaik
Kyunhla
Shwebo
Mong Yu
Lashio
Kawnro

Kushtia
Haridaspur
Balla
TRIPURA
Aijal
Tiddim
Kalewa
Budalin
Mokteik
Pangyang
693

Narayanganj
Comilla
Belonia
Diphu
Kennedy Peak
Taungdeik 2704
Falam
Mingin
Madaya
Mong Yai
Mong Hsu
Mong Pawk

Jessore
Dhaka
Madaripur
Lungleh
Karnaphuli Res.
Alon
Monywa
Mandalay
Kyaukse
Mong Kung
Mong Wa

bara
Khulna
Bhola Maindi (Noakhali)
Gangaw
Yinmabin
Sagaing
S   H   A   N
Keng Tung
G

KATA
Barisal
Patuakhali
Hatia
CHIN
Pauk
Myingyan
Thazi
Meiktila
2519
Keng Tawng

Canning
Sandwip Chan
Chittagong
Dohazari
Victoria Taungdeik
(Mt. Victoria)
3053
Kanpetlet
Yamethin
Taunggyi
Inle L.
Mong Nai
Mong Ton
2296

ndarbans
Haringhata
Cox's Bazar
Kaladan
Paletwa
B   U   R   M   A
(M Y A N M A R)
Pakokku
Minbu
Magwe
Taungdwingyi
Pyinmana
Loikaw 216
Chiang Rai

hs
of
the Ganga
Akyab
Kyaukpyu
Letpan
Thayetmyo
Arakan
Irrawaddy
Pegu Yoma
KAYAH
Mae Hong Son
Chiengmai
H

O C E A N
B   E   N   G   A   L
Ramree I.
Taungup Taunggy
168
Sandoway
Myanaung
Prome
Toungoo
2620
2576
THAILAND
Lamphun

Cheduba I.
Sandoway Coast
Henzada
Letpadan
Pyu
Sittang Myit
Papun
Lampang
18

Gwa
Kyonpyaw
Tharrawaddy
Madauk
Pegu
Tak (Raheng)
J

Myaungmya
Yandoon
Insein
Rangoon
Thaton
Martaban
Maulamyaing (Moulmein)
16

Bassein
Pyapon
Rangon Myit
Amherst
Kalegauk Kyun
Lamaing

Maudin Sun
Myitwanya
Gulf of Martaban
Yeb
Nam Tok
Mae Klong
K

Erawadi
Nat Kyizing
Tavoy
14

O   C   E   A   N
Preparis North Channel
Pariparit Kyun (Burma)
Preparis South Channel
Koko Kyunzu (Burma)
Heinze Is.
Moscos
Maungmagan Is.
Islands
Lauingan Bok Is.
Zebyu

CARTOGRAPHY BY PHILIP'S.

7        8        9        10        11        12

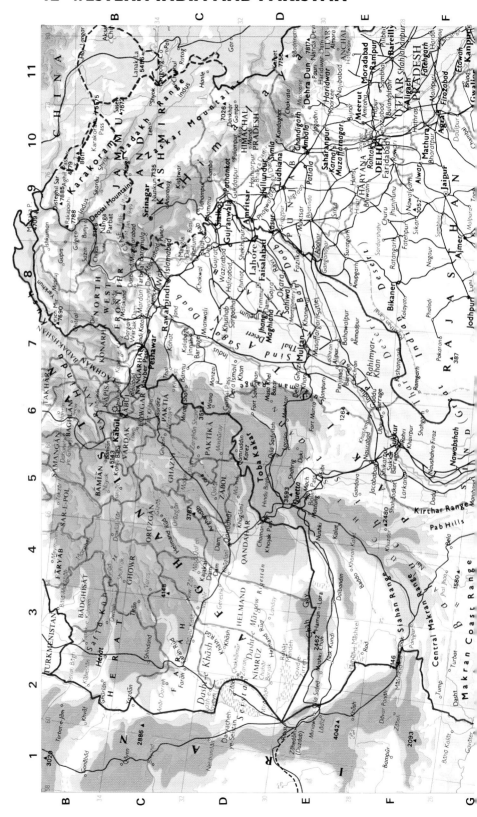

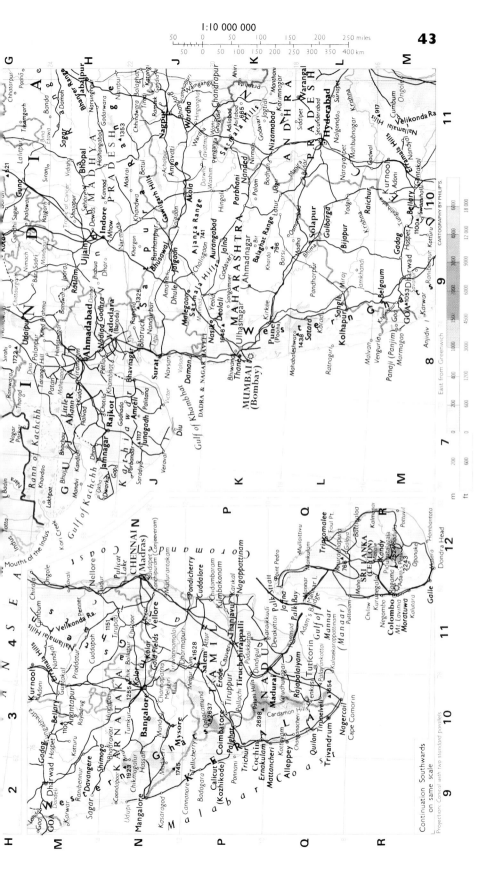

1:10 000 000

50    0    50    100    150    200    250 miles
50   0   50   100  150  200  250  300  350  400 km

CARTOGRAPHY BY PHILIPS.

Continuation Southwards
on same scale

Projection Conical with two standard parallels

East from Greenwich

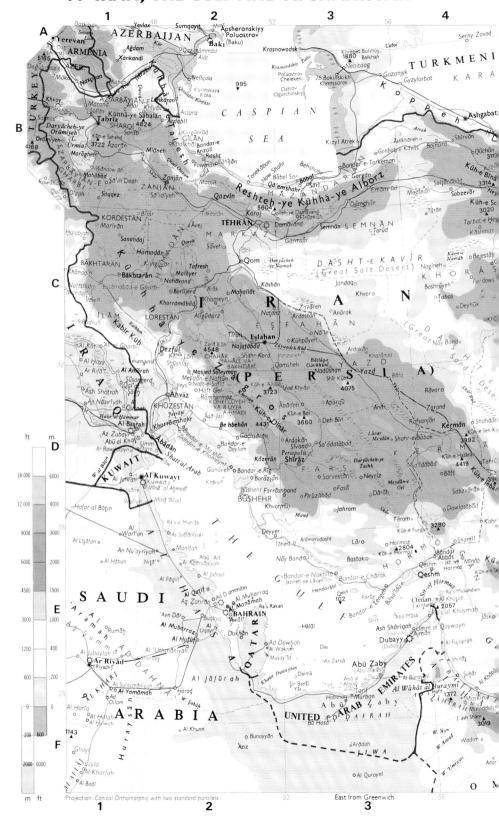

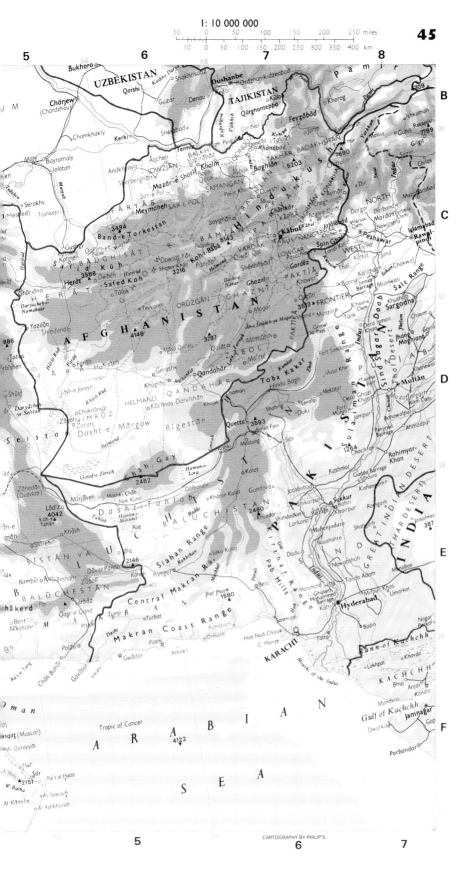

1:10 000 000

50    0    50    100    150    200    250 miles
50   0   50  100  150  200  250  300  350  400 km

5                6                7                8

B

Bukhoro
UZBEKISTAN
Qarshi
Kashka Darya
Shakhrisabz
Denau
Guzar
Qarshi
Dushanbe
Ordzhonikidzeabad
TAJIKISTAN
Qürghonteppa
Kŭlob
Khorog
Pamir
709
B

Chärjew
(Chardzhou)
Chamkhakly
Kerki
Shaartuz
Termiz
Kofarnihon
Pyandzh
Jzh.
Qondoz
Kakhka
Jorm
Mir
Yashkun
Feyzâbâd
Khandud
Ishkuman
Rakaposhi
Gubis
7189
Gilgit
36

Mary
Bayramaly
Iolotan
Andkhvoy
Āqcheh
Sheberghan
Mazār-e Sharif
Khulm
Balkh
Vazirabad
Termiz
Boyn
Pol-e Khomri
Baghlān
5203
TAKHAR
BADAKHSHAN
7690
Chitrāl
Dargai
Dir
Chilas
Muzaffarabad
NORTH
C

Serakhs
Tashkepri
(Meshed)
FĀRYĀB
Meymaneh
SAR-E POL
Sayghān
Bāmī
Charikār
KĀPĪSĀ
Kabul
NANGAR
Jalālābād
Khyber
Peshawar
Mardan
Nowshera
Islāmābād
Rawal-
pindi
WEST
C

Yazdān
Shindand
HERĀT
Owbeh
Harirud
Safed Koh
3588
Tālok
Teyvoreh
ORŪZGĀN
GHAZNĪ
Mogor
Qalāt
3787
Māruf
Hindu Bagh
Toba Kakar
Duki
Fort
Munro
Salt Range
Sargodha
32

AFGHANISTAN
4148
Māsa Qal'eh
HELMAND
Geresk
Qandahār
Khūgiāni
QANDAHĀR
Kūchnay Darvīshān
Chaman
Shahrig
Quetta
3593
Bolan Pass
Sibi
Multān
D

Shūst
Daryācheh-
ye Seistan
Zābol
NIMRŪZ
Zaranj
Dasht-e Mārgow
Helmand
Rigestān
Kalat
Mastung
Chachran
Rahimyar-
Khan
Ahmadpur
GREAT INDIAN DESERT
28

Zāhedān
(Duzdab)
Mirjāveh
Māshki Chāh
Nok Kundi
Dālbandin
Kharan Kalat
Gandava
Jacobabad
Shikarpur
Sukkur
Khairpur
Jaisalmer
387
INDIA
E

Lādīz
4042
Tiz
Khāsh
Dasht-i-Tahlab
Taftan
Rod
Baddo
2480
Khuzdar
Larkana
Mohenjodaro
Naushahro
Shahdadkot
Dadu
Nawabshah
N

SĪSTĀN VA
2146
Siahan Range
Rakhshan
Saka Kalat
Kirthar Ra.
Pab Hills
Tando Adam
Manchar
E

Bampūr
Īrānshahr
Zābolī
Dāvar Panāh
Kāhak
Panjgūr
Kharan
Mashkel
Bela
Porali
Mīrpur Khas
Umarkot
BALŪCHESTĀN
Central Makran Range
1580
Turbat
Kandrach
Hyderabad
Manjhand
Mohammed
Barrage
Katri
KACHCHH
Bhuj
Anjar
F

Pip
Qasr-e Qand
Dasht
Tump
Pasni
Ormara
Sonmiani
Hab Nadi Chauk
C. Monze
KARACHI
Mouths of the Indus
Tatta
Lakhpat
Khavda
Nagar
Parkar
Mandvia
Jamnagar

Ra's e Tang
Chāh Bahār
Gavāter
Jiwani
Gwādar
Astola I.
Rann of Kachchh

Oman
Tropic of Cancer
A  R  A  B  I  A  N
4122
ARABIAN
N
Gulf of Kachchh
Dwarka
Porbandar
F

sqaţ (Muscat)
Al Qurayyāt
Tiwi
Sūr
2151
Ra's al Hadd
W. Barha
As Suwayh
Al Kāmil
Al Ashkharah
S  E  A

5                6                7

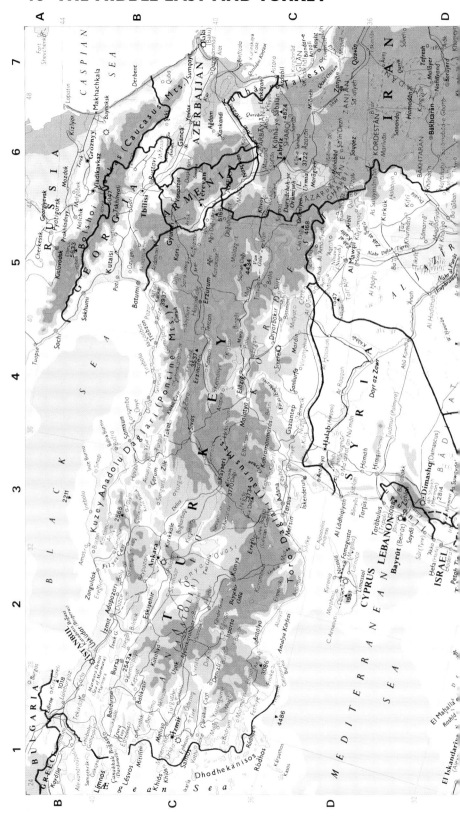

**47**

1:10 000 000

50  0  50  100  150  200  250 miles
50  0  50  100  150  200  250  300  350  400 km

East from Greenwich

5  - - - - - -  Division between Greeks and Turks  6  CARTOGRAPHY BY PHILIPS.
in Cyprus; Turks to the North.

Projection: Conical Orthomorphic with two standard parallels

m  2000  600  0  200  400  1000  1500  2000  3000  4000
ft  6000  0  600  1200  3000  4500  6000  9000  12 000

THE GULF

KHUZESTAN

MESOPOTAMIA

IRAQ

KUWAIT

Al Kuwayt

Ar Riyāḍ

NAJD

S A U D I   A R A B I A

HEJAZ

AL HIJĀRAH

AN NAFŪD

JABAL SHAMMAR

Ḥarrat Khaybar

Al Madīnah

Makkah (Mecca)

Jiddah

R E D   S E A

E G Y P T

EL QAHIRA (CAIRO)

Es Sahrâ esh Sharqiya

Gebel el Tîh

SINAI

Nahr en Nîl (Nile)

Buheiret en Naser (Lake Nasser)

S U D A N

ES SAHRÂ EN NÛBIYA (NUBIAN DESERT)

At Tubayq

SHAM

SYRIA

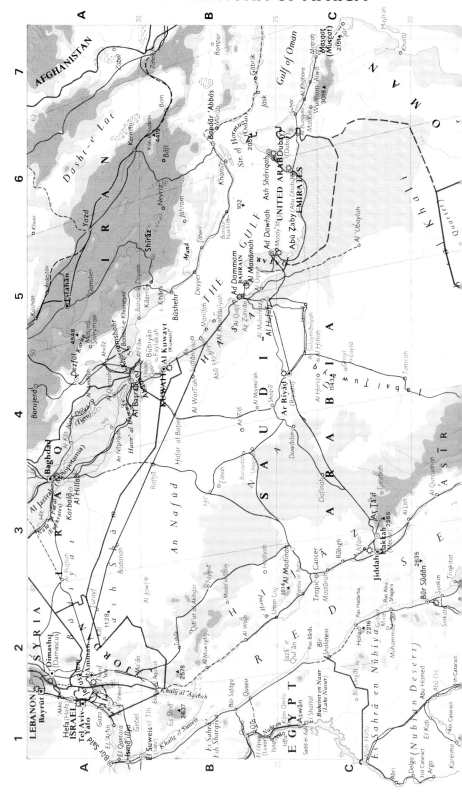

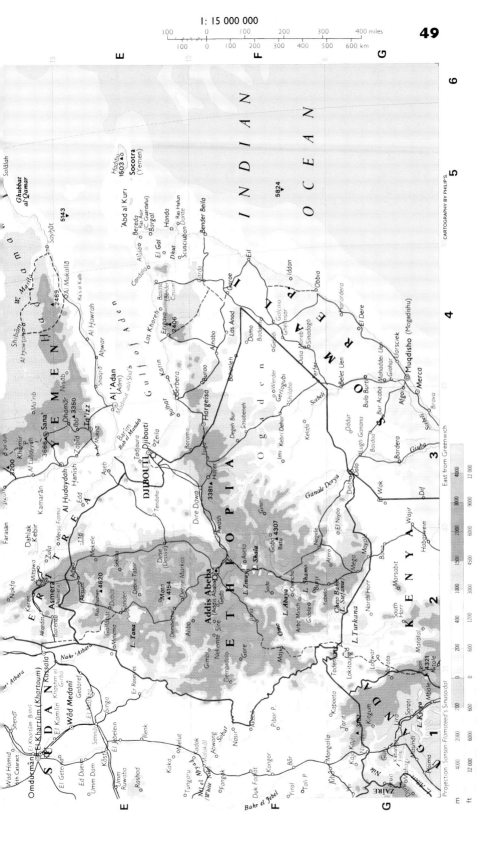

1: 15 000 000

100   0   100   200   300   400 miles
100   0   100   200   300   400   500   600 km

CARTOGRAPHY BY PHILIP'S.

East from Greenwich

Projection Sanson-Flamsteed's Sinusoidal

m   4000   2000   0   200   400   1000   1500   2000   3000   4000
ft   12 000   6000   0   600   1200   3000   4500   6000   9000   12 000

INDIAN   OCEAN

Socotra (Yemen)
Hadbu 1503

5824

Abd al Kuri

Y E M E N

Sana'
Al 'Izz   3350
Al Hudaydah

DJIBOUTI
Djibouti

E R I T R E A

Asmera

Addis Abeba (Adis Abeba)

E T H I O P I A

Ogaden

S O M A L I A

Muqdisho (Mogadishu)
Merca

Hargeisa

S U D A N

El Khartûm (Khartoum)
Omdurman   El Khartûm Bahrî
Wâd Medanî

K E N Y A

L. Turkana

U G A N D A

ZAIRE

Bahr el Jebel

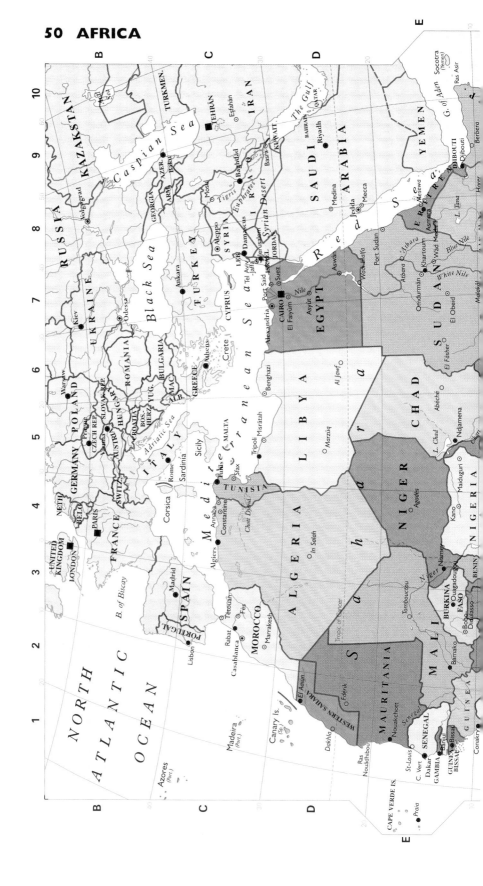

1 : 56 000 000

200   0   200   400   600   800   1000   1200 miles
200   0   200   400   600   800   1000   1200   1400   1600   1800   km

CARTOGRAPHY BY PHILIP'S

**INDIAN**

**OCEAN**

SEYCHELLES

SOMALIA

Mogadishu

Kismayu

Juba

Tana

KENYA

Kismayu

Mombasa

Nairobi

Kisumu

L. Turkana

L. Victoria

Kampala

UGANDA

Kigali

RWANDA

BURUNDI

Bujumbura

Kisangani

L. Albert

L. Edward

L. Kivu

Lualaba

CONGO

(DEM. REP. OF THE)

Mbandaka

Kananga

Congo

Kasai

Kwa

Bangui

Brazzaville

Kinshasa

Matadi

GABON

Libreville

Pointe Noire

CABINDA (Angola)

Luanda

Lobito

C. Lopez

Annobon

EQUATORIAL GUINEA

SÃO TOMÉ & PRÍNCIPE

Malabo

Port Harcourt

Douala

Yaounde

CAMEROON

Bangui

Ogun

Ubangi

Bight of Benin

Gulf of Guinea

Porto Novo

Accra

Sekondi-Takoradi

Abidjan

ASCENSION I.
(U.K.)

St. Helena
(U.K.)

Tristan da Cunha
(U.K.)

**SOUTH**

**ATLANTIC**

**OCEAN**

Aldabra Is.

COMOROS

Mayotte
(Fr.)

C. Delgado

Moçambique

Mozambique Channel

MOZAMBIQUE

Beira

ZIMBABWE

Harare

Bulawayo

Limpopo

TANZANIA

Dodoma

Dar es Salaam

Zanzibar

L. Tanganyika

L. Malawi

Mtwara

MALAWI

Lilongwe

Blantyre

Zambezi

ZAMBIA

Lusaka

Lubumbashi

Ndola

Likasi

Livingstone

ANGOLA

Huambo

Cubango

Cunene

C. Fria

Namibe

Cuango

Cuanza

NAMIBIA

Windhoek

BOTSWANA

Gaborone

Orange

Vaal

SOUTH AFRICA

Johannesburg

Pretoria

Mbabane

SWAZ.

Maputo

Kimberley

Maseru

LESOTHO

Durban

East London

Port Elizabeth

Cape Town

C. of Good Hope

Equator

Tropic of Capricorn

SEYCHELLES

MADAGASCAR

Antsiranana

Mahajanga

Antananarivo

Toamasina

Fianarantsoa

Réunion
(Fr.)

MAURITIUS

• Dakar   Capital Cities

West from Greenwich   East from Greenwich

Projection: Azimuthal Equidistant

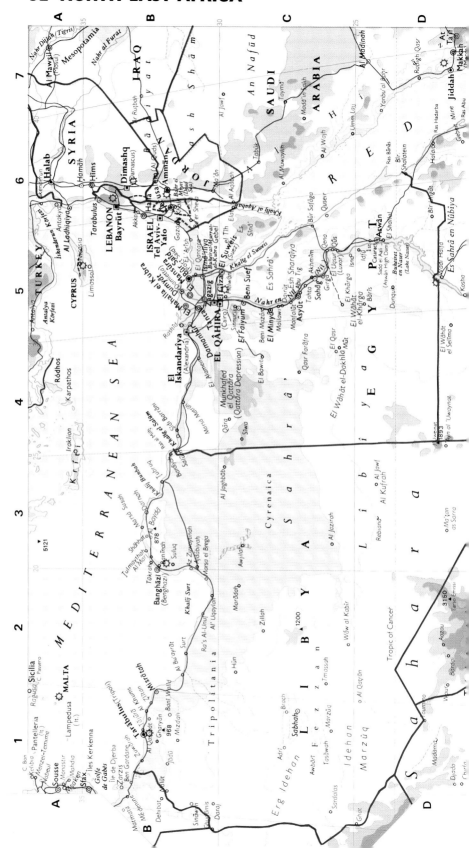

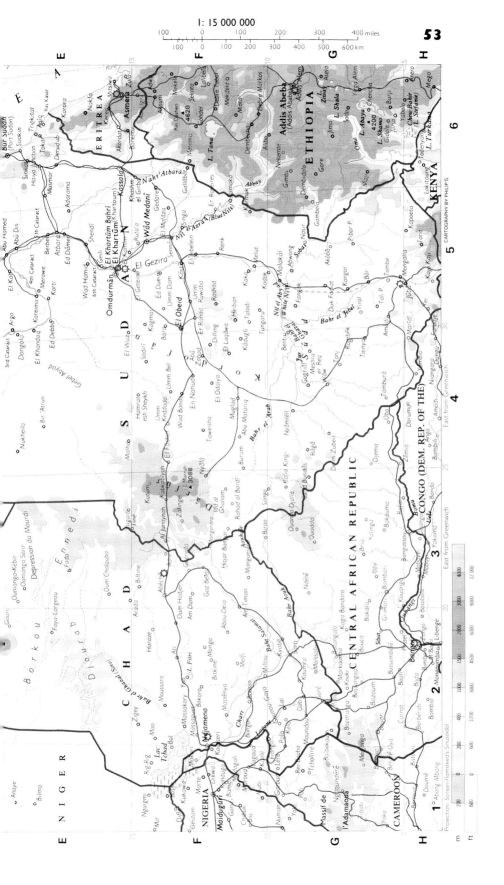

1: 15 000 000

**53**

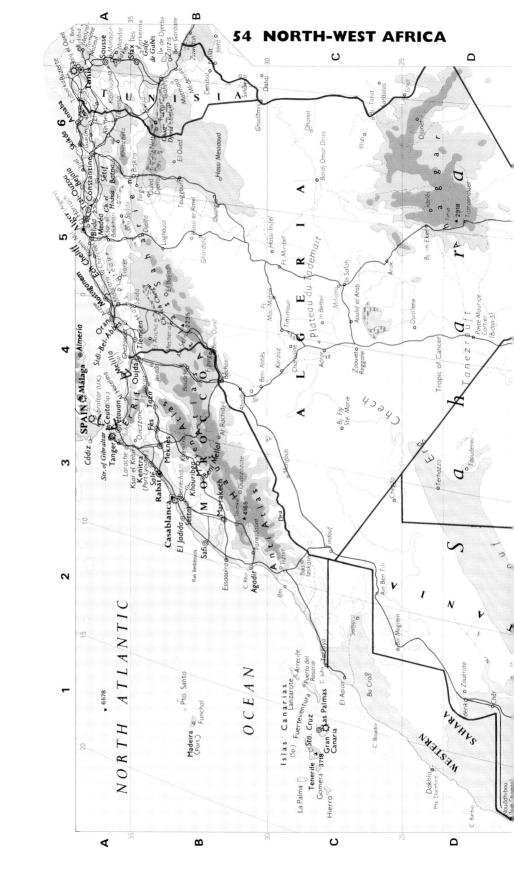

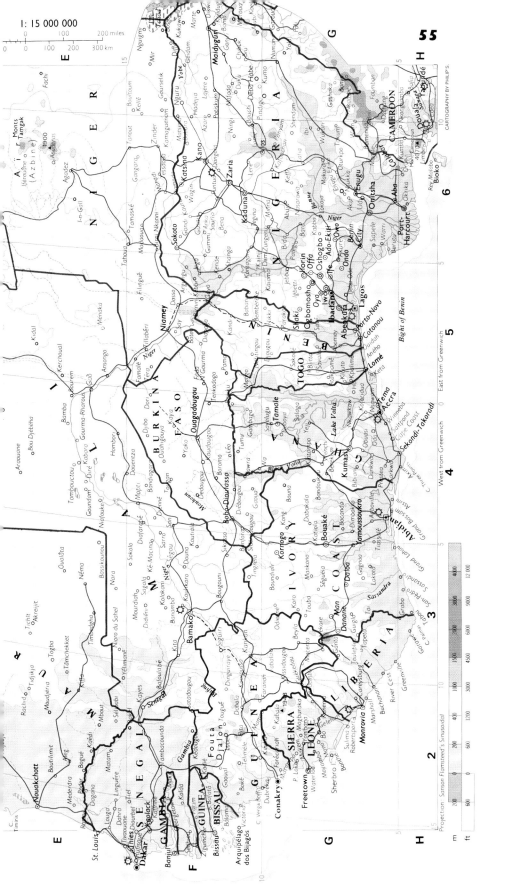

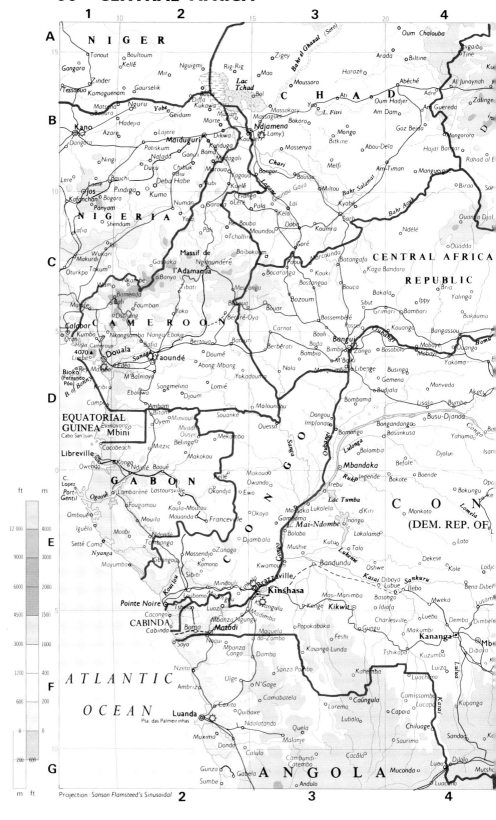

1: 15 000 000

100 0 100 200 300 400 miles
100 0 100 200 300 400 500 600 km

5 6 7 8

30 35 40

**A**

Omdurmân  El Khartûm Bahrî  Kerena  Mitsiwa  Dahlak Kebir
El Wuz  El Khartûm (Khartoum)  Kassala  Akordat  Asmera  Zula  ERITREA
El Kamlin  Khashm el Girba  Barentu  Um Ugri  Mersa Fatma
Sodirî  Rufa'a  Adwa  Aksum  Edd
Hamrat esh Sheykh  Kagmar  Ed Dueim  Gedaref  -116
Umm Keddada  Umm Bel  Bara  Umm Dam  Sennâr  El Mafâza  Ras Dashen 4620  Mekele
Umm Ruwaba  El Jebelein  Singa  Gallâbât  Metema  Gonder  Sekota
El Obeid  Kôstî  Gondar  Lalibela  Tendaho
Abū Zabad  Er Rahad  Umm  Renk  L. Tana  Debre Tabor  Mekdela  Dese
En Nahud  Dilling  Rashad  Er Roseires  Debre Markos  Mota
Taweisha  El Odaiya  El Laqâwa  Heiban  Kaka  Dembecha (Blue Nile)  Ankober
Muglad  Kâdugli  Talodi  Melut  Alibo  Gedo  Addis Abeba
Abu Matariq  Tungaru  Kodok  Abbay (Blue Nile)  Nekemte  Addis Alem  Awash
Nyâmlêll  Bentiu  Ntl el Abyad (White Nile)  Malakâl  Gimbi  Asela
Gogrial  Jur  Bahr el Ghazal  Abwong  Dembidolo  E T H I O P I A
Meshra er Req  Sûdd  Fangak  Nasir  Gore  Jima  Ziway  Asela
Wâw  Bahr el Jebel  Gambela  Sodo  Ginir
Tonj  Duk Fadiat  Akôbo  Maji  Omo  L. Abaya  Yirga Alem  Goba 4307
Zuber  Rumbêk  Yirol  Bôr  L. Shamo  Gidole  Burji  Negele
Tamburâ  Tainya  Kongor  Pibor P.  Chencha  Yarso  Yabelo  Arero
Dorumo  Amadi  Tali P  Tombe  Lotagipi Swamp  Chew Bahir (L. Stefanie)  Mega  El Niybo
Maridî  Jûba  Mongalla  Kapoeta  Todenyang  Mega  El Wak

**B**

**C**

**D**

**E**

S U D A N

**Kisangani**  Wamba  Bomili  Isiro  Dungu  Watsa  Nimule  Kitgum  Lokitaung  L. Turkana (L. Rudolf)  Buna  El Wak  Wajir  Diff
Banalia  Bafwasende  Mungbere  Mahagi  Gulu  Lira  Moroto  Lodwar  South Horr  Marsabit  Habaswein
Irumu  Bunia  Kaparega Falls  Masindi  Soroti  Mt. Elgon  Maralal  Garissa  Lamu
Equator  Beni  Butembo  Hoima  L. Kyoga  Mbale  Kitale  Eldoret  Nyahururu  Isiolo  Meru  Nanyuki  Mt. Kenya 5199  Embu
Kirundu  Lubutu  Kasese  Fort Portal  Mubende  Jinja  Kakamega  Nakuru  Kericho  Murang'a  Kitui  Garissa
Ubundu  Luofu  George  Masaka  Entebbe  Kisumu  Kisii  Naivasha  Limuru  Thika  Machakos
L. Edward  Mbarara  L. Victoria  Bukoba  Musoma  Loliondo  Nairobi  Konza  Kibwezi  Garsen
Kalima  Rutshuru  Kabale  Ukerewe I.  Nyahanga  Geita  L. Natron  Magadi  Makindu  Formosa Bay
Lokandu  Lac Kivu  Gisenyi  RWANDA  Kigali  Mwanza  Ngudu  Arusha  Moshi  Kilimanjaro 5895  Malindi
Shabunda  Bukavu  Butare  BURUNDI  Bujumbura  Kibondo  Kahama  Shinyanga  Nzega  Lake Eyasi  Lake Manyara  Same  Taveta  Voi  Mombasa
Kindu  Mwenga  Fizi  Kasulu  Usoke  Bukene  Mbulu  Kilindini
Kibombo  Kasongo  Kigoma-Ujiji  Kaliua  Tabora  Singida  Kondoa  Korogwe  Pangani  Tanga  Pemba I.
Kongolo  Kabambare  Uvinza  Ugalla  Manyoni  Dodoma  Kibaya  Handeni  Zanzibar  Zanzibar I.
Kiseng wa  Kalemie  Kibwesa  Mpanda  Rungwa  Mpwapwa  Saadani  Bagamoyo
Ankoro  Manono  Karema  Iringa  Morogoro  Dar-es-Salaam
Kabongo  Kiambi  Moba  Kipili  Sumbawanga  Kasanga  L. Rukwa  Kipembawe  Gt. Ruaha  Rufiji  Utete  Mafia I.
Mwanza  Molira  Mbala  Chunya  Mahenge  Kilwa Kivinje
Mitwaba  L. Mweru  Chiengi  Mbeya  Tukuyu  Njombe  Liwale  Lindi
Bukama  Kilwa  Kajulwe  Rosa  Kapenga  Isoka  Manda  Nachingwea  Mtwara  Cabo Delgado
Likasi  Kasenga  Mambilima Falls  Kasama  Livingstonia  L. Nyasa  Songea  Tunduru  Masasi  Newala  Palma  Moçimboa da Praia
Luwingu  Chinsali  ZAMBIA  Mbamba Bay  Nkhata Bay  MALAWI  Ruvuma

U G A N D A
K E N Y A
T A N Z A N I A
L. Albert
Albert Nile
Ruwenzori 5119
Kampala
L. George
L. Victoria
Lake Natron

**F**

**G**

5 6

CARTOGRAPHY BY PHILIP'S.

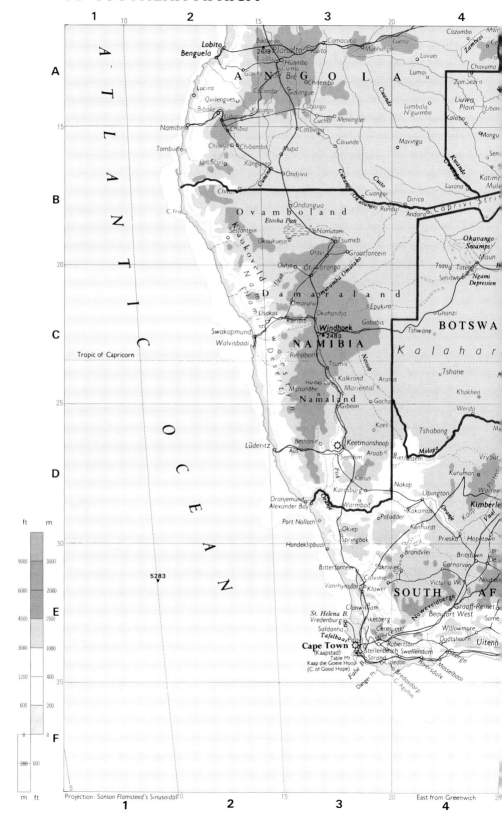

**A T L A N T I C   O C E A N**

A N G O L A

Lobito
Benguela
Lucira
Quilengues
Bibala
Namibe
Tombua

2619 Planalto
Cáala
Huambo
Cuimo
Galangue
Lubango
Kikupgo
Chibia
Chianje
Chibemba
Oncocua
Xangongo

Balombo
Ngunza Bié
Chitembo
Citconda
Cuchi
Cassinga

Camacuta
Luena
Munhango
Luvuei
Cubango
Menongue
Caiundo
Mupa
Mavinga

Cazombo
Zambezi
Chavuma
Zambezi
Lumbala N'guimbo
Kalabo
Cuando

Mwi
Co

Liuwa Plain
Libon

Lumai

Mongu
Sen

C. Fria
Sesfontein
Kaokoveld

Ondjiva
Ondangua
Etosha Pan
Okaukuejo
Namutoni

O v a m b o l a n d

Tsumeb
Grootfontein
Otavi

Cunene
Cubango
Cuito
Cuangar
Dirico
Rundu
Andara

Katime
Mul

Caprivi Strip

Okavango Swamps
Maun
Tsau Toteng
Sehitwe Ngami
Depression

Luiana
Kwando

Ngami

BOTSWA

Outjo
Otjiwarongo
Onzaruru
Usakos
Swakopmund
Walvisbaai

Kaokoveld

Otjiwarongo
Onzaruru
Omaruru
Okahandja
Karibib
Windhoek
2483
Rehoboth
Tsumis

Ntoeskuppe

Namib Desert

Omuramba Omatako

D a m a r a l a n d

Epukiro
Gobabis
Tshwane

N A M I B I A

K a l a h a r

Ghanzi

Tropic of Capricorn

Hardap Dam
Maltohöhe
Gibeon

Kalkrand
Mariental

N a m a l a n d

Gochas

Tsumis
Nossob
Aranos
Koes
Tshabong

Tshane
Khakhea
Werda

N

Lüderitz
Aus
Bethanie
Seeheim
Aroab
Rietfontein
Kanus
Keetmanshoop
Fish
Molopo
Nakop
Upington

Werda

M

Tshabong

Vryburg
Kuruman
Plateau
Warren

Kimberle

Oranjemund
Alexander Bay
Port Nolloth
Okiep
Springbok
Hondeklipbaai

Warmbad
Karasburg
Orange
Pofadder
Kakamas
Kenhardt

Prieska
Hopetown
Britstown
Carnarvon

Vaal
Kaap

De

5283

Bitterfontein
Calvinia
Vanrhynsdorp
Klawer
Clanwilliam
St. Helena B.
Vredenburg
Saldanha
Tafelbaai
Cape Town
(Kaapstad)
Kaap die Goeie Hoop
(C. of Good Hope)

Sakrivier
Victoria W.
Nuweveldberge

Piketberg
Ceres
Worcester
Robertson
Stellenbosch Swellendam
Strand
Caledon
Table Mt
Danger Pt.
C. Agulhas
Bredasdorp
Riversdale

Brandvlei

**SOUTH   AF**

Graaff-Reinet
Beaufort West
Willowmore
Oudtshoorn
George
Mosselbaai

Some
Uitenh

**Scale legend (left):**

ft   m

9000   3000

6000   2000

4500   1500

3000   1000

1200   400

600   200

0   0

200   600

m   ft

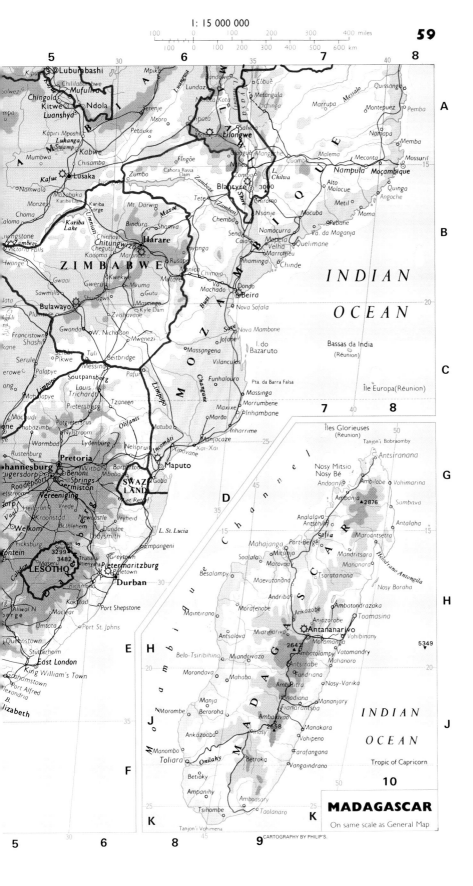

1: 15 000 000

100    0    100    200    300    400 miles
100  0  100  200  300  400  500  600 km

5                    6                    7                    8

Lubumbashi
Mpika
Chililabombwe
Mufulira
Kibuye
Chingola
Kitwe    Ndola
Lukanga
Luanshya
Kápiri Mposhi
Lusaka
Kafue
Namwala
Mazabuka
Monze
Kariba
Lake
Choma
Kalomo

**Z I M B A B W E**

Chitungwiza  Harare

Bulawayo

Gwanda

Francistown
Shashi
Serule
Palapye
Soutpansberg
Louis
Trichardt
Pietersburg
Tzaneen

Pretoria
hannesburg
Germiston
Vereeniging
Welkom
LESOTHO
3299
3482

Durban
Pietermaritzburg

East London
King William's Town
lizabeth

Lilongwe

Cahora Bassa
Dam
Tete
Blantyre  3000

**M O Z A M B I Q U E**

Nampula  Moçambique

Quelimane

Beira

Nova Sofala

Bassas da India
(Réunion)

**I N D I A N**

**O C E A N**

Île Europa(Réunion)

Maputo
SWAZI
LAND

Îles Glorieuses
(Réunion)

Nosy Mitsio
Nosy Bé

Antsiranana

Antananarivo

5349

**M A D A G A S C A R**

Toliara

**I N D I A N**

**O C E A N**

Tropic of Capricorn

**10**

**MADAGASCAR**

On same scale as General Map

CARTOGRAPHY BY PHILIP'S.

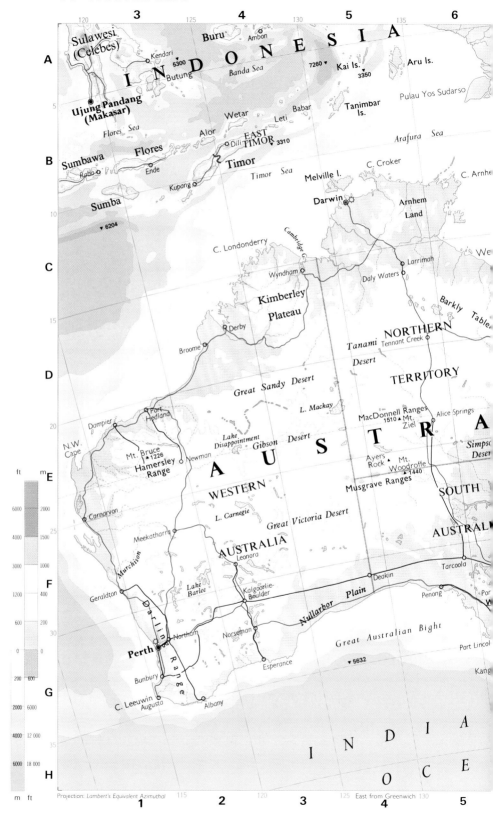

Projection: Lambert's Equivalent Azimuthal    East from Greenwich

1:20 000 000

100  0  100  200  300  400  500 miles
100  0  200  400  600  800 km

7          8          9          10          11

Mount Hagen○  4508  Mt.
              ●Mt.  Wilhelm
              ○Lae
**PAPUA NEW GUINEA**          New Britain     Mt.  Bougainville   **SOLOMON**
                                              Balbi
Owen Stanley Range   Solomon          New      Choiseul   **ISLANDS**
Fly                  9140             Georgia
Gulf of                               Sea                          Santa Isabel        B
Papua
                                                        Honiara○              Malaita
**Port** ○◎     D'Entrecasteaux Arch.                        ▲2331
**Moresby**                                         **Guadalcanal**
Torres Strait                                        **San Cristobal**
        C. York              Louisiade                              10
                            **Archipelago**                Rennell
                                                                                C
**Cape**                    C o r a l    S e a
Weipa○ **York**
**Peninsula**                                        **P    A    C    I    F    I    C**      15
                                                                                D
Cooktown○                              Coral
Mitchell                                Sea       Chesterfield Is.
○Normanton   1611 ▲  ○**Cairns**        Islands
        Bartle Frere                                                                    20
Forsayth○                              Territory    **O    C    E    A    N**
Flinders                                                                                E
unt Isa    **Townsville**◎
           Charters Towers○
Hughenden○         **Mackay**                                                    25
Winton○                                          Tropic of Capricorn
**QUEENSLAND**   **Rockhampton**
Longreach○        **Gladstone**
Diamantina  Yaraka○    **Bundaberg**
                      Maryborough○                                              F
Creek   Charleville○  Roma○  Gympie○
        Quilpie○              **BRISBANE**                Lord Howe
Cunnamulla○  **Toowoomba**○    Ipswich       (Austr.)
Thargomindah○ Dirrabandi○      Gold         ▼734
                              Coast
Walgett○        **Lismore**                                                      G
Bourke○   **NEW SOUTH**   Round ▲1615
**Broken Hill**○  Tamworth○   Mt.|
        Cobar○          ○**Taree**
**WALES**  **Newcastle**
t Pirie  Orange○ Bathurst○
Murray  Mildura○      ■**SYDNEY**
**Adelaide**          **Wollongong**
Wagga Wagga○  **Canberra**  **Shellharbour**
Shepparton○  CAPITAL TERRITORY   T a s m a n   S e a
Albury○  Mt.Kosciuszko                                                          H
Horsham○ ●**Bendigo**  2237▲
**VICTORIA**   ○Bombala
Ballarat○ ■**MELBOURNE**  C. Howe
unt Gambier  ●**Geelong**
Warrnambool                                        ▼5267
                Bass Strait
King I.    Furneaux Group                                                       J
N
        Burnie○ ○**Launceston**
        1617
        Mt.Ossa
**TASMANIA**   ◎**Hobart**

## NORTH ISLAND

Three Kings Is.
C. Renga
North C.
C. Maria van Diemen
Houhora
Rangaunu Bay
Whangaroa Bay
Doubtless Bay
Ahipara B.
Kaitaia
Tauroa Pt.
Hokianga Harb.
Donnelly's Crossing
Dargaville
Rawene
Opanake
Kaihu
Northland
Waipoua
C. Brett
Bay of Islands
Whangarei
Hikurangi
Maungaturoto
Kaipara Harb.
Helensville
Workworth
Waiwera
Whangarei Harb.
Whangaparoa
Bream Hd.
Bream Bay
C. Rodney
Gt. Barrier I.
Lit. Barrier I.
Cuvier I.
C. Colville
Coromandel
Whitianga
Whangaparaoa
Hauraki Gulf
Takapuna Devonport
AUCKLAND
Manukau
Onehunga
Papakura
Thames
Pukekohe
Mercer
Waiuku
Waikato
Raglan
Morrinsville
Huntly
Te Aroha
Kohakura
Mayor I.
Bay of Plenty
White I.
C. Runaway
East C.
Hicks Bay
Te Puke
Whakatane
Opotiki
Motu
Cambridge
Hamilton
Te Awamutu
Putaruru
Kinleith
Te Kuiti
Mokau
L. Taupo
Ongarue
Rotorua
Tauranga
Waihi
Tauranga Harb.
Mt. Maunganui
Kawerau
Rotomahana
Waikaremoana
Urewera
Gisborne
Poverty Bay
Waikokopu
Mahia Peninsula
Nuhaka
Wairoa
Hawke Bay
Te Karaka
Tolaga Bay
Ormond
Waipiro
Tokomaru
Napier
Hastings
C. Kidnappers
Raukumara Ra.
Waihirere
Te Kaha
Kawhia Harb.
Kawhia
Marokopa
Otorohanga
Taumarunu
Waiouru
Waiuru
Ohakune
Taihape
Kaimanawa Mts.
Ruahine Ra.
Mangaweka
Hunterville
Waipawa
Waipukurau
Dannevirke
Woodville
Feilding
Pahiatua
Marton
Palmerston N.
Fox ...
North Taranaki Bight
New Plymouth
Inglewood
Mt. Egmont (Taranaki) 2518
Opunake
Kaponga
Eltham
Stratford
Hawera
Patea
Waverley
Waitotara
Wanganui
South Taranaki Bight
Waitara

---

## SOUTH-WEST PACIFIC

1: 54 000 000

International Date Line

NORTHERN MARIANAS (U.S.)
Saipan
GUAM (U.S.)
Mariana Trench
M i c r o n e s i a
Caroline Islands
FEDERATED STATES OF MICRONESIA
Truk
Pohnpei
MARSHALL IS.
Bikini Atoll
Enewetak Atoll
Jaluit
Butaritari
Gilbert Is.
KIRIBATI
Baker I. (U.S.)
Banaba
Equator
NAURU
TUVALU
Rotuma
Wallis & Futuna (Fr.)
FIJI
Vanua Levu
Viti Levu
Suva
M e l a n e s i a
Admiralty Is.
Bismarck Arch.
New Ireland
New Britain
Rabaul
9103
Lae
PAPUA NEW GUINEA
Port Moresby
SOLOMON IS.
Guadalcanal
Honiara
9165
Sta. Cruz I.
VANUATU
NEW CALEDONIA (Fr.)
Is. Chesterfield
7570
Nouméa
Is. Loyauté
Louisiade Arch.
Coral Sea
Cairns
Townsville
AUSTRALIA
Rockhampton
Brisbane
Great Divide
Norfolk I. (Aust.)
Tropic of Capricorn
Kermadec Is. (N.Z.)
NEW ZEALAND
10 047

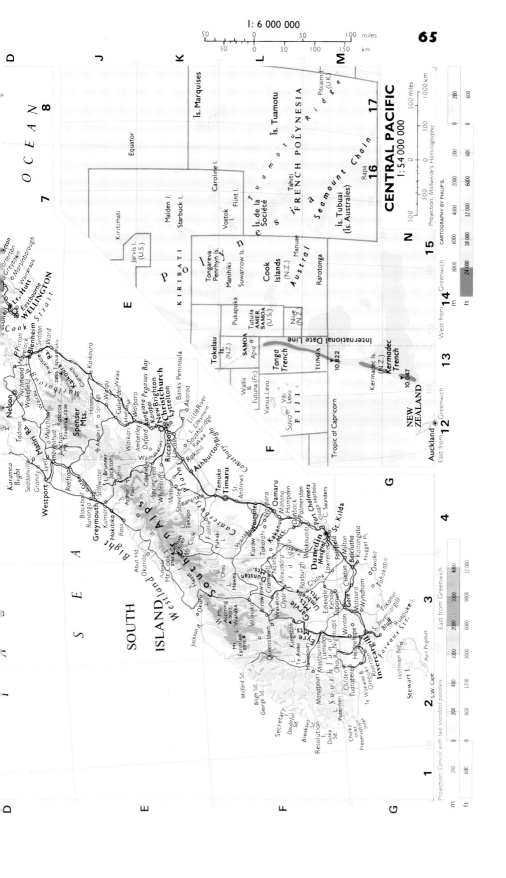

1: 35 000 000

CARTOGRAPHY BY PHILIP'S

7 ■ MÉXICO  Capital Cities  8

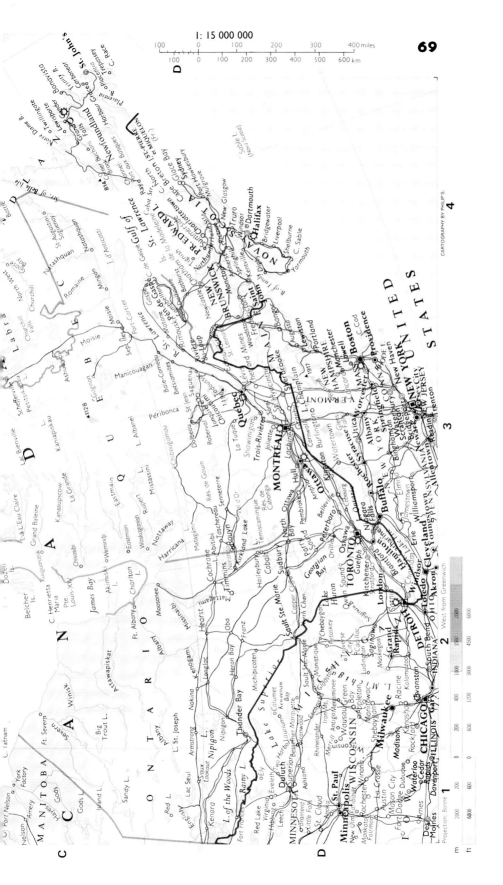

1: 15 000 000

100        0        100        200        300        400 miles
100        0        100        200        300        400        500        600 km

D

CARTOGRAPHY BY PHILIPS.

Projection Bonne        West from Greenwich

m
ft

2000        0        200        400        1000        1500        2000        6000
6000        0        600        1200        3000        4500        6000

1        2        3        4

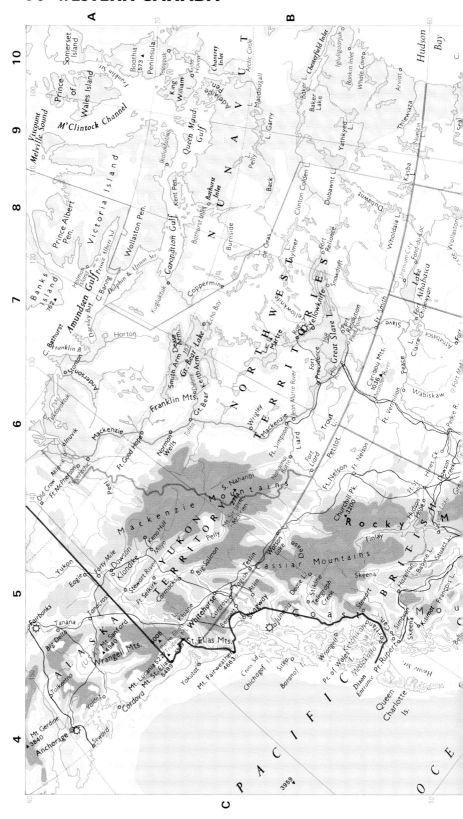

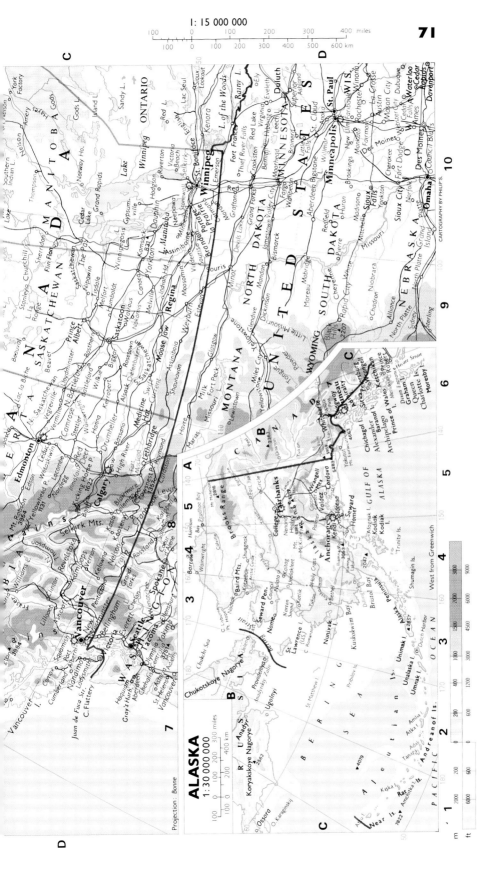

1: 15 000 000

CARTOGRAPHY BY PHILIPS.

ALASKA
1: 30 000 000

Projection: Bonne

West from Greenwich

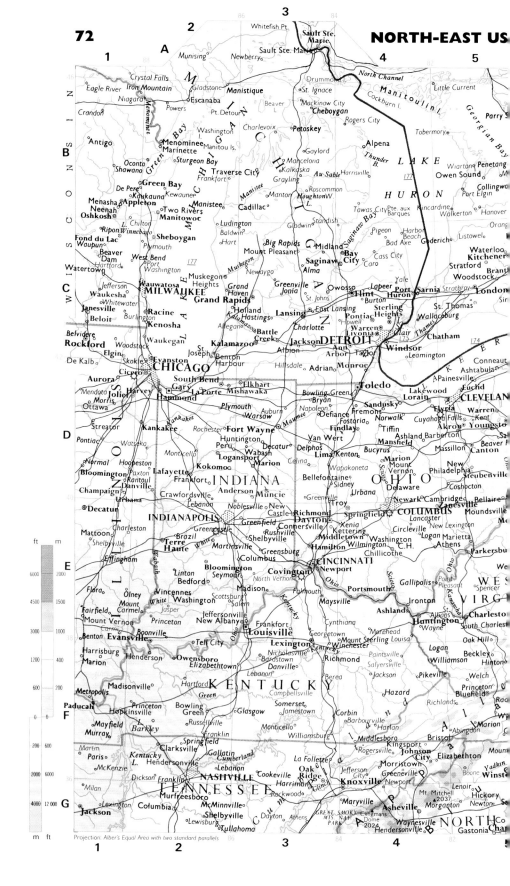

6          7          8          9          10

Pembroke    Fort
Coulonge    Buckingham    Hawkesbury    Ottawa    MONTREAL    Granby    Sherbrooke
Eganville    Hull    Ottawa    Lachine    Magog    Coaticook    Richardson
Barry's    Renfrew    Arnprior    St-Jean    Cowansville    Newport    Island Pond    Colebrook    Lakes
Bay                Carleton    Cornwall    Beauharnois            B
Huntsville    Bancroft    Place    Malone    St. Albans    Lancaster
Bracebridge    Smiths Falls    Massena    Plattsburg    L.    Johnsbury    Mt.    Berlin
Gravenhurst        Perth    Prescott    Ogdensburg    Champlain    Burlington    Montpelier    White    Washington    Conway
and    Bobcaygeon    Brockville    Potsdam    Canton    Winooski    Barre    Mts.    1917
Simcoe    Marmora    Gananoque    Saranac Lakes            Middlebury            Laconia
Lindsay    Kingston    Gouverneur    1629    Ticonderoga    Rutland    Lebanon    Franklin
Peterborough    Belleville    Watertown    Lowville    L.    Claremont    Concord    Rochester    Dover
Oshawa    Trenton    Picton    Lake Pleasant    George    Glens    Hudson    Springfield    Keene    Manchester    Portsmouth
Cobourg    75    Oswego    Oneida    Rome    Falls    Saratoga Springs    Brattleboro    Nashua    Haverhill    Newburyport
TORONTO        Fulton    Utica    Amsterdam    Greenfield    Fitchburg    Lowell    C. Ann
LAKE ONTARIO    Rochester    Newark    Syracuse    Gloversville    Schenectady    Troy    Leominster    Salem
Niagara    Batavia    Auburn    Cayuga    Cortland    Norwich    Albany    Pittsfield    Worcester    Cambridge    BOSTON
Falls    Amherst    Geneva    Seneca            Northampton        MASS.    Quincy
gara Falls    Buffalo    Canandaigua            Oneonta    Catskill    Hudson    Springfield    Chicopee    Brockton
elland    West Seneca    Penn Yan        Ithaca    NEW    YORK    Catskill    Springfield    Hartford    Providence    Taunton    Fall River
edonia    Dunkirk    Bath        Johnson City    1281    Kingston    New Britain    Pawtucket    New
orry    Salamanca    Hornell    Corning    Endicott    Binghamton    Mts.        Waterbury    Meriden    Warwick    R.I.    Bedford
Jamestown    Olean    Wellsville    Elmira    Sayre    Delaware        Poughkeepsie    New    London    Martha's
Warren    Bradford        Towanda    Susquehanna    Carbondale    Newburgh    Beacon    Haven    New    Vineyard
ville    Kane    Coudersport    Wellsboro        Dunmore    Middletown    Danbury    Bridgeport    Stamford
lle    Ridgway    St. Marys    759    Emporium    Scranton    Wilkes    Paterson    Yonkers    Mount    Long Island    Riverhead
Franklin    Du    Williamsport    Lock    Nanticoke    Barre    Shenandoah    Jersey City    Vernon
Brookville    Bois    Clearfield    Haven    Bloomsburg    Sunbury    Hazleton    Newark    D
Butler    Punxsutawney    State College    Lewistown    Berwick    Pottsville    Easton    Elizabeth    NEW YORK
nning    Penn Hills    956    Indiana    Altoona    Harrisburg    Blue Mt.    Allentown    Reading    New Brunswick
ppa    PITTSBURGH    Johnstown        Carlisle    Lebanon    Pottstown    Trenton    Long Branch
Greensburg        Chambersburg    PHILADELPHIA    Lancaster    Norristown    Asbury Park    E
hington    Connellsville    Hanover    York    Camden    NEW
Uniontown    Hagerstown    Westminster    Bridgeton    Chester    JERSEY
nesburg    Cumberland    Frederick    Columbia    Newark    Wilmington    Hammonton
irmont    Keyser    Martinsburg    Towson    Vineland    Atlantic City
sburg    Romney    Winchester    BALTIMORE    Dover    Millville    Ocean City
ckhannon    1482    Front Royal    Arlington    Annapolis    C. May
Elkins    Franklin    Luray    WASHINGTON D.C.    Easton    DELAWARE    C. Henlopen
er    Harrisonburg    Culpeper    Alexandria    Lexington    Cambridge    Salisbury
Waynesboro    Staunton    Fredericksburg    Park    Chesapeake    Snow Hill
Clifton    Buena    Orange    Tappahannock    Potomac    Bay    Accomac
Forge    Vista    Charlottesville    VIRGINIA    West    Bay
Lynchburg    Lakeside        Point    Cape Charles
Roanoke    Bedford    Richmond    Williamsburg    C. Charles
sburg    Farmville    Colonial Heights    Hampton
R    Danville    John H. Kerr    Petersburg    Nottoway    Newport News    Virginia Beach
Eden    Reservoir    Emporia    Franklin    Portsmouth    Norfolk
eidsville    Roxboro    Roanoke    Winton    Elizabeth    Chesapeake
sboro    Oxford    Rapids    City    Currituck Sd.
High    Burlington    Henderson    Roanoke    Edenton    Albemarle Sd.    Manteo
Point    Graham    Durham    Rocky Mount    Williamston
e    Chapel Hill    Raleigh    Wilson    Greenville
Lexington    Ham    Smithfield    Washington    Pamlico
olis    Asheboro    Sanford        Goldsboro    Kinston    Pamlico Sound    Hatteras
AROLINA    Dunn    Neuse    New Bern
lbemarle
West from Greenwich

### Maine inset

CANADA    Edmundston
Fort    Van    A
Eagle    Kent    Buren    Grand
St. John    Lake    Allagash    Caribou    Falls
Presque Isle    St. John
Eagle L.
Chamberlain    Houlton
Chesuncook    L.    Patten
Mt. Katahdin    1605    Chiputneticook
Moosehead    Lakes
L.    Millinocket
Greenville    Mattawamkeag    B
MAINE    Lincoln
Richardson    Dover    Calais
Lakes    Foxcroft    East-port
Rangeley    Bangor    Old Town
Farmington        Brewer    Machias
Berlin    Rumford    Waterville    Ellsworth
Mt. Washington    Augusta    Belfast    Bar
1917    Gardiner    Harbor
Conway    Auburn    Lewiston    Rockland    Mt. Desert
Brunswick    Bath    Penobscot B.
Westbrook    Portland
Laconia    Saco    Biddeford
Dover    C
Rochester
Portsmouth
Haverhill    NEW HAMPSHIRE

Continuation
Eastwards
On same scale

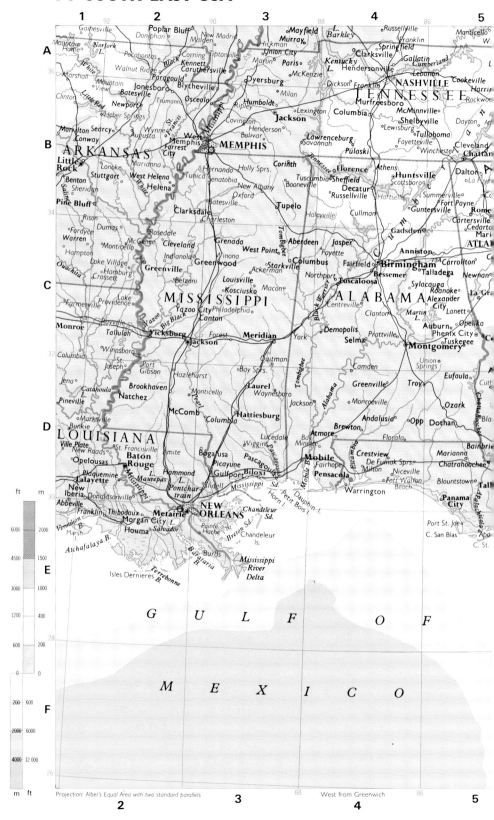

Projection: Alber's Equal Area with two standard parallels    West from Greenwich

50    0    50    100 miles
50    0    50    100    150 km

6        7        8        9        10

**A**

Currituck Sd.

Harlan
Middlesboro    Marion
Kingsport  Bristol    Galax  Martinsville    Danville    Emporia
Rogersville  Johnson    Abingdon  S.    Eden    Roxboro  Roanoke
Jefferson  Morristown  City  Elizabethton  Mount Airy  Reidsville  Oxford  Rapids  Winton  Elizabeth
City  Greeneville  Boone  Yadkin    Burlington  Henderson  Edenton  City
Knoxville  Newport  Lenoir    Greensboro  Durham    Albemarle Sd.  Manteo
Maryville  Mt. Mitchell  Hickory  Thomasville  High  Graham  Chapel Hill  Rocky Mount  Williamston  Roanoke I.
SMOKY  2037  Statesville  Lexington  Raleigh  Wilson  Greenville
Asheville  Morganton  Newton  Salisbury  Asheboro  Smithfield  Washington  Pamlico
Waynesville  Clingmans  Concord  Kannapolis  Sanford  Dunn  Goldsboro  Kinston
Hendersonville  Dome  Shelby  Gastonia  NORTH  CAROLINA  New Bern

**B**

Brevard  2024  Charlotte  Albemarle  Southern  Fayetteville  C. Hatteras
Murphy  Gaffney  Monroe  Pines  Clinton  Beaufort  Raleigh
Spartanburg  Rock Hill  Lancaster  Laurinburg  Jacksonville  B.  C. Lookout
Greenville  Easley  Union  Chester  Bennettsville  Lumberton  Onslow
Toccoa  Seneca  Hartsville  Dillon  Whiteville  Wilmington  B.
Anderson  Laurens  Darlington  Mullins
Hartwell  Greenwood  Newberry  Camden  Florence  Southport
Gainesville  Abbeville  Saluda  Murray  Columbia  Sumter  Lake City  Conway  C. Fear

**C**

Elberton  Clark  SOUTH  CAROLINA  Myrtle Beach
Athens  Hill L.  Orangeburg  Manning  Kingstree
Lawrenceville  Covington  Augusta  Aiken  Marion  Georgetown
Sparta  Bamberg  Moultrie
Milledgeville  Waynesboro  Summerville  North Charleston
GEORGIA  Millen  Walterboro  Charleston  Mt. Pleasant
Macon  Swainsboro  Hampton  Ridgeland  Beaufort
Warner  Dublin  Parris I.
Robins  Statesboro
Perry  Cochran  Vidalia

**D**

Eastman  Savannah
Cardele  Hazlehurst  Hinesville  Ossabaw I.
Fitzgerald  Baxley  St. Catherines I.
Sylvester  Douglas  Jesup  Sapelo I.
Tifton  Waycross  Brunswick
Adel  Okefenokee  Folkston  Cumberland I.
Valdosta  Swamp  Fernandina Beach
Quitman  ATLANTIC

**E**

Monticello  Jacksonville
Madison  JACKSONVILLE  Beach
Live Oak  Lake  Green Cove Springs
Perry  City  St. Augustine  OCEAN
FLORIDA  High Springs  Starke
Cross City  Palatka  Bunnell
Gainesville  Ormond
L.  Beach  New
Ocala  George  Smyrna
Crystal River  Daytona Beach  Beach
Inverness  De Land  Eustis  Sanford
Leesburg  Titusville  C. Canaveral

**F**

Brooksville  Winter Park
Dade City  Orlando  Cocoa  Merritt Island
Kissimmee  Haines City  Melbourne
Tarpon Springs  Lakeland  Winter Haven
Clearwater  TAMPA  Bartow  Vero Beach
Largo  St. Petersburg  Grand Cays
Tampa Bay  Little Abaco  Gt. Guana Cay
Bradenton  Sebring  Fort Pierce  Hope
Sarasota  Istokpoga  Stuart  Settlement  Town
Arcadia  Okeechobee  Pt.
Punta Gorda  Okeechobee  Pahokee  Freeport  Grand  Great
La Belle  Belle  West Palm  Bahama I.  Abaco I.

**G**

Charlotte Harb.  Glade  Beach  BAHAMAS
Cape  Fort  Delray Beach
Coral  Myers  Immokalee  Boca Raton
Naples  Big Cypress Swamp  Pompano Beach
Everglades  Fort Lauderdale
Carol City  Hollywood
Hialeah  Miami Beach  CARTOGRAPHY BY PHILIP'S.
EVERGLADES  MIAMI
NAT. PARK  Biscayne
B.
Homestead

6        8        9

1　2　3　4　5

**A**

Scobey　Plentywood　Crosby　Bowbells　Mohall　Bottineau　Rolla　Langdon　Cavalier　Grafton　Park River

Kenmare　Souris　Cando　Wa

MONTANA

Wolf Point　Missouri　Williston　Stanley　Minot　Towner　Rugby　Devils Lake

Fort Peck L.　Fairview　New Town　Velva　Lakota　Larimore　Grand Forks

Sidney　Watford City　L. Sakakawed　Garrison　Harvey　New Rockford　Northwood

Circle　Manning　Fessenden　Sheyenne　Cooperstown　Mo

N O R T H°　D A K O T A　McClusky　Carrington　Hillsbor

**B**

Glendive　Stanton　Washburn　Steele　Jamestown　Valley City

Terry　Wibaux　Beach　Center　Hebron　Mandan　Bismarck　Napoleon　Lisbon　Fa

Miles City　Dickinson　Heart　James　La Moure

Yellowstone　Baker　White Butte 1069　Mott　Carson　Cannonball　Linton　Ashley　Ellendale　Wal

Tongue　Powder　Bowman　Fort Yates　Selfridge　Lake　Missouri　Forman

Ekalaka　Hettinger　Lemmon　McIntosh　Grand　Mound City　Eureka　Leola　Britton　Sisseton

Broadus　Buffalo　Bison　Timber Lake　Mobridge　Oahe　Selby　Ipswich　Aberdeen　Webster

**C**

Little　Missouri　Moreau　Dupree　Eagle Butte　Gettysburg　Faulkton　Clark　Coteau

Belle Fourche　S O U T H　D A K O T A　Redfield　James　De Smet

Spearfish　Cheyenne　Onida　Highmore　Miller　Huron

Gillette　Sundance　Sturgis　Deadwood　Oahe Dam　Pierre　Howa

Belle　Lead　Bad　Fort Pierre　Wessington Sprs.　Woonsocket　Madiso

Newcastle　Black Hills 2207　Rapid City　Philip　Kadoka　Murdo　Kennebec　Chamberlain　Mitchell　Salem

Custer　Harney Pk.　White　L. Francis Case　Alexandria　Parker

**D**

Hot Springs　B a d l a n d s　White River　Winner　Missouri　Armour　Lake Andes

Edgemont　White　Martin　Little White　Yankton

Douglas　Pine Ridge　Chadron　Niobrara　Butte　South

Lusk　Harrison　Crawford　Rushville　Valentine　Bassett　Atkinson

WYOMING　Hemingford　North Loup　Ainsworth　O'Neill　Elkhorn　Neligh　Wayn　Nor

Torrington　Wheatland　Alliance　Sand Hills 1036　Mullen　Taylor　Burwell　Madison　Wes

Laramie Mountains 3131　Scottsbluff　Hyannis　Thedford　Middle　Albion

Gering　Bridgeport　N E B R A S K A　Greeley　Col

Harrisburg　Kimball　Oshkosh　Stapleton　Broken Bow　Fullerton　Sc

Laramie　Lodgepole Cr.　Loup City　David City

**E**

Cheyenne　Sidney　Ogallala　L. McConaughy　North Platte　South Loup　St. Paul　Central　Platte

Fort Collins　Sterling　South Platte　Julesburg　Grant　Gothenburg　Cozad　Grand Island　York　Seware

Loveland　Evans　Greeley　Holyoke　Imperial　Curtis　Elwood　Lexington　Kearney　Aurora

Boulder　Longmont　Fort Morgan　Akron　Frenchman Cr.　Hastings　Geneva

**F**

Lafayette　Golden　Brighton　Trenton　McCook　Republican　Holdrege

DENVER　Byers　Wray　Benkelman　Beaver City　Alma　Franklin　Red Cloud　Hebron　Fairbury

Lakewood　Aurora　Englewood　Atwood　Oberlin　Norton　Phillipsburg　Smith Center　Mankato　Belleville

Castle Rock　St. Francis　N. Fork　Solomon　Concordia　Republica

C O L O R A D O　Limon　Burlington　Colby　Stockton　Solomon　Beloit

Hugo　Goodland　Oakley　S. Fork　Hill City　Osborne　Minneapolis　Ma Junct

Pikes Pk. 4300　Colorado Springs　Cheyenne Wells　Smoky Hills　Saline　Lincoln　Abilene

Fountain　Big Sandy Cr.　Smoky Hill　Hays　Russell　Salina

Canon City　Sharon Springs　Leoti　Scott City　La Crosse　Ellsworth

Pueblo　Eads　K A N S A

Ordway　Tribune　Dighton　Great Bend　Lyons　McPhers

Las Animas　Lamar　Larned

Projection: Alber's Equal Area with two standard parallels　West from Greenwich

2　3　4　5

| ft | m |
|---|---|
| 12 000 | 4000 |
| 9000 | 3000 |
| 6000 | 2000 |
| 4500 | 1500 |
| 3000 | 1000 |
| 1200 | 400 |
| 600 | 200 |
| 0 | 0 |
| 200 | 600 |

m ft

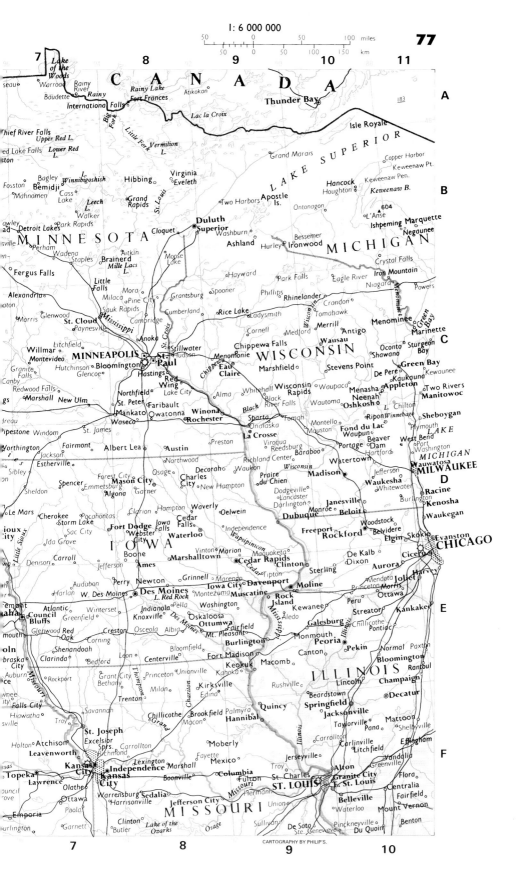

1: 6 000 000

50     0     50     100   miles

50    0    50    100   150   km

**7**     **8**     **9**     **10**     **11**

**C A N A D A**

Lake of the Woods
seau
Warroad
Rainy River
Baudette
International Falls
Rainy Lake
Fort Frances
Atikokan
**Thunder Bay**
183
**A**

Thief River Falls
Upper Red L.
ed Lake Falls
Lower Red L.
ston
Fosston
Bagley
Mahnomen
Bemidji
Cass Lake
Winnibigoshish
Hibbing
Virginia
Eveleth
Lac la Croix
Isle Royale
Grand Marais
Copper Harbor
Keweenaw Pt.
Keweenaw Pen.
Hancock
Houghton
Keweenaw B.
**B**

LAKE SUPERIOR

awley
ad
sville
Detroit Lakes
Park Rapids
Walker
Leech L.
Grand Rapids
St. Louis
Two Harbors
Apostle Is.
Ontonagon
L'Anse
604
Ishpeming
Marquette
Negaunee

**M I N N E S O T A**
Cloquet
**Duluth**
**Superior**
Washburn
Ashland
Hurley
Ironwood
Bessemer
**M I C H I G A N**

Perham
Wadena
Aitkin
Moose Lake
Hayward
Park Falls
Eagle River
Iron Mountain
Crystal Falls
Niagara
Powers

**Fergus Falls**
Alexandria
aton
Morris
Glenwood
Staples
Brainerd
Mille Lacs L.
Little Falls
Mora
Milaca
Pine City
Grantsburg
Spooner
Phillips
Rhinelander
Crandon
Tomahawk
Menominee
Marinette
Green Bay

Sauk Rapids
**St. Cloud**
Paynesville
Cambridge
Cumberland
Rice Lake
Ladysmith
Cornell
Medford
Merrill
Antigo
Oconto
Shawano
Sturgeon Bay

Litchfield
**MINNEAPOLIS**
Montevideo
Hutchinson
Anoka
Stillwater
Hudson
Chippewa Falls
Menomonie
**WISCONSIN**
**Wausau**
Stevens Point
De Pere
**Green Bay**
Kewaunee

Granite Falls
Glencoe
**St. Paul**
Hastings
Red Wing
Lake City
**Eau Claire**
Marshfield
Menasha
Neenah
**Appleton**
Two Rivers
**Manitowoc**

Canby
Redwood Falls
Northfield
St. Peter
Faribault
Alma
Whitehall
Wisconsin Rapids
Waupaca
Wautoma
Oshkosh
L. Chilton
Winnebago
Sheboygan

gs
Marshall
New Ulm
Mankato
Owatonna
Winona
Rochester
Black River Falls
Sparta
Onalaska
Tomah
Montello
Mauston
Ripon
Fond du Lac
Waupun
Plymouth
Port Washington

Worthington
Windom
St. James
Preston
**La Crosse**
Viroqua
Reedsburg
Baraboo
Portage
Beaver Dam
Hartford
**LAKE MICHIGAN**

Pipestone
Fairmont
Jackson
Albert Lea
Austin
Northwood
Richland Center
Prairie du Chien
Wisconsin
**Madison**
Watertown
Jefferson
Waukesha
Whitewater
**MILWAUKEE**
Wauwatosa

Sibley
Estherville
Decorah
Waukon
Dodgeville
Lancaster
Darlington
Janesville
Monroe
Beloit
Burlington
**Racine**
Kenosha

Sheldon
Spencer
Emmetsburg
Algona
Garner
Mason City
Charles City
New Hampton
Dubuque
Freeport
Woodstock
Belvidere
Elgin
Skokie
Evanston
Waukegan

Le Mars
Cherokee
Pocahontas
Clarion
Hampton
Waverly
Oelwein
Independence
Rockford
De Kalb
Dixon
Aurora
Cicero
**CHICAGO**

ioux
ity
Storm Lake
Sac City
Ida Grove
**I O W A**
Cedar Falls
**Fort Dodge**
Webster City
Waterloo
Wapsipinicon
Sterling
Mendota
Princeton
Morris
**Joliet**
Harvey

wl
Denison
Carroll
Boone
Ames
Marshalltown
Marion
Maquoketa
Cedar Rapids
**Clinton**
Tipton
Peru
Ottawa

Audubon
Perry
Newton
Grinnell
Marengo
**Iowa City**
**Davenport**
Moline
Streator
Kankakee

Harlan
W. Des Moines
**Des Moines**
L. Red Rock
Montezuma
Washington
**Rock Island**
Kewanee
Pontiac

emont
aha
Atlantic
Council Bluffs
Winterset
Indianola
Knoxville
Oskaloosa
Ottumwa
Aledo
Galesburg
Chillicothe
Normal
Paxton

Greenfield
Osceola
Albia
Fairfield
Mt. Pleasant
Monmouth
**Peoria**
Pekin
Paxton

mouth
Glenwood
Red Oak
Creston
Corning
Bloomfield
**Burlington**
Canton
**Bloomington**

oln
braska City
ce
Shenandoah
Clarinda
Bedford
Leon
Centerville
Fort Madison
Macomb
**ILLINOIS**
Lincoln
Champaign
Rantoul

Auburn
Rockport
Princeton
Unionville
Keokuk
Kahoka
Rushville
Beardstown
**Decatur**

ymee
ity
Falls City
Bethany
Milan
Kirksville
Edina
Quincy
**Springfield**
Jacksonville
Taylorville
Pana
Mattoon
Shelbyville

sville
Hiawatha
Troy
Savannah
Trenton
Chillicothe
Brookfield
Palmyra
Macon
**Hannibal**
Carrollton
Carlinville
Litchfield
Effingham

Holton
Atchison
**St. Joseph**
Excelsior Sprs.
Richmond
Carrollton
Moberly
Jerseyville
Vandalia
Greenville

**Topeka**
Leavenworth
**Kansas City**
**Independence**
**Kansas City**
Lexington
Marshall
Mexico
Fayette
Columbia
Fulton
Troy
St. Charles
**Alton**
**Granite City**
**E. St. Louis**
Flora

Lawrence
Olathe
Ottawa
Warrensburg
Sedalia
Boonville
Jefferson City
Hermann
**ST. LOUIS**
Belleville
Centralia
Fairfield

ounci
rove
Emporia
Paola
Harrisonville
**M I S S O U R I**
Union
Waterloo
Mount Vernon
Benton

urlington
Garnett
Clinton
Butler
Lake of the Ozarks
Osage
Sullivan
De Soto
Ste. Genevieve
Pincknayville
Du Quoin

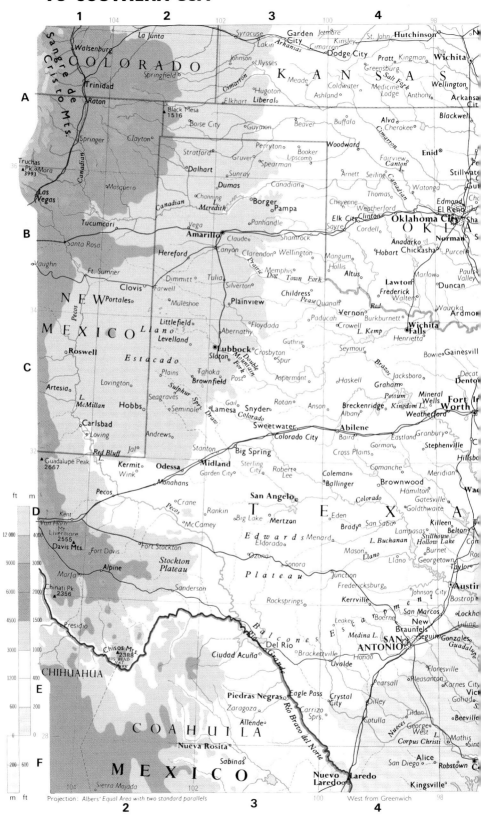

Projection: Albers' Equal Area with two standard parallels    West from Greenwich

A

B

C

D

E

F

Yates
Center    Iola    Nevada    Camdenton    Rolla    Steelville    Murphysboro    Marion
ado    Chanute    Fort Scott    Lebanon    Perryville    Carbondale
Center    Buffalo    Salem    Ironton    Fredericktown    Anna
Fredonia    Girard    Stockton    Bolivar    Houston    Cape Girardeau    Metropolis
Howard    Pittsburg    Lamar    Greenfield    Marshfield    a  u    Paducah
Parsons    Carthage    Springfield    a    Cairo
Sedan    Independence    Toplin    Aurora    Ozark    a    Charleston    Mayfield
Coffeyville    Joplin    Monett    Cabool    Van    Sikeston    Hickman
Bartlesville    Miami    Neosho    Bull Shoals    West Plains    Poplar Bluff    New Madrid    Union City
Vinita    Cassville    Gainesville    Doniphan    Malden    Tiptonville
Sprs    Tulsa    Lake O'    Jay    Berryville    Mountain    Norfork    Corning    McKenzie
ulpa    The Cherokees    Rogers    Home    L.    Pocahontas    Black    Caruthersville    Dyersburg
Claremore    Springdale    White    Walnut Ridge    Paragould    Blytheville    TENNESSEE

MISSOURI

ARKANSAS

TENNESSEE

MEMPHIS

MISSISSIPPI

LOUISIANA

TEXAS

GULF    OF    MEXICO

MEXICO

Continuation
Southwards
on same scale

Projection: Alber's Equal Area with two standard parallels

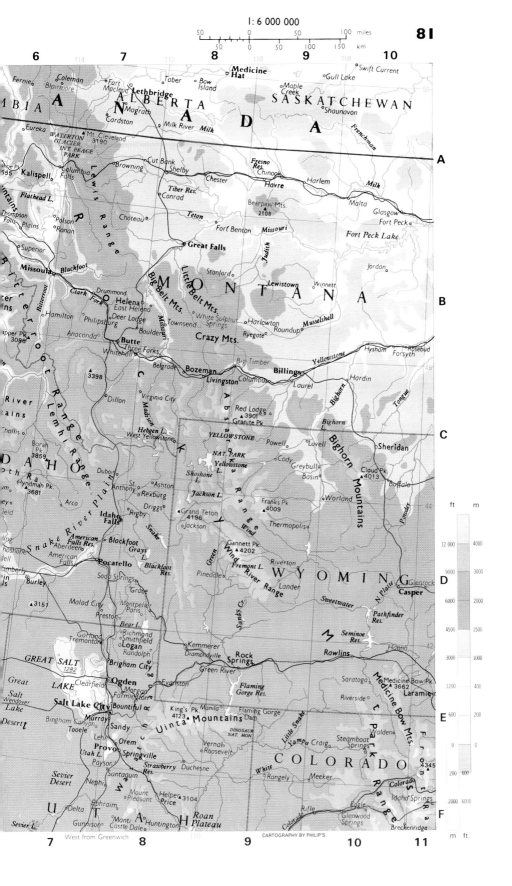

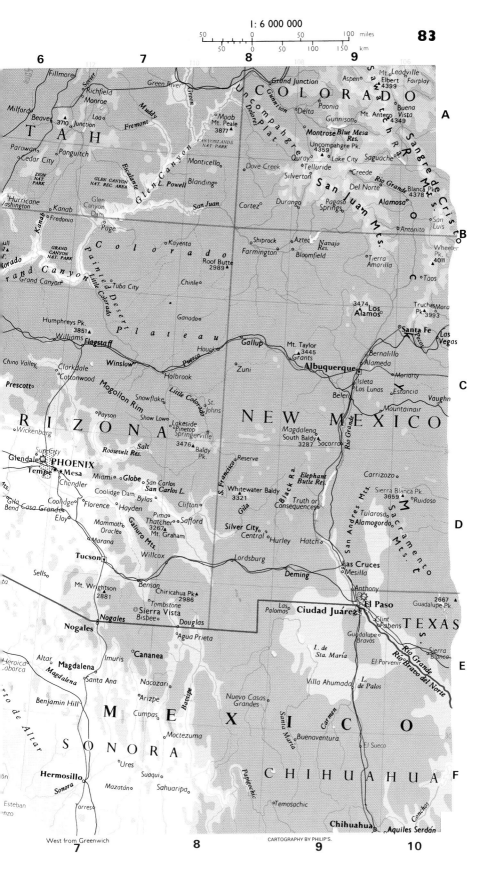

1: 6 000 000

50    0    50    100 miles

50    0    50    100   150 km

**6**          **7**          **8**          **9**

Fillmore
Sevier
Green River
Green
Grand Junction
C O L O R A D O
Aspen
Mt. Leadville
Elbert Fairplay
4399
Richfield
Monroe
Gunnison
Paonia
Buena
Delta
Vista
**A**
Milford
Beaver
3710
Loa
Junction
Muddy
Fremont
Moab
Mt. Peale
3877
Gunnison
Montrose Blue Mesa
Mt. Antero
4349
Res.

T          A          H
Parowan
Panguitch
Cedar City
ZION
NAT.
PARK
Escalante
Glen
Canyon
GLEN CANYON
NAT. REC. AREA
Monticello
Dove Creek
Uncompahgre
Ouray
Uncompahgre Pk.
4359
Montrose Blue Mesa
Res.
Telluride
Lake City
Saguache

Hurricane
Washington
Kanab
Fredonia
Page
Glen
Canyon
Dam
L. Powell
Blanding
San Juan
Cortez
Durango
Silverton
San Juan Mts.
Creede
Del Norte
Rio Grande
Pagosa
Springs
Alamosa
Blanca Pk.
4378
San
Luis
**B**
GRAND
CANYON
NAT. PARK
Colorado
Kayenta
Shiprock
Aztec
Navajo
Res.
Farmington
Bloomfield
Tierra
Amarilla
Taos
Wheeler
Pk.
4011
Grand Canyon
Painted
Roof Butte
2989
Chinle
Tuba City
Grand Canyon
Little Colorado
Desert
Humphreys Pk.
3851
Williams Flagstaff
Winslow
Ganado
Gallup
Mt. Taylor
3445
Grants
Los
Alamos
3474
Truchas
Pk.
3993
Mora
Santa Fe
Las
Vegas
Pecos
**C**
Chino Valley
Clarkdale
Cottonwood
Prescott
R          I          Z          O          N          A
Holbrook
Snowflake
Show Low
Little Colorado
St.
Johns
Houck
Puerco
Zuni
Bernalillo
Alameda
Albuquerque
Isleta
Los Lunas
Moriarty
Estancia
Vaughn
Mountainair
Belen
Payson
Wickenburg
Lakeside
Pinetop
Springerville
3476
Baldy
Pk.
N          E          W          M          E          X          I          C          O
Magdalena
South Baldy
3287 Socorro
Rio Grande
San Andres Mts.
Carrizozo
Mogollon Rim
Roosevelt Res.
Salt
Sun City
Glendale PHOENIX
Tempe Mesa
Chandler
Miami Globe
San Carlos
San Carlos L.
Reserve
S. Francisco
Whitewater Baldy
3321
Elephant
Butte Res.
Black R.
Truth or
Consequences
Sierra Blanca Pk.
3659
Ruidoso
Tularosa
Alamogordo
Sacramento
Mts.
**D**
Coolidge Dam
Bylas
Clifton
Gila
Coolidge
Florence
Hayden
Casa Grande
Eloy
Pima
Thatcher
Safford
Mammoth
Oracle
3267
Mt. Graham
Galiuro Mts.
Silver City
Central
Hurley
Hatch
Tucson
Willcox
Lordsburg
Deming
Las Cruces
Mesilla
2667
Guadalupe Pk.
Sells
Mt. Wrightson
2881
Benson
Chiricahua Pk.
2986
Tombstone
Anthony
Las
Palomas
Ciudad Juárez
El Paso
Clint
Fabens
T E X A S
Nogales
Sierra Vista
Bisbee
Douglas
Agua Prieta
Guadalupe
Bravos
Rio Grande
Sierra
Blanco
**E**
Heroica
Caborca
Altar
Magdalena
Magdalena
Santa Ana
Imuris
Cananea
Nacozari
Arizpe
L. de
Sta. María
El Porvenir
Rio Bravo del Norte
Benjamin Hill
M          E          X          I          C          O
Cumpas
Moctezuma
Santa María
Nuevo Casas
Grandes
Villa Ahumada
L.
de Palos
El Sueco
Carmen
S          O          N          O          R          A
Ures
Suaqui
Sahuaripa
Buenaventura
C H I H U A H U A
**F**
Hermosillo
Sonora
Mazatán
Torres
Temosachic
Chihuahua
Aquiles Serdán
Conchos

San Diego
Tijuana
Ensenada
Pta.Baja
S.Quintin
3078
Pta. Sta.
Eugenia
Sta. Rosalia
B. Ballenas
Pta.S.Juanico
C. San Lucas
La Paz
2406
Is. Tres
Marías
Is. de
Revillagigedo
(Mex.)

Yuma
Mexicali
Phoenix
Tucson
Deming
Bisbee
Nogales
Cananea
Nacozari
Galeana
Agua Prieta
Ciudad Juárez
El Paso
U N I T E
3658
Carlsbad
Wichita Falls
Abilene
Fort Wo
Pecos
Pecos
S. Angelo
Brow
Tem
Austin

Golfo
de California
Tiburón
Hermosillo
Torres
Empalme
Guaymas
Ciudad
Obregón
Muleje
La Purísima
Navojoa
Huatabampo
Fuerte
El Fuerte
Los Mochis
Sinaloa
Guamúchil
Topolobampo
Culiacán
Elota
Mazatlán
Rosario
Escuinapa
Acaponeta
Tuxpan
Tepic

Villa Ahumada
Madera
Chihuahua
Sta. Maria
Rio Grande
San Carlos
2896
Piedras Negras
Eagle Pass
San Antonio
Ciudad
Camargo
Delicias
Jimenez
3150
Hidalgo del
Parral
Nueva Rosita
Sabinas
Monclova
Falcon Res.
Lerdo
Nazas
Gómez Palacio
S. Pedro
Torreón
Matamoros
Saltillo
Durango
Sombrerete
Concepcion
del Oro
4054
Matehuala
Catorce
Fresnillo
Charcas
Zacatecas
3353
San Luis
Potosí
Aguascalientes
León
Guanajuato
Irapuato
Celaya
Querétaro

Laredo
Nuevo Laredo
Sabino
Hidalgo
Reynosa
Monterrey
S. Ferr
Linares
Monterrelos
Ciudad
Victoria
Ciudad
Tula
Panuco
Ciudad Mante
Ciuda
Made
Tam
Papantla
Tu
Pachuca
Tulancingo
Tlaxcala

Manzanillo

C. Corrientes
Guadalajara
Ameca
Zacoalco
Colima Vol.
4339
Zamora
Morelia
Colima
Santiago
L.de Chapala
MEXICO
Toluca
Cuernavaca
Iguala
Balsas
Chilpancingo
3703
Popocatepetl
5462
Mexcala
Chilapa
Acapulco
Ayutla
Ometepec
Verde
Puebla
Or
Oaxaca
Tlaxia
Tehu
Sa

Mazatlán

P A C I F I C

O C E A N

Projection: Bonne

ft    m
12 000  4000
9000   3000
6000   2000
4500   1500
3000   1000
1200   400
600    200
0      0
200    600
2000   6000
m    ft

1: 15 000 000

100    0    100    200    300    400 miles
100  0  100  200  300  400  500  600 km

6        7             8            9

C. Royal
Columbia
Birmingham        Atlanta        Augusta
Marshall                                    Charleston        A
esville    Shreveport          Macon
allas    Tyler    Monroe    Vicksburg    Jackson    Montgomery    Columbus
S    T    A    Meridian    T    E    Albany    Savannah
Natchez    Hattiesburg    Dothan
Alexandria    Lake Charles    Baton Rouge    Pensacola    Altamaha
Beaumont    Mobile
Lafayette                                          Jacksonville
Port Arthur B.    New Orleans        Tallahassee
Galveston    Atchafalaya B.    Mississippi    C. San    Daytona Beach
gorda I.    Delta    Blas    Apalachee B.    C. Canaveral
Christi                                          Orlando
                                          Tampa    Lakeland        C. Canaveral
G    U    L    F    O    F    M    E    X    I    C    O    St. Petersburg    W. Palm Beach    Grand    B
re                              Sarasota    L. Okeechobee    Bahama
de del Norte                                    Miami    Fort
                                          Lauderdale
                                          C. Sable
Tropic of Cancer    Key West    Andros I.
                              Florida Str.
                    Canal    La Habana    Matanzas    Sagua la Grande
                    de    (Havana)    Cárdenas    Sta. Clara    C
                    C. Catoche    Marianao    Colón    Caibarién
                    El Cuyo    Pinar del Río    G. de    C    U    B    A
Progreso        C.    Batabanó    Cienfuegos    Trinidad    Ciego de Ávila
            Temax    San    Guane        Sancti Spíritus    Júcaro
            El Díaz    Antonio    I. de Juventud            C
uez    Mérida    Puerto    Yucatán        Grand Cayman
Golfo de    Valladolid    Morelos    (U.K.)
            i. de
ruz    Peto    Cozumel
Campeche    Felipe
C a m p e c h e    Carrillo Puerto    Vigía Chico
rado    Ciudad del Carmen    Yucatan
cotalpan    Laguna        Ciudad Chetumal
Coatzacoalcos    de Terminos    Coroza
Villahermosa        Corozal    Ambergris Cay    D
e de    Tuxtla    Belize    Turneffe Is.    Golfo de Honduras
antepec    Gutiérrez    Belmopan    Middlesex
chitlán    Usumacinta    BELIZE    Barrios
Chiapa    San    Pto. Cortés
Tonalá    Cristóbal        Pto. Tela    Trujillo
    Chiapa    GUATEMALA        La Ceiba    Iriona    D
de    Huixtla    4217        Zacapa    S. Pedro Sula    L. Caratasca
antepec    Guatemala        HONDURAS    or Coco    C. Gracias á Dios
        Sta. Rosa    Comayagua    Wanks
    Sonsonate    San    Tegucigalpa    Jinotega
    San Salvador    Vicente    Nacaome    Matagalpa    Puerto Cabezas
    EL SALVADOR    S. Miguel    Choluteca    El Gallo    Providencia
    San José    G. de Fonseca    NICARAGUA        (Col.)    E
        Chinandega    León        Bluefields    San Andrés
        Managua    Granada            (Col.)
        Masaya    L. Nicaragua
            S. Juan    Irazú
    Pen. de Nicoya    COSTA    Limón    Colón
        Puntarenas    Aldjuel    3432        Panama
        San José    RICA    3374    P A N A M A    La
West from Greenwich    CARTOGRAPHY BY PHILIP'S.    Cartago    383    Chitré    Arch. de    Palma
                        David    Pen. de    las Perlas    El
6            Coiba    Azuero    G. de    Real    F
                        Panama

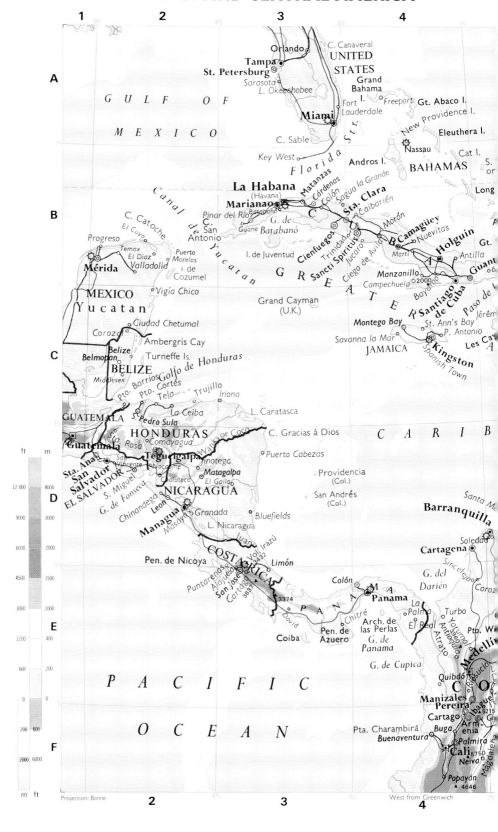

1: 15 000 000

100      0      100      200      300      400 miles
100   0   100   200   300   400   500   600 km

A

ATLANTIC

OCEAN

B

Tropic of Cancer

aguana

Caicos I. (U.K.)

Turks Is. (U.K.)

de Paix

Cap Haitien
Monte Cristi
Valverde
Pto. Plata
Santiago
S. Francisco de Macoris
Sanchez

C

Canal de la Mona
PUERTO RICO (U.S.A.)
San Juan
Aguadilla
Arecibo
St. Thomas (U.S.A.)
Charlotte Amalie
Virgin Is. (U.K.)
Sombrero (U.K.)
Anguilla (U.K.)
St. Martin (Fr. & Neth.)

de la Vega
DOMINICAN
REP.
La Romana
1338
Caguas
St. Croix
(U.S.A.)
Basseterre
ST. KITTS-NEVIS
ANTIGUA &
BARBUDA

ince
2680
S. Pedro de Macoris
Guayama
Ponce
Mayagüez
Christiansted
Charlestown
St. John's
Montserrat (U.K.)

Azua
Bani
Barahona
Santo Domingo
Duverge
Plymouth
Guadeloupe (Fr.)
Pointe à Pitre

Hispaniola

Leeward
Islands

Martinique (Fr.)

TILLES

LESSER

DOMINICA
Roseau

AN        SEA

Fort de France
Castries
ANTILLES
ST. LUCIA
Windward
BARBADOS
ST. VINCENT

D

& Kingstown
Bridgetown

THE GRENADINES

Islands
GRENADA

Gallinas

Golfo de Venezuela
Aruba (Neth.)
Curacao
Willemstad
Bonaire

La Blanquilla
(Ven.)
St. George's

de la
ajira

NETH.
ANTILLES

Pto. Cabello
Maiquetia

Margarita
Asunción
La

Tobago
Port of Spain
TRINIDAD & TOBAGO
San Fernando

Coro
Dabajuro

La Tortuga
(Ven.)
Carúpano
Carípito

G. de
Paria

evada
Marta
Maracaibo
Cabimas

Caracas
Cumaná
2596

E

L. de
Maracaibo
Trujillo
San Felipe
Valencia
Maracay
Barcelona
Maturín
Tucupita

Georgetown

Valera
Barquisimeto
Calabozo
Las Mercedes
El Tigre
Ciudad
Guayana

New
Amsterdam
Wismare

Cord. de Mérida
5007
Portuguesa
Guanare
San Fernando
de Apure
Orinoco
Ciudad Bolívar

Cuyuni
Bartic.

SURINAM

San Cristóbal
Apure
Caicara
El Callao
Tumeremo

GUYANA

Rubio
Pamplona
Arauca
Arauca
VENEZUELA

Corentyne

Bucaramanga
ncabermeja
Pto. Páez
Pto. Carreño
2285
Meta
Pto. Ayacucho

Caura
Caroní
2560
Roraima
2810

Essequibo

1280

OMBIA

Sierra Pacaraima

quirá
gotá

Sa. Parima

Guaviare
Casiquiare

BRAZIL

F

5                 6                 7                 8

CARTOGRAPHY BY PHILIP'S.

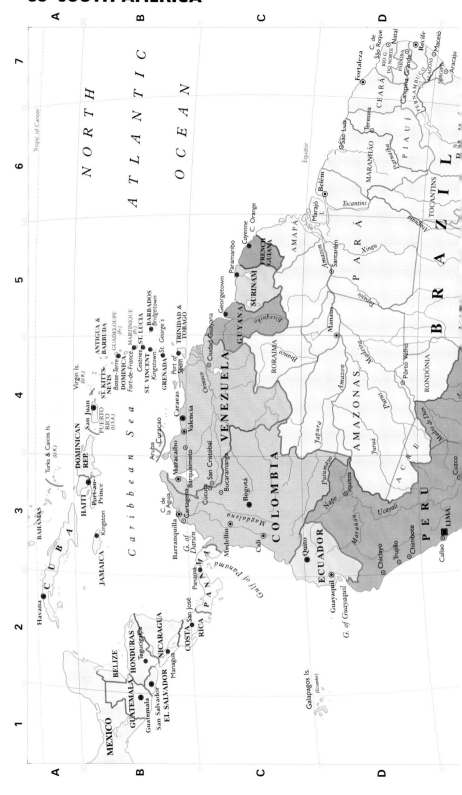

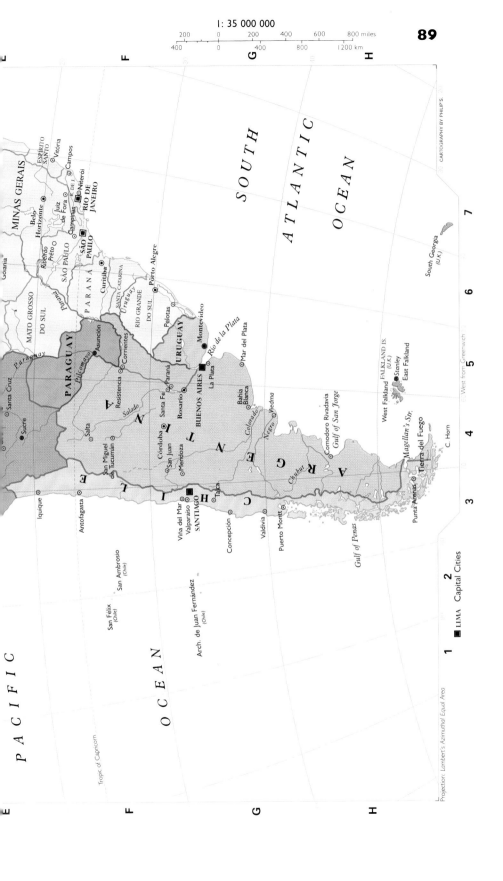

1 : 35 000 000

| 200 | 0 | 200 | 400 | 600 | 800 miles |
| 400 | 0 | 400 | 800 | | 1200 km |

**89**

CARTOGRAPHY BY PHILIP'S

PACIFIC

OCEAN

Tropic of Capricorn

San Félix *(Chile)*

San Ambrosio *(Chile)*

Arch. de Juan Fernández *(Chile)*

Projection: Lambert's Azimuthal Equal Area

Iquique

Antofagasta

Santa Cruz

Sucre

MINAS GERAIS

ESPIRITO SANTO

Goiania

MATO GROSSO DO SUL

Belo Horizonte

Ribeirão Preto

Juiz de Fora

Vitória

Campos

Niterói

RIO DE JANEIRO

R. DE J.

SÃO PAULO

Campinas

SÃO PAULO

PARANÁ

Paraná

Paraguay

PARAGUAY

Asunción

Pilcomayo

Curitiba

SANTA CATARINA

Uruguay

RIO GRANDE DO SUL

Pôrto Alegre

Pelotas

Corrientes

Resistencia

Salta

San Miguel de Tucumán

Salado

Córdoba

San Juan

Mendoza

ARGENTINA

CHILE

Santa Fe

Paraná

Rosario

URUGUAY

Montevideo

Río de la Plata

BUENOS AIRES

La Plata

Mar del Plata

Viña del Mar

Valparaíso

SANTIAGO

Talca

Concepción

Valdivia

Puerto Montt

Colorado

Bahía Blanca

Negro

Viedma

Chubut

Comodoro Rivadavia

Gulf of San Jorge

Gulf of Peñas

Magellan's Str.

Punta Arenas

Tierra del Fuego

C. Horn

SOUTH

ATLANTIC

OCEAN

West from Greenwich

FALKLAND IS. (U.K.)

West Falkland

Stanley

East Falkland

South Georgia (U.K.)

■ LIMA   Capital Cities

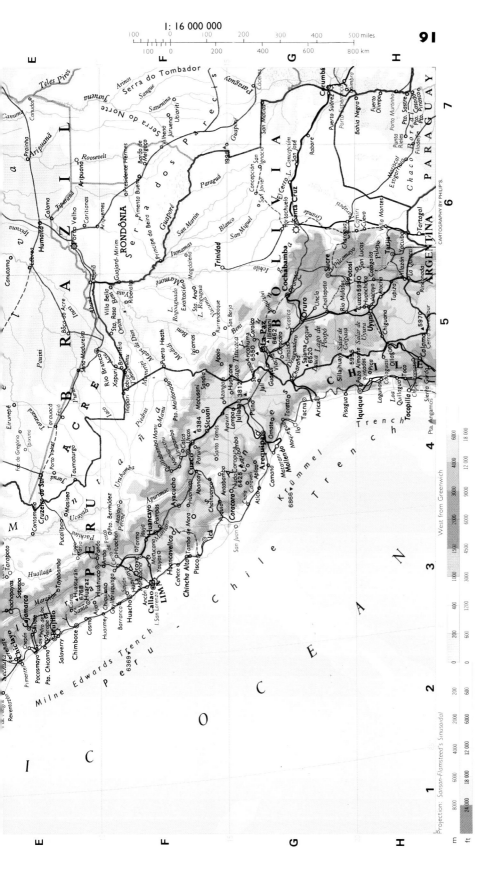

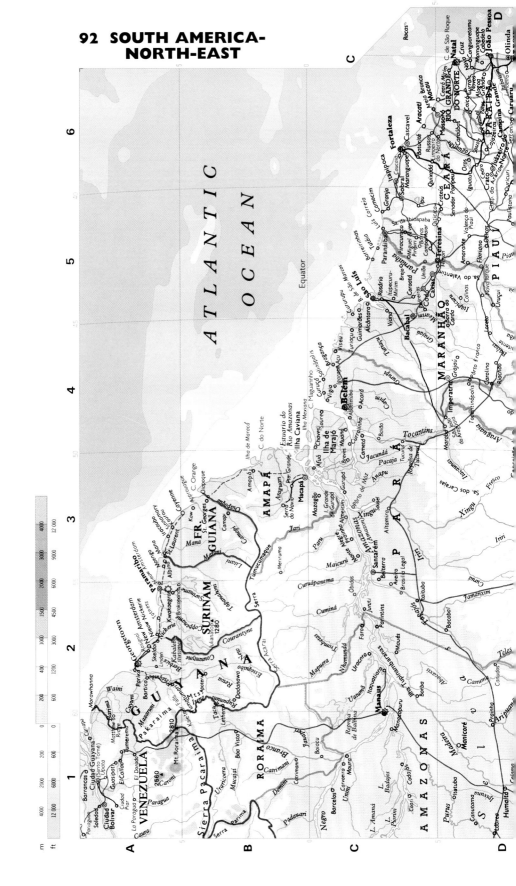

ATLANTIC

OCEAN

Equator

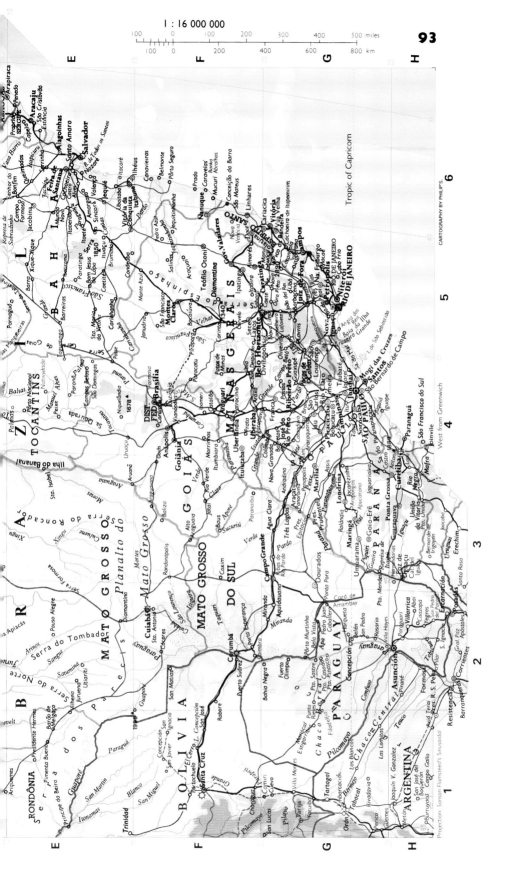

1 : 16 000 000

100    0    100    200    300    400    500 miles

100    0    200    400    600    800 km

CARTOGRAPHY BY PHILIP'S

Tropic of Capricorn

West from Greenwich

Projection: Sanson-Flamsteed's Sinusoidal

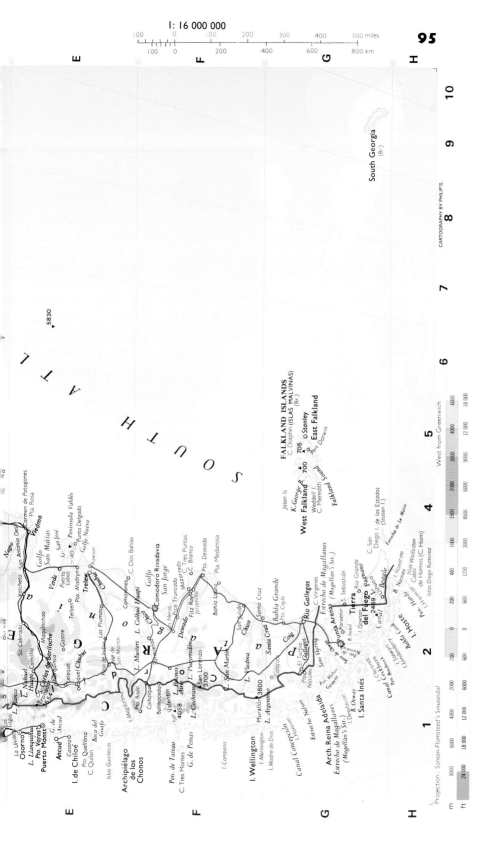

# Index to Map Pages

The index contains the names of all principal places and features shown on the maps. Physical features composed of a proper name (Erie) and a description (Lake) are positioned alphabetically by the proper name. The description is positioned after the proper name and is usually abbreviated:

Erie, L. . . . . . . **72 C5**

Where a description forms part of a settlement or administrative name however, it is always written in full and put in its true alphabetical position:

Lake Charles **79 D7**

Names beginning St. are alphabetized under Saint, but Sankt, Sint, Sant, Santa and San are all spelt in full and are alphabetized accordingly.

The number in bold type which follows each name in the index refers to the number of the map page where that feature or place will be found. This is usually the largest scale at which the place or feature appears.

The letter and figure which are in bold type immediately after the page number give the grid square on the map page, within which the feature is situated.

Rivers carry the symbol ↪ after their names. A solid square ■ follows the name of a country while an open square □ refers to a first order administrative area.

## A

| | | |
|---|---|---|
| A Coruña = La Coruña | 18 | A1 |
| Aachen | 14 | C4 |
| Aalborg = Ålborg | 9 | G9 |
| Aalen | 14 | D6 |
| Aarau | 13 | C8 |
| Aare ↪ | 13 | C8 |
| Aarhus = Århus | 9 | G10 |
| Aba | 55 | G6 |
| Ābādān | 47 | E7 |
| Ābādeh | 44 | D3 |
| Abadla | 54 | B4 |
| Abaetetuba | 92 | C4 |
| Abakan | 30 | D7 |
| Abancay | 91 | F4 |
| Abarqū | 44 | D3 |
| Abashiri | 32 | F12 |
| Abay | 29 | E8 |
| Abaya, L. | 53 | G6 |
| Abbay = Nîl el Azraq ↪ | 53 | E5 |
| Abbeville | 12 | A4 |
| Abbieglassie | 63 | A4 |
| Abbot Ice Shelf | 96 | B1 |
| Abbottabad | 42 | B8 |
| Abd al Kūrī | 49 | E5 |
| Abéché | 53 | F3 |
| Abeokuta | 55 | G5 |
| Abercorn = Mbala | 57 | F6 |
| Abercorn | 63 | A5 |
| Aberdeen, Australia | 63 | B5 |
| Aberdeen, U.K. | 10 | C5 |
| Aberdeen, S. Dak., U.S.A. | 76 | C5 |

| | | |
|---|---|---|
| Aberdeen, Wash., U.S.A. | 80 | B2 |
| Aberystwyth | 11 | E4 |
| Abidjan | 55 | G4 |
| Abilene | 78 | C4 |
| Abitibi L. | 69 | D3 |
| Abkhaz Republic □ = Abkhazia □ | 25 | E5 |
| Abkhazia □ | 25 | E5 |
| Abminga | 62 | A1 |
| Åbo = Turku | 9 | F12 |
| Abohar | 42 | D9 |
| Aboméy | 55 | G5 |
| Abong-Mbang | 56 | D2 |
| Abou-Deïa | 53 | F2 |
| Abri | 52 | D5 |
| Abrolhos, Banka | 93 | F6 |
| Abrud | 17 | E6 |
| Absaroka Range | 81 | C9 |
| Abū al Khaṣīb | 47 | E6 |
| Abū 'Alī | 47 | F7 |
| Abu 'Arīsh | 49 | D3 |
| Abu Dhabi = Abū Ẓaby | 44 | E3 |
| Abū Dīs | 53 | E5 |
| Abu Hamed | 53 | E5 |
| Abū Kamāl | 46 | D5 |
| Abū Madd, Ra's | 47 | F4 |
| Abu Matariq | 53 | F4 |
| Abu Rudeis | 47 | E3 |
| Abu Tig | 52 | C5 |
| Abū Zabad | 53 | F4 |
| Abū Ẓaby | 44 | E3 |
| Abuja | 55 | G6 |
| Abukuma-Gawa ↪ | 33 | G12 |
| Abunã | 91 | E5 |
| Abunã ↪ | 91 | E5 |

| | | |
|---|---|---|
| Abut Hd. | 65 | E4 |
| Abwong | 53 | G5 |
| Acaponeta | 84 | C3 |
| Acapulco | 84 | D5 |
| Acarigua | 90 | B5 |
| Accra | 55 | G4 |
| Aceh □ | 36 | D1 |
| Achalpur | 43 | J10 |
| Achill I. | 11 | E1 |
| Achinsk | 30 | D7 |
| Acireale | 21 | F5 |
| Acklins I. | 86 | B5 |
| Aconcagua, Cerro | 94 | C3 |
| Aconquija, Mt. | 94 | B3 |
| Açores, Is. dos = Azores | 50 | C1 |
| Acraman, L. | 62 | B2 |
| Acre = 'Akko | 46 | D3 |
| Acre □ | 91 | E4 |
| Acre ↪ | 91 | E5 |
| Ad Dahnā | 47 | F7 |
| Ad Dammām | 47 | F7 |
| Ad Dawhah | 44 | E2 |
| Ad Dilam | 47 | G6 |
| Ad Dīwānīyah | 47 | E6 |
| Ada | 79 | B5 |
| Adaja ↪ | 18 | B3 |
| Adam | 44 | F4 |
| Adamaoua, Massif de l' | 53 | G1 |
| Adamawa Highlands = Adamaoua, Massif de l' | 53 | G1 |
| Adamello, Mte. | 20 | A3 |
| Adaminaby | 63 | C4 |
| Adam's Bridge | 43 | Q11 |
| Adams Mt. | 80 | B3 |

| | | |
|---|---|---|
| Adana | 46 | C3 |
| Adapazarı | 46 | B2 |
| Adarama | 53 | E5 |
| Adare, C. | 96 | B15 |
| Adaut | 39 | F4 |
| Adavale | 63 | A3 |
| Adda ↪ | 20 | B2 |
| Addis Ababa = Addis Abeba | 53 | G6 |
| Addis Abeba | 53 | G6 |
| Addis Alem | 53 | G6 |
| Adelaide | 62 | B2 |
| Adelaide I. | 96 | A3 |
| Adelaide Pen. | 70 | B10 |
| Adélie, Terre | 96 | A14 |
| Adélie Land = Adélie, Terre | 96 | A14 |
| Aden = Al 'Adan | 49 | E4 |
| Aden, G. of | 49 | E4 |
| Adi | 39 | E4 |
| Adi Ugri | 53 | F6 |
| Adige ↪ | 20 | B4 |
| Adilabad | 43 | K11 |
| Adirondack Mts. | 73 | C8 |
| Admer | 54 | D6 |
| Admiralty I. | 71 | C6 |
| Admiralty Is. | 64 | K9 |
| Ado-Ekiti | 55 | G6 |
| Adonara | 39 | F2 |
| Adoni | 43 | M10 |
| Adour ↪ | 12 | E3 |
| Adra | 18 | D4 |
| Adrano | 21 | F5 |
| Adrar | 54 | C4 |
| Adré | 53 | F3 |
| Adrī | 52 | C1 |
| Adriatic Sea | 20 | C5 |
| Adua | 39 | E3 |

| | | |
|---|---|---|
| Adwa | 53 | F6 |
| Adzhar | | |
| Republic □ = | | |
| Ajaria □ | 25 | E5 |
| Ægean Sea | 23 | E5 |
| Aerhtai Shan | 34 | B4 |
| Afghanistan ■ | 45 | C6 |
| Afgoi | 49 | G3 |
| 'Afif | 47 | G5 |
| Afognak I. | 71 | C4 |
| Afuá | 92 | C3 |
| Afyonkarahisar | 46 | C2 |
| Agadès = | | |
| Agadez | 55 | E6 |
| Agadez | 55 | E6 |
| Agadir | 54 | B3 |
| Agapa | 30 | B6 |
| Agartala | 41 | F8 |
| Agats | 39 | F5 |
| Agboville | 55 | G4 |
| Agde | 13 | E5 |
| Agen | 12 | D4 |
| Agra | 42 | F10 |
| Agri → | 21 | D6 |
| Ağrı Dağı | 46 | C6 |
| Ağrı Karakose | 46 | C5 |
| Agrigento | 21 | F4 |
| Agrinion | 23 | E3 |
| Água Clara | 93 | G3 |
| Agua Prieta | 84 | A3 |
| Aguadas | 90 | B3 |
| Aguadilla | 87 | C6 |
| Aguarico → | 90 | D3 |
| Aguas Blancas | 94 | A3 |
| Aguascalientes | 84 | C4 |
| Aguilas | 19 | D5 |
| Agulhas, C. | 58 | E4 |
| Agung | 37 | F5 |
| Agusan → | 38 | C3 |
| Ahaggar | 54 | D6 |
| Ahar | 46 | C6 |
| Ahipara B. | 64 | A5 |
| Ahiri | 43 | K12 |
| Ahmadabad | 43 | H8 |
| Ahmadnagar | 43 | K9 |
| Ahmadpur | 42 | E7 |
| Ahmedabad = | | |
| Ahmadabad | 43 | H8 |
| Ahmednagar = | | |
| Ahmadnagar | 43 | K9 |
| Ahvāz | 47 | E7 |
| Ahvenanmaa = | | |
| Åland | 9 | F11 |
| Aḥwar | 49 | E4 |
| Aigues-Mortes | 13 | E6 |
| Aihui | 35 | A7 |
| Aija | 91 | E3 |
| Aiken | 75 | C7 |
| Aimere | 39 | F2 |
| Aimorés | 93 | F5 |
| Ain Banaiyan | 44 | F2 |
| Aïn Beïda | 54 | A6 |
| Aïn Ben Tili | 54 | C3 |
| Aïn-Sefra | 54 | B4 |
| Ainabo | 49 | F4 |
| Aïr | 55 | E6 |
| Aisne → | 13 | B5 |
| Aiud | 17 | E6 |
| Aix-en-Provence | 13 | E6 |
| Aix-la-Chapelle | | |
| = Aachen | 14 | C4 |
| Aix-les-Bains | 13 | D6 |
| Aiyion | 23 | E4 |
| Aizawl | 41 | F9 |
| Ajaccio | 13 | F8 |
| Ajanta Ra. | 43 | J9 |
| Ajari Rep. = | | |
| Ajaria □ | 25 | E5 |
| Ajaria □ | 25 | E5 |
| Ajdâbiyah | 52 | B3 |
| Ajka | 16 | E3 |
| 'Ajmān | 44 | E3 |
| Ajmer | 42 | F9 |
| Ajo, C. de | 18 | A4 |
| Akaroa | 65 | E5 |
| Akashi | 32 | B4 |
| Akelamo | 39 | D3 |
| Aketi | 56 | D4 |
| Akharnaí | 23 | E4 |
| Akhelóös → | 23 | E3 |
| Akhisar | 23 | E6 |
| Akhmîm | 52 | C5 |
| Akimiski I. | 69 | C2 |
| Akita | 33 | G12 |
| Akjoujt | 55 | E2 |
| 'Akko | 46 | D3 |
| Akkol | 29 | E8 |
| Aklavik | 70 | B6 |
| Akmolinsk = | | |
| Astana | 29 | D8 |
| Akobo → | 53 | G5 |
| Akola | 43 | J10 |
| Akordat | 53 | E6 |
| Akpatok I. | 68 | B4 |
| Akreïjit | 55 | E3 |
| Akron | 72 | D5 |
| Aksai Chin | 42 | B11 |
| Aksaray | 46 | C3 |
| Aksarka | 28 | C7 |
| Akşehir | 46 | C2 |
| Aksu | 34 | B3 |
| Aksum | 53 | F6 |
| Aktogay | 29 | E8 |
| Aktsyabrski | 17 | B9 |
| Aktyubinsk = | | |
| Aqtöbe | 29 | D6 |
| Aku | 55 | G6 |
| Akure | 55 | G6 |
| Akyab = Sittwe | 41 | G9 |
| Al 'Adan | 49 | E4 |
| Al Aḥsā | 47 | F7 |
| Al Amādīyah | 46 | C5 |
| Al Amārah | 47 | E6 |
| Al 'Aqabah | 47 | E3 |
| Al 'Aramah | 47 | F6 |
| Al Ashkhara | 45 | F4 |
| Al Badï' | 47 | G6 |
| Al Başrah | 47 | E6 |
| Al Bayḍā | 52 | B3 |
| Al Bu'ayrāt al | | |
| Ḥasūn | 52 | B2 |
| Al Fallūjah | 46 | D5 |
| Al Fāw | 47 | E7 |
| Al Fujayrah | 44 | E4 |
| Al Hābah | 47 | F6 |
| Al Haddār | 47 | G6 |
| Al Hāmad | 47 | E4 |
| Al Ḥamar | 47 | G6 |
| Al Ḥamrā' | 47 | F4 |
| Al Ḥarīq | 47 | G6 |
| Al Ḥasakah | 46 | C5 |
| Al Ḥawrah | 49 | E4 |
| Al Ḥayy | 47 | D6 |
| Al Ḥijāz | 47 | F4 |
| Al Ḥillah, Iraq | 47 | D6 |
| Al Ḥillah, | | |
| Si. Arabia | 47 | G6 |
| Al Hindīyah | 47 | D6 |
| Al Hoceïma | 54 | A4 |
| Al Ḥudaydah | 49 | E3 |
| Al Hufūf | 47 | F7 |
| Al Ḥulwah | 47 | G6 |
| Al Ittihad = | | |
| Madīnat ash | | |
| Sha'b | 49 | E3 |
| Al Jāfūrah | 47 | F7 |
| Al Jaghbūb | 52 | C3 |
| Al Jahrah | 47 | E6 |
| Al Jalāmīd | 47 | E4 |
| Al Jawf, Libya | 52 | D3 |
| Al Jawf, | | |
| Si. Arabia | 47 | E4 |
| Al Jazirah, Iraq | 46 | D5 |
| Al Jazirah, Libya | 52 | C3 |
| Al Jubayl | 47 | F7 |
| Al Jubaylah | 47 | F6 |
| Al Junaynah | 53 | F3 |
| Al Khābūra | 44 | F4 |
| Al Khalīl | 47 | E3 |
| Al Kharfah | 47 | G6 |
| Al Kharj | 47 | F6 |
| Al Khasab | 44 | E4 |
| Al Kufrah | 52 | D3 |
| Al Kūt | 47 | D6 |
| Al Kuwayt | 47 | E7 |
| Al Lādhiqīyah | 46 | D3 |
| Al Luḥayyah | 49 | D3 |
| Al Madīnah | 47 | F4 |
| Al Majma'ah | 47 | F6 |
| Al Manāmah | 44 | E2 |
| Al Marj | 52 | B3 |
| Al Mawşil | 46 | C5 |
| Al Midhnab | 47 | F6 |
| Al Mish'āb | 47 | E7 |
| Al Mubarraz | 47 | F7 |
| Al Muḥarraq | 44 | E2 |
| Al Mukallā | 49 | E4 |
| Al Mukhā | 49 | E3 |
| Al Musayyib | 47 | D6 |
| Al Muwayliḥ | 47 | F3 |
| Al Qaḍimah | 47 | G4 |
| Al Qā'iyah | 47 | F5 |
| Al Qāmishli | 46 | C5 |
| Al Qaşabát | 52 | B1 |
| Al Qaşīm | 47 | F5 |
| Al Qaţif | 47 | F7 |
| Al Qaţrūn | 52 | D2 |
| Al Qayşūmah | 47 | E6 |
| Al Quaisūmah | 47 | E6 |
| Al Quds = | | |
| Jerusalem | 47 | E3 |
| Al Qurayyāt | 45 | F4 |
| Al Qurnah | 47 | E6 |
| Al 'Ulā | 47 | F4 |
| Al Uqaylah ash | | |
| Sharqīgah | 52 | B2 |
| Al Uqayr | 47 | F7 |
| Al 'Uthmānīyah | 47 | F7 |
| Al 'Uwaynid | 47 | F6 |
| Al 'Uwayqilah | 47 | E5 |
| Al 'Uyūn | 47 | F5 |
| Al Wakrah | 44 | E2 |
| Al Wari'ah | 47 | F5 |
| Al Yamāmah | 47 | F6 |
| Alabama □ | 74 | C4 |
| Alabama → | 74 | D4 |
| Alaçam Dağları | 23 | E7 |
| Alagoa Grande | 92 | D6 |
| Alagoas □ | 93 | D6 |
| Alagoinhas | 93 | E6 |
| Alajuela | 86 | D3 |
| Alamosa | 83 | B10 |
| Åland | 9 | F11 |
| Alania = North | | |
| Ossetia □ | 25 | E5 |
| Alanya | 46 | C2 |
| Alapayevsk | 29 | D7 |
| Alaşehir | 23 | E7 |
| Alaska □ | 71 | B4 |
| Alaska, G. of | 71 | C5 |
| Alaska Peninsula | 71 | C4 |
| Alaska Range | 71 | B4 |
| Alataw Shankou | 34 | B3 |
| Alatyr | 24 | C6 |
| Alausi | 90 | D3 |
| Alawoona | 62 | B3 |
| Alba | 20 | B2 |
| Alba-Iulia | 17 | E6 |
| Albacete | 19 | C5 |
| Albacutya, L. | 62 | C3 |
| Albania ■ | 23 | D3 |
| Albany, | | |
| Australia | 60 | H2 |
| Albany, Ga., | | |
| U.S.A. | 75 | D5 |
| Albany, N.Y., | | |
| U.S.A. | 73 | C9 |
| Albany, Oreg., | | |
| U.S.A. | 80 | C2 |
| Albany → | 69 | C2 |
| Albardón | 94 | C3 |
| Albemarle | 75 | B7 |
| Alberche → | 18 | C3 |
| Albert, L. | 62 | C2 |
| Albert L. | 57 | D6 |
| Albert Nile → | 57 | D6 |
| Albertville | 13 | D7 |
| Albi | 12 | E5 |
| Albina | 92 | A3 |
| Alborán | 18 | E4 |
| Ålborg | 9 | G9 |
| Alborz, Reshteh- | | |
| ye Kūhhā-ye | 44 | B3 |
| Albuquerque | 83 | C9 |
| Albury | 63 | C4 |
| Alcalá de | | |
| Henares | 18 | B4 |
| Alcalá la Real | 18 | D4 |
| Alcamo | 21 | F4 |
| Alcaníz | 19 | B5 |
| Alcântara | 92 | C5 |
| Alcántara, | | |
| Embalse de | 18 | C2 |
| Alcantarilla | 19 | D5 |
| Alcaraz, Sierra | | |
| de | 19 | C4 |
| Alcaudete | 18 | D3 |
| Alcázar de San | | |
| Juan | 18 | C4 |
| Alchevsk | 25 | D4 |
| Alcira | 19 | C5 |
| Alcoy | 19 | C5 |
| Aldabra Is. | 51 | G8 |
| Aldan → | 31 | C10 |
| Alderney | 11 | G5 |
| Aleg | 55 | E2 |
| Alegrete | 94 | B5 |
| Aleisk | 29 | D9 |
| Aleksandriya = | | |
| Oleksandriya | 17 | C8 |
| Aleksandrovskoye | | |
| | 29 | C8 |
| Alemania | 94 | B3 |
| Alençon | 12 | B4 |
| Aleppo = Ḥalab | 46 | C4 |
| Alès | 13 | D6 |
| Alessándria | 20 | B2 |
| Ålesund | 8 | F9 |
| Aleutian Is. | 71 | C6 |
| Alexander Arch. | 71 | C6 |
| Alexander I. | 96 | A3 |
| Alexandra, | | |
| Australia | 63 | C4 |
| Alexandra, N.Z. | 65 | F3 |
| Alexandria = El | | |
| Iskandarîya | 52 | B4 |
| Alexandria, | | |
| Canada | 71 | C7 |
| Alexandria, | | |
| Romania | 22 | C5 |
| Alexandria, | | |
| S. Africa | 59 | E5 |
| Alexandria, La., | | |
| U.S.A. | 79 | D7 |
| Alexandria, Va., | | |
| U.S.A. | 73 | E7 |

| | | |
|---|---|---|
| Alexandrina, L. | 62 | C2 |
| Alexandroúpolis | 22 | D5 |
| Alga | 29 | E6 |
| Algarve | 18 | D1 |
| Algeciras | 18 | D3 |
| Algemesi | 19 | C5 |
| Alger | 54 | A5 |
| Algeria ■ | 54 | C5 |
| Alghero | 21 | D2 |
| Algiers = Alger | 54 | A5 |
| Algoa B. | 59 | E5 |
| Alhucemas = Al | | |
| Hoceïma | 54 | A4 |
| 'Alī al Gharbī | 47 | D6 |
| 'Alī Khēl | 42 | C6 |
| Aliağa | 23 | E6 |
| Alibo | 53 | G6 |
| Alicante | 19 | C5 |
| Alice Springs | 94 | E5 |
| Aligarh | 42 | F11 |
| Aligüdarz | 46 | D7 |
| Alipur | 42 | E7 |
| Alipur Duar | 41 | D7 |
| Aliwal North | 59 | E5 |
| Aljustrel | 18 | D1 |
| Alkmaar | 14 | B3 |
| All American | | |
| Canal | 82 | D5 |
| Allahabad | 40 | E3 |
| Allanmyo | 41 | H10 |
| Allegheny → | 73 | D5 |
| Allegheny | | |
| Plateau | 73 | F5 |
| Allentown | 73 | D8 |
| Alleppey | 43 | Q10 |
| Aller → | 14 | B5 |
| Allier → | 13 | C5 |
| Allora | 63 | A5 |
| Alma Ata = | | |
| Almaty | 29 | E8 |
| Almada | 18 | C1 |
| Almadén | 18 | C3 |
| Almansa | 19 | C5 |
| Almanzor, Pico | | |
| del Moro | 18 | B3 |
| Almanzora → | 19 | D5 |
| Almaty | 29 | E8 |
| Almazán | 19 | B4 |
| Almeirim | 92 | C3 |
| Almelo | 14 | B4 |
| Almendralejo | 18 | C2 |
| Almería | 19 | D4 |
| Almora | 42 | E11 |
| Alnwick | 10 | D6 |
| Alon | 41 | F10 |
| Alor | 39 | F2 |
| Alor Setar | 36 | C2 |
| Alps | 14 | E5 |
| Alsace | 13 | B7 |
| Alsask | 71 | C9 |
| Alsásua | 19 | A4 |
| Alta Gracia | 94 | C4 |
| Altagracia | 90 | A4 |
| Altai = Aerhtai | | |
| Shan | 34 | B4 |
| Altamira | 92 | C3 |
| Altamura | 21 | D6 |
| Altanbulag | 35 | A5 |
| Altay | 34 | B3 |
| Altea | 19 | C5 |
| Alto Araguaia | 93 | F3 |
| Alto Molocue | 59 | B7 |
| Alton | 77 | F9 |
| Alton Downs | 62 | A2 |
| Altoona | 73 | D6 |
| Altun Shan | 34 | C3 |
| Alùla | 49 | E5 |
| Alusi | 39 | F4 |
| Alvarado | 85 | D5 |
| Alvear | 94 | B5 |
| Alvie | 62 | C3 |
| Alwar → | 42 | F10 |
| Alxa Zuoqi | 35 | C5 |
| Am Dam | 53 | F3 |
| Am-Timan | 53 | F3 |
| Amâdi, Sudan | 53 | G5 |
| Amadi, | | |
| Dem. Rep. of the Congo | | |
| | 57 | D5 |
| Amadjuak | 68 | B3 |
| Amadjuak L. | 68 | B3 |
| Amagasaki | 32 | B4 |
| Amakusa-Shotō | 32 | C2 |
| Amaliás | 23 | F3 |
| Amalner | 43 | J9 |
| Amambay, | | |
| Cordillera de | 94 | A5 |
| Amangeldy | 29 | D7 |
| Amapá | 92 | B3 |
| Amapá □ | 92 | B3 |
| Amarante | 92 | D5 |
| Amargosa | 93 | E6 |
| Amarillo | 78 | B3 |
| Amaro, Mte. | 20 | C5 |
| Amasra | 46 | B3 |
| Amasya | 46 | B3 |
| Amazon = | | |
| Amazonas → | 92 | C3 |
| Amazonas □ | 90 | D6 |
| Amazonas → | 92 | C3 |
| Ambala | 42 | D10 |
| Ambalavao | 59 | J9 |
| Ambam | 56 | D2 |
| Ambanja | 59 | G9 |
| Ambartsevo | 29 | D9 |
| Ambato | 90 | D3 |
| Ambatolampy | 59 | H9 |
| Ambatondrazaka | 59 | H9 |
| Amberg | 15 | D6 |
| Ambergris Cay | 85 | D7 |
| Amberley | 65 | E5 |
| Ambikapur | 40 | F4 |
| Ambilobé | 59 | G9 |
| Ambo | 91 | F3 |
| Amboise | 12 | C4 |
| Ambon | 39 | E3 |
| Ambositra | 59 | J9 |
| Amboyna I. | 36 | C4 |
| Ambriz | 56 | F2 |
| Amby | 63 | A4 |
| Amchitka I. | 71 | C1 |
| Amderma | 28 | C7 |
| Ameca | 84 | C4 |
| Ameland | 14 | B3 |
| American | | |
| Highland | 96 | B10 |
| American | | |
| Samoa ■ | 65 | L13 |
| Americus | 75 | C5 |
| Amery | 71 | C10 |
| Amery Ice Shelf | 96 | A10 |
| Ames | 77 | D8 |
| Amherst, Burma | 41 | J11 |
| Amherst, | | |
| Canada | 69 | D4 |
| Amiata, Mte. | 20 | C3 |
| Amiens | 12 | B5 |
| Amirante Is. | 26 | K9 |
| 'Ammān | 47 | E3 |
| Amorgós | 23 | F5 |
| Amoy = Xiamen | 35 | D6 |
| Ampanihy | 59 | J8 |
| Ampenan | 37 | F5 |
| Amper → | 15 | D6 |
| Amravati | 43 | J10 |
| Amreli | 43 | J7 |
| Amritsar | 42 | D9 |
| Amroha | 42 | E11 |
| Amsterdam | 14 | B3 |
| Amstetten | 15 | D8 |
| Amudarya → | 29 | E6 |
| Amundsen Gulf | 70 | A7 |
| Amundsen Sea | 96 | B1 |
| Amuntai | 37 | E5 |
| Amur → | 31 | D12 |
| Amurang | 39 | D2 |
| Amuri Pass | 65 | E5 |
| Amyderya = | | |
| Amudarya → | 29 | E6 |
| An Nafūd | 47 | E5 |
| An Najaf | 47 | D6 |
| An Nhon | 36 | B3 |
| An Nu'ayrīyah | 47 | F7 |
| Anabar → | 30 | B9 |
| Anaconda | 81 | B7 |
| Anadolu | 46 | C2 |
| 'Ānah | 46 | D5 |
| Anaheim | 82 | D4 |
| Anakapalle | 40 | J4 |
| Analalava | 59 | G9 |
| Anambas, | | |
| Kepulauan | 37 | D3 |
| Anambas Is. = | | |
| Anambas, | | |
| Kepulauan | 37 | D3 |
| Anamur | 46 | C3 |
| Anan | 32 | C4 |
| Anantnag | 42 | C9 |
| Ananyiv | 17 | E9 |
| Anápolis | 93 | F4 |
| Anār | 44 | D3 |
| Anārak | 44 | C3 |
| Anatolia = | | |
| Anadolu | 46 | C2 |
| Añatuya | 94 | B4 |
| Anaye | 53 | E1 |
| Anchorage | 71 | B5 |
| Ancohuma, | | |
| Nevada | 91 | G5 |
| Ancón | 91 | F3 |
| Ancona | 20 | C4 |
| Ancud | 95 | E2 |
| Ancud, G. de | 95 | E2 |
| Andalgalá | 94 | B3 |
| Andalucía □ | 18 | D3 |
| Andalucía | 74 | D4 |
| Andalusia □ = | | |
| Andalucía □ | 18 | D3 |
| Andaman Is. | 27 | H13 |
| Andaman Sea | 36 | B1 |
| Andara | 58 | B4 |
| Anderson | 72 | D3 |
| Anderson → | 70 | B7 |
| Andes = Andes, | | |
| Cord. de los | 91 | G4 |
| Andes, Cord. de | | |
| los | 91 | G4 |
| Andhra | | |
| Pradesh □ | 43 | L11 |
| Andijon | 29 | E8 |
| Andikíthira | 23 | G4 |
| Andizhan = | | |
| Andijon | 29 | E8 |
| Andkhvoy | 45 | B6 |
| Andoany | 59 | G9 |
| Andorra ■ | 19 | A6 |
| Andorra La Vella | 19 | A6 |
| Andreanof Is. | 71 | C2 |
| Andrewilla | 62 | A2 |
| Ándria | 20 | D6 |
| Andriba | 59 | H9 |
| Andropov = | | |
| Rybinsk | 24 | B4 |
| Ándros | 23 | F5 |
| Andros I. | 86 | B4 |
| Andújar | 18 | C3 |
| Andulo | 56 | G3 |
| Aného | 55 | G5 |
| Aneto, Pico de | 19 | A6 |
| Angamos, Punta | 94 | A2 |
| Ang'angxi | 35 | B7 |
| Angara → | 30 | D7 |
| Angarsk | 30 | D8 |
| Angaston | 62 | B2 |
| Ånge | 8 | F11 |
| Angeles | 38 | A2 |
| Angellala | 63 | A4 |
| Ångermanälven → | | |
| | 8 | F11 |
| Angers | 12 | C3 |
| Anglesey | 11 | E4 |
| Ango | 57 | D5 |
| Angola ■ | 58 | A3 |
| Angoulême | 12 | D4 |
| Angoumois | 12 | D4 |
| Angra dos Reis | 94 | A8 |
| Angren | 29 | E8 |
| Anguilla ■ | 87 | C7 |
| Anhui □ | 35 | C6 |
| Anhwei □ = | | |
| Anhui □ | 35 | C6 |
| Anjidiv I. | 43 | M9 |
| Anjou | 12 | C3 |
| Anjozorobe | 59 | H9 |
| Anju | 35 | C7 |
| Anka | 55 | F6 |
| Ankang | 35 | C5 |
| Ankara | 46 | C3 |
| Ankazoabo | 59 | J8 |
| Ankazobe | 59 | H9 |
| Ankoro | 57 | F5 |
| Ann Arbor | 72 | C4 |
| Annaba | 54 | A6 |
| Annan | 11 | D5 |
| Annapolis | 73 | E7 |
| Annecy | 13 | D7 |
| Anning | 34 | D5 |
| Anniston | 74 | C5 |
| Annobón | 51 | G4 |
| Annuello | 62 | B3 |
| Anqing | 35 | C6 |
| Ansbach | 14 | D6 |
| Anshan | 35 | B7 |
| Anshun | 35 | D5 |
| Ansirabe | 59 | H9 |
| Ansongo | 55 | E5 |
| Ansudu | 39 | E5 |
| Antabamba | 91 | F4 |
| Antakya | 46 | C4 |
| Antalaha | 59 | G10 |
| Antalya | 46 | C2 |
| Antalya Körfezi | 46 | C2 |
| Antananarivo | 59 | H9 |
| Antarctic Pen. | 96 | A4 |
| Antarctica | 96 | C |
| Antequera | 18 | D3 |
| Anti Atlas | 54 | C3 |
| Antibes | 13 | E7 |
| Anticosti, I. d' | 69 | D4 |
| Antigua & | | |
| Barbuda ■ | 87 | C7 |
| Antilla | 86 | B4 |
| Antioquia | 90 | B3 |
| Antofagasta | 94 | A2 |
| Antofagasta de | | |
| la Sierra | 94 | B3 |
| Antongila, | | |
| Helodrano | 59 | H9 |
| Antonina | 94 | B7 |
| Antrim | 11 | D3 |
| Antsalova | 59 | H8 |
| Antsiranana | 59 | G9 |
| Antsohihy | 59 | G9 |
| Antwerp = | | |
| Antwerpen | 14 | C3 |
| Antwerpen | 14 | C3 |

Anupgarh ..... 42 E8
Anvers =
Antwerpen . . 14 C3
Anvers I. ..... 96 A3
Anxi ......... 34 B4
Anxious B. .... 62 B1
Anyang ...... 35 C6
Anzhero-
Sudzhensk . . 29 D9
Ánzio ........ 20 D4
Aomori ....... 33 F12
Aoraki
Mt. Cook ..... 65 E4
Aosta ........ 20 B1
Aoudéras .... 55 E6
Aoulef el Arab . 54 C5
Apalachicola → 74 E5
Apaporis → . . 90 D5
Aparri ........ 38 A2
Apeldoorn .... 14 B3
Apennines =
Appennini . . 20 B3
Apia ......... 65 L13
Apiacás, Serra
dos ....... 91 E7
Aplao ........ 91 G4
Apo, Mt. ...... 38 C3
Apollonia =
Marsá Susah 52 B3
Apolo ........ 91 F5
Apoteri ....... 90 C7
Appalachian
Mts. ........ 73 F5
Appennini .... 20 B3
Appleton ..... 72 B1
Approuague . . 92 B3
Aprília ....... 20 D4
Apucarana ... 94 A6
Apure → ..... 90 B5
Apurimac → . . 91 F4
Aqabah = Al
'Aqabah .... 47 E3
'Aqabah, Khalīj
al ......... 47 E3
Āqcheh ....... 45 B6
Aqîq ......... 53 ꞌE6
Aqmola =
Astana ..... 29 D8
Aqrah ........ 46 C5
Aqtöbe ....... 29 D6
Aquidauana ... 93 G2
Aquitain, Bassin 12 D3
Ar Rachidiya . . 54 B4
Ar Ramādī .... 46 D5
Ar Raqqah .... 46 D4
Ar Rass ...... 47 F5
Ar Rifā'ī ..... 47 E6
Ar Riyāḍ ...... 47 F6
Ar Ruṭbah .... 46 D5
Ar Ruwayḍah . 47 G6
Ara ......... 40 E5
'Arab, Bahr el → 53 G4
'Arab, Shatt al → 47 E7
Arabian Desert
= Es Sahrâ'
Esh Sharqîya 52 C5
Arabian Gulf =
Gulf, The ... 44 E2
Arabian Sea ... 26 H10
Araç ........ 46 B3
Aracaju ....... 93 E6
Aracataca ..... 90 A4
Aracati ....... 92 C6
Araçatuba .... 93 G3
Aracena ...... 18 D2
Araçuaí ....... 93 F5
Arad ......... 16 E5
Arada ........ 53 F3
Arafura Sea ... 39 F4
Aragón □ ..... 19 B5

Aragón → .... 19 A5
Araguacema . . 92 D4
Araguaia → .. 92 D4
Araguari ..... 93 F4
Araguari → .. 92 B4
Arak ........ 54 C5
Arakan Coast . . 41 H9
Arakan Yoma . 41 H10
Araks = Aras,
Rūd-e → ... 46 B7
Aral ......... 29 E7
Aral Sea ...... 29 E6
Aral Tengizi =
Aral Sea .... 29 E6
Aralsk = Aral . . 29 E7
Aralskoye More
= Aral Sea .. 29 E6
Aran I. ....... 10 D2
Aran Is. ...... 11 E2
Aranda de
Duero ..... 18 B4
Aranjuez ..... 18 B4
Aranos ....... 58 C3
Araouane ..... 55 E4
Arapgir ...... 46 C4
Arapiraca .... 93 D6
Arapongas ... 94 A6
Araranguá .... 94 B7
Araraquara ... 93 G4
Ararat ....... 62 C3
Ararat, Mt. =
Ağrı Dağı ... 46 C6
Araripe,
Chapada do . 92 D6
Aras, Rūd-e → 46 B7
Arauca ....... 90 B4
Arauca → ..... 90 B5
Arauco ....... 94 D2
Araxá ........ 93 F4
Araya, Pen. de . 90 A6
Arbatax ...... 21 E2
Arbīl ........ 46 C6
Arbroath ..... 10 C5
Arcachon ..... 12 D3
Archangel =
Arkhangelsk . 28 C5
Arcila = Asilah 54 A3
Arckaringa .... 62 A1
Arckaringa
Cr. → ...... 62 A2
Arcos de la
Frontera .... 18 D3
Arcot ........ 43 N11
Arcoverde .... 92 D6
Arctic Bay .... 68 A2
Arctic Red River 70 B6
Arda → ...... 22 D6
Ardabīl ....... 46 C7
Ardahan ...... 46 B5
Ardakān =
Sepīdān .... 44 D3
Ardenne .... 14 D3
Ardennes =
Ardenne ... 14 D3
Ardestān .... 44 C3
Ardlethan ..... 63 B4
Ardmore ..... 78 B5
Ardrossan .... 62 B2
Arecibo ...... 87 C6
Areia Branca . 92 C6
Arendal ...... 9 G9
Arequipa ..... 91 G4
Arero ........ 53 H6
Arévalo ...... 18 B3
Arezzo ....... 20 C3
Argamakmur . 37 E2
Arganda ..... 18 B4
Argentan ..... 12 B3
Argentário, Mte. 20 C3

Argentina ■ ... 94 D3
Argentina Is. .. 96 A3
Argentino, L. .. 95 G2
Argeş → ...... 22 B6
Arghandab → 42 D4
Argo ......... 53 E5
Argolikós
Kólpos ..... 23 F4
Árgos ........ 23 F4
Argostólion ... 23 E3
Argungu ..... 55 F5
Århus ........ 9 G10
Arica, Chile .. 91 G4
Arica, Colombia 90 D4
Aridh ........ 47 F6
Arinos → ..... 91 F7
Aripuanã ..... 91 E6
Aripuanã → .. 90 E6
Ariquemes ... 91 E6
Arizona ...... 94 D3
Arizona □ .... 83 C7
Arjona ....... 90 A3
Arkalyk =
Arqalyk ..... 29 D7
Arkansas □ ... 79 B7
Arkansas → .. 79 C8
Arkansas City . 78 A5
Arkhangelsk ... 28 C5
Arklow ....... 11 E3
Arkticheskiy,
Mys ........ 30 A7
Arlanzón → .. 18 A3
Arlberg P. .... 14 E6
Arles ........ 13 E6
Arlington, Va.,
U.S.A. ..... 73 E7
Arlington,
Wash., U.S.A. 80 A2
Arlon ........ 14 D3
Armagh ...... 11 D3
Armavir ...... 25 D5
Armenia ...... 90 C3
Armenia ■ ... 25 E5
Armidale ..... 63 B5
Armstrong ... 69 C2
Arnaud → .... 68 B3
Arnauti, C. .... 46 D3
Arnhem ...... 14 C3
Arnhem, C. ... 60 C6
Arnhem Land . 60 C5
Arno → ...... 20 C3
Arno Bay ..... 62 B2
Arnsberg .... 14 C5
Aroab ........ 58 D3
Arqalyk ...... 29 D7
Arrabury .... 62 A3
Arrah = Ara ... 40 E5
Arran ........ 10 D4
Arras ........ 13 A5
Arrecife ...... 54 C2
Arrée, Mts. d' . 12 B2
Arrowtown ... 65 F3
Árta ......... 23 E3
Arthur → ..... 62 D3
Arthur's Pass . 65 E4
Artigas ....... 94 C5
Artois ....... 12 A5
Artsyz ....... 17 E9
Artvin → ..... 46 B5
Aru, Kepulauan 39 F4
Aru Is. = Aru,
Kepulauan .. 39 F4
Arua ......... 57 D6
Aruanã ....... 93 E3
Aruba ■ ...... 87 D6
Arumpo ...... 62 B3
Arunachal
Pradesh □ .. 41 C10
Arusha ....... 57 E7

Aruwimi → .... 56 D
Arviat ........ 70 B1⁣
Arxan ........ 35 B⁣
Arys ......... 29 E⁣
Arzamas ...... 24 B⁣
Arzew ........ 54 A⁣
'As Saffānīyah . 47 E
As Samāwah . . 47 E⁣
As
Sulaymānīyah,
Iraq ....... 46 D⁣
As
Sulaymānīyah,
Si. Arabia ... 47 F⁣
As Summān . . 47 F⁣
As Sūq ....... 47 G⁣
As Suwaydā' . 46 D⁣
As Suwayh ... 45 F⁣
As Şuwayrah .. 47 E⁣
Asahigawa ... 32 F1⁣
Asansol ...... 40 F⁣
Ascension I. .. 51 G⁣
Aschaffenburg . 14 D⁣
Aschersleben . . 15 C⁣
Áscoli Piceno .. 20 C⁣
Ascope ....... 91 E⁣
Aseb ......... 49 E⁣
Asela ........ 53 G⁣
Asenovgrad .. 22 C⁣
Ash Shām,
Bādiyat .... 47 D⁣
Ash Shāmīyah . 47 E⁣
Ash Shāriqah . 44 E⁣
Ash Shaṭrah .. 47 E⁣
Ash Shaykh, J. 46 D⁣
Ash Shu'aybah 47 F⁣
Ash Shu'bah .. 47 E⁣
Ashburton ... 65 E⁣
Ashcroft ..... 71 C⁣
Asheville ..... 75 B⁣
Ashford,
Australia .... 63 A⁣
Ashford, U.K. .. 11 F⁣
Ashgabat .... 29 F⁣
Ashikaga .... 32 A⁣
Ashizuri-Zaki . 32 C⁣
Ashkhabad =
Ashgabat ... 29 F⁣
Ashmyany .... 17 A⁣
Ashqelon .... 47 E⁣
Ashtabula ... 72 D⁣
Ashuanipi, L. . 69 C⁣
Asia, Kepulauan 39 D⁣
Asifabad ..... 43 K11
Asike ........ 39 F⁣
Asilah ....... 54 A⁣
Asinara ...... 20 D⁣
Asinara, G. dell' 20 D⁣
Asino ........ 29 D⁣
Asipovichy ... 17 B⁣
'Asīr □ ...... 48 D⁣
Asir, Ras .... 49 E⁣
Asmara =
Asmera ..... 53 E⁣
Asmera ...... 53 E⁣
Aspiring, Mt. .. 65 F⁣
Assam □ ..... 41 D⁣
Assen ....... 14 B⁣
Assini ....... 55 G⁣
Assiniboia → .. 71 D⁣
Assiniboine → 71 D10
Assis ........ 94 A⁣
Assisi ........ 20 C⁣
Astana ....... 29 D⁣
Asti ......... 20 B⁣
Astipálaia .... 23 F⁣
Astorga ...... 18 A⁣
Astoria ....... 80 B⁣
Astrakhan .... 25 D⁣
Astrakhan-Bazàr 25 F⁣

Asturias □ .... 18 A3
Asunción ..... 94 B5
Aswân ........ 52 D5
Aswân High
  Dam = Sadd
  el Aali ...... 52 D5
Asyût ........ 52 C5
At Țafilah ..... 47 E3
At Țā'if ....... 48 C3
Atacama,
  Desierto de . 94 A3
Atacama, Salar
  de .......... 94 A3
Atakpamé .... 55 G5
Atalaya ....... 91 F4
Atami ........ 32 B6
Atapupu ...... 39 F2
Atâr ......... 54 D2
Atasu ........ 29 E8
Atauro ....... 39 F3
Atbara ....... 53 E5
'Atbara → ... 53 E5
Atbasar ...... 29 D7
Athabasca .... 71 C8
Athabasca → . 70 C8
Athabasca, L. .. 70 C8
Athens =
  Athínai ..... 23 F4
Athens, Ala.,
  U.S.A. ...... 74 B4
Athens, Ga.,
  U.S.A. ...... 75 C6
Athínai ....... 23 F4
Athlone ...... 11 E3
Athos ........ 23 D5
Athy ......... 11 E3
Ati .......... 53 F2
Atico ........ 91 G4
Atlanta ....... 75 C5
Atlantic City ... 73 E8
Atlas Mts. =
  Haut Atlas .. 54 B3
Atrak =
  Atrek → .... 44 B3
Atrek → ...... 44 B3
Attawapiskat → 69 C2
Attock ....... 42 C8
Atopeu ....... 36 B3
Attur ........ 43 P11
Atuel → ...... 94 D3
Atyraū ....... 29 E6
Aubagne ..... 13 E6
Aube → ...... 13 B5
Auburn ...... 74 C5
Auburn Ra. ... 63 A5
Aubusson .... 12 D5
Auch ........ 12 E4
Auckland ..... 64 B6
Aude → ...... 13 E5
Augathella .... 63 A4
Augsburg .... 14 D6
Augusta, Italy . 21 F5
Augusta, Ga.,
  U.S.A. ...... 75 C7
Augusta, Maine,
  U.S.A. ...... 73 B11
Aunis ........ 12 C3
Auponhia .... 39 E3
Aurangabad,
  Bihar, India . 40 E5
Aurangabad,
  Maharashtra,
  India ....... 43 K9
Aurich ....... 14 B4
Aurillac ...... 12 D5
Aurora, Colo.,
  U.S.A. ...... 76 F2
Aurora, Ill.,
  U.S.A. ...... 72 D1

Aus .......... 58 D3
Auschwitz =
  Oświęcim ... 16 C4
Austin, Minn.,
  U.S.A. ...... 77 D8
Austin, Tex.,
  U.S.A. ...... 78 D5
Austral Is. =
  Tubuai Is. ... 65 M16
Austral
  Seamount
  Chain ...... 65 M16
Australia ■ ... 60 E6
Australian
  Capital
  Territory □ .. 63 C4
Austria ■ ..... 15 E8
Autun ........ 13 C6
Auvergne ..... 13 D5
Auvergne, Mts.
  d' .......... 13 D5
Auxerre ...... 13 C5
Avallon ...... 13 C5
Aveiro, Brazil .. 92 C2
Aveiro, Portugal 18 B1
Āvej ......... 46 D7
Avellaneda .... 94 C5
Avellino ...... 21 D5
Aversa ....... 21 D5
Avezzano ..... 20 C4
Aviá Terai .... 94 B4
Aviemore ..... 10 C5
Avignon ...... 13 E6
Ávila ........ 18 B3
Avilés ........ 18 A3
Avoca → ..... 62 C3
Avola ........ 21 F5
Avranches .... 12 B3
'Awālī ....... 44 E2
Awash ....... 49 F3
Awatere → ... 65 D6
Awbārī ...... 52 C1
Awjilah ...... 52 C3
Axim ........ 55 H4
Axiós → ..... 23 D4
Ayabaca ..... 90 D3
Ayabe ....... 32 B4
Ayacucho,
  Argentina .. 94 D5
Ayacucho,
  Peru ....... 91 F4
Ayaguz ...... 29 E9
Ayamonte .... 18 D2
Ayaviri ...... 91 F4
Āybak ....... 45 B7
Aydın ....... 23 F6
Ayers Rock ... 60 F5
Áyios Evstrátios 23 E5
Aylmer, L. .... 70 B8
Ayn Dār ..... 47 F7
Ayn Zālah .... 46 C5
Ayr ......... 10 D4
Aytos ....... 22 C6
Ayu, Kepulauan 37 D4
Ayutla ....... 84 D5
Ayvacık ..... 23 E6
Ayvalık ...... 23 E6
Az Zahrān .... 47 F7
Az Zarqā ..... 46 D4
Az-Zilfi ...... 47 F6
Az Zubayr .... 47 E6
Az Zuwaytīnah 52 B3
Azamgarh .... 40 D4
Azärbayjan =
  Azerbaijan ■ 25 E6
Āzarbāyjān-e
  Gharbī □ ... 46 C6
Āzarbāyjān-e
  Sharqī □ .... 46 C6

Azare ........ 55 F7
Azbine = Aïr .. 55 E6
Azerbaijan ■ .. 25 E6
Azerbaijchan =
  Azerbaijan ■ 25 E6
Azogues ...... 90 D3
Azores ....... 50 C1
Azov ........ 25 D4
Azov, Sea of .. 25 D4
Azovskoye More
  = Azov, Sea
  of .......... 25 D4
Azovy ....... 28 C7
Azúa ........ 87 C5
Azuaga ...... 18 C3
Azuero, Pen. de 86 E3
Azul ........ 94 D5

## B

Ba Don ....... 36 A3
Ba Ria ....... 36 B3
Bab el Mandeb 49 E3
Baba Burnu ... 23 E6
Babadag ...... 22 B7
Babadayhan .. 29 F7
Babaeski ..... 22 D6
Babahoyo .... 90 D3
Babana ...... 55 F5
Babar ........ 39 F3
Babo ........ 39 E4
Bābol ....... 44 B3
Bābol Sar .... 44 B3
Baboua ...... 56 C2
Babruysk .... 17 B9
Babura ...... 55 F7
Babuyan Chan. 38 A2
Babylon ...... 47 D6
Bacabal ...... 92 C5
Bacan,
  Kepulauan . 39 E3
Bacan, Pulau .. 39 E3
Bacarra ...... 38 A2
Bacău ....... 17 E8
Bachelina .... 29 D7
Back → ...... 70 B9
Backstairs
  Passage .... 62 C2
Bacolod ...... 38 B2
Bad Ischl .... 15 E7
Bad Kissingen . 14 C6
Bad Lands ... 76 D3
Badagara .... 43 P9
Badajoz ..... 18 C2
Badalona .... 19 B7
Badalzai ..... 42 E4
Badampahar .. 40 F6
Badanah ..... 47 E5
Badarinath ... 42 D11
Badas ....... 36 D4
Badas,
  Kepulauan .. 37 D3
Baddo → .... 42 E4
Bade ........ 39 F5
Baden ....... 15 D9
Baden-Baden .. 14 D5
Baden-
  Württemberg □
  ........... 14 D5
Badgastein ... 15 E7
Bādghīsāt □ .. 42 B3
Badin ....... 43 G6
Baduen ...... 49 F4
Baena ....... 18 D3
Baeza ....... 18 D4
Bafatá ....... 55 F2

Baffin B. ...... 68 A4
Baffin I. ...... 68 B3
Bafia ........ 56 D2
Bafing → ..... 55 F2
Bafoulabé .... 55 F2
Bāfq ........ 44 D3
Bafra ........ 46 B3
Bāft ........ 44 D4
Bafwasende .. 57 D5
Bagamoyo ... 57 F7
Baganga ..... 38 C3
Bagansiapiapi . 37 D2
Bagdarin .... 30 D9
Bagé ........ 94 C6
Baghdād ..... 46 D6
Bagheria ..... 21 E4
Baghlān ..... 42 A6
Baghlān □ .... 45 C7
Baguio ...... 38 A2
Bahamas ■ ... 86 A4
Baharampur .. 40 E7
Bahawalpur ... 42 E7
Bahía =
  Salvador .... 93 E6
Bahía □ ..... 93 E5
Bahía Blanca . 94 D4
Bahía de
  Caráquez ... 90 D2
Bahía Laura .. 95 F3
Bahía Negra . 91 H7
Bahr Aouk → . 56 C3
Bahr
  Salamat → . 53 G2
Bahraich ..... 40 D3
Bahrain ■ .... 44 E2
Baia Mare .... 17 E6
Baïbokoum .. 53 G2
Baidoa ...... 49 G3
Baie Comeau . 69 D4
Ba'ījī ....... 46 D5
Baikal, L. =
  Baykal, Oz. .. 30 D8
Baile Atha Cliath
  = Dublin ... 11 E3
Băileşti ...... 22 B4
Bailundo ..... 58 A3
Bā'ir ........ 47 E4
Baird Mts. .... 71 B3
Bairnsdale ... 63 C4
Baitadi ...... 40 C3
Baiyin ....... 35 C5
Baja ........ 16 E4
Baja, Pta. .... 84 B1
Baja California . 84 A1
Bajimba, Mt. . 63 A5
Bakala ...... 56 C4
Bakchar ..... 29 D9
Bakel ....... 55 F2
Baker, L. .... 70 B10
Baker I. ..... 64 J13
Baker Lake .. 70 B10
Baker Mt. ... 80 A3
Baker's Dozen
  Is. ......... 69 C3
Bakersfield ... 82 C3
Bākhtarān ... 46 D6
Bakı ........ 25 E6
Bakony Forest =
  Bakony
  Hegyseg ... 16 E3
Bakony Hegyseg 16 E3
Bakouma .... 56 C4
Baku = Bakı .. 25 E6
Bakutis Coast . 96 B1
Baky = Bakı .. 25 E6
Balabac I. .... 36 C5
Balabac Str. .. 36 C5
Balabalangan,
  Kepulauan .. 37 E5

# Balaghat Ra.

| | | |
|---|---|---|
| Balaghat Ra. . . | 43 | K10 |
| Balaguer . . . . . | 19 | B6 |
| Balaklava, | | |
|   *Australia* . . . . | 62 | B2 |
| Balaklava, | | |
|   *Ukraine* . . . . . | 25 | E3 |
| Balakovo . . . . . | 24 | C6 |
| Balashov . . . . . | 24 | C5 |
| Balasore = | | |
|   Baleshwar . . | 40 | G6 |
| Balaton . . . . . . . | 16 | E3 |
| Balbina, Reprêsa | | |
|   de . . . . . . . . . | 90 | D7 |
| Balchik . . . . . . . | 22 | C7 |
| Balclutha . . . . . | 65 | G3 |
| Baleares, Is. . . | 19 | C7 |
| Balearic Is. = | | |
|   Baleares, Is. . | 19 | C7 |
| Baler . . . . . . . . . | 38 | A2 |
| Baleshwar . . . . | 40 | G6 |
| Bali, *Cameroon* | 55 | G7 |
| Bali, *Indonesia* | 37 | F5 |
| Bali ☐ . . . . . . . | 37 | F5 |
| Balikeşir . . . . . . | 23 | E6 |
| Balikpapan . . . | 37 | E5 |
| Balimbing . . . . | 38 | C1 |
| Balipara . . . . . . | 41 | D9 |
| Baliza . . . . . . . . | 93 | F3 |
| Balkan Mts. = | | |
|   Stara Planina | 22 | C4 |
| Balkh . . . . . . . . | 45 | B6 |
| Balkhash = | | |
|   Balqash . . . . | 29 | E8 |
| Balkhash, Ozero | | |
|   = Balqash Köl | 29 | E8 |
| Balla . . . . . . . . . | 41 | E8 |
| Ballarat . . . . . . . | 62 | C3 |
| Ballater . . . . . . | 10 | C5 |
| Ballina, *Australia* | 63 | A5 |
| Ballina, *Ireland* | 11 | D2 |
| Ballinasloe . . . . | 11 | E2 |
| Ballymena . . . . | 11 | D3 |
| Balmaceda . . . . | 95 | F2 |
| Balmoral . . . . . | 62 | C3 |
| Balonne → . . . | 63 | A4 |
| Balqash . . . . . . | 29 | E8 |
| Balqash Köl . . | 29 | E8 |
| Balrampur . . . . | 40 | D4 |
| Balranald . . . . | 62 | B3 |
| Balsas → . . . . | 84 | D4 |
| Balta . . . . . . . . . | 17 | D9 |
| Bălţi . . . . . . . . . | 17 | E8 |
| Baltic Sea . . . | 9 | G11 |
| Baltimore . . . . . | 73 | E7 |
| Baluchistan ☐ . | 42 | F4 |
| Balya . . . . . . . . | 23 | E6 |
| Bam . . . . . . . . . | 44 | D4 |
| Bama . . . . . . . . | 53 | F1 |
| Bamako . . . . . . | 55 | F3 |
| Bamba . . . . . . . | 55 | E4 |
| Bambari . . . . . . | 56 | C4 |
| Bamberg . . . . . | 14 | D6 |
| Bambili . . . . . . . | 57 | D5 |
| Bamenda . . . . | 55 | G7 |
| Bāmiān ☐ . . . . | 42 | B5 |
| Bampūr . . . . . . | 45 | E5 |
| Ban Don = | | |
|   Surat Thani . | 36 | C1 |
| Ban Mê Thuôt = | | |
|   Buon Me | | |
|   Thuot . . . . . . | 36 | B3 |
| Banaba . . . . . . | 64 | K11 |
| Banalia . . . . . . | 57 | D5 |
| Banam . . . . . . . | 36 | B3 |
| Banamba . . . . . | 55 | F3 |
| Bananal, I. do . | 93 | E3 |
| Banaras = | | |
|   Varanasi . . . . | 40 | E4 |
| Band-e | | |
|   Torkestān . . . | 45 | C6 |
| Banda, | | |
|   Kepulauan . . | 39 | E3 |
| Banda Aceh . . . | 36 | C1 |
| Banda Banda, | | |
|   Mt. . . . . . . . . | 63 | B5 |
| Banda Elat . . . . | 39 | F4 |
| Banda Is. = | | |
|   Banda, | | |
|   Kepulauan . . | 39 | E3 |
| Banda Sea . . . . | 39 | F3 |
| Bandanaira . . . | 39 | E3 |
| Bandar = | | |
|   Machilipatnam | 40 | J3 |
| Bandār 'Abbās | 44 | E4 |
| Bandar-e Anzalī | 46 | C7 |
| Bandar-e | | |
|   Bushehr = | | |
|   Būshehr . . . . | 44 | D2 |
| Bandar-e Chārak | 44 | E3 |
| Bandar-e | | |
|   Deylam . . . . . | 47 | E7 |
| Bandar-e | | |
|   Khomeynı . . . | 47 | E7 |
| Bandar-e | | |
|   Lengeh . . . . . | 44 | E3 |
| Bandar-e | | |
|   Ma'shur . . . . | 47 | E7 |
| Bandar-e | | |
|   Nakhīlū . . . . | 44 | E3 |
| Bandar-e Rīg . . | 44 | D2 |
| Bandar-e | | |
|   Torkeman . . . | 44 | B3 |
| Bandar | | |
|   Maharani = | | |
|   Muar . . . . . . . | 37 | D2 |
| Bandar | | |
|   Penggaram = | | |
|   Batu Pahat . | 37 | D2 |
| Bandar Seri | | |
|   Begawan . . . | 36 | D5 |
| Bandawe . . . . . | 59 | A6 |
| Bandeira, Pico | | |
|   da . . . . . . . . . | 93 | G5 |
| Bandera . . . . . . | 94 | B4 |
| Bandiagara . . . | 55 | F4 |
| Bandırma . . . . . | 23 | D7 |
| Bandon . . . . . . | 11 | F2 |
| Bandundu . . . . | 56 | E3 |
| Bandung . . . . . | 37 | F3 |
| Banff, *Canada* . | 71 | C8 |
| Banff, *U.K.* . . . . | 10 | C5 |
| Banfora . . . . . . | 55 | F4 |
| Bang Saphan . . | 36 | B1 |
| Bangalore . . . . | 43 | N10 |
| Bangassou . . . . | 56 | D4 |
| Banggai, | | |
|   Kepulauan . . | 39 | E2 |
| Banggi, P. . . . . | 36 | C5 |
| Banghāzī . . . . . | 52 | B3 |
| Bangka, P., | | |
|   *Sulawesi,* | | |
|   *Indonesia* . . . | 39 | D3 |
| Bangka, P., | | |
|   *Sumatera,* | | |
|   *Indonesia* . . . | 37 | E3 |
| Bangka, Selat . | 37 | E3 |
| Bangkinang . . . | 37 | D2 |
| Bangko . . . . . . | 37 | E2 |
| Bangkok . . . . . | 36 | B2 |
| Bangladesh ■ . | 41 | E7 |
| Bangong Co . . | 42 | B11 |
| Bangor, *Down,* | | |
|   *U.K.* . . . . . . . | 11 | D4 |
| Bangor, | | |
|   *Gwynedd,* | | |
|   *U.K.* . . . . . . . | 11 | E4 |
| Bangor, *U.S.A.* | 73 | B11 |
| Bangued . . . . . | 38 | A2 |
| Bangui . . . . . . . | 56 | D3 |
| Bangweulu, L. . | 57 | G6 |
| Bani . . . . . . . . . | 87 | C5 |
| Banī Walīd . . . . | 52 | B1 |
| Banīnah . . . . . . | 52 | B3 |
| Bāniyās . . . . . . | 46 | D3 |
| Banja Luka . . . | 20 | B6 |
| Banjarmasin . . | 37 | E4 |
| Banjul . . . . . . . . | 55 | F1 |
| Bankipore . . . . | 40 | E5 |
| Banks I. . . . . . . | 70 | A7 |
| Banks Pen. . . . | 65 | E5 |
| Banks Str. . . . . | 62 | D4 |
| Bankura . . . . . . | 40 | F6 |
| Banningville = | | |
|   Bandundu . . | 56 | E3 |
| Bannu . . . . . . . | 42 | C7 |
| Banská Bystrica | 16 | D4 |
| Banswara . . . . . | 43 | H9 |
| Bantry . . . . . . . | 11 | F2 |
| Banu . . . . . . . . | 42 | B6 |
| Banyak, | | |
|   Kepulauan . . | 37 | D1 |
| Banyo . . . . . . . | 55 | G7 |
| Banzare Coast . | 96 | A13 |
| Banzyville = | | |
|   Mobayi . . . . . | 56 | D4 |
| Baoding . . . . . . | 35 | C6 |
| Baoji . . . . . . . . | 35 | C5 |
| Baoshan . . . . . | 34 | D4 |
| Baotou . . . . . . . | 35 | B6 |
| Bapatla . . . . . . | 40 | K3 |
| Ba'qūbah . . . . | 46 | D6 |
| Bar, | | |
|   *Montenegro, Yug.* | | |
|   . . . . . . . . . . . | 22 | C2 |
| Bar, *Ukraine* . . | 17 | D8 |
| Bar-le-Duc . . . . | 13 | B6 |
| Barabai . . . . . . | 37 | E5 |
| Barabinsk . . . . | 29 | D8 |
| Baracaldo . . . . | 19 | A4 |
| Baracoa . . . . . . | 86 | B5 |
| Barahona . . . . . | 87 | C5 |
| Barail Range . . | 41 | E9 |
| Barakhola . . . . | 41 | E9 |
| Barakpur . . . . . | 41 | F7 |
| Barakula . . . . . | 63 | A5 |
| Baramula . . . . . | 42 | B9 |
| Baran . . . . . . . . | 43 | G10 |
| Baranavichy . . . | 17 | B8 |
| Baranof I. . . . . . | 71 | C6 |
| Barão de | | |
|   Melgaço . . . . | 91 | F6 |
| Barapasi . . . . . | 39 | E5 |
| Barat Daya, | | |
|   Kepulauan . . | 39 | F3 |
| Barbacena . . . . | 93 | G5 |
| Barbacoas . . . . | 90 | C3 |
| Barbados ■ . . . | 87 | D8 |
| Barbastro . . . . . | 19 | A6 |
| Barberton . . . . | 59 | D6 |
| Barcellona Pozzo | | |
|   di Gotto . . . . | 21 | E5 |
| Barcelona, *Spain* | 19 | B7 |
| Barcelona, | | |
|   *Venezuela* . . | 90 | A6 |
| Barcelos . . . . . | 90 | D6 |
| Bardai . . . . . . . | 52 | D2 |
| Barddhaman . . | 40 | F6 |
| Bardejov . . . . . | 16 | D5 |
| Bardera . . . . . . | 49 | G3 |
| Bardi, Ra's . . . | 47 | F4 |
| Bardīyah . . . . . | 52 | B4 |
| Bareilly . . . . . . | 42 | E11 |
| Barentu . . . . . . | 53 | E6 |
| Barfleur, Pte. de | 12 | B3 |
| Barga . . . . . . . . | 34 | C3 |
| Bargal . . . . . . . | 49 | E5 |
| Barhi . . . . . . . . | 40 | E5 |
| Bari . . . . . . . . . | 20 | D6 |
| Bari Doab . . . . | 42 | D8 |
| Barīm . . . . . . . . | 49 | E3 |
| Barinas . . . . . . | 90 | B4 |
| Baring, C. . . . . | 70 | B8 |
| Bârîs . . . . . . . . | 52 | D5 |
| Barisal . . . . . . . | 41 | F8 |
| Barisan, Bukit . | 37 | E2 |
| Barito → . . . . . | 37 | E4 |
| Barkly Tableland | 60 | D6 |
| Barlee, L. . . . . . | 60 | F2 |
| Barletta . . . . . . | 20 | D6 |
| Barmedman . . . | 63 | B4 |
| Barmer . . . . . . . | 42 | G7 |
| Barmera . . . . . . | 62 | B3 |
| Barnato . . . . . . | 63 | B4 |
| Barnaul . . . . . . | 29 | D9 |
| Barnsley . . . . . | 11 | E6 |
| Barnstaple . . . . | 11 | F4 |
| Baro . . . . . . . . | 55 | G6 |
| Baroda = | | |
|   Vadodara . . . | 43 | H8 |
| Barpeta . . . . . . | 41 | D8 |
| Barquísimeto . . | 90 | A5 |
| Barra, *Brazil* . . . | 93 | E5 |
| Barra, *U.K.* . . . | 10 | C3 |
| Barra do Corda | 92 | D4 |
| Barra do Piraí . | 93 | G5 |
| Barra Falsa, Pta. | | |
|   da . . . . . . . . . | 59 | C7 |
| Barraba . . . . . . | 63 | B5 |
| Barrackpur = | | |
|   Barakpur . . . . | 41 | F7 |
| Barraigh = | | |
|   Barra . . . . . . | 10 | C3 |
| Barranca, *Lima,* | | |
|   *Peru* . . . . . . . | 91 | F3 |
| Barranca, | | |
|   *Loreto, Peru* . | 90 | D3 |
| Barrancabermeja | | |
|   . . . . . . . . . . . | 90 | B4 |
| Barrancas . . . . | 90 | B6 |
| Barrancos . . . . | 18 | C2 |
| Barranqueras . . | 94 | B5 |
| Barranquilla . . . | 90 | A4 |
| Barras . . . . . . . | 92 | C5 |
| Barreiras . . . . . | 93 | E5 |
| Barreirinhas . . . | 92 | C5 |
| Barreiro . . . . . . | 18 | C1 |
| Barreiros . . . . . | 92 | D6 |
| Barretos . . . . . . | 93 | G4 |
| Barrier Ra. . . . . | 62 | B3 |
| Barrington Tops | 63 | B5 |
| Barringun . . . . . | 63 | A4 |
| Barrow . . . . . . . | 71 | A4 |
| Barrow-in- | | |
|   Furness . . . . | 11 | D5 |
| Barry . . . . . . . . | 11 | F5 |
| Barsi . . . . . . . . | 43 | K9 |
| Barsoi . . . . . . . | 40 | E6 |
| Barstow . . . . . . | 82 | C4 |
| Bartica . . . . . . . | 90 | B7 |
| Bartin . . . . . . . | 46 | B3 |
| Bartle Frere . . . | 61 | D8 |
| Bartlesville . . . | 79 | A6 |
| Barysaw . . . . . . | 17 | A9 |
| Bāsa'idū . . . . . | 44 | E3 |
| Basankusa . . . . | 56 | D3 |
| Basarabeasca . | 17 | E9 |
| Basel . . . . . . . . | 13 | C7 |
| Bashi Channel . | 35 | D7 |
| Bashkir Republic | | |
|   = | | |
|   Bashkortostan ☐ | | |
|   . . . . . . . . . . . | 29 | D6 |
| Bashkortostan ☐ | 29 | D6 |
| Basilan . . . . . . | 38 | C2 |
| Basilan Str. . . . | 38 | C2 |
| Basildon . . . . . | 11 | F7 |
| Basim = | | |
|   Washim . . . . | 43 | J10 |

102

| Name | Page | Ref |
|---|---|---|
| Basingstoke ... | 11 | F6 |
| Basle = Basel . | 13 | C7 |
| Basoka ....... | 56 | D4 |
| Basongo ...... | 56 | E4 |
| Basque Provinces = País Vasco □ | 19 | A4 |
| Basra = Al Başrah ..... | 47 | E6 |
| Bass Str. ..... | 61 | H8 |
| Bassano ...... | 71 | C8 |
| Bassano del Grappa .... | 20 | B3 |
| Bassas da India | 59 | C7 |
| Bassein ...... | 41 | J10 |
| Basseterre .... | 87 | C7 |
| Bassikounou .. | 55 | E3 |
| Bastak ....... | 44 | E3 |
| Bastar ....... | 40 | H3 |
| Basti ........ | 40 | D4 |
| Bastia ........ | 13 | E8 |
| Bastogne .... | 14 | C3 |
| Bata ......... | 56 | D1 |
| Bataan ....... | 38 | B2 |
| Batabanó .... | 86 | B3 |
| Batabanó, G. de | 86 | B3 |
| Batac ........ | 38 | A2 |
| Batagoy ...... | 31 | C11 |
| Batamay .... | 31 | C10 |
| Batang ....... | 34 | C4 |
| Batangafo .... | 56 | C3 |
| Batangas .... | 38 | B2 |
| Batanta ...... | 39 | E4 |
| Bateman's B. .. | 63 | C5 |
| Batemans Bay . | 63 | C5 |
| Bath ......... | 11 | F5 |
| Bathurst, Australia .... | 63 | B4 |
| Bathurst, Canada ..... | 69 | D4 |
| Bathurst, C. .. | 70 | A7 |
| Bathurst Harb. . | 62 | D4 |
| Bathurst Inlet . | 70 | B9 |
| Batinah ...... | 44 | F4 |
| Batlow ....... | 63 | C4 |
| Batman ...... | 46 | C5 |
| Batna ........ | 54 | A6 |
| Baton Rouge .. | 79 | D8 |
| Batouri ...... | 56 | D2 |
| Battambang ... | 36 | B2 |
| Battipáglia ... | 21 | D5 |
| Battle Creek .. | 72 | C3 |
| Battle Harbour . | 69 | C5 |
| Battleford ..... | 71 | C9 |
| Batu ......... | 49 | F2 |
| Batu, Kepulauan | 37 | E1 |
| Batu Is. = Batu, Kepulauan . | 37 | E1 |
| Batu Pahat ... | 37 | D2 |
| Batuata ...... | 39 | F2 |
| Batumi ...... | 25 | E5 |
| Baturaja ..... | 37 | E2 |
| Baturité ...... | 92 | C6 |
| Bau ......... | 37 | D4 |
| Baubau ...... | 39 | F2 |
| Bauchi ....... | 55 | F6 |
| Bauer, C. .... | 62 | B1 |
| Baukau ...... | 39 | F3 |
| Bauru ........ | 93 | G4 |
| Baús ......... | 93 | F3 |
| Bautzen ..... | 15 | C8 |
| Bavaria = Bayern □ ... | 15 | D6 |
| Bawdwin .... | 41 | F11 |
| Bawean ..... | 37 | F4 |
| Bawku ...... | 55 | F4 |
| Bawlake ..... | 41 | H11 |
| Bay, L. de .... | 38 | B2 |
| Bay City ..... | 72 | C4 |
| Bay View ..... | 64 | C7 |
| Bayamo ...... | 86 | B4 |
| Bayan Har Shan | 34 | C4 |
| Bayan Hot = Alxa Zuoqi .. | 35 | C5 |
| Bayanaūyl .... | 29 | D8 |
| Bayanhongor .. | 35 | B5 |
| Bayázeh ...... | 44 | C3 |
| Baybay ....... | 38 | B2 |
| Bayburt ...... | 46 | B5 |
| Bayern □ ..... | 15 | D6 |
| Bayeux ....... | 12 | B3 |
| Bayındır ...... | 23 | E6 |
| Baykal, Oz. .. | 30 | D8 |
| Baykit ........ | 30 | C7 |
| Baykonur = Bayqongyr .. | 29 | E7 |
| Bayombong ... | 38 | A2 |
| Bayonne ...... | 12 | E3 |
| Bayovar ...... | 91 | E2 |
| Bayqongyr .... | 29 | E7 |
| Bayram-Ali = Bayramaly .. | 29 | F7 |
| Bayramaly ... | 29 | F7 |
| Bayramiç .... | 23 | E6 |
| Bayreuth ..... | 15 | D6 |
| Bayrūt ....... | 46 | D3 |
| Baytown ..... | 79 | E6 |
| Baza ......... | 19 | D4 |
| Bazaruto, I. do . | 59 | C7 |
| Beachport .... | 62 | C2 |
| Beagle, Canal . | 95 | G3 |
| Beardmore Glacier ..... | 96 | C14 |
| Béarn ....... | 12 | E3 |
| Beauce, Plaine de la ...... | 12 | B4 |
| Beaudesert ... | 63 | A5 |
| Beaufort ..... | 36 | C5 |
| Beaufort Sea .. | 66 | B6 |
| Beaufort West . | 58 | E4 |
| Beaumont ... | 79 | D6 |
| Beaune ...... | 13 | C6 |
| Beauvais .... | 12 | B5 |
| Beauval ..... | 71 | C9 |
| Beaver ...... | 71 | B5 |
| Beaver → ... | 71 | C9 |
| Beawar ...... | 42 | F9 |
| Bečej ........ | 22 | B3 |
| Béchar ...... | 54 | B4 |
| Bedford ...... | 11 | E6 |
| Beenleigh .... | 63 | A5 |
| Be'er Sheva ... | 47 | E3 |
| Beersheba = Be'er Sheva . | 47 | E3 |
| Befale ....... | 56 | D4 |
| Bega ......... | 63 | C4 |
| Behbehān .... | 47 | E7 |
| Behshahr .... | 44 | B3 |
| Bei Jiang → . | 35 | D6 |
| Bei'an ....... | 35 | B7 |
| Beibei ....... | 35 | D5 |
| Beihai ....... | 35 | D5 |
| Beijing ....... | 35 | C6 |
| Beilpajah .... | 63 | B3 |
| Beinn na Faoghla = Benbecula .. | 10 | C3 |
| Beira ........ | 59 | B6 |
| Beirut = Bayrūt | 46 | D3 |
| Beitbridge ... | 59 | C6 |
| Beja, Portugal . | 18 | C2 |
| Béja, Tunisia . | 54 | A6 |
| Bejaia ....... | 54 | A6 |
| Béjar ........ | 18 | B3 |
| Bejestān ..... | 44 | C4 |
| Békéscsaba .. | 16 | E5 |
| Bela, India ... | 40 | E4 |
| Bela, Pakistan . | 42 | F5 |
| Bela Crkva .... | 22 | B3 |
| Bela Vista ..... | 94 | A5 |
| Belarus ■ ..... | 24 | C2 |
| Belau = Palau ■ | 38 | C4 |
| Belawan ...... | 37 | D1 |
| Belaya Tserkov = Bila Tserkva | 17 | D10 |
| Belcher Is. .... | 69 | C3 |
| Belém ........ | 92 | C4 |
| Belén ........ | 94 | A5 |
| Belet Uen ..... | 49 | G4 |
| Belev ........ | 24 | C4 |
| Belfast ....... | 11 | D4 |
| Belfort ....... | 13 | C7 |
| Belgaum ..... | 43 | M9 |
| Belgium ■ .... | 14 | C3 |
| Belgorod ..... | 24 | C4 |
| Belgorod-Dnestrovskiy = Bilhorod-Dnistrovskyy | 25 | D3 |
| Belgrade = Beograd .... | 22 | B3 |
| Beli Drim → . | 22 | C3 |
| Belinga ...... | 56 | D2 |
| Belinyu ...... | 37 | E3 |
| Beliton Is. = Belitung .... | 37 | E3 |
| Belitung ..... | 37 | E3 |
| Belize ■ ..... | 85 | D7 |
| Belize City .... | 85 | D7 |
| Belkovskiy, Ostrov ..... | 30 | B11 |
| Bell Bay ..... | 62 | D4 |
| Bell Peninsula . | 68 | B2 |
| Bell Ville ..... | 94 | C4 |
| Bella Unión ... | 94 | C5 |
| Bella Vista ... | 94 | B5 |
| Bellary ...... | 43 | M10 |
| Bellata ...... | 63 | A4 |
| Belle-Ile ..... | 12 | C2 |
| Belle Isle .... | 69 | C5 |
| Belle Isle, Str. of | 69 | C5 |
| Belleville, Canada ..... | 69 | D3 |
| Belleville, U.S.A. | 77 | F10 |
| Bellin = Kangirsuk ... | 68 | C4 |
| Bellingen .... | 63 | B5 |
| Bellingham ... | 80 | A2 |
| Bellingshausen Sea ....... | 96 | A2 |
| Bellinzona .... | 13 | C8 |
| Belluno ...... | 20 | A4 |
| Belmont ..... | 63 | B5 |
| Belmonte .... | 93 | F6 |
| Belmopan .... | 85 | D7 |
| Belo Horizonte . | 93 | F5 |
| Belo-Tsiribihina | 59 | H8 |
| Beloit ....... | 77 | D10 |
| Belokorovichi . | 17 | C9 |
| Belomorsk ... | 28 | C4 |
| Belonia ...... | 41 | F8 |
| Belorussia ■ = Belarus ■ .. | 24 | C2 |
| Belovo ....... | 29 | D9 |
| Beloye, Ozero . | 24 | A4 |
| Beloye More .. | 28 | C4 |
| Belozersk ..... | 24 | A4 |
| Beltana ...... | 62 | B2 |
| Belterra ..... | 92 | C3 |
| Beltsy = Bălţi . | 17 | E8 |
| Belukha ...... | 29 | E9 |
| Beluran ...... | 36 | C5 |
| Belyy, Ostrov . | 28 | B8 |
| Belyy Yar .... | 29 | D9 |
| Bembéréke ... | 55 | F5 |
| Bemidji ...... | 77 | B7 |
| Ben Gardane . | 52 | B1 |
| Ben Lomond, N.S.W., Australia .... | 63 | B5 |
| Ben Lomond, Tas., Australia | 62 | D4 |
| Ben Nevis .... | 10 | C4 |
| Bena ........ | 55 | F6 |
| Bena Dibele .. | 56 | E4 |
| Benagerie .... | 62 | B3 |
| Benalla ...... | 63 | C4 |
| Benambra, Mt. . | 63 | C4 |
| Benares = Varanasi .... | 40 | E4 |
| Benavente ... | 18 | A3 |
| Benbecula ... | 10 | C3 |
| Benbonyathe .. | 62 | B2 |
| Bend ........ | 80 | C3 |
| Bender Beila . | 49 | F5 |
| Bendery = Tighina ..... | 17 | E9 |
| Bendigo ...... | 63 | C3 |
| Benevento ... | 20 | D5 |
| Bengal, Bay of . | 41 | J7 |
| Bengbu ...... | 35 | C6 |
| Benghazi = Banghāzī .. | 52 | B3 |
| Bengkalis .... | 37 | D2 |
| Bengkulu .... | 37 | E2 |
| Bengkulu □ .. | 37 | E2 |
| Benguela .... | 58 | A2 |
| Beni → ...... | 57 | D5 |
| Beni → ...... | 91 | F5 |
| Beni Abbès .. | 54 | B4 |
| Beni Mazâr .. | 52 | C5 |
| Beni Mellal .. | 54 | B3 |
| Beni Ounif ... | 54 | B4 |
| Beni Suef ... | 52 | C5 |
| Benidorm .... | 19 | C5 |
| Benin ■ ...... | 55 | G5 |
| Benin, Bight of . | 55 | H5 |
| Benin City .... | 55 | G6 |
| Benjamin Constant .... | 90 | D4 |
| Benoni ...... | 59 | D5 |
| Bent ........ | 44 | E4 |
| Benteng ..... | 39 | F2 |
| Benton Harbor . | 72 | C2 |
| Benue → .... | 55 | G6 |
| Benxi ....... | 35 | B7 |
| Beo ......... | 38 | D3 |
| Beograd ..... | 22 | B3 |
| Beppu ....... | 32 | C2 |
| Berati ....... | 23 | D2 |
| Berau, Teluk . | 39 | E4 |
| Berber ...... | 53 | E5 |
| Berbera ..... | 49 | E4 |
| Berbérati .... | 56 | D3 |
| Berbice → ... | 90 | B7 |
| Berdichev = Berdychiv .. | 17 | D9 |
| Berdsk ...... | 29 | D9 |
| Berdyansk ... | 25 | D4 |
| Berdychiv ... | 17 | D9 |
| Berebere .... | 39 | D3 |
| Bereda ...... | 49 | E5 |
| Berehove .... | 17 | D6 |
| Berekum ..... | 55 | G4 |
| Berestechko .. | 17 | C7 |
| Bereza ....... | 17 | B7 |
| Berezhany ... | 17 | D7 |
| Berezina = Byarezina → | 17 | B10 |
| Berezniki .... | 28 | D6 |
| Berezovo .... | 28 | C7 |
| Berga ....... | 19 | A6 |
| Bergama ..... | 23 | E6 |
| Bérgamo .... | 20 | B2 |
| Bergen ...... | 8 | F9 |
| Bergerac ..... | 12 | D4 |

| | | | |
|---|---|---|---|
| Berhala, Selat . 37 E2 | Bhatpara ..... 41 F7 | Bilbao ........ 19 A4 | Bistriţa → .... 17 E8 |
| Berhampore = Baharampur . 40 E7 | Bhaunagar = Bhavnagar .. 43 J8 | Bilbo = Bilbao . 19 A4 | Bitam ........ 56 D2 |
| Berhampur = Brahamapur . 40 H5 | Bhavnagar .... 43 J8 | Bilecik ........ 46 B2 | Bitkine ....... 53 F2 |
| Bering Sea .... 71 C1 | Bhawanipatna . 40 H3 | Bilhorod-Dnistrovskyy 25 D3 | Bitlis ........ 46 C5 |
| Bering Strait .. 71 B3 | Bhilsa = Vidisha 43 H10 | Bilir .......... 31 C11 | Bitola ........ 22 D3 |
| Berja ......... 19 D4 | Bhilwara ..... 43 G9 | Billings ....... 81 C9 | Bitolj = Bitola . 22 D3 |
| Berkeley ..... 80 G2 | Bhima → .... 43 L10 | Billiton Is. = Belitung .... 37 E3 | Bitter L. = Buheirat-Murrat-el-Kubra ..... 52 B5 |
| Berkner I. .... 96 B4 | Bhimavaram .. 40 J3 | Bilma ........ 53 E1 | Bitterfontein .. 58 E3 |
| Berlin ........ 15 B7 | Bhind ........ 42 F11 | Biloxi ........ 79 D9 | Bitterroot Range 81 B6 |
| Bermejo →, Formosa, Argentina ... 94 B5 | Bhiwandi ..... 43 K8 | Biltine ....... 53 F3 | Biu .......... 53 F1 |
| Bermejo →, San Juan, Argentina ... 94 C3 | Bhiwani ...... 42 E10 | Bima ......... 39 F1 | Biwa-Ko ..... 32 B5 |
| Bermuda ■ ... 67 F13 | Bhola ........ 41 F8 | Bimbo ....... 56 D3 | Biysk ........ 29 D9 |
| Bern ......... 13 C7 | Bhopal ....... 43 H10 | Bina-Etawah .. 43 G11 | Bizerte ....... 54 A6 |
| Bernardo de Irigoyen .... 94 B6 | Bhubaneshwar 40 G5 | Binalbagan ... 38 B2 | Bjelovar ...... 20 B5 |
| Bernburg .... 15 C6 | Bhuj ......... 43 H6 | Binalong ..... 63 B4 | Black Forest = Schwarzwald 14 D5 |
| Berne = Bern . 13 C7 | Bhumiphol Dam = Phumiphon, Khuan ...... 36 A1 | Bīnālūd, Kūh-e 44 B4 | Black Hills ... 76 D3 |
| Bernina, Piz ... 13 C8 | Bhusaval ..... 43 J9 | Binatang ..... 37 D4 | Black Sea ..... 25 E3 |
| Beroroha ..... 59 J9 | Bhutan ■ ..... 41 D8 | Binda ........ 63 A4 | Black Volta → 55 G4 |
| Beroun ....... 16 D2 | Biafra, B. of = Bonny, Bight of .......... 56 D1 | Bindle ....... 63 A4 | Blackball ..... 65 E4 |
| Berrechid .... 54 B3 | Biak ......... 39 E5 | Bindura ...... 59 B6 | Blackburn ... 11 E5 |
| Berri ......... 62 B3 | Biała Podlaska . 17 B6 | Bingara, N.S.W., Australia .... 63 A5 | Blackpool .... 11 E5 |
| Berry, Australia 63 B5 | Białogard ..... 16 A2 | Bingara, Queens., Australia .... 63 A3 | Blackwater → . 11 E2 |
| Berry, France .. 12 C5 | Białystok ..... 17 B6 | Bingham Canyon ..... 81 E7 | Blagodarnoye = Blagodarnyy 25 D5 |
| Bershad ...... 17 D9 | Biaro ........ 39 D3 | Binghamton ... 73 C8 | Blagodarnyy .. 25 D5 |
| Bertoua ...... 56 D2 | Biarritz ...... 12 E3 | Bingöl ....... 46 C5 | Blagoevgrad .. 22 C4 |
| Berwick-upon-Tweed ...... 10 D6 | Bibala ........ 58 A2 | Binh Dinh = An Nhon ....... 36 B3 | Blagoveshchensk ..... 31 D10 |
| Besalampy ... 59 H8 | Biberach ..... 14 D5 | Binh Son ..... 36 A3 | Blairmore .... 71 D8 |
| Besançon .... 13 C7 | Bibiani ....... 55 G4 | Binjai ........ 37 D1 | Blanc, Mont ... 13 D7 |
| Besar ........ 37 E5 | Bida ......... 55 G6 | Binnaway .... 63 B4 | Blanca, B. .... 95 D4 |
| Besni ........ 46 C4 | Bidar ........ 43 L10 | Binongko ..... 39 F2 | Blanca Peak .. 83 B10 |
| Bessarabiya ... 17 E9 | Biddeford .... 73 C10 | Bintan ....... 37 D2 | Blanche, C. ... 62 B1 |
| Bessarabka = Basarabeasca 17 E9 | Bidon 5 = Poste Maurice Cortier ..... 54 D5 | Bintulu ....... 37 D4 | Blanche, L. ... 62 A2 |
| Bessemer ..... 74 C4 | Bié, Planalto de 58 A3 | Bintuni ....... 39 E4 | Blanes ....... 19 B7 |
| Betanzos .... 18 A1 | Biel .......... 13 C7 | Binzert = Bizerte 54 A6 | Blantyre ...... 59 B6 |
| Bétaré Oya .... 56 C2 | Bielefeld ..... 14 B5 | Bioko ........ 56 D1 | Blayney ...... 63 B4 |
| Bethanien .... 58 D3 | Biella ........ 20 B2 | Bir .......... 43 K9 | Blednaya, Gora 28 B7 |
| Bethel ........ 71 B3 | Bielsk Podlaski 17 B6 | Bir Autrun .... 53 E4 | Blenheim ..... 65 D5 |
| Bethlehem, S. Africa .... 59 D5 | Bielsko-Biała .. 16 D4 | Bir Mogrein ... 54 C2 | Blida ........ 54 A5 |
| Bethlehem, U.S.A. ...... 73 D8 | Bien Hoa ..... 36 B3 | Bîr Ungât .... 52 D5 | Bligh Sound .. 65 F2 |
| Béthune ...... 13 A5 | Bienne = Biel . 13 C7 | Bira ......... 39 E4 | Blitta ........ 55 G5 |
| Bethungra ... 63 B4 | Bienville, L. ... 69 C3 | Birao ........ 53 F3 | Blodgett Iceberg Tongue ... 96 A13 |
| Betioky ....... 59 J8 | Big Horn Mts. = Bighorn Mts. 81 C10 | Birchip ....... 62 C3 | Bloemfontein . 59 D5 |
| Betroka ...... 59 J9 | Big Spring .... 78 C3 | Birecik ....... 46 C4 | Bloemhof .... 59 D5 |
| Betsiamites ... 69 D4 | Big Trout L. ... 69 C2 | Bireuen ...... 36 C1 | Blois ........ 12 C4 |
| Bettiah ....... 40 D5 | Biğa ......... 23 D6 | Bîrlad ........ 17 E8 | Bloomington, Ill., U.S.A. ... 77 E10 |
| Betul ......... 43 J10 | Bigadiç ...... 23 E7 | Bîrlad → ..... 17 F8 | Bloomington, Ind., U.S.A. .. 72 E2 |
| Betung ....... 37 D4 | Biggar ....... 71 C9 | Birmingham, U.K. ...... 11 E6 | Blue Mts., Oreg., U.S.A. ...... 80 C4 |
| Beverley ...... 11 E6 | Biggenden .... 63 A5 | Birmingham, U.S.A. ...... 74 C4 | Blue Mts., Pa., U.S.A. ...... 73 D7 |
| Beverly Hills . 82 C3 | Bighorn → ... 81 B10 | Birmitrapur ... 40 F5 | Blue Nile = Nîl el Azraq → . 53 E5 |
| Beyla ........ 55 G3 | Bighorn Mts. .. 81 C10 | Birni Nkonni .. 55 F6 | Blue Ridge Mts. 75 A7 |
| Beyneu ....... 29 E6 | Bihać ........ 20 B5 | Birnin Kebbi .. 55 F5 | Bluefields .... 86 D3 |
| Beypazarı .... 46 B2 | Bihar ........ 40 E5 | Birr .......... 11 E3 | Bluff ........ 65 G3 |
| Beyşehir Gölü . 46 C2 | Bihar □ ...... 40 E5 | Birrie → ..... 63 A4 | Blumenau .... 94 B7 |
| Bezhitsa ..... 24 C3 | Bihor, Munţii . 17 E6 | Birsk ........ 29 D6 | Bo ........... 55 G2 |
| Béziers ....... 13 E5 | Bijagós, Arquipélago dos ........ 55 F1 | Birur ........ 43 N9 | Bo Duc ....... 36 B3 |
| Bezwada = Vijayawada . 40 J3 | Bijapur, Karnataka, India ..... 43 L9 | Bisa ......... 39 E3 | Bo Hai ....... 35 C6 |
| Bhachau ...... 43 H7 | Bijapur, Mad. P., India ..... 40 H3 | Biscay, B. of .. 12 D2 | Boa Vista .... 90 C6 |
| Bhadrakh .... 40 G6 | Bījār ........ 46 D6 | Biscoe Bay ... 96 B17 | Boatman ..... 63 A4 |
| Bhadravati ... 43 N9 | Bijeljina ..... 20 B7 | Biscoe Is. ..... 96 A3 | Bobadah ..... 63 B4 |
| Bhagalpur .... 40 E6 | Bijnor ....... 42 E11 | Bishkek ...... 29 E8 | Bobbili ....... 40 H4 |
| Bhakra Dam .. 42 D10 | Bikaner ...... 42 E8 | Biskra ....... 54 B6 | Bobo-Dioulasso 55 F4 |
| Bhamo ....... 41 E11 | Bikini Atoll .... 64 H11 | Bislig ........ 38 C3 | Bóbr → ...... 16 B2 |
| Bhandara .... 43 J11 | Biła Tserkva ... 17 D10 | Bismarck ..... 76 B4 | Bobraomby, Tanjon' i .... 59 G9 |
| Bhanrer Ra. ... 43 H11 | Bilara ........ 42 F8 | Bismarck Arch. 64 K9 | Bobruysk = Babruysk ... 17 B9 |
| Bharat = India ■ .... 43 J10 | Bilaspur ..... 40 F4 | Bissagos = Bijagós, Arquipélago dos ........ 55 F1 | Bôca do Acre .. 91 E5 |
| Bharatpur .... 42 F10 | Bilauk Taungdan 36 B1 | Bissau ....... 55 F1 | |
| | | Bistriţa ....... 17 E7 | |

Boca Raton ... 75 F7
Bocaiúva ..... 93 F5
Bocanda ...... 55 G4
Bocaranga .... 56 C3
Bochnia ...... 16 D5
Bochum ...... 14 C4
Boda ......... 56 D3
Bodaybo ..... 30 D9
Boden ........ 8 E12
Bodensee .... 13 C8
Bodhan ...... 43 K10
Bodø ......... 8 E10
Bodrog → .... 16 D5
Bodrum ...... 23 F6
Boende ....... 56 E4
Boffa ........ 55 F2
Bogalusa ..... 79 D9
Bogan Gate ... 63 B4
Boggabilla .... 63 A5
Boggabri ..... 63 B5
Bogo ......... 38 B2
Bogong, Mt. .. 63 C4
Bogotá ....... 90 C4
Bogotol ...... 29 D9
Bogra ........ 41 E7
Bogué ........ 55 E2
Bohemian
  Forest =
  Böhmerwald  15 D7
Bohena Cr. → . 63 B4
Böhmerwald .. 15 D7
Bohol ........ 38 C2
Bohol Sea .... 38 C2
Bohotleh ..... 49 F4
Boise ........ 80 D5
Boise City .... 78 A2
Bojador C. .... 54 C2
Bojana → .... 22 D2
Bojnūrd ...... 44 B4
Boké ......... 55 F2
Bokhara → ... 63 A4
Bokoro ....... 53 F2
Bokote ....... 56 E4
Bokungu ..... 56 E4
Bol .......... 53 F1
Bolama ....... 55 F1
Bolan Pass ... 42 E5
Bolbec ....... 12 B4
Bole ......... 34 B3
Bolekhiv ...... 17 D6
Bolekhov =
  Bolekhiv .... 17 D6
Bolesławiec ... 16 C2
Bolgrad =
  Bolhrad .... 17 F9
Bolhrad ...... 17 F9
Bolinao C. .... 38 A1
Bolívar,
  Argentina ... 94 D4
Bolívar,
  Colombia ... 90 C3
Bolivia ■ ..... 91 G6
Bollon ........ 63 A4
Bolobo ....... 56 E3
Bologna ...... 20 B3
Bologoye ..... 24 B3
Bolomba ..... 56 D3
Bolong ....... 38 C2
Bolsena, L. di . 20 C3
Bolshereche .. 29 D8
Bolshevik,
  Ostrov ...... 30 B8
Bolshoi Kavkas
  = Caucasus
  Mountains .. 25 E5
Bolshoy Atlym  28 C7
Bolshoy
  Begichev,
  Ostrov ...... 30 B9

Bolshoy
  Lyakhovskiy,
  Ostrov ...... 31 B12
Bolton ....... 11 E5
Bolu ......... 46 B2
Bolvadin ..... 46 C2
Bolzano ...... 20 A3
Bom Despacho 93 F4
Bom Jesus da
  Lapa ....... 93 E5
Boma ........ 56 F2
Bomaderry ... 63 B5
Bombala ..... 63 C4
Bombay ...... 43 K8
Bomboma .... 56 D3
Bomili ........ 57 D5
Bomongo ..... 56 D3
Bomu → ..... 56 D4
Bon, C. ...... 52 A1
Bonaire ...... 87 D6
Bonang ...... 63 C4
Bonavista .... 69 D5
Bondo ....... 56 D4
Bondoukou ... 55 G4
Bone, Teluk .. 39 E2
Bonerate ..... 39 F2
Bonerate,
  Kepulauan .. 39 F2
Bong Son =
  Hoai Nhon .. 36 B3
Bongandanga . 56 D4
Bongor ....... 53 F2
Bonifacio .... 13 F8
Bonn ......... 14 C4
Bonney, L. ... 62 C3
Bonny, Bight of 56 D1
Bonoi ........ 39 E5
Bontang ...... 37 D5
Bonthain ..... 39 F1
Bonthe ....... 55 G2
Bontoc ....... 38 A2
Boolaboolka L. 62 B3
Booligal ...... 63 B3
Boonah ...... 63 A5
Boorindal .... 63 B4
Boorowa ..... 63 B4
Boothia, Gulf of 68 A2
Boothia Pen. .. 70 A10
Booué ........ 56 E2
Bor,
  Serbia, Yug. . 22 B4
Bôr, Sudan ... 53 G5
Borama ...... 49 F3
Borås ........ 9 G10
Borāzjān ..... 44 D2
Borba ........ 90 D7
Borda, C. ..... 62 C2
Bordeaux .... 12 D3
Bordertown ... 62 C3
Bordj Fly Ste.
  Marie ...... 54 C4
Bordj-in-Eker . 54 D6
Bordj Omar
  Driss ...... 54 C6
Bordj-Tarat ... 54 C6
Borger ....... 78 B3
Borisoglebsk .. 24 C5
Borisov =
  Barysaw .... 17 A9
Borja ........ 90 D3
Borkou ....... 53 E2
Borkum ...... 14 B4
Borley, C. .... 96 A9
Borneo ....... 37 D4
Bornholm ..... 9 G11
Boromo ...... 55 F4
Borongan .... 38 B3
Borovichi .... 24 B3
Borşa ........ 17 E7

Borūjerd ...... 46 D7
Boryslav ...... 17 D6
Bosa ......... 21 D2
Bosanska
  Gradiška .... 20 B6
Bosaso ....... 49 E4
Boshan ....... 35 C6
Boshrūyeh .... 44 C4
Bosna → ..... 20 B7
Bosna i
  Hercegovina
  = Bosnia-
  Herzegovina ■ 20 B6
Bosnia-
  Herzegovina ■ 20 B6
Bosnik ....... 39 E5
Bosobolo ..... 56 D3
Bosporus =
  Karadeniz
  Boğazı ...... 22 D7
Bossangoa .... 56 C3
Bossembélé .. 53 G2
Bosso ........ 53 F1
Bosten Hu .... 34 B3
Boston, U.K. .. 11 E6
Boston, U.S.A. . 73 C10
Botany B. ..... 63 B5
Bothnia, G. of . 8 F12
Bothwell ..... 62 D4
Botletle → ... 58 C4
Botoşani ..... 17 E8
Botswana ■ ... 58 C4
Botucatu ..... 94 A7
Bou Djébéha .. 55 E4
Bou Izakarn .. 54 C3
Bouaké ...... 55 G3
Bouar ........ 56 C3
Bouârfa ...... 54 B4
Bouca ........ 56 C3
Bougie = Bejaia 54 A6
Bougouni ..... 55 F3
Boulder ...... 76 E2
Boulder Dam =
  Hoover Dam  82 B5
Boulogne-sur-
  Mer ........ 12 A4
Boultoum ..... 55 F7
Bouna ........ 55 G4
Boundiali ..... 55 G3
Bourbonnais . 13 C5
Bourem ...... 55 E4
Bourg-en-Bresse 13 C6
Bourg-St.-
  Maurice .... 13 D7
Bourges ...... 12 C5
Bourgogne ... 13 C6
Bourke ....... 63 B4
Bournemouth . 11 F6
Bousso ....... 53 F2
Boutilimit .... 55 E2
Bowen Mts. .. 63 C4
Bowman I. .... 96 A12
Bowmans ..... 62 B2
Bowral ....... 63 B5
Bowraville .... 63 B5
Boyne → .... 11 E3
Boyni Qara ... 45 B6
Boz Dağları .. 23 E7
Bozburun .... 23 F7
Bozcaada .... 23 E6
Bozdoğan .... 23 F7
Bozeman ..... 81 C8
Bozen =
  Bolzano .... 20 A3
Bozoum ...... 56 C3
Bra .......... 20 B1
Brač ......... 20 C6
Bracciano, L. di 20 C4
Brach ........ 52 C1

Bräcke ....... 8 F11
Brad ......... 17 E6
Bradenton .... 75 F6
Bradford ..... 11 E6
Braemar ...... 62 B2
Braga ........ 18 B1
Bragança, Brazil 92 C4
Bragança,
  Portugal .... 18 B2
Brahamapur .. 40 H5
Brahmanbaria . 41 F8
Brahmani → .. 40 G6
Brahmaputra → 41 F7
Braidwood .... 63 C4
Brăila ........ 17 F8
Branco → .... 90 D6
Brandenburg =
  Neubrandenburg
  ........... 15 B7
Brandenburg .. 15 B7
Brandenburg □ 15 B7
Brandon ...... 71 D10
Brandvlei ..... 58 E4
Braniewo ..... 16 A4
Bransfield Str. . 96 A4
Brantford .... 69 D2
Branxholme ... 62 C3
Brasiléia ...... 91 F5
Brasília ...... 93 F4
Braşov ....... 17 F7
Brassey,
  Banjaran ... 36 D5
Bratislava .... 16 D3
Bratsk ....... 30 D8
Braunau ...... 15 D7
Braunschweig . 14 B6
Brava ........ 49 G3
Bravo del Norte,
  R. → =
  Grande,
  Rio → ..... 79 F5
Brawley ...... 82 D5
Bray ......... 11 E3
Bray, Pays de . 12 B4
Brazil ■ ...... 93 E4
Brazos → .... 79 E6
Brazzaville ... 56 E3
Brčko ........ 20 B7
Breaksea Sd. .. 65 F2
Bream B. ..... 64 A6
Bream Hd. .... 64 A6
Brecon ....... 11 F5
Breda ........ 14 C3
Bredasdorp ... 58 E4
Bredbo ....... 63 C4
Bregenz ...... 14 E5
Brejo ........ 92 C5
Bremen ...... 14 B5
Bremerhaven . 14 B5
Bremerton ... 80 B2
Brenner P. ... 15 E6
Bréscia ...... 20 B3
Breslau =
  Wrocław .... 16 C3
Bressanone ... 20 A3
Brest, Belarus . 17 B6
Brest, France .. 12 B1
Brest-Litovsk =
  Brest ...... 17 B6
Bretagne ..... 12 B2
Brett, C. ..... 64 A6
Brewarrina ... 63 A4
Brezhnev =
  Naberezhnyye
  Chelny ..... 29 D6
Bria ......... 56 C4
Briançon ..... 13 D7
Bribie I. ...... 63 A5
Bridgeport ... 73 D9

# Bridgetown

Bridgetown ... 87 D8
Bridgewater ... 69 D4
Bridgewater, C. 62 C3
Bridlington .... 11 D6
Bridport ...... 62 D4
Brig ......... 13 C7
Brigham City .. 81 E7
Bright ...... 63 C4
Brighton,
*Australia* .... 62 C2
Brighton, *U.K.* . 11 F6
Bríndisi ...... 21 D6
Brinkworth ... 62 B2
Brisbane .... 63 A5
Brisbane → .. 63 A5
Bristol,
*U.K.* ........ 11 F5
Bristol,
*U.S.A.* ...... 75 A6
Bristol B. .... 71 C3
Bristol Channel 11 F4
Britstown ..... 58 E4
Brittany =
Bretagne .... 12 B2
Brive-la-
Gaillarde ... 12 D4
Brixen =
Bressanone . 20 A3
Brlik ......... 29 E8
Brno ...... 16 D3
Brocken ...... 14 C6
Brodeur Pen. .. 68 A2
Brodnica ...... 16 B4
Brody ........ 17 C7
Broken Hill =
Kabwe .... 59 A5
Broken Hill .... 62 B3
Bronte Park ... 62 D4
Brooks Ra. ... 71 B5
Brooloo ...... 63 A5
Broome ...... 60 D3
Brown, Pt. .... 62 B1
Brownsville ... 78 G5
Brownwood ... 78 D4
Bruay-en-Artois 13 A5
Bruce, Mt. ... 60 E2
Bruck an der
Mur ........ 15 E8
Bruges =
Brugge ..... 14 C2
Brugge ....... 14 C2
Brumado .. 93 E5
Brunei = Bandar
Seri Begawan 36 D5
Brunei ■ ... 36 D4
Brunner, L. .. 65 E4
Brunswick =
Braunschweig 14 B6
Brunswick ... 75 D7
Brunswick, Pen.
de ......... 95 G2
Brusque .. 94 B7
Brussel ....... 14 C3
Brussels =
Brussel ..... 14 C3
Bruthen ...... 63 C4
Bruxelles =
Brussel ..... 14 C3
Bryan ........ 79 D5
Bryan, Mt. .... 62 B2
Bryansk ...... 24 C3
Bu Craa ...... 54 C2
Buapinang .... 39 E2
Buayan ....... 38 C3
Bucak ........ 46 C2
Bucaramanga . 90 B4
Buchach ...... 17 D7
Buchanan ..... 55 G3
Buchans ...... 69 D5

Bucharest =
Bucureşti ... 22 B6
Buckie ....... 10 C5
Buckleboo .... 62 B2
Bucureşti ..... 22 B6
Budalin ....... 41 F10
Budapest .... 16 E4
Budd Coast ... 96 A12
Bude ......... 11 F4
Budennovsk ... 25 E5
Budgewoi .... 63 B5
Budjala ....... 56 D3
Buenaventura . 90 C3
Buenos Aires . 94 C5
Buenos Aires, L. 95 F2
Buffalo ....... 73 C6
Bug → =
Buh → ..... 25 D3
Bug → ..... 16 B5
Buga ........ 90 C3
Bugel, Tanjung 37 F4
Bugsuk ....... 36 C5
Bugun Shara .. 35 B5
Buguruslan ... 29 D6
Buh → ..... 25 D3
Buheirat-Murrat-
el-Kubra ... 52 B5
Buir Nur ...... 35 B6
Bujumbura ... 57 E5
Bukama ...... 57 F5
Bukavu ...... 57 E5
Bukene ...... 57 E6
Bukhara =
Bukhoro .... 29 F7
Bukhoro ..... 29 F7
Bukittinggi ... 37 E2
Bukoba ...... 57 E6
Bula ........ 39 E4
Bulahdelah ... 63 B5
Bulan ........ 38 B2
Bulandshahr .. 42 E10
Bulawayo .... 59 C5
Buldan ....... 23 E7
Bulgan ....... 35 B5
Bulgaria ■ ... 22 C5
Bulgroo ...... 63 A3
Bulgunnia .... 62 B1
Bulhar ....... 49 E3
Buli, Teluk ... 39 D3
Buliluyan, C. .. 36 C5
Bulli ........ 63 B5
Bulloo → .... 63 A3
Bulloo Downs . 62 A3
Bulloo L. ..... 62 A3
Bulls ........ 64 D6
Bulo Burti .... 49 G4
Bulsar = Valsad 43 J8
Bulukumba ... 39 F2
Bulun ........ 30 B10
Bumba ....... 56 D4
Bumhpa Bum . 41 D11
Buna ........ 57 D7
Bunbah, Khalīj . 52 B3
Bunbury ...... 60 G2
Buncrana ..... 11 D3
Bundaberg .... 63
Bundi ........ 43 G9
Bundoran ..... 11 D2
Bungo-Suidō .. 32 C3
Bunia ........ 57 D6
Bunji ........ 42 B9
Buntok ....... 37 E4
Bunyu ........ 37 D5
Buol ........ 39 D2
Buon Me Thuot 36 B3
Buorkhaya, Mys 31 B11
Buqayq ...... 47 F7
Bur Acaba .... 49 G3
Bûr Safâga ... 52 C5

Bûr Sa'îd ... 52 B5
Bûr Sûdân ... 53 E6
Burao ........ 49 F4
Buraydah ..... 47 F6
Buraymī, Al
Wāhāt al .... 44 E3
Burcher ...... 63 B4
Burdur ....... 46 C2
Burdwan =
Barddhaman 40 F6
Burgas ....... 22 C6
Burgersdorp .. 59 E5
Burgos ...... 18 A4
Burgundy =
Bourgogne .. 13 C6
Burhaniye .... 23 E6
Burhanpur ... 43 J10
Burias ........ 38 B2
Buriram ...... 36 A2
Burji ........ 53 G6
Burkina Faso ■ 55 F4
Burlington,
*Iowa, U.S.A.* . 77 E9
Burlington, *N.C.,*
*U.S.A.* ...... 75 A8
Burlington, *Vt.,*
*U.S.A.* ...... 73 B9
Burlyu-Tyube .. 29 E8
Burma ■ ..... 41 G11
Burnie ....... 62 D4
Burnley ...... 11 E5
Burnside → .. 70 B9
Burqān ....... 47 E6
Burqin ....... 34 B3
Burra ........ 62 B2
Burren Junction 63 B4
Burrendong
Dam ...... 63 B4
Burrinjuck Res. 63 C4
Burruyacú .... 94 B4
Bursa ........ 23 D7
Burtundy ..... 62 B3
Buru ......... 39 E3
Burundi ■ ... 57 E6
Burutu ....... 55 G6
Bury St.
Edmunds .. 11 E7
Buşayyah .... 47 E6
Büshehr ...... 44 D2
Büshehr □ .... 44 D2
Bushire =
Büshehr .... 44 D2
Businga ...... 56 D4
Busra ash Shām 46 D4
Busto Arsízio . 20 B2
Busu-Djanoa .. 56 D4
Busuanga .... 38 B1
Buta ......... 57 D4
Butare ....... 57 E5
Butaritari ..... 64 J12
Butembo ...... 57 D5
Butha Qi ..... 35 B7
Buton ........ 39 E2
Butte ........ 81 B7
Butterworth .. 36 C2
Butuan ....... 38 C3
Butung = Buton 39 E2
Buturlinovka .. 24 C5
Buxtehude ... 14 B5
Buy ......... 24 B5
Büyük
Menderes → 23 F6
Büyükçekmece 22 D7
Buzău ....... 17 F8
Buzău → .... 17 F8
Buzen ........ 32 C2
Buzi → ..... 59 B6
Buzi → ...... 59 B6
Buzuluk ...... 29 D6
Byarezina → .. 17 B10

Bydgoszcz .... 16 B3
Byelarus =
Belarus ■ ... 24 C2
Byelorussia =
Belarus ■ ... 24 C2
Bykhaw ...... 17 B10
Bykhov =
Bykhaw .... 17 B10
Bylot I. ....... 68 A3
Byrd, C. ...... 96 A3
Byrock ...... 63 B4
Byron Bay .... 63 A5
Byrranga, Gory 30 B8
Byrranga Mts. =
Byrranga,
Gory ...... 30 B8
Bytom ...... 16 C4
Bytów ........ 16 A3

## C

Ca Mau = Quan
Long ....... 36 C3
Caála ........ 58 A3
Cabanatuan ... 38 A2
Cabedelo ..... 92 D7
Cabimas ...... 90 A4
Cabinda ...... 56 F2
Cabinda □ .... 56 F2
Cabinet Mts. .. 81 B6
Cabo Blanco .. 95 F3
Cabo Frio .... 93 G5
Cabo Pantoja .. 90 D3
Cabonga,
Réservoir ... 69 D3
Caboolture .... 63 A5
Cabora Bassa
Dam =
Cahora Bassa
Dam ...... 59 B6
Cabot Str. .... 69 D5
Cabra ........ 18 D3
Cabrera ...... 19 C7
Cabriel → .... 19 C5
Čačak ...... 22 C3
Cáceres, *Brazil* . 91 G7
Cáceres, *Spain* 18 C2
Cachimbo, Serra
do ......... 93 D2
Cachoeira .... 93 E6
Cachoeira de
Itapemirim .. 93 G5
Cachoeira do
Sul ........ 94 C6
Cacólo ...... 56 G3
Caconda ..... 58 A3
Cacongo ..... 56 F2
Cadibarrawirracanna,
L. ......... 62 A2
Cadiz, *Phil.* .... 38 B2
Cádiz, *Spain* .. 18 D2
Cádiz, G. de .. 18 D2
Cadney Park .. 62 A1
Caen ........ 12 B3
Caeté ....... 93 F5
Caetité ...... 93 E5
Cagayan → .. 38 A2
Cagayan de Oro 38 C2
Cágliari ...... 21 E2
Cágliari, G. di . 21 E2
Caguas ...... 87 C6
Cahora Bassa
Dam ...... 59 B6
Cahors ...... 12 D4
Cahuapanas .. 91 E3
Cahul ........ 17 F9

| Name | Map | Grid |
|---|---|---|
| Caia | 59 | B7 |
| Caibarién | 86 | B4 |
| Caicara | 90 | B5 |
| Caicó | 92 | D6 |
| Caicos Is. | 87 | B5 |
| Caird Coast | 96 | B5 |
| Cairns | 61 | D8 |
| Cairo = El Qâhira | 52 | B5 |
| Cairo | 79 | A9 |
| Caiundo | 58 | B3 |
| Caiza | 91 | H5 |
| Cajamarca | 91 | E3 |
| Cajàzeiras | 92 | D6 |
| Calabar | 55 | H6 |
| Calábria □ | 21 | A4 |
| Calafate | 95 | G2 |
| Calahorra | 19 | A5 |
| Calais | 12 | A4 |
| Calama, *Brazil* | 91 | E6 |
| Calama, *Chile* | 94 | A3 |
| Calamar, *Bolívar, Colombia* | 90 | A4 |
| Calamar, *Vaupés, Colombia* | 90 | C4 |
| Calamian Group | 38 | B1 |
| Calamocha | 19 | B5 |
| Calang | 36 | D1 |
| Calapan | 38 | B2 |
| Călăraşi | 22 | B6 |
| Calatayud | 19 | B5 |
| Calauag | 38 | B2 |
| Calavite, C. | 38 | B2 |
| Calbayog | 38 | B2 |
| Calca | 91 | F4 |
| Calcutta | 41 | F7 |
| Caldas da Rainha | 18 | C1 |
| Caldera | 94 | B2 |
| Caldwell | 80 | D5 |
| Caledon | 58 | E3 |
| Caledon → | 59 | E5 |
| Calgary | 71 | C8 |
| Cali | 90 | C3 |
| Calicut | 43 | P9 |
| California □ | 82 | B3 |
| California, G. de | 84 | B2 |
| Calingasta | 94 | C3 |
| Callabonna, L. | 62 | A3 |
| Callao | 91 | F3 |
| Caloundra | 63 | A5 |
| Caltagirone | 21 | F5 |
| Caltanissetta | 21 | F5 |
| Calulo | 56 | G2 |
| Calunda | 58 | A4 |
| Calvi | 13 | E8 |
| Calviá | 19 | C7 |
| Calvinia | 58 | E3 |
| Camabatela | 56 | F4 |
| Camacupa | 58 | A3 |
| Camagüey | 86 | B4 |
| Camaná | 91 | G4 |
| Camargo | 91 | H5 |
| Camargue | 13 | E6 |
| Camarones | 95 | E3 |
| Cambay = Khambhat | 43 | H8 |
| Cambay, G. of = Khambat, G. of | 43 | J8 |
| Cambodia ■ | 36 | B3 |
| Cambrai | 13 | A5 |
| Cambrian Mts. | 11 | E5 |
| Cambridge, *N.Z.* | 64 | B6 |
| Cambridge, *U.K.* | 11 | E7 |
| Cambridge, *U.S.A.* | 73 | C10 |
| Cambridge Bay = Ikaluktutiak | 70 | B9 |
| Cambridge G. | 60 | C4 |
| Cambundi-Catembo | 56 | G3 |
| Camden, *Ark., U.S.A.* | 79 | C7 |
| Camden, *N.J., U.S.A.* | 73 | E8 |
| Cameroon ■ | 56 | C2 |
| Cameroun, Mt. | 56 | D1 |
| Cametá | 92 | C4 |
| Caminha | 18 | B1 |
| Camira Creek | 63 | A5 |
| Camissombo | 56 | F4 |
| Camocim | 92 | C5 |
| Camopi → | 92 | B3 |
| Campana, I. | 95 | F1 |
| Campánia □ | 21 | D5 |
| Campbell Town | 62 | D4 |
| Campbellton | 69 | D4 |
| Campbelltown | 63 | B5 |
| Campbeltown | 10 | D4 |
| Campeche | 85 | D6 |
| Campeche, B. de | 85 | D6 |
| Camperdown | 62 | C3 |
| Campina Grande | 92 | D6 |
| Campinas | 94 | A7 |
| Campo | 56 | D1 |
| Campo Belo | 93 | G4 |
| Campo Formoso | 93 | E5 |
| Campo Grande | 93 | G3 |
| Campo Maíor | 92 | C5 |
| Campo Mourão | 93 | G3 |
| Campoalegre | 90 | C3 |
| Campobasso | 20 | D5 |
| Campos | 93 | G5 |
| Campos Belos | 93 | E4 |
| Campuya → | 90 | D4 |
| Camrose | 71 | C8 |
| Çan | 23 | D6 |
| Can Tho | 36 | B3 |
| Canada ■ | 70 | C8 |
| Cañada de Gómez | 94 | C4 |
| Çanakkale | 23 | D6 |
| Çanakkale Boğazı | 23 | D6 |
| Cananea | 84 | A2 |
| Canarias, Is. | 54 | C1 |
| Canary Is. = Canarias, Is. | 54 | C1 |
| Canavieiras | 93 | F6 |
| Canbelego | 63 | B4 |
| Canberra | 63 | C4 |
| Candala | 49 | E4 |
| Candelo | 63 | C4 |
| Candia = Iráklion | 23 | G5 |
| Canea = Khaniá | 23 | G5 |
| Canelones | 94 | C5 |
| Cañete, *Chile* | 94 | D2 |
| Cañete, *Peru* | 91 | F3 |
| Cangas de Narcea | 18 | A2 |
| Canguaretama | 92 | D6 |
| Canguçu | 94 | C6 |
| Canicattì | 21 | F4 |
| Canigou, Mt. | 12 | E5 |
| Canipaan | 36 | C5 |
| Çankırı | 46 | B3 |
| Cann River | 63 | C4 |
| Cannanore | 43 | P9 |
| Cannes | 13 | E7 |
| Canoas | 94 | B6 |
| Canora | 71 | C9 |
| Canowindra | 63 | B4 |
| Cantabria □ | 18 | A4 |
| Cantabrian Mts. = Cantábrica, Cordillera | 18 | A3 |
| Cantábrica, Cordillera | 18 | A3 |
| Cantal, Plomb du | 13 | D5 |
| Canterbury | 11 | F7 |
| Canterbury □ | 65 | E4 |
| Canterbury Bight | 65 | F4 |
| Canterbury Plains | 65 | E4 |
| Canton = Guangzhou | 35 | D6 |
| Canton | 72 | D5 |
| Canudos | 91 | E7 |
| Canutama | 91 | E6 |
| Cap-Haïtien | 87 | C5 |
| Cap St.-Jacques = Vung Tau | 36 | B3 |
| Capaia | 56 | F4 |
| Capanaparo → | 90 | B5 |
| Cape Barren I. | 62 | D4 |
| Cape Breton I. | 69 | D4 |
| Cape Coast | 55 | G4 |
| Cape Dorset | 68 | B3 |
| Cape Girardeau | 79 | A9 |
| Cape Jervis | 62 | C2 |
| Cape Town | 58 | E3 |
| Cape Verde Is. ■ | 50 | E1 |
| Cape York Peninsula | 61 | C7 |
| Capela | 93 | E6 |
| Capim → | 92 | C4 |
| Capraia | 20 | C2 |
| Capri | 21 | D5 |
| Caprivi Strip | 58 | B4 |
| Captain's Flat | 63 | C4 |
| Caquetá → | 90 | D5 |
| Caracal | 22 | B5 |
| Caracas | 90 | A5 |
| Caracol | 93 | D5 |
| Caradoc | 62 | B3 |
| Carajás, Serra dos | 92 | D3 |
| Carangola | 93 | G5 |
| Caransebeş | 17 | F6 |
| Caratasca, L. | 86 | C3 |
| Caratinga | 93 | F5 |
| Caraúbas | 92 | D6 |
| Caravaca | 19 | C5 |
| Caravelas | 93 | F6 |
| Caraveli | 91 | G4 |
| Carballo | 18 | A1 |
| Carbonara, C. | 21 | E2 |
| Carbondale | 79 | A9 |
| Carbonear | 69 | D5 |
| Carbonia | 21 | E2 |
| Carcassonne | 12 | E5 |
| Carcross | 70 | B6 |
| Cardamon Hills | 43 | Q10 |
| Cárdenas | 86 | B3 |
| Cardiff | 11 | F5 |
| Cardigan B. | 11 | E4 |
| Cardston | 71 | D8 |
| Carei | 17 | E6 |
| Careysburg | 55 | G2 |
| Carhué | 94 | D4 |
| Caria | 23 | F7 |
| Cariacica | 93 | G5 |
| Caribbean Sea | 86 | D5 |
| Cariboo Mts. | 71 | C7 |
| Carinda | 63 | B4 |
| Carinhanha | 93 | E5 |
| Carinthia □ = Kärnten □ | 15 | E7 |
| Caripito | 90 | A6 |
| Caritianas | 91 | E6 |
| Carlisle | 11 | D5 |
| Carlow | 11 | E3 |
| Carlsbad | 78 | C1 |
| Carmacks | 70 | B6 |
| Carman | 71 | D10 |
| Carmarthen | 11 | F4 |
| Carmaux | 12 | D5 |
| Carmelo | 94 | C5 |
| Carmen | 90 | B3 |
| Carmen de Patagones | 95 | E4 |
| Carmona | 18 | D3 |
| Carnac | 12 | C2 |
| Carnarvon, *Australia* | 60 | E1 |
| Carnarvon, *S. Africa* | 58 | E4 |
| Carnegie, L. | 60 | F3 |
| Carnic Alps = Karnische Alpen | 20 | A4 |
| Carniche Alpi = Karnische Alpen | 20 | A4 |
| Carnot | 56 | D3 |
| Carnot, C. | 62 | B2 |
| Carolina | 92 | D4 |
| Caroline I. | 65 | K15 |
| Caroline Is. | 64 | J10 |
| Caroni → | 90 | B6 |
| Caronie = Nébrodi, Monti | 21 | F5 |
| Caroona | 63 | B5 |
| Carpathians | 16 | D5 |
| Carpaţii Meridionali | 17 | F7 |
| Carpentaria, G. of | 60 | C6 |
| Carpentras | 13 | D6 |
| Carpi | 20 | B3 |
| Carpolac = Morea | 62 | C3 |
| Carrara | 20 | B3 |
| Carrauntoohill | 11 | E2 |
| Carrick-on-Suir | 11 | E3 |
| Carrieton | 62 | B2 |
| Carrizal Bajo | 94 | B2 |
| Çarşamba | 46 | B4 |
| Carson City | 80 | F4 |
| Cartagena, *Colombia* | 90 | A3 |
| Cartagena, *Spain* | 19 | D5 |
| Cartago, *Colombia* | 90 | C3 |
| Cartago, *Costa Rica* | 86 | E3 |
| Carterton | 65 | D6 |
| Carthage | 79 | A6 |
| Cartwright | 68 | C5 |
| Caruaru | 92 | D6 |
| Carúpano | 90 | A6 |
| Carvoeiro | 90 | D6 |
| Carvoeiro, C. | 18 | C1 |
| Casablanca | 54 | B3 |
| Cascade Ra. | 80 | B3 |
| Cascais | 18 | C1 |
| Cascavel | 94 | A6 |
| Cáscina | 20 | C3 |
| Caserta | 20 | D5 |
| Casiguran | 38 | A2 |
| Casilda | 94 | C4 |
| Casino | 63 | A5 |
| Casiquiare → | 90 | C5 |
| Casma | 91 | E3 |
| Caspe | 19 | B5 |
| Casper | 81 | D10 |

| | | |
|---|---|---|
| Caspian Sea | 29 | E6 |
| Cassinga | 58 | B3 |
| Castellammare | | |
| di Stábia | 21 | D5 |
| Castellón de la | | |
| Plana | 19 | C5 |
| Castelo Branco | 18 | C2 |
| Castelsarrasin | 12 | D4 |
| Castelvetrano | 21 | F4 |
| Casterton | 62 | C3 |
| Castilla La | | |
| Mancha □ | 18 | C4 |
| Castilla y | | |
| Leon □ | 18 | A3 |
| Castlebar | 11 | E2 |
| Castleblaney | 11 | D3 |
| Castlemaine | 63 | C3 |
| Castlereagh → | 63 | B4 |
| Castres | 12 | E5 |
| Castries | 87 | D7 |
| Castro | 95 | E2 |
| Castro Alves | 93 | E6 |
| Castuera | 18 | C3 |
| Cat I. | 86 | B4 |
| Catacáos | 91 | E2 |
| Catalão | 93 | F4 |
| Çatalca | 22 | D7 |
| Catalonia = | | |
| Cataluña □ | 19 | B6 |
| Cataluña □ | 19 | B6 |
| Catamarca | 94 | B3 |
| Catanduanes | 38 | B2 |
| Catanduva | 93 | G4 |
| Catánia | 21 | F5 |
| Catanzaro | 21 | E6 |
| Catarman | 38 | B2 |
| Cateel | 38 | C3 |
| Catoche, C. | 85 | C7 |
| Catrimani | 90 | C6 |
| Catskill Mts. | 73 | C8 |
| Cauca → | 90 | B4 |
| Caucaia | 92 | C6 |
| Caucasus | | |
| Mountains | 25 | E5 |
| Caúngula | 56 | F3 |
| Cauquenes | 94 | D2 |
| Caura → | 90 | B6 |
| Cauvery → | 43 | P11 |
| Caux, Pays de | 12 | B4 |
| Cavan | 11 | D3 |
| Cavendish | 62 | C3 |
| Caviana, I. | 92 | B3 |
| Cavite | 38 | B2 |
| Cawndilla L. | 62 | B3 |
| Cawnpore = | | |
| Kanpur | 40 | D3 |
| Caxias | 92 | C5 |
| Caxias do Sul | 94 | B6 |
| Caxito | 56 | F2 |
| Cayambe | 90 | C3 |
| Cayenne | 92 | A3 |
| Cayman Is. ■ | 67 | H11 |
| Cazombo | 58 | A4 |
| Ceadâr-Lunga | 17 | E9 |
| Ceanannus Mor | 11 | E3 |
| Ceará = | | |
| Fortaleza | 92 | C6 |
| Ceará □ | 92 | D6 |
| Ceará Mirim | 92 | D6 |
| Cebollar | 94 | B3 |
| Cebu | 38 | B2 |
| Cecil Plains | 63 | A5 |
| Cedar L. | 71 | C10 |
| Cedar Rapids | 77 | E9 |
| Cedro | 92 | D6 |
| Ceduna | 62 | B1 |
| Cefalù | 21 | E5 |
| Ceglèd | 16 | E4 |
| Celaya | 84 | C4 |

| | | |
|---|---|---|
| Celebes = | | |
| Sulawesi □ | 39 | E2 |
| Celebes Sea | 39 | D2 |
| Celje | 20 | A5 |
| Celle | 14 | B6 |
| Celtic Sea | 11 | F2 |
| Central, | | |
| Cordillera | 90 | C3 |
| Central African | | |
| Rep. ■ | 56 | C4 |
| Central Makran | | |
| Range | 42 | F4 |
| Cephalonia = | | |
| Kefallinía | 23 | E3 |
| Ceram = Seram | 39 | E3 |
| Ceram Sea = | | |
| Seram Sea | 39 | E3 |
| Ceres, Argentina | 94 | B4 |
| Ceres, S. Africa | 58 | E3 |
| Cerignola | 20 | D5 |
| Cerigo = Kíthira | 23 | F4 |
| Çerkeş | 46 | B3 |
| Çerkeşköy | 22 | D6 |
| Cervera | 19 | B6 |
| Cesena | 20 | B4 |
| Česka Republika | | |
| = Czech | | |
| Rep. ■ | 16 | D2 |
| České | | |
| Budějovice | 16 | D2 |
| Ceskomoravská | | |
| Vrchovina | 16 | D2 |
| Çeşme | 23 | E6 |
| Cessnock | 63 | B5 |
| Cetinje | 22 | C2 |
| Cetraro | 21 | E5 |
| Ceuta | 18 | E3 |
| Cévennes | 13 | D5 |
| Ceyhan | 46 | C3 |
| Ceylon = Sri | | |
| Lanka ■ | 43 | R12 |
| Chachapoyas | 91 | E3 |
| Chachran | 42 | E7 |
| Chad ■ | 53 | E2 |
| Chad, L. = | | |
| Tchad, L. | 53 | F1 |
| Chadileuvú → | 94 | D3 |
| Chadyr-Lunga = | | |
| Ceadâr-Lunga | 17 | E9 |
| Chagai Hills | 42 | E3 |
| Chagos Arch. | 27 | K11 |
| Chāh Bahār | 45 | E5 |
| Chāh Gay Hills | 45 | D6 |
| Chahar Burjak | 42 | D3 |
| Chaibasa | 40 | F5 |
| Chakhānsūr | 42 | D3 |
| Chakradharpur | 40 | F5 |
| Chakwal | 42 | C8 |
| Chala | 91 | G4 |
| Chalcis = | | |
| Khalkís | 23 | E4 |
| Chalhuanca | 91 | F4 |
| Chalisgaon | 43 | J9 |
| Chalky Inlet | 65 | G2 |
| Challapata | 91 | G5 |
| Chalon-sur- | | |
| Saône | 13 | C6 |
| Châlons-en- | | |
| Champagne | 13 | B6 |
| Chaman | 42 | D5 |
| Chamba, India | 42 | C10 |
| Chamba, | | |
| Tanzania | 59 | A7 |
| Chambal → | 42 | F11 |
| Chambéry | 13 | D6 |
| Chamical | 94 | C3 |
| Chamonix-Mont | | |
| Blanc | 13 | D7 |
| Champagne | 13 | B6 |

| | | |
|---|---|---|
| Champaign | 72 | D1 |
| Champlain, L. | 73 | B9 |
| Chañaral | 94 | B2 |
| Chandigarh | 42 | D10 |
| Chandler | 62 | A1 |
| Chandmani | 34 | B4 |
| Chandpur | 41 | F8 |
| Chandrapur | 43 | K11 |
| Chang Jiang → | 35 | C7 |
| Changanacheri | 43 | Q10 |
| Changane → | 59 | C6 |
| Changchiak'ou | | |
| = Zhangjiakou | 35 | B6 |
| Ch'angchou = | | |
| Changzhou | 35 | C6 |
| Changchun | 35 | B7 |
| Changde | 35 | D6 |
| Changhai = | | |
| Shanghai | 35 | C7 |
| Changjiang | 35 | E5 |
| Changsha | 35 | D6 |
| Changting | 35 | D6 |
| Changzhi | 35 | C6 |
| Changzhou | 35 | C6 |
| Channapatna | 43 | N10 |
| Channel Is. | 11 | G5 |
| Chantada | 18 | A2 |
| Chanthaburi | 36 | B2 |
| Chantrey Inlet | 70 | B10 |
| Chanute | 79 | A6 |
| Chao Phraya → | 36 | B2 |
| Chao'an | 35 | D6 |
| Chaoyang | 35 | D6 |
| Chapala, L. de | 84 | C4 |
| Chapayevsk | 24 | C6 |
| Chapra = | | |
| Chhapra | 40 | E5 |
| Châr | 54 | D2 |
| Chara | 31 | D9 |
| Charadai | 94 | B5 |
| Charagua | 91 | G6 |
| Charaña | 91 | G5 |
| Chardara | 29 | E7 |
| Chardzhou = | | |
| Chärjew | 29 | F7 |
| Charente → | 12 | D3 |
| Chari → | 53 | F1 |
| Chārīkār | 42 | B6 |
| Chärjew | 29 | F7 |
| Charleroi | 14 | C3 |
| Charles, C. | 73 | F8 |
| Charleston, S.C., | | |
| U.S.A. | 75 | C8 |
| Charleston, | | |
| W. Va., U.S.A. | 72 | E5 |
| Charlesville | 56 | F4 |
| Charleville | 63 | A4 |
| Charleville- | | |
| Mézières | 13 | B6 |
| Charlotte | 75 | B7 |
| Charlotte Amalie | 87 | C7 |
| Charlottesville | 73 | E6 |
| Charlottetown | 69 | D4 |
| Charlton | 62 | C3 |
| Charolles | 13 | C6 |
| Charouine | 54 | C4 |
| Charters Towers | 61 | E8 |
| Chartres | 12 | B4 |
| Chascomús | 94 | D5 |
| Châteaubriant | 12 | C3 |
| Châteaulin | 12 | B1 |
| Châteauroux | 12 | C4 |
| Châtellerault | 12 | C4 |
| Chatham, N.B., | | |
| Canada | 69 | D4 |
| Chatham, Ont., | | |
| Canada | 69 | D2 |
| Chatham, U.K. | 11 | F7 |
| Chatrapur | 40 | H5 |

| | | |
|---|---|---|
| Chattahoochee → | | |
| | 74 | D5 |
| Chattanooga | 74 | B5 |
| Chauk | 41 | G10 |
| Chaukan La | 41 | D11 |
| Chaumont | 13 | B6 |
| Chaves, Brazil | 92 | C4 |
| Chaves, Portugal | 18 | B2 |
| Chavuma | 58 | A4 |
| Cheb | 16 | C1 |
| Cheboksary | 24 | B6 |
| Chech, Erg | 54 | D4 |
| Chechenia □ | 25 | E6 |
| Checheno- | | |
| Ingush | | |
| Republic = | | |
| Chechenia □ | 25 | E6 |
| Chechnya = | | |
| Chechenia □ | 25 | E6 |
| Cheduba I. | 41 | H9 |
| Cheepie | 63 | A4 |
| Chegga | 54 | C3 |
| Chegutu | 59 | B6 |
| Chehalis | 80 | B2 |
| Cheju Do | 35 | C7 |
| Chekiang = | | |
| Zhejiang □ | 35 | D7 |
| Cheleken | 29 | F6 |
| Chelforó | 95 | D3 |
| Chelkar | 29 | E6 |
| Chelkar Tengiz, | | |
| Solonchak | 29 | E7 |
| Chelm | 17 | C6 |
| Chelmno | 16 | B4 |
| Chelmsford | 11 | F7 |
| Cheltenham | 11 | F5 |
| Chelyabinsk | 29 | D7 |
| Chemnitz | 15 | C7 |
| Chen Xian | 35 | D6 |
| Chenab → | 42 | D7 |
| Chencha | 53 | G6 |
| Chenchiang = | | |
| Zhenjiang | 35 | C6 |
| Chengde | 35 | B6 |
| Chengdu | 35 | C5 |
| Chengjiang | 34 | D5 |
| Ch'engtu = | | |
| Chengdu | 35 | C5 |
| Chennai = | | |
| Madras | 43 | N12 |
| Cheo Reo | 36 | B3 |
| Cheom Ksan | 36 | B2 |
| Chepén | 91 | E3 |
| Chepes | 94 | C3 |
| Cher → | 12 | C4 |
| Cherbourg | 12 | B3 |
| Cherchell | 54 | A5 |
| Cherdyn | 28 | C6 |
| Cherepanovo | 29 | D9 |
| Cherepovets | 24 | B4 |
| Chergui, Chott | | |
| ech | 54 | B5 |
| Cherikov = | | |
| Cherykaw | 17 | B10 |
| Cherkasy | 24 | D3 |
| Cherlak | 29 | D8 |
| Chernaya | 30 | B6 |
| Chernigov = | | |
| Chernihiv | 24 | C3 |
| Chernihiv | 24 | C3 |
| Chernivtsi | 17 | D7 |
| Chernobyl = | | |
| Chornobyl | 17 | C10 |
| Chernovtsy = | | |
| Chernivtsi | 17 | D7 |
| Chernyakhovsk | 28 | D3 |
| Cherquenco | 94 | D2 |
| Cherrapunji | 41 | E8 |

Cherven . . . . . . 17 B9
Chervonohrad . 17 C7
Cherykaw . . . . 17 B10
Chesapeake . . 73 F7
Chesapeake B. . 73 E7
Cheshskaya
Guba . . . . 28 C5
Chester, U.K. . . 11 E5
Chester, U.S.A. 73 E8
Chesterfield . . . 11 E6
Chesterfield, Is. 64 L10
Chesterfield Inlet 70 B10
Chesterton Ra. 63 A4
Cheviot Hills . . 10 D5
Chew Bahir . . . 53 H6
Cheyenne . . . . 76 E2
Cheyenne ⟶ . 76 C4
Chhapra . . . . . . 40 E5
Chhatarpur . . . 43 G11
Chhattisgarh
□ . . . . . . . . 40 G3
Chhindwara . . 43 H11
Chhlong . . . . . 36 B3
Chi ⟶ . . . . . . 36 A2
Chiamussu =
Jiamusi . . . . . 35 B8
Chiange . . . . . . 58 B2
Chiapa ⟶ . . . 85 D6
Chiávari . . . . . . 20 B2
Chiavenna . . . 20 A2
Chiba . . . . . . . . 32 B7
Chibemba . . . . 58 B2
Chibia . . . . . . . 58 B2
Chibougamau . 69 D3
Chibuk . . . . . . . 53 F1
Chicacole =
Srikakulam . . 40 H4
Chicago . . . . . . 72 D2
Chichagof I. . . 71 C6
Chichibu . . . . . 32 A6
Chickasha . . . . 78 B5
Chiclana de la
Frontera . . . 18 D2
Chiclayo . . . . . . 91 E3
Chico . . . . . . . . 80 F3
Chico ⟶,
Chubut,
Argentina . . . 95 E3
Chico ⟶,
Santa Cruz,
Argentina . . . 95 F3
Chicoutimi . . . 69 D3
Chidambaram . 43 P11
Chidley, C. . . . 68 B4
Chiemsee . . . . 15 E7
Chiengi . . . . . . 57 F5
Chiese ⟶ . . . 20 B3
Chieti . . . . . . . . 20 C5
Chiguana . . . . . 91 H5
Chihli, G. of =
Bo Hai . . . 35 C6
Chihuahua . . . . 84 B3
Chiili . . . . . . . . 29 E7
Chik Bollapur . 43 N10
Chikmagalur . 43 N9
Chilapa . . . . . . 84 D5
Chilas . . . . . . . . 42 B9
Chilaw . . . . . . 43 R11
Childers . . . . . . 63 A5
Chile ■ . . . . . . . 94 D2
Chilete . . . . . . . 91 E3
Chililabombwe 59 A5
Chilin = Jilin . . 35 B7
Chilka L. . . . . . 40 H5
Chillán . . . . . . . 94 D2
Chiloé, I. de . . . 95 E2
Chilpancingo . . 84 D5
Chiluage . . . . . 56 F4
Chilwa, L. . . . . 59 B7

Chimbay . . . . . 29 E6
Chimborazo . . . 90 D3
Chimbote . . . . . 91 E3
Chimkent =
Shymkent . . . 29 E7
Chimoio . . . . . . 59 B6
Chin □ . . . . . . . 41 F9
China ■ . . . . . . 35 C5
Chinan = Jinan 35 C6
Chinandega . . 85 E7
Chincha Alta . . 91 F3
Chinchilla . . . . . 63 A5
Chinchou =
Jinzhou . . . . 35 B7
Chinde . . . . . . . 59 B7
Chindwin ⟶ . . 41 G10
Chingola . . . . . 59 A5
Ch'ingtao =
Qingdao . . . . 35 C7
Chinguetti . . . 54 D2
Chinhoyi . . . . . 59 B6
Chiniot . . . . . . . 42 D8
Chinju . . . . . . . 35 C7
Chinnampo . . . 35 C7
Chinon . . . . . . . 12 C4
Chinsali . . . . . . 57 G6
Chióggia . . . . . 20 B4
Chíos = Khíos . 23 E6
Chipata . . . . . . 59 A6
Chiquián . . . . . 91 F3
Chiquinquira . . 90 B4
Chirchiq . . . . . . 29 E7
Chirmiri . . . . . . 40 F4
Chiromo . . . . . . 59 B7
Chisamba . . . . 59 A5
Chisapani Garhi 40 D5
Chişinău . . . . . 17 E9
Chistopol . . . . 24 B7
Chita . . . . . . . . 30 D9
Chitado . . . . . . 58 B2
Chitembo . . . . . 58 A3
Chitral . . . . . . . 42 B7
Chitré . . . . . . . 86 E3
Chittagong . . . . 41 F8
Chittagong □ . . 41 E8
Chittaurgarh . . 43 G9
Chittoor . . . . . . 43 N11
Chiusi . . . . . . . 20 C3
Chivasso . . . . . 20 B1
Chivilcoy . . . . . 94 B4
Chkalov =
Orenburg . . . 29 D6
Choele Choel . . 95 D3
Chojnice . . . . . 16 B3
Cholet . . . . . . . 12 C3
Choluteca . . . . 85 E7
Choma . . . . . . . 59 B5
Chomutov . . . . 16 C1
Chon Buri . . . . 36 B2
Chone . . . . . . . . 90 D3
Chŏngjin . . . . . 35 B7
Chŏngju . . . . . 35 C7
Chongqing . . . . 35 D5
Chŏnju . . . . . . 35 C7
Chonos, Arch.
de los . . . . . 95 F2
Chop . . . . . . . . 17 D6
Chornobyl . . . . 17 C10
Chortkiv . . . . . . 17 D7
Chorzów . . . . . 16 C4
Chos-Malal . . . 94 D2
Chōshi . . . . . . . 32 B7
Choszczno . . . . 16 B2
Choybalsan . . . 35 B6
Christchurch . . 65 E5
Christiana . . . . 59 D5
Christmas I. =
Kiritimati . . . 65 J15

Chu = Shu . . . . 29 E8
Ch'uanchou =
Quanzhou . . . 35 D6
Chubut ⟶ . . . 95 E3
Chudskoye, Oz. 24 B2
Chūgoku-Sanchi 32 B3
Chula Vista . . . 82 D4
Chulucanas . . . 90 E2
Chulym ⟶ . . . 29 D9
Chumbicha . . . 94 B3
Chumphon . . . . 36 B1
Chuna ⟶ . . . . 30 D7
Chunchŏn . . . . 35 C7
Chungking =
Chongqing . . 35 D5
Chunya . . . . . . 57 F6
Chuquibamba . 91 G4
Chuquicamata . 94 A3
Chur . . . . . . . . 13 C8
Churachandpur 41 E9
Churchill . . . . . 70 C10
Churchill ⟶,
Man., Canada 70 C10
Churchill ⟶,
Nfld., Canada 69 C4
Churchill, C. . . 70 C10
Churchill Falls . 69 C4
Churchill L. . . . 71 C9
Churu . . . . . . . 42 E9
Chushal . . . . . . 42 C11
Chusovoy . . . . 28 D6
Chuvash
Republic □ =
Chuvashia . . 24 B6
Chuvashia □ . . 24 B6
Cicero . . . . . . . 72 D2
Ciechanów . . . . 16 B5
Ciego de Avila . 86 B4
Ciénaga . . . . . . 90 A4
Cienfuegos . . . 86 B3
Cieszyn . . . . . . 16 D4
Cieza . . . . . . . . 19 C5
Cijara, Pantano
de . . . . . . . . 18 C3
Cilician Gates P. 46 C3
Cill Chainnigh =
Kilkenny . . . . 11 E3
Cimişlia . . . . . . 17 E9
Cimone, Mte. . . 20 B3
Cîmpina . . . . . . 17 F7
Cîmpulung . . . . 17 F7
Cinca ⟶ . . . . . 19 B6
Cincar . . . . . . . 20 C6
Cincinnati . . . . 72 E3
Çine . . . . . . . . 23 F7
Cinto, Mte. . . . . 13 E8
Circle . . . . . . . . 71 B5
Cirebon . . . . . . 37 F3
Citlaltépetl . . . . 84 D5
Città di Castello 20 C4
Ciudad Bolívar . 90 B6
Ciudad
Chetumal . . . 85 D7
Ciudad del
Carmen . . . . . 85 D6
Ciudad Delicias
= Delicias . . . 84 B3
Ciudad Guayana 90 B6
Ciudad Juárez . 84 A3
Ciudad Madero 84 C5
Ciudad Mante . 84 C5
Ciudad Obregón 84 B3
Ciudad Real . . 18 C4
Ciudad Rodrigo 18 B2
Ciudad Trujillo
= Santo
Domingo . . . 87 C6
Ciudad Victoria 84 C5
Civitanova
Marche . . . . . 20 C4

Civitavécchia . . 20 C3
Cizre . . . . . . . . 46 C5
Clanwilliam . . . 58 E3
Clare . . . . . . . . 62 B2
Clarence ⟶,
Australia . . . . 63 A5
Clarence ⟶,
N.Z. . . . . . . . 65 E5
Clarence, I. . . . . 95 G2
Clarence I. . . . . 96 A4
Clarie Coast . . 96 A13
Clarke I. . . . . . . 62 D4
Clarksdale . . . . 79 B8
Clarksville . . . . 74 A4
Claveria . . . . . . 38 A2
Clear, C. . . . . . 11 F2
Clearwater . . . . 75 F6
Clearwater Mts. 81 B6
Clermont-
Ferrand . . . . 13 D5
Cleveland,
Australia . . . . 63 A5
Cleveland,
U.S.A. . . . . 72 D5
Clifden . . . . . . . 65 G2
Clifton . . . . . . . 63 A5
Clifton Hills . . . 62 A2
Clinton, Canada 71 C7
Clinton, N.Z. . . 65 G3
Clinton, U.S.A. . 77 E9
Clinton Colden
L. . . . . . . . . 70 B9
Clones . . . . . . . 11 D3
Clonmel . . . . . . 11 E3
Clovis . . . . . . . 78 B2
Cluj-Napoca . . . 17 E6
Clunes . . . . . . . 62 C3
Clutha ⟶ . . . . 65 G3
Clyde . . . . . . . . 65 F3
Clyde ⟶ . . . . . 10 D4
Clyde, Firth of . 10 D4
Clyde River . . . 68 A4
Coari . . . . . . . . 90 D6
Coast Mts. . . . . 70 C7
Coast Ranges . 80 F2
Coats I. . . . . . . 68 B2
Coats Land . . . 96 B5
Coatzacoalcos . 85 D6
Cobalt . . . . . . . 69 D3
Cobar . . . . . . . . 63 B4
Cóbh . . . . . . . . 11 F2
Cobham . . . . . . 62 B3
Cobija . . . . . . . 91 F5
Cobourg . . . . . . 69 D3
Cobram . . . . . . 63 C4
Cóbué . . . . . . . 59 A6
Coburg . . . . . . 15 C6
Cocanada =
Kakinada . . . 40 J4
Cochabamba . . 91 G5
Cochin . . . . . . 43 Q10
Cochin China =
Nam-Phan . . 36 B3
Cochrane . . . . . 69 D2
Cochrane, L. . . 95 F2
Cockburn . . . . . 62 B3
Cockburn, Canal 95 G2
Coco ⟶ . . . . . 86 D3
Cocobeach . . . . 56 D1
Cod, C. . . . . . . 73 C10
Codajás . . . . . . 90 D6
Codó . . . . . . . . 92 C5
Cœur d'Alene . 80 B5
Coffeyville . . . . 79 A6
Coffin B. . . . . . 62 B2
Coffin Bay
Peninsula . . . 62 B2
Coffs Harbour . 63 B5
Cognac . . . . . . 12 D3

| | | |
|---|---|---|
| Cohuna | 63 | C3 |
| Coiba, I. | 86 | E3 |
| Coig ~→ | 95 | G3 |
| Coihaique | 95 | F2 |
| Coimbatore | 43 | P10 |
| Coimbra, *Brazil* | 91 | G7 |
| Coimbra, | | |
| *Portugal* | 18 | B1 |
| Coín | 18 | D3 |
| Cojimies | 90 | C3 |
| Colac | 62 | C3 |
| Colatina | 93 | F5 |
| Colbeck, C. | 96 | B17 |
| Colbinabbin | 63 | C3 |
| Colchester | 11 | F7 |
| Colebrook | 62 | D4 |
| Coleman | 71 | D8 |
| Coleraine, | | |
| *Australia* | 62 | C3 |
| Coleraine, *U.K.* | 11 | D3 |
| Coleridge, L. | 65 | E4 |
| Colesberg | 59 | E5 |
| Colhué Huapi, L. | 95 | F3 |
| Colima | 84 | D4 |
| Colinas | 92 | D5 |
| Coll | 10 | C3 |
| Collaguasi | 91 | H5 |
| Collarenebri | 63 | A4 |
| Collingwood | 64 | D5 |
| Colmar | 13 | B7 |
| Colo ~→ | 63 | B5 |
| Cologne = Köln | 14 | C4 |
| Colomb-Béchar | | |
| = Béchar | 54 | B4 |
| Colômbia | 93 | G4 |
| Colombia ■ | 90 | C4 |
| Colombo | 43 | R11 |
| Colón, *Cuba* | 86 | B3 |
| Colón, *Panama* | 85 | F9 |
| Colonia | 94 | C5 |
| Colonia Dora | 94 | B4 |
| Colonsay | 10 | C3 |
| Colorado □ | 83 | A10 |
| Colorado ~→, | | |
| *Argentina* | 95 | D4 |
| Colorado ~→, | | |
| *N. Amer.* | 82 | E5 |
| Colorado | | |
| Plateau | 83 | B7 |
| Colorado | | |
| Springs | 76 | F2 |
| Columbia, *Mo.,* | | |
| *U.S.A.* | 77 | F8 |
| Columbia, *S.C.,* | | |
| *U.S.A.* | 75 | B7 |
| Columbia, | | |
| *Tenn., U.S.A.* | 74 | B4 |
| Columbia ~→ | 80 | B1 |
| Columbia, | | |
| District of □ | 73 | E7 |
| Columbia Basin | 80 | B4 |
| Columbretes, Is. | 19 | C6 |
| Columbus, *Ga.,* | | |
| *U.S.A.* | 74 | C5 |
| Columbus, | | |
| *Miss., U.S.A.* | 74 | C3 |
| Columbus, *Ohio,* | | |
| *U.S.A.* | 72 | E4 |
| Colville ~→ | 71 | A4 |
| Colville, C. | 64 | B6 |
| Colwyn Bay | 11 | E5 |
| Comácchio | 20 | B4 |
| Comallo | 95 | E2 |
| Comilla | 41 | F8 |
| Comino, C. | 21 | D2 |
| Committee B. | 68 | B2 |
| Commonwealth | | |
| B. | 96 | A14 |
| Commoron | | |
| Cr. ~→ | 63 | A5 |

| | | |
|---|---|---|
| Communism Pk. | | |
| = | | |
| Kommunizma, | | |
| Pik | 29 | F8 |
| Como | 20 | B2 |
| Como, L. di | 20 | B2 |
| Comodoro | | |
| Rivadavia | 95 | F3 |
| Comorin, C. | 43 | Q10 |
| Comoro Is. = | | |
| Comoros ■ | 51 | H8 |
| Comoros ■ | 51 | H8 |
| Comox | 71 | D7 |
| Compiègne | 13 | B5 |
| Compton Downs | 63 | B4 |
| Comrat | 17 | E9 |
| Conakry | 55 | G2 |
| Conara Junction | 62 | D4 |
| Concarneau | 12 | C2 |
| Conceiçâo da | | |
| Barra | 93 | F6 |
| Concepción, | | |
| *Bolivia* | 91 | G6 |
| Concepción, | | |
| *Chile* | 94 | D2 |
| Concepción, | | |
| *Paraguay* | 94 | A5 |
| Concepción, L. | 91 | G6 |
| Concepción del | | |
| Oro | 84 | C4 |
| Concepción del | | |
| Uruguay | 94 | C5 |
| Conchos ~→ | 84 | B3 |
| Concord, *N.C.,* | | |
| *U.S.A.* | 75 | B7 |
| Concord, *N.H.,* | | |
| *U.S.A.* | 73 | C10 |
| Concordia, | | |
| *Argentina* | 94 | C5 |
| Concórdia, *Brazil* | 90 | D5 |
| Condamine | 63 | A5 |
| Condeúba | 93 | E5 |
| Condobolin | 63 | B4 |
| Conegliano | 20 | B4 |
| Confuso ~→ | 94 | B5 |
| Congo ■ | 56 | E3 |
| Congo ~→ | 56 | F2 |
| Congo, Dem. | | |
| Rep. of the ■ | 56 | E4 |
| Conjeeveram = | | |
| Kanchipuram | 43 | N11 |
| Conlea | 63 | B3 |
| Conn, L. | 11 | D2 |
| Connacht □ | 11 | E2 |
| Connecticut □ | 73 | D9 |
| Connecticut ~→ | 73 | D9 |
| Connemara | 11 | E2 |
| Conoble | 63 | B3 |
| Cononaco ~→ | 90 | D3 |
| Conran, C. | 63 | C4 |
| Conselheiro | | |
| Lafaiete | 93 | G5 |
| Constance = | | |
| Konstanz | 14 | E5 |
| Constance, L. = | | |
| Bodensee | 13 | C8 |
| Constanţa | 22 | B7 |
| Constantine | 54 | A6 |
| Constitución | 94 | D2 |
| Contai | 40 | G6 |
| Contamana | 91 | E4 |
| Contas ~→ | 93 | E6 |
| Conway, L. | 62 | A2 |
| Coober Pedy | 62 | A1 |
| Cooch Behar = | | |
| Koch Bihar | 41 | D7 |
| Cook, B. | 95 | H2 |
| Cook, Aoraki Mt. | 65 | E4 |
| Cook Inlet | 71 | C4 |

| | | |
|---|---|---|
| Cook Is. | 65 | L14 |
| Cook Strait | 65 | D6 |
| Cooktown | 61 | D8 |
| Coolabah | 63 | B4 |
| Cooladdi | 63 | A4 |
| Coolah | 63 | B4 |
| Coolamon | 63 | B4 |
| Coolangatta | 63 | A5 |
| Cooma | 63 | C4 |
| Coonabarabran | 63 | B4 |
| Coonamble | 63 | B4 |
| Coondapoor | 43 | N9 |
| Coongie | 62 | A3 |
| Coongoola | 63 | A4 |
| Cooninie, L. | 62 | A2 |
| Cooper Cr. ~→, | | |
| *N. Terr.,* | | |
| *Australia* | 60 | C5 |
| Cooper Cr. ~→, | | |
| *S. Austral.,* | | |
| *Australia* | 62 | A2 |
| Cooroy | 63 | A5 |
| Cootamundra | 63 | B4 |
| Cooyar | 63 | A5 |
| Copenhagen = | | |
| København | 9 | G10 |
| Copiapó | 94 | B2 |
| Copiapó ~→ | 94 | B2 |
| Copley | 62 | B2 |
| Copper Center | 71 | B5 |
| Copper Cliff | 69 | D2 |
| Coppermine = | | |
| Kugluktuk | 70 | B8 |
| Coppermine ~→ | 70 | B8 |
| Coquimbo | 94 | C2 |
| Corabia | 22 | C5 |
| Coracora | 91 | G4 |
| Coral Harbour = | | |
| Salliq | 68 | B2 |
| Coral Sea | 64 | L10 |
| Corato | 21 | D6 |
| Corby | 11 | E6 |
| Corcaigh = Cork | 11 | F2 |
| Corcubión | 18 | A1 |
| Córdoba, | | |
| *Argentina* | 94 | C4 |
| Córdoba, *Spain* | 18 | D3 |
| Córdoba, Sierra | | |
| de | 94 | C4 |
| Cordon | 38 | A2 |
| Cordova | 71 | B5 |
| Corfu = Kérkira | 23 | E2 |
| Coria | 18 | C2 |
| Corigliano | | |
| Cálabro | 21 | E6 |
| Corinna | 62 | D4 |
| Corinth = | | |
| Kórinthos | 23 | F4 |
| Corinth, G. of = | | |
| Korinthiakós | | |
| Kólpos | 23 | E4 |
| Corinto | 93 | F5 |
| Cork | 11 | F2 |
| Çorlu | 22 | D6 |
| Corner Brook | 69 | D5 |
| Corneşti | 17 | E9 |
| Cornwall | 69 | D3 |
| Corny Pt. | 62 | B2 |
| Coro | 90 | A5 |
| Coroatá | 92 | C5 |
| Corocoro | 91 | G5 |
| Coroico | 91 | G5 |
| Coromandel | 64 | B6 |
| Corona | 26 | B2 |
| Coronation Gulf | 70 | B8 |
| Coronation I. | 96 | A4 |
| Coronel | 94 | D2 |
| Coronel Dorrego | 94 | D4 |
| Coronel Suárez | 94 | D4 |

| | | |
|---|---|---|
| Corowa | 63 | C4 |
| Corpus Christi | 78 | F5 |
| Corque | 91 | G5 |
| Corrib, L. | 11 | E2 |
| Corrientes | 94 | B5 |
| Corrientes ~→ | 90 | D4 |
| Corrientes, C., | | |
| *Colombia* | 90 | B3 |
| Corrientes, C., | | |
| *Mexico* | 84 | C3 |
| Corse | 13 | E8 |
| Corse, C. | 13 | E8 |
| Corsica = Corse | 13 | E8 |
| Corsicana | 79 | C5 |
| Corte | 13 | E8 |
| Çorum | 46 | B3 |
| Corumbá | 91 | G7 |
| Corumbá de | | |
| Goiás | 93 | F4 |
| Corunna = La | | |
| Coruña | 18 | A1 |
| Corvallis | 80 | C2 |
| Cosenza | 21 | E6 |
| Costa Blanca | 19 | C5 |
| Costa Brava | 19 | B7 |
| Costa del Sol | 18 | D3 |
| Costa Dorada | 19 | B6 |
| Costa Rica ■ | 86 | E3 |
| Cotabato | 38 | C2 |
| Cotagaita | 91 | H5 |
| Côte d'Azur | 13 | E7 |
| Côte-d'Ivoire ■ | | |
| = Ivory | | |
| Coast ■ | 55 | G3 |
| Cotentin | 12 | B3 |
| Cotonou | 55 | G5 |
| Cotopaxi | 90 | D3 |
| Cotswold Hills | 11 | F5 |
| Cottbus | 15 | C8 |
| Couedic, C. du | 62 | C2 |
| Coulman I. | 96 | B15 |
| Council | 71 | B3 |
| Council Bluffs | 77 | E7 |
| Courantyne ~→ | 90 | B7 |
| Courtrai = | | |
| Kortrijk | 14 | C2 |
| Coventry | 11 | E6 |
| Covilhã | 18 | B2 |
| Covington | 72 | E3 |
| Cowal, L. | 63 | B4 |
| Cowangie | 62 | C3 |
| Cowarie | 62 | A2 |
| Cowell | 62 | B2 |
| Cowra | 63 | B4 |
| Coxim | 93 | F3 |
| Cox's Bazar | 41 | G4 |
| Cozumel, I. de | 85 | C7 |
| Craboon | 63 | B4 |
| Cracow = | | |
| Kraków | 16 | C4 |
| Cracow | 63 | A5 |
| Cradock | 59 | E5 |
| Craigavon | 11 | D3 |
| Crailsheim | 14 | D6 |
| Craiova | 22 | B4 |
| Cranbrook, | | |
| *Australia* | 62 | D4 |
| Cranbrook, | | |
| *Canada* | 71 | D8 |
| Crateús | 92 | D5 |
| Crato | 92 | D6 |
| Crawley | 11 | F6 |
| Crazy Mts. | 81 | B8 |
| Crema | 20 | B2 |
| Cremona | 20 | B3 |
| Cres | 20 | B5 |
| Cressy | 62 | C3 |
| Crete = Kríti | 23 | G5 |
| Créteil | 12 | B5 |

Creus, C. de ... 19 A7
Creuse ↦ .... 12 C4
Crewe ....... 11 E5
Criciúma ..... 94 B7
Crimean Pen. =
 Krymskyy
 Pivostriv .... 25 D3
Crişul Alb ↦ . 16 E5
Crişul Negru ↦ 16 E5
Crna Gora =
 Montenegro □ 22 C2
Crna Gora .... 22 C3
Crna Reka ↦ . 22 D3
Croatia ■ ..... 20 B6
Crocker,
 Banjaran ... 36 C5
Croker, C. .... 60 C5
Cromer ....... 11 E7
Cromwell .... 65 F3
Cronulla ..... 63 B5
Crookwell .... 63 B4
Cross Sound .. 71 C6
Crotone ...... 21 E6
Crows Nest ... 63 A5
Crowsnest Pass 71 D8
Cruz Alta .... 94 B6
Cruz del Eje ... 94 C4
Cruzeiro ...... 93 G5
Cruzeiro do Sul 91 E4
Crystal Brook . 62 B2
Csongrád ..... 16 E5
Cuamba ...... 59 A7
Cuando ↦ ... 58 B4
Cuarto ↦ .... 94 C4
Cuba ■ ...... 86 B4
Cubango ↦ .. 58 B4
Cuchi ....... 58 A3
Cúcuta ...... 90 B4
Cuddalore ... 43 P11
Cuddapah .... 43 M11
Cudgewa ..... 63 C4
Cuenca, Ecuador 90 D3
Cuenca, Spain . 19 B4
Cuenca,
 Serranía de . 19 C5
Cuernavaca ... 84 D5
Cuevas del
 Almanzora .. 19 D5
Cuevo ....... 91 H6
Cuiabá ....... 93 F2
Cuiabá ↦ .... 93 F2
Cuima ....... 58 A3
Cuito ↦ ..... 58 B4
Cukai ....... 36 D2
Culcairn ..... 63 C4
Culgoa ↦ .... 63 A4
Culiacán ..... 84 C3
Culion ....... 38 B2
Cullarin Ra. .. 63 B4
Cullera ...... 19 C5
Culuene ↦ ... 93 E3
Culverden .... 65 E5
Cumaná ...... 90 A6
Cumberland,
 Canada ..... 71 D7
Cumberland,
 U.S.A. ..... 73 E6
Cumberland
 Pen. ....... 68 B4
Cumberland
 Plateau ..... 72 F3
Cumberland Sd. 68 B4
Cumborah .... 63 A4
Cumbum ..... 43 M11
Cummins ..... 62 B2
Cumnock ..... 63 B4
Cunene ↦ ... 58 B2
Cúneo ....... 20 B1
Cunnamulla ... 63 A4

Cupica, G. de .. 90 B3
Curaçao ...... 87 D6
Curaray ↦ ... 90 D4
Curiapo ...... 90 B6
Curicó ....... 94 C2
Curitiba ..... 94 B7
Currabubula .. 63 B5
Currais Novos . 92 D6
Curralinho ... 92 C4
Curraweena ... 63 B4
Currie ....... 62 C3
Curtea de Argeş 17 F7
Curtis Group .. 62 C4
Curuápanema ↦
 .......... 92 C2
Curuçá ...... 92 C4
Curup ....... 37 E2
Cururupu ..... 92 C5
Curuzú Cuatiá . 94 B5
Cuttaburra ↦ . 63 A3
Cuttack ...... 40 G5
Cuvier I. ..... 64 B6
Cuxhaven ..... 14 B5
Cuyo ........ 38 B2
Cuzco, Bolivia . 91 H5
Cuzco, Peru .. 91 F4
Cwmbran .... 11 F5
Cyclades =
 Kikládhes .. 23 F5
Cygnet ...... 62 D4
Cyprus ■ .... 46 D3
Cyrenaica =
 Shaḥḥāt .... 52 B3
Czech Rep. ■ .. 16 D2
Częstochowa . 16 C4

## D

Da Hinggan Ling 35 B7
Da Lat ...... 36 B3
Da Nang ..... 36 A3
Da Qaidam ... 34 C4
Da Yunhe ↦ . 35 C7
Daba Shan .... 35 C5
Dabakala ..... 55 G4
Dabo ........ 37 E2
Dabola ...... 55 F2
Daboya ...... 55 G4
Dacca = Dhaka 41 F8
Dacca =
 Dhaka □ .... 41 E8
Dachau ...... 15 D6
Dadanawa .... 90 C7
Dadra and
 Nagar
 Haveli □ .... 43 J8
Dadu ........ 42 F5
Daet ........ 38 B2
Dagana ...... 55 E1
Dagestan □ ... 25 E6
Daghestan
 Republic =
 Dagestan □ . 25 E6
Dagö = Hiiumaa 24 B1
Dagupan ..... 38 A2
Dahlak Kebir .. 49 D3
Dahod ...... 43 H9
Dahomey =
 Benin ■ .... 55 G5
Dahra ....... 55 E1
Daiō-Misaki .. 32 B5
Dairût ....... 52 C5
Dakar ....... 55 F1
Dakhla ...... 54 D1

Dakhla, El
 Wâhât el- ... 52 C4
Dakhovskaya .. 25 E5
Đakovica ..... 22 C3
Dalaman ↦ .. 23 F7
Dalandzadgad . 35 B5
Dālbandīn .... 42 E4
Dalby ........ 63 A5
Dalhousie .... 69 D4
Dali ......... 34 D5
Dalian ....... 35 C7
Daliang Shan .. 34 D5
Dallarnil ..... 63 A5
Dallas ....... 79 C5
Dalmacija .... 20 C6
Dalmatia =
 Dalmacija ... 20 C6
Daloa ....... 55 G3
Dalton ....... 74 B5
Dalton Iceberg
 Tongue ..... 96 A13
Daly Waters .. 60 D5
Daman ...... 43 J8
Damanhûr .... 52 B5
Damar ....... 39 F3
Damaraland .. 58 C3
Damascus =
 Dimashq .... 46 D4
Damāvand ... 44 C3
Damāvand,
 Qolleh-ye .. 44 C3
Damba ...... 56 F3
Dāmghān .... 44 B3
Damiel ...... 18 C4
Damietta =
 Dumyât ..... 52 B5
Dammam = Ad
 Dammām ... 47 F7
Damoh ...... 43 H11
Dampier ...... 60 E2
Dampier, Selat 39 E4
Danbury ..... 73 D9
Dandeldhura .. 40 C3
Dandeli ...... 43 M9
Dandenong ... 63 C4
Dandong ..... 35 B7
Danger Is. =
 Pukapuka ... 65 L14
Danger Pt. .... 58 E3
Dangora ..... 55 F6
Danilov ...... 24 B5
Dankhar Gompa 42 C11
Dannemora ... 9 F11
Dannevirke ... 64 D7
Dante ....... 49 E5
Danube =
 Dunărea ↦ . 17 F9
Danville ..... 75 A8
Danzig =
 Gdańsk .... 16 A4
Dao ......... 38 B2
Daoud = Aïn
 Beïda ...... 54 A6
Dar el Beida =
 Casablanca . 54 B3
Dar es Salaam . 57 F7
Dārāb ....... 44 D3
Daraj ....... 54 B7
Darband ..... 42 B8
Darbhanga ... 40 D5
Dardanelles =
 Çanakkale
 Boğazı ..... 23 D6
Dârfûr ....... 53 F3
Dargai ...... 42 B7
Dargan Ata ... 29 E7
Dargaville .... 64 A5
Danca ....... 22 D7
Darién, G. del . 90 B3

Darjeeling =
 Darjiling .... 40 D7
Darjiling ...... 40 D7
Darling ↦ ... 62 B3
Darling Downs 63 A5
Darling Ra. ... 60 G2
Darlington ... 11 D6
Darłowo ...... 16 A3
Darmstadt ... 14 D5
Darnah ...... 52 B3
Darnley, C. .... 96 A10
Darnley B. .... 70 B7
Dart, C. ..... 96 B18
Dartmoor ..... 11 F5
Dartmouth .... 69 D4
Dartmouth, L. . 63 A4
Darvaza ...... 29 E6
Darvel, Teluk . 38 D1
Darwha ...... 43 J10
Darwin ...... 60 C5
Daryoi Amu =
 Amudarya ↦ 29 E6
Dās ......... 44 E3
Dashhowuz ... 29 E6
Dasht ↦ .... 42 G2
Dasht-e Kavīr . 44 C3
Dasht-e Mārgow 42 D3
Datça ....... 23 F6
Datia ........ 43 G11
Datong ...... 35 B6
Datu, Tanjung . 37 D3
Datu Piang ... 38 C2
Daugava ↦ .. 24 B1
Daugavpils ... 24 B2
Daulpur ..... 42 F10
Dauphin ..... 71 C9
Dauphiné ..... 13 D6
Davangere ... 43 M9
Davao ....... 38 C3
Davao, G. of .. 38 C3
Dāvar Panāh .. 45 E5
Davenport .... 77 E9
David ....... 86 E3
David Gorodok
 = Davyd
 Haradok .... 17 B8
Davis Sea ..... 96 A11
Davis Str. .... 68 B5
Davos ....... 13 C8
Davyd Haradok 17 B8
Dawson ..... 70 B6
Dawson, I. ... 95 G2
Dax ......... 12 E3
Daxian ...... 35 C5
Daxue Shan .. 34 C5
Daylesford ... 62 C3
Dayr az Zawr .. 46 D5
Dayton ...... 72 E3
Daytona Beach 75 E7
Dead Sea ..... 47 E3
Deakin ...... 60 G4
Deal I. ...... 62 C4
Deán Funes .. 94 C4
Death Valley .. 82 B4
Deba Habe ... 55 F7
Debar ....... 22 D3
Dębica ...... 16 C5
Debre Markos . 53 F6
Debre Tabor .. 53 F6
Debrecen .... 16 E5
Decatur, Ala.,
 U.S.A. ..... 74 B4
Decatur, Ill.,
 U.S.A. ..... 77 F10
Deccan ...... 43 L11
Děčín ....... 16 C2
Dedéagach =
 Alexandroúpolis
 .......... 22 D5

Dédougou .... 55 F4
Dee -→ ....... 10 C5
Deepwater .... 63 A5
Degeh Bur ... 49 F3
Deggendorf ... 15 D7
Deh Bīd ...... 44 D3
Dehi Titan .. 42 C3
Dehibat ...... 54 B7
Dehkareqan .. 46 C6
Dehra Dun .... 42 D11
Dej .......... 17 E6
Dekese ....... 56 E4
Delano ....... 82 C3
Delaware □ ... 73 E8
Delaware -→ .. 73 E8
Delegate ..... 63 C4
Delgado, C. .. 57 G8
Delgo ....... 53 D5
Delhi ......... 42 E10
Delice -→ .... 46 C3
Delicias ...... 84 B3
Déline ....... 70 B7
Delmenhorst .. 14 B5
Delmiro Gouveia 93 D6
Deloraine ..... 62 D4
Delungra ..... 63 A5
Delvinë ....... 23 E3
Demanda, Sierra
  de la ....... 18 A4
Demavand =
  Damāvand .. 44 C3
Demba ....... 56 F4
Dembecha .. 53 F6
Dembidolo .... 53 G5
Demini -→ .... 90 D6
Demirci ...... 23 E7
Demirköy ..... 22 D6
Dempo ....... 37 E2
Den Haag = 's-
  Gravenhage . 14 B3
Den Helder .. 14 B3
Denau ....... 29 F7
Dendang ..... 37 E3
Denia ........ 19 C6
Denial B. ..... 62 B1
Deniliquin .... 63 C3
Denman Glacier 96 A11
Denmark ■ ... 9 G9
Denmark Str. .. 66 C17
Denpasar ..... 37 F5
Denton ....... 78 C5
D'Entrecasteaux
  Is. ......... 61 B9
Denver ....... 76 F2
Deoghar ...... 40 E6
Deolali ....... 43 K8
Deoria ....... 40 D4
Deosai Mts. ... 42 B9
Dêqên ........ 34 D4
Dera Ghazi Khan 42 D7
Dera Ismail
  Khan ...... 42 D7
Derbent ...... 25 E6
Derby, Australia 60 D3
Derby, U.K. .. 11 E6
Derg, L. ...... 11 E2
Dergaon ...... 41 D9
Derry =
  Londonderry 11 D3
Derudub ...... 53 E6
Des Moines .. 77 E8
Des Moines -→ 77 E9
Desaguadero -→ 91 G5
Dese ......... 49 E2
Desna -→ ..... 17 C10
Desolación, I. .. 95 G2
Despeñaperros,
  Paso ....... 18 C4
Dessau ....... 15 C7

D'Estrees B. ... 62 C2
Detmold ...... 14 C5
Detroit ....... 72 C4
Deutsche Bucht 14 A5
Deva ......... 17 F6
Devakottai .... 43 Q11
Deventer ..... 14 B4
Devonport,
  Australia ... 62 D4
Devonport, N.Z. 64 B6
Dewas ....... 43 H10
Deyhük ....... 44 C4
Deyyer ....... 44 E2
Dezfūl ........ 47 D7
Dezhneva, Mys 31 C16
Dhafra ....... 44 F3
Dhahira ...... 44 F4
Dhahran = Aẓ
  Ẕahrān ..... 47 F7
Dhaka ........ 41 F8
Dhaka □ ..... 41 E8
Dhamar ...... 49 E3
Dhamtari ..... 40 G3
Dhanbad ..... 40 F6
Dhangarhi .... 40 C3
Dhankuta ..... 40 D6
Dhar ......... 43 H9
Dharmapuri ... 43 N11
Dharwad ..... 43 M9
Dhaulagiri .... 40 C4
Dhenkanal ... 40 G5
Dhíkti Óros .. 23 G5
Dhírfis ....... 23 E4
Dhodhekánisos 23 F6
Dhrol ........ 43 H7
Dhubaibah .... 44 F3
Dhuburi ...... 41 D7
Dhule ........ 43 J9
Dhut -→ ...... 49 E5
Diafarabé .... 55 F4
Diamantina .. 93 F5
Diamantina -→ 62 A2
Diamantino ... 93 E2
Diamond
  Harbour .... 40 F7
Diapaga ..... 55 F5
Dībā ........ 44 E4
Dibaya ....... 56 F4
Dibaya-Lubue . 56 E3
Dibbi ........ 49 G3
Dibrugarh .... 41 D10
Dickson ..... 28 B9
Didiéni ...... 55 F3
Diébougou ... 55 F4
Diefenbaker L. . 71 C9
Dieppe ....... 12 B4
Digby ........ 69 D4
Digges Is. ..... 68 B3
Dighinala .... 41 F9
Digne-les-Bains 13 D7
Digos ........ 38 C3
Digul -→ ..... 39 F5
Dihang -→ .... 41 D10
Dijlah, Nahr -→ 47 E6
Dijon ........ 13 C6
Dikimdya ..... 31 D10
Dikson =
  Dickson ..... 28 B9
Dikwa ....... 53 F1
Dili ......... 39 F3
Dilling ....... 53 F4
Dillingham .... 71 C4
Dilolo ....... 56 G4
Dilston ...... 62 D4
Dimashq ..... 46 D4
Dimbokro .... 55 G4
Dimboola ..... 62 C3
Dîmbovița -→ . 22 B6
Dimitrovgrad,
  Bulgaria .... 22 C5

Dimitrovgrad,
  Russia ...... 24 C6
Dimitrovo =
  Pernik ...... 22 C4
Dinagat ...... 38 B3
Dinajpur ..... 41 E7
Dinan ....... 12 B2
Dinant ....... 14 C3
Dinar ........ 46 C2
Dīnār, Kūh-e .. 44 D2
Dinara Planina . 20 B6
Dinard ....... 12 B2
Dinaric Alps =
  Dinara Planina 20 B6
Dindigul ...... 43 P11
Dingle ....... 11 E1
Dinguiraye ... 55 F2
Dingwall ..... 10 C4
Dinosaur
  National
  Monument .. 81 E9
Diourbel ..... 55 F1
Dipolog ...... 38 C2
Dir .......... 42 B7
Diré ......... 55 E4
Dire Dawa .... 49 F3
Dirico ....... 58 B4
Dirranbandi ... 63 A4
Disa ......... 43 G8
Disappointment,
  L. ......... 60 E3
Disaster B. ... 63 C4
Discovery B. .. 62 C3
Disteghil Sar .. 42 A9
Distrito
  Federal □ ... 93 F4
Diu .......... 43 J7
Divinópolis ... 93 G5
Divnoye ...... 25 D5
Diwāl Kol .... 42 B5
Diyarbakır .... 46 C5
Diz Chah ..... 44 C3
Djado ........ 52 D1
Djakarta =
  Jakarta ..... 37 F3
Djambala ..... 56 E2
Djanet ....... 54 D6
Djawa = Jawa . 37 F3
Djelfa ....... 54 B5
Djema ....... 57 C5
Djenné ...... 55 F4
Djerba, I. de .. 52 B1
Djerid, Chott .. 54 B6
Djibo ........ 55 F4
Djibouti ..... 49 E3
Djibouti ■ .... 49 E3
Djolu ........ 56 D4
Djougou ..... 55 G5
Djoum ....... 56 D2
Djourab ...... 53 E2
Djugu ....... 57 D6
Dmitriya
  Lapteva, Proliv 31 B12
Dnepr -→ =
  Dnipro -→ .. 25 D3
Dneprodzerzhinsk
  =
  Dniprodzerzhynsk
  ........... 25 D3
Dnepropetrovsk
  =
  Dnipropetrovsk
  ........... 25 D4
Dnestr -→ =
  Dnister -→ .. 17 E10
Dnestrovski =
  Belgorod ... 24 C4
Dnieper =
  Dnipro -→ .. 25 D3

Dniester =
  Dnister -→ .. 17 E10
Dnipro -→ .... 25 D3
Dniprodzerzhynsk
  ........... 25 D3
Dnipro
  petrovsk..... 25 D4
Dnister -→ .... 17 E10
Dnistrovskyy
  Lyman ..... 17 E10
Dnyapro =
  Dnipro -→ .. 25 D3
Doba ....... 53 G2
Doberai,
  Jazirah ...... 39 E4
Doblas ....... 94 D4
Dobo ........ 39 F4
Doboj ....... 20 B7
Dobrich ...... 22 C6
Dobruja ...... 22 B7
Dobrush ...... 17 B10
Dodecanese =
  Dhodhekánisos
  ........... 23 F6
Dodge City ... 78 A3
Dodoma ...... 57 F7
Dogi ......... 42 C3
Doha = Ad
  Dawhah .... 44 E2
Dohazari ...... 41 F9
Doi .......... 39 D3
Dois Irmãos, Sa. 93 D5
Dolbeau ...... 69 D3
Dole ......... 13 C6
Dolomites =
  Dolomiti .... 20 A3
Dolomiti ...... 20 A3
Dolores ...... 94 D5
Dolphin, C. .. 95 C5
Dolphin and
  Union Str. .. 70 B8
Dombarovskiy . 29 D6
Dominica ■ ... 87 C7
Dominican
  Rep. ■ ..... 87 C5
Domo ....... 49 F4
Domodóssola . 20 A2
Domville, Mt. .. 63 A5
Don -→, Russia 25 D4
Don -→, U.K. .. 10 C5
Don Benito .. 18 C3
Donald ...... 62 C3
Donau =
  Dunărea -→ . 17 F9
Donauwörth .. 14 D6
Doncaster .... 11 E6
Dondo, Angola 56 F2
Dondo, Mozam. 59 B6
Dondo, Teluk . 39 D2
Donegal ..... 11 D2
Donets -→ .... 25 D5
Donetsk ..... 25 D4
Donggala ..... 39 E1
Dongola ...... 53 E5
Dongou ...... 56 D3
Dongting Hu .. 35 D6
Dongxing ..... 35 D5
Donington, C. . 62 B2
Donnelly's
  Crossing ... 64 A5
Donostia = San
  Sebastián ... 19 A5
Dora Báltea -→ 20 B2
Dorchester, C. . 68 B3
Dordogne -→ . 12 D3
Dordrecht .... 14 C3
Dori ......... 55 F4
Dornbirn ..... 14 E5
Dorohoi ...... 17 E8

| | | |
|---|---|---|
| Döröö Nuur ... | 34 | B4 |
| Dorrigo ....... | 63 | B5 |
| Dortmund .... | 14 | C4 |
| Doruma ....... | 57 | D5 |
| Dos Bahías, C. . | 95 | E3 |
| Dos Hermanas | 18 | D3 |
| Dosso ........ | 55 | F5 |
| Dothan ....... | 74 | D5 |
| Douai ........ | 13 | A5 |
| Douala ....... | 56 | D1 |
| Douarnenez ... | 12 | B1 |
| Double Island | | |
| Pt. ......... | 63 | A5 |
| Doubs ⟶ .... | 13 | C6 |
| Doubtful Sd. .. | 65 | F2 |
| Doubtless B. . | 64 | A5 |
| Douentza ..... | 55 | F4 |
| Douglas, U.K. . | 11 | D4 |
| Douglas, U.S.A. | 83 | E8 |
| Doumé ....... | 56 | D2 |
| Dourados .... | 94 | A6 |
| Douro ⟶ ..... | 18 | B1 |
| Dover, Australia | 62 | D4 |
| Dover, U.K. ... | 11 | F7 |
| Dover, Str. of .. | 11 | F7 |
| Dovrefjell ..... | 8 | F9 |
| Dowlat Yār .... | 45 | C6 |
| Dowlatābād .. | 44 | D4 |
| Dowshī ....... | 45 | C7 |
| Draa, Oued ⟶ | 54 | C2 |
| Drăgăşani .... | 22 | B5 |
| Dragichyn .... | 17 | B7 |
| Dragoman, | | |
| Prokhod ... | 22 | C4 |
| Draguignan ... | 13 | E7 |
| Drake ........ | 63 | A5 |
| Drakensberg . | 59 | E5 |
| Dráma ....... | 22 | D5 |
| Drammen ..... | 9 | G10 |
| Drau = | | |
| Drava ⟶ ... | 20 | B7 |
| Drava ⟶ .... | 20 | B7 |
| Dresden ...... | 15 | C7 |
| Dreux ........ | 12 | B4 |
| Drina ⟶ ..... | 20 | B7 |
| Drini ⟶ ...... | 22 | C2 |
| Drobeta- | | |
| Turnu-Severin | 22 | B4 |
| Drochia ...... | 17 | D8 |
| Drogheda ..... | 11 | E3 |
| Drogobych = | | |
| Drohobych .. | 17 | D6 |
| Drohobych .... | 17 | D6 |
| Droichead Atha | | |
| = Drogheda . | 11 | E3 |
| Dromedary, C. . | 63 | C5 |
| Drumheller .... | 71 | C8 |
| Drummond Pt. | 62 | B2 |
| Drut ⟶ ...... | 17 | B10 |
| Drygalski I. .... | 96 | A11 |
| Dschang ..... | 55 | G7 |
| Dubā ......... | 47 | F3 |
| Dubai = Dubayy | 44 | E3 |
| Dubăsari ..... | 17 | E9 |
| Dubăsari Vdkhr. | 17 | E9 |
| Dubawnt ⟶ .. | 70 | B9 |
| Dubawnt, L. .. | 70 | B9 |
| Dubayy ....... | 44 | E3 |
| Dubbo ........ | 63 | B4 |
| Dublin, Ireland | 11 | E3 |
| Dublin, U.S.A. . | 75 | C6 |
| Dubno ........ | 17 | C7 |
| Dubossary = | | |
| Dubăsari .... | 17 | E9 |
| Dubossary | | |
| Vdkhr. = | | |
| Dubăsari | | |
| Vdkhr. ...... | 17 | E9 |
| Dubovka ...... | 24 | D5 |

| | | |
|---|---|---|
| Dubréka ...... | 55 | G2 |
| Dubrovitsa = | | |
| Dubrovytsya | 17 | C8 |
| Dubrovnik .... | 20 | C7 |
| Dubrovytsya .. | 17 | C8 |
| Dudhi ........ | 40 | E4 |
| Dudinka ...... | 30 | C6 |
| Duero = | | |
| Douro ⟶ ... | 18 | B1 |
| Dugi Otok .... | 20 | B5 |
| Duisburg ..... | 14 | C4 |
| Dukelský | | |
| Průsmyk .. | 16 | D5 |
| Dukhān ....... | 44 | E2 |
| Duki ......... | 42 | D6 |
| Duku ......... | 55 | F7 |
| Dulce ⟶ ..... | 94 | C4 |
| Dulit, Banjaran | 37 | D4 |
| Duluth ....... | 77 | B8 |
| Dum Duma ... | 41 | D10 |
| Dum Hadjer .. | 53 | F2 |
| Dumaguete ... | 38 | C2 |
| Dumai ........ | 37 | D2 |
| Dumaran ..... | 38 | B1 |
| Dumfries ..... | 11 | D5 |
| Dumyât ...... | 52 | B5 |
| Dún Dealgan = | | |
| Dundalk ..... | 11 | D3 |
| Dun Laoghaire | 11 | E3 |
| Duna = | | |
| Dunărea ⟶ . | 17 | F9 |
| Dunaj = | | |
| Dunărea ⟶ . | 17 | F9 |
| Dunakeszi .... | 16 | E4 |
| Dunărea ⟶ .. | 17 | F9 |
| Dunaújváros .. | 16 | E4 |
| Dunav = | | |
| Dunărea ⟶ . | 17 | F9 |
| Dunback ...... | 65 | F4 |
| Dunbar ....... | 10 | D5 |
| Duncan ....... | 78 | B5 |
| Dundalk ...... | 11 | D3 |
| Dundee, | | |
| S. Africa .... | 59 | D6 |
| Dundee, U.K. .. | 10 | C5 |
| Dundoo ...... | 63 | A3 |
| Dunedin ..... | 65 | F4 |
| Dunfermline .. | 10 | C5 |
| Dungarvan .... | 11 | E3 |
| Dungog ...... | 63 | B5 |
| Dungu ........ | 57 | D5 |
| Dunhuang .... | 34 | B4 |
| Dunkerque ... | 12 | A5 |
| Dunkirk = | | |
| Dunkerque .. | 12 | A5 |
| Dunkwa ...... | 55 | G4 |
| Dúnleary = Dun | | |
| Laoghaire .. | 11 | E3 |
| Dunolly ...... | 62 | C3 |
| Dunqul ....... | 52 | D5 |
| Dunstan Mts. .. | 65 | F3 |
| Durance ⟶ ... | 13 | E6 |
| Durango, | | |
| Mexico ..... | 84 | C4 |
| Durango, Spain | 19 | A4 |
| Durazno ...... | 94 | C5 |
| Durazzo = | | |
| Durrësi ...... | 22 | D2 |
| Durban ....... | 59 | D6 |
| Düren ........ | 14 | C4 |
| Durg ......... | 40 | G3 |
| Durgapur ..... | 40 | F6 |
| Durham, U.K. .. | 11 | D6 |
| Durham, U.S.A. | 75 | B8 |
| Durham Downs | 63 | A4 |
| Durmitor ..... | 22 | C2 |
| Durrësi ....... | 22 | D2 |
| Dursunbey .... | 23 | E7 |

| | | |
|---|---|---|
| D'Urville, | | |
| Tanjung .... | 39 | E5 |
| D'Urville I. .... | 65 | D5 |
| Dusa Mareb ... | 49 | F4 |
| Dushak ....... | 29 | F7 |
| Dushanbe .... | 29 | F7 |
| Dusky Sd. .... | 65 | F2 |
| Düsseldorf .... | 14 | C4 |
| Dutch Harbor .. | 71 | C3 |
| Duwādimi .... | 47 | F6 |
| Duyun ....... | 35 | D5 |
| Düzce ........ | 46 | B2 |
| Duzdab = | | |
| Zāhedān .... | 45 | D5 |
| Dvina, | | |
| Severnaya ⟶ | 28 | C5 |
| Dvinsk = | | |
| Daugavpils .. | 24 | B2 |
| Dwarka ....... | 43 | H6 |
| Dyatlovo = | | |
| Dzyatlava ... | 17 | B7 |
| Dyer, C. ..... | 68 | B4 |
| Dyer Plateau .. | 96 | B3 |
| Dyersburg ... | 79 | A9 |
| Dymer ....... | 17 | C10 |
| Dynevor Downs | 63 | A3 |
| Dzamin Üüd .. | 35 | B6 |
| Dzerzhinsk .... | 24 | B5 |
| Dzhambul = | | |
| Taraz........ | 29 | E8 |
| Dzhankoy ..... | 25 | D3 |
| Dzhardzhan ... | 30 | C10 |
| Dzhezkazgan = | | |
| Zhezqazghan | 29 | E7 |
| Dzhizak = | | |
| Jizzakh .... | 29 | E7 |
| Działdowa .... | 16 | B5 |
| Dzierzoniów ... | 16 | C3 |
| Dzungaria = | | |
| Junggar Pendi | 34 | B3 |
| Dzungarian Gate | | |
| = Alataw | | |
| Shankou ... | 34 | B3 |
| Dzuumod ..... | 35 | B5 |
| Dzyarzhynsk .. | 17 | B8 |
| Dzyatlava ..... | 17 | B7 |

**E**

| | | |
|---|---|---|
| Earnslaw, Mt. . | 65 | F3 |
| East Bengal ... | 41 | E7 |
| East Beskids = | | |
| Vychodné | | |
| Beskydy ... | 17 | D5 |
| East C. ....... | 64 | B8 |
| East China Sea | 35 | C7 |
| East Falkland . | 95 | G5 |
| East Kilbride . | 10 | D4 |
| East London .. | 59 | E5 |
| East Orange .. | 73 | D8 |
| East St. Louis . | 77 | F9 |
| East Sea = | | |
| Japan, Sea of | 31 | G11 |
| East Timor .... | 39 | F3 |
| East Toorale .. | 63 | B4 |
| Eastbourne, N.Z. | 65 | D6 |
| Eastbourne, U.K. | 11 | F7 |
| Eastern Ghats . | 43 | N11 |
| Eastmain ..... | 69 | C3 |
| Eastmain ⟶ .. | 69 | C3 |
| Eau Claire .... | 77 | C9 |
| Eberswalde- | | |
| Finow ...... | 15 | B7 |
| Ebolowa ..... | 56 | D2 |
| Ebro ⟶ ...... | 19 | B6 |
| Eceabat ...... | 23 | D6 |
| Ech Cheliff .... | 54 | A5 |

| | | |
|---|---|---|
| Echo Bay ..... | 70 | B8 |
| Echuca ...... | 63 | C3 |
| Ecija ........ | 18 | D3 |
| Ecuador ■ ... | 90 | D3 |
| Ed Dâmer .... | 53 | E5 |
| Ed Debba .... | 53 | E5 |
| Ed Dueim .... | 53 | F5 |
| Edd ......... | 49 | E3 |
| Eddystone Pt. . | 62 | D4 |
| Édea ........ | 56 | D2 |
| Eden ........ | 63 | C4 |
| Eder ⟶ ...... | 14 | C5 |
| Édhessa ...... | 23 | D4 |
| Edievale ...... | 65 | F3 |
| Edinburg ..... | 78 | F4 |
| Edinburgh .... | 10 | D5 |
| Ediniţa ...... | 17 | D8 |
| Edirne ....... | 22 | D6 |
| Edithburgh ... | 62 | C2 |
| Edmonton .... | 71 | C8 |
| Edmundston .. | 69 | D4 |
| Edremit ...... | 23 | E6 |
| Edremit Körfezi | 23 | E6 |
| Edson ....... | 71 | C8 |
| Edward ⟶ ... | 62 | C3 |
| Edward, L. .... | 57 | E5 |
| Edward VII Land | 96 | C17 |
| Edwards Plateau | 78 | D3 |
| Égadi, Ísole .. | 21 | F4 |
| Eger = Cheb .. | 16 | C1 |
| Eger ........ | 16 | E5 |
| Egersund ..... | 9 | G9 |
| Egmont, C. ... | 64 | C5 |
| Egmont, Mt. .. | 64 | C6 |
| Eğridir ....... | 46 | C2 |
| Eğridir Gölü ... | 46 | C2 |
| Egypt ■ ..... | 52 | C5 |
| Eibar ........ | 19 | A4 |
| Eidsvold ...... | 63 | A5 |
| Eifel ........ | 14 | C4 |
| Eigg ........ | 10 | C3 |
| Eil ......... | 49 | F4 |
| Eildon, L. .... | 63 | C4 |
| Eindhoven .... | 14 | C3 |
| Eire = Ireland ■ | 11 | E3 |
| Eirunepé ..... | 91 | E5 |
| Eisenach ..... | 14 | C6 |
| Eisenerz ..... | 15 | E8 |
| Eivissa = Ibiza . | 19 | C6 |
| Eketahuna ... | 64 | D6 |
| Ekibastuz .... | 29 | D8 |
| El Aaiún ..... | 54 | C2 |
| El Alamein ... | 52 | B4 |
| El Aricha ..... | 54 | B4 |
| El 'Arîsh ..... | 52 | B5 |
| El Asnam = Ech | | |
| Cheliff ...... | 54 | A5 |
| El Bawiti ..... | 52 | C4 |
| El Bayadh .... | 54 | B5 |
| El Callao ..... | 90 | B6 |
| El Centro ..... | 82 | D5 |
| El Cerro ..... | 91 | G6 |
| El Cuy ....... | 95 | D3 |
| El Cuyo ...... | 85 | C7 |
| El Dere ...... | 49 | G4 |
| El Diviso ..... | 90 | C3 |
| El Djouf ..... | 55 | D3 |
| El Dorado, Ark., | | |
| U.S.A. ..... | 79 | C7 |
| El Dorado, | | |
| Kans., U.S.A. | 78 | A5 |
| El Dorado, | | |
| Venezuela .. | 90 | B6 |
| El Escorial ... | 18 | B3 |
| El Faiyûm .... | 52 | C5 |
| El Fâsher .... | 53 | F4 |
| El Ferrol ..... | 18 | A1 |
| El Fuerte ..... | 84 | B3 |
| El Gal ........ | 49 | E5 |

# El Geneina

El Geneina = Al
  Junaynah ... 53 F3
El Geteina .... 53 F5
El Gîza ....... 52 C5
El Iskandarîya . 52 B4
El Jadida ..... 54 B3
El Jebelein ... 53 F5
El Kab ....... 53 E5
El Kala ....... 54 A6
El Kamlin .... 53 E5
El Kef ....... 54 A6
El Khandaq ... 53 E5
El Khârga .... 52 C5
El Khartûm ... 53 E5
El Khartûm
  Bahrî ....... 53 E5
El Laqâwa .... 53 F4
El Mafâza .... 53 F5
El Mahalla el
  Kubra ..... 52 B5
El Mansûra ... 52 B5
El Minyâ ..... 52 C5
El Obeid ..... 53 F5
El Odaiya .... 53 F4
El Oued ...... 54 B6
El Paso ...... 83 E9
El Prat de
  Llobregat ... 19 B7
El Puerto de
  Santa María . 18 D2
El Qâhira .... 52 B5
El Qantara ... 52 B5
El Qasr ...... 52 C4
El Reno ...... 78 B5
El Salvador ■ . 85 E7
El Shallal .... 52 D5
El Suweis .... 52 B5
El Tigre ..... 90 B6
El Tocuyo .... 90 B5
El Turbio .... 95 G2
El Uqsur ..... 52 C5
El Vigía ...... 90 B4
El Wak ...... 57 D8
El Wuz ...... 53 E5
Elat ......... 47 E3
Elâzığ ....... 46 C4
Elba ........ 20 C3
Elbasani ..... 22 D3
Elbe ➔ ..... 14 B5
Elbert, Mt. ... 83 A9
Elbeuf ....... 12 B4
Elbidtan ..... 46 C4
Elbing = Elbląg 16 A4
Elbląg ....... 16 A4
Elbrus ....... 25 E5
Elburz Mts. =
  Alborz,
  Reshteh-ye
  Kühhā-ye .. 44 B3
Elche ........ 19 C5
Elda ......... 19 C5
Elde ➔ ...... 15 B6
Eldoret ...... 57 D7
Elektrostal ... 24 B4
Elephant I. ... 96 A4
Eleuthera .... 86 A4
Elgin, U.K. ... 10 C5
Elgin, U.S.A. .. 72 C1
Elgon, Mt. ... 57 D6
Eliase ....... 39 F4
Elisabethville =
  Lubumbashi . 59 A5
Elista ........ 25 D5
Elizabeth,
  Australia .... 62 B2
Elizabeth, U.S.A. 73 D8
Elizabeth City . 75 A9
Elizabethton ... 75 A6
Ełk ......... 16 B6

Elkhart ....... 72 D3
Elkhovo ...... 22 C6
Elko ........ 80 E6
Ellery, Mt. ... 63 C4
Ellesmere, L. .. 65 G5
Ellice Is. =
  Tuvalu ■ ... 64 K12
Elliston ..... 62 B1
Ellore = Eluru . 40 J3
Ellsworth Land 96 B2
Ellsworth Mts. . 96 B2
Elmore ....... 63 C3
Elmshorn .... 14 B5
Eltham ...... 64 C6
Eluru ........ 40 J3
Elvas ........ 18 C2
Elx = Elche ... 19 C5
Ely ......... 11 E7
Emâmrûd ..... 44 B3
Emba = Embi . 29 E6
Emba ➔ =
  Embi ➔ .... 29 E6
Embarcación .. 94 A4
Embi ........ 29 E6
Embi ➔ ..... 29 E6
Embrun ...... 13 D7
Embu ....... 57 E7
Emden ...... 14 B4
Emerson ..... 71 D10
Emet ........ 23 E7
Emi Koussi ... 53 E2
Emine, Nos .. 22 C6
Emmen ...... 14 B4
Empalme ..... 84 B2
Empangeni ... 59 D6
Empedrado .. 94 B5
Empty Quarter
  = Rub' al
  Khali ...... 48 D4
Ems ➔ ...... 14 B4
En Nahud ..... 53 F4
Enaratoli .... 39 E5
Enare =
  Inarijärvi .... 8 E13
Encanto, C. .. 38 A2
Encarnación .. 94 B5
Encounter B. .. 62 C2
Ende ........ 39 F2
Enderby Land . 96 A9
Enewetak Atoll 64 H11
Enez ........ 23 D6
Engadin ..... 13 C9
Engaño, C. ... 38 A2
Engels ....... 24 C6
Enggano ..... 37 F2
Engkilili ..... 37 D4
England □ .... 11 E6
Englewood ... 76 F2
English Bazar =
  Ingraj Bazar . 40 E7
English Channel 11 F5
Enid ........ 78 A5
Enna ........ 21 F5
Ennedi ...... 53 E3
Enngonia .... 63 A4
Ennis ....... 11 E2
Enniskillen ... 11 D3
Enns ➔ ..... 15 D8
Enschede .... 14 B4
Ensenada ..... 84 A1
Entebbe ...... 57 D6
Entroncamento 18 C1
Enugu ....... 55 G6
Enugu Ezike .. 55 G6
Eólie, Ís. .... 21 E5
Épernay ..... 13 B5
Ephesus ..... 23 F6
Épinal ....... 13 B7
Epukiro ...... 58 C3

Equatorial
  Guinea ■ ... 56 D1
Er Rahad ..... 53 F5
Er Rif ....... 54 A4
Er Roseires ... 53 F5
Erāwadī Myit =
  Irrawaddy ➔ 41 K10
Erbil = Arbīl .. 46 C6
Erciyaş Dağı ... 46 C3
Érd ......... 16 E4
Erdek ....... 23 D6
Erebus, Mt. ... 96 B15
Erechim ..... 94 B6
Ereğli, Konya,
  Turkey .... 46 C3
Ereğli,
  Zonguldak,
  Turkey ..... 46 B2
Eresma ➔ .. 18 B3
Erewadi
  Myitwanya .. 41 K10
Erfurt ........ 15 C6
Ergani ....... 46 C4
Érice ........ 21 E4
Erie ........ 73 C5
Erie, L. ...... 72 C5
Erigavo ...... 49 E4
Erímanthos ... 23 F3
Erimo-misaki .. 32 F12
Eritrea ■ ..... 49 E2
Erlangen ..... 15 D6
Ermenak ..... 46 C3
Ermoúpolis =
  Síros ...... 23 F5
Ernakulam =
  Cochin .... 43 Q10
Erne, Lower L. . 11 D3
Erode ........ 43 P10
Eromanga .... 63 A3
Erramala Hills . 43 M11
Ertis ➔ =
  Irtysh ➔ ... 28 C7
Erzgebirge ... 15 C7
Erzincan ..... 46 C4
Erzurum ..... 46 C5
Es Sahrâ' Esh
  Sharqîya ... 52 C5
Es Sînâ' ..... 52 C5
Esbjerg ...... 9 G9
Esch-sur-Alzette 13 B6
Escuinapa .... 84 C3
Eşfahān ..... 44 C2
Esh Sham =
  Dimashq .... 46 D4
Esil ➔ =
  Ishim ➔ .... 29 D8
Eskilstuna .... 9 G11
Eskimo Pt. =
  Arviat ...... 70 B10
Eskişehir ..... 46 C2
Esla ➔ ..... 18 B2
Eslāmābād-e
  Gharb ..... 46 D6
Eşme ........ 23 E7
Esmeraldas .. 90 C3
Esperance ... 60 G3
Esperanza .... 94 C4
Espichel, C. .. 18 C1
Espinal ...... 90 C4
Espinazo, Sierra
  del = ......
  Espinhaço,
  Serra do .... 93 F5
Espinhaço, Serra
  do ......... 93 F5
Espírito Santo □ 93 G5
Esquel ...... 95 E2
Esquina ...... 94 C5
Essaouira ..... 54 B3

Essen ........ 14 C4
Essequibo ➔ . 90 B7
Esslingen ..... 14 D5
Estados, I. de
  Los ....... 95 G4
Estância ...... 93 E6
Estevan ...... 71 D9
Estonia ■ .... 24 B2
Estrêla, Serra da 18 B2
Estremoz ..... 18 C2
Estrondo, Serra
  do ......... 92 D4
Esztergom ... 16 E4
Etadunna .... 62 A2
Étampes ..... 12 B5
Etawah ...... 42 F11
Ethiopia ■ ... 49 F2
Etna ........ 21 F5
Etosha Pan ... 58 B3
Euboea =
  Évvoia ..... 23 E5
Eucumbene, L. 63 C4
Eufaula ...... 74 D5
Eugene ...... 80 C2
Eugowra ..... 63 B4
Eulo ........ 63 A4
Euphrates =
  Furāt, Nahr
  al ➔ ...... 47 E6
Eureka ....... 80 E1
Euroa ....... 63 C4
Europa, I. .... 59 J8
Europa, Picos de 18 A3
Europa, Pta. de 18 D3
Europa Pt. =
  Europa, Pta.
  de ........ 18 D3
Evans Head .. 63 A5
Evanston .... 72 C2
Evansville .... 72 F2
Everard, L. ... 62 B1
Everest, Mt. .. 40 C6
Everett ...... 80 B2
Everglades
  National Park 75 G7
Evinayong ... 56 D2
Évora ....... 18 C2
Évreux ...... 12 B4
Évros ➔ .... 22 D6
Evry ........ 12 B5
Évvoia ...... 23 E5
Ewo ........ 56 E2
Exaltación ... 91 F5
Exeter ...... 11 F5
Exmoor ..... 11 F5
Exmouth ..... 11 F5
Extremadura □ 18 C2
Eyasi, L. ..... 57 E6
Eyre (North), L. 62 A2
Eyre (South), L. 62 A2
Eyre, L. ..... 60 F6
Eyre Cr. ➔ .. 62 A2
Eyre Mts. .... 65 F3
Eyre Pen. .... 62 B2
Ezine ....... 23 E6

# F

F.Y.R.O.M. =
  Macedonia ■ 22 D3
Fabriano ..... 20 C4
Facatativá ... 90 C4
Fachi ....... 55 E7
Fada ........ 53 E3
Fada-n-Gourma 55 F5
Faddeyevskiy,
  Ostrov ...... 31 B12

Fāḏilī ........ 47 F7
Faenza ....... 20 B3
Færoe Is. =
  Føroyar ..... 6 C4
Fāgāras ...... 17 F7
Fagnano, L. ... 95 G3
Fahraj ........ 45 D4
Fahūd ........ 44 F4
Fair Isle ...... 10 B6
Fairbanks ..... 71 B5
Fairfield, *Ala.,*
  *U.S.A.* ...... 74 C4
Fairfield, *Calif.,*
  *U.S.A.* ...... 80 F2
Fairlie ........ 65 F4
Fairweather, Mt. 71 C6
Faisalabad .... 42 D8
Faizabad ..... 40 D4
Fakfak ........ 39 E4
Falaise ....... 12 B3
Falam ........ 41 F9
Falconara
  Maríttima ... 20 C4
Falcone, C. .... 20 D2
Faleshty =
  Fălești ...... 17 E8
Fălești ....... 17 E8
Falkland Is. □ . 95 G5
Falkland Sd. ... 95 G5
Fall River ..... 73 D10
Falmouth ..... 11 F4
False B. ...... 58 E3
Fălticeni ...... 17 E8
Falun ........ 9 F11
Famagusta .... 46 D3
Fandriana ..... 59 J9
Fano ......... 20 C4
Fao = Al Fāw . 47 E7
Faradje ....... 57 D5
Farafangana .. 59 J9
Farāh ........ 42 C3
Farāh □ ...... 42 C3
Faranah ...... 55 F2
Farasān, Jazā'ir 49 D3
Farasan Is. =
  Farasān,
  Jazā'ir ...... 49 D3
Fareham ...... 11 F6
Farewell, C. ... 64 D5
Farewell C. =
  Farvel, Kap .. 68 C6
Farghona ..... 29 E8
Fargo ........ 76 B6
Farim ........ 55 F1
Farīmān ...... 45 C4
Farina ........ 62 B2
Faro, *Brazil* ... 92 C2
Faro, *Portugal* . 18 D2
Farrāshband .. 44 D3
Farrell Flat .... 62 B2
Farrukhabad-
  cum-
  Fatehgarh ... 42 F11
Fārs □ ....... 44 D3
Fársala ....... 23 E4
Fartak, Râs .... 47 E3
Farvel, Kap ... 68 C6
Fāryāb □ ..... 45 B6
Fasā ......... 44 D3
Fasano ....... 21 D6
Fastiv ........ 17 C9
Fastov = Fastiv 17 C9
Fatagar, Tanjung 39 E4
Fatehgarh .... 42 F11
Fatehpur, *Raj.,*
  *India* ....... 42 F9
Fatehpur, *Ut. P.,*
  *India* ....... 40 E3
Favara ........ 21 F4

Favignana .... 21 F4
Faya-Largeau .. 53 E2
Fayd ......... 47 F5
Fayetteville,
  *Ark., U.S.A.* . 79 A6
Fayetteville,
  *N.C., U.S.A.* . 75 B8
Fazilka ....... 42 D9
Fdérik ........ 54 D2
Feather → .... 80 F3
Featherston ... 65 D6
Fécamp ...... 12 B4
Fehmarn ...... 15 A6
Feilding ...... 64 D6
Feira de Santana 93 E6
Feldkirch ..... 14 E5
Felipe Carrillo
  Puerto ...... 85 D7
Felixstowe .... 11 F7
Fengjie ....... 35 C5
Fenyang ...... 35 C6
Feodosiya .... 25 D4
Ferdows ...... 44 C4
Ferfer ........ 49 F4
Fergana =
  Farghona ... 29 E8
Fermo ........ 20 C4
Fernando de
  Noronha .... 92 C7
Fernando Póo =
  Bioko ...... 56 D1
Ferozepore =
  Firozpur .... 42 D9
Ferrara ....... 20 B3
Ferreñafe ..... 91 E3
Ferret, C. ..... 12 D3
Ferrol = El
  Ferrol ...... 18 A1
Fès ......... 54 B4
Feshi ........ 56 F3
Fetești ....... 22 B6
Fetlar ........ 10 A6
Feuilles → ... 68 C3
Fezzan ....... 52 C2
Fianarantsoa .. 59 J9
Fianga ....... 53 G2
Ficksburg ..... 59 D5
Fieri ......... 23 D2
Figeac ....... 12 D5
Figueira da Foz 18 B1
Figueras ...... 19 A7
Figuig ........ 54 B4
Fiji ■ ........ 64 L12
Filiatrá ....... 23 F3
Filyos → ..... 46 B3
Fíngōe ....... 59 A6
Finike ........ 46 C2
Finisterre, C. .. 18 A1
Finke → ..... 62 A2
Finland ■ ..... 8 F13
Finland, G. of . 9 G13
Finlay → ..... 70 C7
Finley ........ 63 C4
Finniss, C. .... 62 B1
Fiora → ...... 20 C3
Firat = Furāt,
  Nahr al → .. 47 E6
Firenze ....... 20 C3
Firozabad .... 42 F11
Firozpur ...... 42 D9
Firūzābād .... 44 D3
Firūzkūh ..... 44 C3
Fish → ...... 58 D3
Fishguard .... 11 E4
Fitri, L. ...... 53 F2
Fitz Roy ...... 95 F3
Fiume = Rijeka 20 B5
Fizi ......... 57 E5
Flagstaff ..... 83 C7

Flaming Gorge
  Reservoir ... 81 E9
Flamingo, Teluk 39 F5
Flandre ....... 14 C2
Flathead L. .... 81 B6
Flattery, C. .... 80 A1
Flensburg ..... 14 A5
Flers ......... 12 B3
Flesko, Tanjung 39 D2
Flin Flon ...... 71 C9
Flinders → .... 61 D7
Flinders I. ..... 62 C4
Flinders Ras. .. 62 B2
Flint ......... 72 C4
Flint I. ........ 65 L15
Flinton ....... 63 A4
Florence =
  Firenze ..... 20 C3
Florence, *Ala.,*
  *U.S.A.* ...... 74 B4
Florence, *S.C.,*
  *U.S.A.* ...... 75 B8
Florence, L. ... 62 A2
Flores ........ 39 F2
Flores Sea .... 39 F2
Floreşti ....... 17 E9
Floriano ...... 92 D5
Florianópolis .. 94 B7
Florida ....... 94 C5
Florida □ ..... 75 F6
Florida, Straits
  of ......... 86 B3
Flórina ....... 23 D3
Florø ......... 8 F9
Fluk ......... 39 E3
Flushing =
  Vlissingen .. 14 C2
Fly → ....... 61 B7
Flying Fish, C. . 96 B1
Foça ......... 23 E6
Focşani ...... 17 F8
Fóggia ....... 20 D5
Föhr ......... 14 A5
Foix ......... 12 E4
Foligno ....... 20 C4
Folkestone .... 11 F7
Fond du Lac .. 77 D10
Fondi ........ 20 D4
Fonsagrada ... 18 A2
Fonseca, G. de 85 E7
Fontainebleau . 13 B5
Fonte Boa .... 90 D5
Fontenay-le-
  Comte ..... 12 C3
Foochow =
  Fuzhou .... 35 D6
Forbes ....... 63 B4
Ford's Bridge .. 63 A4
Forécariah .... 55 G2
Forestier Pen. . 62 D4
Forfar ........ 10 C5
Forlì ......... 20 B4
Formentera ... 19 C6
Formentor, C. de 19 C7
Former
  Yugoslav
  Republic of
  Macedonia =
  Macedonia ■ 22 D3
Fórmia ....... 20 D4
Formosa =
  Taiwan ■ ... 35 D7
Formosa ...... 94 B5
Formosa, Serra 93 E3
Formosa Bay .. 57 E8
Føroyar =
  Føroyar ..... 6 C4
Føroyar ...... 6 C4
Forrest ....... 62 C3

Forsayth ...... 61 D7
Forst ......... 15 C8
Forster ....... 63 B5
Fort Albany ... 69 C2
Fort Collins ... 76 E2
Fort-de-France . 87 D7
Fort de Possel =
  Possel ...... 56 C3
Fort Dodge ... 77 D7
Fort
  Good-Hope .. 70 B7
Fort Hertz =
  Putao ..... 41 D11
Fort Lauderdale 75 F7
Fort Liard ..... 70 B7
Fort Macleod .. 71 D8
Fort MacMahon 54 C5
Fort McPherson 70 B6
Fort Miribel ... 54 C5
Fort Myers .... 75 F7
Fort Peck L. ... 81 B10
Fort Pierce .... 75 F7
Fort Portal .... 57 D6
Fort Providence 70 B8
Fort Resolution 70 B8
Fort Rosebery =
  Mansa ..... 57 G5
Fort Rupert =
  Waskaganish 69 C3
Fort Sandeman 42 D6
Fort Scott ..... 79 A6
Fort Severn ... 69 C2
Fort
  Shevchenko .. 29 E6
Fort Simpson . 70 B7
Fort Smith,
  *Canada* ..... 70 B8
Fort Smith,
  *U.S.A.* ...... 79 B6
Fort Trinquet =
  Bir Mogrein . 54 C2
Fort Walton
  Beach ..... 74 D4
Fort Wayne ... 72 D3
Fort William .. 10 C4
Fort Worth ... 78 C5
Fort Yukon ... 71 B5
Fortaleza ..... 92 C6
Forūr ........ 44 E3
Foshan ....... 35 D6
Fossano ...... 20 B1
Fouçamou ... 56 E2
Fougères ..... 12 B3
Foula ........ 10 A5
Foumban ..... 55 G7
Foúrnoi ...... 23 F6
Fouta Djalon .. 55 F2
Foveaux Str. .. 65 G3
Foxe Basin ... 68 B3
Foxe Chan. ... 68 B2
Foxe Pen. .... 68 B3
Foxton ....... 64 D6
Foz do Gregório 91 E4
Foz do Iguaçu . 94 B6
Franca ....... 93 G4
Francavilla
  Fontana .... 21 D6
France ■ ..... 13 C5
Frances ...... 62 C3
Franceville .... 56 E2
Franche-Comté 13 C6
Francistown .. 59 C5
Frankfurt,
  *Brandenburg,*
  *Germany* ... 15 B8
Frankfurt,
  *Hessen,*
  *Germany* ... 14 C5
Fränkische Alb 15 D6

# Franklin B.

Franklin B. .... 70 B7
Franklin I. ...... 96 B15
Franklin Mts. .. 70 B7
Franklin Str. ... 70 A10
Frankston ..... 63 C4
Frantsa Iosifa,
  Zemlya ..... 28 A6
Franz ........ 69 D2
Franz Josef
  Land =
  Frantsa Iosifa,
  Zemlya ..... 28 A6
Fraser → ..... 71 D7
Fraser I. ...... 63 A5
Fraserburgh ... 10 C5
Fray Bentos ... 94 C5
Fredericksburg 73 E7
Fredericton ... 69 D4
Fredrikstad .... 9 G10
Freeport,
  Bahamas ... 86 A4
Freeport, U.S.A. 77 D10
Freetown ..... 55 G2
Fregenal de la
  Sierra ...... 18 C2
Freibourg =
  Fribourg .... 13 C7
Freiburg ..... 14 E4
Freire ........ 95 D2
Freising ...... 15 D6
Freistadt ...... 15 D8
Fréjus ........ 13 E7
Fremont ...... 82 B2
French
  Guiana ■ ... 92 B3
French
  Polynesia ■ . 65 M16
Fresco → .... 92 D3
Freshfield, C. .. 96 A14
Fresnillo ...... 84 C4
Fresno ....... 82 B3
Freycinet Pen. . 62 D4
Fria, C. ....... 58 B2
Frías ......... 94 B3
Fribourg ...... 13 C7
Friedrichshafen 14 E5
Friendly Is. =
  Tonga ■ .... 65 L13
Frobisher B. ... 68 B4
Frobisher Bay =
  Iqaluit ...... 68 B4
Frome, L. ..... 62 B2
Frome Downs . 62 B2
Front Range ... 81 E11
Frosinone ..... 20 D4
Frunze =
  Bishkek ..... 29 E8
Frutal ........ 93 F4
Frýdek-Místek . 16 D4
Fuchou =
  Fuzhou .... 35 D6
Fuengirola .... 18 D3
Fuentes de
  Oñoro ...... 18 B2
Fuerte → .... 84 B3
Fuerte Olimpo . 91 H7
Fuerteventura . 54 C2
Fuhai ........ 34 B3
Fuji-San ...... 32 B6
Fujian □ ..... 35 D6
Fujinomiya .... 32 B6
Fujisawa ..... 32 B6
Fukien =
  Fujian □ .... 35 D6
Fukuchiyama .. 32 B4
Fukui ........ 32 A5
Fukuoka ..... 32 C2
Fukushima ... 33 G12
Fukuyama .... 32 B3

Fulda ........ 14 C5
Fulda → ..... 14 C5
Fullerton ..... 82 D4
Funabashi ... 32 B7
Funchal ..... 54 B1
Fundación .... 90 A4
Fundão ...... 18 B2
Fundy, B. of .. 69 D4
Funtua ....... 55 F6
Furāt, Nahr
  al → ..... 47 E6
Furneaux Group 62 D4
Fürstenwalde . 15 B8
Fürth ........ 14 D6
Fury and Hecla
  Str. ........ 68 B2
Fusagasuga ... 90 C4
Fushun ...... 35 B7
Futuna ...... 64 L12
Fuxin ........ 35 B7
Fuyuan ...... 35 B8
Fuzhou ...... 35 D6
Fyn .......... 9 G10

# G

Gabela ....... 56 G2
Gabès ........ 54 B7
Gabès, G. de . 52 B1
Gabon ■ ..... 56 E2
Gaborone .... 59 C5
Gabrovo ..... 22 C5
Gachsārān ... 44 D2
Gadag ....... 43 M9
Gadarwara ... 43 H11
Gadhada .... 43 J7
Gadsden .... 74 B4
Gadwal ..... 43 L10
Gafsa ....... 54 B6
Gagnoa ..... 55 G3
Gagnon ..... 69 C4
Gaillimh =
  Galway .... 11 E2
Gainesville, Fla.,
  U.S.A. ..... 75 E6
Gainesville, Ga.,
  U.S.A. ..... 75 B6
Gainesville,
  Tex., U.S.A. . 78 C5
Gairdner, L. ... 62 B2
Galangue .... 58 A3
Galashiels ... 10 D5
Galați ........ 17 F9
Galatina ..... 21 D7
Galcaio ...... 49 F4
Galdhøpiggen . 8 F9
Galela ....... 39 D3
Galesburg ... 77 E9
Galich ....... 24 B5
Galicia □ ..... 18 A2
Galilee, Sea of
  = Yam
  Kinneret ... 46 D3
Gallabat ..... 53 F6
Gállego → ... 19 B5
Gallegos → .. 95 G3
Gallinas, Pta. . 90 A4
Gallipoli =
  Gelibolu ... 23 D6
Gallípoli ..... 21 D6
Gällivare .... 8 E12
Galloway, Mull
  of ........ 11 D4
Galong ....... 63 B4
Galveston .... 79 E6
Gálvez ....... 94 C4

Galway ....... 11 E2
Galway B. .... 11 E2
Gambaga ..... 55 F4
Gambela ..... 53 G5
Gambia ■ .... 55 F1
Gambia → ... 55 F1
Gambier Is. ... 62 C2
Gamboma .... 56 E3
Gan Jiang → . 35 D6
Ganāveh ..... 44 D2
Gäncä ....... 25 E6
Gand = Gent .. 14 C2
Ganda ....... 58 A2
Gandak → ... 40 E5
Gandava ..... 42 E5
Gander ....... 69 D5
Gandhi Sagar . 43 G9
Gandi ........ 55 F6
Gandía ....... 19 C5
Ganedidalem =
  Gani ....... 39 E3
Ganga → ... 41 F8
Ganganagar .. 42 E8
Gangara ..... 55 F6
Gangaw ..... 41 F10
Gangdisê Shan 40 B3
Ganges =
  Ganga → . 41 F8
Gangtok ..... 41 D7
Gani ......... 39 E3
Gansu □ ..... 34 C5
Ganta ........ 55 G3
Gantheaume, C. 62 C2
Gantsevichi =
  Hantsavichy . 17 B8
Ganyem ..... 39 E6
Ganzhou ..... 35 D6
Gaoua ....... 55 F4
Gaoual ...... 55 F2
Gaoxiong .... 35 D7
Gap ......... 13 D7
Gar ......... 34 C2
Garabogazköl
  Aylagy ..... 29 E6
Garanhuns ... 92 D6
Garawe ...... 55 H3
Gard ......... 49 F4
Garda, L. di ... 20 B3
Garden City .. 78 A3
Garden Grove . 82 D4
Gardēz ...... 42 C6
Gargano, Mte. . 20 D5
Gariglianp → . 20 D4
Garland ...... 81 E7
Garm ........ 29 F8
Garmisch-
  Partenkirchen 14 E6
Garmsār ..... 44 C3
Garoe ....... 49 F4
Garonne → .. 12 D3
Garoua ...... 53 G1
Garrison Res. =
  Sakakawea, L. 76 B4
Garry, L. ...... 70 B9
Garsen ...... 57 E8
Garvie Mts. ... 65 F3
Garwa =
  Garoua .... 53 G1
Gary ......... 72 D2
Garzê ........ 34 C5
Garzón ...... 90 C3
Gasan Kuli =
  Hasan Kuli .. 29 F6
Gascogne ..... 12 E4
Gascogne, G. de 12 D2
Gascony =
  Gascogne .. 12 E4
Gashaka ..... 55 G7
Gaspé ........ 69 D4

Gaspé, C. de .. 69 D4
Gaspé, Pén. de 69 D4
Gasteiz = Vitoria 19 A4
Gastonia ..... 75 B7
Gastre ....... 95 E3
Gata, C. de .... 19 D4
Gata, Sierra de 18 B2
Gateshead .... 11 D6
Gauhati ...... 41 D9
Gaváter ...... 45 E5
Gávdhos ..... 23 G5
Gävle ........ 8 F11
Gawilgarh Hills 43 J10
Gawler ....... 62 B2
Gaxun Nur ... 34 B5
Gaya, India ... 40 E5
Gaya, Niger .. 55 F5
Gayndah ..... 63 A5
Gaysin =
  Haysyn ..... 17 D9
Gayvoron =
  Hayvoron ... 17 D9
Gaza ........ 47 E3
Gaziantep ... 46 C4
Gazli ........ 29 E7
Gdańsk ...... 16 A4
Gdańska, Zatoka 16 A4
Gdov ........ 24 B2
Gdynia ...... 16 A4
Gebe ........ 39 D3
Gebeit Mine .. 52 D6
Gebze ....... 22 D7
Gedaref ...... 53 F6
Gede, Tanjung 37 F3
Gediz → .... 23 E6
Gedser ....... 9 H10
Geelong ..... 63 C3
Geesthacht ... 14 B6
Geidam ...... 53 F1
Geili ........ 53 E5
Geita ........ 57 E6
Gejiu ........ 34 D5
Gela ......... 21 F5
Geladi ....... 49 F4
Gelehun ..... 55 G2
Gelibolu ..... 23 D6
Gelsenkirchen . 14 C4
Gemas ....... 37 D2
Gemena ..... 56 D3
Gemerek .... 46 C4
Gemlik ...... 23 D7
General Acha . 94 D4
General Alvear,
  Buenos Aires,
  Argentina ... 94 D5
General Alvear,
  Mendoza,
  Argentina ... 94 D3
General Artigas 94 B5
General
  Belgrano ... 94 D5
General Guido . 94 D5
General Juan
  Madariaga .. 94 D5
General La
  Madrid ..... 94 D4
General
  MacArthur .. 38 B3
General Martin
  Miguel de
  Güemes ... 94 A4
General Paz ... 94 B5
General Pico .. 94 D4
General Pinedo 94 B4
General Santos 38 C3
General Villegas 94 D4
Geneva =
  Genève .... 13 C7

116

Geneva, L. =
Léman, L. ... 13 C7
Genève ...... 13 C7
Genil → ..... 18 D3
Gennargentu,
Mti. del ..... 21 D2
Genoa =
Génova ..... 20 B2
Genoa ....... 63 C4
Génova ...... 20 B2
Génova, G. di . 20 C2
Gent ........ 14 C2
Georga, Zemlya 28 A5
George ...... 58 E4
George → .... 68 C4
George, L.,
N.S.W.,
Australia .... 63 C4
George, L.,
S. Austral.,
Australia .... 62 C3
George, L.,
Uganda ..... 57 D6
George River =
Kangiqsualujjuaq
.......... 68 C4
George Sound . 65 F2
George Town . 36 C2
George V Land 96 A14
George VI
Sound ..... 96 B3
Georgetown,
Gambia ..... 55 F2
Georgetown,
Guyana .... 90 B7
Georgia □ .... 75 C6
Georgia ■ .... 25 E5
Georgian B. ... 69 D2
Georgiu-Dezh =
Liski ...... 24 C4
Georgiyevsk .. 25 E5
Gera ........ 15 C7
Geral de Goiás,
Serra ...... 93 E4
Geraldton .... 60 F1
Gerede ...... 46 B3
Gereshk ..... 42 D4
Gerlogubi .... 49 F4
Germany ■ ... 14 C6
Germiston .... 59 D5
Gerona ...... 19 B7
Geser ....... 39 E4
Getafe ...... 18 B4
Gettysburg ... 73 E7
Getz Ice Shelf . 96 B18
Ghaghara → . 40 E5
Ghana ■ ..... 55 G4
Ghanzi ...... 58 C4
Ghardaïa ..... 54 B5
Gharyān ..... 52 B3
Ghat ........ 54 D7
Ghawdex =
Gozo ...... 21 F5
Ghayl ....... 47 G6
Ghazal, Bahr
el →, Chad . 53 F2
Ghazâl, Bahr
el →, Sudan 57 C6
Ghazaouet .... 54 A4
Ghaziabad .... 42 E10
Ghazipur .... 40 E4
Ghaznī ...... 42 C6
Ghaznī □ .... 42 C6
Ghèlinsor .... 49 F4
Ghent = Gent . 14 C2
Ghizao ...... 42 C4
Ghowr □ .... 42 C4
Ghugus ...... 43 K11
Ghūriān ..... 42 B2

Gia Lai = Pleiku 36 B3
Gian ........ 38 C3
Giarabub = Al
Jaghbūb .... 52 C3
Giarre ....... 21 F5
Gibraltar ■ ... 18 D3
Gibraltar, Str. of 18 E3
Gibson Desert . 60 E4
Gidole ....... 53 G6
Giessen ...... 14 C5
Gifu ........ 32 B5
Giglio ....... 20 C3
Gijón ....... 18 A3
Gila → ...... 82 D5
Gīlān □ ...... 46 C7
Gilbert Is. .... 64 J12
Gilgandra .... 63 B4
Gilgit ....... 42 B9
Gilles, L. .... 62 B2
Gilmore ..... 63 C4
Gimbi ....... 53 G6
Gin Gin ..... 63 A5
Ginir ........ 49 F3
Giohar ...... 49 G4
Gióna, Óros .. 23 E4
Girardot ..... 90 C4
Giresun ..... 46 B4
Girga ....... 52 C5
Giridih ...... 40 E6
Girilambone .. 63 B4
Girne = Kyrenia 46 D3
Girona =
Gerona ..... 19 B7
Gironde → ... 12 D3
Girvan ...... 10 D4
Gisborne ..... 64 C8
Gisenyi ...... 57 E5
Gitega ...... 57 E5
Giuba → ..... 49 G3
Giurgiu ...... 22 C5
Giza = El Gîza . 52 C5
Giżycko ..... 16 A5
Gjirokastra ... 23 D3
Gjoa Haven .. 70 B10
Glace Bay ... 69 D5
Gladstone,
Queens.,
Australia .... 61 E9
Gladstone,
S. Austral.,
Australia .... 62 B2
Glåma =
Glomma → . 9 G10
Glasgow .... 10 D4
Glazov ...... 28 D6
Gleiwitz =
Gliwice .... 16 C4
Glen Canyon
National
Recreation
Area ...... 83 B7
Glen Innes ... 63 A5
Glendale .... 82 C3
Glenelg ...... 62 B2
Glenelg → ... 62 C3
Glenmorgan .. 63 A4
Glenorchy ... 62 D4
Glenreagh ... 63 B5
Glenrothes ... 10 C5
Glens Falls .. 73 C9
Gliwice ..... 16 C4
Głogów ...... 16 C3
Glomma → .. 9 G10
Glorieuses, Is. . 59 G9
Gloucester,
Australia .... 63 B5
Gloucester, U.K. 11 F5
Glusk ....... 17 B9
Gmünd ...... 15 D8

Gmunden ..... 15 E7
Gniezno ...... 16 B3
Go Cong ..... 36 B3
Goa ......... 43 M8
Goa □ ....... 43 M8
Goalen Hd. ... 63 C5
Goalpara ..... 41 D8
Goba, Ethiopia 49 F2
Goba, Mozam. . 59 D6
Gobabis ..... 58 C3
Gobi ........ 35 B6
Gochas ...... 58 C3
Godavari → .. 40 J4
Godavari Point 40 J4
Godhra ...... 43 H8
Gods → ..... 71 C10
Gods L. ...... 71 C10
Godthåb = Nuuk . 68 B5
Godwin Austen
= K2 ....... 42 B10
Goeie Hoop,
Kaap die =
Good Hope, C.
of ......... 58 E3
Gogra =
Ghaghara → 40 E5
Goiânia ...... 93 F4
Goiás ....... 93 F3
Goiás □ ..... 93 E4
Goio-Ere ..... 94 A6
Gojra ....... 42 D8
Gökçeada ... 23 D5
Gokteik ..... 41 F11
Gold Coast .. 63 A5
Golden Gate .. 80 G2
Goldsboro ... 75 B9
Goleniów .... 16 B2
Golfo Aranci .. 20 D2
Golspie ..... 10 C5
Goma ....... 57 E5
Gomel =
Homyel .... 17 B10
Gomera ..... 54 C1
Gómez Palacio 84 B4
Gomogomo ... 39 F4
Gomoh ...... 40 F6
Gompa = Ganta 55 G3
Gonābād ..... 44 C4
Gonaïves .... 87 C5
Gonbad-e Kāvūs 44 B3
Gonda ....... 40 D3
Gonder ...... 53 F6
Gönen ....... 23 D6
Gonghe ...... 34 C5
Gongolgon ... 63 B4
Goniri ....... 53 F1
Good Hope, C.
of ......... 58 E3
Goodooga ... 63 A4
Goolgowi .... 63 B4
Goombalie ... 63 A4
Goondiwindi .. 63 A5
Gooray ...... 63 A5
Gop ........ 43 H6
Göppingen .. 14 D5
Gorakhpur ... 40 D4
Goražde .... 20 C7
Gordon → ... 62 D4
Gore, Australia 63 A5
Goré, Chad .. 53 G2
Gore, Ethiopia . 53 G6
Gore, N.Z. ... 65 G3
Gorgān ...... 44 B3
Gorgona, I. .. 90 C3
Gorízia ..... 20 B4
Gorki = Nizhniy
Novgorod .. 24 B5
Gorkiy =
Nizhniy
Novgorod ... 24 B5

Gorkovskoye
Vdkhr. ...... 24 B5
Görlitz ...... 15 C8
Gorlovka =
Horlivka .... 25 D4
Gorna
Dzhumayo =
Blagoevgrad 22 C4
Gorna
Oryakhovitsa 22 C5
Gorno-Altay □ . 29 D9
Gorno-Altaysk . 29 D9
Gorno Slinkino
=
Gornopravdinsk
.......... 29 C8
Gornopravdinsk 29 C8
Gorodenka =
Horodenka .. 17 D7
Gorodok =
Horodok .... 17 D6
Gorokhov =
Horokhiv .... 17 C7
Gorontalo .... 39 D2
Gorzów
Wielkopolski 16 B2
Gosford ...... 63 B5
Goslar ...... 14 C6
Gospič ...... 20 B5
Göta kanal .... 9 G11
Göteborg ..... 9 G10
Gotha ....... 14 C6
Gothenburg =
Göteborg ... 9 G10
Gotland ...... 9 G11
Göttingen ..... 14 C5
Gottwaldov =
Zlin ........ 16 D3
Gouda ...... 14 B3
Gouin, Rés. .. 69 D3
Goulburn .... 63 B4
Gounou-Gaya . 53 G2
Gourma
Rharous .... 55 E4
Gourock Ra. ... 63 C4
Governador
Valadares ... 93 F5
Gowd-e Zirreh . 42 E3
Goya ....... 94 B5
Goyder Lagoon 62 A2
Goyllarisquisga 91 F3
Goz Beïda ... 53 F3
Gozo ....... 21 F5
Graaff-Reinet .. 58 E4
Gračac ....... 20 B5
Gracias a Dios,
C. ........ 86 D3
Grado ....... 18 A2
Gradule ..... 63 A4
Grafton ..... 63 A5
Graham Bell,
Os. ....... 28 A7
Graham Land . 96 A3
Grahamstown . 59 E5
Grajaú ...... 92 D4
Grajaú → .... 92 C5
Grampian
Highlands =
Grampian
Mts. ...... 10 C4
Grampian Mts. 10 C4
Gran Canaria . 54 C1
Gran Chaco .. 94 B4
Gran Paradiso . 20 B1
Gran Sasso
d'Italia ..... 20 C4
Granada, Nic. . 85 E7
Granada, Spain 18 D4

# Granby

Granby . . . . . . . 69 D3
Grand Bahama 86 A4
Grand Bassam 55 G4
Grand Canyon . 83 B6
Grand Cayman 86 C3
Grand Coulee
Dam . . . . . . . 80 B4
Grand Forks,
Canada . . . . . 71 D8
Grand Forks,
U.S.A. . . . . . . 76 B6
Grand Island . . 76 E5
Grand Lahou . . 55 G3
Grand Rapids,
Canada . . . . . 71 C10
Grand Rapids,
U.S.A. . . . . . . 72 C3
Grand St.-
Bernard, Col
du . . . . . . . . 13 D7
Grand Teton . . 81 D8
Grande →,
Argentina . . . 94 A3
Grande →,
Bolivia . . . . . 91 G6
Grande →,
Bahia, Brazil . 93 E5
Grande →,
Minas Gerais,
Brazil . . . . . . . 93 G3
Grande, B. . . . . 95 G3
Grande, Rio → 79 F5
Grande Baleine,
R. de la → . . 69 C3
Grande de
Santiago → 84 C3
Granite City . . . 77 F9
Granity . . . . . . . 65 D4
Granja . . . . . . . 92 C5
Granollers . . . . 19 B7
Grantham . . . . 11 E6
Granville . . . . . 12 B3
Gras, L. de . . . . 70 B8
Grasse . . . . . . . 13 E7
Grassmere . . . . 62 B3
Graulhet . . . . . . 12 E4
's-Gravenhage . 14 B3
Gravesend . . . . 63 A5
Graz . . . . . . . . . 15 E8
Great Abaco I. . 86 A4
Great Australian
Bight . . . . . . 60 G4
Great Barrier I. 64 B6
Great Barrier
Reef . . . . . . . 61 D8
Great Basin . . . 80 F5
Great Bear → . 70 B7
Great Bear L. . . 70 B7
Great Belt =
Store Bælt . . 9 G10
Great Dividing
Ra. . . . . . . . . 61 E8
Great Falls . . . . 81 B8
Great Inagua I. 86 B5
Great Indian
Desert = Thar
Desert . . . . . 42 F7
Great Karoo . . . 58 E4
Great Lake . . . . 62 D4
Great Ouse → 11 E7
Great Ruaha → 57 F7
Great Saint
Bernard P. =
Grand St.-
Bernard, Col
du . . . . . . . . . 13 D7
Great Salt L. . . 81 E7
Great Salt Lake
Desert . . . . . . 81 E7

Great Sandy
Desert . . . . . . 60 E3
Great Sangi =
Sangihe, P. . . 39 D3
Great Slave L. . 70 B8
Great Smoky
Mts. Nat. Pk. 75 B6
Great Victoria
Desert . . . . . . 60 F4
Great Wall . . . . 35 C5
Great Yarmouth 11 E7
Greater Antilles 86 C5
Greater Sunda
Is. . . . . . . . . . 37 F4
Gredos, Sierra
de . . . . . . . . . 18 B3
Greece ■ . . . . . 23 E4
Greeley . . . . . . 76 E2
Green → . . . . . 83 A8
Green Bay . . . . 72 B2
Green C. . . . . . 63 C5
Greenland ■ . . 66 C9
Greenock . . . . . 10 D4
Greensboro . . . 75 A8
Greenville,
Liberia . . . . . 55 G3
Greenville, Ala.,
U.S.A. . . . . . . 74 D4
Greenville,
Miss., U.S.A. 79 C8
Greenville, N.C.,
U.S.A. . . . . . . 75 B9
Greenville, S.C.,
U.S.A. . . . . . . 75 B6
Greenwood,
Miss., U.S.A. 79 C8
Greenwood,
S.C., U.S.A. . 75 B6
Gregory, L. . . . 62 A2
Greifswald . . . . 15 A7
Greiz . . . . . . . . 15 C7
Gremikha . . . . . 28 C4
Grenada ■ . . . . 87 D7
Grenfell . . . . . . 63 B4
Grenoble . . . . . 13 D6
Grey → . . . . . . 65 E4
Grey Ra. . . . . . . 63 A3
Greymouth . . . 65 E4
Greytown, N.Z. 65 D6
Greytown,
S. Africa . . . . 59 D6
Griffin . . . . . . . 75 C5
Griffith . . . . . . . 63 B4
Grimari . . . . . . . 56 C4
Grimaylov =
Hrymayliv . . . 17 D8
Grimsby . . . . . . 11 E6
Gris-Nez, C. . . . 12 A4
Grodno =
Hrodna . . . . . 17 B6
Grodzyanka =
Hrodzyanka . 17 B9
Grójec . . . . . . . 16 C5
Groningen . . . . 14 B4
Grootfontein . . 58 B3
Gross Glockner 15 E7
Grosser Arber . 15 D7
Grosseto . . . . . 20 C3
Groznyy . . . . . . 25 E6
Grudziądz . . . . . 16 B4
Gryazi . . . . . . . 24 C4
Gryazovets . . . . 28 D5
Gua . . . . . . . . . 40 F5
Guadalajara,
Mexico . . . . . 84 C4
Guadalajara,
Spain . . . . . . 18 B4
Guadalcanal . . 64 K11
Guadalete → . 18 D2
Guadalquivir → 18 D2

Guadalupe =
Guadeloupe ■ 87 C7
Guadalupe,
Sierra de . . . 18 C3
Guadarrama,
Sierra de . . . 18 B4
Guadeloupe ■ . 87 C7
Guadiana → . . 18 D2
Guadix . . . . . . . 18 D4
Guafo, Boca del 95 E2
Guaíra . . . . . . . 94 A6
Guaitecas, Is. . . 95 E2
Guam ■ . . . . . . 64 H9
Guamúchil . . . . 84 B3
Guan Xian . . . . 34 C5
Guanahani =
San Salvador 86 B5
Guanajuato . . . 84 C4
Guandacol . . . . 94 B3
Guane . . . . . . . 86 B3
Guangdong □ . 35 D6
Guanghua . . . . 35 C6
Guangxi
Zhuangzu
Zizhiqu □ . . . 35 D5
Guangzhou . . . 35 D6
Guanipa → . . . 90 B6
Guantánamo . . 86 B4
Guaporé → . . . 91 F5
Guaqui . . . . . . . 91 G5
Guarapuava . . . 94 B6
Guarda . . . . . . . 18 B2
Guardafui, C. =
Asir, Ras . . . . 49 E5
Guasdualito . . . 90 B4
Guasipati . . . . . 90 B6
Guatemala ■ . . 85 E6
Guatemala ■ . . 85 D6
Guatire . . . . . . 90 A5
Guaviare □ . . . 90 C4
Guaviare → . . . 90 C5
Guaxupé . . . . . 93 G4
Guayama . . . . . 87 C6
Guayaquil . . . . 90 D3
Guayaquil, G. de 90 D2
Guaymas . . . . . 84 B2
Guddu Barrage 42 E6
Gudivada . . . . . 40 J3
Gudur . . . . . . . 43 M11
Guecho . . . . . . 19 A4
Guékédou . . . . 55 G2
Guelma . . . . . . 54 A6
Guelph . . . . . . 69 D2
Guéréda . . . . . . 53 F3
Guéret . . . . . . . 12 C4
Guernica . . . . . 19 A4
Guernsey . . . . . 11 G5
Guidónia-
Montecélio . . 20 C4
Guiglo . . . . . . . 55 G3
Guildford . . . . . 11 F6
Guilin . . . . . . . 35 D6
Guimarães,
Brazil . . . . . . 92 C5
Guimarães,
Portugal . . . . 18 B1
Guimaras . . . . . 38 B2
Guinea ■ . . . . . 55 F2
Guinea, Gulf of 51 F3
Guinea-Bissau ■ 55 F1
Guingamp . . . . 12 B2
Guiping . . . . . . 35 D6
Güiria . . . . . . . 90 A6
Guiuan . . . . . . 38 B3
Guiyang . . . . . . 35 D5

Guizhou □ . . . . 35 D5
Gujarat □ . . . . . 43 H7
Gujranwala . . . 42 C9
Gujrat . . . . . . . 42 C9
Gulbarga . . . . . 43 L10
Gulf, The . . . . . 44 E2
Gulgong . . . . . . 63 B4
Güllük . . . . . . . 23 F6
Gulshad . . . . . . 29 E8
Gulu . . . . . . . . 57 D6
Gum Lake . . . . 62 B3
Gummi . . . . . . . 55 F6
Gunnedah . . . . 63 B5
Gunningbar
Cr. → . . . . . . 63 B4
Guntakal . . . . . 43 M10
Guntur . . . . . . . 40 J3
Gunungapi . . . . 39 F3
Gunungsitoli . . 37 D1
Gunza . . . . . . . 56 G2
Gupis . . . . . . . 42 A8
Gürchān . . . . . 46 D7
Gurdaspur . . . . 42 C9
Gurgaon . . . . . 42 E10
Gurkha . . . . . . 40 C5
Gurley . . . . . . . 63 A4
Gurupá . . . . . . 92 C3
Gurupá, I.
Grande de . . 92 C3
Gurupi → . . . . . 92 C4
Guryev =
Atyraū . . . . . 29 E6
Gusau . . . . . . . 55 F6
Güstrow . . . . . . 15 B7
Gütersloh . . . . 14 C5
Guthrie . . . . . . 78 B5
Guyana ■ . . . . . 90 B7
Guyane
française ■ =
French
Guiana ■ . . . 92 B3
Guyenne . . . . . 12 D4
Guyra . . . . . . . 63 B5
Gwa . . . . . . . . . 41 J10
Gwaai . . . . . . . 59 B5
Gwabegar . . . . 63 B4
Gwādar . . . . . . 42 G3
Gwalior . . . . . . 42 F11
Gwanda . . . . . . 59 C5
Gweru . . . . . . . 59 B5
Gwydir → . . . . 63 A4
Gyandzha =
Gäncä . . . . . 25 E6
Gyaring Hu . . . 34 C4
Gydanskiy P-ov. 28 B8
Gympie . . . . . . 63 A5
Gyöngyös . . . . 16 E4
Györ . . . . . . . . 16 E3
Gypsumville . . 71 C10
Gyula . . . . . . . 16 E5
Gyumri . . . . . . 25 E5
Gyzylarbat . . . . 29 F6

# H

Ha 'Arava → . 47 E3
Haarlem . . . . . . 14 B3
Haast → . . . . . 65 E3
Habaswein . . . . 57 D7
Hachinohe . . . . 33 F12
Hadarba, Ras . . 52 D6

118

Hadd, R'as al . . 45 F4
Hadejia . . . . . . . 55 F7
Haden . . . . . . . 63 A5
Hadera . . . . . . . 46 D3
Hadhramaut =
  Hadramawt . 49 D4
Hadramawt . . . 49 D4
Haeju . . . . . . . . 35 C7
Haerhpin =
  Harbin . . . . . . 35 B7
Hafar al Bāṭin . 47 E6
Hafizabad . . . . . 42 C8
Haflong . . . . . . 41 E9
Haft Gel . . . . . . 47 E7
Hafun, Ras . . . . 49 E5
Hagen . . . . . . . 14 C4
Hagerstown . . . 73 E7
Hagi . . . . . . . . 32 B2
Hagondange-
  Briey . . . . . . . 13 B7
Hague, C. de la 12 B3
Hague, The = 's-
  Gravenhage . 14 B3
Haguenau . . . . 13 B7
Hai'an . . . . . . . 35 C7
Haifa = Ḥefa . 46 D3
Haikou . . . . . . 35 D6
Ḥā'il . . . . . . . . 47 F5
Hailar . . . . . . . 35 B6
Haileybury . . . . 69 D3
Hailun . . . . . . . 35 B7
Hainan □ . . . . . 35 E5
Haiphong . . . . . 35 D5
Haiti ■ . . . . . . . 87 C5
Haiya Junction 53 E6
Hajar Bangar . . 53 F3
Hajdúböszörmény
  . . . . . . . . . . 16 E5
Hajnówka . . . . . 17 B6
Hakken-Zan . . 32 B4
Hakodate . . . . 32 F12
Hala . . . . . . . . 42 G6
Ḥalab . . . . . . . 46 C4
Ḥalabjah . . . . . 46 D6
Halaib . . . . . . . 52 D6
Halberstadt . . . 15 C6
Halcombe . . . . 64 D6
Halcon, Mt. . . . 38 B2
Halden . . . . . . . 9 G10
Haldia . . . . . . . 40 F7
Haldwani . . . . . 42 E11
Halifax, Canada 69 D4
Halifax, U.K. . . . 11 E6
Ḥalīl → . . . . . 44 E4
Hall Beach =
  Sanirajak . . . 68 B2
Halle . . . . . . . . 15 C6
Hallett . . . . . . . 62 B2
Halmahera . . . . 39 D3
Halmstad . . . . . 9 G10
Halq el Oued . 52 A1
Hälsingborg =
  Helsingborg . 9 G10
Halul . . . . . . . . 44 E3
Hamada . . . . . . 32 B3
Hamadān . . . . 46 D7
Hamadān □ . . . 46 D7
Hamāh . . . . . . 46 D4
Hamamatsu . . 32 B5
Hamar . . . . . . . 8 F10
Hamburg . . . . . 14 B5
Hameln . . . . . . 14 B5
Hamersley Ra. . 60 E2
Hamhung . . . . 35 C7
Hami . . . . . . . . 34 B4
Hamilton,
  Australia . . . 62 C3
Hamilton,
  Canada . . . . 69 D3

Hamilton, N.Z. . 64 B6
Hamilton, U.K. . 10 D4
Hamley Bridge 62 B2
Hamlin =
  Hameln . . . . . 14 B5
Hamm . . . . . . . 14 C4
Hammerfest . . . 8 D12
Hammond . . . . 72 D2
Hampden . . . . . 65 F4
Hampton . . . . . 73 F7
Hamrat esh
  Sheykh . . . . . 53 F4
Han Pijesak . . . 20 B7
Hanamaki . . . . 33 G12
Hanau . . . . . . . 14 C5
Hancock . . . . . 77 C7
Handa . . . . . . . 49 E5
Handan . . . . . . 35 C6
Handeni . . . . . . 57 F7
Hangayn Nuruu 34 B4
Hangchou =
  Hangzhou . . . 35 C7
Hangu . . . . . . . 35 C6
Hangzhou . . . . 35 C7
Hangzhou Wan 35 C7
Ḥanīsh . . . . . . 49 E3
Hanle . . . . . . . 42 C11
Hanmer Springs 65 E5
Hanna . . . . . . . 71 C8
Hannibal . . . . . 77 F9
Hannover . . . . . 14 B5
Hanoi . . . . . . . 35 D5
Hanover =
  Hannover . . . 14 B5
Hanover, I. . . . . 95 G2
Hansi . . . . . . . 42 E9
Hanson, L. . . . . 62 B2
Hantsavichy . . . 17 B8
Hanzhong . . . . 35 C5
Haora . . . . . . . 40 F7
Haparanda . . . 8 E12
Happy Valley-
  Goose Bay . . 69 C4
Hapur . . . . . . . 42 E10
Ḥaql . . . . . . . . 47 E3
Har . . . . . . . . . 39 F4
Har Hu . . . . . . 34 C4
Har Us Nuur . . 34 B4
Ḥaraḍ . . . . . . . 47 F7
Haraisan Plateau
  = Hurayṣān . 47 G6
Harardera . . . . 49 G4
Harare . . . . . . 59 B6
Harazé . . . . . . 53 F2
Harbin . . . . . . 35 B7
Harbour Grace 69 D5
Hardangerfjorden
  . . . . . . . . . . 8 F9
Hardap Dam . . 58 C3
Hardwar =
  Haridwar . . . 42 E11
Hardy, Pen. . . . 95 H3
Harer . . . . . . . 49 F3
Hargeisa . . . . . 49 F3
Hari → . . . . . . 37 E2
Haridwar . . . . 42 E11
Haringhata → . 41 G7
Harīrūd . . . . . . 45 C5
Harīrūd → . . . 42 A2
Harlingen . . . . 78 F5
Harlow . . . . . . 11 F7
Harney Basin . 80 D4
Härnösand . . . 8 F11
Ḥarrat al Kishb 47 G5
Harrat al
  'Uwairidh . . . 47 F4
Harris . . . . . . . 10 C3
Harris L. . . . . . 62 B2
Harrisburg . . . . 73 D7

Harrison, C. . . . 68 C5
Harrison Bay . . 71 A4
Harrogate . . . . 11 D6
Hart, L. . . . . . . 62 B2
Hartford . . . . . 73 D9
Hartlepool . . . . 11 D6
Harvey . . . . . . 72 D2
Harwich . . . . . . 11 F7
Haryana □ . . . . 42 E10
Haryn → . . . . . 17 B8
Harz . . . . . . . . 14 C6
Hasa . . . . . . . . 47 F7
Hasan Kuli . . . 29 F6
Hassi Inifel . . . 54 C5
Hassi Messaoud 54 B6
Hastings, N.Z. . 64 C7
Hastings, U.K. . 11 F7
Hastings, U.S.A. 78 E5
Hastings Ra. . . 63 B5
Hatay = Antalya 46 C2
Hatfield P.O. . . 62 B3
Hatgal . . . . . . . 34 A5
Hathras . . . . . . 42 F11
Hatia . . . . . . . 41 F8
Hattah . . . . . . 62 B3
Hatteras, C. . . . 75 B10
Hattiesburg . . . 79 D9
Hatvan . . . . . . 16 E4
Hau Bon = Cheo
  Reo . . . . . . . 36 B3
Haugesund . . . 9 G9
Hauraki G. . . . 64 B6
Haut Atlas . . . 54 B3
Hautah, Waḥat
  al . . . . . . . . 47 G6
Hauts Plateaux 54 B4
Havana = La
  Habana . . . . 86 B3
Havant . . . . . . 11 F6
Havel → . . . . . 15 B7
Havelock . . . . . 65 D5
Haverfordwest . 11 F4
Havlíčkův Brod 16 D2
Havre . . . . . . . 81 A9
Havza . . . . . . . 46 B3
Hawaii □ . . . . . 82 J12
Hawaiian Is. . . . 82 H12
Hawea, L. . . . . 65 F3
Hawera . . . . . . 64 C6
Hawick . . . . . . 10 D5
Hawke B. . . . . . 64 C7
Hawker . . . . . . 62 B2
Hawkwood . . . 63 A5
Hay . . . . . . . . . 63 B3
Hay River . . . . 70 B8
Haya . . . . . . . . 39 E3
Hayes → . . . . . 71 C10
Hayrabolu . . . . 22 D6
Haysyn . . . . . . 17 D9
Hayvoron . . . . 17 D9
Hazaribag . . . . 40 F5
Healesville . . . . 63 C4
Hearst . . . . . . . 69 D2
Hebei □ . . . . . . 35 C6
Hebel . . . . . . . 63 A4
Hebron = Al
  Khalīl . . . . . . 47 E3
Hebron . . . . . . 68 C4
Hechi . . . . . . . 35 D5
Hechuan . . . . . 35 C5
Heerlen . . . . . . 13 A6
Ḥefa . . . . . . . . 46 D3
Hefei . . . . . . . 35 C6
Hegang . . . . . . 35 B8
Heidelberg . . . 14 D5
Heilbron . . . . . 59 D5
Heilbronn . . . . 14 D5
Heilongjiang □ 35 B7

Heilunkiang =
  Heilongjiang □
  . . . . . . . . . . 35 B7
Heinze Is. . . . . 41 K11
Hejaz = Al Ḥijāz 47 F4
Hekımhan . . . . 46 C4
Hekou . . . . . . . 34 D5
Helena, Ark.,
  U.S.A. . . . . . . 79 B8
Helena, Mont.,
  U.S.A. . . . . . . 81 B7
Helensville . . . . 64 B6
Helgoland . . . . 14 A4
Heligoland =
  Helgoland . . . 14 A4
Heligoland B. =
  Deutsche
  Bucht . . . . . . 14 A5
Hellín . . . . . . . 19 C5
Helmand □ . . . 42 D3
Helmand → . . . 42 D2
Helmand,
  Hamun . . . . . 45 D5
Helmsdale . . . . 10 B5
Helsingborg . . 9 G10
Helsingfors =
  Helsinki . . . . . 9 F13
Helsinki . . . . . 9 F13
Helwân . . . . . . 52 C5
Hemel
  Hempstead . . 11 F6
Henan □ . . . . . 35 C6
Henares → . . . 18 B4
Henderson . . . . 75 A8
Hendon . . . . . . 63 A5
Hengyang . . . . 35 D6
Henrietta Maria,
  C. . . . . . . . . 69 C2
Hentiyn Nuruu 35 B5
Henty . . . . . . . 63 C4
Henzada . . . . . 41 J10
Herāt . . . . . . . 42 B3
Herāt □ . . . . . . 42 B3
Hercegnovi . . . 22 C2
Hereford . . . . . 11 E5
Herford . . . . . . 14 B5
Hermidale . . . . 63 B4
Hermitage . . . . 65 E4
Hermite, I. . . . . 95 H3
Hermon, Mt. =
  Ash Shaykh,
  J. . . . . . . . . 46 D3
Hermosillo . . . . 84 B2
Hernád → . . . . 16 E5
Hernandarias . . 94 B6
Heroica Nogales
  = Nogales . . 84 A2
Heron Bay . . . . 69 D2
Herrick . . . . . . 62 D4
's-
  Hertogenbosch
  . . . . . . . . . . 14 C3
Hesse =
  Hessen □ . . . 14 C5
Hessen □ . . . . . 14 C5
Hewett, C. . . . . 68 A4
Hexham . . . . . 11 D5
Heyfield . . . . . . 63 C4
Heywood . . . . 62 C3
Hibbing . . . . . . 77 B8
Hibbs B. . . . . . 62 D4
Hickory . . . . . . 75 B7
Hicks, Pt. . . . . . 63 C4
Hida-Sammyaku 32 A5
Hidalgo del
  Parral . . . . . 84 B3
Higashiōsaka . . 32 B4
High Atlas =
  Haut Atlas . . 54 B3

# High Point

High Point . . . . 75 B8
High River . . . . 71 C8
High Tatra =
   Tatry . . . . . . . 16 D4
High Wycombe 11 F6
Hiiumaa . . . . . . 24 B1
Ḥijārah, Ṣaḥrā'
   al . . . . . . . . . 47 E6
Ḥijāz □ . . . . . . 48 C2
Hijo = Tagum . 38 C3
Hikone . . . . . . . 32 B5
Hikurangi . . . . 64 A6
Hikurangi, Mt. . 64 C7
Hildesheim . . . 14 B5
Hillston . . . . . . . 63 B4
Hilo . . . . . . . . 82 J13
Hilversum . . . . 14 B3
Himachal
   Pradesh □ . . 42 D10
Himalaya . . . . . 40 C5
Himatnagar . . 43 H8
Himeji . . . . . . . . 32 B4
Himi . . . . . . . . . 32 A5
Ḥimṣ . . . . . . . . 46 D4
Hindmarsh, L. . 62 C3
Hindu Kush . . 42 B7
Hindubagh . . . . 42 D5
Hindupur . . . . 43 N10
Hinganghat . . 43 J11
Hingoli . . . . . . 43 K10
Hinna = Imi . . . 49 F3
Hinojosa del
   Duque . . . . . . 18 C3
Hirakud Dam . . 40 G4
Hiratsuka . . . . 32 B6
Hirosaki . . . . . 33 F12
Hiroshima . . . . 32 B3
Hisar . . . . . . . . 42 E9
Hispaniola . . . . 87 C5
Hita . . . . . . . . . 32 C2
Hitachi . . . . . . . 32 A7
Hjälmaren . . . . 9 G11
Hlyboka . . . . . . 17 D7
Ho . . . . . . . . . . 55 G5
Ho Chi Minh
   City = Phanh
   Bho Ho Chi
   Minh . . . . . . 36 B3
Hoai Nhon . . . . 36 B3
Hoare B. . . . . . . 68 B4
Hobart . . . . . . . 62 D4
Hobbs Coast . . 96 B18
Hodgson . . . . . 71 C10
Hódmezővásárhely
   . . . . . . . . . . . 16 E5
Hodna, Chott el 54 A5
Hodonín . . . . . 16 D3
Hoek van
   Holland . . . . 14 B3
Hof . . . . . . . . . . 15 C6
Hōfu . . . . . . . . 32 B2
Hogan Group . 62 C4
Hoggar =
   Ahaggar . . . . 54 D6
Hoh Xil Shan . . 34 C3
Hohe Rhön . . . 14 C5
Hohhot . . . . . . 35 B6
Hoi An . . . . . . . 36 A3
Hokianga
   Harbour . . . 64 A5
Hokitika . . . . . . 65 E4
Hokkaidō □ . . . 32 F12
Holbrook . . . . 63 C4
Holguín . . . . . . 86 B4
Hollandia =
   Jayapura . . . 39 E6
Holman Island . 70 A8
Holy Cross . . . 71 B4
Holyhead . . . . . 11 E4

Homalin . . . . . . 41 E10
Hombori . . . . . . 55 E4
Home B. . . . . . . 68 B4
Homer . . . . . . . 71 C4
Homs = Ḥimṣ . 46 D4
Homyel . . . . . . 17 B10
Hon Chong . . . 36 B2
Honan =
   Henan □ . . . . 35 C6
Honda . . . . . . . 90 B4
Hondeklipbaai . 58 E3
Honduras ■ . . . 85 E7
Honduras, G. de 85 D7
Honfleur . . . . . 12 B4
Hong Kong . . . 35 D6
Hongjiang . . . . 35 D5
Hongshui He → 35 D5
Hongze Hu . . . 35 C6
Honiara . . . . . 64 K10
Honolulu . . . . 82 H12
Honshū . . . . . 32 G11
Hood, Mt. . . . . 80 C3
Hooghly → =
   Hughli → . . . 40 G7
Hook of Holland
   = Hoek van
   Holland . . . . 14 B3
Hoorn . . . . . . . 14 B3
Hoover Dam . . 82 B5
Hope, L. . . . . . . 62 A2
Hope, Pt. . . . . . 71 B3
Hopedale . . . . . 68 C4
Hopei =
   Hebei □ . . . . 35 C6
Hopetoun . . . . . 62 C3
Hopetown . . . . 58 D4
Hoquiam . . . . . 80 B2
Horlick Mts. . . . 96 C1
Horlivka . . . . . . 25 D4
Hormoz . . . . . . 44 E3
Hormoz, Jaz. ye 44 E4
Hormozgān □ . 44 E3
Hormuz, Str. of 44 E4
Horn . . . . . . . 15 D8
Horn, Cape =
   Hornos, C. de 95 H3
Hornavan . . . . 8 E11
Hornos, C. de . 95 H3
Hornsby . . . . . 63 B5
Horodenka . . . . 17 D7
Horodok,
   *Khmelnytskyy,*
   *Ukraine* . . . . 17 D8
Horodok, *Lviv,*
   *Ukraine* . . . . 17 D6
Horokhiv . . . . . 17 C7
Horqin Youyi
   Qianqi . . . . . 35 B7
Horqueta . . . . 94 A5
Horsham . . . . . 62 C3
Horton → . . . . 70 B7
Hose, Gunung-
   Gunung . . . 37 D4
Hoshangabad . 43 H10
Hoshiarpur . . . 42 D9
Hospet . . . . . 43 M10
Hospitalet de
   Llobregat . . 19 B7
Hoste, I. . . . . . 95 H3
Hot Springs . . 79 B7
Hotan . . . . . . 34 C2
Houhora Heads 64 A5
Houlton . . . . 73 A12
Houma . . . . . . 79 E8
Houston . . . . . 79 E6
Hovd . . . . . . . . 34 B4
Hövsgöl Nuur . 34 A5
Howard . . . . . 63 A5
Howe, C. . . . . . 63 C5

Howitt, L. . . . . . 62 A2
Howrah = Haora 40 F7
Höxter . . . . . . 14 C5
Hoy . . . . . . . . . 10 B5
Høyanger . . . . 8 F9
Hoyerswerda . 15 C8
Hpungan Pass . 41 D11
Hradec Králové 16 C2
Hrodna . . . . . 17 B6
Hrodzyanka . . 17 B9
Hron → . . . . . 16 E4
Hrvatska =
   Croatia ■ . . . 20 B6
Hrymayliv . . . . 17 D8
Hsenwi . . . . 41 F11
Hsiamen =
   Xiamen . . . . . 35 D6
Hsian = Xi'an . 35 C5
Hsinhailien =
   Lianyungang 35 C6
Hsisha Chuntao 36 A4
Hsüchou =
   Xuzhou . . . . 35 C6
Hua Hin . . . . . 36 B1
Huacho . . . . . 91 F3
Huachón . . . . 91 F3
Huai He → . . . 35 C6
Huainan . . . . 35 C6
Huallaga → . . 90 E3
Huambo . . . . . 58 A3
Huancabamba . 91 E3
Huancane . . . . 91 G5
Huancapi . . . . 91 F4
Huancavelica . 91 F3
Huancayo . . . 91 F3
Huang Hai =
   Yellow Sea . . 35 C7
Huang He → . . 35 C6
Huangliu . . . . 35 E5
Huangshi . . . . 35 C6
Huánuco . . . . 91 E3
Huaraz . . . . . 91 E3
Huarmey . . . . 91 F3
Huascarán . . . 91 E3
Huasco . . . . . 94 B2
Huatabampo . . 84 B3
Huayllay . . . . 91 F3
Hubei □ . . . . . 35 C6
Hubli-Dharwad
   = Dharwad . 43 M9
Huddersfield . 11 E6
Hudiksvall . . . 8 F11
Hudson → . . . 73 D8
Hudson Bay . . 68 B2
Hudson Mts. . 96 B2
Hudson Str. . . 68 B4
Hue . . . . . . . . 36 A3
Huelva . . . . . . 18 D2
Huesca . . . . . 19 A5
Hughenden . . 61 E7
Hughli → . . . . 40 G7
Huila, Nevado
   del . . . . . . . 90 C3
Huinca Renancó 94 C4
Huize . . . . . . . 34 D5
Hukawng Valley 41 D11
Hulan . . . . . . 35 B7
Ḥulayfā' . . . . 47 F5
Huld . . . . . . . 35 B5
Hull = Kingston
   upon Hull . . 11 E6
Hull . . . . . . . 69 D3
Hulun Nur . . . 35 B6
Humahuaca . . 94 A3
Humaitá, *Brazil* 91 E6
Humaitá,
   *Paraguay* . . 94 B5
Humber → . . . 11 E6
Humboldt . . . . 71 C9

Humboldt → . 80 F4
Hume, L. . . . . 63 C4
Humenné . . . . 16 D5
Hūn . . . . . . . . 52 C2
Hunan □ . . . . 35 D6
Hunedoara . . . 17 F6
Hungary ■ . . . 16 E4
Hungerford . . . 63 A3
Hŭngnam . . . 35 C7
Hunsrück . . . 14 D4
Hunter I. . . . . 62 D3
Hunter Ra. . . . 63 B5
Hunterville . . . 64 C6
Huntington . . 72 E4
Huntington
   Beach . . . . 82 D3
Huntly, *N.Z.* . . 64 B6
Huntly, *U.K.* . . 10 C5
Huntsville . . . 74 B4
Huonville . . . . 62 D4
Hupeh =
   Hubei □ . . . 35 C6
Ḥuraysān . . . 47 G6
Huron, L. . . . . 72 B4
Hurunui → . . . 65 E5
Huşi . . . . . . . 17 E9
Hutchinson . . 78
Hutton, Mt. . . 63 A4
Hvar . . . . . . . 20 C7
Hwang Ho =
   Huang He → 35 C6
Hwange . . . . . 59 B5
Hyargas Nuur . 34 B4
Hyderabad,
   *India* . . . . 43 L11
Hyderabad,
   *Pakistan* . . 42 G6
Hyères . . . . . 13 E7
Hyères, Is. d' . 13 E7

## I

I-n-Gall . . . . . 55 E6
Iaco → . . . . . . 91 E5
Ialomiţa → . . . 22 B6
Iaşi . . . . . . . . 17 E8
Iba . . . . . . . . 38 A2
Ibadan . . . . . 55 G5
Ibagué . . . . . 90 C3
Ibar → . . . . . 22 C3
Ibarra . . . . . . 90 C3
Ibi . . . . . . . . 55 G6
Ibiá . . . . . . . 93 F4
Ibicuy . . . . . . 94 C5
Ibioapaba, Sa.
   da . . . . . . . 92 C5
Ibiza . . . . . . 19 C6
Ibonma . . . . . 39 E4
Ibotirama . . . 93 E5
Ibu . . . . . . . . 39 D3
Icá . . . . . . . . 91 F3
Içá → . . . . . . 90 D5
Içana . . . . . . 90 C5
İçel = Mersin . 46 C3
Iceland ■ . . . . 8 D4
Ich'ang =
   Yichang . . . 35 C6
Ichchapuram . 40 H5
Ichihara . . . . 32 B7
Ichikawa . . . . 32 B6
Ichilo → . . . . 91 G6
Ichinomiya . . 32 B5
Idaho □ . . . . 81 C6
Idaho Falls . . 81 D7
Idar-Oberstein . 14 D4
Idd el Ghanam 53 F3

120

Iddan ....... 49 F4
Idehan ...... 52 C1
Idehan Marzūq 52 D1
Idelès ....... 54 D6
Idfû ........ 52 D5
Ídhi Óros .... 23 G5
Ídhra ........ 23 F4
Idi .......... 36 C1
Idiofa ....... 56 E3
Idlip ........ 46 D4
Ierápetra .... 23 G5
Iesi ......... 20 C4
Ifanadiana ... 59 J9
Ife .......... 55 G5
Ifni ......... 54 C2
Iforas, Adrar des 54
Igarapava .... 93 G4
Igarapé Açu .. 92 C4
Igarka ....... 28 C9
Igbetti ...... 55 G5
Iglésias ..... 21 E2
Igli ......... 54 B4
Igloolik ..... 68 B2
Igluligaarjuk .. 68 B2
Iğneada Burnu 22 D7
Igoumenítsa .. 23 E3
Iguaçu → .... 94 B6
Iguaçu, Cat. del 94 B6
Iguaçu Falls =
  Iguaçu, Cat.
  del ........ 94 B6
Iguala ....... 84 D5
Igualada ..... 19 B6
Iguassu =
  Iguaçu → .. 94 B6
Iguatu ....... 92 D6
Iguéla ....... 56 E1
Ihosy ........ 59 J9
Iida ......... 32 B5
Iisalmi ...... 8 F13
Iizuka ....... 32 C2
Ijebu-Ode .... 55 G5
IJsselmeer .... 14 B3
Ikaluktutiak .. 70 B9
Ikaría ....... 23 F6
Ikela ........ 56 E4
Iki .......... 32 C1
Ilagan ....... 38 A2
Ilām ........ 46 D6
Ilawa ........ 16 B4
Île-de-France .. 12 B5
Ilebo ........ 56 E4
Ilhéus ....... 93 E6
Ili → ........ 29 E8
Ilich ........ 29 E7
Iligan ....... 38 C2
Illampu =
  Ancohuma,
  Nevada .... 91 G5
Illana B. ..... 38 C2
Illapel ...... 94 C2
Iller → ...... 14 D5
Illimani ..... 91 G5
Ilium = Troy .. 23 E6
Ilmen, Ozero .. 24 B3
Ilo .......... 91 G4
Iloilo ....... 38 B2
Ilorin ....... 55 G5
Ilwaki ....... 39 F3
Imabari ...... 32 B3
Imandra, Ozero 28 C4
Imari ........ 32 C1
imeni 26
  Bakinskikh
  Komissarov =
  Neftçala ... 46 C7
Imeri, Serra .. 90 C5
Imi .......... 49 F3
Imola ........ 20 B3

Imperatriz ... 92 D4
Impéria ...... 20 C2
Imperial Dam . 82 D5
Impfondo ..... 56 D3
Imphal ....... 41 E9
İmroz =
  Gökçeada ... 23 D5
Imuruan B. ... 38 B1
In Belbel ..... 54 C5
In Salah ..... 54 C5
Ina .......... 32 B5
Inangahua
  Junction .... 65 D4
Inanwatan ... 39 E4
İñapari ...... 91 F5
Inarijärvi .... 8 E13
Inca ......... 19 C7
İnce-Burnu ... 46 B3
Inchon ....... 35 C7
İncirliova .... 23 F6
Incomáti → .. 59 D6
Indalsälven → 8 F11
Indaw ....... 41 E11
Independence,
  Kans., U.S.A. 79 A6
Independence,
  Mo., U.S.A. . 77 F7
India ■ ....... 43 J10
Indian → ..... 75 F7
Indian Harbour 68 C5
Indian Head .. 71 C9
Indiana □ .... 72 D3
Indianapolis ... 72 E2
Indiga ....... 28 C5
Indigirka → .. 31 B12
Indonesia ■ ... 37 E4
Indore ....... 43 H9
Indravati → .. 40 H3
Indre → ...... 12 C4
Indus → ...... 43 G5
İnebolu ...... 46 B3
Ingende ...... 56 E3
Inglewood,
  Queens.,
  Australia .... 63 A5
Inglewood, Vic.,
  Australia .... 62 C3
Inglewood, N.Z. 64 C6
Ingolstadt .... 15 D6
Ingraj Bazar ... 40 E7
Ingrid
  Christensen
  Coast ...... 96 A10
Ingulec =
  Inhulec ..... 25 D3
Inhambane .... 59 C7
Inhaminga ... 59 B7
Inharrime .... 59 C7
Inhulec ...... 25 D3
Ining = Yining . 34 B3
Inírida → .... 90 C5
Injune ....... 63 A4
Inle L. ....... 41 G11
Inn → ........ 15 D7
Innamincka ... 62 A3
Inner Hebrides 10 C3
Inner Mongolia
  = Nei
  Monggol
  Zizhiqu □ ... 35 B6
Innisfail ..... 71 C8
Innsbruck .... 15 E6
Inongo ....... 56 E3
Inoucdjouac =
  Inukjuak .... 68 C3
Inowrocław .. 16 B4
Inquisivi ..... 91 G5
Insein ....... 41 J11
Interlaken .... 13 C7

International
  Falls ...... 77 A8
Intiyaco ..... 94 B4
Inukjuak ..... 68 C3
Inútil, B. ..... 95 G2
Inuvik ....... 70 B6
Invercargill .... 65 G3
Inverell ...... 63 A5
Invergordon ... 10 C4
Inverness ... 10 C4
Inverurie ..... 10 C5
Investigator
  Group ...... 62 B1
Investigator Str. 62 C2
Inya ......... 29 D9
Inza ......... 24 C6
Ioánnina ..... 23 E3
Ionian Is. =
  Iónioi Nísoi . 23 E3
Ionian Sea .... 21 F6
Iónioi Nísoi ... 23 E3
Íos .......... 23 F5
Iowa □ ....... 77 D8
Iowa City ..... 77 E9
Ipameri ...... 93 F4
Ipatinga ..... 93 F5
Ipiales ....... 90 C3
Ipin = Yibin ... 35 D5
Ipixuna ...... 91 E4
Ipoh ......... 36 D2
Ippy ......... 56 C4
Ipsala ....... 22 D6
Ipswich,
  Australia ... 63 A5
Ipswich, U.K. .. 11 E7
Ipu .......... 92 C5
Iqaluit ....... 68 B4
Iquique ...... 91 H4
Iquitos ...... 90 D4
Iracoubo ..... 92 A3
Iráklion ...... 23 G5
Iran ■ ....... 44 C3
Iran, Gunung-
  Gunung ... 37 D4
Iran Ra. = Iran,
  Gunung-
  Gunung ... 37 D4
İrānshahr ..... 45 E5
Irapuato ..... 84 C4
Iraq ■ ....... 46 D5
Irbid ........ 46 D3
Irebu ........ 56 E3
Ireland ■ ..... 11 E3
Irian Jaya □ ... 39 E5
Iringa ....... 57 F7
Iriri → ....... 92 C3
Irish Sea ..... 11 E4
Irkineyeva ... 30 D7
Irkutsk ...... 30 D8
Iron Baron ... 62 B2
Iron Gate =
  Portile de Fier 22 B4
Iron Knob .... 62 B2
Ironwood ..... 77 B9
Irpin ........ 17 C10
Irrara Cr. .... 63 A4
Irrawaddy □ .. 41 J10
Irrawaddy → .. 41 K10
Irtysh → ..... 28 C7
Irumu ....... 57 D5
Irún ......... 19 A5
Irunea =
  Pamplona ... 19 A5
Irvine ....... 10 D4
Irymple ...... 62 B3
Isabella ..... 38 C2
Isangi ....... 56 D4
Isar → ....... 15 D7
Íschia ....... 21 D4

Ise .......... 32 B5
Ise-Wan ..... 32 B5
Isère → ...... 13 D6
Isérnia ...... 20 D5
Ishikari-Wan .. 32 F12
Ishim → ..... 29 D8
Ishinomaki ... 33 G12
Ishkuman .... 42 A8
Isil Kul ...... 29 D8
Isiolo ....... 57 D7
Isiro ........ 57 D5
İskenderun ... 46 C4
Iskŭr → ...... 22 C5
Islamabad .... 42 C8
Island L. ..... 71 C10
Island Lagoon . 62 B2
Islay ........ 10 D3
Isle → ....... 12 D3
Isle of Wight □ 11 F6
Ismail = Izmayil 17 F9
Ismâ'ilîya .... 47 E3
Isna ......... 52 C5
İsparta ...... 46 C2
Íspica ....... 21 F5
Israel ■ ...... 46 E3
Issoire ...... 13 D5
Issyk-Kul, Ozero
  = Ysyk-Köl,
  Ozero ...... 29 E8
İstanbul ..... 22 D7
Istiaía ...... 23 E4
Istra ........ 20 B4
İstranca Dağları 22 D6
Istres ....... 13 E6
Istria = Istra . 20 B4
Itabaiana .... 92 D6
Itaberaba .... 93 E5
Itabira ...... 93 F5
Itabuna ...... 93 E6
Itaipú, Reprêsa
  de ........ 94 B6
Itaituba ..... 92 C2
Itajaí ....... 94 B7
Italy ■ ...... 20 C4
Itapecuru-Mirim 92 C5
Itaperuna .... 93 G5
Itapicuru →,
  Bahia, Brazil . 93 E6
Itapicuru →,
  Maranhão,
  Brazil ...... 92 C5
Itapipoca .... 92 C6
Itaquatiara ... 90 D7
Itaquí ....... 94 B5
Itatuba ...... 91 E6
Ithaca = Itháki . 23 E3
Itháki ....... 23 E3
Ito .......... 32 B6
Itonamas → .. 91 F6
Ituaçu ...... 93 E5
Ituiutaba .... 93 F4
Itumbiara .... 93 F4
Iturbe ....... 94 A3
Itzehoe ...... 14 B5
Ivanava ...... 17 B7
Ivanhoe ..... 63 B3
Ivano-Frankivsk 17 D7
Ivano-Frankovsk
  = Ivano-
  Frankivsk .. 17 D7
Ivanovo =
  Ivanava ..... 17 B7
Ivanovo ...... 24 B5
Ivatsevichy ... 17 B7
Ivory Coast ■ . 55 G3
Ivrea ........ 20 B1
Ivujivik ...... 68 B3
Iwahig ....... 36 C5
Iwaki ........ 33 G12

Iwakuni ...... 32 B3
Iwata ........ 33 H11
Iwate-San ..... 33 G12
Iwo ......... 55 G5
Ixiamas ....... 91 F5
Izhevsk ....... 28 D6
Izmayil ....... 17 F9
Izmir ......... 23 E6
İzmit ........ 25 E2
İznik Gölü ..... 23 D7
Izumi-sano ... 32 B4
Izumo ....... 32 B3
Izyaslav ...... 17 C8

## J

Jabalpur ...... 43 H11
Jablah ....... 46 D4
Jablanica ..... 22 D3
Jablonec ..... 16 C2
Jaboatão ..... 92 D6
Jaca ......... 19 A5
Jacareí ....... 94 A7
Jacarèzinho ... 94 A7
Jackson,
  Australia .... 63 A4
Jackson, Mich.,
  U.S.A. ...... 72 C3
Jackson, Miss.,
  U.S.A. ...... 79 C8
Jackson, Tenn.,
  U.S.A. ...... 74 B3
Jackson B. .... 65 E3
Jacksons ..... 65 E4
Jacksonville,
  Fla., U.S.A. .. 75 D7
Jacksonville, Ill.,
  U.S.A. ...... 77 F9
Jacksonville,
  N.C., U.S.A. . 75 B9
Jacmel ....... 87 C5
Jacobabad .... 42 E6
Jacobina ..... 93 E5
Jacundá → ... 92 C3
Jadotville =
  Likasi ...... 57 G5
Jädü ........ 52 B1
Jaén, Peru ... 91 E3
Jaén, Spain ... 18 D4
Jaffa = Tel Aviv-
  Yafo ...... 46 D3
Jaffa, C. ...... 62 C2
Jaffna ....... 43 Q12
Jagadhri ...... 42 D10
Jagdalpur .... 40 H3
Jagraon ...... 42 D9
Jagtial ....... 43 K11
Jaguariaíva ... 94 A7
Jaguaribe → . 92 C6
Jahrom ...... 44 D3
Jailolo ....... 39 D3
Jailolo, Selat .. 39 D3
Jaipur ........ 42 F9
Jakarta ...... 37 F3
Jalalabad ..... 42 B7
Jalapa Enríquez 84 D5
Jalas, Jabal al . 47 F4
Jalgaon,
  Maharashtra,
  India ....... 43 J10
Jalgaon,
  Maharashtra,
  India ....... 43 J9
Jalna ........ 43 K9
Jalón → ..... 19 B5
Jalpaiguri ..... 41 D7

Jalq ......... 45 E5
Jaluit I. ........ 64 J11
Jamaica ■ .... 86 C4
Jamalpur,
  Bangla. ..... 41 E7
Jamalpur, India 40 E6
Jamanxim → . 92 C2
Jambe ........ 39 E4
Jambi ........ 37 E2
Jambi □ ...... 37 E2
James → .... 76 D6
James B. ..... 69 C2
James Ross I. . 96 A4
Jamestown,
  Australia .... 62 B2
Jamestown,
  N. Dak., U.S.A. 76 B5
Jamestown,
  N.Y., U.S.A. . 73 C6
Jamkhandi .... 43 L9
Jammu ....... 42 C9
Jammu &
  Kashmir □ .. 42 B10
Jamnagar .... 43 H7
Jamrud ...... 42 C7
Jamshedpur .. 40 F6
Jand ......... 42 C8
Jandaq ....... 44 C3
Jandowae .... 63 A5
Janesville .... 77 D10
Januária ..... 93 F5
Jaora ........ 43 H9
Japan ■ .... 33 G11
Japan, Sea of . 33 G11
Japen = Yapen 39 E5
Japurá → .... 90 D5
Jaque ....... 90 B3
Jarama → .... 18 B4
Jargalant =
  Hovd ....... 34 B4
Jarosław ..... 17 C6
Jarso ........ 53 G6
Jarvis I. ...... 65 K15
Jarwa ........ 40 D4
Jāsk ......... 44 E4
Jasło ........ 16 D5
Jasper ....... 74 C4
Jászberény ... 16 E4
Jataí ........ 93 F3
Játiva ....... 19 C5
Jaú ......... 93 G4
Jauja ....... 91 F3
Jaunpur ..... 40 E4
Java = Jawa .. 37 F3
Java Sea ..... 37 E3
Javhlant =
  Ulyasutay ... 34 B4
Jawa ........ 37 F3
Jaya, Puncak .. 39 E5
Jayanti ....... 41 D7
Jayapura ..... 39 E6
Jayawijaya,
  Pegunungan 39 E5
Jaynagar ..... 40 D6
Jean Marie
  River ....... 70 B7
Jebba ....... 55 G5
Jebel, Bahr
  el → ...... 53 G5
Jedburgh .... 10 D5
Jedda = Jiddah 47 G4
Jędrzejów .... 16 C5
Jefferson City . 77 F8
Jega ........ 55 F5
Jelenia Góra .. 16 C2
Jelgava ...... 24 B1
Jemaja ...... 37 D3
Jembongan ... 36 C5
Jena ........ 15 C6

Jeparit ....... 62 C3
Jequié ....... 93 E5
Jequitinhonha . 93 F5
Jequitinhonha→ 93 F6
Jerada ....... 54 B4
Jerantut ..... 37 D2
Jérémie ...... 86 C5
Jerez de la
  Frontera .... 18 D2
Jerez de los
  Caballeros .. 18 C2
Jerilderie .... 63 C4
Jersey ....... 11 G5
Jersey City .... 73 D8
Jerusalem .... 47 E3
Jervis B. ...... 63 C5
Jesselton =
  Kota Kinabalu 36 C5
Jessore ...... 41 F7
Jeypore ...... 40 H4
Jhal Jhao .... 42 F4
Jhalawar .... 43 G10
Jhang Maghiana 42 D8
Jhansi ...... 43 G11
Jharkand □ ... 40 F5
Jharsaguda ... 40 G5
Jhelum ...... 42 C8
Jhelum → ... 42 D8
Jhunjhunu ... 42 E9
Jiamusi ...... 35 B8
Ji'an ........ 35 D6
Jianchuan ... 34 D4
Jiangling .... 35 C6
Jiangmen ... 35 D6
Jiangsu □ ... 35 C6
Jiangxi □ ... 35 D6
Jian'ou ...... 35 D6
Jianshui .... 34 D5
Jiao Xian ..... 35 C7
Jiaozuo ...... 35 C6
Jiaxing ...... 35 C7
Jiayi ........ 35 D7
Jibuti =
  Djibouti ■ .. 49 E3
Jiddah ....... 47 G4
Jido ........ 41 C10
Jihlava ...... 16 D2
Jihlava → .... 16 D3
Jijel .......... 54 A6
Jijiga ....... 49 F3
Jilin ........ 35 B7
Jilong ....... 35 D7
Jima ........ 53 G6
Jiménez ..... 84 B4
Jinan ....... 35 C6
Jindabyne .... 63 C4
Jindřichův
  Hradeç .... 16 D2
Jingdezhen ... 35 D6
Jinggu ...... 34 D5
Jingxi ....... 35 D5
Jinhua ...... 35 D6
Jining,
  Nei Mongol Zizhiqu,
  China ...... 35 B6
Jining,
  Shandong,
  China ...... 35 C6
Jinja ........ 57 D6
Jinnah Barrage 42 C7
Jinotega ..... 85 E7
Jinshi ....... 35 D6
Jinzhou ..... 35 B7
Jiparaná → . 91 E6
Jipijapa ...... 90 D2
Jisr ash
  Shughūr .. 46 D4
Jiu → ...... 22 C4
Jiujiang ..... 35 D6

Jiuquan ...... 34 C4
Jixi .......... 35 B8
Jizzakh ...... 29 E7
Joaçaba ...... 94 B6
João Pessoa .. 92 D7
Joaquín V.
  González .... 94 B4
Jodhpur .... 42 F8
Jofane ...... 59 C6
Jogjakarta =
  Yogyakarta .. 37 F4
Johannesburg . 59 D5
Johnson City .. 75 A6
Johnston Falls
  = Mambilima
  Falls ....... 57 G5
Johnstown .... 73 D6
Johor Baharu . 37 D2
Joinvile ...... 94 B6
Joinville I. .... 96 A4
Joliet ....... 72 D1
Joliette ...... 69 D3
Jolo ........ 38 C2
Jome ........ 39 E3
Jonesboro ... 79 B8
Jönköping ... 9 G10
Jonquière ... 69 D3
Joplin ....... 79 A6
Jordan ■ ... 47 E4
Jorhat ...... 41 D10
Jorong ...... 37 E4
Jos ......... 55 G6
Jowzjän □ .... 45 B6
Juan de Fuca
  Str. ....... 80 A1
Juan de Nova . 59 H8
Juan Fernández,
  Arch. de .... 89 G3
Juárez ...... 94 D5
Juàzeiro ..... 93 D5
Juàzeiro do
  Norte ...... 92 D6
Jubbulpore =
  Jabalpur ... 43 H11
Juby, C. ..... 54 C2
Júcar → .... 19 C5
Juchitán .... 85 D5
Jugoslavia =
  Yugoslavia ■ 22 B3
Juiz de Fora .. 93 G5
Juli ........ 91 G5
Juliaca ...... 91 G4
Jullundur ... 42 D9
Jumilla ...... 19 C5
Jumla ...... 40 C4
Jumna =
  Yamuna → . 40 E3
Junagadh .... 43 J7
Jundiaí ...... 94 A7
Juneau ...... 71 C6
Junee ....... 63 B4
Jungfrau ..... 13 C7
Junggar Pendi . 34 B3
Junín ....... 94 C4
Junín de los
  Andes ..... 95 D2
Jūniyah ..... 46 D3
Jur, Nahr el → 53 G4
Jura = Jura,
  Mts. du .... 13 C7
Jura =
  Schwäbische
  Alb ....... 14 D5
Jura ........ 10 D4
Jura, Mts. du .. 13 C7
Jurado ...... 90 B3
Juruá → .... 90 D4
Juruena → ... 91 E7
Juruti ....... 92 C2

Justo Daract .. 94 C3
Jutland =
Jylland ..... 9 G9
Juventud, I. de
  la .......... 86 B3
Juwain ....... 42 D2
Jylland ....... 9 G9
Jyväskylä ..... 8 F13

**K**

K2 .......... 42 B10
Kaapkruis .... 58 C2
Kaapstad =
  Cape Town . 58 E3
Kabaena ...... 39 F2
Kabala ....... 55 G2
Kabale ....... 57 E6
Kabalo ....... 57 F5
Kabambare ... 57 E5
Kabanjahe .... 37 D1
Kabara ....... 55 E4
Kabardino-
  Balkar
  Republic =
  Kabardino
  Balkaria □ .. 25 E5
Kabardino
  Balkaria □ .. 25 E5
Kabare ....... 39 E4
Kabarega Falls 57 D6
Kabasalan .... 38 C2
Kabba ........ 55 G6
Kabīr, Zab al ⟶ 46 C5
Kabīr Kūh .... 47 D6
Kabkabīyah ... 53 F3
Kabompo ⟶ .. 58 A4
Kabongo ...... 57 F5
Kabūd Gonbad 44 B4
Kābul ........ 42 B6
Kābul □ ...... 42 B6
Kabul ⟶ ..... 42 C8
Kaburuang .... 39 D3
Kabwe ........ 59 A5
Kachchh, Gulf of 43 H6
Kachchh, Rann
  of .......... 43 G6
Kachin □ ..... 41 D11
Kachiry ...... 29 D8
Kaçkar ....... 46 B5
Kadan Kyun ... 36 B2
Kadina ....... 62 B2
Kadirli ........ 46 C4
Kadiyevka =
  Stakhanov .. 25 D4
Kadoma ...... 59 B5
Kâdugli ...... 53 F4
Kaduna ...... 55 F6
Kaédi ........ 55 E2
Kaelé ........ 53 F1
Kaesŏng ...... 35 C7
Kāf .......... 47 E4
Kafakumba ... 56 F4
Kafan = Kapan 25 F6
Kafanchan ... 55 G6
Kaffrine ...... 55 F1
Kafia Kingi ... 53 G3
Kafirévs, Ákra . 23 E5
Kafue ⟶ ..... 59 B5
Kafulwe ..... 57 F5
Kaga Bandoro . 56 C3
Kagan ........ 29 F7
Kağizman ..... 46 B5
Kagoshima ... 33 D2
Kagoshima-Wan 33 D2
Kagul = Cahul . 17 F9

Kahama ...... 57 E6
Kahayan ⟶ .. 37 E4
Kahemba ..... 56 F3
Kahnūj ....... 44 E4
Kahoolawe .... 82 H12
Kahramanmaraş 46 C4
Kai, Kepulauan 39 F4
Kai Besar ..... 39 F4
Kai Is. = Kai,
  Kepulauan .. 39 F4
Kai Kecil ...... 39 F4
Kaiama ....... 55 G5
Kaiapoi ...... 65 E5
Kaieteur Falls . 90 B7
Kaifeng ....... 35 C6
Kaikohe ...... 64 A5
Kaikoura ..... 65 E5
Kaikoura Ra. .. 65 D5
Kaimana ..... 39 E4
Kaimanawa Mts. 64 C6
Kaingaroa
  Forest ...... 64 C7
Kainji Res. .... 55 F5
Kaipara Harbour 64 B6
Kaironi ....... 39 E4
Kairouan ..... 54 A7
Kaiserslautern . 14 D4
Kaitaia ....... 64 A5
Kaitangata .... 65 G3
Kajaani ....... 8 F13
Kajabbi ....... 61 D6
Kajana =
  Kajaani .... 8 F13
Kajo Kaji .... 53 H5
Kaka ........ 53 F5
Kakamas ..... 58 D4
Kakamega .... 57 D6
Kakanui Mts. .. 65 F4
Kakhovka .... 25 D3
Kakhovske
  Vdskh. ...... 25 D3
Kakinada ..... 40 J4
Kalaallit Nunaat
  =
  Greenland ■ 66 C9
Kalabagh ..... 42 C7
Kalabahi ...... 39 F2
Kalabo ....... 58 A4
Kalach ....... 24 C5
Kaladan ⟶ ... 41 G9
Kalahari ...... 58 C4
Kalakan ...... 31 D9
Kalámai ...... 23 F4
Kalamata =
  Kalámai .... 23 F4
Kalamazoo ... 72 C3
Kalan ........ 46 C4
Kalao ........ 39 F2
Kalaotoa ..... 39 F2
Kalat ........ 42 E5
Kalce ........ 20 B5
Kale ......... 23 F7
Kalegauk Kyun 41 K11
Kalemie ...... 57 F5
Kalewa ....... 41 F10
Kalgan =
  Zhangjiakou . 35 B6
Kalgoorlie-
  Boulder ..... 60 G3
Kaliakra, Nos .. 22 C7
Kalianda ..... 37 F3
Kalibo ....... 38 B2
Kalima ....... 57 E5
Kalimantan ... 37 E4
Kalimantan
  Barat □ .... 37 D4
Kalimantan
  Selatan □ ... 37 E5

Kalimantan
  Tengah □ ... 37 E4
Kalimantan
  Timur □ .... 37 D5
Kálimnos ..... 23 F6
Kalinin = Tver . 24 B4
Kaliningrad,
  *Kaliningd.,*
  *Russia* ..... 24 C1
Kaliningrad,
  *Moskva,*
  *Russia* ...... 24 B4
Kalinkavichy .. 17 B9
Kalinkovichi =
  Kalinkavichy . 17 B9
Kalispell ...... 81 A6
Kalisz ........ 16 C4
Kaliua ........ 57 F6
Kalkrand ..... 58 C3
Kalmar ....... 9 G11
Kalmyk Republic
  = Kalmykia □ 25 D6
Kalmykia □ ... 25 D6
Kalocsa ...... 16 E4
Kalomo ...... 59 B5
Kaluga ....... 24 C4
Kalush ....... 17 D7
Kalutara ..... 43 R11
Kama ⟶ ..... 29 D6
Kamaishi ..... 33 G12
Kamaran ..... 49 D3
Kamchatka, P-
  ov. ......... 31 D13
Kamchatka Pen.
  = Kamchatka,
  P-ov. ....... 31 D13
Kamchiya ⟶ . 22 C6
Kamen ....... 29 D9
Kamenjak, Rt. . 20 B4
Kamenka
  Bugskaya =
  Kamyanka-
  Buzka ...... 17 C7
Kamensk
  Uralskiy .... 29 D7
Kamin-
  Kashyrskyy .. 17 C7
Kamina ...... 57 F5
Kamloops .... 71 C7
Kampala ..... 57 D6
Kampar ⟶ ... 37 D2
Kampen ...... 14 B3
Kampot ...... 36 B2
Kampuchea =
  Cambodia ■ 36 B3
Kampung ⟶ .. 39 F5
Kampungbaru =
  Tolitoli ..... 39 D2
Kamrau, Teluk . 39 E4
Kamsack ..... 71 C9
Kamyanets-
  Podilskyy ... 17 D8
Kamyanka-Buzka 17 C7
Kamyshin .... 24 C6
Kanaaupscow . 69 C3
Kananga ..... 56 F4
Kanash ...... 24 B6
Kanastraíon,
  Ákra =
  Palioúrion,
  Ákra ....... 23 E4
Kanazawa .... 32 A5
Kanchanaburi . 36 B1
Kanchenjunga . 40 D7
Kanchipuram .. 43 N11
Kanda Kanda . 56 F4
Kandahar =
  Qandahār ... 42 D4
Kandalaksha .. 28 C4

Kandalu ...... 42 E3
Kandangan ... 37 E5
Kandi ........ 55 F5
Kandla ....... 43 H7
Kandos ....... 63 B4
Kandy ........ 43 R12
Kangaroo I. ... 62 C2
Kangávar ..... 46 D7
Kangean,
  Kepulauan .. 37 F5
Kangean Is. =
  Kangean,
  Kepulauan .. 37 F5
Kangiqsualujjuaq
  ............. 68 C4
Kangiqsujuaq . 68 B3
Kangirsuk .... 68 C4
Kangnŭng ... 35 C7
Kango ........ 56 D2
Kangto ....... 41 D9
Kaniapiskau ⟶ 68 C4
Kaniapiskau L. . 69 C4
Kanin,
  Poluostrov .. 28 C5
Kanin Nos, Mys 28 C5
Kanin Pen. =
  Kanin,
  Poluostrov .. 28 C5
Kaniva ....... 62 C3
Kankakee .... 72 D2
Kankan ...... 55 F3
Kankendy =
  Xankändi ... 25 F6
Kanker ....... 40 G3
Kannapolis ... 75 B7
Kannauj ...... 42 F11
Kannod ...... 43 H10
Kano ........ 55 F6
Kanowit ...... 37 D4
Kanoya ...... 33 D2
Kanpetlet .... 41 G9
Kanpur ...... 40 D3
Kansas □ .... 76 F5
Kansas City,
  *Kans., U.S.A.* 77 F7
Kansas City,
  *Mo., U.S.A.* . 77 F7
Kansk ........ 30 D7
Kansu =
  Gansu □ .... 34 C5
Kantang ...... 36 C1
Kanuma ...... 32 A6
Kanye ....... 59 C5
Kaohsiung =
  Gaoxiong ... 35 D7
Kaokoveld .... 58 B2
Kaolack ...... 55 F1
Kapan ....... 25 F6
Kapanga ..... 56 F4
Kapchagai =
  Qapshaghay . 29 E8
Kapfenberg ... 15 E8
Kapiri Mposhi . 59 A5
Kāpīsā □ ..... 45 C7
Kapit ........ 37 D4
Kapoeta ...... 53 H5
Kaposvár ..... 16 E3
Kapuas ⟶ ... 37 E3
Kapuas Hulu,
  Pegunungan 37 D4
Kapuas Hulu Ra.
  = Kapuas
  Hulu,
  Pegunungan 37 D4
Kapunda ..... 62 B2
Kapuni ....... 64 C6
Kaputar ...... 63 B5
Kara ........ 28 C7

# Kara Bogaz Gol, Zaliv

Kara Bogaz Gol,
Zaliv =
Garabogazköl
Aylagy ..... 29 E6
Kara Kalpak
Republic □ =
Karakalpakstan □
.......... 29 E6
Kara Kum ..... 29 F6
Kara Sea ..... 28 B8
Karabiğa ..... 23 D6
Karabük ...... 46 B3
Karaburun .... 23 E6
Karabutak =
Qarabutaq .. 29 E7
Karacabey .... 23 D7
Karacasu ..... 23 F7
Karachi ....... 43 G5
Karad ........ 43 L9
Karadeniz
Boğazı ...... 22 D7
Karaganda = 
Qaraghandy . 29 E8
Karagayly .... 29 E8
Karaikal ...... 43 P11
Karaikkudi .... 43 P11
Karaj ......... 44 C2
Karakalpakstan □
.......... 29 E6
Karakas ...... 29 E9
Karakelong ... 38 D3
Karakitang .... 39 D3
Karaklis =
Vanadzor ... 25 E5
Karakoram Pass 42 B10
Karakoram Ra. 42 B10
Karalon ...... 30 D9
Karaman ..... 46 C3
Karamay ..... 34 B3
Karambu ..... 37 E5
Karamea Bight 65 D4
Karasburg .... 58 D3
Karasino ..... 28 C9
Karasuk ...... 29 D8
Karatau =
Qarataū .... 29 E8
Karatau, Khrebet 29 E7
Karawanken ... 20 A5
Karazhal ..... 29 E8
Karbalā ...... 47 D6
Karcag ....... 16 E5
Kardhítsa ..... 23 E3
Karelia □ ..... 28 C4
Karelian
Republic □ =
Karelia □ ... 28 C4
Kargänrüd .... 46 C7
Kargasok ..... 29 D9
Kargat ....... 29 D9
Kargil ........ 42 B10
Kariba, L. ..... 59 B5
Kariba Dam ... 59 B5
Kariba Gorge . 59 B5
Karibib ....... 58 C3
Karimata,
Kepulauan .. 37 E3
Karimata, Selat 37 E3
Karimata Is. =
Karimata,
Kepulauan .. 37 E3
Karimnagar ... 43 K11
Karimunjawa,
Kepulauan .. 37 F4
Karin ......... 49 E4
Karkaralinsk =
Qarqaraly ... 29 E8
Karkinitska
Zatoka ...... 25 D3

Karkinitskiy Zaliv
= Karkinitska
Zatoka ...... 25 D3
Karl-Marx-Stadt
= Chemnitz . 15 C7
Karlovac ..... 20 B5
Karlovo ...... 22 C5
Karlovy Vary .. 16 C1
Karlsbad =
Karlovy Vary 16 C1
Karlskrona .... 9 G11
Karlsruhe .... 14 D5
Karlstad ..... 9 G10
Karnal ........ 42 E10
Karnali ─→ .... 40 C3
Karnaphuli Res. 41 F9
Karnataka □ .. 43 N10
Karnische Alpen 20 A4
Kärnten □ .... 15 E7
Karonga ...... 57 F6
Karoonda ..... 62 C2
Karora ....... 53 E6
Kárpathos .... 23 G6
Kars ......... 46 B5
Karsakpay .... 29 E7
Karshi = Qarshi 29 F7
Karsun ....... 24 C6
Karufa ....... 39 E4
Karungu ...... 57 E6
Karviná ...... 16 D4
Karwar ....... 43 M9
Kasai ─→ ..... 56 E3
Kasama ...... 57 G6
Kasanga ..... 57 F6
Kasangulu .... 56 E3
Kasaragod .... 43 N9
Kasba L. ..... 70 B9
Kasempa ..... 59 A5
Kasenga ..... 57 G5
Kāshān ...... 44 C2
Kashi ........ 34 C2
Kashk-e Kohneh 42 B3
Kāshmar ..... 44 C4
Kashun Noerh =
Gaxun Nur .. 34 B5
Kasimov ...... 24 C5
Kasiruta ..... 39 E3
Kasongo ..... 57 E5
Kasongo Lunda 56 F3
Kásos ........ 23 G6
Kassalâ ...... 53 E6
Kassel ....... 14 C5
Kassue ...... 39 F5
Kastamonu ... 46 B3
Kasulu ....... 57 E6
Kasur ........ 42 D9
Katako Kombe . 56 E4
Katamatite ... 63 C4
Katanga =
Shaba □ ... 57 F4
Katangi ...... 43 J11
Kateríni ...... 23 D4
Katha ........ 41 E11
Kathiawar .... 43 H7
Katihar ....... 40 E6
Katima Mulilo . 58 B4
Katingan =
Mendawai ─→ 37 E4
Katiola ....... 55 G3
Katmandu .... 40 D5
Katoomba .... 63 B5
Katowice ..... 16 C4
Katsina ...... 55 F6
Kattegat ..... 9 G10
Kauai ........ 82 G11
Kaunas ...... 24 C1
Kaura Namoda 55 F6
Kavála ....... 22 D5
Kaw .......... 92 B3

Kawagoe ..... 32 B6
Kawaguchi .... 32 B6
Kawambwa ... 57 F5
Kawardha .... 40 G3
Kawasaki ..... 32 B6
Kawerau ..... 64 C7
Kawhia Harbour 64 C6
Kawio,
Kepulauan . 38 D3
Kawnro ...... 41 F12
Kawthoolei =
Kawthule □ . 41 H11
Kawthule □ ... 41 H11
Kaya ......... 55 F4
Kayah □ ..... 41 H11
Kayan ─→ .... 37 D5
Kayeli ....... 39 E3
Kayes ....... 55 F2
Kayoa ....... 39 D3
Kayrunnera ... 62 B3
Kayseri ...... 46 C3
Kayuagung ... 37 E2
Kazachye ..... 31 B11
Kazakstan ■ .. 29 E7
Kazan ....... 24 B6
Kazanlůk ..... 22 C5
Kazatin =
Kozyatyn ... 17 D9
Kãzerün ..... 44 D2
Kazumba ..... 56 F4
Kazym ─→ .... 28 C7
Ké-Macina ... 55 F3
Kéa .......... 23 F5
Kebnekaise ... 8 E11
Kebri Dehar .. 49 F3
Kecskemét .... 16 E4
Kediri ....... 37 F4
Kédougou ... 55 F2
Keetmanshoop 58 D3
Kefallinía ..... 23 E3
Kefamenanu .. 39 F2
Keffi ........ 55 G6
Keighley ...... 11 E6
Keith ........ 62 C3
Keith Arm .... 70 B7
Kekri ........ 42 G9
Kël ......... 30 C10
Kelang ....... 37 D2
Kelibia ....... 52 A1
Kellé ........ 56 E2
Kells =
Ceanannus
Mor ...... 11 E3
Kélo ........ 53 G2
Kelowna ..... 71 D8
Kelso ........ 65 F3
Keluang ..... 37 D2
Kem ........ 28 C4
Kema ....... 39 D3
Kemah ...... 46 C4
Kemerovo ... 29 D9
Kemi ........ 8 E12
Kemi älv = 
Kemijoki ─→ . 8 E12
Kemijoki ─→ .. 8 E12
Kemp Land ... 96 A9
Kempsey ..... 63 B5
Kempten ..... 14 E6
Kendal ....... 37 F4
Kendall ...... 63 B5
Kendari ...... 39 E2
Kendawangan . 37 E4
Kende ....... 55 F5
Kendrapara .. 40 G6
Kenema ..... 55 G2
Keng Tawng .. 41 G12
Keng Tung ... 41 G12
Kenge ....... 56 E3
Kenhardt .... 58 D4

Kenitra ....... 54 B3
Kennedy
Taungdeik .. 41 F9
Kennewick .... 80 B4
Kenogami ─→ . 69 C2
Kenosha ..... 72 C2
Kent Group ... 62 C4
Kent Pen. ..... 70 B9
Kentau ...... 29 E7
Kentucky □ ... 72 F3
Kentville ...... 69 D4
Kenya ■ ..... 57 D7
Kenya, Mt. ... 57 E7
Kepi ......... 39 F5
Kerala □ ..... 43 P10
Kerang ...... 62 C3
Kerch ........ 25 D4
Kerchoual .... 55 E5
Keren ....... 53 E6
Kericho ...... 57 E7
Kerinci ...... 37 E2
Kerki ........ 29 F7
Kérkira ...... 23 E2
Kermadec Is. .. 64 M13
Kermadec
Trench ...... 65 N13
Kermān □ .... 44 D4
Kermān □ ... 44 D4
Kermānshāh =
Bākhtarān ... 46 D6
Kerme Körfezi . 23 F6
Kerrobert .... 71 C7
Kerulen ─→ ... 35 B6
Kerzaz ...... 54 C4
Keşan ....... 22 D6
Kestenga ..... 28 C4
Ket ─→ ....... 29 D9
Keta ........ 55 G5
Ketapang .... 37 E4
Ketchikan .... 71 C6
Kętrzyn ..... 16 A5
Keweenaw B. . 69 D2
Key West .... 86 B3
Khabarovo ... 28 C7
Khabarovsk .. 31 E11
Khābūr ─→ ... 46 D5
Khairpur ..... 42 F6
Khakassia □ .. 30 D6
Khakhea .... 58 C4
Khalkhāl .... 46 C7
Khalkís ...... 23 E4
Khalmer-Sede =
Tazovskiy ... 28 C8
Khalmer Yu ... 28 C7
Khalturin .... 24 B6
Khalûf ....... 48 C6
Khambat, G. of 43 J8
Khambhat .... 43 H8
Khamir ...... 49 D3
Khānābād .... 45 B7
Khānaqīn .... 46 D6
Khandwa .... 43 J10
Khanewal .... 42 D7
Khaniá ...... 23 G5
Khaníon, Kólpos 23 G4
Khankendy =
Xankändi ... 25 F6
Khanty-
Mansiysk ... 29 C7
Khapcheranga . 30 E9
Kharagpur ... 40 F6
Kharan Kalat .. 42 E4
Khārānaq .... 44 C3
Kharda ...... 43 K9
Khârga, El
Wâhât el ... 52 C5
Khargon ..... 43 J9
Khārk, Jazireh . 47 E7
Kharkiv ...... 24 D4

Kharkov =
Kharkiv ..... 24 D4
Kharovsk ..... 24 B5
Kharsäniya .... 47 F7
Kharta ....... 22 D7
Khartoum = El
Khartûm .... 53 E5
Khâsh ....... 42 E2
Khashm el Girba 53 F6
Khaskovo ..... 22 D5
Khatanga .... 30 B8
Khatanga → .. 30 B8
Khaybar, Harrat 47 F5
Khed Brahma . 43 G8
Khemmarat ... 36 A3
Khenchela .... 54 A6
Khenifra ..... 54 B3
Kherson ...... 25 D3
Kheta → ..... 30 B8
Khilok ....... 30 D9
Khíos ....... 23 E6
Khiuma =
Hiiumaa .... 24 B1
Khiva ....... 29 E7
Khīyāv ...... 46 C6
Khmelnik .... 17 D8
Khmelnitskiy =
Khmelnytskyy 17 D8
Khmelnytskyy . 17 D8
Khmer Rep. =
Cambodia ■ . 36 B3
Khodoriv ..... 17 D7
Khodzent =
Khudzhand .. 29 E7
Khojak P. ..... 42 D5
Kholm, Afghan. 45 B6
Kholm, Russia . 24 B3
Khomeyn ..... 44 C2
Khon Kaen ... 36 A2
Khoper → ... 29 E5
Khóra Sfakíon . 23 G5
Khorat =
Nakhon
Ratchasima . 36 B2
Khorramābād . 46 D7
Khorrämshahr . 47 E7
Khotyn ....... 17 D8
Khouribga .... 54 B3
Khowai ...... 41 E8
Khoyniki ..... 17 C9
Khu Khan .... 36 B2
Khudzhand .. 29 E7
Khūgiāni ..... 42 D4
Khulna ...... 41 F7
Khulna □ .... 41 F7
Khūr ........ 44 C4
Khuraуş ...... 47 F7
Khūrīyā Mūrīyā,
Jazā 'ir ..... 48 D6
Khush ....... 42 C3
Khushab ..... 42 C8
Khust ....... 17 D6
Khuzdar ..... 42 F5
Khvor ....... 44 C3
Khvormūj ..... 44 D2
Khvoy ....... 46 C6
Khyber Pass .. 42 B7
Kiama ....... 63 B5
Kiamba ...... 38 C2
Kiangsi =
Jiangxi □ ... 35 D6
Kiangsu =
Jiangsu □ .. 35 C6
Kibangou .... 56 E2
Kibombo .... 57 E5
Kibondo ..... 57 E6
Kibwesa ..... 57 F5
Kibwezi ...... 57 E7
Kicking Horse
Pass ...... 71 C8

Kidal ........ 55 E5
Kidnappers, C. . 64 C7
Kiel ......... 14 A6
Kiel Canal =
Nord-Ostsee-
Kanal → ... 14 A5
Kielce ....... 16 C5
Kieler Bucht .. 14 A6
Kiev = Kyyiv .. 17 C10
Kiffa ........ 55 E2
Kifrī ........ 46 D6
Kigali ....... 57 E6
Kigoma-Ujiji . . 57 E5
Kihee ....... 62 A3
Kii-Suidō .... 32 C4
Kikinda ...... 22 B3
Kikládhes .... 23 F5
Kikwit ....... 56 E3
Kilcoy ....... 63 A5
Kilimanjaro ... 57 E7
Kilindini ..... 57 E7
Kilis ........ 46 C4
Kiliya ....... 17 F9
Kilkenny ..... 11 E3
Kilkís ....... 23 D4
Killarney,
Australia .... 63 A5
Killarney, Ireland 11 E2
Killeen ...... 78 D5
Killíni ....... 23 F4
Kilmarnock .. 10 D4
Kilmore ...... 63 C3
Kilosa ....... 57 F7
Kilrush ...... 11 E2
Kilwa Kivinje .. 57 F7
Kimaam ..... 39 F5
Kimba ....... 62 B2
Kimberley .... 58 D4
Kimberley
Plateau .... 60 D4
Kimry ....... 24 B4
Kinabalu,
Gunong ... 36 C5
Kindia ....... 55 G2
Kindu ....... 57 E5
Kineshma .... 24 B5
King George B. . 95 G4
King George I. . 96 A4
King George II. . 69 C2
King I. = Kadan
Kyun ..... 36 B1
King I. ....... 62 C3
King William I. . 70 B10
King William's
Town ...... 59 E5
Kingaroy ..... 63 A5
Kingoonya .... 62 B2
Kings Canyon
National Park 82 B3
King's Lynn ... 11 E7
Kingscote .... 62 C2
Kingsport .... 75 A6
Kingston,
Canada ..... 69 D3
Kingston,
Jamaica .... 86 C4
Kingston, N.Z. . 65 F3
Kingston South
East ....... 62 C2
Kingston upon
Hull ....... 11 E6
Kingstown .... 87 D7
Kingsville .... 78 F5
Kınık ....... 23 E6
Kinkala ...... 56 E2
Kinleith ...... 64 C6
Kinsale ...... 11 F2
Kinshasa ..... 56 E3
Kinston ...... 75 B9

Kintampo ..... 55 G4
Kintap ........ 37 E5
Kiparissía ..... 23 F3
Kiparissiakós
Kólpos ..... 23 F3
Kipembawe ... 57 F6
Kipili ........ 57 F6
Kipushi ...... 59 A5
Kirghizia ■ =
Kyrgyzstan ■ 29 E8
Kirghizstan =
Kyrgyzstan ■ 29 E8
Kiri ......... 56 E3
Kiribati ■ ..... 64 K12
Kınıkkale ..... 46 C3
Kirillov ....... 24 B4
Kirin = Jilin ... 35 B7
Kiritimati ..... 65 J15
Kirkcaldy .... 10 C5
Kirkcudbright .. 11 D4
Kirkee ....... 43 K8
Kirkenes ..... 8 E14
Kirkland Lake .. 69 D2
Kırklareli ..... 22 D6
Kirkūk ....... 46 D6
Kirkwall ..... 10 B5
Kirov ....... 28 D5
Kirovabad =
Gäncä ..... 25 E6
Kirovakan =
Vanadzor ... 25 E5
Kirovograd =
Kirovohrad .. 25 D3
Kirovohrad ... 25 D3
Kirovsk =
Babadayhan . 29 F7
Kirovsk ...... 28 C4
Kirsanov ..... 24 C5
Kırşehir ...... 46 C3
Kīrteh ....... 45 C5
Kirthar Range . 42 F5
Kiruna ....... 8 E12
Kirundu ...... 57 E5
Kiryū ....... 32 A6
Kisangani .... 57 D5
Kisar ....... 39 F3
Kiselevsk .... 29 D9
Kishanganj ... 40 D7
Kishangarh ... 42 F7
Kishinev =
Chişinău .... 17 E9
Kishiwada ... 32 B4
Kishtwar .... 42 C9
Kisii ........ 57 E6
Kisiju ....... 57 F7
Kiska I. ...... 71 C1
Kiskörös ..... 16 E4
Kiskunfélegyháza
........... 16 E4
Kiskunhalas ... 16 E4
Kislovodsk .... 25 E5
Kiso-Sammyaku 32 B5
Kissidougou .. 55 G2
Kisumu ... 57 E6
Kita ....... 55 F3
Kitab ....... 29 F7
Kitakami-
Gawa → ... 33 G12
Kitakyūshū ... 32 C2
Kitale ....... 57 D7
Kitchener .... 69 D2
Kitega = Gitega 57 E5
Kitgum ...... 57 D6
Kíthira ...... 23 F4
Kíthnos ..... 23 F5
Kittakittaooloo,
L. .......... 62 A2
Kitui ........ 57 E7
Kitwe ....... 59 A5

Kivertsi ...... 17 C7
Kivu, L. ...... 57 E5
Kiyev = Kyyiv . 17 C10
Kiyevskoye
Vdkhr. =
Kyyivske
Vdskh. ..... 17 C10
Kızıl Irmak → . 25 E4
Kizlyar ....... 25 E6
Kizyl-Arvat =
Gyzylarbat . 29 F6
Kladno ....... 16 C2
Klagenfurt ... 15 E8
Klaipeda ..... 24 B1
Klamath Falls . 80 D3
Klamath Mts. .. 80 E2
Klarälven → .. 9 G10
Klatovy ...... 16 D1
Klawer ...... 58 E3
Klerksdorp ... 59 D5
Kletsk = Klyetsk 17 B8
Klin ......... 28 D4
Kłodzko ...... 16 C3
Klondike ..... 70 B6
Klouto ....... 55 G5
Kluane L. .... 70 B6
Kluczbork .... 16 C4
Klyetsk ...... 17 B8
Knossós ..... 23 G5
Knox Coast ... 96 A12
Knoxville ..... 75 B6
Koartac =
Quaqtaq .... 68 B4
Koba, Aru,
Indonesia .. 39 F4
Koba, Bangka,
Indonesia .. 37 E3
Kobarid ..... 20 A4
Kobdo = Hovd 34 B4
Kōbe ........ 32 B4
København .. 9 G10
Koblenz ..... 14 C4
Kobroor,
Kepulauan . 39 F4
Kobryn ...... 17 B7
Kocaeli = İzmit 25 E2
Kočani ...... 22 D4
Koch Bihar ... 41 D7
Kōchi ....... 32 C3
Kochiu = Gejiu 34 D5
Kodiak ...... 71 C4
Kodiak I. ..... 71 C4
Koes ........ 58 D3
Kofiau ...... 39 E3
Koforidua ... 55 G4
Kōfu ....... 32 B6
Kogan ...... 63 A5
Koh-i-Bābā ... 42 B5
Kohat ....... 42 C7
Kohima ..... 41 E10
Kohkīlūyeh va
Būyer
Aḥmadi □ .. 44 D2
Kohler Ra. ... 96 B1
Kokand =
Qŭqon ..... 29 E8
Kokas ...... 39 E4
Kokchetav =
Kökshetaū .. 29 D7
Koko Kyunzu . 41 K9
Kokomo ..... 72 D2
Kokonau .... 39 E5
Kökshetaū ... 29 D7
Koksoak → .. 68 C4
Kokstad ..... 59 E5
Kola, Indonesia 39 F4
Kola, Russia .. 28 C4
Kola Pen. =
Kolskiy
Poluostrov .. 28 C4

Kolaka ....... 39 E2
Kolar ......... 43 N11
Kolar Gold Fields 43 N11
Kolayat ....... 42 F8
Kolchugino =
  Leninsk-
  Kuznetskiy .. 29 D9
Kolda ........ 55 F2
Kole ......... 56 E4
Kolepom = Yos
  Sudarso,
  Pulau ...... 39 F5
Kolguyev,
  Ostrov ...... 28 C5
Kolhapur ..... 43 L9
Kolín ......... 16 C2
Kolkata ........ 41 F7
Köln ......... 14 C4
Koło ......... 16 B4
Kołobrzeg ..... 16 A2
Kolokani ...... 55 F3
Kolomna ..... 24 B4
Kolomyya .... 17 D7
Kolonodale ... 39 E2
Kolosib ....... 41 E9
Kolpashevo ... 29 D9
Kolpino ...... 24 B3
Kolskiy
  Poluostrov .. 28 C4
Kolwezi ...... 57 G5
Kolyma → .. 31 C13
Komárno ..... 16 E4
Komatsu ..... 32 A5
Komi □ ...... 28 C6
Kommunarsk =
  Alchevsk .... 25 D4
Kommunizma,
  Pik ......... 29 F8
Komodo ...... 39 F1
Komono ...... 56 E2
Komoran, Pulau 39 F5
Komotini ..... 22 D5
Kompong Cham 36 B3
Kompong
  Chhnang .... 36 B2
Kompong Som 36 B2
Komrat =
  Comrat ..... 17 E9
Komsomolets,
  Ostrov ...... 30 A7
Konarhá □ .... 42 B7
Konch ........ 42 G11
Kondoa ...... 57 E7
Konduga ..... 53 F1
Köneürgench .. 29 E6
Kong ........ 55 G4
Kong, Koh ... 36 B2
Konglu ....... 41 D11
Kongolo ...... 57 F5
Kongor ...... 53 G5
Königsberg =
  Kaliningrad . 24 C1
Konin ........ 16 B4
Konjic ........ 20 C6
Konosha ..... 28 C5
Konotop ..... 24 C3
Konqi He → .. 34 B4
Końskie ..... 16 C5
Konstanz .... 14 E5
Kontagora ... 55 F6
Kontum ...... 36 B3
Konya ....... 46 C3
Konya Ovası . 46 C3
Konza ....... 57 E7
Kooloonong .. 62 B3
Koondrook .. 63 C3
Koonibba .... 62 B1
Koorawatha .. 63 B4
Kootenay L. ... 71 D8

Kopaonik ..... 22 C3
Koper ........ 20 B4
Kopeysk ...... 29 D7
Kopi ......... 62 B2
Koprivnica ... 20 A6
Kopychyntsi ... 17 D7
Korab ........ 22 D3
Korça ........ 23 D3
Korce = Korça . 23 D3
Korčula ...... 20 C6
Kordestan ... 46 D5
Kordestān □ .. 46 D6
Kordofân ..... 53 F4
Korea, North ■ 35 C7
Korea, South ■ 35 C7
Korea Bay .... 35 C7
Korea Strait ... 35 C7
Korets ....... 17 C8
Korhogo ..... 55 G3
Korim ........ 39 E5
Korinthiakós
  Kólpos ..... 23 E4
Kórinthos .... 23 F4
Kōriyama ..... 33 G12
Korneshty =
  Corneşti .... 17 E9
Koro, Ivory C. .. 55 G3
Koro, Mali ... 55 F4
Korogwe ..... 57 F7
Koroit ....... 62 C3
Koror ........ 38 C4
Körös → ..... 16 E5
Korosten .... 17 C9
Korostyshev .. 17 C9
Korti ........ 53 E5
Kortrijk ...... 14 C2
Kos .......... 23 F6
Kościan ..... 16 B3
Kosciuszko, Mt. 63 C4
Kosha ........ 52 D5
K'oshih = Kashi 34 C2
Košice ....... 16 D5
Kosovo □ ..... 22 C3
Kosovska-
  Mitrovica ... 22 C3
Kôstî ........ 53 F5
Kostopil ..... 17 C8
Kostroma ..... 24 B5
Kostrzyn .... 16 B2
Koszalin ..... 16 A3
Kota ......... 43 G9
Kota Baharu .. 36 C2
Kota Belud ... 36 C5
Kota Kinabalu . 36 C5
Kota Tinggi ... 37 D2
Kotaagung ... 37 F2
Kotabaru .... 37 E5
Kotabumi .... 37 E2
Kotamobagu .. 39 D2
Kotawaringin .. 37 E4
Kotelnich .... 24 B6
Kotelnyy, Ostrov 31 B11
Kotka ........ 9 F13
Kotlas ....... 28 C5
Kotli ........ 42 C8
Kotor ........ 22 C2
Kotovsk ..... 17 E9
Kotri ........ 42 G6
Kottayam .... 43 Q10
Kotturu ...... 43 M10
Kotuy → .... 30 B8
Kotzebue .... 71 B3
Kouango .... 56 D4
Koudougou ... 55 F4
Kouilou → ... 56 E2
Kouki ....... 56 C3
Koula Moutou . 56 E2
Koulen ....... 36 B2
Koulikoro .... 55 F3

Koumra ...... 53 G2
Kounradskiy .. 29 E8
Kouroussa .... 55 F3
Kousseri ..... 53 F1
Koutiala ..... 55 F3
Kovel ........ 17 C7
Kovrov ...... 24 B5
Kowloon .... 35 D6
Köyceğiz ..... 23 F7
Koyuk ....... 71 B3
Koyukuk → .. 71 B4
Kozan ....... 46 C3
Kozáni ....... 23 D3
Kozhikode =
  Calicut .... 43 P9
Kozyatyn ..... 17 D9
Kpalimé ..... 55 G5
Kra, Isthmus of
  = Kra, Kho
  Khot ....... 36 B1
Kra, Kho Khot . 36 B1
Kragujevac ... 22 B3
Krajina ...... 20 B6
Krakatau =
  Rakata, Pulau 37 F3
Kraków ...... 16 C4
Kraljevo ..... 22 C3
Kramatorsk ... 25 D4
Kranj ........ 20 A5
Kraśnik ...... 16 C6
Krasnoarmeysk 29 D5
Krasnodar ... 25 D4
Krasnoperekopsk
  ........... 25 D3
Krasnoselkupsk 28 C9
Krasnoturinsk . 28 D7
Krasnoufimsk . 29 D6
Krasnouralsk .. 29 D7
Krasnovodsk =
  Krasnowodsk 29 E6
Krasnowodsk .. 29 E6
Krasnoyarsk .. 30 D7
Krasnyy Luch . 25 D4
Krasnyy Yar ... 25 D6
Kratie ........ 36 B3
Krau ......... 39 E6
Krefeld ...... 14 C4
Kremen ...... 20 B5
Kremenchug =
  Kremenchuk . 24 D3
Kremenchuk .. 24 D3
Kremenchuksk
  Vdskh. ...... 24 D3
Kremenets .... 17 C7
Krems ....... 15 D8
Kribi ........ 56 D1
Krichev =
  Krychaw ... 17 B10
Krishna → .. 40 K3
Krishnanagar .. 41 F7
Kristiansand .. 9 G9
Kristiansund .. 8 F9
Kríti ......... 23 G5
Krivoy Rog =
  Kryvyy Rih . 25 D3
Krk ......... 20 B5
Kronprins Olav
  Kyst ........ 96 A9
Kronshtadt ... 24 B2
Kroonstad .... 59 D5
Kropotkin,
  Irkutsk, Russia 30 D9
Kropotkin,
  Krasnodar,
  Russia ...... 25 D5
Krosno ...... 16 D5
Krotoszyn .... 16 C3
Krugersdorp .. 59 D5

Krung Thep =
  Bangkok .... 36 B2
Krupki ........ 17 A9
Kruševac ..... 22 C3
Krychaw .... 17 B10
Krymskiy
  Poluostrov =
  Krymskyy
  Pivostriv .... 25 D3
Krymskyy
  Pivostriv .... 25 D3
Kryvyy Rih .... 25 D3
Ksar el Boukhari 54 A5
Ksar el Kebir . 54 B3
Ksar es Souk =
  Ar Rachidiya 54 B4
Kuala ........ 37 D2
Kuala Kubu
  Baharu ..... 37 D2
Kuala Lipis ... 37 D2
Kuala Lumpur . 37 D2
Kuala
  Terengganu . 36 C2
Kualajelai .... 37 E4
Kualakapuas .. 37 E4
Kualakurun ... 37 E4
Kualapembuang 37 E4
Kualasimpang . 37 D1
Kuandang .... 39 D2
Kuangchou =
  Guangzhou . 35 D6
Kuantan ...... 37 D2
Kuba = Quba . 25 E6
Kuban → .... 25 D4
Kucing ....... 37 D4
Kuda ........ 43 H7
Kudat ....... 36 C5
Kudymkar ... 28 D6
Kueiyang =
  Guiyang ... 35 D5
Kufra Oasis = Al
  Kufrah ..... 52 D3
Kufstein ..... 15 E7
Kugluktuk ... 70 B8
Küh-e 'Alījūq .. 44 D2
Küh-e-Hazārān . 44 D4
Küh-e Sorkh .. 44 C4
Küh-e Taftān . 45 D5
Kühak ....... 42 F3
Kühhā-ye-
  Bashäkerd .. 45 E4
Kühpäyeh .... 44 C3
Kuito ........ 58 A3
Kujū-San .... 32 C2
Kukawa ..... 53 F1
Kukësi ...... 22 C3
Kula ......... 23 E7
Kulasekarappattinam
  ........... 43 Q11
Kuldja = Yining 34 B3
Külob ....... 29 F7
Kulsary ...... 29 E6
Kulunda ..... 29 D8
Kulwin ....... 62 C3
Kulyab = Külob 29 F7
Kum Tekei ... 29 E8
Kuma → .... 25 E6
Kumagaya ... 32 A6
Kumai ....... 37 E4
Kumamba,
  Kepulauan . 39 E5
Kumamoto ... 32 C2
Kumanovo ... 22 C3
Kumara ...... 65 E4
Kumasi ...... 55 G4
Kumayri =
  Gyumri .... 25 E5
Kumba ....... 56 D1
Kumbakonam . 43 P11

Kumbarilla .... 63 A5
Kumo ........ 55 F7
Kumon Bum .. 41 D11
Kunama ...... 63 C4
Kungala ...... 63 A5
Kungrad =
  Qŭnghirot ... 29 E6
Kungur ....... 29 D6
Kunlong ..... 41 F12
Kunlun Shan .. 34 C3
Kunming .... 34 D5
Kunsan ....... 35 C7
Kunya-Urgench
  =
  Köneürgench 29 E6
Kuopio ....... 8 F13
Kupa ─► ..... 20 B6
Kupyansk .... 28 E4
Kuqa ......... 34 B3
Kür ─► ....... 25 E6
Kura = Kür ─► 25 E6
Kurashiki ..... 32 B3
Kurayoshi .... 32 B3
Kŭrdzhali .... 22 D5
Kure ........ 32 B3
Kurgaldzhinskiy 29 D8
Kurgan ...... 29 D7
Kuria Maria Is.
  = Khūrīyā
  Mūrīyā, Jazā
  'ir ....... 48 D6
Kurigram ..... 41 E7
Kuril Is. =
  Kurilskiye
  Ostrova ..... 31 E12
Kurilskiye
  Ostrova ..... 31 E12
Kurmuk ..... 53 F5
Kurnool ..... 43 L11
Kurow ...... 65 F4
Kurrajong .... 63 B5
Kurri Kurri .... 63 B5
Kursk ....... 24 C4
Kuruktag .... 34 B3
Kuruman ..... 58 D4
Kurume ...... 32 C2
Kus Gölü .... 23 D6
Kuşadası .... 23 F6
Kushiro ..... 32 F12
Kushtia ..... 41 F7
Kuskokwim ─► 71 B3
Kuskokwim B. . 71 C3
Kustanay =
  Qostanay ... 29 D7
Kütahya ...... 46 C2
Kutaisi ...... 25 E5
Kutaraja =
  Banda Aceh . 36 C1
Kutch, Gulf of =
  Kachchh, Gulf
  of .......... 43 H6
Kutch, Rann of
  = Kachchh,
  Rann of ..... 43 G6
Kutno ........ 16 B4
Kutu ....... 56 E3
Kutum ...... 53 F3
Kuujjuaq ..... 68 C4
Kuwait = Al
  Kuwayt .... 47 E7
Kuwait ■ .... 47 E6
Kuwana .... 32 B5
Kuybyshev =
  Samara .... 24 C7
Kuybyshev ... 29 D8
Kuybyshevskoye
  Vdkhr. ...... 24 B6
Küysanjaq .... 46 C6
Kuyumba .... 30 C7

Kuzey Anadolu
  Dağları ..... 46 B3
Kuznetsk ..... 24 C6
Kvarner ...... 20 B5
Kvarnerič .... 20 B5
Kwakoegron .. 92 A2
Kwamouth ... 56 E3
Kwando ─► .. 58 B4
Kwangju ...... 35 C7
Kwangsi-Chuang
  = Guangxi
  Zhuangzu
  Zizhiqu □ ... 35 D5
Kwangtung =
  Guangdong □ 35 D6
Kwatisore ..... 39 E4
Kweichow =
  Guizhou □ .. 35 D5
Kwekwe ...... 59 B5
Kwidzyn ..... 16 B4
Kwoka ...... 39 E4
Kyabé ........ 53 G2
Kyabra Cr. ─► . 63 A3
Kyabram ..... 63 C4
Kyancutta .... 62 B2
Kyangin ...... 41 H10
Kyaukpadaung 41 G10
Kyaukpyu .... 41 H9
Kyaukse ..... 41 G11
Kyle Dam .... 59 C6
Kyneton ..... 63 C3
Kyō-ga-Saki .. 32 B4
Kyoga, L. .... 57 D6
Kyogle ...... 63 A5
Kyongpyaw ... 41 J10
Kyōto ........ 32 B4
Kyrenia ...... 46 D3
Kyrgyzstan ■ .. 29 E8
Kystatyam ... 30 C10
Kytal Ktakh .. 31 C10
Kyunhla ..... 41 F10
Kyūshū ..... 32 C2
Kyūshū-Sanchi 32 C2
Kyustendil ... 22 C4
Kyusyur ...... 30 B10
Kywong ..... 63 B4
Kyyiv ....... 17 C10
Kyyivske Vdskh. 17 C10
Kyzyl Kum ... 29 E7
Kyzyl-Kyya ... 29 E8
Kzyl-Orda =
  Qyzylorda ... 29 E7

**L**

La Albufera ... 19 C5
La Alcarria ... 19 B4
La Asunción .. 90 A6
La Banda .... 94 B4
La Calera .... 94 C2
La Carlota .... 94 C4
La Ceiba ...... 85 D7
La Chaux de
  Fonds ...... 13 C7
La Cocha .... 94 B3
La Coruña ... 18 A1
La Crosse ..... 77 D9
La Dorada .... 90 B4
La Estrada ... 18 A1
La Grange .... 74 C5
La Guaira .... 90 A5
La Güera .... 54 D1
La Habana ... 86 B3
La Línea de la
  Concepción . 18 D3
La Mancha .... 19 C4

La Palma,
  Canary Is. ... 54 C1
La Palma,
  Panama .... 86 E4
La Palma del
  Condado .... 18 D2
La Paragua ... 90 B6
La Paz,
  Entre Ríos,
  Argentina ... 94 C5
La Paz, San Luis,
  Argentina ... 94 C3
La Paz, Bolivia . 91 G5
La Paz, Mexico 84 C2
La Pedrera ... 90 D5
La Plata ...... 94 D5
La Quiaca .... 94 A3
La Rioja ...... 94 B3
La Rioja □ .... 19 A4
La Robla ...... 18 A3
La Roche-sur-
  Yon ....... 12 C3
La Rochelle ... 12 C3
La Roda ..... 19 C4
La Romana ... 87 C6
La Serena .... 94 B2
La Seyne-sur-
  Mer ....... 13 E6
La Spézia ..... 20 B2
La Tortuga ... 87 D6
La Tuque ..... 69 D3
La Unión ..... 95 E2
La Urbana .... 90 B5
La Vega ...... 87 C5
Labe = Elbe ─► 14 B5
Labé ....... 55 F2
Labis ......... 37 D2
Laboulaye .... 94 C4
Labrador
  □.......... 69 C4
Lábrea ....... 91 E6
Labuan....... 36 C5
Labuha ...... 39 E3
Labuhanbajo .. 39 F2
Labuk, Telok .. 36 C5
Labyrinth, L. .. 62 B2
Labytnangi ... 28 C7
Lac La Biche .. 71 C8
Lac la Martre .. 70 B8
Lacanau ..... 12 D3
Laccadive Is. =
  Lakshadweep
  Is. .......... 26 H11
Lacepede B. ... 62 C2
Lachine ─► ... 69 D3
Lachlan ─► .. 63 B3
Lackawanna ... 73 C6
Lacombe ..... 71 C8
Ladakh Ra. ... 42 B10
Lādīz ....... 45 D5
Ladoga, L. =
  Ladozhskoye
  Ozero ..... 28 C4
Ladozhskoye
  Ozero ..... 28 C4
Ladysmith,
  Canada ..... 71 D7
Ladysmith,
  S. Africa ... 59 D5
Lae ....... 61 B8
Lafayette ..... 79 D7
Lafia ....... 55 G6
Laghmān □ .. 45 C7
Laghouat ..... 54 B5
Lagonoy Gulf . 38 B2
Lagos, Nigeria . 55 G5
Lagos, Portugal 18 D1
Laguna ....... 94 B7
Lagunas, Chile 91 H5

Lagunas, Peru . 90 E3
Lahad Datu ... 38 C1
Lahat ........ 37 E2
Lahewa ...... 37 D1
Lāhījān ...... 46 C7
Lahn ─► ...... 14 C4
Lahore ...... 42 D9
Lahti ....... 8 F13
Lahtis = Lahti . 8 F13
Laï ........... 53 G2
Laibin ....... 35 D5
Laidley ....... 63 A5
Laila = Laylá . 47 G6
Lairg ......... 10 B4
Lajere ....... 55 F7
Lajes ....... 94 B6
Lake Cargelligo 63 B4
Lake Charles . 79 D7
Lake City .... 75 D6
Lake Worth .. 75 F7
Lakeland ..... 75 E7
Lakes Entrance 63 C4
Lakewood .... 72 D5
Lakonikós
  Kólpos ..... 23 F4
Lakor ....... 39 F3
Lakselv ..... 55 G3
Lakshadweep
  Is. .......... 26 H11
Lala Ghat .... 41 E9
Lalibela ...... 53 F6
Lalín ....... 18 A1
Lalitapur =
  Patan ..... 40 D5
Lamaing ..... 41 K11
Lamas ....... 91 E3
Lambaréné ... 56 E2
Lambert Glacier 96 B10
Lame ....... 55 F6
Lamego ..... 18 B2
Lameroo ..... 62 C3
Lamía ....... 23 E4
Lamon Bay ... 38 B2
Lampa ....... 91 G4
Lampedusa ... 21 G4
Lampione .... 21 G4
Lampung □ ... 37 F2
Lamu ....... 57 E8
Lanai I. ...... 82 H12
Lanak La .... 42 B11
Lanak'o
  Shank'ou =
  Lanak La ... 42 B11
Lanao, L. ..... 38 C2
Lancaster, U.K. 11 D5
Lancaster,
  U.S.A. ...... 73 D7
Lancaster Sd. . 68 A2
Lanchow =
  Lanzhou ... 35 C5
Lanciano ..... 20 C5
Landeck ..... 14 E6
Landes ...... 12 D3
Landi Kotal ... 42 B7
Land's End ... 11 F4
Landshut .... 15 D7
La'nga Co .... 40 B3
Langkawi, P. . 36 C1
Langkon .... 36 C5
Langres ..... 13 C6
Langres, Plateau
  de ........ 13 C6
Langsa ..... 36 D1
Languedoc .... 13 E5
Langzhong ... 35 C5
Lannion .... 12 B2
Lansdowne ... 63 B5
Lansing .... 72 C3
Lanusei ...... 21 E2

# Lanzarote

Lanzarote ..... 54 C2
Lanzhou ...... 35 C5
Laoag ........ 38 A2
Laoang ....... 38 B3
Laon ......... 13 B5
Laos ■ ...... 36 A3
Lapa ......... 94 B7
Laparan ...... 38 C1
Lapland =
 Lappland ... 8 E12
Lappland ..... 8 E12
Lapseki ...... 23 D6
Laptev Sea ... 30 B10
L'Áquila ..... 20 C4
Lär .......... 44 E3
Larache ...... 54 A3
Laramie ...... 76 E2
Larantuka .... 39 F2
Larap ........ 38 B2
Larat ........ 39 F4
Laredo ....... 78 F4
Lariang ...... 39 E1
Lárisa ....... 23 E4
Larnaca ...... 46 D3
Larne ........ 11 D4
Larrimah ..... 60 D5
Larsen Ice Shelf 96 A3
Larvik ....... 9 G9
Laryak ....... 29 C8
Las Anod ..... 49 F4
Las Cruces ... 83 D9
Las Flores .... 94 D5
Las Khoreh ... 49 E4
Las Lajas .... 94 D2
Las Lomitas ... 94 A4
Las Palmas ... 54 C1
Las Pipinas ... 94 D5
Las Plumas ... 95 E3
Las Rosas .... 94 C4
Las Varillas ... 94 C4
Las Vegas .... 82 B5
Lashio ....... 41 F11
Lassen Pk. .... 80 E3
Lastoursville . 56 E2
Lastovo ...... 20 C6
Latacunga .... 90 D3
Latakia = Al
 Lādhiqīyah .. 46 D3
Latina ........ 20 D4
Latium =
 Lazio □ ..... 20 C4
Latrobe ....... 62 D4
Latvia ■ ...... 24 B1
Lauchhammer . 15 C7
Launceston ... 62 D4
Laurel ....... 79 D9
Lauria ........ 21 D5
Laurium ...... 69 D2
Lausanne ..... 13 C7
Laut ......... 36 D3
Laut Kecil,
 Kepulauan .. 37 E5
Laval ........ 12 B3
Lávrion ...... 23 F5
Lawas ........ 36 D5
Lawele ....... 39 F2
Lawng Pit ..... 41 E11
Lawrence, N.Z. 65 F3
Lawrence,
 U.S.A. ..... 77 F7
Lawton ....... 78 B4
Laylá ........ 47 G6
Lazio □ ...... 20 C4
Le Creusot .... 13 C6
Le Havre ..... 12 B4
Le Mans ...... 12 C4
Le Mont-St.-
 Michel ..... 12 B3
Le Moule ..... 87 C7

Le Puy-en-Velay 13 D5
Le Touquet-
 Paris-Plage .. 12 A4
Le Tréport .... 12 A4
Le Verdon-sur-
 Mer ........ 12 D3
Leamington Spa
 = Royal
 Leamington
 Spa ........ 11 E6
Leandro Norte
 Alem ....... 94 B5
Leavenworth .. 77 F7
Lebak ........ 38 C2
Lebanon ■ .... 46 D3
Lębork ....... 16 A3
Lebrija ....... 18 D2
Lebu ......... 94 D2
Lecce ........ 23 D2
Lecco ........ 20 B2
Lech → ...... 14 D6
Łęczyca ...... 16 B4
Leduc ........ 71 C8
Leeds ........ 11 E6
Leer ......... 14 B4
Leeton ....... 63 B4
Leeuwarden ... 14 B3
Leeuwin, C. ... 60 G2
Leeward Is. ... 87 C7
Leganés ...... 18 B4
Legazpi ...... 38 B2
Leghorn =
 Livorno .... 20 C3
Legionowo .... 16 B5
Legnago ...... 20 B3
Legnica ...... 16 C3
Legume ...... 63 A5
Leh .......... 42 B10
Leicester ..... 11 E6
Leiden ....... 14 B3
Leie → ...... 14 C2
Leine → ..... 14 B5
Leinster □ .... 11 E3
Leipzig ...... 15 C7
Leiria ........ 18 C1
Leitrim ...... 11 D2
Leizhou Bandao 35 D6
Leksula ...... 39 E3
Lékva Ori .... 23 G5
Leleque ...... 95 E2
Léman, L. .... 13 C7
Lemhi Ra. .... 81 C7
Lena → ...... 30 B10
Leninabad =
 Khudzhand .. 29 E7
Leninakan =
 Gyumri ..... 25 E5
Leningrad =
 Sankt-
 Peterburg .. 24 B3
Leninogorsk =
 Ridder ...... 29 D9
Leninsk ...... 25 D6
Leninsk-
 Kuznetskiy .. 29 D9
Lenmalu ...... 39 E4
Lens ......... 13 A5
Lentini ...... 21 F5
Leoben ....... 15 E8
Leodhas =
 Lewis ...... 10 B3
León, Mexico .. 84 C4
León, Nic. .... 85 E7
León, Spain .. 18 A3
León, Montañas
 de ......... 18 A2
Leongatha .... 63 C4
Léopold II, Lac
 = Mai-
 Ndombe, L. . 56 E3

Léopoldville =
 Kinshasa .... 56 E3
Leova ........ 17 E9
Lepel = Lyepyel 24 C2
Lepikha ...... 31 C10
Léré ......... 53 G1
Lérida ....... 19 B6
Lerwick ...... 10 A6
Les Cayes .... 86 C5
Les Sables-
 d'Olonne ... 12 C3
Lesbos =
 Lésvos ..... 23 E6
Leskovac ..... 22 C3
Lesotho ■ .... 59 D5
Lesser Antilles . 87 D7
Lesser Sunda Is. 39 F2
Lésvos ....... 23 E6
Leszno ....... 16 C3
Lethbridge ... 71 D8
Leti, Kepulauan 39 F3
Leti Is. = Leti,
 Kepulauan .. 39 F3
Leticia ....... 90 D4
Letpadan ..... 41 J10
Letpan ....... 41 H10
Letterkenny ... 11 D3
Leuser, G. ... 37 D1
Leuven ....... 14 C3
Levádhia ..... 23 E4
Levice ....... 16 D4
Levin ........ 64 D6
Lévis ........ 69 D3
Levkás ....... 23 E3
Levkôsia =
 Nicosia .... 46 D3
Levskigrad =
 Karlovo .... 22 C5
Lewis ........ 10 B3
Lewisporte ... 69 D5
Lewiston, Idaho,
 U.S.A. ..... 80 B5
Lewiston,
 Maine, U.S.A. 73 B10
Lexington, Ky.,
 U.S.A. ..... 72 E3
Lexington, N.C.,
 U.S.A. ..... 75 B7
Leyte ........ 38 B2
Lezha ........ 22 D2
Lhasa ........ 34 D4
Lhazê ........ 34 D3
Lhokkruet .... 36 D1
Lhokseumawe . 36 C1
Lhuntsi Dzong . 41 D8
Lianga ....... 38 C3
Lianyungang .. 35 C6
Liaoning □ ... 35 B7
Liaoyuan ..... 35 B7
Liard → ..... 70 B7
Libau = Liepāja 24 B1
Libenge ...... 56 D3
Liberal ...... 78 A3
Liberec ...... 16 C2
Liberia ■ .... 55 G3
Lîbîya, Sahrâ' . 52 C4
Libobo, Tanjung 39 E3
Libonda ...... 58 A4
Libourne ..... 12 D3
Libreville .... 56 D1
Libya ■ ...... 52 C2
Libyan Desert =
 Lîbîya, Sahrâ' 52 C4
Licantén ..... 94 D2
Licata ........ 21 F4
Lichinga ..... 59 A7
Lichtenburg ... 59 D5
Lida ......... 17 B7
Liechtenstein ■ 14 E5

Liège ........ 14 C3
Liegnitz =
 Legnica .... 16 C3
Lienyünchiangshih
 =
 Lianyungang 35 C6
Lienz ........ 15 E7
Liepāja ...... 24 B1
Liffey → ..... 11 E3
Lifford ....... 11 D3
Lightning Ridge 63 A4
Liguria □ .... 20 B2
Ligurian Sea .. 20 C2
Lijiang ....... 34 D5
Likasi ....... 57 G5
Lille ......... 13 A5
Lillehammer .. 8 F10
Lilongwe ..... 59 A6
Liloy ........ 38 C2
Lim → ...... 20 C7
Lima, Indonesia 39 E3
Lima, Peru .... 91 F3
Lima, U.S.A. .. 72 D3
Lima → ..... 18 B1
Limassol ..... 46 D3
Limay Mahuida 94 D3
Limbang ..... 36 D5
Limbe ....... 56 D1
Limbri ....... 63 B5
Limburg ..... 14 C5
Limeira ...... 94 A7
Limerick ..... 11 E2
Limfjorden ... 9 G9
Limia =
 Lima → .... 18 B1
Límnos ...... 23 E5
Limoeiro do
 Norte ...... 92 D6
Limoges ..... 12 D4
Limón ....... 86 E3
Limousin ..... 12 D4
Limoux ...... 12 E5
Limpopo → .. 59 D6
Limuru ...... 57 E7
Linares, Chile . 94 D2
Linares, Mexico 84 C5
Linares, Spain . 18 C4
Linchuan .... 35 D6
Lincoln,
 Argentina ... 94 C4
Lincoln, N.Z. .. 65 E5
Lincoln, U.K. .. 11 E6
Lincoln, U.S.A. 77 E6
Linden ....... 90 B7
Líndhos ...... 23 F7
Lindi ........ 57 F7
Lingayen ..... 38 A2
Lingayen G. .. 38 A2
Lingen ....... 14 B4
Lingga ....... 37 E2
Lingga,
 Kepulauan .. 37 E2
Lingga Arch. =
 Lingga,
 Kepulauan .. 37 E2
Linguéré ..... 55 E1
Lingyun ...... 35 D5
Linhai ....... 35 D7
Linhares ..... 93 F5
Linköping .... 9 G11
Linosa, I. .... 21 G4
Lins ......... 94 A7
Linville ...... 63 A5
Linxia ....... 34 C5
Linz ......... 15 D8
Lion, G. du ... 13 E6
Lions, G. of =
 Lion, G. du .. 13 E6
Lipa ......... 38 B2

Lípari ........ 21 E5
Lípari, Is. =
  Eólie, Ís. .... 21 E5
Lipcani ....... 17 D8
Lipetsk ....... 24 C4
Lipkany =
  Lipcani ..... 17 D8
Lipovets ...... 17 D9
Lippe → ..... 14 C4
Liptrap C. .. 63 C4
Lira ......... 57 D6
Liria ........ 19 C5
Lisala ....... 56 D4
Lisboa ....... 18 C1
Lisbon = Lisboa 18 C1
Lisburn ...... 11 D3
Lisburne, C. ... 71 B3
Lishui ....... 35 D6
Lisichansk =
  Lysychansk . 25 D4
Lisieux ...... 12 B4
Liski ........ 24 C4
Lismore ...... 63 A5
Lister, Mt. .... 96 B15
Liston ....... 63 A5
Listowel ..... 11 E2
Litang ....... 38 C1
Litani → ..... 46 D3
Lithgow ...... 63 B5
Líthinon, Ákra . 23 G5
Lithuania ■ ... 24 B1
Litoměřice .... 16 C2
Little Barrier I. . 64 B6
Little Laut Is. =
  Laut Kecil,
  Kepulauan .. 37 E5
Little
  Missouri → . 76 B3
Little River .... 65 E5
Little Rock .... 79 B7
Liukang
  Tenggaja ... 39 F1
Liuwa Plain .. 58 A4
Liuzhou ...... 35 D5
Liverpool,
  Australia .... 63 B5
Liverpool,
  Canada ..... 69 D4
Liverpool, U.K. 11 E5
Liverpool Plains 63 B5
Liverpool Ra. .. 63 B5
Livingstone ... 59 B5
Livingstonia .. 57 G6
Livny ........ 24 C4
Livorno ...... 20 C3
Livramento ... 94 C5
Liwale ....... 57 F7
Ljubljana .... 20 A5
Ljungan → ... 8 F11
Ljusnan → ... 8 F11
Llancanelo,
  Salina ..... 94 D3
Llanelli ...... 11 F4
Llanes ....... 18 A3
Llano Estacado 78 C2
Llanos ....... 90 C4
Lleida = Lérida 19 B6
Llobregat → .. 19 B7
Lloret de Mar . 19 B7
Lluchmayor ... 19 C7
Llullaillaco,
  Volcán .... 94 A3
Loa → ....... 94 A2
Lobatse ..... 59 D5
Lobería ...... 94 D5
Lobito ....... 58 A2
Locarno ...... 13 C8
Loch Garman =
  Wexford .... 11 E3

Loches ....... 12 C4
Lock ......... 62 B2
Lodhran ...... 42 E7
Lodi, Italy ... 20 B2
Lodi, U.S.A. .. 80 F3
Lodja ........ 56 E4
Lodwar ...... 57 D7
Łódź ......... 16 C4
Lofoten ...... 8 E10
Logan ........ 81 E8
Logan, Mt. =
  Pierre Elliott
  Trudeau, Mt. .. 70 B5
Logone → .... 53 F2
Logroño ...... 19 A4
Lohardaga .... 40 F5
Loi-kaw ...... 41 H11
Loir → ....... 12 C3
Loire → ...... 12 C2
Loja, Ecuador . 90 D3
Loja, Spain ... 18 D3
Loji .......... 39 E3
Lokandu ...... 57 E5
Lokitaung .... 57 D7
Lokoja ....... 55 G6
Lokolama ..... 56 E3
Loliondo ..... 57 E7
Lom ......... 22 C4
Lomami → ... 56 D4
Lombardy =
  Lombárdia □ 20 B2
Lomblen ...... 39 F2
Lombok ...... 37 F5
Lomé ........ 55 G5
Lomela ...... 56 E4
Lomela → .... 56 E4
Lomié ........ 56 D2
Lomond, L. ... 10 C4
Lompobatang . 39 F1
Łomza ....... 16 B6
Loncoche ..... 95 D2
Londa ........ 43 M9
London ....... 11 F6
Londonderry .. 11 D3
Londonderry, C. 60 C4
Londonderry, I. 95 H2
Londrina ..... 94 A6
Long Beach .. 82 D3
Long I.,
  Bahamas ... 86 B4
Long I., U.S.A. . 73 D9
Long Xuyen .. 36 B3
Longford,
  Australia .... 62 D4
Longford,
  Ireland ..... 11 E3
Longiram ..... 37 E5
Longlac ...... 69 D2
Longnawan ... 37 D4
Longreach .... 61 E7
Longview, Tex.,
  U.S.A. ...... 79 C6
Longview,
  Wash., U.S.A. 80 B2
Lons-le-Saunier 13 C6
Lop Nor = Lop
  Nur ........ 34 B4
Lopez, C. ..... 56 E1
Lora → ....... 42 D4
Lora, Hamun-i- 42 E4
Lora Cr. → ... 62 A2
Lora del Río .. 18 D3
Lorain ....... 72 D4
Loralai ...... 42 D6
Lorca ....... 19 D5
Lorestán □ .... 46 D6
Loreto ....... 92 D4
Lorient ...... 12 C2
Lorne ........ 62 C3

Lorraine ...... 13 B7
Los Alamos ... 83 C9
Los Andes ... 94 C2
Los Angeles,
  Chile ...... 94 D2
Los Angeles,
  U.S.A. ...... 82 C3
Los Blancos ... 94 A4
Los Hermanos . 90 A6
Los Mochis .. 84 B3
Los Roques .. 90 A5
Los Testigos .. 90 A6
Los Vilos .... 94 C2
Lošinj ....... 20 B5
Lot → ....... 12 D4
Lota ......... 94 D2
Loubomo ..... 56 E2
Louga ....... 55 E1
Louis Trichardt 59 C5
Louis XIV, Pte. . 69 C3
Louisiade Arch. 61 C9
Louisiana □ ... 79 D8
Louisville ..... 72 E3
Loulé ........ 18 D1
Lourdes ...... 12 E3
Louth, Australia 63 B4
Louth, U.K. ... 11 E6
Louvain =
  Leuven .... 14 C3
Lovech ....... 22 C5
Low Tatra =
  Nízké Tatry .. 16 D4
Lowell ....... 73 C10
Lower California
  = Baja
  California ... 84 A1
Lower Hutt .... 65 D6
Lower Saxony =
  Niedersachsen □
  ............ 14 B5
Lower Tunguska
  = Tunguska,
  Nizhnyaya → 30 C6
Lowestoft ..... 11 E7
Łowicz ....... 16 B4
Lowyar □ ..... 45 C7
Loxton ....... 62 B3
Loyalty Is. =
  Loyauté, Is. . 64 M11
Loyang =
  Luoyang ... 35 C6
Loyauté, Is. ... 64 M11
Loyev = Loyew 17 C10
Loyew ........ 17 C10
Luachimo ..... 56 F4
Luacono ..... 56 G4
Lualaba → ... 57 D5
Luanda ....... 56 F2
Luangwa ..... 59 B6
Luangwa → .. 59 A6
Luanshya .... 59 A5
Luapula → ... 57 F5
Luarca ....... 18 A2
Luashi ....... 56 G4
Luau ........ 56 G4
Lubalo ....... 56 F3
Lubang Is. ... 38 B2
Lubbock ..... 78 C3
Lübeck ...... 15 B6
Lubefu ...... 56 E4
Lubero = Luofu 57 E5
Lubin ....... 16 C3
Lublin ....... 17 C6
Lubuagan ... 38 A2
Lubuk Antu .. 37 D4
Lubuklinggau . 37 E2
Lubuksikaping . 37 D2
Lubumbashi .. 59 A5
Lubutu ....... 57 E5

Lucca ........ 20 C3
Lucena, Phil. .. 38 B2
Lucena, Spain . 18 D3
Lučenec ...... 16 D4
Lucerne =
  Luzern ..... 13 C8
Lucira ....... 58 A2
Luckenwalde .. 15 B7
Lucknow ..... 40 D3
Lüda = Dalian . 35 C7
Lüderitz ..... 58 D3
Ludhiana .... 42 D9
Ludwigsburg .. 14 D5
Ludwigshafen . 14 D5
Luebo ....... 56 F4
Lufira → ..... 57 F5
Lufkin ....... 79 D6
Luga ........ 24 B2
Lugano ...... 13 C8
Lugansk =
  Luhansk .... 25 D4
Lugh Ganana .. 49 G3
Lugo, Italy ... 20 B3
Lugo, Spain ... 18 A2
Lugoj ....... 17 F5
Lugovoy ..... 29 E8
Luhansk ..... 25 D4
Luiana ....... 58 B4
Luimneach =
  Limerick .... 11 E2
Luís Correia .. 92 C5
Luitpold Coast . 96 B5
Luiza ....... 56 F4
Luján ....... 94 C5
Lukanga Swamp 59 A5
Lukenie → ... 56 E3
Lukolela ..... 56 E3
Łuków ....... 17 C6
Lule älv → ... 8 E12
Luleå ....... 8 E12
Lüleburgaz .... 22 D6
Lulonga → ... 56 D3
Lulua → ..... 56 E4
Luluabourg =
  Kananga .... 56 F4
Lumai ....... 58 A4
Lumbala
  N'guimbo ... 58 A4
Lumsden .... 65 F3
Lumut, Tg. ... 37 E3
Lundazi ..... 59 A6
Lundu ....... 37 D3
Lüneburg .... 14 B6
Lüneburg Heath
  = Lüneburger
  Heide ..... 14 B6
Lüneburger
  Heide ..... 14 B6
Lunéville .... 13 B7
Lunglei ...... 41 F9
Luni ........ 42 G8
Luni → ...... 43 G7
Luninets =
  Luninyets ... 17 B8
Luninyets ..... 17 B8
Luofu ....... 57 E5
Luoyang ..... 35 C6
Luozi ....... 56 E2
Luremo ..... 56 F3
Lurgan ...... 11 D3
Lusaka ...... 59 B5
Lusambo ..... 56 E4
Lushnja ..... 23 D2
Lushoto ..... 57 E7
Luta = Dalian . 35 C7
Luton ....... 11 F6
Lutong ...... 36 D4
Lutsk ........ 17 C7

# Lützow Holmbukta

Lützow
  Holmbukta .. 96 A8
Luwuk ....... 39 E2
Luxembourg .. 13 B7
Luxembourg ■ 14 D4
Luxor = El
  Uqsur ..... 52 C5
Luza ......... 24 A6
Luzern ....... 13 C8
Luzhou ...... 35 D5
Luziânia ...... 93 F4
Luzon ........ 38 A2
Lviv ......... 17 D7
Lvov = Lviv ... 17 D7
Lyakhavichy ... 17 B8
Lyakhovskiye,
  Ostrova ..... 31 B12
Lyallpur =
  Faisalabad .. 42 D8
Lydenburg .... 59 D6
Lydia ........ 23 E7
Lyell ......... 65 D5
Lyepyel ...... 24 C2
Łyna → ...... 16 A5
Lynchburg ... 73 F6
Lynd Ra. .... 63 A4
Lyndhurst .... 62 B2
Lynn Lake ... 71 C9
Lyon ........ 13 D6
Lyonnais .... 13 D6
Lyons = Lyon . 13 D6
Lys = Leie → . 14 C2
Lysychansk ... 25 D4
Lyttelton ...... 65 E5
Lyubertsy ..... 24 B4
Lyuboml ...... 17 C7

# M

Ma'alah ...... 47 F6
Ma'ān ........ 47 E3
Ma'anshan ... 35 C6
Ma'arrat an
  Nu'mān .... 46 D4
Maas → ...... 14 C3
Maastricht ... 13 A6
Mabrouk ..... 55 E4
Macaé ....... 93 G5
McAllen ...... 78 F4
Macao =
  Macau ■ ... 35 D6
Macapá ...... 92 B3
Macau ....... 92 D6
Macau ■ .... 35 D6
M'Clintock Chan. 70 A9
McComb .... 79 D8
MacDonnell Ras. 60 E5
McDouall Peak 62 A1
Macdougall L. . 70 B10
Macedonia =
  Makedhonía □ 23 D4
Macedonia ■ .. 22 D3
Maceió ....... 93 D6
Macenta ..... 55 G3
Macerata ..... 20 C4
Macfarlane, L. . 62 B2
Macgillycuddy's
  Reeks ...... 11 F2
McGregor Ra. . 62 A3
Mach ........ 42 E5
Machado =
  Jiparaná → . 91 E6
Machakos .... 57 E7
Machala ...... 90 D3
Machilipatnam 40 J3
Machiques .... 90 A4

Machupicchu .. 91 F4
Macintyre → . 63 A5
Mackay ....... 61 E8
Mackay, L. .... 60 E4
Mackenzie → . 70 B6
Mackenzie City
  = Linden ... 90 B7
Mackenzie Mts. 70 B6
McKinley, Mt. . 71 B4
McKinney .... 79 C5
Macksville .... 63 B5
Maclean ..... 63 A5
Maclear ..... 59 E5
Macleay → .. 63 B5
McMurdo Sd. . 96 B15
Mâcon, France 13 C6
Macon, U.S.A. . 75 C6
Macondo ..... 58 A4
McPherson Ra. 63 A5
Macquarie
  Harbour .... 62 D4
MacRobertson
  Land ....... 96 B10
Madagali ..... 53 F1
Madagascar ■ . 59 J9
Madā'in Sālih . 47 F4
Madama ..... 52 D1
Madang ...... 61 B8
Madaoua .... 55 F6
Madaripur .... 41 F8
Madauk ..... 41 J11
Madaya ..... 41 F11
Maddalena .... 20 D2
Madeira ..... 54 B1
Madeira → .. 90 D7
Madha ...... 43 L9
Madhya
  Pradesh □ . 43 H10
Madikeri ...... 43 N9
Madimba .... 56 E3
Madīnat ash
  Sha'b ...... 49 E3
Madingou .... 56 E2
Madison ..... 77 D10
Madiun ...... 37 F4
Madras = Tamil
  Nadu □ ..... 43 P10
Madras ...... 43 N12
Madre, Laguna 78 F5
Madre, Sierra . 38 A2
Madre de
  Dios → .... 91 F5
Madre de Dios,
  I. .......... 95 G1
Madre
  Occidental,
  Sierra ...... 84 B3
Madrid ....... 18 B4
Madurai ..... 43 Q11
Madurantakam 43 N11
Mae Sot ..... 36 A1
Maebashi ..... 32 A6
Maestrazgo,
  Mts. del .... 19 B5
Maevatanana .. 59 H9
Mafeking =
  Mafikeng ... 59 D5
Maffra ....... 63 C4
Mafia I. ...... 57 F7
Mafikeng ..... 59 D5
Mafra, Brazil . 94 B7
Mafra, Portugal 18 C1
Magadan .... 31 D13
Magadi ...... 57 E7
Magallanes,
  Estrecho de . 95 G2
Magangué .... 90 B4
Magburaka ... 55 G2
Magdalena,
  Argentina ... 94 D5

Magdalena,
  Bolivia ..... 91 F6
Magdalena,
  Malaysia .... 36 D5
Magdalena → 90 A4
Magdeburg .. 15 B6
Magelang ... 37 F4
Magellan's Str.
  = Magallanes,
  Estrecho de . 95 G2
Maggiore, L. .. 20 B2
Magnetic Pole
  (South) =
  South
  Magnetic Pole 96 A13
Magnitogorsk . 29 D6
Magosa =
  Famagusta .. 46 D3
Maguarinho, C. 92 C4
Maģusa =
  Famagusta .. 46 D3
Magwe ....... 41 G10
Mahābād ..... 46 C6
Mahabo ..... 59 J8
Mahagi ...... 57 D6
Mahajanga ... 59 H9
Mahakam → . 37 E5
Mahalapye ... 59 C5
Maḥallāt .... 44 C2
Mahanadi → . 40 G6
Mahanoro ... 59 H9
Maharashtra □ 43 J9
Mahbubnagar . 43 L10
Mahdia ...... 52 A1
Mahenge .... 57 F7
Maheno ..... 65 F4
Mahesana .... 43 H8
Mahia Pen. .. 64 C7
Mahilyow .... 17 B10
Mahón ....... 19 C8
Mai-Ndombe, L. 56 E3
Maicurú → .. 92 C3
Maidstone ... 11 F7
Maiduguri ... 53 F1
Maijdi ....... 41 F8
Maikala Ra. .. 40 G3
Main → ...... 14 D5
Maine ....... 12 C3
Maingkwan ... 41 D11
Mainit, L. ..... 38 C3
Mainland,
  Orkney, U.K. 10 B5
Mainland, Shet.,
  U.K. ........ 10 A6
Maintirano .... 59 H8
Mainz ....... 14 C5
Maipú ....... 94 D5
Maiquetía .... 90 A5
Mairabari .... 41 D9
Maitland,
  N.S.W.,
  Australia .... 63 B5
Maitland,
  S. Austral.,
  Australia .... 62 B2
Maizuru ...... 32 B4
Majene ...... 39 E1
Maji ......... 53 G6
Majorca =
  Mallorca ... 19 C7
Maka ........ 55 F2
Makale ...... 39 E1
Makari ...... 56 B2
Makarikari =
  Makgadikgadi
  Salt Pans .. 59 C5
Makasar =
  Ujung
  Pandang .... 39 F1

Makasar, Selat 39 E1
Makasar, Str. of
  = Makasar,
  Selat ....... 39 E1
Makat ........ 29 E6
Makedhonía □ 23 D4
Makedonija =
  Macedonia ■ 22 D3
Makeni ...... 55 G2
Makeyevka =
  Makiyivka ... 25 D4
Makgadikgadi
  Salt Pans ... 59 C5
Makhachkala . 25 E6
Makian ....... 39 D3
Makindu ..... 57 E7
Makinsk ..... 29 D8
Makiyivka ..... 25 D4
Makkah ...... 47 G4
Makó ....... 16 E5
Makokou .... 56 D2
Makoua ..... 56 E3
Makrai ...... 43 H10
Makran ..... 45 E5
Makran Coast
  Range ..... 42 G4
Maksimkin Yar 29 D9
Mākū ....... 46 C6
Makumbi .... 56 F4
Makurazaki .. 33 D2
Makurdi ..... 55 G6
Malabang .... 38 C2
Malabar Coast . 43 P9
Malabo = Rey
Malabo ..... 56 D1
Malacca, Str. of 36 D1
Maladzyechna . 17 A8
Málaga ...... 18 D3
Malakâl ..... 53 G5
Malakand ... 42 B7
Malang ...... 37 F4
Malanje ..... 56 F3
Mälaren ..... 9 G11
Malargüe .... 94 D3
Malaryta .... 17 C7
Malatya ..... 46 C4
Malawi ■ .... 59 A6
Malawi, L. ... 59 A6
Malaybalay .. 38 C3
Malāyer ..... 46 D7
Malaysia ■ ... 36 D4
Malazgirt .... 46 C5
Malbooma ... 62 B1
Malbork ..... 16 A4
Malden I. .... 65 K15
Maldives ■ ... 26 J11
Maldonado .. 94 C6
Malé Karpaty . 16 D3
Maléa, Ákra .. 23 F4
Malegaon ... 43 J9
Malema ..... 59 A7
Malha ...... 53 E4
Mali ■ ....... 55 E4
Mali → ...... 41 E11
Malik ....... 39 E2
Malili ....... 39 E2
Malin Hd. ... 10 D3
Malindi ..... 57 E8
Malines =
  Mechelen ... 14 C3
Malino ...... 39 D2
Malita ...... 38 C3
Malkara ..... 22 D6
Mallacoota ... 63 C4
Mallacoota Inlet 63 C4
Mallaig ...... 10 C4
Mallawi ..... 52 C5
Mallorca ..... 19 C7
Mallow ...... 11 E2

Malmö ....... 9 G10
Malolos ...... 38 B2
Malpelo ...... 90 C2
Malta ■ ...... 21 G5
Maltahöhe .... 58 C3
Maluku ....... 39 E3
Maluku □ .... 39 E3
Maluku Sea =
Molucca Sea 39 E2
Malvan ....... 43 L8
Malvinas, Is. =
Falkland Is. □ 95 G5
Malyn ........ 17 C9
Malyy
Lyakhovskiy,
Ostrov ...... 31 B12
Mamahatun ... 46 C5
Mamanguape . 92 D6
Mamasa ...... 39 E1
Mamberamo ⟶ 39 E5
Mambilima Falls 57 G5
Mamburao .... 38 B2
Mamfe ....... 55 G6
Mamoré ⟶ ... 91 F5
Mamou ...... 55 F2
Mamuju ...... 39 E1
Man ......... 55 G3
Man, I. of .... 11 D4
Man Na ...... 41 F11
Mana ........ 92 A3
Manaar, G. of =
Mannar, G. of 43 Q11
Manacapuru .. 90 D6
Manacor ..... 19 C7
Manado ...... 39 D2
Managua ..... 85 E7
Manakara .... 59 J9
Manama = Al
Manāmah ... 44 E2
Mananara .... 59 H9
Mananjary .... 59 J9
Manaos =
Manaus .... 90 D7
Manapouri .... 65 F2
Manapouri, L. . 65 F2
Manas ....... 34 B3
Manas ⟶ .... 41 D8
Manasir ..... 44 E2
Manaung .... 41 H9
Manaus ...... 90 D7
Manay ....... 38 C3
Manchester,
U.K. ........ 11 E5
Manchester,
U.S.A. ...... 73 C10
Mand ⟶ ..... 44 D3
Manda ....... 57 G6
Mandal ...... 9 G9
Mandalay .... 41 F11
Mandale =
Mandalay ... 41 F11
Mandalī ..... 46 D6
Mandar, Teluk . 39 E1
Mandaue .... 38 B2
Mandi ....... 42 D10
Mandimba ... 59 A7
Mandioli ..... 39 E3
Mandla ...... 40 F3
Mandritsara .. 59 H9
Mandsaur .... 43 G9
Mandvi ...... 43 H6
Mandya ..... 43 N10
Manfalût .... 52 C5
Manfred ..... 63 B3
Manfredónia . 20 D5
Mangalia .... 22 C7
Mangalore ... 43 N9
Mangaweka ... 64 C6
Manggar ..... 37 E3

Manggawitu .. 39 E4
Mangkalihat,
Tanjung .... 39 D1
Mangla Dam .. 42 C8
Mangnai ...... 34 C4
Mango ....... 55 F5
Mangoche .... 59 A7
Mangole ...... 39 E3
Mangonui .... 64 A5
Mangueigne .. 53 F3
Mangueira, L. da 94 C6
Mangyshlak
Poluostrov .. 29 E6
Manhuaçu ... 93 G5
Manica ...... 59 B6
Manicoré ..... 91 E6
Manicouagan ⟶
............. 69 D4
Maniîfah ..... 47 F7
Manihiki ...... 65 L14
Manila ....... 38 B2
Manila B. ..... 38 B2
Manilla ...... 63 B5
Manipur □ .... 41 E9
Manipur ⟶ .. 41 F10
Manisa ...... 23 E6
Manitoba □ .. 71 C10
Manitoba, L. .. 71 C10
Manitowoc ... 72 B2
Manizales .... 90 B3
Manja ........ 59 J8
Manjacaze ... 59 C6
Manjhand .... 42 G6
Manjil ....... 46 C7
Manjra ⟶ .... 43 K10
Mankono .... 55 G3
Manly ....... 63 B5
Manmad ..... 43 J9
Manna ....... 37 E2
Mannahill .... 62 B3
Mannar ...... 43 Q11
Mannar, G. of . 43 Q11
Mannar I. .... 43 Q11
Mannheim .... 14 D5
Mannum ..... 62 B2
Mano ........ 55 G2
Manokwari ... 39 E4
Manombo .... 59 J8
Manono ...... 57 F5
Manosque .... 13 E6
Manresa ..... 19 B6
Mansa ....... 57 G5
Mansel I. ..... 68 B2
Mansfield,
Australia .... 63 C4
Mansfield, U.K. 11 E6
Mansfield,
U.S.A. ...... 72 D4
Manta ....... 90 D2
Mantalingajan,
Mt. ........ 36 C5
Mantes-la-Jolie 12 B4
Manthani .... 43 K11
Mantiqueira,
Serra da ... 93 G5
Mántova ...... 20 B3
Mantua =
Mántova .... 20 B3
Manu ........ 91 F4
Manuae ..... 65 L15
Manuel
Alves ⟶ ... 93 E4
Manui ........ 39 E2
Manyara, L. .. 57 E7
Manych-Gudilo,
Ozero ...... 25 D5
Manyoni ..... 57 F6
Manzai ...... 42 C7
Manzanares .. 18 C4

Manzanillo,
Cuba ...... 86 B4
Manzanillo,
Mexico .... 84 D4
Manzhouli .... 35 B6
Mao ......... 53 F2
Maoke,
Pegunungan 39 E5
Maoming .... 35 D6
Mapam Yumco 40 B3
Mapia,
Kepulauan .. 39 D4
Mapuera ⟶ .. 90 D7
Maputo ...... 59 D6
Maqnā ...... 47 E3
Maquela do
Zombo ..... 56 F3
Maquinchao .. 95 E3
Mar, Serra do . 94 B7
Mar Chiquita, L. 94 C4
Mar del Plata . 94 D5
Mar Menor .. 19 D5
Maraã ....... 90 D5
Marabá ...... 92 D4
Maracá, I. de . 92 B3
Maracaibo .... 90 A4
Maracaibo, L. de 90 B4
Maracay ..... 90 A5
Marādah .... 52 C2
Maradi ...... 55 F6
Marāgheh .... 46 C6
Marāh ...... 47 F6
Marajó, I. de . 92 C4
Maralal ...... 57 D7
Marama ..... 62 C3
Marampa .... 55 G2
Marand ..... 46 C6
Maranguape . 92 C6
Maranhão =
São Luís .... 92 C5
Maranhão □ . 92 D4
Maranoa ⟶ . 63 A4
Marañón ⟶ . 90 D4
Marão ....... 59 C6
Maraş =
Kahramanmaraş
............. 46 C4
Maratua .... 39 D1
Marbella .... 18 D3
Marburg .... 14 C5
Marche ...... 12 C4
Marchena ... 18 D3
Mardan ..... 42 B8
Mardin ..... 46 C5
Marek = Stanke
Dimitrov ... 22 C4
Marek ■ ..... 39 E2
Margarita, I. de 90 A6
Margate ..... 11 F7
Margelan =
Marghilon .. 29 E8
Marghilon ... 29 E8
Mari El □ .... 24 B6
Mari Republic □
= Mari El □ . 24 B6
Maria I. ...... 62 D4
Maria van
Diemen, C. . 64 A5
Mariana Trench 64 H9
Marianao .... 86 B3
Ma'rib ....... 49 D4
Maribor ..... 20 A5
Marîdî ....... 53 H4
Marie Byrd Land 96 B18
Marie-Galante . 87 C7
Mariecourt =
Kangiqsujuaq 68 B3
Mariental .... 58 C3
Mariinsk ..... 29 D9

Marília ....... 93 G3
Marín ........ 18 A1
Marinduque .. 38 B2
Maringá ..... 94 A6
Marion ...... 79 A9
Mariscal
Estigarribia . 91 H6
Maritime Alps =
Maritimes,
Alpes ..... 13 D7
Maritimes, Alpes 13 D7
Maritsa =
Évros ⟶ ... 22 D6
Mariupol .... 25 D4
Marīvān .... 46 D6
Markazi □ ... 44 C2
Markham, Mt. . 96 C15
Marks ...... 24 C6
Marla ....... 62 A1
Marmagao ... 43 M8
Marmara .... 23 D6
Marmara, Sea of
= Marmara
Denizi ..... 22 D7
Marmara Denizi 22 D7
Marmaris .... 23 F7
Marmolada,
Mte. ...... 20 A3
Marne ⟶ ... 12 B5
Maroantsetra . 59 H9
Marondera .. 59 B6
Maroni ⟶ ... 92 A3
Maroochydore . 63 A5
Maroona .... 62 C3
Maroua ..... 53 F1
Marovoay ... 59 H9
Marquesas Is. =
Marquises, Is. 65 K17
Marquette ... 69 D2
Marquises, Is. . 65 K17
Marrakech ... 54 B3
Marrawah ... 62 D3
Marree ...... 62 A2
Marromeu ... 59 B7
Marrowie Cr. ⟶ 63 B4
Marrupa .... 59 A7
Marsá Matrûh . 52 B4
Marsá Susah . 52 B3
Marsabit .... 57 D7
Marsala ..... 21 F4
Marsden .... 63 B4
Marseille .... 13 E6
Marseilles =
Marseille ... 13 E6
Marshall, Liberia 55 G2
Marshall, U.S.A. 79 C6
Marshall Is. ■ . 64 J12
Marshalltown . 77 D8
Martaban .... 41 J11
Martaban, G. of 41 J11
Martapura,
Kalimantan,
Indonesia ... 37 E4
Martapura,
Sumatera,
Indonesia ... 37 E2
Marte ....... 53 F1
Martigny .... 13 C7
Martigues ... 13 E6
Martin ...... 16 D4
Martina Franca 21 D6
Martinborough 65 D6
Martinique ■ .. 87 D7
Martinique
Passage .... 87 C7
Martinsville ... 75 A8
Marton ..... 64 D6
Martos ...... 18 D4
Marudi ...... 37 D4

Ma'ruf ....... 42 D5
Marugame .... 32 B3
Marulan ...... 63 B5
Marwar ...... 42 G8
Mary ......... 29 F7
Maryborough =
  Port Laoise .. 11 E3
Maryborough,
  Queens.,
  Australia .. 63 A5
Maryborough,
  Vic., Australia 62 C3
Maryland □ ... 73 E7
Maryvale .... 63 A5
Marzūq ....... 52 C1
Masaka ...... 57 E6
Masalembo,
  Kepulauan .. 37 F4
Masalima,
  Kepulauan .. 37 F5
Masamba ..... 39 E2
Masan ....... 35 C7
Masandam, Ras 44 E4
Masasi ....... 57 G7
Masaya ...... 85 E7
Masbate ...... 38 B2
Mascara ..... 54 A5
Masela ....... 39 F3
Maseru ...... 59 D5
Mashābih .... 47 F4
Mashhad ..... 44 B4
Mashike ..... 32 F12
Mashkel,
  Hamun-i- ... 42 E3
Mashki Chāh .. 42 E3
Masi Manimba 56 E3
Masindi ...... 57 D6
Masisea ..... 91 E4
Masjed
  Soleyman ... 47 E7
Mask, L. ...... 11 E2
Masohi ....... 39 E3
Mason City ... 77 D8
Masqat ....... 45 F4
Massa ........ 20 B3
Massachusetts □
  .......... 73 C9
Massaguet ... 53 F2
Massakory ... 53 F2
Massangena .. 59 C6
Massawa =
  Mitsiwa ..... 53 E6
Massena ..... 73 B8
Massénya .... 53 F2
Massif Central . 13 D5
Massinga .... 59 C7
Masson I. ..... 96 A11
Mastanli =
  Momchilgrad 22 D5
Masterton .... 65 D6
Mastuj ....... 42 A8
Mastung ..... 42 E5
Masty ........ 17 B7
Masuda ...... 32 B2
Masvingo .... 59 C6
Mataboor ..... 39 E5
Matad ....... 35 B6
Matadi ...... 56 F2
Matagalpa ... 85 E7
Matagami, L. .. 69 D3
Matak, P. .... 37 D3
Matakana .... 63 B4
Matam ....... 55 E2
Matamoros,
  Coahuila,
  Mexico ..... 84 B4
Matamoros,
  Tamaulipas,
  Mexico ..... 84 B5

Ma'ṭan as Sarra 52 D3
Matane ....... 69 D4
Matanzas ..... 86 B3
Matapan, C. =
  Taínaron, Ákra 23 F4
Mataram ..... 37 F5
Matarani ..... 91 G4
Mataró ....... 19 B7
Mataura ...... 65 G3
Matehuala .... 84 C4
Matera ....... 21 D6
Mathura ...... 42 F10
Mati ......... 38 C3
Matiri Ra. .... 65 D5
Matmata ..... 54 B6
Mato Grosso □ 93 E3
Mato Grosso,
  Planalto do .. 93 F3
Mato Grosso do
  Sul □ ....... 93 F3
Matochkin Shar 28 B6
Matosinhos ... 18 B1
Matrah ....... 45 F4
Matsue ....... 32 B3
Matsumoto ... 32 A6
Matsusaka ... 32 B5
Matsuyama ... 32 C3
Mattagami → . 69 C2
Mattancheri ... 43 Q10
Matterhorn ... 13 D7
Matthew's Ridge 90 B6
Matucana .... 91 F3
Matun ....... 42 C6
Maturín ...... 90 B6
Mau Ranipur .. 43 G11
Maubeuge .... 13 A5
Maude ....... 63 B3
Maudin Sun ... 41 K10
Maués ....... 90 D7
Mauganj ..... 40 E3
Maui ......... 82 H12
Maulamyaing =
  Moulmein ... 41 J11
Maumere ..... 39 F2
Maun ........ 58 B4
Maungmagan
  Kyunzu ..... 41 K11
Mauritania ■ .. 55 D2
Mauritius ■ ... 51 H9
Mavinga ..... 58 B4
Mawk Mai ... 41 G11
Mawlaik ..... 41 F10
Mawson Coast 96 A10
Maxixe ....... 59 C7
Mayaguana ... 87 B5
Mayagüez .... 87 C6
Maydena ..... 62 D4
Mayenne → .. 12 C3
Maykop ...... 25 E5
Mayo ........ 70 B6
Mayo L. ...... 70 B6
Mayon Volcano 38 B2
Mayor I. ...... 64 B7
Mayu ........ 39 D3
Mazabuka ... 59 B5
Mazagán = El
  Jadida ...... 54 B3
Mazagão ..... 92 C3
Mazán ....... 90 D4
Māzandarān □ . 44 B3
Mazar-e Sharīf . 45 B6
Mazara del Vallo 21 F4
Mazarredo .... 95 F3
Mazarrón ..... 19 D5
Mazaruni → .. 90 B7
Mazatlán ..... 84 C3
Māzhān ...... 44 C4
Mazīnān ...... 44 B4
Mazoe → .... 59 B6

Mazurian Lakes
  = Mazurski,
  Pojezierze ... 16 B5
Mazurski,
  Pojezierze ... 16 B5
Mazyr ........ 17 C9
Mbabane ..... 59 D6
Mbaïki ....... 56 D3
Mbala ........ 57 F6
Mbale ........ 57 D6
Mbalmayo .... 56 D2
Mbamba Bay .. 57 G6
Mbandaka .... 56 D3
Mbanza Congo 56 F2
Mbanza Ngungu 56 F2
Mbarara ...... 57 E6
Mbeya ....... 57 F6
Mbini □ ...... 56 D2
Mbour ....... 55 F1
Mbout ....... 55 E2
Mbuji-Mayi ... 56 F4
Mbulu ....... 57 E7
Mchinji ...... 59 A6
Mead, L. ...... 82 B5
Mearim → .... 92 C5
Meaux ....... 13 B5
Mecca =
  Makkah .... 47 G4
Mechelen ..... 14 C3
Mecheria ..... 54 B4
Mecklenburg .. 15 B6
Mecklenburger
  Bucht ...... 15 A6
Meconta ...... 59 A7
Medan ....... 37 D1
Medanosa, Pta. 95 F3
Medéa ....... 54 A5
Medellín ..... 90 B3
Mederdra .... 55 E1
Medford ...... 80 D2
Medgidia ..... 22 B7
Mediaş ....... 17 E7
Medicine Bow
  Ra. ......... 81 E10
Medicine Hat .. 71 C8
Medina = Al
  Madīnah .... 47 F4
Medina del
  Campo ..... 18 B3
Medina-Sidonia 18 D3
Medinipur .... 40 F6
Mediterranean
  Sea ........ 50 C5
Médoc ....... 12 D3
Medveditsa → 24 D5
Medvezhyegorsk 28 C4
Meekatharra . 60 F2
Meerut ...... 42 E10
Mega ........ 53 H6
Mégara ...... 23 F4
Meghalaya □ .. 41 E8
Mei Xian ..... 35 D6
Meiganga .... 56 C2
Meiktila ..... 41 G10
Meissen ...... 15 C7
Mejillones ... 94 A2
Mékambo .... 56 D2
Mekdela ..... 53 F6
Mekhtar ..... 42 D6
Meknès ...... 54 B3
Mekong → ... 36 C3
Mekongga .... 39 E2
Mekvari =
  Kür → ..... 25 E6
Melagiri Hills .. 43 N10
Melaka ....... 37 D2
Melalap ...... 36 C5
Melanesia .... 64 K10
Melbourne,
  Australia .... 63 C3

Melbourne,
  U.S.A. ...... 75 E7
Mélèzes → ... 68 C3
Melfi ........ 53 F2
Melfort ...... 71 C9
Melilla ....... 19 E4
Melitopol .... 25 D4
Melk ........ 15 D8
Melo ........ 94 C6
Melolo ....... 39 F2
Melrose ...... 63 B4
Melun ....... 13 B5
Melut ....... 53 F5
Melville ...... 71 C9
Melville I. .... 60 C5
Melville Pen. .. 68 B2
Memba ...... 59 G8
Memboro .... 39 F1
Memel =
  Klaipėda .... 24 B1
Memmingen .. 14 E6
Mempawah ... 37 D3
Memphis, Tenn.,
  U.S.A. ..... 74 B3
Memphis, Tex.,
  U.S.A. ..... 78 B3
Ménaka ...... 55 E5
Menan = Chao
  Phraya → .. 36 B2
Menate ...... 37 E4
Mendawai → . 37 E4
Mende ....... 13 D5
Mendocino, C. . 80 E1
Mendoza ..... 94 C3
Mene Grande . 90 B4
Menemen ... 23 E6
Menggala .... 37 E3
Mengzi ...... 34 D5
Menindee .... 62 B3
Menindee L. .. 62 B3
Meningie .... 62 C2
Menominee ... 72 B2
Menongue ... 58 A3
Menorca ..... 19 C7
Mentawai,
  Kepulauan .. 37 E1
Menton ...... 13 E7
Meppel ...... 14 B4
Merabéllou,
  Kólpos ..... 23 G5
Meran =
  Merano .... 20 A3
Merano ..... 20 A3
Merauke ..... 39 F6
Merbein ..... 62 B3
Merca ....... 49 G3
Merced ...... 82 B2
Mercedes,
  Buenos Aires,
  Argentina ... 94 C4
Mercedes,
  Corrientes,
  Argentina ... 94 B5
Mercedes,
  San Luis,
  Argentina ... 94 C3
Mercedes,
  Uruguay .... 94 C5
Merceditas .... 94 B2
Mercer ...... 64 B6
Mercy C. ..... 68 B4
Meredith, C. .. 95 G4
Merga =
  Nukheila .... 53 E4
Mergui Arch. =
  Myeik Kyunzu 36 B1
Mérida, Mexico 85 C7
Mérida, Spain . 18 C2

Mérida,
  Venezuela ... 90 B4
Mérida, Cord. de 87 E5
Meridian .... 74 C3
Meriruma ..... 92 B3
Merowe ...... 53 E5
Merriwa ...... 63 B5
Merriwagga ... 63 B4
Merrygoen ... 63 B4
Mersa Fatma .. 49 E3
Merseburg .... 15 C6
Mersin ....... 46 C3
Mersing ...... 37 D2
Merthyr Tydfil . 11 F5
Mértola ...... 18 D2
Meru ........ 57 D7
Mesa ........ 83 D7
Meshed =
  Mashhad ... 44 B4
Meshra er Req 53 G4
Mesolóngion .. 23 E3
Mesopotamia =
  Al Jazirah .. 46 D5
Messina, Italy . 21 E5
Messina,
  S. Africa .... 59 C6
Messina, Str. di 21 E5
Messíni ...... 23 F4
Messiniakós
  Kólpos .... 23 F4
Mesta ─► ..... 22 D5
Meta ─► ..... 90 B5
Metairie ...... 79 E8
Metán ........ 94 B4
Metangula .... 59 A6
Metema ...... 53 F6
Methven ..... 65 E4
Metil ........ 59 B7
Metlakatla ... 71 C6
Mettur Dam ... 43 P10
Metz ........ 13 B7
Meulaboh .... 37 D1
Meureudu .... 36 C1
Meuse ─► .... 13 A6
Mexiana, I. ... 92 C4
Mexicali ..... 84 A1
México ....... 84 D5
México □ ... 84 D5
Mexico ■ .... 84 C4
Mexico, G. of . 85 B7
Meymaneh ... 42 B4
Mezen ....... 28 C5
Mezen ─► .... 28 C5
Mézene ...... 13 D6
Mezökövesd .. 16 E5
Mezötúr ...... 16 E5
Mhow ........ 43 H9
Miami ....... 75 G7
Miami Beach .. 75 G7
Miăndowăb .. 46 C6
Miandrivazo .. 59 H9
Miăneh ...... 46 C6
Mianwali ..... 42 C7
Miaoli ....... 35 D7
Miarinarivo .. 59 H9
Miass ........ 29 D7
Michalovce ... 17 D5
Michigan □ .. 72 C3
Michigan, L. ... 72 C2
Michipicoten .. 69 D2
Michurin ..... 22 C6
Michurinsk .... 24 C5
Micronesia,
  Federated
  States of ■ .. 64 J10
Middelburg ... 58 E5
Middlesbrough 11 D6
Midi, Canal
  du ─► ..... 12 E4

Midland ...... 78 D3
Midyat ....... 46 C5
Midzŏr ....... 22 C4
Międzychód ... 16 B2
Międzyrzec
  Podlaski .... 17 C6
Mielec ....... 16 C5
Miercurea Ciuc 17 E7
Mieres ....... 18 A3
Miguel Alves .. 92 C5
Mihara ....... 32 B3
Mikhaylovgrad 22 C4
Míkonos ...... 23 F5
Mikura-Jima .. 32 C6
Milagro ...... 90 D3
Milan = Milano 20 B2
Milang ....... 62 B2
Milano ....... 20 B2
Milâs ........ 23 F6
Milazzo ...... 21 E5
Mildura ...... 62 B3
Miles ........ 63 A5
Miletus ...... 23 F6
Milford Haven . 11 F4
Milford Sd. ... 65 F2
Milḥ, Baḥr al .. 47 D5
Miliana ...... 54 C5
Mill I. ....... 96 A12
Millau ........ 13 D5
Millicent ...... 62 C3
Millinocket .... 73 B11
Millmerran ... 63 A5
Milne Inlet ... 68 A2
Mílos ........ 23 F5
Milparinka P.O. 62 A3
Milton ....... 65 G3
Milton Keynes . 11 E6
Miltou ....... 53 F2
Milwaukee ... 72 C2
Min Chiang ─► 35 D6
Min Jiang ─► .. 35 D5
Mina Pirquitas . 94 A3
Mīnā Su'ud ... 47 E7
Mīnā'al Aḥmadī 47 E7
Mīnāb ....... 44 E4
Minamata .... 32 C2
Minas ........ 94 C5
Minas Gerais □ 93 F4
Minbu ....... 41 G10
Mindanao .... 38 C2
Mindanao Sea =
  Bohol Sea .. 38 C2
Mindanao
  Trench ..... 38 B3
Minden ...... 14 B5
Mindiptana .. 39 F6
Mindoro ..... 38 B2
Mindoro Str. .. 38 B2
Mindouli ..... 56 E2
Mingäçevir Su
  Anbarı ..... 25 E6
Mingan ....... 69 C4
Mingechaurskoye
  Vdkhr. = 
  Mingäçevir Su
  Anbarı ...... 25 E6
Mingin ....... 41 F10
Mingt'iehkaitafan
  = Mintaka
  Pass ....... 42 A9
Minho =
  Miño ─► .... 18 B1
Minho ....... 18 B1
Minna ....... 55 G6
Minneapolis .. 77 C8
Minnedosa .... 71 C10
Minnesota □ .. 77 B7
Minnipa ...... 62 B2
Miño ─► ..... 18 B1

Minorca =
  Menorca .... 19 C7
Minore ....... 63 B4
Minot ........ 76 A4
Minsk ........ 24 C2
Mińsk
  Mazowiecki . 16 B5
Mintaka Pass .. 42 A9
Minto ........ 71 B5
Minutang .... 41 C11
Minvoul ...... 56 D2
Mir .......... 53 F1
Mira ......... 20 B4
Miraj ........ 43 L9
Miram Shah .. 42 C7
Miranda ...... 93 G2
Miranda de Ebro 19 A4
Miranda do
  Douro ...... 18 B2
Miri ......... 36 D4
Mirim, L. ..... 94 C6
Mirpur Khas .. 42 G6
Mirzapur ..... 40 E4
Mirzapur-cum-
  Vindhyachal =
  Mirzapur ... 40 E4
Mish'āb, Ra'as
  al .......... 47 E7
Mishan ...... 35 B8
Miskin ....... 44 F4
Miskolc ...... 16 D5
Misool ....... 39 E4
Misrātah ..... 52 B2
Misriç ....... 46 C5
Missinaibi ─► . 69 C2
Mississippi □ . 79 C9
Mississippi ─► 79 E9
Mississippi River
  Delta ....... 79 E9
Missoula ..... 81 B6
Missouri □ ... 77 F8
Missouri ─► .. 77 F8
Mistassini L. .. 69 C3
Misurata =
  Misrātah .... 52 B2
Mitchell,
  Australia ... 63 A4
Mitchell, U.S.A. 76 D5
Mitchell ─► .. 61 D7
Mitilíni ....... 23 E6
Mito ......... 32 A7
Mitrovica =
  Titova-
  Mitrovica .. 22 C3
Mitsinjo ...... 59 H9
Mitsiwa ...... 53 E6
Mittagong ... 63 B5
Mitú ......... 90 C4
Mitumba,
  Chaîne des . 57 F5
Mitumba Mts. =
  Mitumba,
  Chaîne des . 57 F5
Mitwaba ..... 57 F5
Mitzic ....... 56 D2
Miyake-Jima . 32 B6
Miyako ...... 33 G12
Miyakonojō .. 32 D2
Miyazaki ..... 32 D2
Miyet, Bahr el =
  Dead Sea ... 47 E3
Mizal ........ 47 G6
Mizdah ...... 52 B1
Mizoram □ .. 41 F9
Mjøsa ....... 8 F10
Mladá Boleslav 16 C2
Mlawa ....... 16 B5
Mljet ........ 20 C6
Mmabatho ... 59 D5

Moa ........ 39 F3
Moabi ....... 56 E2
Moalie Park ... 62 A3
Moba ....... 57 F5
Mobaye ..... 56 D4
Mobayi ...... 56 D4
Mobile ...... 74 D3
Mobutu Sese
  Seko, L. =
  Albert L. .... 57 D6
Moçambique .. 59 H8
Moçâmedes =
  Namibe ... 58 B2
Mochudi ..... 59 C5
Mocimboa da
  Praia ...... 57 G8
Mocoa ...... 90 C3
Mocuba ..... 59 B7
Modane ..... 13 D7
Módena ..... 20 B3
Modesto ..... 82 B2
Módica ...... 21 F5
Moe ........ 63 C4
Moengo ..... 92 A3
Mogadishu =
  Muqdisho ... 49 G4
Mogador =
  Essaouira ... 54 B3
Mogami ─► .. 33 G12
Mogaung ..... 41 E11
Mogi das Cruzes 94 A7
Mogi-Mirim ... 94 A7
Mogilev =
  Mahilyow ... 17 B10
Mogilev-
  Podolskiy =
  Mohyliv-
  Podilskyy ... 17 D8
Mogoi ....... 39 E4
Mogok ....... 41 F11
Mohács ...... 16 F4
Moḥammadābād
  ............ 44 B4
Mohoro ...... 57 F7
Mohyliv-
  Podilskyy ... 17 D8
Mointy ...... 29 E8
Moisie ....... 69 C4
Moisie ─► .... 69 C4
Moïssala ..... 53 G2
Mojave Desert . 82 C4
Mokai ....... 64 C6
Mokokchung .. 41 D10
Mokra Gora ... 22 C3
Molchanovo .. 29 D9
Moldavia ■ =
  Moldova ■ .. 17 E9
Molde ....... 8 F9
Moldova ■ ... 17 E9
Moldoveanu, Vf. 17 F7
Molepolole ... 59 C5
Molfetta ...... 20 D6
Moline ....... 77 E9
Moliro ....... 57 F6
Mollendo ..... 91 G4
Molodechno =
  Maladzyechna 17 A8
Molokai ...... 82 H12
Molong ...... 63 B4
Molopo ─► ... 58 D4
Molotov = Perm 29 D6
Moloundou ... 56 D3
Molu ........ 39 F4
Molucca Sea .. 39 E2
Moluccas =
  Maluku .... 39 E3
Moma ....... 59 B7
Mombasa ..... 57 E7
Momchilgrad .. 22 D5

| | | |
|---|---|---|
| Mompós | 90 | B4 |
| Mon → | 41 | G10 |
| Mona, Canal de | | |
| la | 87 | C6 |
| Monaco ■ | 13 | E7 |
| Monahans | 78 | D2 |
| Monastir = | | |
| Bitola | 22 | D3 |
| Monastir | 52 | A1 |
| Moncayo, Sierra | | |
| del | 19 | B5 |
| Mönchengladbach | | |
| | 14 | C4 |
| Monchique | 18 | D1 |
| Monclova | 84 | B4 |
| Mondego → | 18 | B1 |
| Mondeodo | 39 | E2 |
| Mondovì | 20 | B1 |
| Monforte de | | |
| Lemos | 18 | A2 |
| Mong Hsu | 41 | G12 |
| Mong Kung | 41 | G11 |
| Mong Nai | 41 | G11 |
| Mong Pawk | 41 | F12 |
| Mong Ton | 41 | G12 |
| Mong Wa | 41 | G13 |
| Mong Yai | 41 | F12 |
| Mongalla | 53 | G5 |
| Monghyr = | | |
| Munger | 40 | E6 |
| Mongibello = | | |
| Etna | 21 | F5 |
| Mongo | 53 | F2 |
| Mongolia ■ | 35 | B5 |
| Mongororo | 53 | F3 |
| Mongu | 58 | B4 |
| Monkoto | 56 | E4 |
| Monópoli | 21 | D6 |
| Monqoumba | 56 | D3 |
| Monroe, La., | | |
| U.S.A. | 79 | C7 |
| Monroe, N.C., | | |
| U.S.A. | 75 | B7 |
| Monrovia | 55 | G2 |
| Mons | 14 | C2 |
| Monse | 39 | E2 |
| Mont-de-Marsan | 12 | E3 |
| Mont-St.-Michel, | | |
| Le = Le Mont- | | |
| St.-Michel | 12 | B3 |
| Montalbán | 19 | B5 |
| Montana □ | 81 | B9 |
| Montargis | 13 | C5 |
| Montauban | 12 | D4 |
| Montbéliard | 13 | C7 |
| Montceau-les- | | |
| Mines | 13 | C6 |
| Monte Alegre | 92 | C3 |
| Monte Azul | 93 | F5 |
| Monte-Carlo | 20 | C1 |
| Monte Caseros | 94 | C5 |
| Monte Comán | 94 | C3 |
| Monte Santu, C. | | |
| di | 21 | D2 |
| Montecristi | 90 | D2 |
| Montecristo | 20 | C3 |
| Montego Bay | 86 | C4 |
| Montélimar | 13 | D6 |
| Montemorelos | 84 | B5 |
| Montenegro □ | 22 | C2 |
| Montepuez | 59 | A7 |
| Monterey | 82 | B2 |
| Montería | 90 | B3 |
| Monterrey | 84 | B4 |
| Montes Claros | 93 | F5 |
| Montesilvano | | |
| Marina | 20 | C5 |
| Montevideo | 94 | C5 |
| Montgomery = | | |
| Sahiwal | 42 | D8 |
| Montgomery | 74 | C4 |
| Montijo | 18 | C2 |
| Montilla | 18 | D3 |
| Montluçon | 13 | C5 |
| Montmorillon | 12 | C4 |
| Montoro | 18 | C3 |
| Montpellier | 13 | E5 |
| Montréal | 69 | D3 |
| Montreux | 13 | C7 |
| Montrose, U.K. | 10 | C5 |
| Montrose, | | |
| U.S.A. | 83 | A9 |
| Montserrat ■ | 87 | C7 |
| Monveda | 56 | D4 |
| Monywa | 41 | F10 |
| Monza | 20 | B2 |
| Monze | 59 | B5 |
| Monze, C. | 43 | G5 |
| Monzón | 19 | B6 |
| Moolawatana | 62 | A2 |
| Moomin Cr. → | 63 | A4 |
| Moonie | 63 | A5 |
| Moonie → | 63 | A4 |
| Moonta | 62 | B2 |
| Mooroopna | 63 | C4 |
| Moose Jaw | 71 | C9 |
| Moosomin | 71 | C9 |
| Moosonee | 69 | C2 |
| Mopeia Velha | 59 | B7 |
| Mopti | 55 | F4 |
| Moquegua | 91 | G4 |
| Mora | 8 | F10 |
| Moradabad | 42 | E11 |
| Morafenobe | 59 | H8 |
| Moramanga | 59 | H9 |
| Moratuwa | 43 | R11 |
| Morava →, | | |
| Serbia, Yug. | 22 | B3 |
| Morava →, | | |
| Slovak Rep. | 16 | D3 |
| Moravian Hts. = | | |
| Ceskomoravská | | |
| Vrchovina | 16 | D2 |
| Morawhanna | 90 | B7 |
| Moray Firth | 10 | C5 |
| Morden | 71 | D10 |
| Mordovian | | |
| Republic □ = | | |
| Mordvinia □ | 24 | C5 |
| Mordvinia □ | 24 | C5 |
| Morea | 62 | C3 |
| Moree | 63 | A4 |
| Morelia | 84 | D4 |
| Morella | 19 | B5 |
| Morena, Sierra | 18 | C3 |
| Moreton I. | 63 | A5 |
| Morgan | 62 | B2 |
| Morgan City | 79 | E8 |
| Morioka | 33 | G12 |
| Morlaix | 12 | B2 |
| Mornington | 63 | C4 |
| Mornington, I. | 95 | F1 |
| Moro G. | 38 | C2 |
| Morocco ■ | 54 | B3 |
| Morococha | 91 | F3 |
| Morogoro | 57 | F7 |
| Morombe | 59 | J8 |
| Morón | 86 | B4 |
| Mörön → | 35 | B6 |
| Morón de la | | |
| Frontera | 18 | D3 |
| Morondava | 59 | J8 |
| Morotai | 39 | D3 |
| Moroto | 57 | D6 |
| Morphou | 46 | D3 |
| Morrinhos | 93 | F4 |
| Morrinsville | 64 | B6 |
| Morristown | 75 | A6 |
| Morrumbene | 59 | C7 |
| Morshansk | 24 | C5 |
| Morteros | 94 | C4 |
| Mortes, R. | | |
| das → | 93 | E3 |
| Mortlake | 62 | C3 |
| Morundah | 63 | B4 |
| Moruya | 63 | C5 |
| Morvan | 13 | C6 |
| Morven | 63 | A4 |
| Morwell | 63 | C4 |
| Moscos Is. | 41 | L11 |
| Moscow = | | |
| Moskva | 24 | B4 |
| Moscow | 80 | B5 |
| Mosel → | 13 | A7 |
| Moselle = | | |
| Mosel → | 13 | A7 |
| Mosgiel | 65 | F4 |
| Moshi | 57 | E7 |
| Moskva | 24 | B4 |
| Moskva → | 24 | B4 |
| Moson- | | |
| magyaróvar | 16 | E3 |
| Mosquera | 90 | C3 |
| Moss Vale | 63 | B5 |
| Mossaka | 56 | E3 |
| Mossburn | 65 | F3 |
| Mosselbaai | 58 | E4 |
| Mossendjo | 56 | E2 |
| Mossgiel | 63 | B3 |
| Mossoró | 92 | D6 |
| Mossuril | 59 | G8 |
| Most | 16 | C1 |
| Mostaganem | 54 | A5 |
| Mostar | 20 | C6 |
| Mostardas | 94 | C6 |
| Mostiska = | | |
| Mostyska | 17 | D6 |
| Mosty = Masty | 17 | B7 |
| Mostyska | 17 | D6 |
| Mosul = Al | | |
| Mawşil | 46 | C5 |
| Motihari | 40 | D5 |
| Motril | 18 | D4 |
| Motueka | 65 | D5 |
| Motueka → | 65 | D5 |
| Mouanda | 56 | E2 |
| Moúdhros | 23 | E5 |
| Moudjeria | 55 | E2 |
| Mouila | 56 | E2 |
| Moulamein | 63 | C3 |
| Moulins | 13 | C5 |
| Moulmein | 41 | J11 |
| Moundou | 53 | G2 |
| Mount Barker | 62 | C2 |
| Mount Darwin | 59 | B6 |
| Mount Eba | 62 | B2 |
| Mount Gambier | 62 | C3 |
| Mount Hope, | | |
| N.S.W., | | |
| Australia | 63 | B4 |
| Mount Hope, | | |
| S. Austral., | | |
| Australia | 62 | B2 |
| Mount Howitt | 62 | A3 |
| Mount Isa | 61 | E6 |
| Mount Lofty Ra. | 62 | B2 |
| Mount McKinley | | |
| National Park | 71 | B4 |
| Mount Margaret | 63 | A3 |
| Mount | | |
| Maunganui | 64 | B7 |
| Mount Olympus | | |
| = Uludağ | 23 | D7 |
| Mount Perry | 63 | A5 |
| Mount Vernon | 73 | D9 |
| Mountain View | 82 | B1 |
| Moura, Brazil | 90 | D6 |
| Moura, Portugal | 18 | C2 |
| Mourdi, | | |
| Dépression du | 53 | E3 |
| Mourdiah | 55 | F3 |
| Moussoro | 53 | F2 |
| Moutohara | 64 | C7 |
| Moutong | 39 | D2 |
| Moyale | 57 | D7 |
| Moyamba | 55 | G2 |
| Moyen Atlas | 54 | B3 |
| Moyo | 37 | F5 |
| Moyyero → | 30 | C8 |
| Mozambique = | | |
| Moçambique | 59 | H8 |
| Mozambique ■ | 59 | B7 |
| Mozambique | | |
| Chan. | 59 | H8 |
| Mozdok | 25 | E5 |
| Mozyr = Mazyr | 17 | C9 |
| Mpanda | 57 | F6 |
| Mpika | 59 | A6 |
| Mpwapwa | 57 | F7 |
| Msaken | 52 | A1 |
| Msoro | 59 | A6 |
| Mu Us Shamo | 35 | C5 |
| Muaná | 92 | C4 |
| Muar | 37 | D2 |
| Muarabungo | 37 | E2 |
| Muaraenim | 37 | E2 |
| Muarajuloi | 37 | E4 |
| Muarakaman | 37 | E5 |
| Muaratebo | 37 | E2 |
| Muaratembesi | 37 | E2 |
| Muaratewe | 37 | E4 |
| Mubarraz = Al | | |
| Mubarraz | 47 | F7 |
| Mubende | 57 | D6 |
| Mubi | 53 | F1 |
| Muckadilla | 63 | A4 |
| Muconda | 56 | G4 |
| Mucuri | 93 | F6 |
| Mudanjiang | 35 | B7 |
| Mudanya | 23 | D7 |
| Mudgee | 63 | B4 |
| Mufulira | 59 | A5 |
| Muğla | 23 | F7 |
| Mugu | 40 | C4 |
| Muhammad Qol | 52 | D6 |
| Mühlhausen | 14 | C6 |
| Mühlig Hofmann | | |
| fjell | 96 | B7 |
| Mukacheve | 17 | D6 |
| Mukachevo = | | |
| Mukacheve | 17 | D6 |
| Mukah | 37 | D4 |
| Mukden = | | |
| Shenyang | 35 | B7 |
| Mukomuko | 37 | E2 |
| Muktsar | 42 | D9 |
| Mukur | 42 | C5 |
| Mula | 19 | C5 |
| Mulchén | 94 | D2 |
| Mulde → | 15 | C7 |
| Mulgathing | 62 | B1 |
| Mulgrave | 69 | D4 |
| Mulhacén | 18 | D4 |
| Mulhouse | 13 | C7 |
| Mull | 10 | C4 |
| Mullengudgery | 63 | B4 |
| Muller, | | |
| Pegunungan | 37 | D4 |
| Mullingar | 11 | E3 |
| Mullumbimby | 63 | A5 |
| Multan | 42 | D7 |
| Mulwala | 63 | C4 |
| Mumbai = | | |
| Bombay | 43 | K8 |
| Mumbwa | 59 | A5 |
| Muna | 39 | F2 |
| München | 15 | D6 |

Munchen-
Gladbach =
Mönchengladbach
............. 14 C4
Muncie ....... 72 D3
Mundala .... 39 E6
Münden ...... 14 C5
Mundo Novo .. 93 E5
Mungallala .... 63 A4
Mungallala
Cr. → ...... 63 A4
Mungbere .... 57 D5
Munger ...... 40 E6
Mungindi .... 63 A4
Munhango .... 58 A3
Munich =
München ... 15 D6
Muñoz Gamero,
Pen. ...... 95 G2
Münster .... 14 C4
Munster □ .... 11 E2
Muntok ...... 37 E3
Mupa ....... 58 B3
Muqdisho .... 49 G4
Murallón,
Cuerro ..... 95 F2
Murang'a ..... 57 E7
Murashi ..... 24 B6
Muratlı ...... 22 D6
Murchison → . 60 F1
Murchison, Mt. 96 B15
Murchison Falls
= Kabarega
Falls ....... 57 D6
Murcia ..... 19 C5
Murcia □ .... 19 D5
Mureş → .... 16 E5
Mureşul =
Mureş → .... 16 E5
Murfreesboro . 74 B4
Murgab =
Murghob ... 29 F8
Murghob ..... 29 F8
Murgon ...... 63 A5
Müritz-see .... 15 B7
Murmansk ... 28 C4
Murom ....... 24 B5
Muroran .... 32 F12
Muroto-Misaki . 32 C4
Murray → .... 62 C2
Murray Bridge . 62 C2
Murree ...... 42 C8
Murrumbidgee →
............. 62 B3
Murrumburrah 63 B4
Murrurundi ... 63 B5
Murtoa ...... 62 C3
Murwara .... 40 F3
Murwillumbah . 63 A5
Mürzzuschlag . 15 E8
Muş ....... 46 C5
Mûsa, G. .... 47 E3
Musa Khel .... 42 D6
Müsá Qal'eh .. 42 C4
Musaffargarh .. 42 D7
Musala, Bulgaria 22 C4
Musala,
Indonesia ... 37 D1
Musay'īd ..... 44 E2
Muscat =
Masqat ..... 45 F4
Muscat & Oman
= Oman ■ .. 48 C6
Muscatine ... 77 E9
Musgrave Ras. 60 F5
Mushie ....... 56 E3
Musi → ..... 37 E2
Muskogee .... 79 B6
Musmar ...... 53 E6

Musoma ...... 57 E6
Mussoorie .... 42 D11
Mustafakemalpaşa
............. 23 D7
Mustang ...... 40 C4
Musters, L. ... 95 F3
Muswellbrook . 63 B5
Mût, Egypt .... 52 C4
Mut, Turkey ... 46 C3
Mutare ...... 59 B6
Muting ...... 39 F6
Mutoray ..... 30 C8
Muxima ..... 56 F2
Muynak ..... 29 E6
Muzaffarabad . 42 B8
Muzaffarnagar . 42 E10
Muzaffarpur .. 40 D5
Muzhi ........ 28 C7
Muztag ..... 34 C3
Mvuma ..... 59 B6
Mwanza,
Tanzania .... 57 E6
Mwanza,
Dem. Rep. of the Congo
............. 57 F5
Mweka ..... 56 E4
Mwenezi .... 59 C6
Mwenga ..... 57 E5
Mweru, L. .... 57 F5
Mwinilunga ... 58 A4
My Tho ...... 36 B3
Myanaung .... 41 H10
Myanmar =
Burma ■ ... 41 G11
Myaungmya ... 41 J10
Mycenæ ..... 23 F4
Myeik Kyunzu . 36 B1
Myingyan .... 41 G10
Myitkyina .... 41 E11
Mykolayiv .... 25 D3
Mymensingh .. 41 E8
Mysia ...... 23 E6
Mysore =
Karnataka □ . 43 N10
Mysore ..... 43 N10
Myszków ..... 16 C4
Mytishchi ..... 24 B4

## N

Na Hearadh =
Harris ..... 10 C3
Naab → ..... 15 D7
Naberezhnyye
Chelny ..... 29 D6
Nabeul ........ 52 A1
Nabire ....... 39 E5
Nablus =
Nābulus .... 46 D3
Nābulus .... 46 D3
Nachingwea ... 57 G7
Nackara ..... 62 B2
Nacogdoches . 79 D6
Nacozari ...... 84 A3
Nadiad ....... 43 H8
Nadūshan .... 44 C3
Nadvirna ..... 17 D7
Nadvornaya =
Nadvirna ... 17 D7
Nadym ..... 28 C8
Nadym → .... 28 C8
Nafada ....... 55 F7
Nafūd ad Dahy 47 G6
Nafud Desert =
An Nafūd ... 47 E5
Naga ........ 38 B2

Nagaland □ ... 41 E10
Nagano ...... 32 A6
Nagaoka .... 33 G11
Nagappattinam 43 P11
Nagar Parkar .. 43 G7
Nagasaki .... 32 C1
Nagaur ..... 42 F8
Nagercoil .... 43 Q10
Nagīneh ..... 44 C4
Nagoya ..... 32 B5
Nagpur ....... 43 J11
Nagykanizsa .. 16 E3
Nagykörös ... 16 E4
Nahanni Butte . 70 B7
Nahāvand .... 46 D7
Nä'ifah ...... 48 D5
Nain, Canada .. 68 C4
Nā'īn, Iran .... 44 C3
Nairn ...... 10 C5
Nairobi ...... 57 E7
Naivasha ..... 57 E7
Najafābād .... 44 C2
Najd ....... 47 F5
Najibabad .... 42 E11
Nakamura .... 32 C3
Nakfa ...... 53 E6
Nakhichevan =
Naxçıvan ... 25 F6
Nakhichevan
Republic □ =
Naxçıvan □ . 25 F6
Nakhodka .... 31 E11
Nakhon Phanom 36 A2
Nakhon
Ratchasima . 36 B2
Nakhon Sawan 36 A2
Nakhon Si
Thammarat . 36 C2
Nakina ...... 69 C2
Nakuru ..... 57 E7
Nal → ..... 42 G4
Nalchik ..... 25 E5
Nalgonda .... 43 L11
Nallamalai Hills 43 M11
Nālūt ....... 52 B1
Nam Co ..... 34 C4
Nam-Phan .... 36 B3
Namacurra ... 59 B7
Namak,
Daryācheh-ye 44 C3
Namak, Kavir-e 44 C4
Namaland .... 58 C3
Namangan .... 29 E8
Namapa ..... 59 A7
Namber ..... 39 E4
Nambour .... 63 A5
Nambucca
Heads ..... 63 B5
Nameh ...... 37 D5
Namib Desert =
Namibwoestyn
............. 58 C2
Namibe ..... 58 B2
Namibia ■ .... 58 C3
Namibwoestyn 58 C2
Namlea ..... 39 E3
Namoi → ... 63 B4
Nampa ..... 80 D5
Nampula ..... 59 B7
Namrole ..... 39 E3
Namse Shankou 40 C4
Namtu ..... 41 F11
Namur ..... 14 C3
Namutoni .... 58 B3
Namwala .... 59 B5
Nanaimo .... 71 D7
Nanango .... 63 A5
Nanao ..... 32 A5
Nanchang ... 35 D6

Nanching =
Nanjing ..... 35 C6
Nanchong ... 35 C5
Nancy ...... 13 B7
Nanda Devi ... 42 D11
Nanded .... 43 K10
Nandewar Ra. . 63 B5
Nandurbar .... 43 J9
Nandyal .... 43 M11
Nanga-Eboko .. 56 D2
Nanga Parbat . 42 B9
Nangapinoh ... 37 E4
Nangarhár □ .. 42 B7
Nangatayap ... 37 E4
Nanjing ...... 35 C6
Nanking =
Nanjing ..... 35 C6
Nanning .... 35 D5
Nanping .... 35 D6
Nansei-Shotō =
Ryūkyū-rettō 35 D7
Nantes ....... 12 C3
Nanuque .... 93 F5
Nanusa,
Kepulauan .. 38 D3
Nanyang .... 35 C6
Nanyuki ..... 57 D7
Nao, C. de la .. 19 C6
Naoetsu ..... 32 A6
Napa ....... 80 F2
Napier ...... 64 C7
Naples = Nápoli 21 D5
Naples ...... 75 F7
Napo → ..... 90 D4
Nápoli ...... 21 D5
Nappa Merrie . 62 A3
Nara, Japan ... 32 B4
Nara, Mali ... 55 E3
Naracoorte ... 62 C3
Naradhan .... 63 B4
Narasapur .... 40 J3
Narathiwat ... 36 C2
Narayanganj .. 41 F8
Narayanpet ... 43 L10
Narbonne .... 13 E5
Nardò ...... 23 D2
Narew → ... 16 B5
Narin ...... 42 A6
Narmada → .. 43 J8
Narooma .... 63 C5
Narrabri ..... 63 B4
Narran → .... 63 A4
Narrandera ... 63 B4
Narromine ... 63 B4
Narsimhapur .. 43 H11
Narva ..... 24 B2
Narvik ...... 8 E11
Naryan-Mar .. 28 C6
Naryilco ..... 62 A3
Narym ..... 29 D9
Narymskoye .. 29 E9
Naryn ..... 29 E8
Nasarawa ... 55 G6
Naseby ..... 65 F4
Naser, Buheirat
en .......... 52 D5
Nashville .... 74 A4
Nasik ...... 43 K8
Nasirabad .... 42 F9
Nassau ...... 86 A4
Nassau, B. ... 95 H3
Nasser, L. =
Naser,
Buheirat en . 52 D5
Nat Kyizin .... 41 K11
Nata ....... 59 C5
Natagaima ... 90 C3
Natal, Brazil ... 92 D6
Natal, Indonesia 37 D1

135

# Naţanz

Naţanz ....... 44 C2
Natashquan ... 69 C4
Natashquan ─► 69 C4
Natchez ...... 79 D8
Nathalia ...... 63 C4
Nathdwara .... 43 G8
Natitingou .... 55 F5
Natron, L. .... 57 E7
Natuna Besar,
  Kepulauan .. 37 D3
Natuna Is. =
  Natuna Besar,
  Kepulauan .. 37 D3
Natuna Selatan,
  Kepulauan .. 37 D3
Naturaliste, C. . 62 D4
Naumburg .... 15 C6
Nauru ■ ...... 64 K11
Naushahra =
  Nowshera ... 42 B8
Nauta ........ 90 D4
Nautanwa .... 40 D4
Navahrudak ... 17 B7
Navalmoral de
  la Mata ..... 18 C3
Navarino, I. ... 95 H3
Navarra □ ..... 19 A5
Năvodari ..... 22 B7
Navoi = Nawoiy 29 E7
Navojoa ...... 84 B3
Návpaktos .... 23 E3
Návplion ..... 23 F4
Navsari ...... 43 J8
Nawabshah ... 42 F6
Nawakot ..... 40 D5
Nawalgarh .... 42 F9
Nawāsif, Harrat 47 G5
Nawoiy ....... 29 E7
Naxçıvan .... 25 F6
Naxçıvan □ ... 25 F6
Náxos ........ 23 F5
Nāy Band .... 44 E3
Nazas ─► .... 84 B4
Nazilli ........ 23 F7
Nazir Hat ..... 41 F8
Ncheu ....... 59 A6
Ndalatando ... 56 F2
Ndélé ........ 56 C4
Ndendé ...... 56 E2
Ndjamena .... 53 F1
Ndjolé ....... 56 E2
Ndola ........ 59 A5
Neagh, Lough . 11 D3
Near Is. ...... 71 C1
Neath ........ 11 F5
Nebine Cr. ─► . 63 A4
Nebitdag ..... 29 F6
Nebraska □ ... 76 E5
Nébrodi, Monti 21 F5
Neckar ─► .... 14 D5
Necochea ..... 94 D5
Neemuch =
  Nimach .... 43 G9
Neepawa .... 71 C10
Nefta ........ 54 B6
Neftçala ..... 46 C7
Negapatam =
  Nagappattinam
  ........... 43 P11
Negele ....... 49 F2
Negombo ..... 43 R11
Negotin ...... 22 B4
Negra Pt. ..... 38 A2
Negrais, C. =
  Maudin Sun . 41 K10
Negro ─►,
  Argentina ... 95 E4
Negro ─►, Brazil 90 D6

Negro ─►,
  Uruguay .... 94 C5
Negros ....... 38 C2
Nehbandān ... 45 D5
Nei Monggol
  Zizhiqu □ ... 35 B6
Neijiang ...... 35 D5
Neiva ........ 90 C3
Nejd = Najd .. 47 F5
Nekemte ..... 53 G6
Nellore ....... 43 M11
Nelson, Canada 71 D8
Nelson, N.Z. .. 65 D5
Nelson ─► .... 71 C10
Nelson, C. .... 62 C3
Nelson, Estrecho 95 G2
Nelspruit ..... 59 D6
Néma ........ 55 E3
Neman ─► .... 24 B1
Nemunas =
  Neman ─► .. 24 B1
Nemuro ...... 32 F13
Nemuro-Kaikyō 32 F13
Nenagh ...... 11 E2
Nenana ...... 71 B5
Nenjiang ..... 35 B7
Nepal ■ ...... 40 D5
Nepalganj .... 40 C3
Neretva ─► ... 20 C6
Ness, L. ─► ... 10 C4
Nesterov ..... 17 C6
Nesvizh =
  Nyasvizh ... 17 B8
Netherlands ■ . 14 B3
Netherlands
  Antilles ■ ... 87 D6
Nettilling L. ... 68 B3
Neubrandenburg
  ........... 15 B7
Neuchâtel .... 13 C7
Neuchâtel, Lac
  de .......... 13 C7
Neumünster .. 14 A5
Neunkirchen .. 14 D4
Neuquén ..... 94 D3
Neuruppin .... 15 B7
Neustrelitz .... 15 B7
Neva ─► ..... 24 B3
Nevada □ .... 80 F5
Nevada, Sierra,
  Spain ...... 18 D4
Nevada, Sierra,
  U.S.A. ...... 80 F3
Nevers ....... 13 C5
Nevertire ..... 63 B4
Nevinnomyssk 25 E5
Nevis ........ 87 C7
Nevşehir ..... 46 C3
New Amsterdam 90 B7
New Angledool 63 A4
New Bedford .. 73 D10
New Bern .... 75 B9
New Brighton . 65 E5
New Britain,
  Papua N. G. . 64 K10
New Britain,
  U.S.A. ...... 73 D9
New
  Brunswick □ 69 D4
New
  Caledonia ■ . 64 M11
New Delhi .... 42 E10
New England
  Ra. ........ 63 B5
New Glasgow . 69 D4
New Guinea . 64
New
  Hampshire □ 73 C10
New Haven ... 73 D9

New Hebrides =
  Vanuatu ■ .. 64 L11
New Ireland .. 64 K10
New Jersey □ . 73 E9
New London .. 73 D9
New Mexico □ 83 C9
New Norfolk .. 62 D4
New Orleans .. 79 E8
New Plymouth 64 C6
New Providence 86 A4
New Siberian Is.
  =
  Novosibirskiye
  Ostrova ..... 31 B12
New South
  Wales □ .... 63 B4
New
  Westminster 71 D7
New York □ .. 73 C8
New York City . 73 D9
New Zealand ■ 64 D7
Newala ....... 57 G7
Newark ...... 73 D8
Newburgh .... 73 D8
Newbury .... 11 F6
Newcastle,
  Australia .... 63 B5
Newcastle,
  S. Africa .... 59 D5
Newcastle-upon-
  Tyne ....... 11 D6
Newfoundland □
  ........... 69 C5
Newman ..... 60 E2
Newport,
  I. of W., U.K. 11 F6
Newport, Newp.,
  U.K. ....... 11 F5
Newport, U.S.A. 73 D10
Newport News 73 F7
Newquay .... 11 F4
Newry ....... 11 D3
Newton Boyd . 63 A5
Neya ........ 24 B5
Neyrīz ....... 44 D3
Neyshābūr .... 44 B4
Nezhin = Nizhyn 24 C3
Ngabang ..... 37 D3
Ngabordamlu,
  Tanjung .. 39 F4
Ngami
  Depression .. 58 C4
Nganglong
  Kangri ...... 40 A3
Ngaoundéré .. 56 C2
Ngapara ...... 65 F4
Ngoring Hu ... 34 C4
Ngudu ....... 57 E6
Nguigmi ...... 53 F1
Nguru ....... 55 F7
Nha Trang .... 36 B3
Nhill ........ 62 C3
Niafounké .... 55 E4
Niagara Falls,
  Canada .... 69 D3
Niagara Falls,
  U.S.A. ...... 73 C6
Niah ........ 37 D4
Niamey ...... 55 F5
Niangara ..... 57 D5
Nias ........ 37 D1
Nicaragua ■ .. 85 E7
Nicaragua, L. de 85 E7
Nicastro ...... 21 E6
Nice ........ 13 E7
Nichinan ..... 33 D2
Nicobar Is. .... 27 J13
Nicosia ....... 46 D3
Nicoya, Pen. de 85 F7

Niedersachsen □
  ........... 14 B5
Niemen =
  Neman ─► .. 24 B1
Nienburg ..... 14 B5
Nieuw
  Amsterdam . 92 A2
Nieuw Nickerie 92 A2
Niğde ........ 46 C3
Niger ■ ...... 55 E6
Niger ─► ..... 55 G6
Nigeria ■ .... 55 G6
Nightcaps .... 65 F3
Nii-Jima ..... 32 B6
Niigata ...... 33 G11
Niihama ..... 32 C3
Niihau ....... 82
Nijmegen .... 14 C3
Nikiniki ...... 39 F2
Nikki ........ 55 G5
Nikolayev =
  Mykolayiv .. 25 D3
Nikolayevsk .. 24 C6
Nikopol ...... 25 D3
Nīkshahr ..... 45 E5
Nikšić ....... 22 C2
Nîl, Nahr en ─► 52 B5
Nîl el Abyad ─► 53 E5
Nîl el Azraq ─► 53 E5
Nile = Nîl, Nahr
  en ─► ...... 52 B5
Nimach ...... 43 G9
Nîmes ........ 13 E6
Nimfaíon, Ákra
  = Pínnes,
  Ákra ....... 23 D5
Nimmitabel ... 63 C4
Nimrūz □ ..... 45 D5
Nimule ....... 57 D6
Nīnawá ...... 46 C5
Nindigully ... 63 A4
Nineveh =
  Nīnawá .... 46 C5
Ningbo ...... 35 D7
Ningde ....... 35 D6
Ningpo =
  Ningbo .... 35 D7
Ningsia Hui A.R.
  = Ningxia
  Huizu
  Zizhiqu □ ... 35 C5
Ningxia Huizu
  Zizhiqu □ ... 35 C5
Niobrara ─► .. 76 D5
Nioro du Sahel 55 E3
Niort ........ 12 C3
Nipawin ..... 71 C9
Nipigon, L. ... 69 D2
Niquelândia .. 93 E4
Nirmal ....... 43 K11
Nirmali ...... 40 D6
Niš ......... 22 C3
Nişāb, Si. Arabia 47 E6
Nişāb, Yemen . 49 E4
Nishinomiya .. 32 B4
Nistru =
  Dnister ─► .. 17 E10
Niţa' ........ 47 F7
Niterói ....... 93 G5
Nitra ........ 16 D4
Nitra ─► ..... 16 E4
Niue ........ 65 L14
Niut ........ 37 D4
Nivernais .... 13 C5
Nizamabad ... 43 K11
Nizamghat .... 41 C10
Nizhne-Vartovsk 29 C8
Nizhneyansk . 31 B13
Nizhniy
  Novgorod ... 24 B5

Nizhniy Tagil .. **29 D6**
Nizhyn ....... **24 C3**
Nizip ........ **46 C4**
Nízké Tatry .. **16 D4**
Njombe ...... **57 F6**
Nkambe ...... **55 G7**
Nkawkaw .... **55 G4**
Nkhata Bay .. **57 G6**
Nkhota Kota .. **59 A6**
Nkongsamba .. **56 D1**
Nmai → ..... **41 E11**
Noakhali =
Maijdi ...... **41 F8**
Noatak ...... **71 B3**
Nobeoka ..... **32 C2**
Nocera Inferiore **21 D5**
Nockatunga .. **62 A3**
Nogales, *Mexico* **84 A2**
Nogales, *U.S.A.* **83 E7**
Nōgata ...... **32 C2**
Noginsk ...... **30 C7**
Noire, Mts. .... **12 B2**
Noirmoutier, I.
de ....... **12 C2**
Nok Kundi .... **42 E3**
Nokhtuysk .... **30 C9**
Nokomis ..... **71 C9**
Nola ........ **56 D3**
Nome ....... **71 B3**
Nong Khai ... **36 A2**
Noondoo ..... **63 A4**
Nóqui ....... **56 F2**
Noranda ..... **69 D3**
Nord-Ostsee-
Kanal → .. **14 A5**
Nordegg ...... **71 C8**
Norderney ... **14 B4**
Norderstedt ... **14 B5**
Nordfriesische
Inseln .... **14 A5**
Nordhausen .. **14 C6**
Nordkapp ..... **8 D13**
Nordrhein-
Westfalen □ . **14 C4**
Nordvik ...... **30 B9**
Norfolk ...... **73 F7**
Norfolk I. ..... **64 M11**
Norilsk ...... **30 C6**
Norley ....... **63 A3**
Norman ..... **78 B5**
Norman Wells . **70 B7**
Normandie .. **12 B4**
Normandy =
Normandie .. **12 B4**
Normanton ... **61 D7**
Norquinco ... **95 E2**
Norrköping .. **9 G11**
Norrland ..... **8 F11**
Norseman ... **60 G3**
North Battleford **71 C9**
North Bay ... **69 D3**
North Bend ... **80 D1**
North C. ..... **64 A5**
North Cape =
Nordkapp .. **8 D13**
North
Carolina □ .. **75 B7**
North Channel,
*Canada* **69 D2**
North Channel,
*U.K.* ....... **11 D4**
North Dakota □ **76 B4**
North Frisian Is.
=
Nordfriesische
Inseln ... **14 A5**
North I. ....... **64 B5**
North Korea ■ **35 C7**

North
Lakhimpur .. **41 D10**
North Minch .. **10 B4**
North Ossetia □ **25 E5**
North Pagai, I. =
Pagai Utara . **37 E2**
North Platte ... **76 E4**
North Platte → **76 E4**
North Rhine
Westphalia □
= Nordrhein-
Westfalen □ . **14 C4**
North
Saskatchewan →
.......... **71 C8**
North Sea .... **10 D8**
North Sporades
= Voríai
Sporádhes .. **23 E4**
North Taranaki
Bight ....... **64 C6**
North
Thompson → **71 C7**
North Uist .... **10 C3**
North West C. . **60 E1**
North West
Frontier □ .. **42 B8**
North West
Highlands ... **10 C4**
North West
River ....... **69 C4**
North West
Territories □ **70 B7**
Northampton .. **11 E6**
Northern Circars **40 J4**
Northern
Ireland □ ... **11 D3**
Northern
Marianas ■ . **64 H9**
Northern
Territory □ .. **60 D5**
Northland □ .. **64 A5**
Northumberland,
C. .......... **62 C3**
Northumberland
Str. ....... **69 D4**
Norton Sd. ..... **71 B3**
Norway ■ .... **8 F10**
Norway House **71 C10**
Norwegian Sea **6 B5**
Norwich ..... **11 E7**
Nosok ....... **28 B9**
Noşratābād .. **45 D4**
Nossob → .. **58 D4**
Nosy Bé .... **59 G9**
Nosy Boraha .. **59 H9**
Nosy Mitsio .. **59 G9**
Nosy Varika .. **59 J9**
Noteć → ..... **16 B2**
Noto-Hanto .. **33 G11**
Notre Dame B. **69 D5**
Notre Dame de
Koartac =
Quaqtaq .... **68 B4**
Notre Dame
d'Ivugivic =
Ivujivik ..... **68 B3**
Nottaway → .. **69 C3**
Nottingham .. **11 E6**
Nouâdhibou .. **54 D1**
Nouâdhibou,
Ras ..... **54 D1**
Nouakchott .. **55 E1**
Nouméa ...... **64 M11**
Noupoort ..... **58 E4**
Nouveau
Comptoir =
Wemindji ... **69 C3**

Nouvelle-
Calédonie =
New
Caledonia ■ . **64 M11**
Nova Casa Nova **93 D5**
Nova Cruz .. **92 D6**
Nova Friburgo . **93 G5**
Nova Gaia =
Cambundi-
Catembo .... **56 G3**
Nova Iguaçu .. **93 G5**
Nova Iorque .. **92 D5**
Nova Lima ... **93 F5**
Nova Mambone **59 C7**
Nova Scotia □ . **69 D4**
Nova Sofala .. **59 C6**
Nova Venécia . **93 F5**
Nova Zagora .. **22 C5**
Novara ...... **20 B2**
Novaya Ladoga **24 A3**
Novaya Lyalya **29 D7**
Novaya Zemlya **28 B6**
Nové Zámky . **16 D4**
Novgorod .... **24 B3**
Novgorod-
Severskiy =
Novhorod-
Siverskyy ... **24 C3**
Novhorod-
Siverskyy ... **24 C3**
Novi Lígure ... **20 B2**
Novi Pazar ... **22 C3**
Novi Sad ..... **22 B2**
Novo Mesto .. **20 B5**
Novo Remanso **93 D5**
Novoataysk ... **29 D9**
Novocherkassk **25 D5**
Novogrudok =
Navahrudak . **17 B7**
Novohrad-
Volynskyy ... **17 C8**
Novokazalinsk =
Zhangaqazaly **29 E7**
Novokuybyshevsk
......... **24 C6**
Novokuznetsk . **29 D9**
Novomoskovsk **24 C4**
Novorossiysk .. **25 E4**
Novorybnoye . **30 B8**
Novoselytsya . **17 D8**
Novoshakhtinsk **25 D4**
Novosibirsk .. **29 D9**
Novosibirskiye
Ostrova ..... **31 B12**
Novotroitsk ... **29 D6**
Novouzensk ... **24 C6**
Novovolynsk .. **17 C7**
Novska ...... **20 B6**
Novyy Port ... **28 C8**
Now Shahr ... **44 B2**
Nowa Sól .... **16 C2**
Nowgong ..... **41 D9**
Nowra ....... **63 B5**
Nowshera .... **42 B8**
Nowy Sącz .. **16 D5**
Nowy Targ .... **16 D5**
Nowy Tomyśl . **16 B3**
Noyon ....... **13 B5**
Nsanje ....... **59 B7**
Nsawam ..... **55 G4**
Nsukka ...... **55 G6**
Nubian Desert =
Nûbîya, Es
Sahrâ En .. **52 D5**
Nûbîya, Es
Sahrâ En ... **52 D5**
Nuboai ...... **39 E5**
Nueltin L. ..... **70 B10**
Nueva Imperial **94 D2**

Nueva Rosita .. **84 B4**
Nuéve de Julio **94 D4**
Nuevitas ..... **86 B4**
Nuevo, G. .... **95 E4**
Nuevo Laredo . **84 B5**
Nugget Pt. .... **65 G3**
Nuhaka ....... **64 C7**
Nukey Bluff .. **62 B2**
Nukheila ..... **53 E4**
Nukus ...... **29 E6**
Nulato ...... **71 B4**
Nullarbor Plain **60 G4**
Numalla, L. ... **63 A3**
Numan ...... **53 G1**
Numazu ...... **32 B6**
Numfoor .... **39 E4**
Numurkah ... **63 C4**
Nunavut □ .... **66 C10**
Nuneaton .... **11 E6**
Nunivak I. .... **71 B3**
Nunkun ..... **42 C10**
Núoro ...... **21 D2**
Nuremberg =
Nürnberg ... **15 D6**
Nuriootpa .... **62 B2**
Nürnberg ... **15 D6**
Nurran, L. =
Terewah, L. . **63 A4**
Nusa Tenggara
Barat □ ..... **37 F5**
Nusa Tenggara
Timur □ ..... **39 F2**
Nushki ....... **42 E5**
Nutak ....... **68 C4**
Nuuk ....... **68 B5**
Nuwakot .... **40 C4**
Nuweveldberge **58 E4**
Nuyts Arch. ... **62 B1**
Nyah West ... **62 C3**
Nyahanga ... **57 E6**
Nyahururu ... **57 D7**
Nyainqentanglha
Shan ....... **34 C4**
Nyâlâ ....... **53 F3**
Nyasa, L. =
Malawi, L. .. **59 A6**
Nyasvizh ... **17 B8**
Nyda ....... **28 C8**
Nyeri ....... **57 E7**
Nyíregyháza .. **17 E5**
Nylstroom ... **59 C5**
Nymagee .... **63 B4**
Nyngan ..... **63 B4**
Nyoman =
Neman → .. **24 B1**
Nysa ....... **16 C3**
Nysa → ..... **16 B2**
Nyurbe .... **30 C9**
Nzega ....... **57 E6**
N'Zérékoré ... **55 G3**
Nzeto ...... **56 F2**

**O**

Ô-Shima ...... **32 B6**
Oahe, L. ..... **76 C4**
Oahu ....... **82 H12**
Oak Ridge ... **75 A5**
Oakbank .... **62 B3**
Oakey ...... **63 A5**
Oakland ..... **82 B1**
Oamaru ..... **65 F4**
Oates Land .. **96 A15**
Oaxaca ..... **84 D5**
Ob → ....... **28 C7**

Oba .......... 69 D2
Oban ........ 10 C4
Obbia ........ 49 F4
Oberhausen ... 14 C4
Oberon ....... 63 B4
Obi, Kepulauan 39 E3
Obi Is. = Obi,
　Kepulauan .. 39 E3
Óbidos ....... 92 C2
Obihiro ...... 32 F12
Obilatu ...... 39 E3
Obo ......... 57 C5
Obozerskaya =
　Obozerskiy .. 28 C5
Obozerskiy .... 28 C5
Obskaya Guba . 28 C8
Obuasi ....... 55 G4
Ocala ........ 75 E6
Ocaña ........ 18 C4
Occidental,
　Cordillera .. 90 C3
Ocean I. =
　Banaba ..... 64 K11
Oceanside .... 82 D4
Ocniţa ........ 17 D8
Ocumare del
　Tuy ........ 90 A5
Odate ........ 33 F12
Odawara ...... 32 B6
Oddur ........ 49 G3
Ödemiş ...... 23 E7
Odense ....... 9 G10
Oder → ...... 15 B8
Odesa ....... 25 D3
Odessa = Odesa 25 D3
Odessa ....... 78 D2
Odienné ...... 55 G3
Odintsovo .... 24 B4
Odorheiu
　Secuiesc .... 17 E7
Odra = Oder → 15 B8
Odra → ...... 16 B2
Oeiras ....... 92 D5
Ofanto → .... 20 D6
Offa ......... 55 G5
Offenbach .... 14 C5
Offenburg .... 14 D4
Oga-Hantō ... 33 G11
Ōgaki ....... 32 B5
Ogbomosho .. 55 G5
Ogden ....... 81 E8
Ogdensburg .. 73 B8
Oglio → ..... 20 B3
Ogooué → ... 56 E1
Ogowe =
　Ogooué → . 56 E1
Ohai ......... 65 F2
Ohakune ..... 64 C6
Ohanet ....... 54 C6
Ohau, L. ...... 65 F3
Ohio □ ...... 72 D4
Ohio → ...... 72 F1
Ohre → ...... 16 C2
Ohrid ........ 22 D3
Ohridsko Jezero 23 D3
Oise → ...... 12 B5
Ōita ........ 32 C2
Oiticica ...... 92 D5
Ojos del Salado,
　Cerro ...... 94 B3
Oka → ...... 28 D5
Okaba ....... 39 F5
Okahandja .... 58 C3
Okahukura ... 64 C6
Okandja ..... 56 E2
Okanogan → . 80 A4
Okara ........ 42 D8
Okarito ...... 65 E4
Okaukuejo .... 58 B3

Okavango
　Swamps .... 58 B4
Okaya ........ 32 A6
Okayama ..... 32 B3
Okazaki ...... 32 B5
Okeechobee, L. 75 F7
Okefenokee
　Swamp ..... 75 D6
Okhotsk, Sea of 31 D12
Oki-Shotō ... 32 A3
Okiep ........ 58 D3
Okinawa-Jima . 35 D7
Oklahoma □ .. 78 B5
Oklahoma City 78 B5
Okmulgee .... 79 B6
Oknitsa =
　Ocniţa ..... 17 D8
Okrika ........ 55 H6
Oktabrsk =
　Oktyabrsk .. 29 E6
Oktyabrsk .... 29 E6
Oktyabrskiy =
　Aktsyabrski . 17 B9
Oktyabrskoy
　Revolyutsii,
　Os. ........ 30 B7
Oktyabrskoye . 28 C7
Okuru ........ 65 E3
Okushiri-Tō .. 32 F11
Öland ........ 9 G11
Olary ........ 62 B3
Olavarría .... 94 D4
Oława ....... 16 C3
Ólbia ........ 20 D2
Old Crow ..... 70 B6
Oldenburg ... 14 B5
Oldham ...... 11 E5
Olekma → ... 31 C10
Olekminsk ... 31 C10
Oleksandriya .. 17 C8
Olenek ....... 30 C9
Olenek → .... 30 B10
Oléron, I. d' .. 12 D3
Oleśnica ..... 16 C3
Olevsk ...... 17 C8
Olhão ....... 18 D2
Olifants → ... 59 C6
Ólimbos, Óros . 23 D4
Olinda ....... 92 D7
Oliveira ...... 93 G5
Olivenza ..... 18 C2
Ollagüe ...... 91 H5
Olomouc ..... 16 D3
Olongapo .... 38 B2
Olot ......... 19 A7
Olsztyn ...... 16 B5
Olt → ....... 22 C5
Olteniţa ..... 22 B6
Oltu ......... 46 B5
Olympia, Greece 23 F3
Olympia, U.S.A. 80 B2
Olympic Mts. . 80 B2
Olympus, Mt. =
　Ólimbos, Óros 23 D4
Om → ....... 29 D8
Omagh ....... 11 D3
Omaha ....... 77 E7
Oman ■ ..... 48 C6
Oman, G. of .. 45 E4
Omaruru ..... 58 C3
Omate ....... 91 G4
Ombai, Selat . 39 F2
Omboué ...... 56 E1
Ombrone → .. 20 C3
Omdurmân ... 53 E5
Ometepec .... 84 D5
Ōmiya ....... 32 B6
Omo → ...... 53 G6
Omsk ........ 29 D8

Omul, Vf. ..... 17 F7
Ōmura ....... 32 C1
Omuramba
　Omatako → 58 B4
Ōmuta ....... 32 C2
Onang ....... 39 E1
Oncócua ..... 58 B2
Onda ........ 19 C5
Ondangua .... 58 B3
Ondo ........ 55 G5
Öndörhaan ... 35 B6
Onega ....... 28 C4
Onega → ..... 8 F15
Onega, G. of =
　Onezhskaya
　Guba ...... 28 C4
Onega, L. =
　Onezhskoye
　Ozero ..... 28 C4
Onehunga .... 64 B6
Oneşti ....... 17 E8
Onezhskaya
　Guba ...... 28 C4
Onezhskoye
　Ozero ..... 28 C4
Ongarue ...... 64 C6
Onilahy → ... 59 J8
Onitsha ...... 55 G6
Onoda ....... 32 B2
Ontario □ .... 69 D2
Ontario, L. .... 73 C7
Oodnadatta ... 62 A2
Oostende .... 14 C2
Ootacamund . 43 P10
Opala ........ 56 E4
Opava ....... 16 D3
Opole ........ 16 C3
Oporto = Porto 18 B1
Opotiki ...... 64 C7
Opua ........ 64 A6
Opunake ..... 64 C5
Oradea ...... 17 E5
Orai ......... 42 G11
Oral =
　Zhayyq → .. 29 E6
Oral ......... 24 C7
Oran, Algeria .. 54 A4
Oran, Argentina 94 A4
Orange =
　Oranje → . 58 D3
Orange,
　Australia .... 63 B4
Orange, France 13 D6
Orange, U.S.A. 79 D7
Orange, C. .... 92 B3
Orangeburg .. 75 C7
Oranienburg . 15 B7
Oranje → .... 58 D3
Oranjemund .. 58 D3
Oras ......... 38 B3
Oraşul Stalin =
　Braşov ..... 17 F7
Orbetello ..... 20 C3
Orbost ....... 63 C4
Orchila, I. .... 90 A5
Ordos = Mu Us
　Shamo ..... 35 C5
Ordu ........ 46 B4
Ordzhonikidze =
　Vladikavkaz . 25 E5
Ore Mts. =
　Erzgebirge .. 15 C7
Örebro ...... 9 G11
Oregon □ .... 80 C3
Orekhovo-
　Zuyevo ..... 24 B4
Orel ......... 24 C4
Ören ........ 23 F6
Orenburg ..... 29 D6

Orense ....... 18 A2
Orepuki ...... 65 G2
Øresund ..... 9 G10
Orgaz ....... 18 C4
Orgeyev =
　Orhei ...... 17 E9
Orgün ....... 45 C7
Orhaneli ...... 23 E7
Orhangazi .... 23 D7
Orhei ........ 17 E9
Orhon Gol → . 35 A5
Orient ........ 62 A3
Oriental,
　Cordillera ... 90 B4
Orihuela ..... 19 C5
Orinoco → ... 90 B6
Orissa □ ..... 40 G5
Oristano ..... 21 E2
Oristano, G. di . 21 E2
Orizaba ...... 84 D5
Orkney Is. .... 10 B5
Orlando ...... 75 E7
Orléanais .... 12 C5
Orléans ...... 12 C4
Ormara ...... 42 G4
Ormoc ....... 38 B2
Ormond ...... 64 C7
Örnsköldsvik . 8 F11
Orocué ...... 90 C4
Orol Dengizi =
　Aral Sea ... 29 E6
Oroquieta .... 38 C2
Orós ........ 92 D6
Orosháza .... 16 E5
Ororoo ...... 62 B2
Orsha ....... 24 C3
Orsk ........ 29 D6
Orşova ...... 22 B4
Ortaca ....... 23 F7
Ortegal, C. ... 18 A2
Orthez ....... 12 E3
Ortigueira ... 18 A2
Ortles ....... 20 A3
Ortón → ..... 91 F5
Orümīyeh .... 46 C6
Orümīyeh,
　Daryācheh-ye 46 C6
Oruro ....... 91 G5
Oruzgān □ ... 42 C5
Orvieto ...... 20 C4
Oryakhovo ... 22 C4
Ōsaka ....... 32 B4
Ösel =
　Saaremaa ... 24 B1
Osh ......... 29 E8
Oshawa ...... 69 D3
Oshkosh ..... 76 E3
Oshmyany =
　Ashmyany .. 17 A7
Oshogbo ..... 55 G5
Oshwe ...... 56 E3
Osijek ....... 20 B7
Osipenko =
　Berdyansk .. 25 D4
Osipovichi =
　Asipovichy .. 17 B9
Oskarshamn .. 9 G11
Öskemen ..... 29 E9
Oslo ......... 9 G10
Oslob ....... 38 C2
Oslofjorden ... 9 G10
Osmanabad .. 43 K10
Osmaniye .... 46 C6
Osnabrück ... 14 B5
Osorio ....... 94 B6
Osorno ...... 95 E2
Ossa, Mt. .... 62 D4
Óssa, Oros .. 23 E4
Ostend =
　Oostende ... 14 C2

Oster ....... 17 C10
Österdalälven . 8 F10
Östersund .... 8 F10
Ostfriesische
  Inseln ...... 14 B4
Ostrava ...... 16 D4
Ostróda ...... 16 B4
Ostroh ....... 17 C8
Ostrołęka .... 16 B5
Ostrów
  Mazowiecka . 16 B5
Ostrów
  Wielkopolski 16 C3
Ostrowiec-
  Świętokrzyski 16 C5
Ostuni ....... 21 D6
Ōsumi-Kaikyō . 33 D2
Osuna ....... 18 D3
Oswego ...... 73 C7
Oświęcim .... 16 C4
Otago □ ..... 65 F3
Otago Harbour 65 F4
Ōtake ....... 32 B3
Otaki ....... 64 D6
Otaru ....... 32 F12
Otaru-Wan =
  Ishikari-Wan . 32 F12
Otavalo ...... 90 C3
Otavi ....... 58 B3
Otira Gorge ... 65 E4
Otjiwarongo . 58 C3
Otorohanga ... 64 C6
Otranto ...... 23 D2
Otranto, C. d' . 23 D2
Otranto, Str. of 23 D2
Ōtsu ....... 32 B4
Ottawa ...... 69 D3
Ottawa Is. .... 68 C2
Ottumwa .... 77 E8
Oturkpo ..... 55 G6
Otway, B. .... 95 G2
Otway, C. .... 62 C3
Otwock ...... 16 B5
Ouachita Mts. . 79 B6
Ouadâne .... 54 D2
Ouadda ...... 56 C4
Ouagadougou . 55 F4
Ouahran = Oran 54 A4
Ouallene .... 54 D5
Ouanda Djallé . 56 C4
Ouango ...... 56 D4
Ouargla ...... 54 B6
Ouarzazate .... 54 B3
Oubangi → .. 56 E3
Oudtshoorn .. 58 E4
Ouessant, I. d' . 12 B1
Ouesso ...... 56 D3
Ouezzane .... 54 B3
Ouidah ...... 55 G5
Oujda ....... 54 B4
Oujeft ....... 55 D2
Ouled Djellal .. 54 B6
Oulu ....... 8 E13
Oulujärvi .... 8 F13
Oulujoki → ... 8 E13
Oum Chalouba 53 E3
Ounianga-Kébir 53 E3
Ounianga Sérir 53 E3
Ourense =
  Orense ..... 18 A2
Ouricuri ..... 92 D5
Ouro Prêto .... 93 G5
Ouse ....... 62 D4
Outer Hebrides 10 C3
Outjo ....... 58 C3
Ouyen ...... 62 C3
Ovalle ...... 94 C2
Ovamboland .. 58 B3
Oviedo ...... 18 A3

Ovruch ...... 17 C9
Owaka ....... 65 G3
Owambo =
  Ovamboland 58 B3
Owase ...... 32 B5
Owbeh ...... 42 B3
Owen Sound .. 69 D2
Owen Stanley
  Ra. ........ 61 B8
Owendo ..... 56 D1
Owo ........ 55 G6
Owyhee → .. 80 D5
Oxford, N.Z. .. 65 E5
Oxford, U.K. .. 11 F6
Oxley ....... 63 B3
Oxnard ...... 82 C3
Oxus =
  Amudarya → 29 E6
Oya ........ 37 D4
Oyama ...... 32 A6
Oyem ....... 56 D2
Oyo ........ 55 G5
Ozamiz ...... 38 C2
Ozark Plateau . 79 A8
Ózd ........ 16 D5

## P

Paamiut ...... 68 B6
Pa-an ....... 41 J11
Paarl ....... 58 E3
Pab Hills .... 42 F5
Pabianice .... 16 C4
Pabna ....... 41 E7
Pacaja → ... 92 C3
Pacaraima,
  Sierra ...... 90 C6
Pacasmayo ... 91 E3
Pachpadra ... 42 G8
Pachuca ..... 84 C5
Padaido,
  Kepulauan .. 39 E5
Padang ...... 37 E2
Padangpanjang 37 E2
Padangsidempuan
  .......... 37 D1
Paderborn .... 14 C5
Pádova ...... 20 B3
Padua = Pádova 20 B3
Paducah ..... 72 F1
Paeroa ...... 64 B6
Pafúri ....... 59 C6
Pag ........ 20 B5
Pagadian .... 38 C2
Pagai Selatan, P. 37 E2
Pagai Utara .. 37 E2
Pagalu =
  Annobón .. 51 G4
Pagastikós
  Kólpos ..... 23 E4
Pagatan ..... 37 E5
Pahiatua .... 64 D6
Painan ...... 37 E2
Paint Hills =
  Wemindji ... 69 C3
Painted Desert . 83 C7
País Vasco □ .. 19 A4
Paisley ...... 10 D4
Paita ....... 90 E2
Pajares, Puerto
  de ........ 18 A3
Pakaraima Mts. 90 B6
Pakistan ■ .... 42 E7
Pakokku ..... 41 G10
Pakse ....... 36 A3
Paktīā □ ..... 42 C6

Pala ........ 53 G2
Palagruža .... 20 C6
Palam ....... 43 K10
Palampur .... 42 C10
Palana ...... 62 C4
Palanan ..... 38 A2
Palanan Pt. .. 38 A2
Palangkaraya . 37 E4
Palani Hills ... 43 P10
Palanpur .... 43 G8
Palanro ..... 39 E1
Palapye ..... 59 C5
Palau ■ ..... 38 C4
Palawan ..... 36 C5
Palayankottai .. 43 Q10
Paleleh ..... 39 D2
Palembang ... 37 E2
Palencia ..... 18 A3
Palermo ..... 21 E4
Palestine .... 79 D6
Paletwa ..... 41 G9
Palghat ..... 43 P10
Pali ........ 42 G8
Palioúrion, Ákra 23 E4
Palitana ..... 43 J7
Palk Bay ..... 43 Q11
Palk Strait .... 43 Q11
Pallanza =
  Verbánia ... 20 B2
Palm Springs .. 82 D4
Palma ...... 57 G8
Palma → .... 93 E4
Palma, B. de .. 19 C7
Palma de
  Mallorca ... 19 C7
Palmares .... 92 D6
Palmas, C. ... 55 H3
Pálmas, G. di .. 21 E2
Palmeira dos
  Índios ...... 93 D6
Palmeirinhas,
  Pta. das ... 56 F2
Palmer ...... 96 A3
Palmer Arch. .. 96 A3
Palmer Land .. 96 B3
Palmerston .. 65 F4
Palmerston
  North ...... 64 D6
Palmi ....... 21 E5
Palmira ...... 90 C3
Palmyra =
  Tudmur .... 46 D4
Palopo ...... 39 E2
Palos, C. de ... 19 D5
Palu, Indonesia 39 E1
Palu, Turkey .. 46 C5
Paluan ...... 38 B2
Pama ....... 55 F5
Pamiers ..... 12 E4
Pamirs ...... 29 F8
Pamlico Sd. ... 75 B10
Pampa ...... 78 B3
Pampa de las
  Salinas .... 94 C3
Pampanua ... 39 E2
Pampas,
  Argentina .. 94 D4
Pampas, Peru . 91 F4
Pamplona,
  Colombia ... 90 B4
Pamplona,
  Spain ...... 19 A5
Panaji ....... 43 M8
Panamá ..... 85 F9
Panamá ■ .... 86 E4
Panamá, G. de 86 E4
Panama City .. 74 D5
Panão ...... 91 E3
Panay ....... 38 B2

Panay, G. ..... 38 B2
Pančevo ...... 22 B3
Pandan ...... 38 B2
Pandharpur ... 43 L9
Pando ....... 94 C5
Pando, L. =
  Hope, L. .... 62 A2
Panevežys .... 24 B1
Panfilov ..... 29 E8
Pang-Long ... 41 F12
Pang-Yang ... 41 F12
Pangani ..... 57 F7
Pangfou =
  Bengbu ..... 35 C6
Pangkajene .. 39 E1
Pangkalanbrandan
  .......... 37 D1
Pangkalanbuun 37 E4
Pangkalansusu 37 D1
Pangkalpinang 37 E3
Pangkoh ..... 37 E4
Pangnirtung ... 68 B4
Pangutaran
  Group ...... 38 C2
Panjim = Panaji 43 M8
Panjinad
  Barrage ..... 42 E7
Panorama .... 94 A6
Pantar ....... 39 F2
Pante Macassar 39 F2
Pantelleria ... 21 F3
Pánuco ...... 84 C5
Panyam ...... 55 G6
Paoting =
  Baoding ... 35 C6
Paot'ou =
  Baotou .... 35 B6
Paoua ...... 56 C3
Pápa ....... 16 E3
Papakura .... 64 B6
Papantla .... 84 C5
Papar ....... 36 C5
Papua New
  Guinea ■ ... 61 B8
Papudo ..... 94 C2
Papun ...... 41 H11
Pará = Belém . 92 C4
Pará □ ...... 92 C3
Paracatu .... 93 F4
Paracel Is. =
  Hsisha
  Chuntao .... 36 A4
Parachilna ... 62 B2
Parachinar ... 42 C7
Paradip ..... 40 G6
Parado ...... 39 F1
Paragua → ... 90 B6
Paraguaçu → . 93 E6
Paraguaná, Pen.
  de ........ 90 A4
Paraguarí .... 94 B5
Paraguay ■ ... 94 A5
Paraguay → .. 94 B5
Paraíba = João
  Pessoa ..... 92 D7
Paraíba □ .... 92 D6
Paraíba do
  Sul → ..... 93 G5
Parakou ..... 55 G5
Paramaribo ... 92 A2
Paraná,
  Argentina ... 94 C4
Paraná, Brazil . 93 E4
Paraná □ .... 94 A6
Paraná → .... 94 C5
Paranaguá ... 94 B7
Paranaíba → . 93 G3

Paranapanema →
......... 94 A6
Paranapiacaba,
  Serra do .... 94 A7
Parang, Jolo,
  Phil. ........ 38 C2
Parang,
  Mindanao,
  Phil. ........ 38 C2
Paratinga ..... 93 E5
Paratoo ...... 62 B2
Parattah ...... 62 D4
Parbhani ..... 43 K10
Parchim ...... 15 B6
Pardo →,
  Bahia, Brazil . 93 F6
Pardo →,
  Mato Grosso,
  Brazil ....... 93 G3
Pardo →,
  São Paulo,
  Brazil ....... 93 G4
Pardubice ..... 16 C2
Parecis, Serra
  dos ........ 91 F7
Parepare ..... 39 E1
Párga ........ 23 E3
Pariaguán .... 90 B6
Pariaman ..... 37 E2
Parigi ........ 39 E2
Parika ........ 90 B7
Parima, Serra . 90 C6
Parinari ...... 90 D4
Parîngul Mare . 17 F6
Parintins ..... 92 C2
Pariparit Kyun . 41 K9
Paris, France .. 12 B5
Paris, U.S.A. .. 79 C6
Park Range ... 81 F10
Parkersburg ... 72 E5
Parkes ....... 63 B4
Parla ........ 18 B4
Parma ........ 20 B3
Parnaguá ..... 93 E5
Parnaíba, Piauí,
  Brazil ....... 92 C5
Parnaíba,
  São Paulo,
  Brazil ....... 93 F3
Parnaíba → .. 92 C5
Parnassós .... 23 E4
Parnu ........ 24 B1
Paroo → ..... 63 B3
Páros ........ 23 F5
Parral ........ 94 D2
Parramatta .... 63 B5
Parry Sound .. 69 D3
Partinico ..... 21 E4
Paru → ...... 92 C3
Paruro ....... 91 F4
Parvân □ ..... 42 B6
Parvatipuram .. 40 H4
Pasadena, Calif.,
  U.S.A. ...... 82 C3
Pasadena, Tex.,
  U.S.A. ...... 79 E6
Pasaje ....... 90 D3
Pascagoula ... 79 D9
Paşcani ....... 17 E8
Pasco ........ 80 B4
Pasco, Cerro de 91 F3
Pashmakli =
  Smolyan .... 22 D5
Pašman ...... 20 C5
Pasni ........ 42 G3
Paso de Indios 95 E3
Passau ....... 15 D7
Passero, C. ... 21 F5
Passo Fundo .. 94 B6

Passos ....... 93 G4
Pastaza → .... 90 D3
Pasto ........ 90 C3
Patagonia ..... 95 F3
Patan, India ... 43 H8
Patan, Nepal .. 40 D5
Patani ........ 39 D3
Patchewollock . 62 C3
Patea ........ 64 C6
Pategi ........ 55 G6
Paternò ...... 21 F5
Paterson ...... 73 D8
Pathankot .... 42 C9
Patiala ....... 42 D10
Patkai Bum ... 41 D10
Pátmos ....... 23 F6
Patna ........ 40 E5
Patos, L. dos .. 94 C6
Patos de Minas 93 F4
Patquía ...... 94 C3
Pátrai ........ 23 E3
Pátraikós Kólpos 23 E3
Patras = Pátrai 23 E3
Patrocínio .... 93 F4
Pattani ....... 36 C2
Patuakhali .... 41 F8
Pau .......... 12 E3
Pauini → ..... 90 D6
Pauk ........ 41 G10
Paulis = Isiro .. 57 D5
Paulistana .... 92 D5
Paulo Afonso .. 93 D6
Pavia ........ 20 B2
Pavlodar ...... 29 D8
Pavlograd =
  Pavlohrad ... 25 D4
Pavlohrad .... 25 D4
Pavlovo ...... 24 B5
Pavlovsk ..... 24 C5
Pawtucket ... 73 D10
Paxoí ........ 23 E3
Payakumbuh .. 37 E2
Payne Bay =
  Kangirsuk ... 68 C4
Paysandú ..... 94 C5
Paz, B. la ..... 84 C2
Pazar ........ 46 B5
Pazardzhik ... 22 C5
Peace → ..... 70 C8
Peak Hill ..... 63 B4
Peake ........ 62 C2
' Peake Cr. → .. 62 A2
Pebane ....... 59 B7
Pebas ........ 90 D4
Peć .......... 22 C3
Pechenga .... 28 C4
Pechenizhyn .. 17 D7
Pechora → ... 28 C6
Pechorskaya
  Guba ....... 28 C6
Pecos → ..... 78 E3
Pécs ......... 16 E4
Pedder, L. .... 62 D4
Pedirka ...... 62 A2
Pedra Azul ... 93 F5
Pedreiras ..... 92 C5
Pedro Afonso . 93 D4
Pedro Juan
  Caballero ... 94 A5
Peebinga ..... 62 B3
Peel →,
  Australia .... 63 B5
Peel →, Canada 70 B6
Peera Peera
  Poolanna L. . 62 A2
Pegasus Bay .. 65 E5
Pegu ......... 41 J11
Pegu Yoma ... 41 H10
Pehuajó ...... 94 D4

Peine ........ 14 B6
Peip'ing =
  Beijing ..... 35 C6
Peipus, L. =
  Chudskoye,
  Oz. ........ 24 B2
Peixe ........ 93 E4
Pekalongan ... 37 F3
Pekanbaru ... 37 D2
Pekin ........ 77 E10
Peking = Beijing 35 C6
Pelagie, Is. .... 21 G4
Pelaihari ...... 37 E4
Peleaga, Vf. ... 17 F6
Peleng ....... 39 E2
Pelješac ..... 20 C6
Pelly → ...... 70 B6
Pelly Bay .... 68 B2
Pelly L. ...... 70 B9
Peloponnese =
  Pelopónnisos □
  ......... 23 F4
Pelopónnisos □ 23 F4
Peloro, C. ..... 21 E5
Pelorus Sd. ... 65 D5
Pelotas ...... 94 C6
Pelvoux, Massif
  du ........ 13 D7
Pematangsiantar 37 D1
Pemba I. ...... 57 F7
Pembroke,
  Canada ..... 69 D3
Pembroke, U.K. 11 F4
Penang =
  Pinang ... 36 C2
Penápolis ..... 94 A6
Peñarroya-
  Pueblonuevo 18 C3
Peñas, C. de .. 18 A3
Penas, G. de .. 95 F2
Pench'i = Benxi 35 B7
Pend Oreille L. 80 A5
Pendembu .... 55 G2
Pendleton .... 80 C4
Penedo ....... 93 E6
Penguin ...... 62 D4
Peniche ...... 18 C1
Penida ....... 37 F5
Peninsular
  Malaysia □ .. 37 D2
Penmarch, Pte.
  de ........ 12 C1
Pennines ..... 11 D5
Pennsylvania □ 73 D7
Penola ....... 62 C3
Penong ...... 60 G5
Penrith ...... 63 B5
Pensacola .... 74 D4
Pensacola Mts. 96 C4
Penshurst .... 62 C3
Penticton .... 71 D8
Pentland Firth . 10 B5
Penza ....... 24 C6
Penzance .... 11 F4
Peoria ....... 77 E10
Perabumulih .. 37 E2
Perche, Collines
  du ........ 12 B4
Perdido, Mte. .. 19 A6
Perdu, Mt. =
  Perdido, Mte. 19 A6
Pereira ....... 90 C3
Perekerten ... 62 B3
Pereyaslav-
  Khmelnytskyy 24 C3
Pergamino .... 94 C4
Péribonca → . 69 D3
Perico ....... 94 A3
Périgueux .... 12 D4

Perijá,
  Sierra de..... 90 B4
Perlas, Arch. de
  las ........ 86 E4
Perm ........ 29 D6
Pernambuco =
  Recife ...... 92 D7
Pernatty
  Lagoon ...... 62 B2
Pernik ....... 22 C4
Perpendicular
  Pt. ......... 63 B5
Perpignan .... 13 E5
Persepolis .... 44 D3
Pershotravensk 17 C8
Persian Gulf =
  Gulf, The ... 44 E2
Perth, Australia 60 G2
Perth, U.K. .... 10 C5
Perth Amboy .. 73 D8
Peru ■ ....... 90 C3
Perúgia ...... 20 C4
Pervomaysk .. 25 D3
Pervouralsk ... 29 D6
Pésaro ...... 20 C4
Pescara ...... 20 C5
Peshawar ..... 42 B7
Peshkopi .... 22 D3
Pesqueira .... 92 D6
Petah Tiqwa .. 46 D3
Petauke ...... 59 A6
Peter I.s Øy ... 96 A2
Peterborough,
  Australia .... 62 B2
Peterborough,
  Canada ..... 69 D3
Peterborough,
  U.K. ........ 11 E6
Peterhead .... 10 C6
Petersburg,
  Alaska, U.S.A. 71 C6
Petersburg, Va.,
  U.S.A. ...... 73 F7
Petitsikapau, L. 69 C4
Petlad ....... 43 H8
Peto ........ 85 C7
Petone ...... 65 D6
Petrich ...... 22 D4
Petrikov =
  Pyetrikaw ... 17 B9
Petrograd =
  Sankt-
  Peterburg ... 24 B3
Petrolândia .. 93 D6
Petrolina .... 93 D5
Petropavl ..... 29 D7
Petropavlovsk =
  Petropavl ... 29 D7
Petropavlovsk-
  Kamchatskiy 31 D13
Petrópolis ... 93 G5
Petroşani .... 17 F6
Petrovaradin .. 22 B2
Petrovsk ..... 24 C6
Petrozavodsk . 28 C4
Peureulak .... 36 D1
Pforzheim ... 14 D5
Phagwara .... 42 D9
Phalodi ...... 42 F8
Phan Rang ... 36 B3
Phangan, Ko .. 36 C2
Phangnga .... 36 C1
Phatthalung .. 36 C2
Phetchabun .. 36 A2
Philadelphia .. 73 E8
Philippines ■ . 38 B2
Philippopolis =
  Plovdiv .... 22 C5
Phillip I. ...... 63 C4

| | | | |
|---|---|---|---|
| Phillott | 63 | A4 |
| Phitsanulok | 36 | A2 |
| Phnom Dangrek | 36 | B2 |
| Phnom Penh | 36 | B2 |
| Phoenix | 83 | D6 |
| Phra Nakhon Si | | |
| Ayutthaya | 36 | B2 |
| Phuket | 36 | C1 |
| Phumiphon, | | |
| Khuan | 36 | A1 |
| Piacenza | 20 | B2 |
| Pialba | 63 | A5 |
| Pian Cr. → | 63 | B4 |
| Pianosa | 20 | C3 |
| Piatra Neamţ | 17 | E8 |
| Piauí □ | 92 | D5 |
| Piave → | 20 | B4 |
| Pibor Post | 53 | G5 |
| Pica | 91 | H5 |
| Picardie | 13 | B5 |
| Picardy = | | |
| Picardie | 13 | B5 |
| Pichilemu | 94 | C2 |
| Pico Truncado | 95 | F3 |
| Picton, Australia | 63 | B5 |
| Picton, N.Z. | 65 | D6 |
| Pictou | 69 | D4 |
| Picún Leufú | 95 | D3 |
| Piedmont = | | |
| Piemonte □ | 20 | B1 |
| Piedras, R. de | | |
| las → | 91 | F5 |
| Piedras Negras | 84 | B4 |
| Piemonte □ | 20 | B1 |
| Pierre Elliott | | |
| Trudeau, Mt. | 70 | B5 |
| Piet Retief | 59 | D6 |
| Pietermaritzburg | 59 | D6 |
| Pietersburg | 59 | C5 |
| Pietrosul, | | |
| Romania | 17 | E7 |
| Pigüe | 94 | D4 |
| Piketberg | 58 | E3 |
| Piła | 16 | B3 |
| Pilar, Brazil | 93 | D6 |
| Pilar, Paraguay | 94 | B5 |
| Pilas Group | 38 | C2 |
| Pilcomayo → | 94 | B5 |
| Pilibhit | 42 | E11 |
| Pilica → | 16 | C5 |
| Pílos | 23 | F3 |
| Pilsen = Plzeň | 16 | D1 |
| Pimba | 62 | B2 |
| Pimenta Bueno | 91 | F6 |
| Pimentel | 91 | E3 |
| Pinang | 36 | C2 |
| Pinar del Río | 86 | B3 |
| Pınarhisar | 22 | D6 |
| Pińczów | 16 | C5 |
| Pindiga | 55 | G7 |
| Pindos Óros | 23 | E3 |
| Pindus Mts. = | | |
| Pindos Óros | 23 | E3 |
| Pine Bluff | 79 | B7 |
| Pine Point | 70 | B8 |
| Pinega → | 28 | C5 |
| Pinerolo | 20 | B1 |
| Pinetown | 59 | D6 |
| Ping → | 36 | A2 |
| Pingdong | 35 | D7 |
| Pingliang | 35 | C5 |
| Pingwu | 35 | C5 |
| Pingxiang | 35 | D5 |
| Pinhel | 18 | B2 |
| Pini | 37 | D1 |
| Piniós → | 23 | E4 |
| Pinnaroo | 62 | C3 |
| Pinnes, Ákra | 23 | D5 |
| Pinrang | 39 | E1 |
| Pinsk | 17 | B8 |
| Pintados | 91 | H5 |
| Pinyug | 24 | A6 |
| Piombino | 20 | C3 |
| Pioner, Os. | 30 | B7 |
| Piorini, L. | 90 | D6 |
| Piotrków | | |
| Trybunalski | 16 | C4 |
| Pīp | 45 | E5 |
| Piquiri → | 94 | A6 |
| Piracicaba | 94 | A7 |
| Piracuruca | 92 | C5 |
| Piræus = | | |
| Piraiévs | 23 | F4 |
| Piraiévs | 23 | F4 |
| Pirané | 94 | B5 |
| Pirapora | 93 | F5 |
| Pírgos | 23 | F3 |
| Pirin Planina | 22 | D4 |
| Piripiri | 92 | C5 |
| Pirmasens | 14 | D4 |
| Pirot | 22 | C4 |
| Piru | 39 | E3 |
| Pisa | 20 | C3 |
| Pisagua | 91 | G4 |
| Pisciotta | 21 | D5 |
| Pisco | 91 | F3 |
| Písek | 16 | D2 |
| Pishan | 34 | C2 |
| Pising | 39 | F2 |
| Pistóia | 20 | C3 |
| Pisuerga → | 18 | B3 |
| Pitarpunga, L. | 62 | B3 |
| Pitcairn I. | 65 | M17 |
| Piteå | 8 | E12 |
| Piteşti | 22 | B5 |
| Pithapuram | 40 | J4 |
| Pittsburg | 79 | A6 |
| Pittsburgh | 73 | D5 |
| Pittsworth | 63 | A5 |
| Piura | 90 | E2 |
| Placentia | 69 | D5 |
| Placentia B. | 69 | D5 |
| Plainview | 78 | B3 |
| Pláka, Ákra | 23 | G6 |
| Plakhino | 28 | C9 |
| Plasencia | 18 | B2 |
| Plata, Río de la | 94 | C5 |
| Platani → | 21 | F4 |
| Plato | 90 | B4 |
| Platte → | 77 | F7 |
| Plauen | 15 | C7 |
| Pleiku | 36 | B3 |
| Plenty, B. of | 64 | B7 |
| Pleven | 22 | C5 |
| Plevlja | 22 | C2 |
| Płock | 16 | B4 |
| Plöckenstein | 15 | D7 |
| Ploieşti | 22 | B6 |
| Plovdiv | 22 | C5 |
| Plumtree | 59 | C5 |
| Plymouth | 11 | F4 |
| Plzeň | 16 | D1 |
| Po → | 20 | B4 |
| Po Hai = Bo Hai | 35 | C6 |
| Pobedy Pik | 29 | E8 |
| Pocatello | 81 | D7 |
| Poços de Caldas | 93 | G4 |
| Podgorica | 22 | C2 |
| Podilska | | |
| Vysochyna | 17 | D8 |
| Podkamennaya | | |
| Tunguska → | 30 | C7 |
| Podolsk | 24 | B4 |
| Podor | 55 | E1 |
| Pofadder | 58 | D3 |
| Poh | 39 | E2 |
| Pohnpei | 64 | J10 |
| Poinsett, C. | 96 | A12 |
| Pointe-à-Pitre | 87 | C7 |
| Pointe Noire | 56 | E2 |
| Poitiers | 12 | C4 |
| Poitou | 12 | C3 |
| Pokaran | 42 | F7 |
| Pokataroo | 63 | A4 |
| Pokrovsk = | | |
| Engels | 24 | C6 |
| Pola = Pula | 20 | B4 |
| Polan | 45 | E5 |
| Poland ■ | 16 | B5 |
| Polatsk | 24 | B2 |
| Polcura | 94 | D2 |
| Polesye = Pripet | | |
| Marshes | 17 | B9 |
| Poli | 56 | C2 |
| Police | 16 | B2 |
| Polillo Is. | 38 | B2 |
| Políyiros | 23 | D4 |
| Pollachi | 43 | P10 |
| Polnovat | 28 | C7 |
| Polonne | 17 | C8 |
| Polonnoye = | | |
| Polonne | 17 | C8 |
| Poltava | 24 | D3 |
| Polunochnoye | 28 | C7 |
| Polynesia | 65 | L15 |
| Polynésie | | |
| française = | | |
| French | | |
| Polynesia ■ | 65 | M16 |
| Pombal, Brazil | 92 | D6 |
| Pombal, | | |
| Portugal | 18 | C1 |
| Pomézia | 20 | D4 |
| Pomorski, | | |
| Pojezierze | 16 | B3 |
| Ponape = | | |
| Pohnpei | 64 | J10 |
| Ponca City | 78 | A5 |
| Ponce | 87 | C6 |
| Pond Inlet | 68 | A3 |
| Pondicherry | 43 | P11 |
| Ponferrada | 18 | A2 |
| Ponnani | 43 | P9 |
| Ponnyadaung | 41 | F10 |
| Ponoy → | 28 | C5 |
| Ponta Grossa | 94 | B6 |
| Ponta Pora | 94 | A5 |
| Pontarlier | 13 | C7 |
| Pontchartrain L. | 79 | D8 |
| Ponte Nova | 93 | G5 |
| Pontevedra | 18 | A1 |
| Pontiac | 72 | C4 |
| Pontianak | 37 | E3 |
| Pontine Is. = | | |
| Ponziane, | | |
| Ísole | 21 | D4 |
| Pontine Mts. = | | |
| Kuzey | | |
| Anadolu | | |
| Dağları | 46 | B3 |
| Pontivy | 12 | B2 |
| Pontoise | 12 | B5 |
| Ponziane, Ísole | 21 | D4 |
| Poochera | 62 | B1 |
| Poole | 11 | F6 |
| Poona = Pune | 43 | K8 |
| Pooncarie | 62 | B3 |
| Poopelloe L. | 63 | B3 |
| Poopó, L. de | 91 | G5 |
| Popayán | 90 | C3 |
| Popigay | 30 | B9 |
| Popilta, L. | 62 | B3 |
| Popio L. | 62 | B3 |
| Poplar Bluff | 79 | A8 |
| Popocatépetl, | | |
| Volcán | 84 | D5 |
| Popokabaka | 56 | F3 |
| Poprád | 16 | D5 |
| Porbandar | 43 | J6 |
| Porcupine → | 71 | B5 |
| Pordenone | 20 | B4 |
| Pori | 8 | F12 |
| Porkkala | 9 | G12 |
| Porlamar | 90 | A6 |
| Poroshiri-Dake | 32 | F12 |
| Porpoise B. | 96 | A13 |
| Porretta, Passo | | |
| di | 20 | B3 |
| Port Adelaide | 62 | B2 |
| Port Alberni | 71 | D7 |
| Port Alfred | 59 | E5 |
| Port Angeles | 80 | A2 |
| Port Antonio | 86 | C4 |
| Port Arthur, | | |
| Australia | 62 | D4 |
| Port Arthur, | | |
| U.S.A. | 79 | E7 |
| Port-au-Prince | 87 | C5 |
| Port Augusta | 62 | B2 |
| Port Augusta | | |
| West | 62 | B2 |
| Port Bergé | | |
| Vaovao | 59 | H9 |
| Port Bou | 19 | A7 |
| Port Broughton | 62 | B2 |
| Port-Cartier | 69 | C4 |
| Port Chalmers | 65 | F4 |
| Port Darwin | 95 | G5 |
| Port Davey | 62 | D4 |
| Port Dickson | 37 | D2 |
| Port Elizabeth | 59 | E5 |
| Port Fairy | 62 | C3 |
| Port-Gentil | 56 | E1 |
| Port Harcourt | 55 | H6 |
| Port Harrison = | | |
| Inukjuak | 68 | C3 |
| Port | | |
| Hawkesbury | 69 | D4 |
| Port Hedland | 60 | E2 |
| Port Huron | 72 | C4 |
| Port Kembla | 63 | B5 |
| Port Kenny | 62 | B1 |
| Port Lairge = | | |
| Waterford | 11 | E3 |
| Port Laoise | 11 | E3 |
| Port Lincoln | 62 | B2 |
| Port Loko | 55 | G2 |
| Port MacDonnell | 62 | C3 |
| Port Macquarie | 63 | B5 |
| Port Moresby | 61 | B8 |
| Port Nelson | 71 | C10 |
| Port Nolloth | 58 | D3 |
| Port Nouveau- | | |
| Québec = | | |
| Kangiqsualujjuaq | | |
| | 68 | C4 |
| Port of Spain | 87 | D7 |
| Port Pegasus | 65 | G2 |
| Port Phillip B. | 63 | C3 |
| Port Pirie | 62 | B2 |
| Port Safaga = | | |
| Bûr Safâga | 52 | C5 |
| Port Said = Bûr | | |
| Sa'îd | 52 | B5 |
| Port Shepstone | 59 | E6 |
| Port Stanley = | | |
| Stanley | 95 | G5 |
| Port Sudan = | | |
| Bûr Sûdân | 53 | E6 |
| Port Talbot | 11 | F5 |
| Port-Vendres | 13 | E5 |
| Port Wakefield | 62 | B2 |
| Port Weld | 36 | D2 |
| Porta Orientalis | 22 | B4 |

# Portachuelo

Portachuelo ... 91 G6
Portadown .... 11 D3
Portage La
  Prairie ...... 71 D10
Portalegre .... 18 C2
Portile de Fier . 22 B4
Portimão ..... 18 D1
Portland,
  N.S.W.,
  Australia .... 63 B4
Portland, Vic.,
  Australia .... 62 C3
Portland, Maine,
  U.S.A. ...... 73 C10
Portland, Oreg.,
  U.S.A. ...... 80 C2
Portland B. .... 62 C3
Portland Prom. 68 C3
Porto ........ 18 B1
Pôrto Alegre .. 94 C6
Porto Amboim
  = Gunza .. 56 G2
Pôrto de Móz .. 92 C3
Porto
  Empédocle .. 21 F4
Pôrto Esperança 91 G7
Pôrto Franco .. 92 D4
Porto Mendes . 94 A6
Pôrto Murtinho 91 H7
Pôrto Nacional 93 E4
Porto Novo ... 55 G5
Porto Santo .. 54 B1
Pôrto Seguro .. 93 F6
Porto Tórres .. 20 D2
Pôrto União .. 94 B6
Pôrto Válter ... 91 E4
Porto-Vecchio . 13 F8
Pôrto Velho .. 91 E6
Portoferráio ... 20 C3
Portoscuso .... 21 E2
Portoviejo .... 90 D2
Portree ....... 10 C3
Portsmouth,
  U.K. ...... 11 F6
Portsmouth,
  U.S.A. ...... 73 F7
Porttipahtan
  tekojärvi .... 8 E13
Portugal ■ .... 18 C1
Porvenir ...... 95 G2
Posadas ...... 94 B5
Poshan =
  Boshan ..... 35 C6
Poso ......... 39 E2
Posse ........ 93 E4
Possel ....... 56 C3
Possession I. .. 96 B15
Poste Maurice
  Cortier ..... 54 D5
Postojna ...... 20 B5
Potchefstroom . 59 D5
Potenza ...... 21 D5
Poteriteri, L. ... 65 G2
Potgietersrus .. 59 C5
Poti ......... 25 E5
Potiskum ..... 55 F7
Potomac → .. 73 E7
Potosí ....... 91 G5
Pototan ...... 38 B2
Potrerillos .... 94 B3
Potsdam ..... 15 B7
Poughkeepsie . 73 D9
Pouso Alegre .. 93 E2
Považská
  Bystrica .. 16 D4
Povenets ..... 28 C4
Poverty B. .... 64 C8
Póvoa de Varzim 18 B1

Powder → ... 76 B2
Powell L. ..... 83 B7
Poyang Hu .... 35 D6
Požarevac .... 22 B3
Poznań ...... 16 B3
Pozo Almonte . 91 H5
Pozoblanco ... 18 C3
Pozzuoli ..... 21 D5
Prachuap Khiri
  Khan ....... 36 B1
Prado ........ 93 F6
Prague = Praha 16 C2
Praha ........ 16 C2
Prainha,
  Amazonas,
  Brazil ....... 91 E6
Prainha, Pará,
  Brazil ....... 92 C3
Prairies ....... 71 C9
Prapat ....... 37 D1
Prata ........ 93 F4
Prato ........ 20 C3
Pravia ....... 18 A2
Praya ........ 37 F5
Preparis North
  Channel .... 41 K9
Preparis South
  Channel .... 41 K9
Přerov ....... 16 D3
Preservation
  Inlet ....... 65 G2
Presidencia
  Roque Saenz
  Peña ...... 94 B4
Presidente
  Epitácio .... 93 G3
Presidente
  Hermes .... 91 F6
Presidente
  Prudente .... 93 G3
Prešov ....... 16 D5
Prespa, L. =
  Prespansko
  Jezero ...... 23 D3
Prespansko
  Jezero ...... 23 D3
Presque Isle .. 73 A11
Preston ...... 11 E5
Pretoria ...... 59 D5
Préveza ...... 23 E3
Příbram ...... 16 D2
Prichard ...... 74 D3
Prieska ....... 58 D4
Prievidza ..... 16 D4
Prilep ........ 22 D3
Priluki = Pryluky 24 C3
Prime Seal I. .. 62 D4
Prince Albert .. 71 C9
Prince Albert
  Mts. ........ 96 B15
Prince Albert
  Pen. ....... 70 A8
Prince Albert Sd. 70 A8
Prince Charles I. 68 B3
Prince Charles
  Mts. ........ 96 B10
Prince Edward
  I. □ ....... 69 D4
Prince of Wales
  I., Canada .. 70 A10
Prince of Wales
  I., U.S.A. .... 71 C6
Principe da
  Beira ...... 91 F6
Prins Harald
  Kyst ........ 96 B8
Prinsesse Astrid
  Kyst ........ 96 B7

Prinsesse
  Ragnhild Kyst 96 B8
Pripet → =
  Prypyat → .. 17 C10
Pripet Marshes 17 B9
Pripyat Marshes
  = Pripet
  Marshes .... 17 B9
Pripyats =
  Prypyat → .. 17 C10
Priština ....... 22 C3
Privas ........ 13 D6
Privolzhskaya
  Vozvyshennost
  .......... 24 C6
Prizren ....... 22 C3
Proddatur ..... 43 M11
Progreso ..... 85 C7
Prokopyevsk .. 29 D9
Prokuplje ..... 22 C3
Prome = Pyè .. 41 H10
Propriá ...... 93 E6
Prostějov ..... 16 D3
Proston ...... 63 A5
Provence ..... 13 E6
Providence .... 73 D10
Providencia, I.
  de ......... 86 D3
Provins ...... 13 B5
Provo ....... 81 E8
Prozna → .... 16 B3
Pruszków .... 16 B5
Prut → ...... 17 F9
Pruzhany .... 17 B7
Prydz B. ..... 96 A10
Pryluky ...... 24 C3
Prypyat → ... 17 C10
Przemyśl .... 17 D6
Przhevalsk ... 29 E8
Psará ....... 23 E5
Pskov ....... 24 B2
Ptich =
  Ptsich → ... 17 B9
Ptsich → ..... 17 B9
Puán ........ 94 D4
Pucallpa ...... 91 E4
Pudukkottai .. 43 P11
Puebla ....... 84 D5
Pueblo ....... 76 F2
Pueblo Hundido 94 B2
Puelches ..... 94 D3
Puente Alto ... 94 C2
Puente-Genil .. 18 D3
Puerto Aisén . 95 F2
Puerto
  Ayacucho ... 90 B5
Puerto Barrios . 85 D7
Puerto Bermejo 94 B4
Puerto
  Bermúdez .. 91 F4
Puerto Bolívar . 90 D3
Puerto Cabello 90 A5
Puerto Cabezas 86 D3
Puerto Carreño 90 B5
Puerto Chicama 91 E3
Puerto Coig ... 95 G3
Puerto Cortés . 85 D7
Puerto
  Cumarebo . 90 A5
Puerto del
  Rosario .... 54 C2
Puerto Deseado 95 F3
Puerto Heath . 91 F5
Puerto La Cruz 90 A6
Puerto
  Leguízamo . 90 D4
Puerto Lobos . 95 E3
Puerto Madryn 95 E3

Puerto
  Maldonado .. 91 F5
Puerto Montt .. 95 E2
Puerto Morelos 85 C7
Puerto Natales 95 G2
Puerto Páez ... 90 B5
Puerto Pinasco 94 A5
Puerto
  Pirámides ... 95 E4
Puerto Plata ... 87 C5
Puerto Princesa 38 C1
Puerto Quellón 95 E2
Puerto Rico ■ . 87 C6
Puerto Sastre . 91 H7
Puerto Suárez . 91 G7
Puerto Wilches 90 B4
Puertollano ... 18 C3
Pueyrredón, L. . 95 F2
Pugachev ..... 24 C6
Puget Sound .. 80 B2
Puigcerdá .... 19 A6
Pukaki L. ..... 65 F4
Pukapuka .... 65 L14
Pukekohe .... 64 B6
Pula ......... 20 B4
Puławy ...... 16 C5
Pullman ...... 80 B5
Pulog ........ 38 A2
Pułtusk ...... 16 B5
Puna ........ 91 G5
Puná, I. ...... 90 D2
Punakha ..... 41 D7
Punata ...... 91 G5
Punch ....... 42 C9
Pune ........ 43 K8
Punjab □, India 42 D9
Punjab □,
  Pakistan .... 42 D8
Puno ........ 91 G4
Punta Alta ... 94 D4
Punta Arenas .. 95 G2
Punta de Díaz . 94 B2
Puntabie ..... 62 B3
Puntarenas ... 86 E3
Punto Fijo .... 90 A4
Puquio ....... 91 F4
Pur → ....... 28 C8
Purace, Vol. ... 90 C3
Puralia =
  Puruliya ... 40 F6
Puri ......... 40 H5
Purnia ....... 40 E6
Purukcahu ... 37 E4
Puruliya ...... 40 F6
Purus → ..... 90 D6
Pusan ....... 35 C7
Pushkino .... 24 C6
Putao ....... 41 D11
Putaruru ..... 64 C6
Puthein Myit → 41 K10
Putignano .... 21 D6
Puting, Tanjung 37 E4
Putorana, Gory 30 C7
Puttalam ..... 43 Q11
Puttgarden ... 15 A6
Putumayo → . 90 D5
Putussibau .... 37 D4
Puy-de-Dôme . 13 D5
Pweto ....... 57 F5
Pwllheli ...... 11 E4
Pyapon ...... 41 J10
Pyasina → ... 30 B6
Pyatigorsk .... 25 E5
Pyè ......... 41 H10
Pyetrikaw .... 17 B9
Pyinmana .... 41 H11
P'yŏngyang .. 35 C7
Pyrénées ..... 19 A6
Pyu ......... 41 H11

# Q

Qādib ........ 49 E5
Qā'emshahr ... 44 B3
Qahremānshahr
= Bākhtarān . 46 D6
Qaidam Pendi . 34 C4
Qalāt ......... 45 C6
Qal'at al Akhḍar 47 E4
Qal'eh Shaharak 42 B4
Qal'eh-ye Now 45 C5
Qamar, Ghubbat
al .......... 49 D5
Qamruddin
Karez ....... 42 D6
Qandahār ..... 42 D4
Qandahār □ ... 42 D4
Qapshaghay .. 29 E8
Qâra ......... 52 C4
Qarabutaq .... 29 E7
Qarachuk ..... 46 C5
Qaraghandy ... 29 E8
Qārah ........ 47 E5
Qarataū ...... 29 E8
Qarqan ....... 34 C3
Qarqan He → . 34 C3
Qarqaraly ..... 29 E8
Qarshi ....... 29 F7
Qaṣr-e Qand .. 45 E5
Qasr Farâfra . 52 C4
Qatar ■ ...... 44 E2
Qattâra,
Munkhafed el 52 C4
Qattâra
Depression =
Qattâra,
Munkhafed el 52 C4
Qāyen ........ 44 C4
Qazaqstan =
Kazakstan ■ . 29 E7
Qazvin ....... 46 C7
Qena ......... 52 C5
Qeshm ....... 44 E4
Qila Safed .... 42 E2
Qila Saifullāh .. 42 D6
Qilian Shan .. 34 C4
Qingdao ...... 35 C7
Qinghai □ .... 34 C4
Qinghai Hu ... 34 C5
Qinhuangdao .. 35 C6
Qinzhou ...... 35 D5
Qiqihar ....... 35 B7
Qitai ......... 34 B3
Qom .......... 44 C2
Qomsheh ..... 44 C2
Qondūz ...... 45 B7
Qondūz □ .... 45 B7
Qostanay ..... 29 D7
Qu Xian,
*Sichuan,*
*China* ....... 35 C5
Qu Xian,
*Zhejiang,*
*China* ....... 35 D6
Quambatook .. 62 C3
Quambone .... 63 B4
Quan Long .... 36 C3
Quandialla ... 63 B4
Quang Ngai .. 36 A3
Quanzhou .... 35 D6
Quaqtaq ...... 68 B4
Quaraí ....... 94 C5
Quartu
Sant'Elena .. 21 E2
Quatsino ..... 71 C7
Quba ........ 25 E6
Qūchān ...... 44 B4
Queanbeyan .. 63 C4
Québec ....... 69 D3

Québec □ .... 69 D3
Queen
Alexandra Ra. 96 C15
Queen Charlotte
Is. ......... 70 C6
Queen Charlotte
Str. ........ 71 C7
Queen Elizabeth
Is. ......... 66 B9
Queen Mary
Land ....... 96 B11
Queen Maud G. 70 B9
Queen Maud
Land ....... 96 B7
Queen Maud
Mts. ....... 96 C16
Queenscliff ... 63 C3
Queensland □ . 61 E7
Queenstown,
*Australia* .... 62 D4
Queenstown,
*N.Z.* ....... 65 F3
Queenstown,
*S. Africa* .... 59 E5
Queimadas ... 93 E6
Quela ........ 56 F3
Quelimane .... 59 B7
Quelpart =
Cheju Do ... 35 C7
Quequén ..... 94 D5
Querétaro .... 84 C4
Quetta ....... 42 D5
Quezon City .. 38 B2
Qui Nhon ..... 36 B3
Quibaxe ...... 56 F2
Quibdo ....... 90 B3
Quiberon ..... 12 C2
Quilán, C. .... 95 E2
Quilengues ... 58 A2
Quillabamba .. 91 F4
Quillagua .... 91 H5
Quillota ...... 94 C2
Quilon ....... 43 Q10
Quilpie ...... 63 A3
Quimilí ...... 94 B4
Quimper ..... 12 B1
Quimperlé ... 12 C2
Quincy ...... 77 F9
Quines ...... 94 C3
Quinga ...... 59 H8
Quintanar de la
Orden ..... 18 C4
Quintero ..... 94 C2
Quinyambie .. 62 B3
Quipungo .... 58 A2
Quirindi ..... 63 B5
Quissanga ... 59 G8
Quitilipi ..... 94 B4
Quito ........ 90 D3
Quixadá ..... 92 C6
Qŭnghirot ... 29 E6
Quondong ... 62 B3
Quorn ...... 62 B2
Qŭqon ...... 29 E8
Qûs ........ 52 C5
Quseir ...... 52 C5
Qyzylorda ... 29 E7

# R

Raahe ....... 8 F12
Raba ........ 39 F1
Rába → ..... 16 E3
Rabat, *Malta* . 21 G5
Rabat, *Morocco* 54 B3
Rabaul ...... 64 K10

Rābigh ....... 47 G4
Race, C. ...... 69 D5
Rach Gia .... 36 B3
Racibórz ..... 16 C4
Racine ....... 72 C2
Rădăuṭi ...... 17 E7
Radekhiv .... 17 C7
Radekhov =
Radekhiv ... 17 C7
Radhwa, Jabal 47 F4
Radom ...... 16 C5
Radomsko ... 16 C4
Radomyshl ... 17 C9
Radstock, C. ... 62 B1
Rae .......... 70 B8
Rae Bareli ... 40 D3
Rae Isthmus .. 68 B2
Raetihi ...... 64 C6
Rafaela ..... 94 C4
Rafai ....... 56 D4
Rafḥā ....... 47 E5
Rafsanjān ... 44 D4
Ragachow ... 17 B10
Ragama ..... 43 R11
Raglan ...... 64 B6
Ragusa ...... 21 F5
Raha ........ 39 E2
Rahad al Bardī 53 F3
Rahaeng = Tak 36 A1
Rahimyar Khan 42 E7
Raichur ...... 43 L10
Raigarh ..... 40 G4
Railton ...... 62 D4
Rainier, Mt. ... 80 B3
Raipur ...... 40 G3
Ra'is ........ 47 G4
Raj Nandgaon . 40 G3
Raja, Ujung ... 37 D1
Raja Ampat,
Kepulauan .. 39 E3
Rajahmundry .. 40 J3
Rajang → .... 37 D4
Rajapalaiyam .. 43 Q10
Rajasthan □ ... 42 F8
Rajasthan Canal 42 F8
Rajgarh ..... 43 G10
Rajkot ...... 43 H7
Rajpipla ..... 43 J8
Rajshahi .... 41 E7
Rakaia ...... 65 E5
Rakaia → .... 65 E5
Rakan, Ra's .. 44 E2
Rakaposhi ... 42 A9
Rakata, Pulau . 37 F3
Rakhiv ..... 17 D7
Raleigh ..... 75 B8
Ram Hd. ... 63 C4
Ramanathapuram
........... 43 Q11
Ramechhap ... 40 D6
Ramelau .... 39 F3
Ramgarh, *Bihar,*
*India* ....... 40 F5
Ramgarh, *Raj.,*
*India* ....... 42 F7
Rāmhormoz ... 47 E7
Ramnad =
Ramanathapuram
........... 43 Q11
Rampur ..... 42 E11
Rampur Hat .. 40 E6
Ramree I. =
Ramree Kyun 41 H9
Ramree Kyun . 41 H9
Ramtek ..... 43 J11
Ranaghat ... 41 F7
Ranau ...... 36 C5
Rancagua ... 94 C2
Ranchi ...... 40 F5

Randers ...... 9 G10
Rangaunu B. .. 64 A5
Rangia ...... 41 D8
Rangiora .... 65 E5
Rangitaiki → . 64 B7
Rangitata → . 65 E4
Rangon → .. 41 J11
Rangoon .... 41 J11
Rangpur .... 41 E7
Ranibennur ... 43 M9
Raniganj ... 40 F6
Raniwara ... 43 G8
Rankin Inlet .. 70 B10
Rankins Springs 63 B4
Ranong .... 36 C1
Ransiki .... 39 E4
Rantau .... 37 E5
Rantauprapat .. 37 D1
Rantemario .. 39 E1
Rapa ....... 65 M16
Rapallo .... 20 B2
Rāpch ..... 45 E4
Rapid City .. 76 C3
Rarotonga ... 65 M14
Ra's al Khaymah 44 E4
Ra's al-Unuf .. 52 B2
Ras Bânâs .. 52 D6
Ras Dashen .. 57 B7
Râs Timirist .. 55 E1
Rasa, Punta .. 95 E4
Rashad .... 53 F5
Rashîd .... 52 B5
Rasht ...... 46 C7
Rat Islands .. 71 C1
Ratangarh .. 42 E9
Rathenow ... 15 B7
Ratibor =
Racibórz ... 16 C4
Ratlam .... 43 H9
Ratnagiri .... 43 L8
Raukumara Ra. 64 C7
Raurkela ... 40 F5
Rava-Ruska .. 17 C6
Rava Russkaya
= Rava-Ruska 17 C6
Rāvar ..... 44 D4
Ravenna ... 20 B4
Ravensburg .. 14 E5
Ravi → .... 42 D7
Rawalpindi ... 42 C8
Rawāndūz ... 46 C6
Rawene .... 64 A5
Rawlins .... 81 E10
Rawson .... 95 E3
Ray, C. .... 69 D5
Rayadurg .... 43 M10
Rayagada ... 40 H4
Raymond ... 71 D8
Raz, Pte. du .. 12 B1
Razdel'naya =
Rozdilna ... 17 E10
Razelm, Lacul . 22 B7
Razgrad .... 22 C6
Ré, I. de .... 12 C3
Reading, *U.K.* . 11 F6
Reading, *U.S.A.* 73 D8
Realicó .... 94 D4
Rebi ....... 39 F4
Rebiana .... 52 D3
Rebun-Tō ... 32 E12
Rechytsa ... 17 B10
Recife ...... 92 D7
Reconquista ... 94 B5
Recreo .... 94 B3
Red →, *La.,*
*U.S.A.* ....... 79 D8
Red →, *N. Dak.,*
*U.S.A.* .... 76 A6
Red Cliffs .... 62 B3

# Red Deer

Red Deer .... 71 C8
Red Sea ...... 48 C2
Red Tower Pass
= Turnu Roşu,
P. .......... 17 F7
Redcar ....... 11 D6
Redcliffe ...... 63 A5
Redding ...... 80 E2
Redditch ...... 11 E6
Redon ........ 12 C2
Redondela .... 18 A1
Redwood City . 82 B1
Ree, L. ....... 11 E3
Reefton ...... 65 E4
Regensburg ... 15 D7
Réggio di
  Calábria .... 21 E5
Réggio
  nell'Emília .. 20 B3
Reghin ....... 17 E7
Regina ....... 71 C9
Rehoboth ..... 58 C3
Rehovot ...... 46 E3
Rei-Bouba .... 53 G1
Reichenbach .. 15 C7
Reidsville ..... 75 A8
Reigate ....... 11 F6
Reims ........ 13 B6
Reina Adelaida,
  Arch. ...... 95 G2
Reindeer L. ... 71 C9
Reinga, C. .... 64 A5
Reinosa ...... 18 A3
Reliance ...... 70 B9
Remarkable, Mt. 62 B2
Remeshk ..... 45 E4
Rendsburg .... 14 A5
Rengat ....... 37 E2
Reni ......... 17 F9
Renk ........ 53 F5
Renmark ..... 62 B3
Rennes ....... 12 B3
Reno ........ 80 F4
Reno → ..... 20 B4
Rentería ..... 19 A5
Republican → 76 F6
Repulse Bay .. 68 B2
Requena, Peru . 90 E4
Requena, Spain 19 C5
Resadiye =
  Datça ..... 23 F6
Resht = Rasht . 46 C7
Resistencia ... 94 B5
Reşiţa ....... 17 F5
Resolution I.,
  Canada .... 68 B4
Resolution I.,
  N.Z. ...... 65 F2
Réthímnon ... 23 G5
Réunion ■ .... 51 J9
Reus ........ 19 B6
Reutlingen .... 14 D5
Reval = Tallinn 24 B1
Revelstoke ... 71 C8
Rewa ........ 40 E3
Rewari ....... 42 E10
Rey Malabo ... 56 D1
Reykjavík ..... 8 B2
Reynosa ...... 84 B5
Rhein → ..... 14 C4
Rhein-Main-
Donau-
  Kanal → ... 15 D6
Rheine ....... 14 B4
Rheinland-
  Pfalz □ .... 14 C4
Rhin =
  Rhein → ... 14 C4
Rhine =
  Rhein → ... 14 C4

Rhineland-
Palatinate □ =
Rheinland-
  Pfalz □ .... 14 C4
Rhode Island □ 73 D10
Rhodes =
  Ródhos ... 23 F7
Rhodope Mts. =
Rhodopi
  Planina .... 22 D5
Rhodopi Planina 22 D5
Rhön = Hohe
  Rhön ....... 14 C5
Rhondda ..... 11 F5
Rhône → .... 13 E6
Rhum ........ 10 C3
Riachão ...... 92 D4
Riasi ........ 42 C9
Riau □ ....... 37 E2
Riau, Kepulauan 37 D2
Riau Arch. =
Riau,
  Kepulauan .. 37 D2
Ribadeo ...... 18 A2
Ribeirão Prêto . 93 G4
Riberalta ..... 91 F5
Ribniţa ....... 17 E9
Riccarton ..... 65 E5
Richland ...... 80 B4
Richmond,
  Australia .... 63 B5
Richmond, N.Z. 65 D5
Richmond,
  Calif., U.S.A. 80 G2
Richmond, Va.,
  U.S.A. .... 73 F7
Richmond Ra. . 63 A5
Ridder ....... 29 D9
Ried ......... 15 D7
Riesa ........ 15 C7
Rieti ........ 20 C4
Rig Rig ...... 53 F1
Rīga ........ 24 B1
Riga, G. of .... 24 B1
Rīgas Jūras Līcis
  = Riga, G. of 24 B1
Rīgestān □ .... 42 D4
Rigolet ....... 68 C5
Riiser-Larsen-
  halvøya .... 96 A8
Rijeka ........ 20 B5
Rimah, Wadi
  ar → ...... 47 F5
Rímini ........ 20 B4
Rîmnicu Sărat . 17 F8
Rîmnicu Vîlcea 17 F7
Rimouski ..... 69 D4
Rinca ........ 39 F1
Rinconada .... 94 A3
Rinjani ....... 37 F5
Rio Branco,
  Brazil ..... 91 E5
Río Branco,
  Uruguay .... 94 C6
Río Cuarto .... 94 C4
Rio de Janeiro . 93 G5
Rio de
  Janeiro □ ... 93 G5
Rio do Sul .... 94 B7
Río Gallegos .. 95 G3
Río Grande,
  Argentina ... 95 G3
Rio Grande,
  Brazil ...... 94 C6
Rio Grande → 78
Rio Grande do
  Norte □ .... 92 D6
Rio Grande do
  Sul □ ...... 94 B6

Rio Largo ..... 93 D6
Río Mulatos ... 91 G5
Río Muni =
  Mbini □ ... 56 D2
Rio Negro .... 94 B7
Rio Verde ..... 93 F3
Ríobamba .... 90 D3
Ríohacha ..... 90 A4
Ríosucio,
  Caldas,
  Colombia ... 90 B3
Ríosucio, Choco,
  Colombia ... 90 B3
Rishiri-Tō .... 32 E12
Riva del Garda 20 B3
Rivadavia ..... 94 B2
Rivera ....... 94 C5
Riversdale .... 58 E4
Riverside ..... 82 D4
Riverton,
  Australia ... 62 B2
Riverton,
  Canada .... 71 C10
Riverton, N.Z. . 65 G2
Riviera di
  Levante ..... 20 B2
Riviera di
  Ponente .... 20 B2
Rivière-du-Loup 69 D4
Rivne ........ 17 C8
Rívoli ........ 20 B1
Rivoli B. ...... 62 C3
Riyadh = Ar
  Riyāḍ ..... 47 F6
Rize ......... 46 B5
Rizzuto, C. .... 21 E6
Roanne ...... 13 C6
Roanoke ...... 73 F6
Robbins I. .... 62 D4
Robertson .... 58 E3
Robertson I. ... 96 A4
Robertsport ... 55 G2
Robertstown .. 62 B2
Robinvale ..... 62 B3
Roboré ....... 91 G7
Robson, Mt. ... 71 C8
Roca, C. da ... 18 C1
Rocas, I. ...... 92 C7
Rocha ....... 94 C6
Rochefort ..... 12 D3
Rochester,
  Minn., U.S.A. 77 C8
Rochester, N.Y.,
  U.S.A. .... 73 C7
Rock Hill ..... 75 B7
Rock Island ... 77 E9
Rock Springs .. 81 E9
Rockefeller
  Plateau .... 96 C18
Rockford ..... 77 D10
Rockhampton . 61 E9
Rocky Mount .. 75 B9
Rocky Mts. ... 70 C7
Rod ......... 42 E3
Rodez ....... 13 D5
Ródhos ...... 23 F7
Rodney, C. .... 64 B6
Roes Welcome
  Sd. ....... 68 B2
Rogachev =
  Ragachow ... 17 B10
Rogagua, L. ... 91 F5
Rogatyn ...... 17 D7
Rogoaguado, L. 91 F5
Rohri ........ 42 F6
Rohtak ....... 42 E10
Roi Et ....... 36 A2
Rojas ........ 94 C4
Rojo, C. ...... 84 C5

Rokan → ..... 37 D2
Rolândia ...... 94 A6
Roma, Australia 63 A4
Roma, Italy ... 20 D4
Roman ....... 17 E8
Romang ...... 39 F3
Romania ■ ... 22 B5
Romanovka =
  Basarabeasca 17 E9
Romans-sur-
  Isère ...... 13 D6
Romblon ..... 38 B2
Rome = Roma 20 D4
Rome ....... 74 B5
Romorantin-
  Lanthenay .. 12 C4
Roncador, Serra
  do ....... 93 E3
Ronda ....... 18 D3
Rondônia □ ... 91 F6
Rondonópolis . 93 F3
Ronge, L. la ... 71 C9
Ronne Ice Shelf 96 B3
Roodepoort ... 59 D5
Roorkee ...... 42 E10
Roosevelt → .. 91 E6
Roosevelt I. ... 96 B16
Roquetas de
  Mar ....... 19 D4
Roraima □ .... 90 C6
Roraima, Mt. .. 90 B6
Rosa ........ 57 F6
Rosa, Monte .. 13 D7
Rosario,
  Argentina ... 94 C4
Rosário, Brazil . 92 C5
Rosario, Mexico 84 C3
Rosario,
  Paraguay ... 94 A5
Rosario de la
  Frontera .... 94 B3
Rosário do Sul 94 C6
Rosas, G. de .. 19 A7
Roscommon .. 11 E2
Roseau, Domin. 87 C7
Roseau, U.S.A. 77 A7
Rosebery ..... 62 D4
Roseburg ..... 80 D2
Rosenheim ... 15 E7
Rosetown .... 71 C9
Rosetta =
  Rashîd .... 52 B5
Roseville ..... 80 F3
Rosewood .... 63 A5
Rosignano
  Maríttimo .. 20 C3
Rosignol ...... 90 B7
Roşiori-de-Vede 22 B5
Roslavl ....... 24 C3
Roslyn ....... 63 B4
Ross, Australia 62 D4
Ross, N.Z. .... 65 E4
Ross I. ....... 96 B15
Ross Ice Shelf . 96 C16
Ross Sea ..... 96 B15
Rossano Cálabro 21 E6
Rossland ..... 71 D8
Rosslare ...... 11 E3
Rosso ....... 55 E1
Rossosh ...... 24 C4
Rosthern ..... 71 C9
Rostock ...... 15 A7
Rostov, Don,
  Russia .... 25 D4
Rostov, Yarosl.,
  Russia .... 24 B4
Roswell ...... 78 C1
Rotherham .... 11 E6
Roto ........ 63 B4

Rotondo Mte. . 13 E8
Rotorua ...... 64 C7
Rotorua, L. .... 64 C7
Rotterdam .... 14 C3
Rottweil ...... 14 D5
Rotuma ...... 64 L12
Roubaix ...... 13 A5
Rouen ........ 12 B4
Round Mt. .... 63 B5
Roussillon .... 13 E5
Rouyn ........ 69 D3
Rovaniemi .... 8 E13
Rovereto ..... 20 B3
Rovigo ....... 20 B3
Rovinj ........ 20 B4
Rovno = Rivne 17 C8
Rovuma → . . 57 G8
Rowena ...... 63 A4
Roxas ........ 38 B2
Roxburgh .... 65 F3
Royal
  Leamington
  Spa ...... 11 E6
Royan ........ 12 D3
Rozdilna ..... 17 E10
Rozhyshche .. 17 C7
Ruapehu ..... 64 C6
Ruapuke I. .... 65 G3
Rub' al Khali .. 48 D4
Rubio ........ 90 B4
Rubtsovsk .... 29 D9
Rudall ........ 62 B2
Rudolf, Ostrov . 28 A6
Rufa'a ........ 53 F5
Rufiji → . .... 57 F7
Rufino ....... 94 C4
Rufisque ..... 55 F1
Rugby ........ 11 E6
Rügen ....... 15 A7
Ruhr → ...... 14 C4
Rukwa L. ..... 57 F6
Rum = Rhum . 10 C3
Rumāḥ ....... 47 F6
Rumania =
  Romania ■ .. 22 B5
Rumbêk ...... 53 G4
Rumia ....... 16 A4
Rumoi ....... 32 F12
Runanga ..... 65 E4
Runaway, C. .. 64 B7
Rungwa ...... 57 F6
Ruoqiang .... 34 C3
Rupa ........ 41 D9
Rupat ........ 37 D2
Rupert → . .. 69 C3
Rupert House =
  Waskaganish 69 C3
Rurrenabaque . 91 F5
Rusape ...... 59 B6
Ruschuk = Ruse 22 C5
Ruse ......... 22 C5
Rushworth .... 63 C4
Russas ....... 92 C6
Russellkonda .. 40 H5
Russkaya
  Polyana .... 29 D8
Rustavi ...... 25 E6
Rustenburg ... 59 D5
Ruteng ....... 39 F2
Rutshuru ..... 57 E5
Ruwenzori .... 57 D5
Ružomberok .. 16 D4
Rwanda ■ .... 57 E6
Ryazan ....... 24 C4
Ryazhsk ...... 24 C5
Rybache =
  Rybachye ... 29 E9

Rybachye ..... 29 E9
Rybinsk ...... 24 B4
Rybinskoye
  Vdkhr. ...... 24 B4
Rybnitsa =
  Rîbniţa .... 17 E9
Rylstone ..... 63 B4
Rypin ........ 16 B4
Ryūkyū Is. =
  Ryūkyū-rettō 35 D7
Ryūkyū-rettō .. 35 D7
Rzeszów ...... 16 C5
Rzhev ........ 24 B3

## S

Sa Dec ....... 36 B3
Sa'ādatābād .. 44 D3
Saale → ..... 15 C6
Saalfeld ..... 15 C6
Saar → ...... 13 B7
Saarbrücken .. 14 D4
Saaremaa .... 24 B1
Šabac ....... 22 B2
Sabadell ..... 19 B7
Sabah □ ..... 36 C5
Şabāḥ, Wadi → 47 G7
Sabalān, Kūhhā-
  ye ........ 46 C6
Sábanalarga .. 90 A4
Sabang ....... 36 C1
Sabará ....... 93 F5
Saberania .... 39 E5
Sabhah ...... 52 C1
Sabinas ...... 84 B4
Sabinas Hidalgo 84 B4
Sablayan ..... 38 B2
Sable, C.,
  Canada ..... 69 D4
Sable, C., U.S.A. 86 A3
Sable I. ...... 69 D5
Sabrina Coast . 96 A12
Sabulubek ... 37 E1
Sabzevār ..... 44 B4
Sabzvārān ... 44 D4
Săcele ...... 17 F7
Sachsen □ .... 15 C7
Sachsen-
  Anhalt □ .... 15 C7
Sacramento ... 80 F3
Sacramento → 80 F3
Sacramento
  Mts. ....... 83 D10
Sadani ....... 57 F7
Sadd el Aali .. 52 D5
Sado ......... 33 G11
Sadon ....... 41 E11
Safi ......... 54 B3
Safid Küh .... 42 B3
Saga, Indonesia 39 E4
Saga, Japan .. 32 C2
Sagala ....... 55 F3
Sagar ........ 43 M9
Sagil ........ 34 A4
Saginaw ..... 72 C4
Şaġīr, Zāb aş → 46 D5
Saglouc =
  Salluit ..... 68 B3
Sagua la Grande 86 B3
Saguenay → . 69 D3
Sagunto ..... 19 C5
Sahagún ..... 18 A3
Sahand, Küh-e 46 C6
Sahara ....... 54 D6
Saharan Atlas =
  Saharien,
  Atlas ....... 54 B5

Saharanpur ... 42 E10
Saharien, Atlas 54 B5
Sahiwal ...... 42 D8
Sa'id Bundas .. 53 G3
Saïda ........ 54 B5
Sa'īdābād .... 44 D3
Sa'īdīyeh .... 46 C7
Saidpur ...... 41 E7
Saidu ........ 42 B8
Saigon = Phanh
  Bho Ho Chi
  Minh ....... 36 B3
Saijō ........ 32 C3
Saikhoa Ghat .. 41 D10
Saiki ........ 32 C2
Sailolof ..... 39 E4
St. Andrews ... 10 C5
St. Arnaud .... 62 C3
St-Augustin-
  Saguenay → 69 C5
St. Augustine . 75 E7
St. Austell ... 11 F4
St. Boniface .. 71 D10
St.-Brieuc ..... 12 B2
St. Catharines . 69 D3
St.-Chamond . 13 D6
St. Christopher-
  Nevis ■ = St.
  Kitts & Nevis 87 C7
St. Cloud ..... 77 C7
St. Croix ..... 87 C7
St.-Denis ..... 12 B5
St.-Dizier .... 13 B6
St. Elias, Mt. .. 70 B5
St.-Étienne ... 13 D6
St.-Flour .... 13 D5
St. Francis, C. . 58 E4
St. Gallen =
  Sankt Gallen 13 C8
St.-Gaudens ... 12 E4
St. George ... 63 A4
St.-Georges,
  Fr. Guiana .. 92 B3
St. George's,
  Grenada .... 87 D7
St. George's
  Channel .... 11 F3
St. Georges Hd. 63 C5
St. Gotthard P.
  = San
  Gottardo, P.
  del ........ 13 C8
St. Helena ■ .. 51 H3
St. Helena B. . 58 E3
St. Helens .... 62 D4
St. Helens, Mt. . 72 C2
St. Helier .... 11 G5
St-Hyacinthe .. 69 D3
St. John .... 69 D4
St. John's,
  Antigua ..... 87 C7
St. John's,
  Canada ..... 69 D5
St. Johns → .. 75 D7
St. Joseph ... 77 F7
St. Joseph, L. . 69 C1
St. Kilda, N.Z. . 65 F4
St. Kilda, U.K. . 10 C2
St. Kitts & Nevis 87 C7
St.-Laurent .... 92 A3
St. Lawrence → 69 D4
St. Lawrence,
  Gulf of .... 69 D4
St. Lawrence I. . 71 B2
St. Leonard .. 69 D4
St.-Lô ........ 12 B3
St.-Louis .... 55 E1
St. Louis .... 77 F9
St. Lucia ■ .... 87 D7
St. Lucia, L. ... 59 D6

St. Maarten ... 87 C7
St.-Malo ...... 12 B2
St-Marc ...... 87 C5
St. Mary Pk. ... 62 B2
St. Marys .... 62 D4
St.-Mathieu, Pte. 12 B1
St. Matthews, I.
  = Zadetkyi
  Kyun ...... 36 C1
St.-Nazaire ... 12 C2
St.-Omer ..... 12 A5
St. Paul .... 77 C8
St. Peter Port . 11 G5
St. Petersburg =
  Sankt-
  Peterburg .. 24 B3
St. Petersburg . 75 F6
St.-Pierre et
  Miquelon □ . 69 D5
St.-Quentin ... 13 B5
St. Thomas I. .. 87 C7
St.-Tropez .... 13 E7
St. Vincent, G. . 62 C2
St. Vincent &
  the
  Grenadines ■ 87 D7
Saintes ....... 12 D3
Saintonge ... 12 D3
Saipan ....... 64 H9
Sairang ...... 41 F9
Sairecábur,
  Cerro ...... 94 A3
Sajama ....... 91 G5
Sajó ........ 16 D5
Sakai ........ 32 B4
Sakākah ..... 47 E5
Sakakawea, L. . 76 B4
Sakarya =
  Adapazarı .. 46 B2
Sakarya → . . 25 E3
Sakata ....... 33 G11
Sakhalin ..... 31 D12
Sakon Nakhon . 36 A2
Sala ........ 9 G11
Sala Consilina . 21 D5
Saladillo ...... 94 D5
Salado →,
  Buenos Aires,
  Argentina ... 94 D5
Salado →,
  La Pampa,
  Argentina ... 94 D3
Salado →,
  Santa Fe,
  Argentina ... 94 C4
Salaga ...... 55 G4
Salālah ...... 49 D5
Salamanca,
  Chile ...... 94 C2
Salamanca,
  Spain ...... 18 B3
Salamís ...... 23 F4
Salar de
  Atacama ... 94 A3
Salar de Uyuni 91 H5
Salaverry .... 91 E3
Salawati ..... 39 E4
Salayar ...... 39 F2
Saldanha .... 58 E3
Sale, Australia . 63 C4
Salé, Morocco . 54 B3
Salekhard .... 28 C7
Salem, India .. 43 P11
Salem, U.S.A. . 80 C2
Salerno ...... 21 D5
Salgótarján .. 16 D4
Salihli ....... 23 E7
Salihorsk .... 17 B8
Salima ....... 59 A6

# Salina

Salina, *Italy* ... 21 E5
Salina, *U.S.A.* .. 76 F6
Salina Cruz ... 85 D5
Salinas, *Brazil* . 93 F5
Salinas, *Ecuador* 90 D2
Salinas, *U.S.A.* 82 B2
Salinas Grandes 94 C3
Salinópolis .... 92 C4
Salisbury,
   *Australia* .... 62 B2
Salisbury, *U.K.* 11 F6
Salisbury, *U.S.A.* 75 B7
Salliq ........ 68 B2
Salluit ........ 68 B3
Salmäs ...... 46 C6
Salmon → ... 80 C5
Salmon River
   Mts. ........ 81 C6
Salon-de-
   Provence ... 13 E6
Salonica =
   Thessaloníki . 23 D4
Salonta ....... 16 E5
Salsk ......... 25 D5
Salso → ..... 21 F4
Salt Creek .... 62 C2
Salt Lake City . 81 E8
Salta ......... 94 A3
Saltillo ....... 84 B4
Salto ......... 94 C5
Salto → ...... 20 C4
Salton Sea .... 82 D5
Saltpond ..... 55 G4
Salûm ........ 52 B4
Salûm, Khâlig el 52 B4
Salur ........ 40 H4
Salvador ..... 93 E6
Salwa ....... 44 E2
Salween → ... 41 J11
Salyan ...... 25 F6
Salzach → ... 15 D7
Salzburg .... 15 E7
Salzgitter ..... 14 B6
Salzwedel .... 15 B6
Sama ........ 28 C7
Sama de
   Langreo .... 18 A3
Samales Group 38 C2
Samangán □ .. 45 B7
Samar ...... 38 B3
Samara ...... 24 C7
Samarinda .... 37 E5
Samarkand =
   Samarqand . 29 F7
Samarqand ... 29 F7
Sāmarrā ...... 46 D5
Sambalpur .... 40 G5
Sambar,
   Tanjung .... 37 E4
Sambas ...... 37 D3
Sambava ..... 59 G10
Sambhal ..... 42 E11
Sambhar ..... 42 F9
Sambiase ..... 21 E6
Sambir ....... 17 D6
Samoa ■ ...... 65 L13
Samokov ..... 22 C4
Sámos ....... 23 F6
Samothráki,
   *Évros, Greece* 23 D5
Samothráki,
   *Kérkira,
   Greece* ..... 23 E2
Sampacho .... 94 C4
Sampit ....... 37 E4
Sampit, Teluk . 37 E4
Samra ....... 47 F5
Samsun ...... 46 B4
Samui, Ko .... 36 C2

Samut Prakan . 36 B2
Samut
   Songkhram →
   .......... 36 B2
San .......... 55 F4
San → ...... 16 C5
San Agustin, C. 38 C3
San Andrés, I.
   de ......... 86 D3
San Andrés
   Tuxtla ...... 85 D5
San Angelo ... 78 D3
San Antonio,
   *Chile* ...... 94 C2
San Antonio,
   *Spain* ..... 19 C6
San Antonio,
   *U.S.A.* ..... 78 E4
San Antonio, C.,
   *Argentina* ... 94 D5
San Antonio, C.,
   *Cuba* ...... 85 C8
San Antonio
   Oeste ...... 95 E4
San Benedetto
   del Tronto .. 20 C4
San Bernardino 82 C4
San Bernardino
   Str. ........ 38 B2
San Bernardo . 94 C2
San Bernardo, I.
   de ......... 90 B3
San Borja ..... 91 F5
San Carlos,
   *Argentina* ... 94 C3
San Carlos,
   *Chile* ...... 94 D2
San Carlos, *Phil.* 38 B2
San Carlos,
   *Amazonas,
   Venezuela* ... 90 C5
San Carlos,
   *Cojedes,
   Venezuela* ... 90 B5
San Carlos de
   Bariloche ... 95 E2
San Carlos del
   Zulia ....... 90 B4
San Cristóbal,
   *Argentina* ... 94 C4
San Cristóbal,
   *Mexico* ..... 85 D6
San Cristóbal,
   *Venezuela* ... 90 B4
San Diego .... 82 D4
San Diego, C. . 95 G3
San Felipe, *Chile* 94 C2
San Felipe,
   *Venezuela* ... 90 A5
San Felíu de
   Guíxols ..... 19 B7
San Fernando,
   *Chile* ...... 94 C2
San Fernando,
   *La Union, Phil.* 38 A2
San Fernando,
   *Pampanga,
   Phil.* ...... 38 A2
San Fernando,
   *Spain* ...... 18 D2
San Fernando,
   *Trin. & Tob.* . 87 D7
San Fernando,
   *U.S.A.* ...... 82 C3
San Fernando
   de Apure ... 90 B5
San Fernando
   de Atabapo . 90 C5
San Francisco,
   *Argentina* ... 94 C4

San Francisco,
   *U.S.A.* ...... 82 B1
San Francisco
   de Macorîs .. 87 C5
San Francisco
   del Monte de
   Oro ....... 94 C3
San Gil ....... 90 B4
San Gottardo, P.
   del ........ 13 C8
San Ignacio,
   *Bolivia* ..... 91 G6
San Ignacio,
   *Paraguay* ... 94 B5
San Ildefonso,
   C. ......... 38 A2
San Javier,
   *Argentina* ... 94 C5
San Javier,
   *Bolivia* ..... 91 G6
San Joaquin → 82 A2
San Jorge, B. de 84 A2
San Jorge, G. . 95 F3
San Jorge, G. de 19 B6
San José,
   *Bolivia* ..... 91 G6
San José,
   *Costa Rica* .. 86 E3
San José,
   *Guatemala* .. 85 E6
San Jose, *Phil.* 38 A2
San Jose, *U.S.A.* 82 B2
San Jose de
   Buenovista . 38 B2
San José de
   Jáchal ..... 94 C3
San José de
   Mayo ...... 94 C5
San José de
   Ocune ...... 90 C4
San José del
   Guaviare .... 90 C4
San Juan,
   *Argentina* ... 94 C3
San Juan, *Phil.* 38 C3
San Juan,
   *Puerto Rico* . 87 C6
San Juan → ... 86 D3
San Juan, C. .. 56 D1
San Juan de los
   Morros ..... 90 B5
San Juan Mts. . 83 B9
San Julián .... 95 F3
San Justo .... 94 C4
San Leandro .. 82 B1
San Lorenzo .. 90 C3
San Lorenzo, I. 91 F3
San Lorenzo,
   Mt. ........ 95 F2
San Lucas .... 91 H5
San Lucas, C. . 84 C2
San Luis ..... 94 C3
San Luis Obispo 82 C2
San Luis Potosí 84 C4
San Marino ... 20 C4
San Marino ■ . 20 C4
San Martín, L. . 95 F2
San Matías ... 91 G7
San Matías, G. 95 E4
San Miguel ... 85 E7
San Miguel → 91 F6
San Miguel de
   Tucumán ... 94 B3
San Narciso .. 38 A2
San Nicolás de
   los Arroyos . 94 C4
San-Pédro ... 55 H3
San Pedro de
   las Colonias . 84 B4

San Pedro de
   Lloc ........ 91 E3
San Pedro de
   Macorís .... 87 C6
San Pedro del
   Paraná .... 94 B5
San Pedro Sula 85 D7
San Pieto ..... 21 E2
San Rafael,
   *Argentina* ... 94 C3
San Rafael,
   *U.S.A.* ...... 80 G2
San Ramón de
   la Nueva Orán 94 A4
San Remo ... 20 C1
San Roque,
   *Argentina* ... 94 B5
San Roque,
   *Spain* ...... 18 D3
San Rosendo .. 94 D2
San Salvador,
   *Bahamas* ... 86 B5
San Salvador,
   *El Salv.* ..... 85 E7
San Salvador de
   Jujuy ...... 94 A4
San Sebastián,
   *Argentina* ... 95 G3
San Sebastián,
   *Spain* ...... 19 A5
San Severo ... 20 D5
San Valentin,
   Mte. ........ 95 F2
San Vicente de
   la Barquera . 18 A3
Sana' ........ 49 D3
Sana → ...... 20 B6
Sanaga → .... 56 D1
Sanana ...... 39 E3
Sanandaj .... 46 D6
Sanco Pt. .... 38 C3
Sancti-Spíritus . 86 B4
Sancy, Puy de . 13 D5
Sandakan .... 36 C5
Sandanski .... 22 D4
Sanday ....... 10 B5
Sandgate ..... 63 A5
Sandía ....... 91 F5
Sandıklı ..... 46 C2
Sandoa ....... 56 F4
Sandomierz ... 16 C5
Sandoway .... 41 H10
Sandusky ..... 72 D4
Sandwip Chan. 41 F8
Sandy C. ..... 62 D3
Sandy L. ...... 71 C10
Sanford, *Fla.,
   U.S.A.* ...... 75 E7
Sanford, *N.C.,
   U.S.A.* ...... 75 B8
Sanford, Mt. .. 71 B5
Sanga → ..... 56 E3
Sangamner ... 43 K9
Sangar ....... 31 C10
Sangasangadalam
   .......... 37 E5
Sangeang ... 39 F1
Sangerhausen . 15 C6
Sanggau .... 37 D4
Sangihe, P. ... 39 D3
Sangkapura ... 37 F4
Sangli ........ 43 L9
Sangmélina ... 56 D2
Sangre de Cristo
   Mts. ....... 78 A1
Sanirajak ..... 68 B2
Sankt Gallen . 13 C8
Sankt Moritz .. 13 C8
Sankt-Peterburg 24 B3

Sankt Pölten .. 15 D8
Sankuru ⟶ ... 56 E4
Sanliurfa ..... 46 C4
Sanlúcar de
  Barrameda .. 18 D2
Sannicandro
  Gargánico .. 20 D5
Sanok ........ 17 D6
Sanshui ...... 35 D6
Santa Ana,
  Bolivia ..... 91 F5
Santa Ana,
  Ecuador .... 90 D2
Santa Ana,
  El Salv. ..... 85 E7
Santa Ana,
  U.S.A. ...... 82 D4
Santa Barbara . 82 C3
Santa Catalina I. 82 D3
Santa
  Catarina □ .. 94 B7
Santa Clara .. 86 B4
Santa Clotilde . 90 D4
Santa Coloma
  de Gramanet 19 B7
Santa Cruz,
  Argentina ... 95 G3
Santa Cruz,
  Bolivia ..... 91 G6
Santa Cruz, Phil. 38 B2
Santa Cruz,
  U.S.A. ...... 82 B1
Santa Cruz ⟶ . 95 G3
Santa Cruz de
  Tenerife .... 54 C1
Santa Cruz do
  Sul ........ 94 B6
Santa Cruz I. .. 64 L11
Santa Elena ... 90 D2
Santa Eugenia,
  Pta. ........ 84 B1
Santa Fe,
  Argentina ... 94 C4
Santa Fe, U.S.A. 83 C10
Santa Filomena 93 D4
Santa Inés, I. .. 95 G2
Santa Isabel =
  Rey Malabo . 56 D1
Santa Isabel,
  Argentina ... 94 D3
Santa Isabel,
  Brazil ...... 93 E3
Santa Lucia
  Range ...... 82 C2
Santa Maria,
  Brazil ....... 94 B6
Santa Maria,
  U.S.A. ...... 82 C2
Santa María ⟶ 84 A3
Santa Maria da
  Vitória ..... 93 E5
Santa Maria di
  Leuca, C. ... 23 E2
Santa Marta ... 90 A4
Santa Marta,
  Sierra Nevada
  de ........ 90 A4
Santa Maura =
  Levkás ..... 23 E3
Santa Rosa,
  La Pampa,
  Argentina ... 94 D4
Santa Rosa,
  San Luis,
  Argentina ... 94 C3
Santa Rosa,
  Bolivia ..... 91 F5
Santa Rosa,
  Brazil ....... 94 B6

Santa Rosa,
  U.S.A. ...... 80 F2
Santa Rosa de
  Copán ...... 85 E7
Santa Vitória do
  Palmar ..... 94 C6
Santai ........ 35 C5
Santana, Coxilha
  de .......... 94 C5
Santana do
  Livramento .. 94 C5
Santander ... 18 A4
Sant'Antíoco .. 21 E2
Santarém, Brazil 92 C3
Santarém,
  Portugal .... 18 C1
Santiago, Brazil 94 B6
Santiago, Chile 94 C2
Santiago ⟶ .. 90 D3
Santiago de
  Compostela . 18 A1
Santiago de
  Cuba ....... 86 C4
Santiago de los
  Cabelleros . 87 C5
Santiago del
  Estero ...... 94 B4
Santo Amaro .. 93 E6
Santo Ângelo . 94 B6
Santo Antonio . 93 F2
Santo Corazón 91 G7
Santo Domingo 87 C6
Santo Tomás .. 91 F4
Santo Tomé .. 94 B5
Santo Tomé de
  Guayana =
  Ciudad
  Guayana ... 90 B6
Santoña ...... 18 A4
Santoríni =
  Thíra ....... 23 F5
Santos ....... 94 A7
Santos Dumont 94 A8
Sanza Pombo . 56 F3
São Anastácio . 94 A6
São Bernado de
  Campo ..... 93 G4
São Borja ..... 94 B5
São Carlos .... 94 A7
São Cristóvão . 93 E6
São Domingos 93 E4
São Francisco . 93 F5
São
  Francisco ⟶ 93 E6
São Francisco
  do Sul ..... 94 B7
São Gabriel ... 94 C6
São João da
  Madeira .... 18 B1
São João del
  Rei ........ 93 G5
São João do
  Araguaia ... 92 D4
São João do
  Piauí ....... 92 D5
São José do Rio
  Prêto ....... 94 A7
São Leopoldo . 94 B6
São Lourenço . 93 G4
São
  Lourenço ⟶ 93 F2
São Luís ..... 92 C5
São Marcos ⟶ 93 F4
São Marcos, B.
  de .......... 92 C5
São Mateus ... 93 F6
São Paulo .... 94 A7
São Paulo □ .. 94 A7
São Roque, C.
  de ........ 92 D6

São Sebastião, I.
  de ......... 94 A7
São Tomé &
  Principe ■ .. 51 F4
São Vicente, C.
  de ........ 18 D1
Saône ⟶ ... 13 D6
Saonek ...... 39 E4
Saparua ...... 39 E3
Sapele ....... 55 G6
Saposoa ..... 91 E3
Sapporo ..... 32 F12
Sapulpa ..... 79 B5
Saqqez ....... 46 C6
Sar-e Pol .... 45 B6
Sar-e Pol □ ... 45 B6
Sar Planina .. 22 C3
Saráb ........ 46 C6
Sarada ⟶ ... 40 D3
Saragossa =
  Zaragoza ... 19 B5
Saraguro ..... 90 D3
Sarajevo ..... 20 C7
Saran, G. ..... 37 E4
Sarandí del Yi . 94 C5
Sarangani B. .. 38 C3
Sarangani Is. .. 38 C3
Sarangarh .... 40 G4
Saransk ...... 24 C6
Sarapul ...... 29 D6
Sarasota ..... 75 F6
Saratov ...... 24 C6
Saravane ..... 36 A3
Sarawak □ .... 37 D4
Saray ........ 22 D6
Sarayköy ..... 23 F7
Sarbāz ....... 45 E5
Sarbisheh .... 45 C4
Sarda ⟶ =
  Sarada ⟶ .. 40 D3
Sardalas ..... 54 C7
Sardarshahr .. 42 E9
Sardegna □ ... 21 D2
Sardinia =
  Sardegna □ . 21 D2
Sardis ........ 23 E7
Sargodha .... 42 C8
Sarh ......... 53 G2
Sārī ......... 44 B3
Sangöl ....... 23 E7
Sarikamiş .... 46 B5
Sarikei ....... 37 D4
Sark ......... 11 G5
Şarköy ....... 23 D6
Sarlat-la-Canéda 12 D4
Sarmi ....... 39 E5
Sarmiento .... 95 F3
Sarnia ....... 69 D2
Sarny ........ 24 C2
Sarolangun ... 37 E2
Saronikós
  Kólpos ..... 23 F4
Sarre = Saar ⟶ 13 B7
Sarreguemines 13 B7
Sarro ........ 55 F3
Sarthe ⟶ .... 12 C3
Sartynya ..... 28 C7
Sarvestān .... 44 D3
Sary-Tash .... 29 F8
Saryshagan .. 29 E8
Sasabeneh ... 49 F3
Sasaram ..... 40 E5
Sasebo ....... 32 C1
Saser ........ 42 B10
Saskatchewan □ 71 C9
Saskatchewan ⟶
  ............ 71 C9
Saskatoon ... 71 C9
Saskylakh .... 30 B9

Sasovo ....... 24 C5
Sassandra ... 55 H3
Sassandra ⟶ . 55 H3
Sássari ...... 21 D2
Sassnitz ..... 15 A7
Sassuolo .... 20 B3
Sasyk, Ozero . 17 F9
Sata-Misaki ... 33 D2
Satadougou .. 55 F2
Satara ....... 43 L8
Satmala Hills . 43 J9
Satna ....... 40 E3
Sátoraljaújhely 16 D5
Satpura Ra. ... 43 J10
Satu Mare .... 17 E6
Satui ........ 37 E5
Saturnina ⟶ .. 91 F7
Saudi Arabia ■ 47 F6
Sauerland ... 14 C4
Sault Ste. Marie,
  Canada ..... 69 D2
Sault Ste. Marie,
  U.S.A. ...... 72 A3
Saumlaki ..... 39 F4
Saumur ..... 12 C3
Saunders C. ... 65 F4
Sauri ........ 55 F6
Saurimo ..... 56 F4
Sava ⟶ ..... 22 B3
Savage I. =
  Niue ....... 65 L14
Savalou ..... 55 G5
Savanna la Mar 86 C4
Savannah ..... 75 C7
Savannah ⟶ . 75 C7
Savannakhet . 36 A2
Savanur ..... 43 M9
Savé ........ 55 G5
Save ⟶ ..... 59 C6
Sāveh ....... 46 D7
Savelugu .... 55 G4
Savoie □ .... 13 D7
Savona ...... 20 B2
Sawahlunto .. 37 E2
Sawai ....... 39 E3
Sawai
  Madhopur .. 42 F10
Sawara ...... 32 B7
Sawatch Mts. . 83 A9
Sawmills .... 59 B5
Sawu ........ 39 F2
Sawu Sea .... 39 F2
Saxony, Lower
  =
  Niedersachsen □
  ............ 14 B5
Say ......... 55 F5
Sayán ....... 91 F3
Sayan,
  Zapadnyy ... 30 D7
Saydā ....... 46 D3
Sayghān ..... 45 C6
Sayhut ...... 49 D5
Saynshand ... 35 B6
Sazanit ...... 23 D2
Săzava ⟶ ... 16 D2
Sazin ....... 42 B8
Scandicci .... 20 C3
Scandinavia ... 8 F10
Scarborough . 11 D6
Scebeli,
  Wabi ⟶ .... 49 G3
Schaffhausen . 13 C8
Schefferville .. 69 C4
Schelde ⟶ .. 14 C3
Schenectady . 73 C9
Schiermonnikoog
  ............ 14 B4
Schio ........ 20 B3

# Schleswig

Schleswig .... 14 A5
Schleswig-
  Holstein □ .. 14 A5
Schouten I. ... 62 D4
Schouten Is. =
  Supiori ..... 39 E5
Schwäbische
  Alb ........ 14 D5
Schwaner,
  Pegunungan 37 E4
Schwarzwald .. 14 D5
Schwedt ...... 15 B8
Schweinfurt ... 14 C6
Schwenningen
  = Villingen-
  Schwenningen 14 D5
Schwerin ..... 15 B6
Schwyz ....... 13 C8
Sciacca ...... 21 F4
Scilla ........ 21 E5
Scilly, Isles of . 11 G3
Scone ........ 63 B5
Scotland □ ... 10 C4
Scott Glacier .. 96 A12
Scott Inlet .... 68 A3
Scottsbluff .... 76 E3
Scottsdale .... 62 D4
Scranton ..... 73 D8
Scunthorpe ... 11 E6
Scusciuban ... 49 E5
Scutari =
  Üsküdar .... 25 E2
Seaspray ..... 63 C4
Seattle ....... 80 B2
Sebastopol =
  Sevastopol .. 25 E3
Sebha =
  Sabhah ..... 52 C1
Şebinkarahisar 46 B4
Sebta = Ceuta . 18 E3
Sebuku ....... 37 E5
Sebuku, Teluk . 37 D5
Secretary I. ... 65 F2
Secunderabad . 43 L11
Sedalia ....... 77 F8
Sedan, Australia 62 B2
Sedan, France . 13 B6
Seddon ....... 65 D6
Seddonville ... 65 D5
Sedhiou ...... 55 F1
Sedova, Pik ... 28 B6
Seeheim ...... 58 D3
Seferihisar ... 23 E6
Segamat ...... 37 D2
Segesta ...... 21 F4
Seget ........ 39 E4
Ségou ........ 55 F3
Segovia =
  Coco →. ... 86 D3
Segovia ...... 18 B3
Segre →. ..... 19 B6
Séguéla ...... 55 G3
Segura →. .... 19 C5
Sehitwa ...... 58 C4
Sehore ....... 43 H10
Seine →. ..... 12 B4
Seistan ....... 45 D5
Seistan,
  Daryācheh-ye 45 D5
Sekayu ....... 37 E2
Sekondi-
  Takoradi .... 55 H4
Selaru ........ 39 F4
Selçuk ....... 23 F6
Sele →. ...... 21 D5
Selenga =
  Selenge
  Mörön → . 35 A5
Selenge
  Mörön → .. 35 A5

Seletan, Tg. ... 37 E4
Sélibabi ...... 55 E2
Selîma, El
  Wâhât el ... 52 D4
Selkirk ....... 71 C10
Selkirk Mts. ... 71 C8
Selma ........ 75 B8
Selpele ....... 39 E4
Selu ......... 39 F4
Selva ........ 94 B4
Selvas ........ 91 E5
Semani → .... 23 D2
Semarang .... 37 F4
Semey ....... 29 D9
Semiozernoye . 29 D7
Semipalatinsk =
  Semey ..... 29 D9
Semirara Is. ... 38 B2
Semisopochnoi
  I. .......... 71 C1
Semitau ...... 37 D4
Semiyarka .... 29 D8
Semiyarskoye =
  Semiyarka .. 29 D8
Semmering P. . 15 E8
Semnān ...... 44 C3
Semnān □ .... 44 C3
Semporna .... 38 D1
Semuda ...... 37 E4
Sena Madureira 91 E5
Senador
  Pompeu .... 92 D6
Senaja ....... 36 C5
Senanga ...... 58 B4
Sendai,
  Kagoshima,
  Japan ...... 32 D2
Sendai, Miyagi,
  Japan ...... 33 G12
Senegal ■ .... 55 F2
Senegal →. ... 55 E1
Senge Khambab
  = Indus →. . 43 G5
Sengkang .... 39 E2
Senhor-do-
  Bonfim ..... 93 E5
Senigállia .... 20 C4
Senj ......... 20 B5
Senja ........ 8 E11
Senlis ........ 13 B5
Senmonorom . 36 B3
Sennâr ....... 53 F5
Senneterre ... 69 D3
Sens ......... 13 B5
Senta ........ 22 B3
Sentani ....... 39 E6
Seo de Urgel . 19 A6
Seoul = Sŏul . 35 C7
Sepīdān ...... 44 D3
Sept-Îles ..... 69 C4
Sequoia
  National Park 82 B3
Seram ........ 39 E3
Seram Laut,
  Kepulauan .. 39 E4
Seram Sea .... 39 E3
Serasan ...... 37 D3
Serbia □ ..... 22 C3
Serdobsk ..... 24 C5
Seremban .... 37 D2
Serenje ...... 59 A6
Sereth =
  Siret →. .... 17 F9
Sergino ...... 28 C7
Sergipe □ .... 93 E6
Sergiyev Posad 24 B4
Seria ......... 36 D4
Serian ........ 37 D4
Seribu,
  Kepulauan .. 37 F3

Sérifos ....... 23 F5
Sermata ...... 39 F3
Serny Zavod ... 29 F6
Serov ........ 28 D7
Serowe ....... 59 C5
Serpukhov .... 24 C4
Sérrai ........ 22 D4
Serrezuela .... 94 C3
Serrinha ...... 93 E6
Sertânia ...... 92 D6
Serua ........ 39 F4
Serui ......... 39 E5
Serule ........ 59 C5
Sesepe ....... 39 E3
Sesfontein .... 58 B2
Sesheke ...... 58 B4
Sète ......... 13 E5
Sete Lagôas ... 93 F5
Sétif ......... 54 A6
Seto ......... 32 B5
Settat ........ 54 B3
Setté-Cama ... 56 E1
Setúbal ...... 18 C1
Setúbal, B. de . 18 C1
Seulimeum ... 36 C1
Sevan, Ozero =
  Sevana Lich . 25 E6
Sevana Lich ... 25 E6
Sevastopol .... 25 E3
Severn →,
  Canada ..... 69 C2
Severn →, U.K. 11 F5
Severnaya
  Zemlya ..... 30 B7
Severnyye Uvaly 24 B6
Severo-
  Yeniseyskiy . 30 C7
Severodvinsk .. 28 C4
Sevilla ....... 18 D2
Seville = Sevilla 18 D2
Sevlievo ...... 22 C5
Seward ....... 71 B5
Seward Pen. .. 71 B3
Sewer ........ 39 F4
Seychelles ■ .. 26 K9
Seymour ..... 63 C4
Sfax ......... 52 B1
Sfîntu Gheorghe 17 F7
Shaanxi □ ... 35 C5
Shaba □ ...... 57 F4
Shabunda .... 57 E5
Shache ....... 34 C2
Shackleton Ice
  Shelf ....... 96 A11
Shackleton Inlet 96 C15
Shadrinsk .... 29 D7
Shāhābād .... 44 B4
Shahdād ..... 44 D4
Shahdād,
  Namakzār-e . 44 D4
Shahdadkot ... 42 F5
Shahgarh ..... 42 F6
Shahhāt ...... 52 B3
Shahjahanpur . 42 F11
Shahr Kord ... 44 C2
Shahrig ...... 42 D5
Shaikhabad ... 42 B6
Shajapur ..... 43 H10
Shakhty ...... 25 D5
Shakhunya ... 24 B6
Shaki ........ 55 G5
Shala, L. ..... 53 G6
Shalqar ...... 29 E6
Sham, J. ash . 44 F4
Shamil ....... 44 E4
Shammar, Jabal 47 F5
Shamo = Gobi 35 B6
Shamo, L. .... 53 G6
Shamva ...... 59 B6

Shan □ ....... 41 G12
Shandong □ .. 35 C6
Shanghai ..... 35 C7
Shangqiu ..... 35 C6
Shangrao ..... 35 D6
Shangshui .... 35 C6
Shannon ..... 64 D6
Shannon → .. 11 E2
Shansi =
  Shanxi □ ... 35 C6
Shantou ...... 35 D6
Shantung =
  Shandong □ 35 C6
Shanxi □ ..... 35 C6
Shaoguan .... 35 D6
Shaowu ...... 35 D6
Shaoxing ..... 35 C7
Shaoyang .... 35 D6
Shaqra',
  Si. Arabia ... 47 F6
Shaqrā', Yemen 49 E4
Sharjah = Ash
  Shāriqah .... 44 E3
Sharon ....... 72 D5
Sharya ....... 24 B6
Shashi,
  Botswana ... 59 C5
Shashi, China . 35 C6
Shasta, Mt. ... 80 E2
Shatt al'Arab → 47 E7
Shaunavon ... 71 D9
Shawan ...... 34 B3
Shawinigan ... 69 D3
Shcherbakov =
  Rybinsk ..... 24 B4
Shchuchinsk .. 29 D8
Shebele =
  Scebeli,
  Wabi →. .... 49 G3
Sheboygan ... 72 C2
Sheffield ..... 11 E6
Shekhupura .. 42 D8
Shelburne .... 69 D4
Shelby ....... 75 B7
Shelbyville ... 74 B4
Shellharbour .. 63 B5
Shenandoah → 73 E7
Shendam ..... 55 G6
Shendî ....... 53 E5
Shensi =
  Shaanxi □ .. 35 C5
Shenyang .... 35 B7
Sheopur Kalan 42 G10
Shepetivka .... 17 C8
Shepetovka =
  Shepetivka .. 17 C8
Shepparton ... 63 C4
Sherbro I. .... 55 G2
Sherbrooke ... 69 D3
Sheridan ..... 81 C10
Sherman ..... 79 C5
Sherridon .... 71 C9
Shetland Is. ... 10 A6
Shibām ...... 49 D4
Shigaib ...... 53 E3
Shihchiachuangi
  =
  Shijiazhuang 35 C6
Shijiazhuang .. 35 C6
Shikarpur .... 42 F6
Shikoku ...... 32 C3
Shikoku □ .... 33 H10
Shikoku-Sanchi 32 C3
Shilabo ....... 49 F3
Shiliguri ...... 40 D7
Shillong ...... 41 E8
Shilong ...... 35 D6
Shimada ..... 32 B6
Shimizu ...... 32 B6

Shimoga ..... 43 N9
Shimonoseki .. 32 C2
Shinano → ... 32 A6
Shīndand ..... 42 C3
Shingū ....... 32 C4
Shinyanga .... 57 E6
Shipehenski
  Prokhod .. 22 C5
Shipki La ..... 42 D11
Shīr Kūh .... 44 D3
Shirane-San .. 32 A6
Shīrāz ........ 44 D3
Shire → ...... 59 B7
Shiretoko-Misaki 32 F13
Shiriya-Zaki .. 32 F12
Shīrvān ...... 44 B4
Shirwa, L. =
  Chilwa, L. . 59 B7
Shivpuri .... 43 G10
Shizuoka ..... 32 B6
Shklov =
  Shklow ..... 17 A10
Shklow ....... 17 A10
Shkoder =
  Shkodra .... 22 C2
Shkodra ...... 22 C2
Shkumbini → . 23 D2
Shmidta, O. ... 30 A7
Sholapur =
  Solapur ... 43 L9
Shoshone Mts. 80 F5
Shoshong .... 59 C5
Shreveport .... 79 C7
Shrewsbury .. 11 E5
Shrirampur ... 40 F7
Shu .......... 29 E8
Shuangyashan 35 B8
Shule ........ 34 C2
Shumagin Is. .. 71 C4
Shungnak .... 71 B4
Shūr → ...... 44 D3
Shurugwi .... 59 B5
Shūsf ........ 45 D5
Shūshtar ..... 47 D7
Shwebo ...... 41 F10
Shwegu ...... 41 E11
Shweli → .... 41 F11
Shymkent .... 29 E7
Shyok ....... 42 B11
Shyok → ..... 42 B9
Si Kiang = Xi
  Jiang → ... 35 D6
Si-ngan = Xi'an 35 C5
Si Racha .... 36 B2
Siah ......... 47 G6
Siahan Range . 42 F4
Siaksriindrapura 37 D2
Sialkot ...... 42 C9
Siantan, P. ... 37 D3
Sīāreh ....... 45 D5
Siargao ...... 38 C3
Siasi ........ 38 C2
Siau ......... 39 D3
Šiauliai ..... 24 B1
Šibenik ...... 20 C5
Siberut ...... 37 E1
Sibi ......... 42 E5
Sibil ........ 39 E6
Sibiti ....... 56 E2
Sibiu ........ 17 F7
Sibolga ...... 37 D1
Sibsagar .... 41 D10
Sibu ......... 37 D4
Sibuco ...... 38 C2
Sibuguey B. ... 38 C2
Sibut ........ 56 C3
Sibutu ...... 38 D1
Sibutu Passage 38 D1
Sibuyan ...... 38 B2

Sibuyan Sea .. 38 B2
Sichuan □ .... 34 C5
Sicilia ....... 21 F5
Sicily = Sicilia . 21 F5
Sicuani ....... 91 F4
Siddipet ...... 43 K11
Sidéradougou . 55 F4
Sīdi Barrâni ... 52 B4
Sidi-bel-Abbès . 54 A4
Sidley, Mt. .... 96 B18
Sidon = Saydā 46 D3
Sidra, G. of =
  Surt, Khalīj .. 52 B2
Siedlce ...... 17 B6
Sieg → ...... 14 C4
Siegen ....... 14 C5
Siem Reap .... 36 B2
Siena ........ 20 C3
Sieradz ...... 16 C4
Sierra Colorada 95 E3
Sierra Gorda .. 94 A3
Sierra Leone ■ 55 G2
Sífnos ........ 23 F5
Sighetu-
  Marmatiei ... 17 E6
Sighișoara .... 17 E7
Sigli ......... 36 C1
Sigsig ........ 90 D3
Sigüenza ..... 19 B4
Siguiri ....... 55 F3
Sihanoukville =
  Kompong
  Som ...... 36 B2
Siirt ......... 46 C5
Sikar ........ 42 F9
Sikasso ...... 55 F3
Sikhote Alin,
  Khrebet ..... 31 E11
Sikhote Alin Ra.
  = Sikhote
  Alin, Khrebet 31 E11
Síkinos ...... 23 F5
Sikkim □ ..... 40 D7
Sil → ........ 18 A2
Silchar ...... 41 E9
Silesia = Śląsk 16 C3
Silgarhi Doti .. 40 C3
Silghat ...... 41 D9
Silifke ....... 46 C3
Siliguri =
  Shiliguri .... 40 D7
Siling Co .... 34 C3
Silistra ...... 22 B6
Silivri ....... 22 D7
Sillajhuay,
  Cordillera .. 91 G5
Silva Porto =
  Kuito ...... 58 A3
Simanggang .. 37 D4
Simav ........ 23 E7
Simbirsk ..... 24 C6
Simeria ...... 17 F6
Simeulue ..... 37 D1
Simferopol ... 25 E3
Sími ......... 23 F6
Simikot ...... 40 C3
Simla ....... 42 D10
Simplon P. ... 13 C8
Simpson Desert 60 F6
Simunjan .... 37 D4
Sinabang .... 37 D1
Sinadogo .... 49 F4
Sinai = Es Sînâ' 52 C5
Sinai, Mt. =
  Mûsa, G. .. 47 E3
Sinaloa de
  Levya .... 84 B3
Sincelejo .... 90 B3

Sincorá, Serra
  do ........ 93 E5
Sind □ ...... 42 F6
Sind Sagar
  Doab ..... 42 D7
Sindangan ... 38 C2
Sines ........ 18 D1
Sines, C. de .. 18 D1
Singa ........ 53 F5
Singapore ■ .. 37 D2
Singaraja .... 37 F5
Singida ...... 57 E6
Singitikós
  Kólpos .... 23 D5
Singkaling
  Hkamti .... 41 E10
Singkawang .. 37 D3
Singleton .... 63 B5
Singora =
  Songkhla .. 36 C2
Sinjai ....... 39 F2
Sinjār ....... 46 C5
Sinkat ....... 53 E6
Sinkiang Uighur
  = Xinjiang
  Uygur
  Zizhiqu □ ... 34 B3
Sinni → ..... 21 D6
Sinnuris ..... 52 C5
Sinop ........ 46 B3
Sintang ...... 37 D4
Sintra ....... 18 C1
Sinŭiju ...... 35 B7
Siocon ....... 38 C2
Siófok ....... 16 E4
Sioma ....... 58 B4
Sion ......... 13 C7
Sioux City .... 77 D6
Sioux Falls ... 76 D6
Sioux Lookout . 71 C10
Siping ....... 35 B7
Sipura ....... 37 E1
Siquijor ...... 38 C2
Siracusa ..... 21 F5
Sirajganj .... 41 E7
Sirdaryo =
  Syrdarya → 29 E7
Siret → ...... 17 F9
Sirohi ....... 43 G8
Sironj ....... 43 G10
Síros ........ 23 F5
Sirsa ........ 42 E9
Sisak ........ 20 B6
Sisaket ...... 36 A2
Sisophon .... 36 B2
Sīstān va
  Balūchestān □ 45 E5
Sitapur ...... 40 D3
Sitges ....... 19 B6
Sitía ........ 23 G6
Sitka ........ 71 C6
Sittang Myit → 41 J11
Sittwe ....... 41 G9
Siuri ........ 40 F6
Sīvand ...... 44 D3
Sivas ........ 46 C4
Siverek ...... 46 C4
Sivrihisar ... 46 C2
Sīwa ........ 52 C4
Siwalik Range . 40 D4
Siwan ....... 40 D5
Sjælland .... 9 G10
Sjumen =
  Šumen .... 22 C6
Skadarsko
  Jezero ..... 22 C2
Skagerrak .... 9 G9
Skagway .... 71 C6
Skala-Podilska . 17 D8

Skala
  Podolskaya =
  Skala-Podilska 17 D8
Skalat ....... 17 D7
Skardu ....... 42 B9
Skarzysko-
  Kamienna ... 16 C5
Skeena → ... 70 C6
Skegness .... 11 E7
Skeldon ...... 90 B7
Skellefte älv → 8 F12
Skellefteå .... 8 F12
Skíathos ..... 23 E4
Skien ........ 9 G9
Skierniewice .. 16 C5
Skikda ....... 54 A6
Skipton ...... 62 C3
Skíros ....... 23 E5
Skole ........ 17 D6
Skópelos .... 23 E4
Skopje ...... 22 C3
Skvyra ...... 17 D9
Skye ........ 10 C3
Skyros = Skíros 23 E5
Slamet ....... 37 F3
Ślask ....... 16 C3
Slatina ...... 22 B5
Slave → ..... 70 B8
Slavgorod ... 29 D8
Slavonski Brod 20 B7
Slavuta ...... 17 C8
Slavyansk =
  Slovyansk .. 25 D4
Slawharad .... 17 B10
Sleaford B. ... 62 B2
Sleeper Is. ... 68 C2
Sligeach = Sligo 11 D2
Sligo ........ 11 D2
Sliven ....... 22 C6
Slobodskoy .. 24 B7
Slobozia ..... 22 B6
Slonim ...... 17 B7
Slough ...... 11 F6
Slovak Rep. ■ . 16 D5
Slovakia =
  Slovak Rep. ■ 16 D5
Slovakian Ore
  Mts. =
  Slovenské
  Rudohorie .. 16 D4
Slovenia ■ .... 20 B5
Slovenija =
  Slovenia ■ .. 20 B5
Slovenská
  Republika =
  Slovak Rep. ■ 16 D5
Slovenské
  Rudohorie .. 16 D4
Slovyansk .... 25 D4
Sluch → ..... 17 C8
Słupsk ...... 16 A3
Slutsk ....... 17 B8
Smara ....... 54 B3
Smarhon .... 17 A8
Smederevo .. 22 B3
Smith Arm ... 70 B7
Smithton .... 62 D4
Smithtown ... 63 B5
Smoky Bay ... 62 B1
Smolensk .... 24 C3
Smolikas, Óros 23 D3
Smolyan .... 22 D5
Smorgon =
  Smarhon ... 17 A8
Smyrna = İzmir 23 E6
Snake → ..... 80 B4
Snake I. ...... 63 C4
Snake River
  Plain ..... 81 D7

# Sneek

| | | |
|---|---|---|
| Sneek | 14 | B3 |
| Sněžka | 16 | C2 |
| Snøhetta | 8 | F9 |
| Snowdon | 11 | E4 |
| Snowdrift | 70 | B8 |
| Snowtown | 62 | B2 |
| Snowy → | 63 | C4 |
| Snowy Mts. | 63 | C4 |
| Snyatyn | 17 | D7 |
| Snyder | 78 | C3 |
| Soalala | 59 | H9 |
| Sobat, Nahr → | 53 | G5 |
| Sobral | 92 | C5 |
| Soc Trang | 36 | C3 |
| Soch'e = | | |
| Shache | 34 | C2 |
| Sochi | 25 | E4 |
| Société, Is. de la | 65 | L15 |
| Society Is. = | | |
| Société, Is. de | | |
| la | 65 | L15 |
| Socompa, | | |
| Portezuelo de | 94 | A3 |
| Socorro | 90 | B4 |
| Socotra | 49 | E5 |
| Soda Plains | 42 | B11 |
| Söderhamn | 8 | F11 |
| Sodiri | 53 | F4 |
| Sodo | 53 | G6 |
| Sofia = Sofiya | 22 | C4 |
| Sofia → | 59 | H9 |
| Sofiya | 22 | C4 |
| Sogamoso | 90 | B4 |
| Sognefjorden | 8 | F9 |
| Sohâg | 52 | C5 |
| Soissons | 13 | B5 |
| Sokal | 17 | C7 |
| Söke | 23 | F6 |
| Sokhumi | 25 | E5 |
| Sokodé | 55 | G5 |
| Sokol | 24 | B5 |
| Sokółka | 17 | B6 |
| Sokolo | 55 | F3 |
| Sokolów | | |
| Podlaski | 17 | B6 |
| Sokoto | 55 | F6 |
| Solano | 38 | A2 |
| Solapur | 43 | L9 |
| Soledad | 90 | B6 |
| Soligalich | 24 | B5 |
| Soligorsk = | | |
| Salihorsk | 17 | B8 |
| Solikamsk | 28 | D6 |
| Solimões = | | |
| Amazonas → | 92 | C3 |
| Solingen | 14 | C4 |
| Sóller | 19 | C7 |
| Sologne | 12 | C4 |
| Solok | 37 | E2 |
| Solomon Is. ■ | 64 | K10 |
| Solomon Sea | 61 | B9 |
| Solon | 35 | B7 |
| Solor | 39 | F2 |
| Solothurn | 13 | C7 |
| Šolta | 20 | C6 |
| Solţānābād | 44 | B4 |
| Solunska Glava | 22 | D3 |
| Solwezi | 59 | A5 |
| Soma | 23 | E6 |
| Somali Rep. ■ | 49 | F4 |
| Somalia = | | |
| Somali Rep. ■ | 49 | F4 |
| Sombor | 22 | B2 |
| Sombrerete | 84 | C4 |
| Sombrero | 87 | C7 |
| Somerset East | 59 | E5 |
| Somerset I. | 70 | A10 |
| Someş → | 17 | E6 |
| Sommariva | 63 | A4 |
| Somme → | 12 | A4 |
| Somosierra, | | |
| Puerto de | 18 | B4 |
| Somport, Puerto | | |
| de | 12 | E3 |
| Sóndrio | 20 | A2 |
| Sonepur | 40 | G4 |
| Song Cau | 36 | B3 |
| Songea | 57 | G7 |
| Songhua | | |
| Jiang → | 35 | B8 |
| Songkhla | 36 | C2 |
| Songpan | 34 | C5 |
| Sonipat | 42 | E10 |
| Sonmiani | 42 | G5 |
| Sono → | 93 | D4 |
| Sonora → | 84 | B2 |
| Sonsonate | 85 | E7 |
| Soochow = | | |
| Suzhou | 35 | C7 |
| Sopi | 39 | D3 |
| Sopot | 16 | A4 |
| Sopron | 16 | E3 |
| Sør-Rondane | 96 | B8 |
| Sorata | 91 | G5 |
| Sorel | 69 | D3 |
| Sorgono | 21 | D2 |
| Soria | 19 | B4 |
| Sorkh, Kuh-e | 44 | C4 |
| Soroca | 17 | D9 |
| Sorocaba | 94 | A7 |
| Soroki = | | |
| Soroca | 17 | D9 |
| Sorong | 39 | E4 |
| Soroti | 57 | D6 |
| Sørøya | 8 | D12 |
| Sorrento | 63 | C3 |
| Sorsogon | 38 | B2 |
| Sosnowiec | 16 | C4 |
| Souanké | 56 | D2 |
| Soúdhas, Kólpos | 23 | G5 |
| Söul | 35 | C7 |
| Sound, The = | | |
| Øresund | 9 | G10 |
| Sources, | | |
| Mt. aux | 59 | D5 |
| Soure | 92 | C4 |
| Souris | 71 | D9 |
| Souris → | 71 | D10 |
| Sousa | 92 | D6 |
| Sousel | 92 | C3 |
| Sousse | 52 | A1 |
| South Africa ■ | 58 | E4 |
| South | | |
| Australia □ | 62 | B2 |
| South Bend | 72 | D2 |
| South | | |
| Carolina □ | 75 | C7 |
| South China Sea | 36 | C4 |
| South Dakota □ | 76 | C4 |
| South East C. | 62 | D4 |
| South Horr | 57 | D7 |
| South I. | 65 | E3 |
| South | | |
| Invercargill | 65 | G3 |
| South Korea ■ | 35 | C7 |
| South Magnetic | | |
| Pole | 96 | A13 |
| South | | |
| Nahanni → | 70 | B7 |
| South Natuna Is. | | |
| = Natuna | | |
| Selatan, | | |
| Kepulauan | 37 | D3 |
| South Orkney Is. | 96 | A4 |
| South Pagai, I. | | |
| = Pagai | | |
| Selatan, P. | 37 | E2 |
| South Platte → | 76 | E4 |
| South Pole | 96 | C |
| South | | |
| Ronaldsay | 10 | B5 |
| South | | |
| Saskatchewan → | | |
| | 71 | C9 |
| South Shetland | | |
| Is. | 96 | A4 |
| South Shields | 11 | D6 |
| South Taranaki | | |
| Bight | 64 | C6 |
| South Uist | 10 | C3 |
| South West C. | 62 | D4 |
| Southampton | 11 | F6 |
| Southampton I. | 68 | B2 |
| Southbridge | 65 | E5 |
| Southend-on- | | |
| Sea | 11 | F7 |
| Southern Alps | 65 | E4 |
| Southern Indian | | |
| L. | 71 | C10 |
| Southern | | |
| Ocean | 96 | A9 |
| Southern | | |
| Uplands | 10 | D5 |
| Southport | 63 | A5 |
| Southwest C. | 65 | G2 |
| Soutpansberg | 59 | C5 |
| Sovetsk, | | |
| Kaliningd., | | |
| Russia | 24 | B1 |
| Sovetsk, Kirov, | | |
| Russia | 24 | B6 |
| Sōya-Misaki | 32 | E12 |
| Soyo | 56 | F2 |
| Sozh → | 17 | C10 |
| Spain ■ | 18 | C4 |
| Spalding | 62 | B2 |
| Spanish Town | 86 | C4 |
| Sparta = Spárti | 23 | F4 |
| Spartanburg | 75 | B7 |
| Spárti | 23 | F4 |
| Spartivento, C., | | |
| Calabria, Italy | 21 | F6 |
| Spartivento, C., | | |
| Sard., Italy | 21 | E2 |
| Spátha, Ákra | 23 | G4 |
| Spencer, C. | 62 | C2 |
| Spencer G. | 62 | B2 |
| Spenser Mts. | 65 | E5 |
| Spey → | 10 | C5 |
| Speyer | 14 | D5 |
| Split | 20 | C6 |
| Spokane | 80 | B5 |
| Spoleto | 20 | C4 |
| Sporyy Navolok, | | |
| Mys | 28 | B7 |
| Spratly I. | 36 | C4 |
| Spree → | 15 | B7 |
| Springbok | 58 | D3 |
| Springfield, N.Z. | 65 | E4 |
| Springfield, Ill., | | |
| U.S.A. | 77 | F10 |
| Springfield, | | |
| Mass., U.S.A. | 73 | C9 |
| Springfield, Mo., | | |
| U.S.A. | 79 | A7 |
| Springfield, | | |
| Ohio, U.S.A. | 72 | E4 |
| Springfield, | | |
| Oreg., U.S.A. | 80 | C2 |
| Springfontein | 59 | E5 |
| Springhill | 69 | D4 |
| Springhurst | 63 | C4 |
| Springs | 59 | D5 |
| Squamish | 71 | D7 |
| Srbija = | | |
| Serbia □ | 22 | C3 |
| Sre Umbell | 36 | B2 |
| Srebrnica | 20 | B7 |
| Sredinny Ra. = | | |
| Sredinnyy | | |
| Khrebet | 31 | D14 |
| Sredinnyy | | |
| Khrebet | 31 | D14 |
| Srednevilyuysk | 31 | C10 |
| Šrem | 16 | B3 |
| Sremska | | |
| Mitrovica | 22 | B2 |
| Sri Lanka ■ | 43 | R12 |
| Srikakulam | 40 | H4 |
| Srinagar | 42 | B9 |
| Stade | 14 | B5 |
| Stadlandet | 8 | F9 |
| Stafford | 11 | E5 |
| Stakhanov | 25 | D4 |
| Stalingrad = | | |
| Volgograd | 25 | D5 |
| Staliniri = | | |
| Tskhinvali | 25 | E5 |
| Stalino = | | |
| Donetsk | 25 | D4 |
| Stalinogorsk = | | |
| Novomoskovsk | | |
| | 24 | C4 |
| Stalowa Wola | 17 | C6 |
| Stamford | 73 | D9 |
| Stanislav = | | |
| Ivano- | | |
| Frankivsk | 17 | D7 |
| Stanke Dimitrov | 22 | C4 |
| Stanley, | | |
| Australia | 62 | D4 |
| Stanley, Canada | 71 | C9 |
| Stanley, Falk. Is. | 95 | G5 |
| Stanovoy | | |
| Khrebet | 31 | D10 |
| Stanovoy Ra. = | | |
| Stanovoy | | |
| Khrebet | 31 | D10 |
| Stanthorpe | 63 | A5 |
| Stara Planina | 22 | C4 |
| Stara Zagora | 22 | C5 |
| Starachowice | 16 | C5 |
| Staraya Russa | 24 | B3 |
| Starbuck I. | 65 | K15 |
| Stargard | | |
| Szczeciński | 16 | B2 |
| Staritsa | 24 | B3 |
| Starogard | | |
| Gdański | 16 | B4 |
| Starokonstantinov | | |
| = | | |
| Starokonstyantyniv | | |
| | 17 | D8 |
| Starokonstyantyniv | | |
| | 17 | D8 |
| Staryy | | |
| Chartoriysk | 17 | C7 |
| Staryy Oskol | 24 | C4 |
| State College | 73 | D7 |
| Staten, I. = | | |
| Estados, I. de | | |
| Los | 95 | G4 |
| Statesville | 75 | B7 |
| Stavanger | 9 | G9 |
| Staveley | 65 | E4 |
| Stavropol | 25 | D5 |
| Stawell | 62 | C3 |
| Steenkool = | | |
| Bintuni | 39 | E4 |
| Stefanie L. = | | |
| Chew Bahir | 53 | H6 |
| Stefansson Bay | 96 | A9 |
| Steiermark □ | 15 | E8 |
| Steinkjer | 8 | F10 |
| Stellenbosch | 58 | E3 |
| Stendal | 15 | B6 |

Steornabhaigh
= Stornoway 10 B3
Stepanakert =
Xankändi .. 25 F6
Stephens Creek 62 B3
Stepnoi = Elista 25 D5
Stepnyak .... 29 D8
Sterlitamak ... 29 D6
Stettin =
Szczecin .... 16 B2
Stettiner Haff .. 15 B8
Stettler ....... 71 C8
Steubenville .. 72 D5
Stevenage ... 11 F6
Stewart ...... 70 B6
Stewart, I. .... 95 G2
Stewart I. ..... 65 G2
Steyr ......... 15 D8
Stillwater, N.Z. 65 E4
Stillwater,
U.S.A. ...... 78 A5
Štip .......... 22 D4
Stirling ....... 10 C5
Stockerau ..... 15 D9
Stockholm .... 9 G11
Stockport ..... 11 E5
Stockton ...... 82 B2
Stockton-on-
Tees ....... 11 D6
Stoke on Trent 11 E5
Stokes Pt. ..... 62 D3
Stolac ........ 20 C6
Stolbovoy,
Ostrov ...... 30 B11
Stolbtsy =
Stowbtsy ... 17 B8
Stolin ........ 17 C8
Stonehaven .. 10 C5
Stonewall ... 71 C10
Stony Tunguska
=
Podkamennaya
Tunguska → 30 C7
Stora Lulevatten 8 E11
Storavan ..... 8 E11
Store Bælt ... 9 G10
Store Creek ... 63 B4
Storm B. ..... 62 D4
Stormberge .. 59 E5
Stornoway .... 10 B3
Storozhinets =
Storozhynets 17 D7
Storozhynets .. 17 D7
Storsjön ...... 8 F10
Storuman .... 8 E11
Stowbtsy ..... 17 B8
Strahan ...... 62 D4
Stralsund ..... 15 A7
Strand ....... 58 E3
Stranraer ..... 11 D4
Strasbourg .... 13 B7
Stratford,
Canada ..... 69 D2
Stratford, N.Z. . 64 C6
Strathalbyn ... 62 C2
Straubing .... 15 D7
Streaky B. .... 62 B1
Streaky Bay ... 62 B1
Strelka ....... 30 D7
Strezhevoy ... 29 C8
Strimón → ... 23 D4
Strimonikós
Kólpos ..... 23 D5
Strómboli ..... 21 E5
Stronsay ..... 10 B5
Stroud Road .. 63 B5
Strumica ..... 22 D4
Stryy ........ 17 D6
Strzelecki Cr. → 62 A2

Stuart Ra. ..... 62 A1
Stung Treng .. 36 B3
Stutterheim ... 59 E5
Stuttgart ...... 14 D5
Styria =
Steiermark □ 15 E8
Suakin ....... 53 E6
Subansiri → .. 41 D9
Subi ......... 37 D3
Subotica ..... 16 E4
Suceava ...... 17 E8
Suchou =
Suzhou ..... 35 C7
Süchow =
Xuzhou ..... 35 C6
Sucre ........ 91 G5
Sudair ....... 47 F6
Sudan ■ ..... 53 E4
Sudbury ...... 69 D2
Sûdd ........ 53 G4
Sudeten Mts. =
Sudety ..... 16 C3
Sudety ....... 16 C3
Sudirman,
Pegunungan 39 E5
Sueca ....... 19 C5
Suez = El
Suweis ..... 52 C5
Suez, G. of =
Suweis, Khalîg
el .......... 52 C5
Sugluk = Salluit 68 B3
Suhâr ........ 44 E4
Suhbaatar ... 35 A5
Suhl ......... 14 C6
Suihua ....... 35 B7
Sukadana,
Kalimantan,
Indonesia ... 37 E3
Sukadana,
Sumatera,
Indonesia ... 37 F3
Sukaraja ..... 37 E4
Sukarnapura =
Jayapura ... 39 E6
Sukhona → .. 28 C5
Sukhumi =
Sokhumi .... 25 E5
Sukkur ....... 42 F6
Sukkur Barrage 42 F6
Sula, Kepulauan 39 E3
Sulaiman Range 42 D6
Sulawesi □ ... 39 E2
Sulawesi Sea =
Celebes Sea . 39 D2
Sulima ....... 55 G2
Sulina ....... 17 F9
Sulitjelma .... 8 E11
Sullana ...... 90 D2
Sultanpur .... 40 D4
Sulu Arch. ... 38 C2
Sulu Sea .... 38 C2
Suluq ....... 52 B3
Sulzberger Ice
Shelf ...... 96 B17
Sumalata ..... 39 D2
Sumatera □ ... 37 D2
Sumatra =
Sumatera □ . 37 D2
Sumba ....... 39 F1
Sumba, Selat . 39 F1
Sumbawa .... 37 F5
Sumbawa Besar 37 F5
Sumbe ....... 56 G2
Šumen ....... 22 C6
Sumgait =
Sumqayıt ... 25 E6
Summerside .. 69 D4
Šumperk ..... 16 D3

Sumqayıt ..... 25 E6
Sumter ....... 75 C7
Sumy ........ 24 C3
Sunbury ...... 63 C3
Sunda, Selat .. 37 F3
Sunda Str. =
Sunda, Selat 37 F3
Sundarbans,
The ........ 41 G7
Sundargarh ... 40 F5
Sunderland ... 11 D6
Sundsvall ..... 8 F11
Sungaigerong . 37 E2
Sungailiat ... 37 E3
Sungaipakning 37 D2
Sungaipenuh .. 37 E2
Sungaitiram ... 37 E5
Sungari =
Songhua
Jiang → ... 35 B8
Sungguminasa 39 F1
Sunghua Chiang
= Songhua
Jiang → ... 35 B8
Sungurlu ..... 46 B3
Sunnyvale ... 82 B1
Suntar ....... 30 C9
Supaul ....... 40 D6
Superior ...... 77 B8
Superior, L. .. 69 D2
Suphan Dağı .. 46 C5
Supiori ....... 39 E5
Sûr, Lebanon .. 46 D3
Sûr, Oman ... 45 F4
Sura → ..... 24 B6
Surabaja =
Surabaya ... 37 F4
Surabaya .... 37 F4
Surakarta .... 37 F4
Surat, Australia 63 A4
Surat, India ... 43 J8
Surat Thani ... 36 C1
Suratgarh .... 42 E8
Surgut ....... 29 C8
Suriapet ..... 43 L11
Surigao ...... 38 C3
Surinam ■ .... 92 B2
Suriname ■ =
Surinam ■ ... 92 B2
Suriname → .. 92 A2
Surt ......... 52 B2
Surt, Khalīj ... 52 B2
Suruga-Wan .. 32 B6
Süsangerd .... 47 E7
Susanville ... 80 E3
Susquehanna →
............ 73 E7
Susques ..... 94 A3
Susunu ...... 39 E4
Susurluk ..... 23 E7
Sutherland Falls 65 F2
Sutlej → ..... 42 E7
Suva ........ 64 L12
Suva Planina .. 22 C4
Suvorov Is. =
Suwarrow Is. 65 L14
Suwałki ...... 17 A6
Suwarrow Is. .. 65 L14
Suweis, Khalîg
el .......... 52 C5
Suzdal ...... 24 B5
Suzhou ...... 35 C7
Suzu-Misaki ... 32 A5
Svealand □ ... 9 G10
Sverdlovsk =
Yekaterinburg 29 D7
Svetlogorsk =
Svyetlahorsk 17 B9
Svetozarevo ... 22 B3

Svishtov ...... 22 C5
Svislach ...... 17 B7
Svyetlahorsk .. 17 B9
Swabian Alps =
Schwäbische
Alb ........ 14 D5
Swakopmund . 58 C2
Swan Hill ..... 62 C3
Swansea,
Australia .... 63 B5
Swansea, U.K. . 11 F5
Swatow =
Shantou .... 35 D6
Swaziland ■ .. 59 D6
Sweden ■ .... 9 G10
Sweetwater .. 78 C3
Swellendam .. 58 E4
Świdnica ..... 16 C3
Świdnik ...... 17 C6
Świebodzin .. 16 B2
Świecie ...... 16 B4
Swift Current . 71 C9
Swindon ..... 11 F6
Swinemünde =
Świnoujście . 16 B2
Świnoujście .. 16 B2
Switzerland ■ . 13 C8
Sydney,
Australia .... 63 B5
Sydney, Canada 69 D4
Sydra, G. of =
Surt, Khalīj .. 52 B2
Syktyvkar .... 28 C6
Sylhet ....... 41 E8
Sylt ......... 14 A5
Sym ......... 29 C9
Syracuse ..... 73 C7
Syrdarya → .. 29 E7
Syria ■ ...... 46 D4
Syrian Desert =
Ash Shām,
Bādiyat ..... 47 D4
Syzran ...... 24 C6
Szczecin ..... 16 B2
Szczecinek ... 16 B3
Szczytno ..... 16 B5
Szechwan =
Sichuan □ .. 34 C5
Szeged ...... 16 E5
Székesfehérvár . 16 E4
Szekszárd .... 16 E4
Szentes ...... 16 E5
Szolnok ...... 16 E5
Szombathely .. 16 E3

T

Tabacal ...... 94 A4
Tabaco ...... 38 B2
Ṭābah ........ 47 F5
Tabarka ...... 54 A6
Ṭabas,
Khorāsān, Iran 44 C4
Ṭabas,
Khorāsān, Iran 45 C5
Tabatinga, Serra
da ......... 93 E5
Tablas ....... 38 B2
Table B. =
Tafelbaai ... 58 E3
Table Mt. ... 58 E3
Tábor ....... 16 D2
Tabora ...... 57 F6
Tabou ....... 55 H3
Tabrīz ....... 46 C6
Tabūk ....... 47 E4

# Tacheng

| Name | Page | Ref |
|---|---|---|
| Tacheng | 34 | B3 |
| Tacloban | 38 | B2 |
| Tacna | 91 | G4 |
| Tacoma | 80 | B2 |
| Tacuarembó | 94 | C5 |
| Tademaït, Plateau du | 54 | C5 |
| Tadjoura | 49 | E3 |
| Tadmor | 65 | D5 |
| Tadoussac | 69 | D4 |
| Tadzhikistan = Tajikistan ■ | 29 | F8 |
| Taegu | 35 | C7 |
| Taejŏn | 35 | C7 |
| Tafalla | 19 | A5 |
| Tafelbaai | 58 | E3 |
| Tafermaar | 39 | F4 |
| Taft | 38 | B3 |
| Taga Dzong | 41 | D7 |
| Taganrog | 25 | D4 |
| Tagbilaran | 38 | C2 |
| Tagish | 70 | B6 |
| Tagish L. | 70 | B6 |
| Tagliamento ▸ | 20 | B4 |
| Taguatinga | 93 | E5 |
| Tagum | 38 | C3 |
| Tagus = Tejo ▸ | 18 | C1 |
| Tahakopa | 65 | G3 |
| Tahan, Gunong | 36 | D2 |
| Tahat | 54 | D6 |
| Tāherī | 44 | E3 |
| Tahiti | 65 | L16 |
| Tahoe, L. | 80 | F3 |
| Tahoua | 55 | F6 |
| Tahta | 52 | C5 |
| Tahulandang | 39 | D3 |
| Tahuna | 39 | D3 |
| Taï | 55 | G3 |
| Tai Hu | 35 | C7 |
| Taibei | 35 | D7 |
| T'aichung = Taizhong | 35 | D7 |
| Taidong | 35 | D7 |
| Taieri ▸ | 65 | G4 |
| Taihape | 64 | C6 |
| Tailem Bend | 62 | C2 |
| Taimyr Peninsula = Taymyr, Poluostrov | 30 | B7 |
| Tain | 10 | C4 |
| Tainan | 35 | D7 |
| Taínaron, Ákra | 23 | F4 |
| T'aipei = Taibei | 35 | D7 |
| Taiping | 36 | D2 |
| Taitao, Pen. de | 95 | F1 |
| Taiwan ■ | 35 | D7 |
| Taïyetos Óros | 23 | F4 |
| Taiyuan | 35 | C6 |
| Taizhong | 35 | D7 |
| Ta'izz | 49 | E3 |
| Tajikistan ■ | 29 | F8 |
| Tajo = Tejo ▸ | 18 | C1 |
| Tājūrā | 52 | B1 |
| Tak | 36 | A1 |
| Takada | 32 | A6 |
| Takaka | 65 | D5 |
| Takamatsu | 32 | B4 |
| Takaoka | 32 | A5 |
| Takapuna | 64 | B6 |
| Takasaki | 32 | A6 |
| Takatsuki | 32 | B4 |
| Takaungu | 57 | E7 |
| Takayama | 32 | A5 |
| Takefu | 32 | B5 |
| Takengon | 36 | D1 |
| Takeo | 36 | B2 |
| Tākestān | 46 | D7 |
| Takhār □ | 45 | B7 |
| Takum | 55 | G6 |
| Talara | 90 | D2 |
| Talas | 29 | E8 |
| Talaud, Kepulauan | 38 | D3 |
| Talaud Is. = Talaud, Kepulauan | 38 | D3 |
| Talavera de la Reina | 18 | C3 |
| Talayan | 38 | C2 |
| Talbragar ▸ | 63 | B4 |
| Talca | 94 | D2 |
| Talcahuano | 94 | D2 |
| Talcher | 40 | G5 |
| Taldy Kurgan = Taldyqorghan | 29 | E8 |
| Taldyqorghan | 29 | E8 |
| Ţalesh, Kūhhā-ye | 46 | C7 |
| Tali Post | 53 | G5 |
| Talibon | 38 | B2 |
| Taliwang | 37 | F5 |
| Tall 'Afar | 46 | C5 |
| Talladega | 74 | C4 |
| Tallahassee | 75 | D5 |
| Tallangatta | 63 | C4 |
| Tallarook | 63 | C4 |
| Tallinn | 24 | B1 |
| Talodi | 53 | F5 |
| Taltal | 94 | B2 |
| Talwood | 63 | A4 |
| Talyawalka Cr. ▸ | 62 | B3 |
| Tamale | 55 | G4 |
| Tamanrasset | 54 | D6 |
| Tamarang | 63 | B5 |
| Tamaské | 55 | F6 |
| Tambacounda | 55 | F2 |
| Tambelan, Kepulauan | 37 | D3 |
| Tambo de Mora | 91 | F3 |
| Tambora | 37 | F5 |
| Tambov | 24 | C5 |
| Tamburâ | 53 | G4 |
| Tâmchekket | 55 | E2 |
| Tamega ▸ | 18 | B1 |
| Tamenglong | 41 | E9 |
| Tamgak, Mts. | 55 | E6 |
| Tamil Nadu □ | 43 | P10 |
| Tammerfors = Tampere | 8 | F12 |
| Tamo Abu, Pegunungan | 37 | D5 |
| Tampa | 75 | F6 |
| Tampere | 8 | F12 |
| Tampico | 84 | C5 |
| Tamrida = Qādib | 49 | E5 |
| Tamsagbulag | 35 | B6 |
| Tamu | 41 | E10 |
| Tamworth | 63 | B5 |
| Tana ▸, Kenya | 57 | E8 |
| Tana ▸, Norway | 8 | D13 |
| Tana, L. | 53 | F6 |
| Tanahbala | 37 | E1 |
| Tanahgrogot | 37 | E5 |
| Tanahjampea | 39 | F2 |
| Tanahmasa | 37 | E1 |
| Tanahmerah | 39 | F6 |
| Tanami Desert | 60 | D5 |
| Tanana | 71 | B4 |
| Tanana ▸ | 71 | B4 |
| Tananarive = Antananarivo | 59 | H9 |
| Tánaro ▸ | 20 | B2 |
| Tandag | 38 | C3 |
| Tandil | 94 | D5 |
| Tandil, Sa. del | 94 | D5 |
| Tando Adam | 42 | G6 |
| Tandou L. | 62 | B3 |
| Tane-ga-Shima | 33 | D2 |
| Taneatua | 64 | C7 |
| Tanen Tong Dan | 41 | J12 |
| Tanezrouft | 54 | D5 |
| Tanga | 57 | F7 |
| Tanganyika, L. | 57 | F5 |
| Tanger = Tangier | 54 | A3 |
| Tanggula Shan | 34 | C4 |
| Tangier | 54 | A3 |
| Tangshan | 35 | C6 |
| Tanimbar, Kepulauan | 39 | F4 |
| Tanimbar Is. = Tanimbar, Kepulauan | 39 | F4 |
| Tanjay | 38 | C2 |
| Tanjore = Thanjavur | 43 | P11 |
| Tanjung | 37 | E5 |
| Tanjungbalai | 37 | D1 |
| Tanjungbatu | 37 | D5 |
| Tanjungkarang Telukbetung | 37 | F3 |
| Tanjungpandan | 37 | E3 |
| Tanjungpinang | 37 | D2 |
| Tanjungredeb | 37 | D5 |
| Tanjungselor | 37 | D5 |
| Tanout | 55 | F6 |
| Tanta | 52 | B5 |
| Tantung = Dandong | 35 | B7 |
| Tanunda | 62 | B2 |
| Tanzania ■ | 57 | F6 |
| Taolanaro | 59 | K9 |
| Taoudenni | 54 | D4 |
| Taourirt | 54 | B4 |
| Tapa Shan = Daba Shan | 35 | C5 |
| Tapah | 37 | D2 |
| Tapajós ▸ | 92 | C3 |
| Tapaktuan | 37 | D1 |
| Tapanui | 65 | F3 |
| Tapauá ▸ | 91 | E6 |
| Tapeta | 55 | G3 |
| Tapi ▸ | 43 | J8 |
| Tapirapecó, Serra | 90 | C6 |
| Tapuaenuku, Mt. | 65 | D5 |
| Tapul Group | 38 | C2 |
| Taquari ▸ | 91 | G7 |
| Tara, Australia | 63 | A5 |
| Tara, Russia | 29 | D8 |
| Tara ▸, Montenegro, Yug. | 22 | C2 |
| Tara ▸, Russia | 29 | D8 |
| Tarabagatay, Khrebet | 29 | E9 |
| Tarābulus, Lebanon | 46 | D3 |
| Tarābulus, Libya | 52 | B1 |
| Tarakan | 37 | D5 |
| Taralga | 63 | B4 |
| Taranaki □ | 64 | C6 |
| Tarancón | 19 | B4 |
| Taranga Hill | 43 | H8 |
| Táranto | 21 | D6 |
| Táranto, G. di | 21 | D6 |
| Tarapacá | 90 | D5 |
| Tararua Ra. | 64 | D6 |
| Tarashcha | 17 | D10 |
| Tarauacá | 91 | E4 |
| Tarauacá ▸ | 91 | E5 |
| Tarawera | 64 | C7 |
| Tarawera L. | 64 | C7 |
| Taraz | 29 | E8 |
| Tarbela Dam | 42 | B8 |
| Tarbes | 12 | E4 |
| Tarcoola | 62 | B1 |
| Tarcoon | 63 | B4 |
| Taree | 63 | B5 |
| Tarfaya | 54 | C2 |
| Tarija | 94 | A4 |
| Tariku ▸ | 39 | E5 |
| Tarim Basin = Tarim Pendi | 34 | C3 |
| Tarim He ▸ | 34 | C3 |
| Tarim Pendi | 34 | C3 |
| Taritatu ▸ | 39 | E5 |
| Tarkhankut, Mys | 25 | D3 |
| Tarko Sale | 28 | C8 |
| Tarkwa | 55 | G4 |
| Tarlac | 38 | A2 |
| Tarma | 91 | F3 |
| Tarn ▸ | 12 | D4 |
| Tarnobrzeg | 16 | C5 |
| Tarnów | 16 | C5 |
| Tarnowskie Góry | 16 | C4 |
| Taroom | 63 | A4 |
| Taroudannt | 54 | B3 |
| Tarragona | 19 | B6 |
| Tarrasa | 19 | B7 |
| Tarso Emissi | 52 | D2 |
| Tarsus | 46 | C3 |
| Tartagal | 94 | A4 |
| Tartu | 24 | B2 |
| Tarţūs | 46 | D3 |
| Tarutung | 37 | D1 |
| Tasāwah | 52 | C1 |
| Taschereau | 69 | D3 |
| Tash-Kömür | 29 | E8 |
| Tash-Kumyr = Tash-Kömür | 29 | E8 |
| Tashauz = Dashhowuz | 29 | E6 |
| Tashi Chho Dzong = Thimphu | 41 | D7 |
| Tashkent = Toshkent | 29 | E7 |
| Tashtagol | 29 | D9 |
| Tasman B. | 65 | D5 |
| Tasman Mts. | 65 | D5 |
| Tasman Pen. | 62 | D4 |
| Tasmania □ | 62 | D4 |
| Tatabánya | 16 | E4 |
| Tatar Republic □ = Tatarstan □ | 29 | D6 |
| Tatarbunary | 17 | F9 |
| Tatarsk | 29 | D8 |
| Tatarstan □ | 29 | D6 |
| Tateyama | 32 | B6 |
| Tathra | 63 | C4 |
| Tatra = Tatry | 16 | D4 |
| Tatry | 16 | D4 |
| Tatta | 43 | G5 |
| Tatuï | 94 | A7 |
| Tat'ung = Datong | 35 | B6 |
| Tatvan | 46 | C5 |
| Taubaté | 94 | A7 |
| Tauern | 15 | E7 |
| Taumarunui | 64 | C6 |
| Taumaturgo | 91 | E4 |
| Taungdwingyi | 41 | G10 |
| Taunggyi | 41 | G11 |
| Taungup | 41 | H10 |
| Taungup Pass | 41 | H10 |
| Taungup Taunggya | 41 | H9 |
| Taunton | 11 | F5 |

| | | |
|---|---|---|
| Taunus | 14 | C5 |
| Taupo | 64 | C7 |
| Taupo, L. | 64 | C6 |
| Tauranga | 64 | B7 |
| Tauranga Harb. | 64 | B7 |
| Taurianova | 21 | E6 |
| Taurus Mts. = | | |
| Toros Dağları | 46 | C3 |
| Tavda | 29 | D7 |
| Tavda → | 29 | D7 |
| Taveta | 57 | E7 |
| Tavira | 18 | D2 |
| Tavoy | 36 | B1 |
| Tawau | 36 | D5 |
| Tawitawi | 38 | C2 |
| Tay → | 10 | C5 |
| Tayabamba | 91 | E3 |
| Taylakova | 29 | D8 |
| Taylakovy = | | |
| Taylakova | 29 | D8 |
| Taymä | 47 | F4 |
| Taymyr, Oz. | 30 | B8 |
| Taymyr, | | |
| Poluostrov | 30 | B7 |
| Taytay | 38 | B1 |
| Taz → | 28 | C8 |
| Taza | 54 | B4 |
| Tazovskiy | 28 | C8 |
| Tbilisi | 25 | E5 |
| Tchad = Chad ■ | 53 | E2 |
| Tchad, L. | 53 | F1 |
| Tch'eng-tou = | | |
| Chengdu | 35 | C5 |
| Tchibanga | 56 | E2 |
| Tch'ong-k'ing = | | |
| Chongqing | 35 | D5 |
| Tczew | 16 | A4 |
| Te Anau, L. | 65 | F2 |
| Te Aroha | 64 | B6 |
| Te Awamutu | 64 | C6 |
| Te Kuiti | 64 | C6 |
| Te Puke | 64 | B7 |
| Te Waewae B. | 65 | G2 |
| Tebakang | 37 | D4 |
| Tébessa | 54 | A6 |
| Tebicuary → | 94 | B5 |
| Tebingtinggi | 37 | D1 |
| Tecuci | 22 | B6 |
| Tedzhen = | | |
| Tejen | 29 | F7 |
| Tefé | 90 | D6 |
| Tegal | 37 | F3 |
| Tegina | 55 | F6 |
| Tegucigalpa | 85 | E7 |
| Tehachapi | 82 | C3 |
| Tehrān | 44 | C2 |
| Tehuantepec | 85 | D5 |
| Tehuantepec, G. | | |
| de | 85 | D5 |
| Tehuantepec, | | |
| Istmo de | 85 | D6 |
| Tejen | 29 | F7 |
| Tejo → | 18 | C1 |
| Tekapo, L. | 65 | E4 |
| Tekeli | 29 | E8 |
| Tekirdağ | 22 | D6 |
| Tekkali | 40 | H5 |
| Tel Aviv-Yafo | 46 | D3 |
| Tela | 85 | D7 |
| Telanaipura = | | |
| Jambi | 37 | E2 |
| Telavi | 25 | E6 |
| Telekhany = | | |
| Tsyelyakhany | 17 | B7 |
| Teles Pires → | 91 | E7 |
| Telford | 11 | E5 |
| Télimélé | 55 | F2 |
| Tellicherry | 43 | P9 |
| Telsen | 95 | E3 |
| Teluk Anson | 37 | D2 |
| Teluk Betung = | | |
| Tanjungkarang | | |
| Telukbetung | 37 | F3 |
| Teluk Intan = | | |
| Teluk Anson | 37 | D2 |
| Telukbutun | 37 | D3 |
| Telukdalem | 37 | D1 |
| Tema | 55 | G4 |
| Temax | 85 | C7 |
| Temerloh | 37 | D2 |
| Temir | 29 | E6 |
| Temirtau, | | |
| *Kazakstan* | 29 | D8 |
| Temirtau, *Russia* | 29 | D9 |
| Temma | 62 | D3 |
| Temora | 63 | B4 |
| Tempe | 83 | D7 |
| Temple | 78 | D5 |
| Temuco | 94 | D2 |
| Temuka | 65 | F4 |
| Tenali | 40 | J3 |
| Tenasserim | 36 | B1 |
| Tenda, Col di | 20 | B1 |
| Tendaho | 49 | E3 |
| Tenerife | 54 | C1 |
| Teng Xian | 35 | C6 |
| Tengah □ | 39 | E2 |
| Tengah | | |
| Kepulauan | 37 | F5 |
| Tengchong | 34 | D4 |
| Tenggara □ | 39 | E2 |
| Tenggarong | 37 | E5 |
| Tengiz, Ozero | 29 | D7 |
| Tenkasi | 43 | Q10 |
| Tenke | 57 | G5 |
| Tenkodogo | 55 | F4 |
| Tennessee □ | 74 | B4 |
| Tennessee → | 72 | F1 |
| Tenom | 36 | C5 |
| Tenryū- | | |
| Gawa → | 32 | B5 |
| Tenterfield | 63 | A5 |
| Teófilo Otoni | 93 | F5 |
| Tepa | 39 | F3 |
| Tepessa | 39 | F3 |
| Tepic | 84 | C4 |
| Teplice | 16 | C1 |
| Ter → | 19 | A7 |
| Téra | 55 | F5 |
| Téramo | 20 | C4 |
| Terang | 62 | C3 |
| Terebovlya | 17 | D7 |
| Terek → | 25 | E6 |
| Teresina | 92 | D5 |
| Terewah, L. | 63 | A4 |
| Terhazza | 54 | D3 |
| Teridgerie | | |
| Cr. → | 63 | B4 |
| Termez = | | |
| Termiz | 29 | F7 |
| Términi Imerese | 21 | F4 |
| Termiz | 29 | F7 |
| Térmoli | 20 | C5 |
| Ternate | 39 | D3 |
| Terni | 20 | C4 |
| Ternopil | 17 | D7 |
| Ternopol = | | |
| Ternopil | 17 | D7 |
| Terowie, *N.S.W.,* | | |
| *Australia* | 63 | B4 |
| Terowie, | | |
| *S. Austral.,* | | |
| *Australia* | 62 | B2 |
| Terracina | 20 | D4 |
| Terralba | 21 | E2 |
| Terranova = | | |
| Ólbia | 20 | D2 |
| Terrassa = | | |
| Tarrasa | 19 | B7 |
| Terre Haute | 72 | E2 |
| Terschelling | 14 | B3 |
| Teruel | 19 | B5 |
| Teryaweyna L. | 62 | B3 |
| Teshio- | | |
| Gawa | 32 | F12 |
| Tesiyn | | |
| Gol | 34 | A4 |
| Teslin | 70 | B6 |
| Tessalit | 54 | D5 |
| Tessaoua | 55 | F6 |
| Tetas, Pta. | 94 | A2 |
| Tete | 59 | B6 |
| Teterev → | 17 | C10 |
| Teteven | 22 | C5 |
| Tetiyev | 17 | D9 |
| Tétouan | 54 | A3 |
| Tetovo | 22 | C3 |
| Teuco → | 94 | B4 |
| Teun | 39 | F3 |
| Teutoburger | | |
| Wald | 14 | B5 |
| Tévere → | 20 | D4 |
| Tewantin | 63 | A5 |
| Texarkana | 79 | C6 |
| Texas □ | 63 | A5 |
| Texas □ | 78 | D4 |
| Texas City | 79 | E6 |
| Texel | 14 | B3 |
| Teyvareh | 45 | C6 |
| Tezpur | 41 | D9 |
| Thabana | | |
| Ntlenyana | 59 | D5 |
| Thabazimbi | 59 | C5 |
| Thailand ■ | 36 | A2 |
| Thailand, G. of | 36 | B2 |
| Thakhek | 36 | A2 |
| Thal | 42 | C7 |
| Thala La | 41 | C11 |
| Thallon | 63 | A4 |
| Thames | 64 | B6 |
| Thames → | 11 | F7 |
| Thane | 43 | K8 |
| Thanh Pho Ho | | |
| Chi Minh | 36 | B3 |
| Thanjavur | 43 | P11 |
| Thar Desert | 42 | F7 |
| Tharad | 43 | G7 |
| Thargomindah | 63 | A3 |
| Tharrawaddy | 41 | J10 |
| Thásos | 23 | D5 |
| Thaton | 41 | J11 |
| Thaungdut | 41 | E10 |
| Thayetmyo | 41 | H10 |
| Thazi | 41 | G11 |
| The Alberga → | 62 | A2 |
| The Coorong | 62 | C2 |
| The Frome → | 62 | A2 |
| The Grampians | 62 | C3 |
| The Great Divide | | |
| = Great | | |
| Dividing Ra. | 61 | E8 |
| The Hague = 's- | | |
| Gravenhage | 14 | B3 |
| The | | |
| Hamilton → | 62 | A2 |
| The | | |
| Macumba → | 62 | A2 |
| The Neales → | 62 | A2 |
| The Pas | 71 | C9 |
| The Rock | 63 | C4 |
| The Salt L. | 62 | B3 |
| The | | |
| Stevenson → | 62 | A2 |
| The | | |
| Warburton → | 62 | A2 |
| Thebes = Thívai | 23 | E4 |
| Theebine | 63 | A5 |
| Thermaïkós | | |
| Kólpos | 23 | D4 |
| Thermopylae P. | 23 | E4 |
| Thessaloníki | 23 | D4 |
| Thessaloníki,. | | |
| Gulf of = | | |
| Thermaïkós | | |
| Kólpos | 23 | D4 |
| Thetford | 11 | E7 |
| Thetford Mines | 69 | D3 |
| Thevenard | 62 | B1 |
| Thiel Mts. | 96 | C2 |
| Thiers | 13 | D5 |
| Thies | 55 | F1 |
| Thika | 57 | E7 |
| Thimphu | 41 | D7 |
| Thionville | 13 | B7 |
| Thíra | 23 | F5 |
| Thistle I. | 62 | C2 |
| Thívai | 23 | E4 |
| Thomas, L. | 62 | A2 |
| Thomasville, | | |
| *Ga., U.S.A.* | 75 | D6 |
| Thomasville, | | |
| *N.C., U.S.A.* | 75 | B7 |
| Thompson | 71 | C10 |
| Thomson's Falls | | |
| = Nyahururu | 57 | D7 |
| Thrace | 22 | D6 |
| Three Hummock | | |
| I. | 62 | D3 |
| Three Points, C. | 55 | H4 |
| Thun | 13 | C7 |
| Thunder Bay | 69 | D2 |
| Thung Song | 36 | C1 |
| Thunkar | 41 | D8 |
| Thüringer Wald | 14 | C6 |
| Thurles | 11 | E3 |
| Thurloo Downs | 63 | A3 |
| Thurso | 10 | B5 |
| Thurston I. | 96 | B2 |
| Thylungra | 63 | A3 |
| Tia | 63 | B5 |
| Tian Shan | 34 | B3 |
| Tianjin | 35 | C6 |
| Tianshui | 35 | C5 |
| Tiaret | 54 | A5 |
| Tiassalé | 55 | G4 |
| Tibati | 53 | G1 |
| Tiber = | | |
| Tévere → | 20 | D4 |
| Tiberias, L. = | | |
| Yam Kinneret | 46 | D3 |
| Tibesti | 52 | D2 |
| Tibet = | | |
| Xizang □ | 34 | C3 |
| Tibooburra | 62 | A3 |
| Tiburón | 84 | B2 |
| Tîchît | 55 | E3 |
| Ticino → | 20 | B2 |
| Tiddim | 41 | F9 |
| Tidjikja | 55 | E2 |
| Tidore | 39 | D3 |
| Tiel | 55 | F1 |
| Tierra de | | |
| Campos | 18 | A3 |
| Tierra del | | |
| Fuego, I. Gr. | | |
| de | 95 | G3 |
| Tiétar → | 18 | C2 |
| Tieyon | 62 | A1 |
| Tiflis = Tbilisi | 25 | E5 |
| Tifu | 39 | E3 |
| Tighina | 17 | E9 |
| Tignish | 69 | D4 |
| Tigre → | 90 | D4 |
| Tigris = Dijlah, | | |
| Nahr → | 47 | E6 |
| Tigyaing | 41 | F11 |

# Tîh, Gebel el

| | | |
|---|---|---|
| Tîh, Gebel el . . | 52 | C5 |
| Tijuana . . . . . . . | 84 | A1 |
| Tikamgarh . . . . | 43 | G11 |
| Tikhoretsk . . . . | 25 | D5 |
| Tikrīt . . . . . . . . . | 46 | D5 |
| Tiksi . . . . . . . . . | 30 | B10 |
| Tilamuta . . . . . | 39 | D2 |
| Tilburg . . . . . . . | 14 | C3 |
| Tillabéri . . . . . . | 55 | F5 |
| Tílos . . . . . . . . . | 23 | F6 |
| Tilpa . . . . . . . . . | 63 | B3 |
| Tilsit = Sovetsk | 24 | B1 |
| Timaru . . . . . . . | 65 | F4 |
| Timbedgha . . . . | 55 | E3 |
| Timboon . . . . . | 62 | C3 |
| Timbuktu = | | |
| Tombouctou | 55 | E4 |
| Timimoun . . . . | 54 | C5 |
| Timişoara . . . . . | 16 | F5 |
| Timmins . . . . . | 69 | D2 |
| Timok → . . . . . | 22 | B4 |
| Timon . . . . . . . | 92 | D5 |
| Timor . . . . . . . | 39 | F2 |
| Tinaca Pt. . . . . . | 38 | C3 |
| Tindouf . . . . . . | 54 | C3 |
| Tingo Maria . . | 91 | E3 |
| Tinjoub . . . . . . . | 54 | C3 |
| Tinnevelly = | | |
| Tirunelveli . . | 43 | Q10 |
| Tinogasta . . . . . | 94 | B3 |
| Tínos . . . . . . . . | 23 | F5 |
| Tintinara . . . . . | 62 | C3 |
| Tioman, Pulau . | 37 | D2 |
| Tipongpani . . . | 41 | D10 |
| Tipperary . . . . . | 11 | E2 |
| Tīrān . . . . . . . . | 44 | C2 |
| Tirana . . . . . . . . | 22 | D2 |
| Tiranë = Tirana | 22 | D2 |
| Tiraspol . . . . . . | 17 | E9 |
| Tire . . . . . . . . . . | 23 | E6 |
| Tirebolu . . . . . . | 46 | B4 |
| Tiree . . . . . . . . . | 10 | C3 |
| Tîrgovişte . . . . . | 22 | B5 |
| Tîrgu-Jiu . . . . . | 17 | F6 |
| Tîrgu Mureş . . . | 17 | E7 |
| Tirich Mir . . . . | 42 | A7 |
| Tîrnăveni . . . . . | 17 | E7 |
| Tírnavos . . . . . . | 23 | E4 |
| Tirodi . . . . . . . . | 43 | J11 |
| Tirol □ . . . . . . . | 14 | E6 |
| Tirso → . . . . . . | 20 | D7 |
| Tiruchchirappalli | 43 | P11 |
| Tirunelveli . . . . | 43 | Q10 |
| Tirupati . . . . . . | 43 | N11 |
| Tiruppur . . . . . | 43 | P10 |
| Tiruvannamalai | 43 | N11 |
| Tisa → . . . . . . | 22 | B3 |
| Tisdale . . . . . . . | 71 | C9 |
| Tisza = Tisa → | 22 | B3 |
| Tit-Ary . . . . . . . | 30 | B10 |
| Titicaca, L. . . . . | 91 | G5 |
| Titograd = | | |
| Podgorica . . . | 22 | C2 |
| Titov Veles . . . . | 22 | D3 |
| Titova-Mitrovica | | |
| = Kosovska- | | |
| Mitrovica . . . | 22 | C3 |
| Titovo Užice . . . | 22 | C2 |
| Titule . . . . . . . . | 57 | D5 |
| Tivaouane . . . . | 55 | F1 |
| Tívoli . . . . . . . . | 20 | D4 |
| Tiwī . . . . . . . . . | 45 | F4 |
| Tizi-Ouzou . . . . | 54 | A5 |
| Tiznit . . . . . . . . | 54 | C3 |
| Tjirebon = | | |
| Cirebon . . . . . | 37 | F3 |
| Tlaxcala . . . . . . | 84 | D5 |
| Tlaxiaco . . . . . . | 84 | D5 |
| Tlemcen . . . . . . | 54 | B4 |

| | | |
|---|---|---|
| Tmassah . . . . . | 52 | C2 |
| Toamasina . . . . | 59 | H9 |
| Toay . . . . . . . . . | 94 | D4 |
| Toba . . . . . . . . . | 32 | B5 |
| Toba Kakar . . . | 42 | D6 |
| Tobago . . . . . . . | 87 | D7 |
| Tobelo . . . . . . . | 39 | D3 |
| Tobermory . . . . | 10 | C3 |
| Toboali . . . . . . . | 37 | E3 |
| Tobol → . . . . | 29 | D7 |
| Toboli . . . . . . . . | 39 | E2 |
| Tobolsk . . . . . . | 29 | D7 |
| Tobruk = | | |
| Tubruq . . . . . | 52 | B3 |
| Tobyl = | | |
| Tobol → . . . | 29 | D7 |
| Tocantinópolis | 92 | D4 |
| Tocantins □ . . . | 93 | E4 |
| Tocantins → . . | 92 | C4 |
| Tochigi . . . . . . . | 32 | A6 |
| Tocopilla . . . . . | 94 | A2 |
| Tocumwal . . . . | 63 | C4 |
| Tocuyo → . . . | 90 | A5 |
| Todeli . . . . . . . . | 39 | E2 |
| Todenyang . . . | 57 | D7 |
| Todos os | | |
| Santos, B. de | 93 | E6 |
| Togba . . . . . . . . | 55 | E2 |
| Togian, | | |
| Kepulauan . . | 39 | E2 |
| Togliatti . . . . . . | 24 | C6 |
| Togo ■ . . . . . . . | 55 | G5 |
| Toinya . . . . . . . | 53 | G4 |
| Tojikiston = | | |
| Tajikistan ■ . | 29 | F8 |
| Tojo . . . . . . . . . | 39 | E2 |
| Tokala . . . . . . . | 39 | E2 |
| Tōkamachi . . . . | 32 | A6 |
| Tokanui . . . . . . | 65 | G3 |
| Tokar . . . . . . . . | 53 | E6 |
| Tokarahi . . . . . . | 65 | F4 |
| Tokat . . . . . . . . | 46 | B4 |
| Tokelau Is. . . . . | 65 | K13 |
| Tokmak . . . . . . | 29 | E8 |
| Tokushima . . . . | 32 | B4 |
| Tokuyama . . . . | 32 | B2 |
| Tōkyō . . . . . . . . | 32 | B6 |
| Tolaga Bay . . . | 64 | C8 |
| Tolbukhin = | | |
| Dobrich . . . . . | 22 | C6 |
| Toledo, Spain . | 18 | C3 |
| Toledo, U.S.A. . | 72 | D4 |
| Toledo, Montes | | |
| de . . . . . . . . . . | 18 | C3 |
| Tolga . . . . . . . . | 54 | B6 |
| Toliara . . . . . . . | 59 | J8 |
| Tolima . . . . . . . | 90 | C3 |
| Tolitoli . . . . . . . | 39 | D2 |
| Tolo . . . . . . . . . | 56 | E3 |
| Tolo, Teluk . . . . | 39 | E2 |
| Toluca . . . . . . . | 84 | D5 |
| Tomakomai . . . | 32 | F12 |
| Tomar . . . . . . . | 18 | C1 |
| Tomaszów | | |
| Mazowiecki . | 16 | C4 |
| Tombé . . . . . . . | 53 | G5 |
| Tombouctou . . | 55 | E4 |
| Tombua . . . . . . | 58 | B2 |
| Tomelloso . . . . | 18 | C4 |
| Tomingley . . . . | 63 | B4 |
| Tomini . . . . . . . | 39 | D2 |
| Tomini, Teluk . | 39 | E2 |
| Tomorit . . . . . . | 23 | D3 |
| Tomsk . . . . . . . | 29 | D9 |
| Tonantins . . . . | 90 | D5 |
| Tonawanda . . . | 73 | C6 |
| Tondano . . . . . | 39 | D2 |
| Tonekābon . . . | 44 | B2 |
| Tong Xian . . . . | 35 | C6 |

| | | |
|---|---|---|
| Tonga ■ . . . . . . | 65 | L13 |
| Tonga Trench . | 65 | L13 |
| Tongareva . . . . | 65 | K15 |
| Tongchuan . . . | 35 | C5 |
| Tonghua . . . . . | 35 | B7 |
| Tongjiang . . . . | 35 | B8 |
| Tongking, G. of | | |
| = Tonkin, G. | | |
| of . . . . . . . . . . | 35 | D5 |
| Tongoy . . . . . . | 94 | C2 |
| Tongren . . . . . . | 35 | D5 |
| Tongsa Dzong . | 41 | D8 |
| Tongue → . . . | 76 | B2 |
| Tonk . . . . . . . . | 42 | F9 |
| Tonkin, G. of . . | 35 | D5 |
| Tonlé Sap . . . . | 36 | B2 |
| Toompine . . . . | 63 | A3 |
| Toora . . . . . . . . | 63 | C4 |
| Toowoomba . . | 63 | A5 |
| Topeka . . . . . . | 77 | F7 |
| Topki . . . . . . . . | 29 | D9 |
| Topol'čany . . . . | 16 | D4 |
| Topolobampo . | 84 | B3 |
| Torata . . . . . . . | 91 | G4 |
| Torbalı . . . . . . . | 23 | E6 |
| Torbat-e | | |
| Heydārīyeh . . | 44 | C4 |
| Torbat-e Jām . . | 45 | C5 |
| Torbay . . . . . . . | 11 | F5 |
| Tordesillas . . . . | 18 | B3 |
| Torgau . . . . . . . | 15 | C7 |
| Torino . . . . . . . | 20 | B1 |
| Torit . . . . . . . . . | 53 | H5 |
| Tormes → . . . | 18 | B2 |
| Torne älv → . . | 8 | E12 |
| Torneå = Tornio | 8 | E12 |
| Torneträsk . . . | 8 | E11 |
| Tornio . . . . . . . | 8 | E12 |
| Tornquist . . . . . | 94 | D4 |
| Toro, Cerro del | 94 | B3 |
| Toroníios | | |
| Kólpos . . . . . | 23 | D4 |
| Toronto, | | |
| *Australia* . . . . | 63 | B5 |
| Toronto, *Canada* | 69 | D3 |
| Toropets . . . . . | 24 | B3 |
| Tororo . . . . . . . | 57 | D6 |
| Toros Dağları . . | 46 | C3 |
| Tôrre de | | |
| Moncorvo . . . | 18 | B2 |
| Torre del Greco | 21 | D5 |
| Torrejón de | | |
| Ardoz . . . . . . | 18 | B4 |
| Torrelavega . . . | 18 | A3 |
| Torremolinos . . | 18 | D3 |
| Torrens, L. . . . . | 62 | B2 |
| Torrente . . . . . . | 19 | C5 |
| Torreón . . . . . . | 84 | B4 |
| Torres . . . . . . . | 84 | B2 |
| Torres Vedras . | 18 | C1 |
| Torrevieja . . . . | 19 | D5 |
| Tortosa . . . . . . | 19 | B6 |
| Tortosa, C. de . | 19 | B6 |
| Toŗūd . . . . . . . | 44 | C3 |
| Toruń . . . . . . . | 16 | B4 |
| Tosa-Wan . . . . | 32 | C3 |
| Toscana □ . . . . | 20 | C3 |
| Toshkent . . . . . | 29 | E7 |
| Tostado . . . . . . | 94 | B4 |
| Tosya . . . . . . . . | 46 | B3 |
| Toteng . . . . . . . | 58 | C4 |
| Totma . . . . . . . | 24 | A5 |
| Totten Glacier . | 96 | A12 |
| Tottenham . . . . | 63 | B4 |
| Tottori . . . . . . . | 32 | B4 |
| Touba . . . . . . . | 55 | G3 |
| Toubkal, Djebel | 54 | B3 |
| Tougan . . . . . . | 55 | F4 |
| Touggourt . . . . | 54 | B6 |

| | | |
|---|---|---|
| Tougué . . . . . . . | 55 | F2 |
| Toul . . . . . . . . . | 13 | B6 |
| Toulepleu . . . . | 55 | G3 |
| Toulon . . . . . . . | 13 | E6 |
| Toulouse . . . . . | 12 | E4 |
| Toummo . . . . . | 52 | D1 |
| Toungoo . . . . . | 41 | H11 |
| Touraine . . . . . | 12 | C4 |
| Tourane = Da | | |
| Nang . . . . . . . | 36 | A3 |
| Tourcoing . . . . | 13 | A5 |
| Touriñán, C. . . . | 18 | A1 |
| Tournai . . . . . . | 14 | C2 |
| Tournon . . . . . . | 13 | D6 |
| Tours . . . . . . . . | 12 | C4 |
| Towamba . . . . | 63 | C4 |
| Towang . . . . . . | 41 | D8 |
| Townsville . . . . | 61 | D8 |
| Toyama . . . . . . | 32 | A5 |
| Toyohashi . . . . | 32 | B5 |
| Toyonaka . . . . | 32 | B4 |
| Toyooka . . . . . | 32 | B4 |
| Toyota . . . . . . . | 32 | B5 |
| Tozeur . . . . . . . | 54 | B6 |
| Trá Li = Tralee | 11 | E2 |
| Trabzon . . . . . . | 46 | B4 |
| Trafalgar, C. . . . | 18 | D2 |
| Trail . . . . . . . . . | 71 | D8 |
| Tralee . . . . . . . . | 11 | E2 |
| Trancas . . . . . . | 94 | B3 |
| Trang . . . . . . . . | 36 | C1 |
| Trangan . . . . . . | 39 | F4 |
| Trangie . . . . . . | 63 | B4 |
| Trani . . . . . . . . | 20 | D6 |
| Transantarctic | | |
| Mts. . . . . . . . . | 96 | C3 |
| Transilvania . . . | 17 | F7 |
| Transilvanian | | |
| Alps = | | |
| Carpaţii | | |
| Meridionali . . | 17 | F7 |
| Transylvania = | | |
| Transilvania . | 17 | F7 |
| Trápani . . . . . . . | 21 | E4 |
| Traralgon . . . . | 63 | C4 |
| Trasimeno, L. . | 20 | C4 |
| Traun . . . . . . . . | 15 | D8 |
| Travemünde . . | 15 | B6 |
| Travers, Mt. . . . | 65 | E5 |
| Travnik . . . . . . | 20 | B6 |
| Trébbia → . . . | 20 | B2 |
| Třebíč . . . . . . . | 16 | D2 |
| Trebinje . . . . . . | 20 | C7 |
| Treinta y Tres . | 94 | C6 |
| Trelew . . . . . . . | 95 | E3 |
| Tremp . . . . . . . | 19 | A6 |
| Trenčín . . . . . . | 16 | D4 |
| Trenque | | |
| Lauquen . . . . | 94 | D4 |
| Trent → . . . . . | 11 | E6 |
| Trento . . . . . . . | 20 | A3 |
| Trenton . . . . . . | 73 | D8 |
| Trepassey . . . . | 69 | D5 |
| Tres Arroyos . . | 94 | D4 |
| Três Corações . | 93 | G4 |
| Três Lagoas . . . | 93 | G3 |
| Tres Montes, C. | 95 | F1 |
| Tres Puentes . . | 94 | B2 |
| Tres Puntas, C. | 95 | F3 |
| Três Rios . . . . . | 93 | G5 |
| Treviso . . . . . . | 20 | B4 |
| Triabunna . . . . | 62 | D4 |
| Trichinopoly = | | |
| Tiruchchirappalli | | |
| . . . . . . . . . . . . | 43 | P11 |
| Trichur . . . . . . | 43 | P10 |
| Trida . . . . . . . . | 63 | B4 |
| Trier . . . . . . . . . | 14 | D4 |
| Trieste . . . . . . . | 20 | B4 |

| | | |
|---|---|---|
| Triglav | 20 | A4 |
| Tríkkala | 23 | E3 |
| Trikora, Puncak | 39 | E5 |
| Trinidad, *Bolivia* | 91 | F6 |
| Trinidad, *Colombia* | 90 | B4 |
| Trinidad, *Cuba* | 86 | B3 |
| Trinidad, *Uruguay* | 94 | C5 |
| Trinidad, *U.S.A.* | 78 | A1 |
| Trinidad, I. | 95 | D4 |
| Trinidad & Tobago ■ | 87 | D7 |
| Trinity → | 79 | E6 |
| Trinity B. | 69 | D5 |
| Trinity Range | 80 | E4 |
| Trinkitat | 53 | E6 |
| Tripoli = Tarābulus, *Lebanon* | 46 | D3 |
| Tripoli = Tarābulus, *Libya* | 52 | B1 |
| Trípolis | 23 | F4 |
| Tripura □ | 41 | F8 |
| Trivandrum | 43 | Q10 |
| Trnava | 16 | D3 |
| Troglav | 20 | C6 |
| Trois-Rivières | 69 | D3 |
| Troitsko Pechorsk | 28 | C6 |
| Trollhättan | 9 | G10 |
| Tronador | 95 | E2 |
| Trondheim | 8 | F10 |
| Trondheimsfjorden | 8 | F10 |
| Trout L. | 70 | B7 |
| Trouville-sur-Mer | 12 | B4 |
| Troy, *Turkey* | 23 | E6 |
| Troy, *Ala., U.S.A.* | 74 | D5 |
| Troy, *N.Y., U.S.A.* | 73 | C9 |
| Troyes | 13 | B6 |
| Trucial States = United Arab Emirates ■ | 44 | F3 |
| Trujillo, *Honduras* | 85 | D7 |
| Trujillo, *Peru* | 91 | E3 |
| Trujillo, *Spain* | 18 | C3 |
| Trujillo, *Venezuela* | 90 | B4 |
| Truk | 64 | J10 |
| Trundle | 63 | B4 |
| Truro, *Canada* | 69 | D4 |
| Truro, *U.K.* | 11 | F4 |
| Truskavets | 17 | D6 |
| Trutnov | 16 | C2 |
| Tsaratanana | 59 | H9 |
| Tsarevo = Michurin | 22 | C6 |
| Tsau | 58 | C4 |
| Tselinograd = Astana | 29 | D8 |
| Tsetserleg | 34 | B5 |
| Tshabong | 58 | D4 |
| Tshane | 58 | C4 |
| Tshela | 56 | E2 |
| Tshikapa | 56 | F4 |
| Tshofa | 57 | F5 |
| Tshwane | 58 | C4 |
| Tsihombe | 59 | K9 |
| Tsimlyansk Res. = Tsimlyanskoye Vdkhr. | 25 | D5 |
| Tsimlyanskoye Vdkhr. | 25 | D5 |

| | | |
|---|---|---|
| Tsinan = Jinan | 35 | C6 |
| Tsinghai = Qinghai □ | 34 | C4 |
| Tsingtao = Qingdao | 35 | C7 |
| Tskhinvali | 25 | E5 |
| Tsna → | 24 | C5 |
| Tsu | 32 | B5 |
| Tsuchiura | 32 | A7 |
| Tsugaru-Kaikyō | 32 | F12 |
| Tsumeb | 58 | B3 |
| Tsumis | 58 | C3 |
| Tsuruga | 32 | B5 |
| Tsurugi-San | 32 | C4 |
| Tsuruoka | 33 | G11 |
| Tsyelyakhany | 17 | B7 |
| Tual | 39 | F4 |
| Tuamotu Arch. = Tuamotu Is. | 65 | L16 |
| Tuamotu Is. | 65 | L16 |
| Tuamotu Ridge | 65 | M17 |
| Tuao | 38 | A2 |
| Tuapse | 25 | E4 |
| Tuatapere | 65 | G2 |
| Tubarão | 94 | B7 |
| Tubau | 37 | D4 |
| Tübingen | 14 | D5 |
| Tubruq | 52 | B3 |
| Tubuai Is. | 65 | M16 |
| Tucacas | 90 | A5 |
| Tucson | 83 | D7 |
| Tucumcari | 78 | B2 |
| Tucupita | 90 | B6 |
| Tucuruí | 92 | C4 |
| Tucuruí, Reprêsa de | 92 | C4 |
| Tudela | 19 | A5 |
| Tudmur | 46 | D4 |
| Tuen | 63 | A4 |
| Tuguegarao | 38 | A2 |
| Tukangbesi, Kepulauan | 39 | F2 |
| Tükrah | 52 | B3 |
| Tuktoyaktuk | 70 | B6 |
| Tukuyu | 57 | F6 |
| Tula, *Mexico* | 84 | C5 |
| Tula, *Russia* | 24 | C4 |
| Tulak | 45 | C5 |
| Tulancingo | 84 | C5 |
| Tulare | 82 | B3 |
| Tulcán | 90 | C3 |
| Tulcea | 17 | F9 |
| Tulchyn | 17 | D9 |
| Tuli, *Indonesia* | 39 | E2 |
| Tuli, *Zimbabwe* | 59 | C5 |
| Tullamore, *Australia* | 63 | B4 |
| Tullamore, *Ireland* | 11 | E3 |
| Tulle | 12 | D4 |
| Tullibigeal | 63 | B4 |
| Tulmaythah | 52 | B3 |
| Tulsa | 79 | A6 |
| Tulua | 90 | C3 |
| Tulungagung | 37 | F4 |
| Tum | 39 | E4 |
| Tumaco | 90 | C3 |
| Tumatumari | 90 | B7 |
| Tumba, L. | 56 | E3 |
| Tumbarumba | 63 | C4 |
| Túmbes | 90 | D2 |
| Tumby Bay | 62 | B2 |
| Tumeremo | 90 | B6 |
| Tumkur | 43 | N10 |
| Tump | 42 | F3 |
| Tumpat | 36 | C2 |
| Tumu | 55 | F4 |
| Tumucumaque, Serra | 92 | B3 |

| | | |
|---|---|---|
| Tumut | 63 | C4 |
| Tuncurry | 63 | B5 |
| Tunduru | 57 | G7 |
| Tundzha → | 22 | D6 |
| Tunga Pass | 41 | C10 |
| Tungabhadra → | 43 | M11 |
| Tungaru | 53 | F5 |
| Tunguska, Nizhnyaya → | 30 | C6 |
| Tunis | 54 | A7 |
| Tunisia ■ | 54 | B6 |
| Tunja | 90 | B4 |
| Tunuyán → | 94 | C3 |
| Tunxi | 35 | D6 |
| Tupelo | 74 | B3 |
| Tupinambaranas | 90 | D7 |
| Tupiza | 94 | A3 |
| Tupungato, Cerro | 94 | C3 |
| Túquerres | 90 | C3 |
| Tura | 30 | C8 |
| Turabah | 47 | E5 |
| Tūrān | 44 | C4 |
| Turayf | 47 | E4 |
| Turda | 17 | E6 |
| Turek | 16 | B4 |
| Turfan = Turpan | 34 | B3 |
| Turfan Depression = Turpan Hami | 34 | B3 |
| Türgovishte | 22 | C6 |
| Turgutlu | 23 | E6 |
| Turhal | 46 | B4 |
| Turia → | 19 | C5 |
| Turiaçu | 92 | C4 |
| Turiaçu → | 92 | C4 |
| Turin = Torino | 20 | B1 |
| Turkana, L. | 57 | D7 |
| Turkestan = Türkistan | 29 | E7 |
| Turkey ■ | 46 | C3 |
| Türkistan | 29 | E7 |
| Turkmenistan ■ | 29 | F6 |
| Turks & Caicos Is. ■ | 87 | B5 |
| Turku | 9 | F12 |
| Turnagain, C. | 64 | D7 |
| Turneffe Is. | 85 | D7 |
| Turnhout | 14 | C3 |
| Tŭrnovo = Veliko Tŭrnovo | 22 | C5 |
| Turnu Măgurele | 22 | C5 |
| Turnu Roşu, P. | 17 | F7 |
| Turpan | 34 | B3 |
| Turpan Hami | 34 | B3 |
| Turukhansk | 30 | C6 |
| Tuscaloosa | 74 | C4 |
| Tuscany = Toscana □ | 20 | C3 |
| Tuticorin | 43 | Q11 |
| Tutóia | 92 | C5 |
| Tutong | 36 | D4 |
| Tutrakan | 22 | B6 |
| Tuttlingen | 14 | E5 |
| Tutuala | 39 | F3 |
| Tutuila | 65 | L13 |
| Tuvalu ■ | 64 | K12 |
| Tuxpan | 84 | C5 |
| Tuxtla Gutiérrez | 85 | D6 |
| Tuy | 18 | A1 |
| Tuz Gölü | 46 | C3 |
| Ţūz Khurmātū | 46 | D6 |
| Tuzla | 20 | B7 |
| Tver | 24 | B4 |
| Tweed Heads | 63 | A5 |
| Twillingate | 69 | D5 |
| Twin Falls | 81 | D6 |

| | | |
|---|---|---|
| Twofold B. | 63 | C4 |
| Tyachiv | 17 | D6 |
| Tychy | 16 | C4 |
| Tyler | 79 | C6 |
| Tyre = Sūr | 46 | D3 |
| Tyrol = Tirol □ | 14 | E6 |
| Tyrrell → | 62 | C3 |
| Tyrrell, L. | 62 | C3 |
| Tyrrhenian Sea | 21 | E4 |
| Tyumen | 29 | D7 |
| Tzaneen | 59 | C6 |
| Tzukong = Zigong | 35 | D5 |

# U

| | | |
|---|---|---|
| U.S.A. = United States of America ■ | 67 | F10 |
| Uarsciek | 49 | G4 |
| Uato-Udo | 39 | F3 |
| Uatumã → | 90 | D7 |
| Uaupés | 90 | D5 |
| Uaupés → | 90 | C5 |
| Ubá | 93 | G5 |
| Ubaitaba | 93 | E6 |
| Ubangi = Oubangi → | 56 | E3 |
| Ubauro | 42 | E6 |
| Ube | 32 | C2 |
| Ubeda | 18 | C4 |
| Uberaba | 93 | F4 |
| Uberlândia | 93 | F4 |
| Ubon Ratchathani | 36 | A2 |
| Ubort → | 17 | B9 |
| Ubundu | 57 | E5 |
| Ucayali → | 90 | D4 |
| Uchiura-Wan | 32 | F12 |
| Udaipur | 43 | G8 |
| Udaipur Garhi | 40 | D6 |
| Udgir | 43 | K10 |
| Udhampur | 42 | C9 |
| Udi | 55 | G6 |
| Údine | 20 | A4 |
| Udmurtia □ | 28 | D6 |
| Udon Thani | 36 | A2 |
| Udupi | 43 | N9 |
| Ueda | 32 | A6 |
| Uele → | 57 | D4 |
| Uelzen | 14 | B6 |
| Ufa | 29 | D6 |
| Ugab → | 58 | C2 |
| Ugalla → | 57 | F6 |
| Uganda ■ | 57 | D6 |
| Ugljane | 20 | B5 |
| Ugolyak | 30 | C10 |
| Uibhist a Deas = South Uist | 10 | C3 |
| Uibhist a Tuath = North Uist | 10 | C3 |
| Uíge | 56 | F2 |
| Uinta Mts. | 81 | E8 |
| Uitenhage | 59 | E5 |
| Ujjain | 43 | H9 |
| Ujung Pandang | 39 | F1 |
| Ukerewe I. | 57 | E6 |
| Ukhrul | 41 | E10 |
| Ukhta | 28 | C6 |
| Ukraine ■ | 25 | D3 |
| Ulaanbaatar | 35 | B5 |
| Ulaangom | 34 | A4 |
| Ulan Bator = Ulaanbaatar | 35 | B5 |
| Ulan Ude | 30 | D8 |
| Ulcinj | 22 | D2 |

# Ulhasnagar

| | | | | | | | | | | |
|---|---|---|---|---|---|---|---|---|---|---|
| Ulhasnagar | ... | 43 | K8 | Urbino | ...... | 20 | C4 | Uttar Pradesh □ | 42 | F11 |
| Ulladulla | ..... | 63 | C5 | Urbión, Picos de | 19 | A4 | Uttaranchal □... | 40 | C2 |
| Ullapool | ...... | 10 | C4 | Urcos | ........ | 91 | F4 | Uttaradit | ...... | 36 | A2 |
| Ulm | ...... | 14 | D5 | Urda | ......... | 25 | D6 | Uummannarsuaq | | |
| Ulmarra | ...... | 63 | A5 | Urdzhar | ...... | 29 | E9 | = Farvel, Kap | 68 | C6 |
| Ulonguè | ...... | 59 | A6 | Ures | ......... | 84 | B2 | Uusikaupunki | . | 8 | F12 |
| Ulster □ | ...... | 11 | D3 | Urfa = Sanliurfa | 46 | C4 | Uvat | ......... | 29 | D7 |
| Ulubat Gölü | .. | 23 | D7 | Urganch | ...... | 29 | E7 | Uvinza | ...... | 57 | F6 |
| Uludağ | ....... | 23 | D7 | Urgench = | | | Uvira | ........ | 57 | E5 |
| Ulungur He → | 34 | B3 | Urganch | ... | 29 | E7 | Uvs Nuur | ..... | 34 | A4 |
| Uluru = Ayers | | | Uribia | ........ | 90 | A4 | Uwajima | ..... | 32 | C3 |
| Rock | ....... | 60 | F5 | Urla | ........ | 23 | E6 | Uyuni | ........ | 91 | H5 |
| Ulutau | ....... | 29 | E7 | Urmia = | | | Uzbekistan ■ .. | 29 | E7 |
| Ulverstone | ... | 62 | D4 | Orūmīyeh | ... | 46 | C6 | Uzerche | ...... | 12 | D4 |
| Ulyanovsk = | | | Urmia, L. = | | | Uzh → | ...... | 17 | C10 |
| Simbirsk | .... | 24 | C6 | Orūmīyeh, | | | Uzhgorod = | | |
| Ulyasutay | ..... | 34 | B4 | Daryācheh-ye | 46 | C6 | Uzhhorod | ... | 17 | D6 |
| Umala | ....... | 91 | G5 | Uroševac | ..... | 22 | C3 | Uzhhorod | ... | 17 | D6 |
| Uman | ........ | 17 | D10 | Uruana | ....... | 93 | F4 | Uzunköprü | .... | 22 | D6 |
| Umaria | ....... | 40 | F3 | Urubamba | .... | 91 | F4 | | | | |
| Umarkot | ...... | 43 | G6 | Urubamba → | . | 91 | F4 | | | | |
| Umba | ........ | 28 | C4 | Uruçuí | ....... | 92 | D5 | **V** | | | |
| Umbrella Mts. .. | 65 | F3 | Uruguai → | ... | 94 | B6 | | | | |
| Ume älv → | . | 8 | F12 | Uruguaiana | ... | 94 | B5 | | | | |
| Umeå | ........ | 8 | F12 | Uruguay ■ | .... | 94 | C5 | Vaal → | ...... | 58 | D4 |
| Umera | ....... | 39 | E3 | Uruguay → | .. | 94 | C5 | Vaasa | ........ | 8 | F12 |
| Umm al | | | Urumchi = | | | Vác | ......... | 16 | E4 |
| Qaywayn | ... | 44 | E3 | Ürümqi | ..... | 34 | B3 | Vach → = | | |
| Umm Bel | .... | 53 | F4 | Ürümqi | ..... | 34 | B3 | Vakh → | ... | 29 | C8 |
| Umm Lajj | .... | 47 | F4 | Usakos | ...... | 58 | C3 | Vadodara | .... | 43 | H8 |
| Umm Ruwaba . | 53 | F5 | Usedom | ..... | 15 | B8 | Vadsø → | .... | 8 | D13 |
| Umnak I. | ..... | 71 | C3 | Ush-Tobe | ..... | 29 | E8 | Vaduz | ....... | 13 | C8 |
| Umniati → | .. | 59 | B5 | Ushant = | | | Váh → | ...... | 16 | E4 |
| Umtata | ...... | 59 | E5 | Ouessant, I. d' | 12 | B1 | Vahsel B. | ..... | 96 | B5 |
| Umuarama | ... | 93 | G3 | Ushuaia | ...... | 95 | G3 | Vaigach | ..... | 28 | B6 |
| Una → | ...... | 20 | B6 | Üsküdar | ..... | 25 | E2 | Vakh → | ..... | 29 | C8 |
| Unalaska | ..... | 71 | C3 | Usman | ...... | 24 | C4 | Val d'Or | ..... | 69 | D3 |
| Uncía | ....... | 91 | G5 | Usoke | ....... | 57 | F6 | Valahia | ...... | 22 | B5 |
| Underbool | .... | 62 | C3 | Uspallata, P. de | 94 | C3 | Valandovo | .... | 22 | D4 |
| Ungarie | ...... | 63 | B4 | Uspenskiy | ... | 29 | E8 | Valcheta | ..... | 95 | E3 |
| Ungarra | ...... | 62 | B2 | Ussuriysk | .... | 31 | E11 | Valdayskaya | | |
| Ungava B. | ... | 68 | C4 | Ust-Aldan = | | | Vozvyshennost | | |
| Ungava Pen. | .. | 68 | B3 | Batamay | .... | 31 | C10 | ........... | 24 | B3 |
| Ungeny = | | | Ust Ilimpeya = | | | Valdepeñas | .. | 18 | C4 |
| Ungheni | .... | 17 | E8 | Yukti | ....... | 30 | C8 | Valdés, Pen. .. | 95 | E4 |
| Ungheni | .... | 17 | E8 | Ust Ishim | ..... | 29 | D8 | Valdez | ....... | 71 | B5 |
| União da Vitória | 94 | B6 | Ust- | | | Valdivia | ..... | 95 | D2 |
| Unimak I. | ..... | 71 | C3 | Kamenogorsk | | | Valdosta | ..... | 75 | D6 |
| United Arab | | | = Öskemen | . | 29 | E9 | Valença | ...... | 93 | E6 |
| Emirates ■ .. | 44 | F3 | Ust-Karenga | . | 31 | D9 | Valença do Piauí | 92 | D5 |
| United | | | Ust Kuyga | .... | 31 | B11 | Valence | ...... | 13 | D6 |
| Kingdom ■ . | 11 | E5 | Ust Muya | ..... | 30 | D9 | Valencia, *Spain* | 19 | C5 |
| United States of | | | Ust Olenek | .... | 30 | B10 | Valencia, | | |
| America ■ .. | 67 | F10 | Ust Port | ..... | 28 | C9 | *Venezuela* | ... | 90 | A5 |
| Unnao | ....... | 40 | D3 | Ust Tsilma | .... | 28 | C6 | Valencia □ | .... | 19 | C5 |
| Unst | ........ | 10 | A6 | Ust Urt = | | | Valencia, G. de | 19 | C6 |
| Ünye | ......... | 46 | B4 | Ustyurt, | | | Valencia de | | |
| Upata | ........ | 90 | B6 | Plateau | ..... | 29 | E6 | Alcántara | ... | 18 | C2 |
| Upemba, L. ... | 57 | F5 | Ust Vorkuta | ... | 28 | C7 | Valencia I. | .... | 11 | F1 |
| Upington | ..... | 58 | D4 | Ústí nad Labem | 16 | C2 | Valenciennes .. | 13 | A5 |
| Upper Hutt | ... | 65 | D6 | Ustica | ........ | 21 | E4 | Valentim, Sa. do | 92 | D5 |
| Upper Volta = | | | Ustinov = | | | Valera | ........ | 90 | B4 |
| Burkina | | | Izhevsk | .... | 28 | D6 | Valjevo | ....... | 22 | B2 |
| Faso ■ | ..... | 55 | F4 | Ustye | ........ | 30 | D7 | Vall de Uxó | ... | 19 | C5 |
| Uppsala | ...... | 9 | G11 | Ustyurt, Plateau | 29 | E6 | Valladolid, | | |
| Ur | ........ | 47 | E6 | Usu | ......... | 34 | B3 | *Mexico* | ..... | 85 | C7 |
| Uracara | ...... | 90 | D7 | Usuki | ........ | 32 | C2 | Valladolid, *Spain* | 18 | B3 |
| Ural = | | | Usumacinta → | 85 | D6 | Valle de la | | |
| Zhayyq → | . | 29 | E6 | Usumbura = | | | Pascua | ..... | 90 | B5 |
| Ural → | ...... | 63 | B4 | Bujumbura | .. | 57 | E5 | Valledupar | ... | 90 | A4 |
| Ural Mts. = | | | Uta | ......... | 39 | E5 | Vallejo | ....... | 80 | F2 |
| Uralskie Gory | 28 | D6 | Utah □ | ....... | 81 | F8 | Vallenar | ..... | 94 | B2 |
| Uralla | ........ | 63 | B5 | Utete | ........ | 57 | F7 | Valletta | ...... | 21 | G5 |
| Uralsk = Oral . | 24 | C7 | Utiariti | ....... | 91 | F7 | Valls | ........ | 19 | B6 |
| Uralskie Gory . | 28 | D6 | Utica | ......... | 73 | C8 | Valognes | ..... | 12 | B3 |
| Uranquinty .. | 63 | C4 | Utrecht ⌂ | .... | 14 | B3 | Valona = Vlóra | 23 | D2 |
| Urawa | ....... | 32 | B6 | Utrera | ........ | 18 | D3 | Valozhyn | ..... | 17 | A8 |
| Uray | ......... | 29 | C7 | Utsunomiya . | 32 | A6 | Valparaíso | .... | 94 | C2 |

| | | | |
|---|---|---|---|
| Vals, Tanjung | . | 39 | F5 |
| Valsad | ....... | 43 | J8 |
| Valverde del | | |
| Camino | ..... | 18 | D2 |
| Van | ......... | 46 | C5 |
| Van, L. = Van | | |
| Gölü | ...... | 46 | C5 |
| Van Gölü | ..... | 46 | C5 |
| Van Rees, | | |
| Pegunungan | 39 | E5 |
| Vanadzor | ... | 25 | E5 |
| Vancouver, | | |
| *Canada* | ..... | 71 | D7 |
| Vancouver, | | |
| *U.S.A.* | ..... | 80 | C2 |
| Vancouver I. | .. | 71 | D7 |
| Vänern | ........ | 9 | G10 |
| Vanga | ....... | 57 | E7 |
| Vangaindrano | . | 59 | J9 |
| Vännäs | ....... | 8 | F11 |
| Vannes | ...... | 12 | C2 |
| Vanrhynsdorp . | 58 | E3 |
| Vanua Levu .. | 64 | L12 |
| Vanuatu ■ ... | 64 | L11 |
| Vapnyarka | ... | 17 | D9 |
| Varanasi | ...... | 40 | E4 |
| Varangerfjorden | 8 | D13 |
| Varaždin | ..... | 20 | A6 |
| Varberg | ...... | 9 | G10 |
| Vardak □ | ..... | 45 | C7 |
| Vardar = | | |
| Axiós → | ... | 23 | D4 |
| Varese | ...... | 20 | B2 |
| Varna | ....... | 22 | C6 |
| Varzaneh | ..... | 44 | C3 |
| Vasa Barris → | 93 | E6 |
| Vascongadas = | | |
| País Vasco □ | 19 | A4 |
| Vasht = Khāsh | 42 | E2 |
| Vasilevichi | .... | 17 | B9 |
| Vasilkov = | | |
| Vasylkiv | .... | 17 | C10 |
| Vaslui | ....... | 17 | E8 |
| Västerås | ...... | 9 | G11 |
| Västervik | ...... | 9 | G11 |
| Vasto | ....... | 20 | C5 |
| Vasylkiv | ..... | 17 | C10 |
| Vatican City ■ . | 20 | D4 |
| Vatomandry | ... | 59 | H9 |
| Vatra-Dornei | . | 17 | E7 |
| Vättern | ...... | 9 | G10 |
| Vaupés = | | |
| Uaupés → | .. | 90 | C5 |
| Vawkavysk | ... | 17 | B7 |
| Vaygach, Ostrov | 28 | C6 |
| Vedea → | ..... | 22 | C5 |
| Vega | ........ | 8 | E10 |
| Vegreville | .... | 71 | C8 |
| Vejer de la | | |
| Frontera | ... | 18 | D3 |
| Velebit Planina | 20 | B5 |
| Vélez | ........ | 90 | B4 |
| Vélez Málaga . | 18 | D3 |
| Vélez Rubio ... | 19 | D4 |
| Velhas → | ..... | 93 | F5 |
| Velika Kapela .. | 20 | B5 |
| Velikaya → | .. | 24 | B2 |
| Veliki Ustyug .. | 24 | A6 |
| Velikiye Luki . | 24 | B3 |
| Veliko Tŭrnovo | 22 | C5 |
| Velikonda Range | 43 | M11 |
| Velletri | ....... | 20 | D4 |
| Vellore | ....... | 43 | N11 |
| Venado Tuerto . | 94 | C4 |
| Vendée □ | .... | 12 | C3 |
| Vendôme | ..... | 12 | C4 |
| Venézia | ..... | 20 | B4 |
| Venézia, G. di . | 20 | B4 |

Venezuela ■ . . **90 B5**
Venezuela, G. de 90 **A4**
Vengurla . . . . . **43 M8**
Venice =
Venézia . . . . . **20 B4**
Venkatapuram . **40 H3**
Ventotene . . . . **21 D4**
Ventoux, Mt. . . **13 D6**
Ventspils . . . . . **24 B1**
Ventuarí → . . . **90 C5**
Ventura . . . . . . **82 C3**
Venus B. . . . . . **63 C4**
Vera, *Argentina* **94 B4**
Vera, *Spain* . . . **19 D5**
Veracruz . . . . . **84 D5**
Veraval . . . . . . . **43 J7**
Verbánia . . . . . **20 B2**
Vercelli . . . . . . . **20 B2**
Verde → . . . . . **95 E3**
Verden . . . . . . . **14 B5**
Verdun . . . . . . . **13 B6**
Vereeniging . . . **59 D5**
Verga, C. . . . . . **55 F2**
Verin . . . . . . . . **18 B2**
Verkhnevilyuysk 30 **C10**
Verkhniy
Baskunchak . **25 D6**
Verkhoyansk . . **31 C11**
Verkhoyansk Ra.
=
Verkhoyanskiy
Khrebet . . . . . **31 C10**
Verkhoyanskiy
Khrebet . . . . . **31 C10**
Vermilion □ . . . . **71 C8**
Vermont □ . . . . **73 C9**
Vernon, *Canada* **71 C8**
Vernon, *U.S.A.* **78 B4**
Véroia . . . . . . . . **23 D4**
Verona . . . . . . . **20 B3**
Versailles . . . . . **12 B5**
Vert, C. . . . . . . . **55 F1**
Verviers . . . . . . **14 C3**
Veselovskoye
Vdkhr. . . . . . . **25 D5**
Vesoul . . . . . . . **13 C7**
Vesterålen . . . . **8 E11**
Vestfjorden . . . **8 E10**
Vesuvio . . . . . . **21 D5**
Vesuvius, Mt. =
Vesuvio . . . . **21 D5**
Veszprém . . . . . **16 E3**
Vetlugu → . . . . **28 D5**
Vettore, Mte. . . **20 C4**
Veys . . . . . . . . . **47 E7**
Vezhen . . . . . . . **22 C5**
Viacha . . . . . . . **91 G5**
Viamão . . . . . . . **94 C6**
Viana . . . . . . . . **92 C5**
Viana do
Alentejo . . . . **18 C2**
Viana do Castelo 18 **B1**
Vianópolis . . . . **93 F4**
Viaréggio . . . . . **20 C3**
Vibo Valéntia . . **21 E6**
Vicenza . . . . . . **20 B3**
Vich . . . . . . . . . **19 B7**
Vichy . . . . . . . . **13 C5**
Vicksburg . . . . . **79 C8**
Viçosa . . . . . . . **93 D6**
Victor . . . . . . . . **43 J7**
Victor Harbor . . **62 C2**
Victoria, *Canada* 71 **D7**
Victoria, *Chile* . **94 D2**
Victoria, *Guinea* 55 **F2**
Victoria = Labuan,
*Malaysia* . . . **36 C5**
Victoria □ . . . . **62 C3**

Victoria, L.,
*Africa* . . . . . . **57 E6**
Victoria, L.,
*Australia* . . . . **62 B3**
Victoria Beach . **71 C10**
Victoria de
Durango =
Durango . . . . **84 C4**
Victoria Falls . **59 B5**
Victoria I. . . . . . **70 A8**
Victoria Ld. . . . **96 B14**
Victoria
Taungdeik . . **41 G9**
Victoria West . . **58 E4**
Victorica . . . . . **94 D3**
Vicuña . . . . . . . **94 C2**
Vidin . . . . . . . . . **22 C4**
Vidisha . . . . . . . **43 H10**
Viedma . . . . . . . **95 E4**
Viedma, L. . . . . **95 F2**
Vienna = Wien **15 D9**
Vienne . . . . . . . **13 D6**
Vienne → . . . . **12 C4**
Vientiane . . . . . **36 A2**
Vierzon . . . . . . . **12 C5**
Vietnam ■ . . . . **36 A3**
Vigan . . . . . . . . **38 A2**
Vigévano . . . . . **20 B2**
Vigia . . . . . . . . . **92 C4**
Vigo . . . . . . . . . **18 A1**
Vijayawada . . . **40 J3**
Vikeke . . . . . . . **39 F3**
Vikna . . . . . . . . **8 F10**
Vila da Maganja 59 **B7**
Vila de João
Belo = Xai-Xai 59 **D6**
Vila do Bispo . . **18 D1**
Vila Franca de
Xira . . . . . . . **18 C1**
Vila Machado . **59 B6**
Vila Nova de
Gaia . . . . . . . **18 B1**
Vila Real . . . . . **18 B2**
Vila Real de
Santo António 18 **D2**
Vila Velha . . . . **93 G5**
Vilaine → . . . . **12 C2**
Vilanculos . . . . **59 C7**
Vileyka . . . . . . **17 A8**
Vilhelmina . . . . **8 F11**
Vilhena . . . . . . **91 F6**
Vilkitskogo,
Proliv . . . . . . **30 B8**
Vilkovo =
Vylkove . . . . **17 F9**
Villa Ahumada **84 A3**
Villa Ángela . . . **94 B4**
Villa Bella . . . . **91 F5**
Villa Bens =
Tarfaya . . . . . **54 C2**
Villa Colón . . . . **94 C3**
Villa de María . **94 B4**
Villa Dolores . . **94 C3**
Villa Hayes . . . **94 B5**
Villa María . . . . **94 C4**
Villa Mazán . . . **94 B3**
Villa Montes . . **94 A4**
Villa Ocampo . **94 B5**
Villacarrillo . . . **18 C4**
Villach . . . . . . . **15 E7**
Villagarcía de
Arosa . . . . . . **18 A1**
Villaguay . . . . . **94 C5**
Villahermosa . . **85 D6**
Villajoyosa . . . **19 C5**
Villalba . . . . . . **18 A2**
Villanueva de la
Serena . . . . . **18 C3**

Villanueva y
Geltrú . . . . . . **19 B6**
Villarreal . . . . . **19 C5**
Villarrica, *Chile* **95 D2**
Villarrica,
*Paraguay* . . . **94 B5**
Villarrobledo . . **19 C4**
Villavicencio . . **90 C4**
Villaviciosa . . . **18 A3**
Villazón . . . . . . **94 A3**
Villena . . . . . . . **19 C5**
Villeneuve-
d'Ascq . . . . . **13 A5**
Villeneuve-sur-
Lot . . . . . . . . **12 D4**
Villingen-
Schwenningen 14 **D5**
Vilnius . . . . . . . **24 C2**
Vilyuy → . . . . . **31 C10**
Vilyuysk . . . . . **31 C10**
Viña del Mar . . **94 C2**
Vinaroz . . . . . . **19 B6**
Vindhya Ra. . . . **43 H10**
Vineland . . . . . **73 E8**
Vinkovci . . . . . **20 B7**
Vinnitsa =
Vinnytsya . . **17 D9**
Vinnytsya . . . . **17 D9**
Virac . . . . . . . . **38 B2**
Viramgam . . . . **43 H8**
Virananşehir . . **46 C4**
Virden . . . . . . . **71 D9**
Vire . . . . . . . . . **12 B3**
Vírgenes, C. . . . **95 G3**
Virgin Is. (*U.K.*
*-U.S.A.*) ■ . . **87 C7**
Virginia □ . . . . **73 F6**
Virginia Beach . **73 F8**
Virovitica . . . . . **20 B6**
Virudunagar . . **43 Q10**
Vis . . . . . . . . . . **20 C6**
Visalia . . . . . . . **82 B3**
Visayan Sea . . . **38 B2**
Visby . . . . . . . . **9 G11**
Višegrad . . . . . **20 C7**
Viseu, *Brazil* . . **92 C4**
Viseu, *Portugal* **18 B2**
Vishakhapatnam 40 **J4**
Viso, Mte. . . . . **20 B1**
Vistula =
Wisła → . . . **16 A4**
Vitebsk =
Vitsyebsk . . . **24 B3**
Viterbo . . . . . . **20 C4**
Viti Levu . . . . . **64 L12**
Vitigudino . . . . **18 B2**
Vitória, *Brazil* . **93 G5**
Vitoria, *Spain* . **19 A4**
Vitória da
Conquista . . . **93 E5**
Vitsyebsk . . . . . **24 B3**
Vittória . . . . . . **21 F5**
Vittório Véneto . **20 B4**
Vivero . . . . . . . **18 A2**
Vize . . . . . . . . . **22 D6**
Vizianagaram . **40 H4**
Vjosa → . . . . . **23 D2**
Vladikavkaz . . . **25 E5**
Vladimir . . . . . **24 B5**
Vladimir
Volynskiy =
Volodymyr-
Volynskyy . . . **17 C7**
Vladivostok . . . **31 E11**
Vlissingen . . . . **14 C2**
Vlóra . . . . . . . . **23 D2**
Vltava → . . . . . **16 C2**
Vogelsberg . . . **14 C5**

Voghera . . . . . . **20 B2**
Vohibinany . . . **59 H9**
Vohimarina . . . **59 G10**
Vohimena,
Tanjon' i . . . **59 K9**
Vohipeno . . . . . **59 J9**
Voi . . . . . . . . . . **57 E7**
Voiron . . . . . . . **13 D6**
Vojvodina □ . . **22 B2**
Volga → . . . . . **25 D6**
Volga Hts. =
Privolzhskaya
Vozvyshennost
. . . . . . . . . . . **24 C6**
Volgodonsk . . . **25 D5**
Volgograd . . . . **25 D5**
Volgogradskoye
Vdkhr. . . . . . . **24 C6**
Volkhov → . . . **24 A3**
Volkovysk =
Vawkavysk . . **17 B7**
Volochanka . . . **30 B7**
Volodymyr-
Volynskyy . . . **17 C7**
Vologda . . . . . **24 B4**
Vólos . . . . . . . . **23 E4**
Volovets . . . . . **17 D6**
Volozhin =
Valozhyn . . . **17 A8**
Volsk . . . . . . . . **24 C6**
Volta → . . . . . **55 G5**
Volta, L. . . . . . **55 G5**
Volta Redonda **93 G5**
Volterra . . . . . . **20 C3**
Volturno → . . . **20 D4**
Volzhskiy . . . . . **25 D5**
Voríai
Sporádhes . . **23 E4**
Vorkuta . . . . . . **28 C7**
Voronezh . . . . . **24 C4**
Voroshilovgrad
= Luhansk . . **25 D4**
Voroshilovsk =
Alchevsk . . . **25 D4**
Vosges . . . . . . **13 B7**
Vostok I. . . . . . **65 L15**
Vouga → . . . . **18 B1**
Voznesensk . . . **25 D3**
Voznesenye . . . **28 C4**
Vrangelya,
Ostrov . . . . . **31 B15**
Vranje . . . . . . . **22 C3**
Vratsa . . . . . . . **22 C4**
Vrbas → . . . . . **20 B6**
Vrede . . . . . . . . **59 D5**
Vredenburg . . . **58 E3**
Vršac . . . . . . . . **22 B3**
Vryburg . . . . . . **58 D4**
Vryheid . . . . . . **59 D6**
Vukovar . . . . . **20 B7**
Vulcan . . . . . . . **17 F6**
Vulcaneşti . . . . **17 F9**
Vulcano . . . . . **21 E5**
Vulkaneshty =
Vulcaneşti . . **17 F9**
Vung Tau . . . . **36 B3**
Vyatka = Kirov 28 **D5**
Vyatskiye
Polyany . . . . **24 B7**
Vyazma . . . . . **24 B3**
Vyborg . . . . . . **28 C3**
Vychegda → . **28 C5**
Vychodné
Beskydy . . . **17 D5**
Vylkove . . . . . **17 F9**
Vynohradiv . . . **17 D6**
Vyshniy
Volochek . . . **24 B3**
Vyškov . . . . . . **16 D3**

| | | |
|---|---|---|
| Wa | 55 | F4 |
| Waal → | 14 | C3 |
| Wabash → | 72 | F1 |
| Waco | 78 | D5 |
| Wad Banda | 53 | F4 |
| Wad Hamid | 53 | E5 |
| Wâd Medanî | 53 | F5 |
| Waddington, Mt. | 71 | C7 |
| Waddy Pt. | 63 | |
| Wadi Halfa | 52 | D5 |
| Wafrah | 47 | E6 |
| Wager B. | 68 | B2 |
| Wager Bay | 68 | B1 |
| Wagga Wagga | 63 | C4 |
| Waghete | 39 | E5 |
| Wah | 42 | C8 |
| Wahai | 39 | E3 |
| Waiau → | 65 | E5 |
| Waibeem | 39 | E4 |
| Waigeo | 39 | E4 |
| Waihi | 64 | B6 |
| Waihou → | 64 | B6 |
| Waikabubak | 39 | F1 |
| Waikari | 65 | E5 |
| Waikato → | 64 | B6 |
| Waikerie | 62 | B2 |
| Waikokopu | 64 | C7 |
| Waikouaiti | 65 | F4 |
| Waimakariri → | 65 | E5 |
| Waimate | 65 | F4 |
| Wainganga → | 43 | K11 |
| Waingapu | 39 | F2 |
| Wainwright, Canada | 71 | C8 |
| Wainwright, U.S.A. | 71 | A3 |
| Waiouru | 64 | C6 |
| Waipara | 65 | E5 |
| Waipawa | 64 | C7 |
| Waipiro | 64 | C8 |
| Waipu | 64 | A6 |
| Waipukurau | 64 | D7 |
| Wairakei | 64 | C7 |
| Wairarapa, L. | 65 | D6 |
| Wairoa | 64 | C7 |
| Waitaki → | 65 | F4 |
| Waitara | 64 | C6 |
| Waiuku | 64 | B6 |
| Wajima | 32 | A5 |
| Wajir | 57 | D8 |
| Wakasa-Wan | 32 | B4 |
| Wakatipu, L. | 65 | F3 |
| Wakayama | 32 | B4 |
| Wakefield | 65 | D5 |
| Wakema | 41 | J10 |
| Wakkanai | 32 | E12 |
| Wakool | 63 | C3 |
| Wakool → | 62 | C3 |
| Wakre | 39 | E4 |
| Wałbrzych | 16 | C3 |
| Walcha | 63 | B5 |
| Wałcz | 16 | B3 |
| Wales □ | 11 | E4 |
| Walgett | 63 | A4 |
| Walgreen Coast | 96 | B1 |
| Walhalla | 63 | C4 |
| Walla Walla | 80 | B4 |
| Wallachia = Valahia | 22 | B5 |
| Wallal | 63 | A4 |
| Wallaroo | 62 | B2 |
| Wallerawang | 63 | B5 |
| Wallis & Futuna, Is. | 64 | L13 |
| Wallowa Mts. | 80 | C5 |
| Wallsend | 63 | B5 |
| Wallumbilla | 63 | A4 |
| Walvisbaai | 58 | C2 |
| Wamba | 57 | D5 |
| Wamena | 39 | E5 |
| Wamulan | 39 | E3 |
| Wana | 42 | C6 |
| Wanaaring | 63 | A3 |
| Wanaka | 65 | F3 |
| Wanaka L. | 65 | F3 |
| Wanapiri | 39 | E5 |
| Wanbi | 62 | B3 |
| Wandoan | 63 | A4 |
| Wangal | 39 | F4 |
| Wanganella | 63 | C3 |
| Wanganui | 64 | C6 |
| Wangaratta | 63 | C4 |
| Wangary | 62 | B2 |
| Wangerooge | 14 | B4 |
| Wangiwangi | 39 | F2 |
| Wanxian | 35 | C5 |
| Warangal | 43 | L11 |
| Waratah | 62 | D4 |
| Waratah B. | 63 | C4 |
| Warburton | 63 | C4 |
| Ward | 65 | D6 |
| Ward → | 63 | A4 |
| Wardha | 43 | J11 |
| Wardha → | 43 | K11 |
| Warialda | 63 | A5 |
| Wariap | 39 | E4 |
| Warkopi | 39 | E4 |
| Warmbad, Namibia | 58 | D3 |
| Warmbad, S. Africa | 59 | C5 |
| Warner Mts. | 80 | E3 |
| Warracknabeal | 62 | C3 |
| Warragul | 63 | C4 |
| Warrego → | 63 | B4 |
| Warren | 63 | B4 |
| Warrenton | 58 | D4 |
| Warrenville | 63 | A4 |
| Warri | 55 | G6 |
| Warrina | 62 | A2 |
| Warrington, U.K. | 11 | E5 |
| Warrington, U.S.A. | 74 | D4 |
| Warrnambool | 62 | C3 |
| Warsa | 39 | E5 |
| Warsaw = Warszawa | 16 | B5 |
| Warszawa | 16 | B5 |
| Warta → | 16 | B2 |
| Warthe = Warta → | 16 | B2 |
| Waru | 39 | E4 |
| Warwick | 63 | A5 |
| Wasatch Ra. | 81 | E8 |
| Wash, The | 11 | E7 |
| Washim | 43 | J10 |
| Washington | 73 | E7 |
| Washington □ | 80 | B3 |
| Washington, Mt. | 73 | B10 |
| Wasian | 39 | E4 |
| Wasior | 39 | E4 |
| Waskaganish | 69 | C3 |
| Wasserkuppe | 14 | C5 |
| Watangpone | 39 | E2 |
| Waterbury | 73 | D9 |
| Waterford | 11 | E3 |
| Waterloo, S. Leone | 55 | G2 |
| Waterloo, U.S.A. | 77 | D8 |
| Waterton-Glacier International Peace Park | 81 | A6 |
| Watertown | 73 | C8 |
| Waterville | 73 | B11 |
| Watford | 11 | F6 |
| Watling I. = San Salvador | 86 | B5 |
| Watrous | 71 | C9 |
| Watsa | 57 | D5 |
| Watson Lake | 70 | B7 |
| Watsonville | 82 | B2 |
| Wattiwarriganna Cr. → | 62 | A2 |
| Watuata = Batuata | 39 | F2 |
| Watubela, Kepulauan | 39 | E4 |
| Watubela Is. = Watubela, Kepulauan | 39 | E4 |
| Wauchope | 63 | B5 |
| Waukegan | 72 | C2 |
| Waukesha | 72 | C1 |
| Wausau | 77 | C10 |
| Wauwatosa | 72 | C2 |
| Waverley | 64 | C6 |
| Wâw | 53 | G4 |
| Wâw al Kabîr | 52 | C2 |
| Waxahachie | 79 | C5 |
| Wayabula Rau | 39 | D3 |
| Wayatinah | 62 | D4 |
| Waycross | 75 | D6 |
| Wazirabad | 42 | C9 |
| We | 36 | C1 |
| Weda | 39 | D3 |
| Weda, Teluk | 39 | D3 |
| Weddell I. | 95 | G4 |
| Weddell Sea | 96 | A4 |
| Wedderburn | 62 | C3 |
| Wee Waa | 63 | B4 |
| Weemelah | 63 | A4 |
| Weiden | 15 | D7 |
| Weifang | 35 | C6 |
| Weimar | 15 | C6 |
| Weipa | 61 | C7 |
| Weir → | 63 | A4 |
| Wejherowo | 16 | A4 |
| Welbourn Hill | 62 | A1 |
| Welkom | 59 | D5 |
| Wellesley Is. | 60 | D6 |
| Wellington, Australia | 63 | B4 |
| Wellington, N.Z. | 65 | D6 |
| Wellington, I. | 95 | F1 |
| Wellington, L. | 63 | C4 |
| Wels | 15 | D8 |
| Welshpool | 11 | E5 |
| Wemindji | 69 | C3 |
| Wenatchee | 80 | B3 |
| Wenchi | 55 | G4 |
| Wenchow = Wenzhou | 35 | D7 |
| Wendesi | 39 | E4 |
| Wensu | 34 | B3 |
| Wentworth | 62 | B3 |
| Wenut | 39 | E4 |
| Wenzhou | 35 | D7 |
| Werda | 58 | D4 |
| Werder | 49 | F4 |
| Weri | 39 | E4 |
| Werra → | 14 | C5 |
| Werribee | 63 | C3 |
| Werrimull | 62 | B3 |
| Werris Creek | 63 | B5 |
| Wersar | 39 | E4 |
| Weser → | 14 | B5 |
| Wesiri | 39 | F3 |
| West Bengal □ | 40 | F7 |
| West Beskids = Západné Beskydy | 16 | D4 |
| West Falkland | 95 | G4 |
| West Fjord = Vestfjorden | 8 | E10 |
| West Ice Shelf | 96 | A11 |
| West Nicholson | 59 | C5 |
| West Palm Beach | 75 | F7 |
| West Pt. | 62 | C2 |
| West Virginia □ | 72 | E5 |
| West Wyalong | 63 | B4 |
| Westall Pt. | 62 | B1 |
| Westbury | 62 | D4 |
| Westerland | 14 | A5 |
| Western Australia □ | 60 | F3 |
| Western Dvina = Daugava → | 24 | B1 |
| Western Ghats | 43 | N9 |
| Western Sahara ■ | 54 | D2 |
| Western Samoa = Samoa ■ | 65 | L13 |
| Westerwald | 14 | C4 |
| Westland Bight | 65 | E4 |
| Weston | 36 | C5 |
| Weston-super-Mare | 11 | F5 |
| Westport, Ireland | 11 | E2 |
| Westport, N.Z. | 65 | D4 |
| Westray | 10 | B5 |
| Wetar | 39 | F3 |
| Wetaskiwin | 71 | C8 |
| Wetzlar | 14 | C5 |
| Wewak | 61 | |
| Wexford | 11 | E3 |
| Weyburn | 71 | D9 |
| Weymouth | 11 | F5 |
| Whakatane | 64 | B7 |
| Whale → | 68 | C4 |
| Whale Cove | 70 | B10 |
| Whales, B. of | 96 | B16 |
| Whangamomona | 64 | C6 |
| Whangarei | 64 | A6 |
| Whangarei Harb. | 64 | A6 |
| Wheeling | 72 | D5 |
| White →, Ark., U.S.A. | 79 | C8 |
| White →, Ind., U.S.A. | 72 | E2 |
| White Cliffs | 62 | B3 |
| White I. | 64 | B7 |
| White Nile = Nîl el Abyad → | 53 | E5 |
| White Russia = Belarus ■ | 24 | C2 |
| White Sea = Beloye More | 28 | C4 |
| Whitecliffs | 65 | E4 |
| Whitehaven | 11 | D5 |
| Whitehorse | 70 | B6 |
| Whitemark | 62 | D4 |
| Whitfield | 63 | C4 |
| Whitianga | 64 | B6 |
| Whitney, Mt. | 82 | B3 |
| Whittlesea | 63 | C4 |
| Wholdaia L. | 70 | B9 |
| Whyalla | 62 | B2 |
| Whyjonta | 62 | A3 |
| Wichita | 78 | A5 |
| Wichita Falls | 78 | C4 |
| Wick | 10 | B5 |
| Wickham, C. | 62 | C3 |
| Wicklow Mts. | 11 | E3 |
| Wieluń | 16 | C4 |
| Wien | 15 | D9 |
| Wiener Neustadt | 15 | E9 |
| Wiesbaden | 14 | C5 |
| Wilcannia | 62 | B3 |
| Wildspitze | 14 | E6 |
| Wilhelm, Mt. | 61 | B8 |
| Wilhelm II Coast | 96 | A11 |

Wilhelmshaven 14 B5
Wilkes-Barre .. 73 D8
Wilkie ........ 71 C9
Willandra
Billabong
Creek → ... 63 B4
Willemstad ... 87 D6
William Creek . 62 A2
Williams Lake . 71 C7
Williamsburg .. 73 F7
Williamsport .. 73 D7
Williamstown . 63 C3
Williston ...... 76 A3
Willowmore ... 58 E4
Willunga ..... 62 C2
Wilmington,
Australia .... 62 B2
Wilmington,
Del., U.S.A. . 73 E8
Wilmington,
N.C., U.S.A. . 75 B9
Wilpena Cr. → 62 B2
Wilson ........ 75 B9
Wilson → .... 62 A3
Wilsons
Promontory . 63 C4
Wimmera → . 62 C3
Winchester ... 11 F6
Wind River
Range ...... 81 D9
Windau =
Ventspils ... 24 B1
Windhoek .... 58 C3
Windsor,
Australia .... 63 B5
Windsor, N.S.,
Canada ... 69 D4
Windsor, Ont.,
Canada ... 69 D2
Windward Is. .. 87
Wingen ....... 63 B5
Wingham ..... 63 B5
Winisk → ... 69 C2
Winneba ..... 55 G4
Winnipeg ..... 71 D10
Winnipeg, L. .. 71 C10
Winnipegosis L. 71 C9
Winona ....... 77 C9
Winston-Salem 75 A7
Winterthur .... 13 C8
Winton,
Australia .... 61 E7
Winton, N.Z. .. 65 G3
Wirrulla ...... 62 B1
Wisconsin □ .. 77 C10
Wisła → ..... 16 A4
Wismar ...... 15 B6
Witbank ...... 59 D5
Wittenberg .... 15 C7
Wittenberge ... 15 B6
Wolin ........ 16 B2
Wollaston, Is. . 95 H3
Wollaston Pen. 70 B8
Wollongong ... 63 B5
Wolseley ..... 62 C3
Wolverhampton 11 E5
Wondai ...... 63 A5
Wongalarroo L. 63 B3
Wŏnsan ...... 35 C7
Wonthaggi .... 63 C4
Woocalla ..... 62 B2
Woodburn .... 63 A5
Woodenbong . 63 A5

Woodend ..... 63 C3
Woodland .... 80 F3
Woodroffe, Mt. 60 F5
Woods, L. of the 71 D10
Woodstock .... 69 D4
Woodville .... 64 D6
Woolamai, C. .. 63 C4
Woolgoolga ... 63 B5
Woombye .... 63 A5
Woomera .... 62 B2
Worcester,
S. Africa .... 58 E3
Worcester, U.K. 11 E5
Worcester,
U.S.A. ...... 73 C10
Workington ... 11 D5
Worms ....... 14 D5
Worthing ..... 11 F6
Wosi ........ 39 E3
Wou-han =
Wuhan ..... 35 C6
Wour ........ 52 D2
Wousi = Wuxi . 35 C7
Wowoni ..... 39 E2
Woy Woy .... 63 B5
Wrangel I. =
Vrangelya,
Ostrov ..... 31 B15
Wrangell ..... 71 C6
Wrangell Mts. . 71 B5
Wrath, C. .... 10 B4
Wrexham .... 11 E5
Wright ....... 38 B3
Wrigley ...... 70 B7
Wrocław ..... 16 C3
Września ..... 16 B3
Wu Jiang → .. 35 D5
Wuhan ...... 35 C6
Wuhsi = Wuxi . 35 C7
Wuhu ....... 35 C6
Wukari ...... 55 G6
Wuliaru ...... 39 F4
Wulumuchi =
Ürümqi ..... 34 B3
Wum ........ 55 G7
Wuntho ...... 41 F10
Wuppertal .... 14 C4
Würzburg .... 14 D5
Wutongqiao ... 34 D5
Wuwei ....... 34 C5
Wuxi ........ 35 C7
Wuyi Shan .... 35 D6
Wuzhi Shan ... 35 E5
Wuzhong .... 35 C5
Wuzhou ...... 35 D6
Wyandotte .... 72 C4
Wyandra ..... 63 A4
Wyangala Res. 63 B4
Wyara, L. .... 63 A3
Wycheproof ... 62 C3
Wynbring .... 62 B1
Wyndham,
Australia .... 60 D4
Wyndham, N.Z. 65 G3
Wynnum ..... 63 A5
Wynyard ..... 62 D4
Wyoming □ ... 81 D10
Wyong ....... 63 B5

## X

Xai-Xai ....... 59 D6
Xainza ....... 34 C3
Xangongo .... 58 B3
Xankändi ..... 25 F6
Xánthi ....... 22 D5
Xapuri ....... 91 F5

Xi Jiang → ... 35 D6
Xiaguan ...... 34 D5
Xiamen ...... 35 D6
Xi'an ........ 35 C5
Xiang Jiang → 35 D6
Xiangfan ..... 35 C6
Xiangtan ..... 35 D6
Xiao Hinggan
Ling ........ 35 B7
Xiapu ....... 35 D6
Xichang ...... 34 D5
Xigazê ...... 34 D3
Xinavane ..... 59 D6
Xing'an ...... 35 D6
Xingren ...... 35 D5
Xingtai ...... 35 C6
Xingu → .... 92 C3
Xining ....... 34 C5
Xinjiang Uygur
Zizhiqu □ ... 34 B3
Xinjin ....... 35 C7
Xinxiang ..... 35 C6
Xinyang ..... 35 C6
Xinzhu ...... 35 D7
Xique-Xique .. 93 E5
Xisha Qundao =
Hsisha
Chuntao .... 36 A4
Xixabangma
Feng ....... 40 C5
Xizang □ .... 34 C3
Xuanhua ..... 35 B6
Xuchang ..... 35 C6
Xuzhou ...... 35 C6

## Y

Ya'an ........ 34 D5
Yaapeet ..... 62 C3
Yabelo ....... 53 H6
Yablonovy Ra. =
Yablonovyy
Khrebet ..... 30 D9
Yablonovyy
Khrebet ..... 30 D9
Yacuiba ...... 94 A4
Yadgir ....... 43 L10
Yagoua ...... 56 B3
Yahuma ..... 56 D4
Yakima ...... 80 B3
Yakutat ...... 71 C6
Yakutsk ...... 31 C10
Yala ........ 36 C2
Yalinga ...... 56 C4
Yalong Jiang → 34 D5
Yalova ....... 22 D7
Yalta ........ 25 E3
Yalutorovsk ... 29 D7
Yam Ha Melah
= Dead Sea . 47 E3
Yam Kinneret . 46 D3
Yamagata .... 33 G12
Yamaguchi ... 32 B2
Yamal,
Poluostrov .. 28 B8
Yamal Pen. =
Yamal,
Poluostrov .. 28 B8
Yamantau, Gora 29 D6
Yamba, N.S.W.,
Australia .... 63 A5
Yamba,
S. Austral.,
Australia .... 62 B3
Yâmbiô ...... 53 H4
Yambol ...... 22 C6

Yamdena ..... 39 F4
Yamethin ..... 41 G11
Yamma-Yamma,
L. ......... 62 A3
Yamoussoukro 55 G3
Yampil ....... 17 D9
Yampol =
Yampil ..... 17 D9
Yamuna → .. 40 E3
Yamzho Yumco 34 D4
Yana → ..... 31 B11
Yanac ....... 62 C3
Yanbu 'al Bahr 47 F4
Yancannia ... 62 B3
Yanco Cr. → . 63 C4
Yandoon ..... 41 J10
Yangambi .... 56 D4
Yangch'ü =
Taiyuan .... 35 C6
Yangchun .... 35 D6
Yangjiang .... 35 D6
Yangon =
Rangoon ... 41 J11
Yangquan .... 35 C6
Yanji ........ 35 B7
Yanna ....... 63 A4
Yanqi ....... 34 B3
Yantabulla ... 63 A4
Yantai ....... 35 C7
Yanykurgan ... 29 E7
Yao ........ 53 F2
Yaoundé ..... 56 D2
Yapen ....... 39 E5
Yapen, Selat . 39 E5
Yaqui → .... 84 B2
Yar-Sale ..... 28 C8
Yaraka ...... 61 E7
Yaransk ...... 24 B6
Yardea P.O. .. 62 B2
Yaremcha .... 17 D7
Yarensk ..... 28 C5
Yari → ..... 90 D4
Yarkand =
Shache .... 34 C2
Yarkhun → ... 42 A8
Yaroslavl .... 24 B4
Yarram ...... 63 C4
Yarraman ... 63 A5
Yarranvale ... 63 A4
Yarras ...... 63 B5
Yartsevo ..... 30 C7
Yaselda ..... 17 B8
Yasinya ..... 17 D7
Yass ........ 63 B4
Yatağan ..... 23 F7
Yathkyed L. ... 70 B10
Yatsushiro ... 32 C2
Yauyos ...... 91 F3
Yavari → .... 90 D4
Yavatmal .... 43 J11
Yavoriv ...... 17 D6
Yavorov =
Yavoriv ..... 17 D6
Yawatahama .. 32 C3
Yazd ........ 44 D3
Yazd □ ..... 44 C3
Yazdän ..... 45 C5
Yazoo → .... 79 C8
Ye Xian ..... 35 C6
Yebyu ...... 41 K12
Yecla ....... 19 C5
Yedintsy =
Edinita ..... 17 D8
Yeelanna .... 62 B2
Yegros ...... 94 B5
Yei ........ 53 H5
Yekaterinburg . 29 D7
Yekaterinodar =
Krasnodar .. 25 D4

Yelarbon ..... 63 A5
Yelets ........ 24 C4
Yelizavetgrad =
  Kirovohrad .. 25 D3
Yell .......... 10 A6
Yellow Sea ... 35 C7
Yellowhead Pass 71 C8
Yellowknife ... 70 B8
Yellowknife → 70 B8
Yellowstone → 76 B3
Yellowstone
  National Park 81 C8
Yelsk ......... 17 C9
Yemen ■ ..... 49 E3
Yenangyaung . 41 G10
Yenbo = Yanbu
  'al Baḥr ..... 47 F4
Yenda ........ 63 B4
Yenice ....... 23 E6
Yenisey → .. 28 B9
Yeniseysk ..... 30 D7
Yeniseyskiy
  Zaliv ....... 28 B9
Yenyuka ...... 31 D10
Yeola ........ 43 J9
Yeovil ....... 11 F5
Yerbent ...... 29 F6
Yerevan ...... 25 E5
Yermak ....... 29 D8
Yershov ...... 24 C6
Yerushalayim =
  Jerusalem .. 47 E3
Yessey ....... 30 C8
Yeu, I. d' ..... 12 C2
Yevpatoriya ... 25 D3
Yeysk ........ 25 D4
Yezd = Yazd .. 44 D3
Yiannitsa ..... 23 D4
Yibin ........ 35 D5
Yichang ...... 35 C6
Yichun ....... 35 B7
Yilan ......... 35 D7
Yinchuan ..... 35 C5
Yingkou ...... 35 B7
Yingtan ...... 35 D6
Yining ....... 34 B3
Yinmabin ..... 41 F10
Yishan ....... 35 D5
Yíthion ...... 23 F4
Yiyang ....... 35 D6
Yog Pt. ...... 38 B2
Yogyakarta ... 37 F4
Yokadouma ... 56 D2
Yokkaichi ..... 32 B5
Yoko ........ 53 G1
Yokohama .... 32 B6
Yokosuka .... 32 B6
Yola ......... 53 G1
Yonago ...... 32 B3
Yongji ........ 35 C6
Yonibana ..... 55 G2
Yonkers ...... 73 D9
Yonne → .... 13 B5
York, U.K. .... 11 E6
York, U.S.A. ... 73 E7
York, C. ...... 61 C7
Yorke Pen. ... 62 B2
Yorkton ...... 71 C9
Yos Sudarso,
  Pulau ...... 39 F5
Yosemite
  National Park 82 B3
Yoshkar Ola ... 24 B6
Youghal ...... 11 F3
Young ....... 63 B4
Younghusband,
  L. ........ 62 B2
Younghusband
  Pen. ....... 62 C2

Youngstown .. 72 D5
Yozgat ....... 46 C3
Ysyk-Köl, Ozero 29 E8
Yu Jiang → .. 35 D6
Yu Shan ...... 35 D7
Yuan Jiang → 35 D6
Yuanling ...... 35 D6
Yuanyang .... 34 D5
Yuba City .... 80 F3
Yūbari ....... 32 F12
Yucatán □ .... 85 C7
Yucatán, Canal
  de ........ 85 C7
Yucatán,
  Península de 85 D7
Yucatan Str. =
  Yucatán,
  Canal de .... 85 C7
Yuci ........ 35 C6
Yugoslavia ■ .. 22 B3
Yukon → .... 71 B3
Yukon
  Territory □ .. 70 B6
Yukti ........ 30 C8
Yuma ........ 82 D5
Yumen ....... 34 C4
Yun Xian ..... 35 C6
Yungas ....... 91 G5
Yunnan □ .... 34 D5
Yunta ....... 62 B2
Yurgao ....... 29 D9
Yuribei ....... 28 B8
Yurimaguas .. 91 E3
Yuryung Kaya . 30 B9
Yushu ....... 34 C4
Yuzhno-
  Sakhalinsk .. 31 E12
Yvetot ........ 12 B4

# Z

Zabid ....... 49 E3
Zābol ........ 45 D5
Zābol □ ...... 45 D6
Zābolī ....... 45 E5
Zabrze ....... 16 C4
Zacapa ....... 85 E7
Zacatecas .... 84 C4
Zacoalco ..... 84 C4
Zadar ........ 20 B5
Zadetkyi Kyun . 36 C1
Zafra ........ 18 C2
Żagań ........ 16 C2
Zagazig ...... 52 B5
Zagorsk =
  Sergiyev
  Posad ...... 24 B4
Zagreb ....... 20 B6
Zāgros, Kūhhā-
  ye ......... 44 C2
Zagros Mts. =
  Zāgros,
  Kūhhā-ye ... 44 C2
Zāhedān ..... 45 D5
Zahlah ....... 46 D3
Zaïre =
  Congo → .. 56 F2
Zaïre = Congo,
  Dem. Rep. of
  the ■ ...... 56 E4
Zaječar ...... 22 C4
Zakhodnaya
  Dzvina =
  Daugava → . 24 B1
Zākhū ....... 46 C5
Zákinthos ..... 23 F3

Zakopane ..... 16 D4
Zalaegerszeg .. 16 E3
Zalău ........ 17 E6
Zaleshchiki =
  Zalishchyky . 17 D7
Zalew Wiślany . 16 A4
Zalingei ...... 53 F3
Zalishchyky ... 17 D7
Zambeze → .. 59 B7
Zambezi =
  Zambeze → 59 B7
Zambezi ...... 58 A4
Zambia ■ .... 59 B5
Zamboanga ... 38 C2
Zamora, Mexico 84 D4
Zamora, Spain 18 B3
Zamość ...... 17 C6
Zanaga ....... 56 E2
Zanesville .... 72 E4
Zanjān ....... 46 C7
Zanjān □ ..... 46 C7
Zante =
  Zákinthos ... 23 F3
Zanzibar ...... 57 F7
Zaouiet El-Kala
  = Bordj Omar
  Driss ...... 54 C6
Zaouiet Reggane 54 C5
Zap Suyu =
  Kabīr, Zab
  al → ....... 46 C5
Zapadnaya
  Dvina ...... 28 D4
Zapadnaya
  Dvina → =
  Daugava → . 24 B1
Západné
  Beskydy .... 16 D4
Zaporizhzhya .. 25 D4
Zaporozhye =
  Zaporizhzhya 25 D4
Zara ........ 46 C4
Zaragoza ..... 19 B5
Zarand ....... 44 D4
Zaranj ....... 42 D2
Zaria ........ 55 F6
Zaruma ....... 90 D3
Żary ........ 16 C2
Zarzis ....... 52 B1
Zaskar Mts. ... 42 C10
Zavāreh ...... 44 C3
Zawiercie ..... 16 C4
Zāyandeh → . 44 C3
Zaysan ....... 29 E9
Zaysan, Oz. ... 29 E9
Zbarazh ...... 17 D7
Zdolbuniv .... 17 C8
Zduńska Wola . 16 C4
Zeebrugge .... 14 C2
Zeehan ....... 62 D4
Zeerust ...... 59 D5
Zeila ........ 49 E3
Zeitz ........ 15 C7
Zelenograd ... 24 B4
Zémio ....... 57 C5
Zemun ....... 22 B3
Zenica ....... 20 B6
Żepce ....... 20 B7
Zêzere → .... 18 C1
Zgorzelec .... 16 C2
Zhabinka ..... 17 B7
Zhailma ...... 29 D7
Zhambyl = Taraz 29 E8
Zhangagazaly . 29 E7
Zhanghua .... 35 D7
Zhangjiakou ... 35 B6
Zhangye ..... 34 C5
Zhangzhou ... 35 D6
Zhanjiang .... 35 D6

Zhanyi ....... 34 D5
Zhaotong ..... 34 D5
Zhashkiv ..... 17 D10
Zhayyq → .. 29 E6
Zhdanov =
  Mariupol .... 25 D4
Zhejiang □ .. 35 D7
Zhengzhou ... 35 C6
Zhenjiang .... 35 C6
Zhenyuan .... 35 D5
Zhezqazghan .. 29 E7
Zhigansk ..... 30 C10
Zhijiang ...... 35 D5
Zhilinda ...... 30 B9
Zhitomir =
  Zhytomyr ... 17 C9
Zhlobin ...... 17 B10
Zhmerinka =
  Zhmerynka .. 17 D9
Zhmerynka .. 17 D9
Zhodino =
  Zhodzina ... 17 A9
Zhodzina .... 17 A9
Zhongdian ... 34 D4
Zhumadian ... 35 C6
Zhuzhou ..... 35 D6
Zhytomyr .... 17 C9
Zibo ........ 35 C6
Zielona Góra .. 16 C2
Zigey ........ 53 F2
Zigong ....... 35 D5
Zigui ........ 35 C6
Ziguinchor ... 55 F1
Zile ......... 46 B3
Žilina ........ 16 D4
Zillah ....... 52 C2
Zimbabwe ■ .. 59 B5
Zimnicea ..... 22 C5
Zinder ....... 55 F6
Zion National
  Park ....... 83 B6
Zipaquirá ..... 90 C4
Ziway, L. ..... 53 G6
Zlatograd .... 22 D5
Zlatoust ..... 29 D6
Zlin ........ 16 D3
Zlītan ....... 52 B1
Zmeinogorsk . 29 D9
Znojmo ...... 16 D3
Zolochev =
  Zolochiv .... 17 D7
Zolochiv ..... 17 D7
Zomba ....... 59 B7
Zongo ....... 56 D3
Zonguldak .... 46 B2
Zorritos ...... 90 D2
Zouar ....... 52 D2
Zouérate ..... 54 D2
Zrenjanin .... 22 B3
Zuetina = Az
  Zuwaytinah . 52 B3
Zufar ........ 48 D5
Zug ........ 13 C8
Zugspitze .... 14 E6
Zula ........ 53 E6
Zumbo ....... 59 B6
Zungeru ..... 55 G6
Zunyi ....... 35 D5
Zürich ....... 13 C8
Zuwārah ..... 52 B1
Zvishavane ... 59 C6
Zvolen ....... 16 D4
Zwettl ....... 15 D8
Zwickau ..... 15 C7
Zwolle ....... 14 B4
Żyrardów .... 16 B5
Zyryan ....... 29 E9
Zyryanovsk =
  Zyryan .... 29 E9
Żywiec ....... 16 D4